Multicriteria Scheduling

Second Edition

Vincent T'kindt
Jean-Charles Billaut

Multicriteria Scheduling

Theory, Models and Algorithms

Translated from French by Henry Scott

Second Edition
with 138 Figures
and 15 Tables

Springer

Associate Professor Vincent T'kindt,
Professor Jean-Charles Billaut

Université François-Rabelais de Tours
Laboratoire d'Informatique
64 avenue Jean Portalis
37200 Tours
France

Translator

Henry Scott
www.hgs-scientific-translations.co.uk

Cataloging-in-Publication Data
Library of Congress Control Number: 2005937590

ISBN-10 3-540-28230-0 2nd ed. Springer Berlin Heidelberg New York
ISBN-13 978-3-540-28230-3 2nd ed. Springer Berlin Heidelberg New York
ISBN 3-540-43617-0 1st ed. Springer Berlin Heidelberg New York

Springer is a part of Springer Science+Business Media
springeronline.com

Printed in Germany

Cover design: Erich Kirchner
Production: Helmut Petri
Printing: Strauss Offsetdruck

SPIN 11538080 Printed on acid-free paper - 42/3153 - 5 4 3 2 1 0

Preface to the second edition

It is a real pleasure for us to present the second edition of this book on multicriteria scheduling. In this preface we would like to introduce the reader with the improvements made over the first edition. During the writing of the first edition of this book we were focused on putting in it all the results, algorithms and models necessary for the reader to tackle correctly the field of multicriteria scheduling, which is at the crossroad of several research domains: from multicriteria optimisation to scheduling. Writing a second edition is a totally different exercise since we concentrate more on refining, augmenting and, in a sense, making growing the existing manuscript.

We received valuable comments that lead us to rewrite, more or less partially, some chapters as Chapters 5 and 7. Besides, new significant research results published since the first edition have been included into existing chapters of that second edition. We review hereafter the most important changes.
Chapters 2 and 4 now include a survey on the complexity of counting and enumeration optimisation problems with application to multicriteria scheduling. These two chapters provide theoretical tools for evaluating the complexity of the enumeration of the set of strict Pareto optima. Chapter 4 also includes new real-life applications of multicriteria scheduling.
Chapter 5 has been drastically revised and now provides a general unified framework for Just-in-Time scheduling problems. Besides, classic *optimal timing* algorithms, which calculate optimal start times of operations when the jobs order is fixed, are now presented.
At last, chapter 6 is a new chapter dealing with robustness in multicriteria scheduling. This research area has been subject to a growing interest in the literature since the last ten years, notably when considering a criterion of flexibility or robustness in addition to a classic scheduling criterion. Henceforth, the aim of some scheduling problems become to increase the robustness of the calculated solution for its pratical use. Providing flexibility is a way to ensure a certain robustness when unexpected events occur in the shop.
We hope that this new edition will become an important tool and a practical guide for novice an senior researchers that work on multicriteria scheduling.

V. T'KINDT and J.-C. BILLAUT
Tours (France), october 15th 2005

Preface to the first edition

From Theory to Practice, there is a world, and scheduling does not escape this immutable rule.
For more than fifty years, theoretical researches on scheduling and complexity theory have improved our knowledge on both a typology of academic problems, mainly involving a single criterion, and on their solving. Though this work is far from being completed, a few famous books have been a major breakthrough. The typology will be all the more useful as it takes more and more realistic constraints into account. This is just a matter of time.
The relevance of some single criteria, their equivalence and their conflict have been studied...
Yet, numerous genuine problems, even outside the realm of scheduling, do not square with these single criterion approaches. For example, in a production shop, minimising the completion time of a set of jobs may be as interesting as retaining a maximum fragmentation of idle times on an easily damaged machine and minimising the storage of in-process orders. Moreover, even though the optimal solutions to the $F2||C_{max}$ yielded by S.M. Johnson's famous algorithm are numerous, they are far from appearing equivalent to the decision maker when their structure is analysed. A genuine scheduling problem, in essence, involves multiple criteria.

Besides, more general books on Decision Aid in a multicriteria environment have been published and a pool of researchers have long tackled the problem. Undoubtedly, a synthesis book offering a state-of-the-art on the intersection of both the fields of Scheduling and Multicriteria Decision Aid and providing a framework for tackling multicriteria scheduling problems is a must.

I am most happy to present this book. It is divided in four parts: - the first one deals with research on scheduling, now an important branch of operational research.
- the second one presents theories on Decision Aid and Multicriteria Optimisation as well as a framework for the resolution of multicriteria scheduling problems.

- the third and fourth parts involve a tremendous work since they contain state-of-the-arts on multicriteria scheduling problems. Numerous works and resolution algorithms are detailed.

In my opinion, this book will become a reference book for researchers working on scheduling. Moreover, I am convinced it will help PhD students suitably and quickly embark on a fascinating adventure in this branch of Operational Research. May they be numerous in joining us...
I very warmly thank MM. Vincent T'kindt and Jean-Charles Billaut for their tenacity in writing this significant book, and Springer-Verlag publishing for entrusting them.

Professor C. PROUST
Tours (France), february 22th 2002

The authors are very grateful to all the people who have directly or indirectly contributed to the birth of this book. Professor Christian Proust is at the root of this research and is undoubtedly the grandfather of this book. We would also like to thank the members of the research team "Scheduling and Control" of the Laboratory of Computer Science of the University of Tours for creating a friendly environment and thus for having promoted the emergence of this book. In this vein, all the technical and administrative persons of the E3i school have also to be thanked.
At last, we would like to thank Professor Jacques Teghem of the "Faculté Polytechnique de Mons" for having provided excellent ideas and remarks which have helped in improving this book.

Contents

List of algorithms and mathematical formulations

Introduction

Scheduling theory first appears in the mid 1950s. Since then the problems addressed become closer to industrial applications, thus increasing in complexity. The layout of the shops taken into account are closer and closer to those met in practice: we encounter shops where the machines are found in different multiple copies, shops where an operation may require several resources simultaneously, or with multipurpose machines, *etc.* At the same time the embedded constraints are more and more concrete: many authors take into account release dates, the preemption of the jobs, the resource availabilities, *etc.*
Paradoxically, the literature shows that in the majority of the problems addressed, schedules are only evaluated by a single criterion. During the different phases of planning different criteria can be considered. At a strategic level, at the long term planning phase with several years in view, the objectives concern minimising the costs related to the investment plans for materials, finance, or personel, related to the choice of new directions, or the launching of publicity campaigns. For tactical planning at the medium term phase with several months in view, the objectives always focus on minimising the costs: stock costs (supply or interruption of stocks), costs of getting supplies, costs of modifying production capacity, launching costs, costs of modifying production systems and certain commercial costs ([Mercé, 1987], [Giard, 1988]). At the short term planning phase (with the order of a week in view), or scheduling phase, several objectives require the attention of the production executive: above all he must consider the delays that satisfy the customer, next, he must minimise the work-in-process costs in the shop, and finally he must minimise the manufacturing costs related to the time spent to set up the machines or idle periods of the machines. Therefore, a scheduling problem involves multiple criteria.

Bernard Roy emphasises ([Roy, 1985]), that taking account of several criteria enables us to propose to the decision maker a more realistic solution. This still holds when solving scheduling problems in an applied context. Literature is dedicated in abundance to the study of multicriteria problems, whatever their field of application. Numerous theoretical works have been developed on multicriteria decision making. The purpose of this book is to provide a survey, based on a proposed methodology, of the existing methods for solving multicriteria scheduling problems, considering both methods of multicriteria optimisation and scheduling fields.

This book is divided into five major parts each devoted to particular themes. The **first two chapters** are devoted to the rudiments. **Chapter 1** sets out the scheduling problems as encountered in the literature. It presents the shop layouts and the classic constraints and criteria. The notation used throughout this book, as well as the notation of scheduling problems, based on that of Graham, Lawler, Lenstra and Rinnooy Kan ([Graham et al., 1979] [Blazewicz et al., 1996]) are provided. We present a new typology, as well as several classifications. **Chapter 2** reviews the basic concepts of the complexity of algorithms and the complexity classes of problems.

The **following two chapters** are devoted to multicriteria decision making and multicriteria optimisation, and introduce multicriteria scheduling problems. It opens up a new approach to the resolution of multicriteria scheduling problems. **Chapter 3** presents some important concepts related to methodologies of multicriteria decision aids. A large part of the difficulty in solving a multicriteria problem is linked to the way in which the criteria are taken into account. Optimisation techniques, which help in taking account of the criteria are also presented. **Chapter 4** presents an approach to the tackling of multicriteria scheduling problems. This approach is divided into three phases. In the first phase the decision maker indicates what constraints define his problem as well as the criteria to be taken into account. The second phase, of taking account of criteria, consists in choosing a resolution approach, *i.e.* the method which is going to be called upon to calculate a solution. The decision maker also indicates the type of algorithm which he wants to implement: *a priori*, *interactive* or *a posteriori* algorithm. This phase enables an objective function to be defined for the scheduling problem. The last phase consists of solving the identified scheduling problem. Its resolution leads to the best trade-off solution.

The **next two chapters** are chapters devoted to a particular thematic, whatever the configuration of the shop. In **Chapter 5** we are concerned with "Just-in-Time" scheduling problems. Both general considerations and technical issues are investigated in this chapter. **Chapter 6** focuses on robustness considerations in scheduling when multiple criteria are involved.

The **next two chapters** of this book are devoted to the presentation of multicriteria scheduling problems depending on the shop configuration. **Chapter 7** is devoted to single machine problems, which category of problems is undoubtly the most addressed in the literature on multicriteria scheduling.

Chapter 8 is devoted to shop problems, *i.e.*, flowshop, jobshop and open-shop problems.

The **last two chapters** are dedicated to the presentation of multicriteria scheduling and assignment problems. **Chapter 9** is devoted to multicriteria parallel machines scheduling problems, whilst **Chapter 10** is devoted to multicriteria hybrid flowshop scheduling problems.

1. Introduction to scheduling

1.1 Definition

Scheduling problems are encountered in all types of systems, since it is necessary to organise and/or distribute the work between many entities. We find in every book in the literature a definition of a scheduling problem as well as its principal components. Among these definitions we can quote the following one [Carlier and Chrétienne, 1988]:
"Scheduling is to forecast the processing of a work by assigning resources to tasks and fixing their start times. [...] The different components of a scheduling problem are the tasks, the potential constraints, the resources and the objective function.[...] The tasks must be programmed to optimise a specific objective [...] Of course, often it will be more realistic in practice to consider several criteria."

Another definition has been put forward by [Pinedo, 1995]:
"Scheduling concerns the allocation of limited resources to tasks over time. It is a decision-making process that has as a goal the optimization of one or more objectives."

A statement of scheduling problems can be found in [Gotha, 1993]. This article sets out the resolution approaches and the traditional scheduling problems. We can find in [Lee et al., 1997] a presentation of the current problems as well as more recent resolution methods.

In the above definitions, the task (or operation) is the entity to schedule. In this book we deal with *jobs* to schedule, each job is broken down into a series of operations. When all the jobs contain only a single operation we speak of a *mono-operation* problem. By contrast, we speak of a *multi-operation* problem. The operations of a job may be connected by precedence constraints. In this case the set of operations of a job and their precedence constraints define the *routing* of this job.
We are also dealing with the *resource* or *machine* (this latter term is more often used in the context of shop scheduling). We consider generally that the resources are of two types: renewable or consumable. Renewable resources become available again after use (machine, file, proces-

sor, personel, *etc.*), whereas non renewable resources disappear after use (money, raw materials, *etc.*). Among the renewable resources we can distinguish between the disjunctive resources, which can only perform one operation at a time and the cumulative resources which can process a limited number of operations simultaneously. The case of cumulative resources is being studied more and more as for example in shop scheduling problems [Carlier and Latapie, 1991], in project scheduling problems and in batch scheduling problems ([Potts and Kovalyov, 2000]).
Frequently, to solve a scheduling problem, we are also caused to solve an *assignment* problem, where it concerns in addition specifying the resources to process the operations.

We can separate the criteria to optimise into two types: those relating to completion time and those relating to costs. In the category of completion time related criteria we find for example those which measure the completion time of the whole schedule and those which measure tardiness of jobs in relation to their due date. In the category of cost related criteria we may cite those which represent cost of machine use and those which represent cost allied to waiting time of operations before and/or after they are processed.

1.2 Some areas of application

Scheduling problems are encountered at all levels and in all sectors of activity. Generally, we can distinguish between those of manufacturing production and those in computer systems or project management.

1.2.1 Problems related to production

We encounter scheduling problems in **Flexible Manufacturing Systems** (FMS). Numerous definitions of an FMS are found in the literature. For [Liu and MacCarthy, 1996]: "*An FMS comprises three principal elements: computer controlled machine tools; an automated transport system and a computer control system.*" These problems are broadly covered in the literature and most often in a well defined application class. Besides, this very broad problem encompasses other problems related to *Robotic Cell Scheduling* and *Scheduling of Automated Guided Vehicles* (AGV).

Equally, **electroplating and chemical shops** have their peculiarities in scheduling problems. The latter are also called Hoist Scheduling Problems. These shops are characterised by the presence of one or more travelling cranes sharing the same physical area and which are ordered to transport the products for treatment in tanks. In general, the soaking time in a tank is bounded by a minimum and a maximum (*the interval processing time*), transport time is not negligible and the operations must be carried out without waiting time. These problems are very common in industry and the "simple" cases (mono-robot, single batch tanks, *etc.*) have been well solved by now.

Scheduling problems in **car production lines**, so called *Car Sequencing Problems*, are encountered in assembly shops where certain equipment (or options) must be assembled in the different models of vehicles. These problems have constraints and peculiarities of their own. Knowing a sequence of vehicles undergoing treatment, the problem is to determine the type of the next vehicle programmed. We have to take account of a group of constraints connected principally to the assembly options for these vehicles and to the limited movement of the tools along the production line.

1.2.2 Other problems

We encounter scheduling problems in **computer systems**. These problems are studied in different forms by considering mono or multi processor systems, with the constraints of synchronisation of operations and resource sharing. In these problems, certain operations are periodic others are not, some are subject to due dates, others to deadlines. The objective is often to find a feasible solution, *i.e.* a solution which satisfies the constraints. Literature abounds on these problems. In fact, in spite of appearances they are very close to those encountered in manufacturing systems ([Blazewicz et al., 1996]).

Timetable scheduling problems concern all educational establishments or universities, since they involve timetabling of courses assuring the availability of teachers, students and classrooms. These problems are just as much the object of studies.

Project scheduling problems comprise a vast literature. We are interested more generally in problems of scheduling operations which use several resources simultaneously (money, personel, equipment, raw materials, *etc.*), these resources being available in known amounts. In other words we deal with the multi-resource scheduling problem with cumulative and non-renewable resources ([Brucker, 2004],[Herroelen et al., 1998b],[Herroelen et al., 2001]).

1.3 Shop environments

When confronted with a scheduling problem, one has to identify it before tackling it. Acknowledging that the problem is complicated and to know if it is already solved in the literature, we must use a recognised notation. For that purpose, shop "models" have been set up, which differ from each other by composition and organisation of their resources. We denote by n the number of jobs to schedule, by J_i the job number i, by n_i the number of operations of job J_i, by $O_{i,j}$ the operation j of job J_i, by m the number of machines and by M_k the machine number k. A complete synthesis of the notations is given in appendix A.

1.3.1 Scheduling problems without assignment

The problem is to find a processing start time for each operation. Several types of arrangement are traditionally encountered:

- **single machine**: Only a single machine is available for the processing of jobs. It concerns a basic shop or one in which a single machine poses a real scheduling problem. Besides, resolution of more complex problems is often achieved by the study of single machine problems. We can find an area of direct application in computing, if we think of the machine as the single processor of the computer. The jobs to be processed are necessarily mono-operation.
- **flowshop** (F): several machines are available in the shop. The characteristic of this type of shop is that the jobs processed in it use machines in the same order: they all have the same processing routing. In a permutation flowshop we find in addition that each machine has the same sequence of jobs: they cannot overtake each other.
- **jobshop** (J): several machines are available in the shop. Each job has a route of its own, *i.e.* it uses the resources in its own order.
- **openshop** (O): several machines are available in the shop. The jobs do not have fixed routings. They can, therefore, use the machines in any order.
- **mixed shop** (X): several machines are available in the shop. Some jobs have their own routing and others do not.

1.3.2 Scheduling and assignment problems with stages

The machines are grouped in well defined stages and a machine belongs to one stage only. In all cases the machines of a stage are capable of performing the same operations. To carry out one operation it is necessary to choose one among the available machines and, therefore, the problem is twofold, assigning one machine to each operation and sequencing the operations on the machines. At each stage we can differentiate between the following configurations:

- the machines are identical (P): an operation has the same processing time on all the machines.
- the machines are uniform (Q): the processing time of an operation $O_{i,j}$ on the machine M_k is equal to $p_{i,j,k} = q_{i,j}/v_k$ where $q_{i,j}$ is for example a number of components in the operation $O_{i,j}$ to be processed, and v_k is the number of components which the machine M_k can process per unit of time.

- the machines are unrelated or even independent (R): the processing time of the operation $O_{i,j}$ on the machine M_k is equal to $p_{i,j,k}$, and is a data of the problem. Of course, just as the assignment of $O_{i,j}$ is unknown, so is its processing time.

Globally, "traditional" scheduling and assignment problems correspond to the following configuration:

- **parallel machines** (P/Q/R): there is only one stage and the jobs are mono-operation.
- **hybrid flowshop** (HF): all the jobs have the same production routing, and therefore use the stages in the same order.
- **general jobshop** (GJ): each job has a route of its own.
- **general openshop** (GO): the jobs do not have a fixed routing.

It is easily possible to generalise these problems by supposing that each operation can only use its own subset of the resources of the performing stage.

1.3.3 General scheduling and assignment problems

This is the most general case where we suppose that each operation has its own set of machines on which it can be processed. No assumption is made on these sets of resources. We can differentiate several cases:

- the jobs are mono-operations, and we are confronted by a problem of **parallel machines with general assignment**. We find these problems in the literature ([Brucker, 2004]) under the name "Multi Purpose Machines Scheduling Problems" (P/Q/R MPM SP).
- the jobs follow a processing order. It is difficult in this case to distinguish between flowshop and jobshop since the groups of machines used by these jobs are not comparable. This is what is called **shops with general assignment problems** (" General Shop MPM SP").
- the jobs do not follow a fixed routing. This is the case in **openshop with general assignment problems** ("Openshop MPM SP").

1.4 Constraints

A solution of a scheduling problem must always satisfy a certain number of constraints, be they explicit or implicit. For example, in a flowshop problem it is implicit that the jobs are processed according to the routing and therefore an operation cannot start while its precedent remains uncompleted. On the other hand, the occurrence of different release dates constitutes a constraint which must be stated precisely. In this section we describe the explicit constraints encountered most frequently in scheduling. A summary is given in appendix A.

There are several types of constraints related to the **due dates**. There are those due dates which we do not wish to pass by, even if we tolerate to completing afterwards. They correspond to an agreed commitment which is negotiable. There are those due dates which are imperatives, also called deadlines, and which cannot be passed. Typically, they correspond to an unveiling date when the manufacturer must present his product, or even the departure date of the delivery lorry. These dates cannot be passed by: therefore, no tardiness can be permitted. Problems where we encounter these constraints are usually decision problems: these dates can or cannot be respected. When we can, either we are satisfied with a feasible solution or in addition we try to minimise a criterion.

Constraints relating to **start times** are equally various. Of course, there is the release date of the product. Sometimes, it corresponds to the date of the order. Equally, we can find a release date associated with a specific operation of a job. This date can correspond to the arrival of supplies for the operation. Finally, it can happen that the start time of a particular operation is imposed. In this case it is a matter of meeting with the customer for him to witness the implementation of the operation which he regards as critical in the manufacturing process. These two latter definitions correspond to problems rarely dealt with in the literature.

We list below some constraints met frequently in the literature.

- **pmtn** indicates that preemption is authorised. Here it is possible to forsee interuption of an operation so that, possibly it can be taken up next by another resource.
- **split** indicates that splitting is authorised. Here it is possible to forsee splitting of the operation into lots, which can be performed on one or several machines, possibly simultaneously.
- **prec** indicates that the operations are connected by precedence constraints. This heading gives different particular cases according to the nature of the constraints: **prec** to describe the most general case, **tree**, **in-tree**, **out-tree**, **chains** and **sp-graph** (for series-parallel graph ; see [Pinedo, 1995] or [Brucker, 2004]) to denote particular cases.
- **batch** indicates that the operations are grouped in batches. Two types of batch constraints are differentiated in the literature: the first called sometimes **s-batch** concerns serial batches where the operations constituting a batch are processed in sequence and the second of type **p-batch** concerns parallel batches where the operations constituting a batch are processed in parallel on a cumulative resource. In both cases, the completion time of an operation is equal to the completion time of the batch. In the first case,

the duration of the batch is equal to the sum of the processing times of the operations which constitute it, whereas in the second case its duration is equal to the longest processing time of the operations in the batch.

- **no-wait** indicates that the operations which constitute each job follow each other without any waiting.
- **prmu** (permutation) indicates that the operations occur on the machines in the same order. In other words, they cannot overtake themselves (this is true solely for flowshop problems).
- $\mathbf{d_i = d}$ indicates that all the due dates are identical. Likewise $\tilde{d}_i = \tilde{d}$ for the deadlines.
- $\mathbf{p_i = p}$ indicates that the processing times are all identical. We often encounter this constraint with $p = 1$.
- $\mathbf{S_{nsd}}$ and $\mathbf{R_{nsd}}$ indicate that the setup and removal times on the resources before and after each processing, respectively, must be taken into account. These preparation times are independent of the sequence of operations.
- $\mathbf{S_{sd}}$ and $\mathbf{R_{sd}}$ indicate that the setup and removal times on the resources before and after each processing, respectively, must be taken into account. These preparation times are dependent of the sequence of operations.
- $\mathbf{a_{i_1,i_2}}$ indicates that a minimum time lag must be respected between the jobs J_{i_1} and J_{i_2}, if the jobs are mono-operation. Otherwise, we use a_{i_1,j_1,i_2,j_2} to indicate a minimum time lag which must be respected between the operation O_{i_1,j_1} and the operation O_{i_2,j_2}. If this value is positive, we model, for example, a drying time between two successive operations, or else a transport time. In the latter case the resource is available to process the following operation during the transport. If this value is negative, it indicates that it is possible to carry out an overlap, *i.e.* to start an operation before its precedent in the routing is completely finished. Of course, this is possible when a job is composed of lots of items and it is not necessary to wait for the end of a lot on a machine to start the operation on the following machine.
- **blcg** (balancing) is a constraint peculiar to parallel machine shops, translating the fact that the machines must complete processing of jobs which are assigned to them at the same time. This constraint may be imposed when it is necessary to change the type of manufacture on all the machines simultaneously.
- **block** (blocking) is a constraint indicating that the shop has a limited stock area between the machines. Then we note b_k the stock capacity between machine M_k and machine M_{k+1}.
- **recrc** (recirculation) is a constraint which indicates that a job may be processed several times on the same machine.
- $\mathbf{unavail}_j$ translates the case where all the resources are not available all the time, but only during well defined periods. It is a matter of timetables translating periods of opening/closing of the factory, periods of planned maintenance, of holidays, *etc.* Two types of operations can be associated

with this problem: interruption and resumption of an operation as soon as possible (**unavail$_j$-resumable**) or else the operation is not started if it is going to be interrupted (**unavail$_j$-nonresumable**). In the latter case we can have problems of unfeasibility.

We now state the difference between *routing* and *precedence constraints*:

- a routing is a document which precisely describes the set of operations necessary for ending up with a final product: machine, processing time, tools, particular conditions, *etc.* This routing contains, of course, the order in which the operations must be processed, possibly with the help of a precedence graph (in the case of non identical routings). Two successive operations in a routing indicate a flow of material between machines or a set of machines.
- precedence relations between operations indicate simply that the start of an operation is conditioned by the end of all the preceding operations. No notion of flow is attached, a priori, to this constraint and it may simply be a matter of severe technological constraints. Two operations linked by a precedence relation may correspond to two distinct jobs.

In computer systems this distinction does not really exist since the routing of a job does not have a strong sense as in production systems. We have only a set of operations to schedule knowing that these ones can be connected by precedence constraints. Often it is assumed that these constraints are associated to communication times between the operations. We can also consider the existence of a communication media, or server, thus inducing disjunctive constraints.

1.5 Optimality criteria

In order to evaluate schedules we can use a certain number of criteria. Occasionally we want a criterion to be close to a certain reference value. Here we are at the frontier between the notions of criteria and constraints. If a constraint represents a fact which definitely must be respected, optimising a criterion allows rather a certain degree of freedom. For example, stating that no job should be late regarding its due date leaves no margin in the schedule calculation. We may even find a situation where no feasible schedule exists. On the other hand, minimising the number of late jobs allows us to guarantee that there will always be a solution even though to achieve this certain operations might be late. From a practical point of view the difference between a criterion and a constraint is only apparent to the decision maker who initiates a schedule calculated by an algorithm.
Certain criteria are equivalent and that is why they are presented jointly: minimising one or the other leads to the same optimal solution even if the criterion value is not the same in the two cases. Some scheduling problems

have no criterion to be minimised. In this case we are dealing with a feasibility problem, also called a decision problem: does a solution which satisfies the constraints exist ?

We can classify criteria into two large families: "*minimax*" criteria, which represent the maximum value of a set of functions to be minimised, and "*minisum*" criteria, which represent a sum of functions to be minimised. A summary of the criteria presented below is given in appendix A.

1.5.1 Minimisation of a maximum function: "minimax" criteria

We present "minimax" criteria which are most frequently met in the literature. The most traditional is without doubt the criterion measuring the completion time of the whole jobs. This criterion is denoted by C_{max} and is called *"makespan"*. We define $C_{\max} = \max_{i=1,...,n}(C_i)$, with C_i being the completion time of the job J_i. To simplify the notation, we write "max" for "$\max_{i=1,...,n}$" when there is no possible ambiguity. $C_{\max}$ is the total length or duration of a schedule, *i.e.* it is the completion time of the last scheduled job.

We also encounter other criteria based solely on the completion times of jobs, such as criteria:

- $F_{\max} = \max(F_i)$ with $F_i = C_i - r_i$: the maximum time spent in the shop, or even yet, the duration of resting, with r_i the release date of the job J_i,
- $I_{\max} = \max(I_k)$: with I_k the sum of idle times on resource M_k.

Equally, we encounter in the literature criteria which are based on the due dates d_i, $\forall i = 1, ..., n$, of jobs. Notably, we find criteria:

- $L_{\max} = \max(L_i)$ with $L_i = C_i - d_i$: the maximum lateness,
- $T_{\max} = \max(T_i)$ with $T_i = \max(0; C_i - d_i)$: the maximum tardiness,
- $E_{\max} = \max(E_i)$ with $E_i = \max(0; d_i - C_i)$: the maximum earliness.

Generally, f_{max} refers to an ordinary "minimax" criterion, which is a non decreasing function of the completion times of jobs. This is not the case for the criterion E_{max}.

1.5.2 Minimisation of a sum function: "minisum" criteria

"Minisum" criteria are usually more difficult to optimise than "minimax" criteria. This is confirmed from a theoretical point of view for certain special problems ([Ehrgott, 1997]). We write "$\sum$" for "$\sum_{i=1}^{n}$" when there is no ambiguity. Among the minisum criteria, we meet criteria:

- $\overline{C}$ to designate $\frac{1}{n}\sum C_i$ or $\sum C_i$. This criterion represents the average completion time or total completion time of jobs.
- $\overline{C}^w$ to designate $\frac{1}{n}\sum w_iC_i$, $\frac{1}{\sum w_i}\sum w_iC_i$ or else $\sum w_iC_i$. This criterion represents the average weighted completion time or total weighted completion time of jobs.
- $\overline{F}$ to designate $\frac{1}{n}\sum F_i$ or $\sum F_i$. Optimising this criterion is equivalent to optimising the criterion $\overline{C}$. It is the same for the criterion $\overline{F}^w$ regarding to the criterion $\overline{C}^w$.
- $\overline{T}$ to designate $\frac{1}{n}\sum T_i$ or $\sum T_i$. This criterion designates the average tardiness or total tardiness of jobs.
- $\overline{T}^w$ to designate $\frac{1}{n}\sum w_iT_i$, $\frac{1}{\sum w_i}\sum w_iT_i$ or $\sum w_iT_i$. This criterion designates the average weighted tardiness or total weighted tardiness of jobs.
- $\overline{U}$ to designate $\sum U_i$ which is the number of late jobs with $U_i = 1$ if the job J_i is late and 0 otherwise.
- $\overline{U}^w$ to designate $\frac{1}{n}\sum w_iU_i$, $\frac{1}{\sum w_i}\sum w_iU_i$or $\sum w_iU_i$ which is the weighted number of late jobs.
- $\overline{E}$ is the average earliness of jobs.
- $\overline{E}^w$ the average weighted earliness of jobs.

In a general way, $\overline{f}$ designates an ordinary "minisum" criterion which is usually a non decreasing function of the completion times of jobs. This is not the case for criterion $\overline{E}$.

1.6 Typologies and notation of problems

Concerning scheduling problems, we distinguish between their typology and their notation. A typology is a classification of the problems according to their nature. In scheduling it is usually based on the machines environment and on the jobs particularities. A notation enables us to refer quickly to a problem. Thus it is possible to construct a database of the set of problems treated in the literature. The traditional notations in scheduling are clearly based on existing typologies.

1.6.1 Typologies of problems

Different typologies of scheduling problems exist in the literature. We present in figure 1.1 a typology which generalises that of [Mac Carthy and Liu, 1993] and which brings together the problems introduced in section 1.3.

Concerning *scheduling problems*, the objective is to determine a sequence on each machine and a start time for each operation. In *scheduling and assignment problems with stages* we can define, independently of each operation, *stages* of machines. A machine belongs to only one stage. Then, we combine

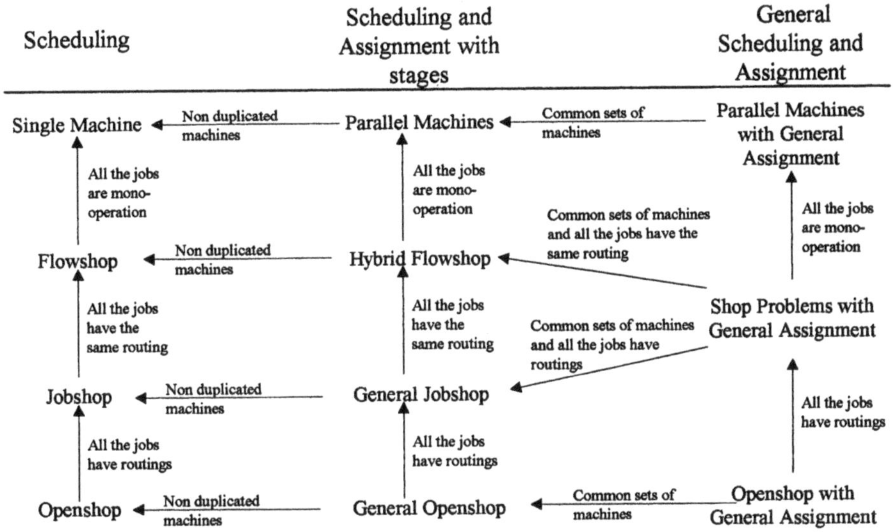

Fig. 1.1. Typology of scheduling problems (1)

each operation with a stage, and an operation can be processed by any machine of its stage. Therefore, we add an assignment problem to the initial scheduling problem. We must then not only find a start time for the operations but also an assignment of the operations on the machines. The same is true for *general scheduling and assignment problems* where a set or *pool* of machines is detailed for each operation. Of course, a machine may participate in several pools. An operation may be processed by any machine in its pool.

The foregoing typology uses the machines environment and operations to differentiate between problems. Other typologies exist ([Blazewicz et al., 1986]). Notably, we can consider problems according to different characteristics (figure 1.2):

1. *deterministic vs. stochastic.* In the case where all the characteristics of the problem (processing time of each operation, release dates, *etc.*) are well known, we speak of a *deterministic* problem. Conversely, some of these characteristics may be random variables of known probability law. In this case we speak of a *stochastic* problem (see [Pinedo, 1995]).
2. *unitary vs. repetitive.* If the operations appear to be cyclical, we are dealing with a *repetitive* problem. Conversely, if each operation corresponds to a unique product the problem is said to be *unitary.*
3. *static vs. dynamic.* If all the data of the problem are known at the same time we speak of a *static* problem. For some problems, a schedule may have been calculated and being processed when new operations arrive in

the system. Then the foregoing schedule has to be re-established in "real time". These problems are said to be *dynamic.*

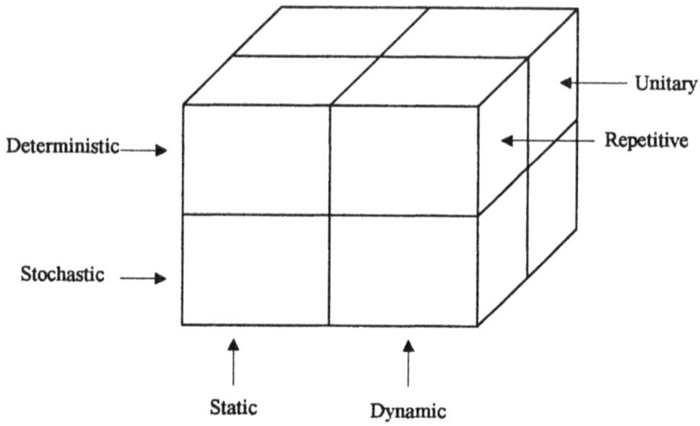

Fig. 1.2. Typology of scheduling problems (2)

These two typologies are complementary since it is possible to handle, for example, a deterministic flowshop problem, whether it be unitary or static. As we shall see in the following section, traditional notation of scheduling problems are the mirror image of these typologies.

1.6.2 Notation of problems

Two notations exist for referencing scheduling problems. Despite the fact that the oldest was proposed by [Conway et al., 1967], the notation most used in the literature was introduced by [Graham et al., 1979] (see a detailed description in [Blazewicz et al., 1996]). This notation is divided into three fields: $\alpha|\beta|\gamma$.

Field α refers to the typology presented in figure 1.1 and describes the structure of the problem (see section 1.3). It breaks down into two fields: $\alpha = \alpha_1\alpha_2$. The values of α_1 and α_2 refer to the machines environment of the problem and possibly to the number of available machines.

Field β contains the explicit constraints of the problem. See section 1.4 for some possible such constraints.

Field γ contains the criterion/criteria to be optimised (see section 1.5). Concerning a more complete presentation of the different possible criteria, the interested reader may refer to [Rinnooy Kan, 1976]. This field is detailed in chapter 4 for the multicriteria case. Appendix A presents a summary of the most current values which can take the fields α, β, and γ.

[Vignier et al., 1999] propose an extension of the notation for hybrid flowshop problems. For these ones the field α breaks down as follows: $\alpha = \alpha_1\alpha_2, (\alpha_3\alpha_4^{(\ell)})_{\ell=1}^{\alpha_2}$. The values $\alpha_3\alpha_4^{(\ell)}$ represent the configuration of each stage. Other extensions of the notation exist. We can quote works, notably the one of [Baptiste et al., 2001] who broaden the notation to hoist scheduling problems. When we address problems where machines are of the type *"batch"*, [Jolai Ghazvini, 1998] and [Oulamara, 2001] similarly propose an extension of the notation.

1.7 Project scheduling problems

Project scheduling problems have been extensively studied in the literature. They are usually separated from problems occuring in shop environments, since they have their own particularities. Several papers review the literature on project scheduling (see [Herroelen et al., 1998a], [Herroelen et al., 1998b], [Brucker et al., 1999], [Kolisch and Padman, 2001], [Tavares, 2002]).

In project scheduling problems we consider the scheduling of a set of operations which are also called *activities*. Each operation has a processing time and the operations are connected by precedence constraints. These ones are usually represented by an "activity-on-the-node" network, where an edge represents a finish-start precedence relationship between two operations. To process the operations we distinguish between two situations.
When the operations can be performed without any resource, we meet two classical problems in the literature. In the first one we have to compute a schedule of the operations which minimises the completion time of the whole project, also called makespan. In the second problem we associate to each operation a cash flow value and we compute a schedule which maximises the net present value of the project.
When operations require resources, we deal with a Resource-Constrained Project Scheduling Problem (RCPSP). We can distinguish between the renewable resources, the non-renewable resources, the partially renewable resources (these are renewable ones during a known time period) and the doubly constrained resources (these are non-renewable resources with the added limitation of consumption for known time periods). Besides, we associate to each resource, whatever its type, a limited capacity per time unit and each operation requires one or several resources in known amounts. In the basic RCPSP we have only renewable resources and the problem is to minimise the makespan. This problem is a generalisation of the jobshop scheduling problem with makespan minimisation. We can consider extensions of this basic problem by allowing the preemption of operations, or by imposing time

lags between the processing of two consecutive operations. Another classical extension of the basic RCPSP consists in defining for each operation a minimum and a maximum processing time. This is related to the presence of at least one non-renewable resource. The more we use of this resource to process an operation, the lower is its processing time. Therefore, the exact processing time of each operation has to be calculated. The aim is to minimise the total requirement of the non-renewable resources, or if this total requirement is limited, to minimise the makespan of the project. A presentation of other classical models can be found in [Herroelen et al., 1998b].

Various extensions to the three-field notation presented in section 1.6.2 exist. The two major are due to [Herroelen et al., 1998b] and [Herroelen et al., 2001] for the first extension and [Brucker et al., 1999] for the second one.

1.8 Some fundamental notions

The notions which are presented in this section refer to the characterisation of *dominant* sets for certain scheduling problems. We say that a subset of schedules is *dominant* for a problem if and only if, whatever the data of the problem, an optimal solution is contained in this subset. Definition 1 introduces the notion of regular criterion in the case of a minimisation problem.

Definition 1
Let S be the set of solutions. A criterion Z is a regular criterion if and only if Z is an increasing function of the completion times of jobs, i.e. if and only if:

$$\forall x, y \in \mathcal{S},\ C_i(x) \leq C_i(y),\ \forall i = 1, ..., n,$$
$$\Rightarrow Z(C_1(x), \ldots, C_n(x)) \leq Z(C_1(y), \ldots, C_n(y))$$

For the criteria presented in section 1.5, we deduce the following result, which is not difficult to prove.

Corollary 1
The criteria C_{max}, $\overline{C}$, $\overline{C}^w$, L_{max}, T_{max}, $\overline{T}$, $\overline{T}^w$, $\overline{U}$ and $\overline{U}^w$ are regular. The criteria I_{max}, E_{max}, $\overline{E}$ and $\overline{E}^w$ are not regular.

We distinguish four classes of schedules (figure 1.3). The schedules *with insertion of machine idle times* constitute an interesting class for the minimisation of certain non regular criteria. This is the case for many Just-in-Time scheduling problems.

Definition 2
A schedule belongs to the class of schedules with insertion of machine idle times if and only if before each scheduled operation, the machines are voluntarily left idle during a positive or null period.

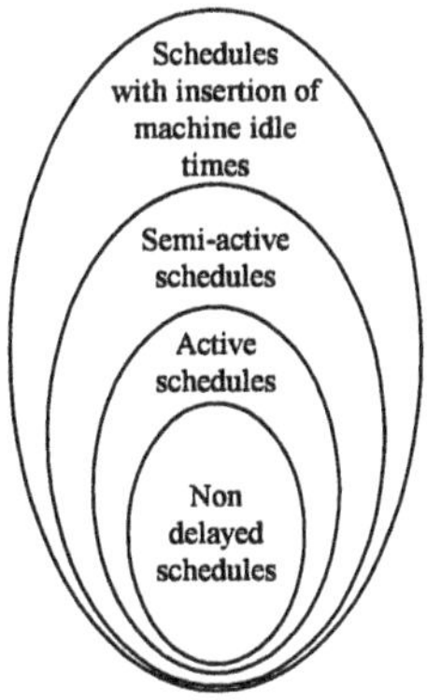

Fig. 1.3. Inclusion of classes of schedules

Some examples of schedules with insertion of machine idle times are presented in figures 1.4a, 1.4b and 1.4c.

Definition 3
Let $x \in S$ be a schedule and S_x be the set of schedules having the same sequences of operations on the machines as x. A schedule x belongs to the class of semi-active schedules if and only if $\nexists y \in S_x$ such that $C_i(y) \leq C_i(x)$, $\forall i = 1, ..., n$, with at least one strict inequality.

We note that the class of *semi-active* schedules is a subclass of the class of schedules with insertion of machine idle times. We say that the semi-active schedules are "left shifted". Figures 1.4b and 1.4c present some semi-active schedules.

Definition 4
A schedule $x \in S$ belongs to the class of active schedules if and only if $\nexists y \in S$ such that $C_i(y) \leq C_i(x)$, $\forall i = 1, ..., n$, with at least one strict inequality.

Active schedules are equally semi-active. Figure 1.4c presents an active schedule. We say also that a schedule is active if it is impossible to start earlier the processing of an operation without delaying another. We can note that the definition of active schedules may be interpreted from a multicriteria point of view: the class of active schedules is the set of solutions which are not dominated for the n completion times C_i.

Definition 5
A schedule $x \in S$ belongs to the class of non delayed schedules if and only if no operation is kept waiting while a machine is available to process it.

Non delayed schedules are equally active schedules. Figure 1.4c presents a non delayed schedule. One important result, presented in lemma 1, relates regular criteria to the class of active schedules.

A P2|prec|C_{max} problem

J_i	p_i
J_1	3
J_2	6
J_3	1
J_4	5
J_5	4

- data -

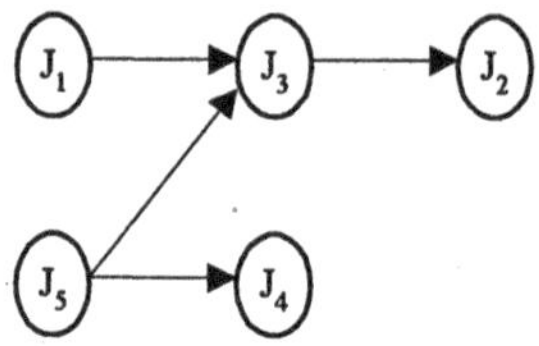

- precedences between jobs -

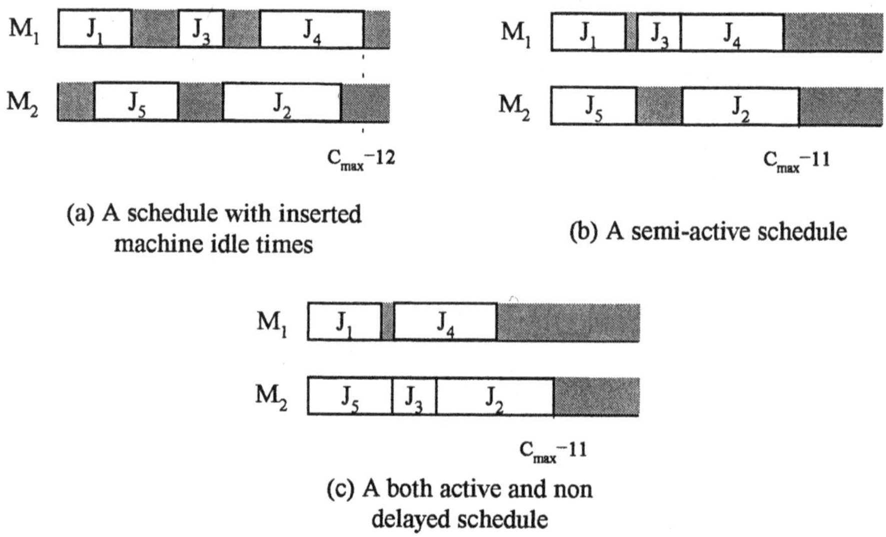

Fig. 1.4. Illustration of different classes of schedules

Lemma 1 *[Baker, 1974]*
For optimisation problems of a regular criterion, the set of active schedules is dominant.

Lemma 1 implies that the search for an optimal solution of the optimisation problem of a regular criterion, may be limited to the set of active schedules. For multicriteria problems this result remains equally true if we optimise several regular criteria. However, it becomes invalid if at least one criterion is not regular, since this is the case for some problems where criteria $\overline{E}$ and $\overline{T}$ are minimised. This is the case in Just-in-Time scheduling.

1.9 Basic scheduling algorithms

This section is intended to present some of the basic scheduling algorithms for single criterion problems. These algorithms are referred to throughout the book. More complex algorithms can be found in books dedicated to scheduling (see for instance [Tanaev et al., 1994a], [Tanaev et al., 1994b], [Pinedo, 1995], [Blazewicz et al., 1996] and [Brucker, 2004]).

1.9.1 Scheduling rules

Several scheduling rules, optimal or heuristic, have been proposed in the literature. They are very often used in heuristic applications to industrial problems, given their simplicity and the little calculation time which they require ([Morton and Pentico, 1993]). Among the most traditional rules, we find the rule SPT which enables us to compute an optimal active schedule for the $1||\overline{C}$ problem.
Rule SPT: (*Shortest Processing Time first*) sequences the jobs in increasing order of their processing time.

The converse rule is the rule LPT (*Longest Processing Time first*). The $1||\overline{C}^w$ problem is solved optimally with the rule WSPT.
Rule WSPT: (*Weighted Shortest Processing Time first*) sequences the jobs in increasing order of their ratio p_i/w_i.

When we consider the due dates and the minimisation of criterion L_{max}, the corresponding single machine problem denoted by $1|d_i|L_{max}$, can be solved optimally by calculating an active schedule using the rule EDD.
Rule EDD: (*Earliest Due Date first*) sequences the jobs in increasing order of their due date d_i.
We notice that this rule also solves the $1|d_i|T_{max}$ problem optimally.

Addition of the release dates r_i, $i = 1, ..., n$, of the jobs no longer enables us to solve these problems optimally by simply considering an adaptation of these rules. For example, the rule EST (*Earliest Start Time first*) sequences the jobs in increasing order of their earliest start time, and breaks ties in favour of the job with the smallest processing time. This rule does not solve optimally the $1|r_i|\overline{C}$ problem. Likewise, no simple sort based on the weights, the processing times or the due dates, can solve optimally the $1|r_i|\overline{C}^w$ and $1|r_i, d_i|L_{max}$ problems, since these problems are $\mathcal{NP}$-hard.

Generalisation of these rules to parallel machines problems necessitates the addition of a job assignment rule to the machines. In the case of identical machines, we generally use the assignment rule FAM (*First Available Machine first*), which assigns a job to the first available machine. The rule SPT-FAM solves optimally the $P||\overline{C}$ problem by considering the jobs in the increasing order of their processing time, and assigning them in turn to the earliest available machine. The rules WSPT-FAM and EDD-FAM give way to the respective heuristic algorithms for the $P||\overline{C}^w$ and $P|d_i|L_{max}$ problems.
In the case of proportional machines, we often consider the assignment rule FM (*Fastest Machine first*) which consists of assigning a job to the fastest machine among those available. The rule SPT-FM solves optimally the $Q||\overline{C}$ problem. The rules WSPT-FM and EDD-FM give heuristic algorithms for the $Q||\overline{C}^w$ and $Q|d_i|L_{max}$ problems, respectively.

When preemption of jobs is authorised, the rule SPT-FM becomes SRPT-FM (*Shortest Remaining Processing Time on Fastest Machine first*) and solves optimally the $Q|pmtn|\overline{C}$ problem. It consists of scheduling the job with the smallest remaining processing time, on the fastest machine among those available, preempting when necessary. The rule LRPT-FM optimally solves the $Q|pmtn|C_{max}$ problem.

1.9.2 Some classical scheduling algorithms

Lawler's algorithm for the $1|prec|f_{max}$ problem

Consider the problem where n jobs have to be scheduled on a single machine. A set of precedence constraints between jobs is defined and no preemption is allowed. Let f_i be an increasing function of the completion time of J_i, $\forall i = 1, ..., n$. The objective is to minimise the maximum cost function defined by $f_{max} = \max_{i=1,...,n}(f_i(C_i))$. [Lawler, 1973] proposes an optimal polynomial time algorithm which iteratively schedules a job by starting from the last position. At the first iteration the jobs that have no successor are candidates and can therefore be scheduled in the last position. Notice that the completion time of the last position is equal to $\overline{P} = p_1+p_2+...+p_n$. Thus, we schedule in the last position the candidate job J_i which has the lowest cost $C_i(\overline{P})$ among the candidate jobs. By setting $\overline{P} = \overline{P} - p_i$ we can iterate this process for the previous position. The complete algorithm, denoted by EEL1, is presented in figure 1.5.

```
ALGORITHM EEL1
/* T is the set of jobs to schedule */
S = ∅;
P̄ = Σ_{i=1}^{n} p_i;
For i = n down to 1 Do
    F = {J_i ∈ T / J_i has no successor in T};
    If (F = ∅) Then
        The problem is not feasible;
    End If;
    Let J_ℓ ∈ F be such that f_ℓ(P̄) = min_{J_k ∈ F} (f_k(P̄));
    /* Break ties by choosing the job with the greatest processing time */
    S = {J_ℓ}//S;
    T = T − {J_ℓ};
    C_ℓ = P̄;
    P̄ = P̄ − p_ℓ;
End For;
Print S;
[Lawler, 1973]
```

Fig. 1.5. An optimal algorithm for the $1|prec|f_{max}$ problem

Moore's algorithm for the $1|d_i|\overline{U}$ problem

Consider the problem where n jobs have to be scheduled on a single machine and each job J_i has a due date d_i. No preemption is allowed. The objective is to minimise the number of late jobs, denoted by $\overline{U}$. [Moore, 1968] provides an optimal polynomial time algorithm to solve this problem. It starts with the schedule obtained by the rule EDD. Let J_k be the first tardy job in this schedule, *i.e.* all jobs scheduled before are early or on time. Moore's algorithm puts J_k on time by removing the preceding job with the greatest processing time. The latter is scheduled late and is not considered anymore. This process is iterated until we have no late jobs in the schedule, except those which have been previously removed and voluntarily put late. The number of late jobs is equal to the number of removed jobs. The algorithm, denoted by EJM1, is presented in figure 1.6.

```
ALGORITHM EJM1
/* T is the set of jobs to schedule */
/* We assume that d_1 ≤ d_2 ≤ ... ≤ d_n */
S = (J_1, J_2, ..., J_n);
Tardy = ∅;
While (∃J_ℓ ∈ S such that C_ℓ > d_ℓ) Do
    Let k be such that C_S[k] > d_S[k] and ∀i < k, C_S[i] ≤ d_S[i];
    Let j be such that j ≤ k and p_S[j] = max_{i=1,...,k} (p_S[i]);
    S = S − {J_j};
    Tardy = Tardy//{J_j};
End While;
Ū = |Tardy|;
Print S//Tardy and Ū;
[Moore, 1968]
```

Fig. 1.6. An optimal algorithm for the $1|d_i|\overline{U}$ problem

Johnson's algorithm for the $F2|prmu|C_{max}$ problem

Consider a two-machine flowshop problem where n jobs have to be scheduled. They first have to be processed on machine M_1 and next on machine M_2. As the makespan criterion is a regular criterion we are restricted to the set of permutation schedules which is a dominant set. [Johnson, 1954] proposes a sufficient condition of optimality and derives an $O(n\log(n))$ time optimal algorithm. It proceeds by scheduling first the jobs such that $p_{i,1} < p_{i,2}$ according to the increasing order of the $p_{i,1}$'s. The remaining jobs are scheduled last according to the decreasing order of the $p_{i,2}$'s. This algorithm, denoted by ESJ1, is presented in figure 1.7. It is often also referred to as algorithm J.

```
ALGORITHM ESJ1
/* T is the set of jobs to schedule */
Let U = {J_i ∈ T/p_i,1 < p_i,2};
Let V = {J_i ∈ T/p_i,1 ≥ p_i,2};
Sort U by increasing values of the values p_i,1;
Sort V by decreasing values of the values p_i,2;
S = U//V;
C*_max = C_max(S);
Print S and C*_max;
[Johnson, 1954]
```

Fig. 1.7. An optimal algorithm for the $F2|prmu|C_{max}$ problem

Campbell, Dudek and Smith's heuristic for the $F|prmu|C_{max}$ problem

Consider a flowshop problem where n jobs have to be scheduled on m machines. The jobs have the same routing, and we assume that they are first processed on machine M_1, next on machine M_2, *etc.* Even if the set of permutation schedules is not dominant for this problem, [Campbell et al., 1970] restrict to this set and propose an heuristic to minimise the makespan criterion. This algorithm proceeds by building $(m-1)$ fictitious two-machine problems and by solving each one using Johnson's algorithm ([Johnson, 1954]). Therefore at most $(m-1)$ distinct permutation schedules are built. The best one regarding the m-machine problem is retained. This detailed heuristic, denoted by HCDS1, is presented in figure 1.8.

```
ALGORITHM HCDS1
/* T is the set of jobs to schedule */
/* J refers to Johnson's algorithm */
For j = 1 to (m − 1) Do
   | /* Building of a fictitious two-machine problem */
   | p'_{i,1} = Σ_{k=1}^{j} p_{i,k} and p'_{i,2} = Σ_{k=m−j+1}^{m} p_{i,k};
   | Let S^j be the sequence obtained by algorithm ESJ1 on
   |     the fictitious problem;
End For;
Let S^ℓ be the schedule such that C_max(S^ℓ) = min_{j=1,...,(m−1)} (C_max(S^j));
/* Notice that the makespan is calculated by considering the m machines */
Print S^ℓ and C_max(S^ℓ);
[Campbell et al., 1970]
```

Fig. 1.8. An heuristic algorithm for the $F|prmu|C_{max}$ problem

Nawaz, Enscore and Ham's heuristic for the $F|prmu|C_{max}$ problem

[Nawaz et al., 1983] consider the same permutation flowshop problem as the one of Campbell, Dudek and Smith. They propose an heuristic based on a job-insertion scheme. Initially, the jobs are sorted by decreasing sums of processing times on the machines, *i.e.* by decreasing order of the values $\sum_{j=1}^{m} p_{i,j}$. The heuristic considers only the two first jobs and retains the permutation schedule, among the two possible ones, which has a minimal value of criterion C_{max}. This is the starting partial schedule. It next inserts the third job of the initial sorting, by trying all the possible positions in the partial schedule. The one which has a minimal makespan value is retained. This process is iterated until all the jobs are scheduled. The heuristic is presented in figure 1.9. Other classical algorithms for flowshop scheduling problems can be found in [Proust, 1992].

ALGORITHM HNEH1

/* T is the set of jobs to schedule */
/* We assume that $\sum_{j=1}^{m} p_{1,j} \geq ... \geq \sum_{j=1}^{m} p_{n,j}$ */
Let S be the best permutation schedule among (J_1, J_2) and (J_2, J_1);
<u>For</u> $i = 3$ <u>to</u> n <u>Do</u>
  /* Insertion of job J_i */
  $\forall k = 1, ..., |S|$, S^k is the partial schedule with job J_i inserted in position k in S;
  $\forall \ell = 1, ..., |S|$, let S^ℓ be such that $C_{max}(S^\ell) = \min_{k=1,...,|S|}(C_{max}(S^k))$;
  $S = S^\ell$;
<u>End For</u>;
<u>Print</u> S and $C_{max}(S)$;

[Nawaz et al., 1983]

Fig. 1.9. An heuristic algorithm for the $F|prmu|C_{max}$ problem

Sahni's algorithm for the $P|pmtn, \tilde{d}_i|-$ problem

Consider a scheduling problem where n independent jobs have to be scheduled on m parallel identical machines. Preemption of jobs is authorised but no job can simultaneously be processed by more than one machine. Each job J_i has associated with it a deadline $\tilde{d}_i$ and the aim is to compute a feasible schedule, if it exists. [Sahni, 1979] proposes an optimal algorithm to solve this problem. This algorithm, denoted by ESS1, is presented in figure 1.10. Notice that this problem can also be solved by reducing it to a network flow problem ([Horn, 1974]).

ALGORITHM ESS1

/* We assume that $\tilde{d}_1 \geq ... \geq \tilde{d}_n$ */
/* C_j^M: the completion time of the last job on M_j, $\forall j = 1, ..., m$ */
$C_j^M = 0, \forall j = 1, ..., m$;
<u>For</u> $i = 1$ <u>to</u> n <u>Do</u>
    /* We schedule job J_i */
    Let $L = \{j / C_j^M < \tilde{d}_i\}$;
    <u>If</u> $((L = \emptyset)$ <u>or</u> $(\tilde{d}_i - \min_{j \in L}(C_j^M) < p_i))$ <u>Then</u>
        <u>Print</u> "No feasible schedule exists";
        END
    <u>End If</u>;
    Let $k \in L$ be such that $C_k^M = \max_{j \in L}(C_j^M)$;
    <u>If</u> $(\tilde{d}_i - C_k^M \geq p_i)$ <u>Then</u>
        /* Job J_i is entirely scheduled on M_j */
        $C_k^M = C_k^M + p_i$;
    <u>Else</u>
        /* Job J_i is processed by more than one machine */
        Let $L_1 = \{j \in L / \tilde{d}_i - C_j^M < p_i\}$;
        Let $L_2 = \{j \in L / \tilde{d}_i - C_j^M \geq p_i\}$;
        Let $\alpha \in L_2$ be such that $C_\alpha^M = \max_{j \in L_2}(C_j^M)$;
        Let $\beta \in L_1$ be such that $C_\beta^M = \min_{j \in L_1}(C_j^M)$;
        $C_\alpha^M = C_\alpha^M + (p_i - \tilde{d}_i + C_\beta^M)$;
        $C_\beta^M = \tilde{d}_i$;
    <u>End If</u>;
<u>End For</u>;
<u>Print</u> the calculated schedule;

[Sahni, 1979]

Fig. 1.10. An optimal algorithm for the $P|pmtn, \tilde{d}_i|-$ problem

2. Complexity of problems and algorithms

This chapter presents an introduction to the theory of complexity. Decision problems, optimisation problems, couting problems and enumeration problems are defined, and complexity classes associated to these problems are introduced. These classes aim at qualifying the difficulty of solving problems. We first start with some considerations on the complexity of solution algorithms.

2.1 Complexity of algorithms

The complexity of an algorithm lies in estimating its processing cost in time (time complexity) or in the required space memory (spatial complexity). Set apart for certain particular algorithms, as for example dynamic programming algorithms which usually take up a lot of memory space, spatial complexity has been less considered than time complexity. In both cases it is possible to propose a *theoretical* complexity and a *practical* complexity. Theoretical complexity reflects an independent estimate on the machine which processes the algorithm. It is less accurate than the practical complexity which enables us to calculate the cost of the algorithm for a given computer. For the latter case, time complexity is obtained using an estimation of the calculation time for each instruction of the program. The advantage of theoretical complexity is that it provides an estimation independent of the calculation time for the machine.

In the remainder of this section we use the term *complexity* to refer to the time complexity of an algorithm. This complexity is established by calculating the number of iterations done by the algorithm during its processing. The number of iterations depends on the size of the data, noted *Length*, and possibly the magnitude of the largest element, noted Max, belonging to these data. If the number of iterations is bounded by a polynomial function of *Length* then the algorithm is of polynomial complexity. If this function is limited by a polynomial of Max and *Length*, then we say that the algorithm is of pseudo-polynomial complexity. In other cases the algorithm is said to be of exponential complexity.

More precisely, we can distinguish minimal, average, and maximal complexities in order to translate complexity in the best case, the average case or in the worst case respectively. These latter two actually are interesting and the easiest to calculate is maximal complexity. On the other hand, average complexity requires a statistical analysis of the processing of the algorithm by function of the input data.

Example.
We can illustrate these notions by the example presented in figure 2.1. The maximum number of iterations is equal to n and the minimum number to 1. The average complexity itself depends on the probability p that the element is found in a given position. We suppose that this probability follows a uniform law, *i.e.* $p = \frac{1}{n}$. Thus, the average complexity is equal to $p(1+2+3+\ldots+n) = \frac{n(n+1)}{2n} = \frac{n+1}{2}$. We notice that the calculation is only valid if we are sure that the element belongs to the list. In the opposite case, the calculation of the average complexity is even more complicated as it causes the law of generation of the elements of the list to intervene.

Search for an element belonging to a list

/* *elt* the searched element */
/* *n* is the list size */
/* *list* is the list of elements */
/* We assume that *elt* belongs to the list */
$i = 0$;
While ($elt \neq list[i]$) Do
    $i = i + 1$;
End While;

Fig. 2.1. Search for an element in a non sorted list

To calculate the complexity of an algorithm, it is possible either to count the number of iterations, as we have done in the above example, or to break up the algorithm into sub-algorithms of known complexity. In this latter case, we can multiply or add the complexities according to the structure of the program. By using the above example, we can propose an algorithm which searches k elements in a list. Its average and maximal complexities are then of the order of $k \times n$. In the case of spatial complexity, the calculation cannot be performed on the algorithm itself -we cannot count the number of iterations- but rather on the data it uses.

The theoretical complexity of an algorithm is usually a function of Max, of *Length* and of addition and multiplying constants. Very often, we resume this complexity by the expression of the term which gives its asymptotic value. For example, if the maximal complexity of an algorithm is $Max^b + a \times Length + c$, we say that it is in $O(Max^b + Length)$. More precisely, the notation $O(b)$ means that the complexity has an upper limit set by a linear function in b whereas the notation $\Theta(b)$ enables to specify that the complexity is equivalent to b. The simplification by the notation $O(b)$ may lead to paradoxical situations. In effect, an algorithm A in $O(Max^2)$ may be slower than an algorithm B in $O(2^{Max})$ for certain problems. Let us take, for example a scheduling problem where Max is the number of jobs n and let us suppose that the complexity of the algorithm A is $2^{1000}n^2$ and that of the algorithm B is 2^n. It is then obvious that for $n \leq 1000$, the algorithm A causes more iterations than the algorithm B. This remark does not imply that the theoretical complexity of an algorithm is lacking in interest. Indeed, algorithm A remains more sensitive to the calculating machines than algorithm B since between two machines of different power, algorithm B attaches little difference regarding the size of the largest problem it can solve, which is not the case with algorithm A.

We give in table 2.1 the complexities of the best algorithms available to solve some classical problems. Notice that for those examples the average complexity is equal to the maximal complexity.

Table 2.1. Some types of algorithms and their complexity

Algorithm to...	**Maximal complexity**
Search an element belonging to a list of n elements	$O(n)$
Add an element in a non sorted list of n elements	$O(1)$
Add an element in a sorted list of n elements	$O(n)$
Perform a dichotomic search in an interval $[\min; \max]$ of integer values	$O(\log(\max - \min))$
Sort a list of n elements (fusion sort)	$O(n \log(n))$

The complexity of a well written algorithm may sometimes be improved to the detriment of the spatial complexity: it is possible to reduce the computational time of an algorithm by increasing the size of the data. However, such a step often leads to adding new functions uniquely dedicated to the management of these data.

So, the equilibrium to find is between the size of the used data and the complexity of the algorithm. It is clear that this complexity cannot be indefinitely broken down in order to get at the end an algorithm which complexity is null. Solving a problem implies a minimum algorithmic complexity. But what is the minimum algorithmic complexity required to solve a given problem ? The algorithm provided in figure 2.1 solves the problem of searching an element in a non sorted list in $O(n)$ time, which is equivalent to say that it is solvable in a polynomial time of the size n. Can we guarantee that this is the case for any problem, *i.e.* there always exists a polynomial time algorithm to solve it ? If the answer to this vaste question is *yes* then all problems are easy to solve: we just have to find the correct algorithm and solve it. Otherwise it means there are some problems which are intractable: do not think about solving in polynomial time these problems. In this case we are only able to solve small-size problems; for the bigger one we should let the computer running for hundred years ! Unfortunately we do not know the answer to the above question. This is quite confusing: given a problem on which we try unsuccessfully to design a polynomial time algorithm, must we continue in this way or should we give up because such an algorithm does not exist? Complexity theory provides useful elements to establish the complexity of problems. This theory assumes that there are some problems which can be solved in polynomial time whilst others cannot. Given this, complexity classes exist which help in deciding if we must look for a polynomial time algorithm or not. This is the matter of the next section.

2.2 Complexity of problems

Complexity theory proposes a set of results and methods to evaluate the intrinsic complexity of the problems. A problem belongs to a *class of complexity*, which informs us of the complexity of the "best algorithm" able to solve it.

Hence, if a given problem is shown to belong to the class of "easy" problems then it means that we are able to exhibit a polynomial time algorithm to solve it. Usually this is a good news but unfortunately this does not often happen for complex problems. Accordingly, if a problem belongs to the class of hard problems, it cannot be solved in polynomial time which, said differently, implies that for some instances the required CPU time to solve it becomes "exponential".

Along the years, numerous complexity classes have been defined and can be separated depending on the type of problems they address to. Basically we distinguish between decision problems, search and optimisation problems, and counting and enumeration problems. In this section we present these kinds of problems and provide the existing complexity classes. Notice that counting and enumeration problems are not often considered in the literature.

2.2.1 The complexity of decision problems

Complexity theory brings our attention to decision problems. Basically, the complexity classes presented in this section have been firstly dedicated to such problems. Complexity theory is based, at the roots, on language theory and Turing machines but can be presented less formally in terms of algorithms. The reader interested in a very detailed presentation of complexity theory is referred to [Garey and Johnson, 1979] or [Papadimitriou, 1995].

Let us first define a decision problem .

Decision problem Π:

- Input data , or instances, noted I. The set of all the instances is noted D_Π,
- Question such that for each instance $I \in D_\Pi$, the answer $R \in \{yes; no\}$.

The set of instances I for the problem Π, for which the answer to the question is *yes*, is noted Y_Π. It is possible to propose a grammar G equivalent to the problem Π, by encoding all the instances by an encoding scheme e (see figure 2.2). For example, with the binary coding scheme all the terminal and non terminal elements will be binary numbers. With set Y_Π of the decision problem, we can associate a set of chains produced by the grammar: the language $L(\Pi, e)$. Thus, we have transformed the decision problem into a grammar. If the answer to the question is *yes* for an instance, then the chain corresponding to this instance belongs to the language $L(\Pi, e)$. In order to know this, we propose a Turing machine. Taking the input chain, this machine exits in an accepting state if the chain belongs to $L(\Pi, e)$. We see that for the decision problem this Turing machine is equivalent to a "*Solve*" procedure which returns *true* or *false*. The complexity of a decision problem thus depends on the "best" Turing machine which we can propose. The encoding scheme used influences equally the efficiency of the proposable Turing machine. In general, we consider a reasonable encoding, *i.e.* which does not pointlessly complicate the obtained grammar. For all reasonable encoding schemes, the proposable Turing machines are judged equivalent ([Garey and Johnson, 1979]).

Before introducing the classes of problems, we must define for the decision problem Π two functions: *Length*$[I]$ and $Max[I]$, with $I \in D_\Pi$. The function *Length* represents the size of the instance I, *i.e.* the length of chains produced by the grammar G. The function Max enables us to know the magnitude of the instance I. In general, we consider that this function returns the magnitude of the largest integer, if it exists, occurring in I. For example, if $I = \{3; 4; 6; 8; 14\}$, we have *Length*$[I] = 5$ and $Max[I] = 14$. The functions *Length* and Max are supposed to be calculable in polynomial time. It is then possible to define several classes of problems according to the difficulty in finding an answer to the decision problem. The definition

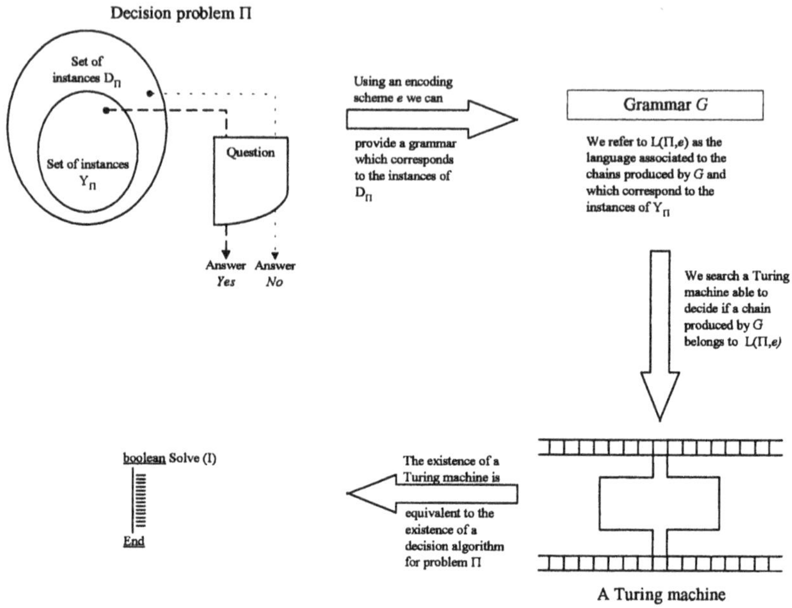

Fig. 2.2. Decision/grammar duality problem

of these classes requires the notion of deterministic and non deterministic Turing machines ([Hopcroft and Ullman, 1979]).

Definition 6
A decision problem Π belongs to the class $\mathcal{P}$ if the following holds: an encoding scheme e exists, such that for all instances I of Π, we can construct for the corresponding grammar a one-tape deterministic Turing machine, capable of checking if the chain corresponding to I belongs to the language. This is equivalent to a "yes" answer to the decision problem Π. In this case the resolution time is a polynomial function of Length[I].

This definition does not prevent the number of possible solutions from being exponential. We simply have the equivalence: a decision problem Π is in $\mathcal{P}$ if and only if an algorithm exists which enables us to calculate in polynomial time a solution which has the answer *yes*. Not all decision problems belong to the class $\mathcal{P}$. A more general class exists, which is introduced in the following definition.

Definition 7
A decision problem Π belongs to the class $\mathcal{NP}$ if a non deterministic polynomial one-tape Turing machine exists which reaches an accepting state in a finite number of iterations when it takes upon entry a chain of language $L(\Pi, e)$. The number of iterations is upper bounded by a polynomial function of Length.

A non deterministic polynomial one-tape Turing machine can be seen as a Turing machine having two modules: a divination module allowing us to construct a solution and an evaluation module capable of calculating if the answer R is *yes* in a time which is a polynomial function of *Length*. Obviously, we have $\mathcal{P} \subseteq \mathcal{NP}$. A conjecture in complexity theory which has never been demonstrated to this day, rests on the non inclusion of $\mathcal{NP}$ in $\mathcal{P}$. We suppose in the following that $\mathcal{P} \neq \mathcal{NP}$, which implies that decision problems which do not belong to $\mathcal{P}$ exist. This leads to the definition of the class $\mathcal{NPC}$ of $\mathcal{NP}$-complete problems, which is a sub-class of $\mathcal{NP}$. For this we must introduce the notion of polynomial reduction (or transformation), denoted by $\propto$.

Definition 8
A polynomial reduction $\propto$ of a decision problem Π' towards a decision problem Π is a function such that:

- *$\forall I'$ instance of Π', $\propto(I')$ is an instance of Π and is calculable in polynomial time.*
- *$\forall I'$ instance of Π', the answer for the instance I' is yes for the problem Π' if and only if the answer for the instance $\propto(I')$ is yes for the problem Π.*

This means that a deterministic one-tape Turing machine exists, which is capable of calculating $\propto$ starting with a chain x generated by the grammar G. Moreover, $x \in L(\Pi', e') \Leftrightarrow \propto(x) \in L(\Pi, e)$.
If we consider two decision problems Π and Π', $\Pi' \propto \Pi$ means that the problem Π' reduces polynomially towards the problem Π, which implies that Π is at least as difficult to solve as Π'.
A polynomial reduction, or transformation, of a problem Π' towards a problem Π can be seen as a function (in the algorithmic sense) which:

1. solves Π', *i.e.* which is able to verify if an instance I' of Π' leads to an answer *yes*.
2. to solve Π', transforms in polynomial time the instance I' in an instance I of Π, and calls a resolution function of Π. The answer returned by this last function is the answer to the problem Π'.

Definition 9
A problem Π is $\mathcal{NP}$-complete if and only if $\Pi \in \mathcal{NP}$ and $\forall \Pi' \in \mathcal{NP}$, $\exists \propto$ such that $\Pi' \propto \Pi$.

This definition implies that the class $\mathcal{NPC}$ of $\mathcal{NP}$-complete problems contains the most difficult problems to solve. Indeed, if an $\mathcal{NP}$-complete problem Π is solvable in polynomial time, then all the problems of $\mathcal{NP}$ are so since all reduce to Π, and therefore $\mathcal{P} = \mathcal{NP}$. We say that an $\mathcal{NP}$-complete problem is solvable in polynomial time if and only if $\mathcal{P}$=$\mathcal{NP}$. The first problem to have been demonstrated $\mathcal{NP}$-complete is due to [Cook, 1971]. In practice, to demonstrate that a problem Π is $\mathcal{NP}$-complete, it is sufficient to demonstrate either that:

1. $\Pi \in \mathcal{NP}$ and that a polynomial reduction $\propto$ and an $\mathcal{NP}$-complete problem Π' exist such that $\Pi' \propto \Pi$, or that
2. there exists an $\mathcal{NP}$-complete sub-problem Π' of Π. Π' is a sub-problem of Π if and only if:
   - Π and Π' have the same question.
   - the set of instances of Π' is included in the set of instances of Π.
   - the set of instances of Π' for which the answer is *yes* is included in the set of instances of Π for which the answer is *yes*.

In the class of $\mathcal{NP}$-complete problems we can distinguish two types of problems: problems $\mathcal{NP}$-complete in the weak sense (or ordinary sense) and problems $\mathcal{NP}$-complete in the strong sense.

Definition 10
A problem Π is weakly $\mathcal{NP}$-complete if it is $\mathcal{NP}$-complete and if it is possible to find an algorithm to solve it such that its complexity is a polynomial function of $Max[I]$ and of $Length[I]$, $\forall I$ instance of Π. We say then that Π is solvable in pseudo-polynomial time.

If an $\mathcal{NP}$-complete problem Π is such that p a polynomial function of *Length* exists, for which $\forall I$ instance of Π, $Max[I] \leq p(Length[I])$, then Π cannot be solved by a pseudo-polynomial time algorithm. Otherwise, this pseudo-polynomial algorithm would be a polynomial algorithm, which contradicts the fact that Π is $\mathcal{NP}$-complete. If such a polynomial p exists, then we say that Π is $\mathcal{NP}$-complete in the strong sense. If p does not exist, then Π is called a *number problem*.

More precisely, the definition of strong $\mathcal{NP}$-completeness can be introduced, extending this result.

Definition 11
Let Π be a decision problem and p a polynomial defined over a set of integer values. We define Π_p the sub-problem of Π which is such that:

1. *The set of instances of Π_p, denoted by D_Π^p, is included in D_Π.*
2. *$\forall I \in D_\Pi^p$, $Max[I] \leq p(Length[i])$.*

The problem Π is $\mathcal{NP}$-complete in the strong sense if:

1. *$\Pi \in \mathcal{NP}$.*
2. *A polynomial p exists such that Π_p is $\mathcal{NP}$-complete.*

A decision problem Π is weakly $\mathcal{NP}$-complete if we can show either that:

1. Π is $\mathcal{NP}$-complete and there exists an algorithm that solves it requiring a computational time upper bounded by a polynomial of $Max[I]$ and $Length[I]$ for every instance I, or that
2. Π is $\mathcal{NP}$-complete and a polynomial reduction $\propto$ of Π exists towards a weakly $\mathcal{NP}$-complete problem Π', or that

3. Π is $\mathcal{NP}$-complete and Π is a sub-problem of a weakly $\mathcal{NP}$-complete problem.

It is different to show that a problem is strongly $\mathcal{NP}$-hard. As for proving $\mathcal{NP}$-completeness in the weak sense, suppose that we have a known strongly $\mathcal{NP}$-complete problem Π' and a polynomial time reduction $\propto$ such that $\Pi' \propto \Pi$. It is not possible to conclude that Π is strongly $\mathcal{NP}$-complete for the following reasons. We note $D_{\Pi}^{\propto} = \{\propto (I'), \forall I' \in D_{\Pi'}\}$. Two cases can occur:

1. A polynomial p exists such that $\forall I \in D_{\Pi}^{\propto}$, $Max[I] \leq p(Length[I])$.
2. A polynomial p does not exist such that $\forall I \in D_{\Pi}^{\propto}$, $Max[I] \leq p(Length[I])$.

In the first case, the corresponding problem Π_p is necessarily strongly $\mathcal{NP}$-complete, otherwise we have found a polynomial time algorithm to solve problem Π'.
In the second case, Π_p is a number problem. Thus, we cannot decide if Π is strongly $\mathcal{NP}$-complete. Therefore, to establish strong $\mathcal{NP}$-completeness we have to consider special reductions. A pseudo-polynomial reduction is one such special reduction and is defined below.

Definition 12
A pseudo-polynomial reduction from a decision problem Π' towards a decision problem Π is a function $\propto_s$ such that:

1. $\forall I' \in D_{\Pi'}$, $I' \in Y_{\Pi'}$ *if and only if* $\propto_s (I') \in Y_{\Pi}$.
2. $\propto_s$ *can be calculated in polynomial time of* $Max[I']$ *and* $Length[I']$.
3. *It exists a polynomial* q_1 *such that* $\forall I' \in D_{\Pi'}$, $q_1(Length[\propto_s (I')]) \geq length'[I']$.
4. *It exists a polynomial* q_2 *such that* $\forall I' \in D_{\Pi'}$, $Max[\propto_s (I')] \leq q_2(Max'[I'], Length'[I'])$.

Conditions 3 and 4 of the above definition ensure that with the instances built by $\propto_s$, Π_p does not correspond to a number problem. Thus, it enables us to prove that if problem Π' is strongly $\mathcal{NP}$-complete, then problem Π is also.

To demonstrate that a decision problem Π is strongly $\mathcal{NP}$-complete, it is thus sufficient to show that either:

1. $\Pi \in \mathcal{NP}$ and that a strongly $\mathcal{NP}$-complete problem Π' and that a pseudo-polynomial transformation $\propto_s$ exist such that $\Pi' \propto_s \Pi$, or that
2. Π is $\mathcal{NP}$-complete and that a polynomial p exists such that $\forall I$ instance of Π, $Max[I] \leq p(Length[I])$, or that
3. $\Pi \in \mathcal{NP}$ possesses a strongly $\mathcal{NP}$-complete sub-problem.

2.2.2 The complexity of optimisation problems

We now turn to a more general class of problems for which the aim is not to decide on the feasibility of an instance but to calculate a solution to that one. These problems are generally referred to as *search problems*. A search problem SP is more formally defined as follows.

Search problem SP:

• Input data, or instances, noted I. The set of instances is noted D_{SP},

• A set of solutions S_I for each instance $I \in D_{SP}$, defined by means of the question.

An algorithm is said to solve a search problem if, given an instance $I \in D_{SP}$, it returns the answer "*no*" if S_I is empty and otherwise returns a solution $s \in S_I$. A decision problem Π can be considered as a particular search problem for which $S_I = \{yes\}$ if $I \in Y_\Pi$ and $S_I = \emptyset$ otherwise.

However, we do not usually search for an arbitrary solution in S_I but for a solution which optimises a given objective function. In this case, the search problem turns to an *optimisation problem* and the aim becomes to calculate any optimal solution. Formally, an optimisation problem O is defined as follows.

Optimisation problem O:

• Input data, or instances, noted I. The set of instances is noted D_O,

• For each instance $I \in D_O$, a set of optimal solutions S_I, *i.e.* solutions which optimise a given objective function (also called criterion).

An algorithm is said to solve an optimisation problem if, given an instance $I \in D_O$, it returns the answer "*no*" if S_I is empty and otherwise returns an optimal solution $s \in S_I$.

It is not difficult to associate a decision problem with an optimisation problem by searching for a solution which has a better value than a given bound K. Henceforth, the question of the decision problem is "*Does a solution exist with a criterion value lower than K ?*", with K an input of the problem. If this decision problem is $\mathcal{NP}$-complete, then at least so is the optimisation problem. Starting from the results presented in section 2.2.1 it is possible to derive straight complexity classes for optimisation problems. This is achieved by using a generalisation of polynomial reductions: the polynomial Turing reductions.

A polynomial Turing reduction $\propto_T$ of a problem O towards a problem O', from the algorithmic point of view, is an algorithm A which verifies the following three properties:

1. A solves O, *i.e.* calculates for an instance I a solution of S_I if it exists.
2. A uses a procedure S which solves the problem O'.
3. If S solves the problem O' in polynomial time, then A solves O in polynomial time.

The complexity of the procedure S is not important in defining the polynomial Turing reduction. What matters is that if S is polynomial then A is also. We notice that the notion of polynomial Turing reduction generalises the notion of polynomial reduction in the sense that procedure S can be used iteratively. In the remainder of this chapter we denote by $\propto_T$ any polynomial reduction or polynomial Turing reduction, if there is no ambiguity.

Definition 13
An optimisation problem O is $\mathcal{NP}$-hard if another optimisation problem O' $\mathcal{NP}$-hard and a polynomial Turing reduction of O' towards O exist. The problem O is at least as difficult to solve as the problem O'.

This definition is also true if O' is an $\mathcal{NP}$-complete decision problem, and the reduction used a polynomial reduction. We say that an $\mathcal{NP}$-hard problem cannot be solved in polynomial time unless $\mathcal{P}$=$\mathcal{NP}$.

An optimisation problem O is $\mathcal{NP}$-hard if we can show that:

1. A polynomial Turing reduction $\propto_T$ and an $\mathcal{NP}$-hard optimisation problem O' exist such that $O' \propto_T O$.
2. A polynomial Turing reduction $\propto_T$ (which is not a simple polynomial reduction) and an $\mathcal{NP}$-complete decision problem Π' exist such that $\Pi' \propto_T O$,
3. O contains an $\mathcal{NP}$-hard sub-problem.

Similarly we can demonstrate that a problem is weakly $\mathcal{NP}$-hard. Besides, we can deduce the following property.

Property 1
Let us consider two optimisation problems O and O'. If

1. *$\forall I'$ instance of $D_{O'}$, $\exists I$ an instance of D_O such that $S_I \subseteq S_{I'}$.*
2. *I can be constructed in polynomial time starting with I'.*

then a polynomial Turing reduction exists such that $O' \propto_T O$.

Considering strong $\mathcal{NP}$-hardness, similar results to those for proving strong $\mathcal{NP}$-completeness have to be stated. Thus polynomial Turing reductions are not sufficient to prove strong $\mathcal{NP}$-hardness, and similarly the notion of pseudo-polynomial Turing reduction must be considered.

$\mathcal{NP}$-hardness is definitely a general complexity state, an $\mathcal{NP}$-hard problem being at least as hard as any problem in class $\mathcal{NP}$. The class of $\mathcal{NP}$-hard

problems is not a class specifically dedicated to optimisation problems and even decision problems can belong to it. For instance, the *Kth largest subset* problem (see [Garey and Johnson, 1979] for a formal definition) is a decision problem which cannot be proved to belong to class $\mathcal{NP}$ but which can be reduced from Partition problem. Consequently, the *Kth largest subset* problem is not $\mathcal{NP}$-complete but $\mathcal{NP}$-hard.
The central question is whether an optimisation problem can belong to $\mathcal{NP}$ or not. If so, it is straightforward that $\mathcal{NP}$-hard optimisation problems are $\mathcal{NP}$-complete and the complexity classes introduced for decision problems are relevant for optimisation problems. But, the definition of class $\mathcal{NP}$ implies that given a solution, we are capable of checking in polynomial time if it is optimal or not. Henceforth, except for polynomialy solvable problems, there are few chance that an optimisation problem belongs to $\mathcal{NP}$ since often this checking step is as hard as solving the optimisation problem itself. This is the main reason why, in the literature, complexity of "hard" optimisation problems is often established in term of $\mathcal{NP}$-hardness instead of $\mathcal{NP}$-completeness. It is remarkable that for optimisation problems, notably, the class $\mathcal{NPO}$ has been introduced to overcome that unsuitability of class $\mathcal{NP}$. A problem belongs to class $\mathcal{NPO}$ if any solution can be evaluated, according to the criteria, in polynomial time. And we still have $\mathcal{P} \subseteq \mathcal{NPO}$. Henceforth, it can be easily seen that a $\mathcal{NP}$-hard optimisation problem is $\mathcal{NPO}$-complete. More formally, the completeness inside class $\mathcal{NPO}$ is, at the lower level, defined by mean of an straigth extension of the polynomial reduction introduced for class $\mathcal{NP}$. Henceforth, a polynomial reduction between an optimisation problem O' towards an optimisation problem O can be seen as an algorithm capable of changing, in a time bounded by a polynomial of *Length*, every instance of I' of O' into an instance I of O. Besides, this reduction can also change in polynomial time *any* solution for instance I into a solution for instance I'. A particular polynomial reduction, namely the AP-reduction, already enables to define the completeness of class $\mathcal{NPO}$ (see [Ausiello et al., 1999]). This reduction has been originally introduced in the context of approximation algorithms.

2.2.3 The complexity of counting and enumeration problems

In terms of complexity, when we introduced the complexity classes dedicated to decision or optimisation problems, we were only interested in deciding of the feasibility or finding one solution. Not to count the number of solutions to the problem, nor to enumerate them. In the literature we commonly distinguish between the problem of counting the number of solutions and the problem of enumerating them. The latter is also referred to as a generation problem. In this section we consider the counting and enumeration problems associated to optimisation problems, even if we can also define versions associated to decision problems. It is quite natural to think that the enumeration of optimal solutions is at least as hard as the calculation of one optimal solution. For instance, if the latter is a strongly $\mathcal{NP}$-complete problem, the former is so. But, can the enumeration be even harder ? Is there any additional complexity classes dedicated to the enumeration of solutions?

And what about the counting problem? A trivial way to count the number of solutions would be to solve the enumeration problem and to count the number of calculated solutions. Henceforth, we can informally derive that enumeration is at least as hard as counting, since when the enumeration is performed the counting of solutions can be polynomially done whilst the converse is false. We first focus on the complexity of counting problems before considering the complexity of enumeration problems.

Let us define the **counting problem**, denoted by C, associated to an optimisation problem O as follows:
Counting problem C

- Input data, or instances, denoted by I. The set of all the instances is denoted by D_O,
- Counting question: how many optimal solutions to the objective of problem O exist ?

A counting problem is basically different from a search, an optimisation or even a decision problem since the outcome is not a solution or a state but a number: counting problems are *function problems* whilst the other mentionned are *set problems.* [Valiant, 1979a] introduced a general complexity class, which could merely be seen as the equivalent of class $\mathcal{NP}$ but for counting problems. Besides, Valiant considered the counting problems associated to decision problems. The following definition is a straight adaptation of this class when dealing with counting problems associated to optimisation problems.

Definition 14
Let e be any reasonable encoding scheme. A counting problem belongs to the class $\#P$ if a non deterministic polynomial Turing machine, with au auxiliary output device, exists which prints the number of accepting states in a finite number of iterations when it takes upon entry a chain of language $L(O, e)$. It is required that the number of iterations induced by the longest verification of a solution is upper bounded by a polynomial function of Length.

Informally speaking, this definition states that a counting problem is $\#P$ if the corresponding decision, search or optimisation problem belongs to $\mathcal{NP}$ or $\mathcal{NPO}$, as soon as any solution to the problem can be checked in polynomial time. As in the case of class $\mathcal{NP}$ it is possible to establish subclasses of counting problems.

Definition 15 *See for instance [Vadhan, 1995]*
We denote by $\mathcal{FP} \subset \#P$ the class of polynomially solvable counting problems.

Class $\#P$ is not assumed to be limited to class $\mathcal{FP}$. Among the counting problems in $\#P$ there are those supposed to be "at least as hard as" all others belonging to $\#P$. Before formally introducing this, we define *parsimonious reductions.*

Definition 16 *See for instance [Ehrgott, 2000a]*
A parsimonious reduction, denoted by $\propto_C$, from a counting problem C^1 towards a counting problem C^2 is a polynomial time reduction such that the number of optimal solutions of every instance I of C^1 is the same as the number of optimal solutions of the instance $\propto_C (I)$ of C^2.

Definition 17 *[Valiant, 1979a]*
A counting problem C is $\#P$-complete if $C \in \#P$, and $\forall C' \in \#P$, $\exists \propto_C$ such that $C' \propto_C C$. The class of $\#P$-complete problems is denoted by $\#PC$.

It is clear from the above definition that the class of $\#P$-complete problems contains the hardest counting problems, as it was the case for the class of $\mathcal{NPO}$-complete optimisation problems. For this reason, study of $\#P$-completeness for counting problems has attracted a lot of attention since the seminal work of Valiant in 1979. A list of $\#P$-complete problems is notably given by [Vadhan, 1995], [Valiant, 1979a] and [Valiant, 1979b]. It is remarkable that decision problems reduce to their counting counterpart ([Vadhan, 1995]), *i.e.* if a decision problem is $\mathcal{NP}$-complete then the associated counting problem is $\mathcal{NP}$-hard. More precisely it is $\#P$-complete: assume that for a $\mathcal{NP}$-complete decision problem we could count in polynomial time the number of "yes" answers, then we would have shown that $\mathcal{P}$=$\mathcal{NP}$. However it appears difficult to establish the same links for $\mathcal{NPO}$-complete optimisation problems and their counting counterparts, since knowing the number of solutions does not necessarily helps in finding one solution.

To achieve this general overview of $\#P$-completeness, we point out that a counting problem C' is $\#P$-hard if another $\#P$-complete problem C reduces to it by means of a polynomial Turing reduction, and if C' has not been shown to be in $\#P$. Notice that if C' can be shown to be in $\#P$ then it is $\#P$-complete. Also notice that to show a counting problem C is $\#P$-complete it is sufficient to show that there exists a parsimonious reduction $\propto_C$ and a $\#P$-complete counting problem C' such that $C' \propto_C C$ (class $\#P$ is closed under parsimonious reductions). When considering counting problems associated to known decision or optimisation problems it is often interesting to first examine existing reductions between these problems in order to determine if they are parsimonious. For example, consider the decision version of the classic knapsack problem, denoted by KP and the decision version of the bicriteria shortest path problem, denoted by $BSPP$. [Serafini, 1987] proves that $BSPP$ is $\mathcal{NP}$-complete by providing a polynomial reduction from KP to $BSPP$. This reduction can be shown to be parsimonious and as the counting problem associated to KP is $\#P$-complete ([Ehrgott, 2000a]) then the counting problem associated to $BSPP$ is also $\#P$-complete. [Simon, 1977] observed that many polynomial reductions between search or optimisation problems were already parsimonious and that, if not, alternative parsimonious reductions can be built. By the way, the informal following statement is often true in practice: "if an optimisation problem is $\mathcal{NPO}$-complete then the associated counting problem is $\#P$-complete". [Vadhan, 1995] presents more complicated techniques for proving $\#P$-completeness.

We now turn our attention to **enumeration problems** associated to optimisation problems. As already stated, *enumeration* is harder than *counting*. "Harder" in the sense that even if we know the number of solutions in polynomial time, calculating all of them may require an exponential time. But also "harder" in the sense that even if we are able to compute *a single* solution in polynomial time, maybe we are not able to calculate all of them due to an exponential number of solutions and huge memory requirements. Henceforth, when dealing with complexity of enumeration problems we have to take account of the *time* and *space* dimensions. Notice that like optimisation problems, enumeration problems are *set problems*. We define the enumeration problem, denoted by E, associated to an optimisation problem O as follows:

Enumeration problem E

- Input data, or instances, denoted by I. The set of all the instances is denoted by D_O,
- Objective: Find all optimal solutions to the objective of problem O. We refer to S_I as the set of all these optimal solutions.

Several classes of complexity dedicated to enumeration problems have been introduced in the literature by various authors, mainly in the case of enumeration problems associated to decision problems. We present hereafter the extension of these classes of complexity to the case of enumeration problems associated to optimisation problems.

Definition 18 *[Fukuda, 1996]*
An enumeration problem E belongs to the class $\mathcal{ENP}$ if for any instance I, there exists an algorithm, which complexity is bounded by a polynomial function of $Length[I]$ and $|S_I|$, capable of checking that any solution of set S_I can be evaluated in polynomial time.

The class $\mathcal{ENP}$ introduced by Fukuda as extended in the above definition, is a direct generalisation of class $\mathcal{NPO}$. Notice that in the original definition of Fukuda, class $\mathcal{ENP}$ is a generalisation of class $\mathcal{NP}$ which, translated in terms of optimisation, would imply that we can check in polynomial time that set S_I is the correct outcome of problem E. However, from a practical viewpoint, checking in polynomial time that set S_I is the correct outcome of problem E is often as hard as calculating this set. This implies that, often, we would not be able to show that a problem belongs to class $\mathcal{ENP}$.

Fukuda also provides a generalisation of class $\mathcal{P}$ which requires first the definition of a bipolynomial algorithm.

Definition 19 *[Fukuda, 1996]*
An algorithm which solves an enumeration problem E is a bipolynomial algorithm if and only if, for any instance I, it requires a number of iterations bounded by a polynomial function of $Length[I]$ and $|S_I|$.

Definition 20 *[Fukuda, 1996]*
An enumeration problem E belongs to the class $\mathcal{EP}$ if there exists a bipolynomial algorithm which solves it.

Notice that the above definition implies that some problems in $\mathcal{EP}$ cannot be solved by a polynomial time algorithm in a similar sense of class $\mathcal{P}$, *i.e.* there are enumeration problems $E \in \mathcal{EP}$ for which we cannot provide the outcome in polynomial time of only *Length*. Nevertheless we have $\mathcal{P} \subseteq \mathcal{EP}$.

Various works have been done to characterise classes inside $\mathcal{EP}$ and how it is "easy" to solve an enumeration problem. [Johnson et al., 1988] introduce different classes of complexity and first consider *polynomial total time* enumeration problems which are in fact exactly the problems inside class $\mathcal{EP}$. Next, they introduce the notion of *incremental polynomial time* algorithms.

Definition 21 *[Johnson et al., 1988]*
Consider an enumeration problem E and, for any instance I, let S be a subset of S_I, i.e. $S \subseteq S_I$. An algorithm for E is an incremental polynomial time algorithm if, starting with S, it is capable of calculating a solution $s \in S_I/S$, or to decide that $S = S_I$, with a time complexity bounded by a polynomial function of $Length[I]$ and $|S|$.

Definition 22 *An enumeration problem E belongs to class IPT if and only if there exists an incremental polynomial time algorithm which solves it.*

From the above definition we can easily deduce that class IPT is a subclass of $\mathcal{EP}$ since with an incremental polynomial time algorithm we can generate S_I with a time complexity bounded by a polynomial function of $Length[I]$ and $|S_I|$, for any instance I. Besides, we have $\mathcal{P} \subseteq IPT$. In his works on the complexity of counting problems, Valiant also introduces a particular class of complexity for enumeration problems which is in fact a subclass of $\mathcal{EP}$.

Definition 23 *[Valiant, 1979a]*
An enumeration problem E belongs to the class of $\mathcal{P}$-enumerable problems if and only if there exists an algorithm which solves it with time complexity bounded by a function $p(Length[I])|S_I|$ for any instance I, where p is a polynomial function.

As function $p(Length[I])|S_I|$ is a polynomial function of $Length[I]$ and $|S_I|$ then we have $\mathcal{P} \subseteq$ $\mathcal{P}$-enumerable$\subseteq \mathcal{EP}$. Notice that the class of $\mathcal{P}$-enumerable problems is slightly more general than the class of problems, introduced by [Johnson et al., 1988], which can be solved by a *polynomial delay* algorithm.

These problems, which form a class referred to as class $\mathcal{PD}$, are solvable in such a way that the time spent to output one solution is upper bounded by a polynomial of n. Henceforth, any problem inside class PD is also $\mathcal{P}$-enumerable whilst the converse is not necessarily true. Johnson, Yannakakis and Papadimitriou also define *polynomial delay algorithms for a specified order* which are no more than algorithms that generates the outcome in a specified order with a polynomial delay.

Up to now we have defined various classes of $\mathcal{EP}$ which gives only measure of the time complexity of the enumeration problem. But the space dimension has also to be taken into account. Consider an enumeration problem $E \in \mathcal{EP}$ such that its time complexity depends on the size of the outcome $|S_I|$ for each instance I. If $|S_I|$ becomes sufficiently high for some instances I, then a solution algorithm for E may require too much memory space to work. And if it holds for any solution algorithm for E, then problem E may become practically unsolvable. This observation leads to the definition of a *compact algorithm.*

Definition 24 *[Fukuda, 1996]*
An algorithm is compact for an enumeration problem E if it solves E using a memory space bounded by a polynomial function of $Length[I]$ *and* $\max_{J \in S_I}(Length[J])$, *for any instance I.*

This definition enables to identify a particular class of $\mathcal{EP}$: the class $\mathcal{CEP}$.

Definition 25 *[Fukuda, 1996]*
An enumeration problem E belongs to the class $\mathcal{CEP}$ *if there exists a compact bipolynomial algorithm which solves it.*

From the above definition it follows that $\mathcal{P} \subseteq \mathcal{CEP} \subseteq \mathcal{EP}$. [Fukuda et al., 1997] introduce the class of strongly $\mathcal{P}$-enumerable problems, based on compact linear-time algorithms where such an algorithm is a compact bipolynomial algorithm with time complexity bounded by a linear function of $|S_I|$.

Definition 26 *[Fukuda et al., 1997]*
An enumeration problem E belongs to the class of strongly $\mathcal{P}$*-enumerable problems if and only if there exists a compact linear-time algorithm which solves it.*

Notice that in [Fukuda et al., 1997], the authors consider a slightly restricted definition of a compact algorithm, by comparison to Definition 24, since they define a compact algorithm as one having space complexity bounded by a polynomial of *Length*, only. However, whatever the considered definition of a compact algorithm, we have $\mathcal{P} \subseteq$strongly $\mathcal{P}$-enumerable$\subseteq \mathcal{CEP}$ and strongly $\mathcal{P}$-enumerable$\subseteq \mathcal{P}$-enumerable.

To complete this section, we need to introduce the class of the hardest problems of $\mathcal{ENP}$, those supposed to be "at least as hard as" all others belonging to $\mathcal{ENP}$. We first define the notion of a bipolynomial reduction.

Definition 27 *A bipolynomial reduction, denoted by $\propto_B$, from an enumeration problem E^1 towards an enumeration problem E^2 is a reduction which time complexity is bounded by a polynomial of Length[I] and $|S_{\propto_B(I)}|$ for any instance I of E^1.*

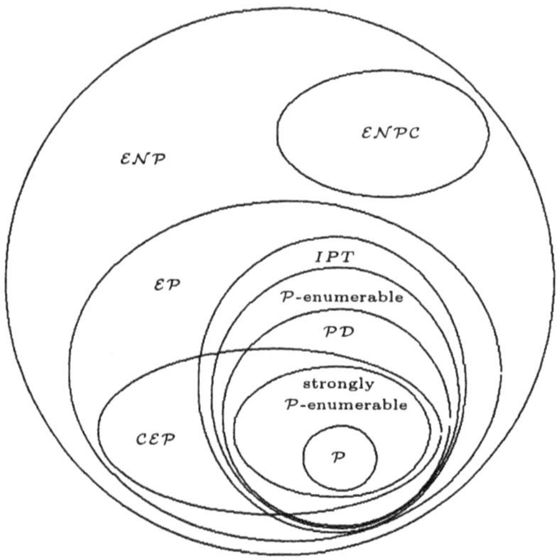

Fig. 2.3. The world of $\mathcal{ENP}$

Definition 28 *An enumeration problem E is $\mathcal{ENP}$-complete if and only if $E \in \mathcal{ENP}$, and $\forall E' \in \mathcal{ENP}$, $\exists \propto_B$ such that $E' \propto_B E$. The class of $\mathcal{ENP}$-complete problems is denoted by $\mathcal{ENPC}$.*

Henceforth, the notion of completeness in class $\mathcal{ENP}$ is defined by mean of bipolynomial reductions which are no more than a straigth adaptation of polynomial reductions to enumeration problems. We now state an important result related to class $\mathcal{ENPC}$.

Theorem 1 *The class $\mathcal{ENPC}$ is not empty.*

Proof.
We do the proof by contradiction. First we recall that a bipolynomial reduction $\propto_B$ from a problem E' toward a problem E is capable of changing in polynomial time any instance I' of E' into an instance I of E, the number of solutions $|S_I| = |S_{I'}|$,

and any solution of S_I can be changed into a unique solution of $S_{I'}$ in polynomial time.
Assume that class $\mathcal{ENPC}$ is empty.
$\Rightarrow \forall E \in \mathcal{ENP}$, $\exists E'$ such that $\nexists \propto_B$ with $E' \propto_B E$.
Let us consider a problem E such that its associated counting problem C is $\#P$-complete and its associated optimisation problem O is $\mathcal{NPO}$-complete. We introduce set $R_p(E') = \{$reductions from E' towards E which are parsimonious but not polynomial$\}$. We have $R_p(E') \neq \emptyset$ since problem C is $\#P$-complete. The previous statement implies:
$\forall E \in \mathcal{ENP}$, $\exists E'$ such that $\forall \propto \in R_p(E')$, $\exists I'$ instance of E' such that $\exists s \in S_{\propto(I')}$ with s non convertible in polynomial time into a solution $s' \in S_{I'}$.
But here we have a contradiction with the fact that problem O is $\mathcal{NPO}$-complete since we can exhibit a polynomial reduction capable of changing in polynomial time a solution of problem E into a solution of problem E' (the solutions of the enumeration problems are all possible solutions of the associated optimisation problems).
Henceforth, class $\mathcal{ENPC}$ is necessarily non empty.□

Figure 2.3 summarizes the world of $\mathcal{ENP}$. In this section, to prove the difficulty of a problem we have suggested the use of reductions. For instance, to show that a counting problem C^1 is in $\mathcal{FP}$ we can provide a parsimonious reduction $\propto_C$ and another $\mathcal{FP}$ counting problem C^2 such that $C^2 \propto_C C^1$. For enumeration, we use the bipolynomial reduction. These reductions have also been used to define the classes of complete problems.
However, it exists some links between an optimisation problem and its counting and enumeration counterparts enabling us to quickly derive, in some cases, the complexity of those problems.

Property 2 *If an enumeration problem E belongs to class $\mathcal{P}$ then so is the corresponding optimisation problem O, and the associated counting problem belongs to class $\mathcal{FP}$.*

The following property states a powerful result which is a consequence of theorem 1.

Property 3 *If an optimisation problem O is $\mathcal{NPO}$-complete and has its counting problem which is $\#P$-complete, then the associated enumeration problem E is $\mathcal{ENP}$-complete.*

Proof.
As problem $O \in \mathcal{NPO}$ it follows that any solution to an instance I can be checked with a time bounded by a polynomial of $Length[I]$ (see Section 2.2.2). From Definition 18, we conclude that problem E necessarily belongs to class $\mathcal{ENP}$. Besides, as problem O is $\mathcal{NPO}$-complete we can exhibit another problem O' belonging to $\mathcal{NPO}$ and a polynomial time reduction $\propto$ such that $O' \propto O$. Assume, without loss of generality, that the associated enumeration problem E' belongs to class $\mathcal{ENPC}$

(otherwise class $\mathcal{ENPC}$ would be empty, see Theorem 1). We now slightly transform the reduction $\propto$ in order to obtain a bipolynomial reduction $\propto_B$. First, notice that the instances of O (resp. O') are also the instances of E (resp. E'). Henceforth, for any instance I' of E', $\propto(I')$ is an instance of E. The difference between problems O and E is that the outcome of E is the whole set of optimal solutions. But, reduction $\propto$ is capable of changing in polynomial time any solution of $S_{\propto(I')}$ into a solution of $S_{I'}$. Besides, as problem C is $\#P$-complete we can state that there exists such a reduction $\propto$ which is parsimonious. This implies that by making reduction $\propto$ changing all solutions of $S_{\propto(I')}$ into solutions of $S_{I'}$ we obtain a bipolynomial reduction $\propto_B$, since the time complexity becomes bounded by a polynomial of $Length[I']$ and $|S_{\propto(I')}| = |S_{I'}|$.$\square$

As already done previously for counting problems, we can informally state that often: "if an optimisation problem is $\mathcal{NPO}$-complete then the associated enumeration problem is $\mathcal{ENP}$-complete". This follows the remark of Simons related to polynomial reductions which often are, or can be transformed into, parsimonious reductions. However, no formal proof of this statement has been proposed.
Several techniques are available to show that an enumeration problem is $\mathcal{ENP}$-complete and they are similar to those useable for optimisation problems. Accordingly, to show that an enumeration problem E is $\mathcal{ENP}$-complete we can show that it is in $\mathcal{ENP}$ and there exists another $\mathcal{ENP}$-complete problem E' which bipolynomially reduces to it. Notice that this kind of proof becomes straightforward if we can exhibit a parsimonious reduction between the two corresponding optimisation problems.

2.3 Application to scheduling

Scheduling problems are optimisation problems. When we address a scheduling problem, we must always look for its complexity, since this determines the nature of the algorithm to implement. If the problem under consideration belongs to the class $\mathcal{P}$, we know that an exact polynomial algorithm exists to solve it. In this case it is convenient to use or to perfect such an algorithm. By contrast, if the problem is $\mathcal{NP}$-hard, two alternatives are possible. The first is to propose an approximated algorithm, therefore an heuristic one, which calculates in polynomial time a solution which is as close as possible to the optimal solution. The second is to propose an algorithm which calculates the optimal solution of the problem, but for which the maximal complexity is exponential. In this case, the challenge is to design an algorithm which can solve problems of the largest possible size.

To calculate the complexity of scheduling problems, a certain amount of traditional results exist in the literature. They show the links between different

single criterion scheduling problems. We can represent them under the form of trees of polynomial Turing reductions (see for example [Pinedo, 1995]) where the vertices characterise the problems and where there is an arc between a vertex A and vertex B if $A \propto_T B$. Such trees exist for types of problems (figure 2.4), types of constraints (figure 2.5) and criteria (figure 2.6). In figure 2.4, the presence of an arc from A towards B means that a polynomial Turing reduction exists from an $A|\beta|\gamma$ problem towards the corresponding $B|\beta|\gamma$ problem. In figure 2.5, the presence of an arc from A towards B means that a polynomial Turing reduction exists from the $\alpha|A|\gamma$ problem towards the corresponding $\alpha|B|\gamma$ problem. Finally, in figure 2.6 the presence of an arc from A towards B means that a polynomial Turing reduction exists from the $\alpha|\beta|A$ problem towards the corresponding $\alpha|\beta|B$ problem.
For example, the arc between $C_{\max}$ and $L_{\max}$ enables us to deduce that the $P||L_{\max}$ problem is $\mathcal{NP}$-hard given that the $P||C_{\max}$ problem is also. In figure 2.4, the arc of the problems $\{P, Q, R\}$ towards the problem HF means that polynomial Turing reductions between these problems exist when the parallel machines are of the same type as those appearing in the stages of machines in workshop problems with assignment. Thus, there is a reduction of problem Q towards the corresponding problem HF if at least one stage of the hybrid flowshop contains proportional machines. It is the same for parallel machines problems with general assignment towards corresponding shop problems.

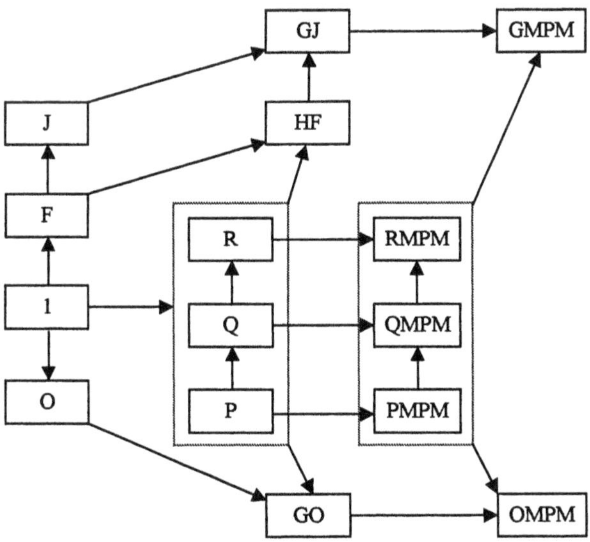

Fig. 2.4. Reduction tree of the problems

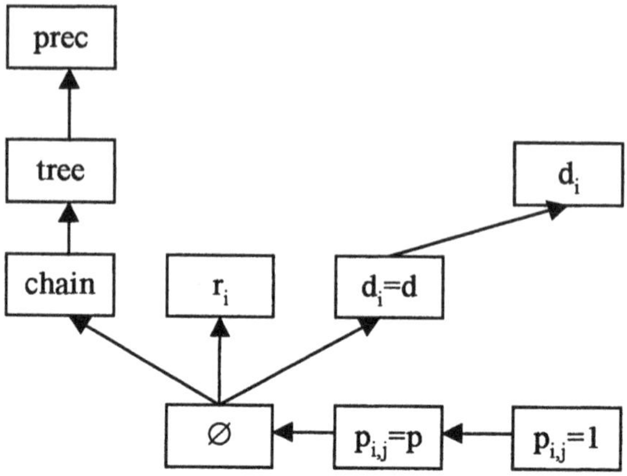

Fig. 2.5. Reduction tree of the constraints

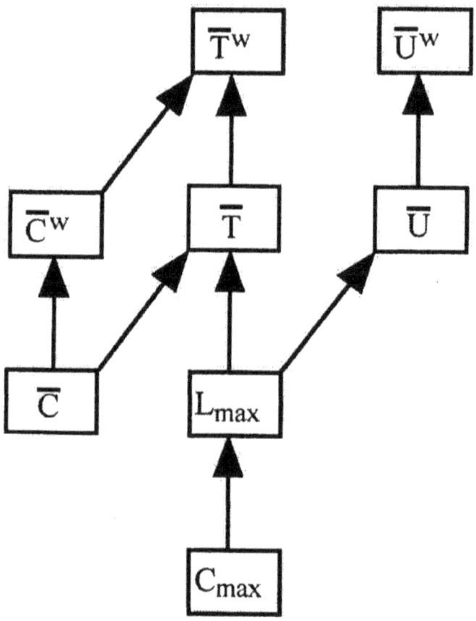

Fig. 2.6. Reduction tree of the criteria

Thus, the reduction trees presented are usable only when we already know the complexity of certain scheduling problems. In order to complete the results presented in this section we therefore recall the complexity of certain basic scheduling problems of the type $\alpha||Z$ where Z refers to any criterion (table 2.2).

Concerning the criteria $E_{\max}$, $\overline{E}$ and $\overline{E}^w$ and whatever the structure of the shop be, the problem is solvable in polynomial time when the insertion of voluntary idle times before each job is authorised. Any schedule such that jobs start after their due date d_i is an optimal schedule for these criteria.

Concerning single machine problems, the minimisation of a function $f_{max} = \max_{i=1,\ldots,n}(f_i(C_i))$ with f_i an increasing function of the completion times is a problem which is solvable in polynomial time. Consequently, the $1||Z$ problems with $Z \in \{C_{max}, F_{max}, T_{max}, L_{max}\}$ are equally so. Notice that any sequence is optimal for the $1||C_{max}$ problem. The $1||\overline{C}^w$ and $1||\overline{C}$ problems are solvable in polynomial time (see [Lawler et al., 1989]) and it is similar for the $1|d_i|\overline{U}$ problem (see [Pinedo, 1995]). Without adding any constraints, the only $\mathcal{NP}$-hard $1||Z$ problems, are the problems $1|d_i|\overline{T}$ in the weak sense, $1|d_i|\overline{U}^w$ in the weak sense and $1|d_i|\overline{T}^w$ in the strong sense (see [Lawler et al., 1989]). As a consequence, all the $\alpha|d_i|\overline{T}^w$ problems are so, whatever the value of α.

For parallel machines problems, the $P||f_{\max}$ problem is strongly $\mathcal{NP}$-hard (see [Lawler et al., 1989] and [Pinedo, 1995]). It is similar for the $P||Z$ problems with $Z \in \{C_{max}, F_{\max}, T_{\max}, L_{\max}\}$ (see [Brucker, 2004]). We note also that to solve the $Rm||C_{\max}$ problem (the number of machines m is fixed), a pseudo-polynomial time dynamic programming algorithm (see [Lawler et al., 1989]) exists. Concerning the criterion $\overline{C}$ its minimisation remains a polynomial time problem whatever the type of considered machines (see [Pinedo, 1995]). On the other hand, the $P||\overline{C}^w$ problem is strongly $\mathcal{NP}$-hard (see [Brucker, 2004]). As for the $R||C_{\max}$ problem a pseudo-polynomial time dynamic programming algorithm exists to solve this problem when the number of machines m is fixed (see [Lawler et al., 1989]).
Knowing that the $\alpha|d_i|L_{\max}$ problems with $\alpha \in \{P, Q, R\}$ are strongly $\mathcal{NP}$-hard we deduce immediately from this that the same problems but with the criteria $\overline{U}$, $\overline{U}^w$ and $\overline{T}$ are equally so. We note that a pseudo-polynomial time dynamic programming algorithm exists to solve the $Rm|d_i|\overline{U}^w$ problem (see [Pinedo, 1995] and [Lawler et al., 1989]).

Finally, we end this complexity survey of scheduling problems with flowshop, jobshop and openshop problems. Beginning with the results presented in [Tanaev et al., 1994b] and the reduction rules presented in this section, we note that all these problems, without adding simplifying hypotheses are strongly $\mathcal{NP}$-hard for the criteria studied. A comprehensive survey of the complexity of single criterion scheduling problems can be found at `www.mathematik.uni-osnabrueck.de/research/OR/class/`.

Table 2.2. Complexity of single criterion problems

	1	P	Q	R	F	HF	J	JG	O	OG
C_{max}	*	** +	** +	** +	** +	** +	** +	** +	** +	** +
F_{max}	*	** +	** +	** +	** +	** +	** +	** +	** +	** +
T_{max}	*	** +	** +	** +	** +	** +	** +	** +	** +	** +
L_{max}	*	** +	** +	** +	** +	** +	** +	** +	** +	** +
f_{max}	*	** +	** +	** +	** +	** +	** +	** +	** +	** +
$\overline{C}$	*	*	*	*	** +	** +	** +	** +	** +	** +
$\overline{C}^w$	*	** +	** +	** +	** +	** +	** +	** +	** +	** +
$\overline{T}$	** −	** +	** +	** +	** +	** +	** +	** +	** +	** +
$\overline{T}^w$	** +	** +	** +	** +	** +	** +	** +	** +	** +	** +
$\overline{U}$	*	** +	** +	** +	** +	** +	** +	** +	** +	** +
$\overline{U}^w$	** −	** +	** +	** +	** +	** +	** +	** +	** +	** +

*: $\mathcal{P}$ / **: $\mathcal{NP}$-hard / ** −: weakly $\mathcal{NP}$-hard / ** +: strongly $\mathcal{NP}$-hard

3. Multicriteria optimisation theory

3.1 MCDA and MCDM: the context

Decision Making arises at all levels in firms. A firm may be described as a "complex system", and we can make the following remarks ([Boldur, 1982]):

- A complex system can be broken down into sub-systems according to the objectives of the first one (production sub-system, human resources management sub-system, *etc.*).
- The methods of management must be arranged in order to propose solutions that fit the actual objectives.
- It is necessary to mix different disciplines such as Operational Research, Management and Psychology in order to thoroughly understand and model a complex system.

These remarks make apparent the complexity of the decision processes in the firms. The desire to rationalise these processes to the extreme leads inevitably to an aberration ([Roy, 1985]) as certain factors, which occur in real time, cannot be taken into account in advance. The multicriteria decision domain proposes a set of tools which enables to model the decision process more or less faithfully ([Boldur, 1982]).

The representation of the decision process, or even simply the search for a correct decision, is conditioned by different elements ([Zionts, 1997]):

- Well defined decisions do not exist all the time, sometimes only "orientations" exist.
- The decision maker is rarely a unique individual. Often there is a group of people that take decisions.
- The set of possible decisions (or actions, or alternatives) is rarely fixed, but tends to evolve in real time.
- Although the decision maker wants to choose the optimal decision, this perhaps does not exist or else he is incapable of differentiating between a good decision and the optimal solution.

Two particular domains, *MultiCriteria Decision Making* and *MultiCriteria Decision Aid*, are found in the literature. The difference lies mainly in the way to model the problems.

3.1.1 MultiCriteria Decision Making

MultiCriteria Decision Making (MCDM), is a *descriptive* approach (see [Roy and Bouyssou, 1993] and [Roy, 1990]) as it consists of describing the problem:

- by defining the possible decisions,
- by defining the attributes (the consequences of these decisions) and the evaluation criteria,
- by incorporating in a utility function f the set of retained criteria.

Finally, we choose the decision which maximises this function. This approach is based on a certain number of fundamental axioms ([Roy, 1985] and [Roy and Bouyssou, 1993]):

- When the decision maker makes a decision he maximises, implicitly or explicity, a utility function.
- An optimal decision exists in every situation.
- Two decisions which might be incomparable do not exist. We can make a choice or a sort between every pair of decisions.
- Formally, the decision maker's preferences hinge upon two binary relations: the preference P and the indifference I. Let us consider two decisions a and b, either a is preferable to b (aPb), or b is preferable to a (bPa) or a and b are indifferent (aIb). These two relationships are transitive.

Different methods classified in the MCDM approach exist (see for example [Olson et al., 1997] and [Guitouni and Martel, 1997]). Among the best known and most used are:

- the methods relating to the MultiAttribute Utility Theory (MAUT, see [VonNeumann and Morgenstern, 1954]) which use a stochastic approach. These methods concern the problems where the different decisions are subject to uncertainty at the criteria level. Finally, these approaches assume that the decision maker is alone.
- the Analytic Hierarchy Process method (AHP, [Saaty, 1986]), which classifies the criteria into groups using a hierarchical analysis in the form of a tree. Each criterion has a weight inside the objective function and to fix these weights the decision maker must compare each pair of criteria and he must give a ratio that reflects his preference.

[Dyer et al., 1992] give a critical presentation of the works in the MultiCriteria Decision Making domain and break it down as shown in figure 3.1.

3.1.2 MultiCriteria Decision Aid

MultiCriteria Decision Aid (MCDA) is an approach known as *constructive* ([Roy and Bouyssou, 1993] and [Roy, 1990]). It does not seek an optimal

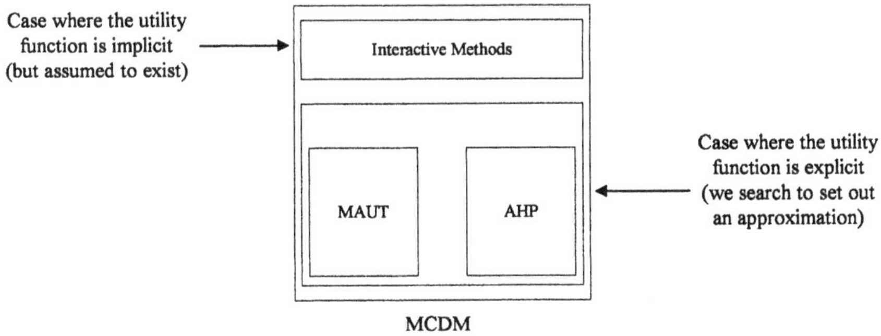

Fig. 3.1. Analysis of the methods of type MCDM

solution but it enables to model the problem by taking account of the preferences and experience of the decision maker. It concerns a flexible approach ([Roy, 1985]) which, by successive dialogues with the decision maker, enables the analyst to propose some response elements (see figure 3.2). The decision process represents in this figure the considerations of the decision maker. In parallel, the decision aid process contains the set of elements highlighted by the analyst to help the decision maker. Thus, from the outset of the questioning by the decision maker, the analyst can construct models of the problem from which he can make a certain number of deductions. These contribute to helping the decision maker to make an explicit choice and therefore make a decision.
The basic axioms for MultiCriteria Decision Aid are the following:

- There are problems for which there is no optimal solution.
- The set of decisions may evolve during the course of the study.
- There is a strong interaction between the decision maker and the analyst.
- The decision maker's preferences may be expressed by means of four basic relationships: the relationship of strict preference, of weak preference, of indifference and of incomparability (these relationships are not necessarily transitive).

More details are presented by [Roy, 1985] and [Roy and Bouyssou, 1993].

3.2 Presentation of multicriteria optimisation theory

Multicriteria Optimisation Theory occurs in the context of MCDA and MCDM. Such theory provides results and methods for calculating best trade-off solutions when the preferences of the decision maker are known.

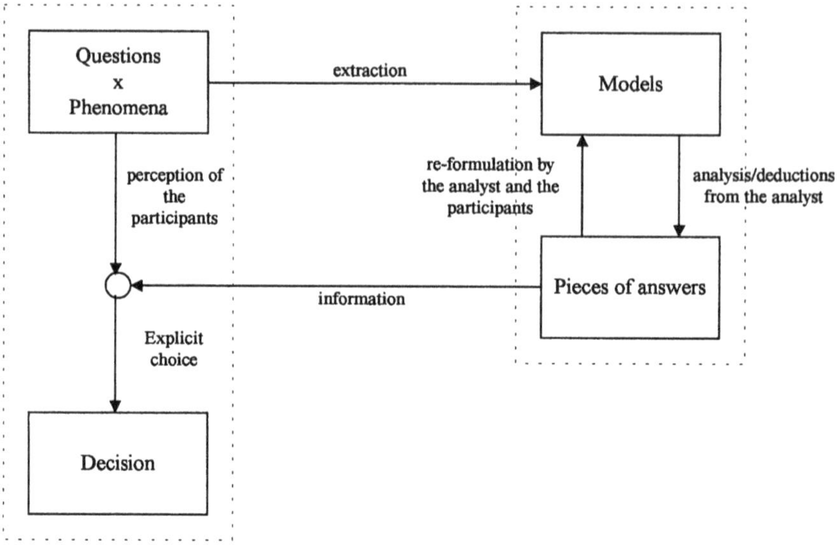

Fig. 3.2. Decision Process and Decision Aid

From a mathematical point of view, multicriteria optimisation problems are a special case of vectors optimisation problems, defined by:

$$\begin{aligned} &\text{Min } Z(x) \quad \text{with } Z(x) = [Z_1(x); \ldots; Z_K(x)]^T \\ &\text{subject to} \\ &\quad x \in \mathcal{S} \\ &\quad \mathcal{S} = \{x/[g_1(x); \ldots; g_M(x)]^T \leq 0\} \end{aligned}$$

Traditionally we can distinguish four axes in the field of vectors optimisation: cone dominance theory, the definition of efficiency, duality theory and the stability analysis of the set of efficient solutions. Cone dominance theory enables us to define order relation in vectorial space on which the sets $\mathcal{S}$ and $Z(\mathcal{S})$ are defined. This leads therefore to the notion of efficiency (or Pareto optimality). Duality theory proposes results which enable us to characterise the efficient solutions. Finally, stability analysis allows us to study the behaviour of the set $Z(\mathcal{S})$ when the definition of $\mathcal{S}$ depends on one or several parameters.

Multicriteria optimisation problems are vectors optimisation problems where solutions space $\mathcal{S}$ and criteria space $Z(\mathcal{S})$ are the vectorial euclidian spaces of finite dimension, Q and K respectively, *i.e.* $\mathcal{S} \subset \mathbb{R}^Q$ and $Z(\mathcal{S}) \subset \mathbb{R}^K$ with $1 \leq Q, K < \infty$.

We firstly present definitions and basic results related to these problems. Afterwards, we study these problems more particularly within the framework of linear problems with real or integer variables defined by:

Min Cx
subject to
$Ax = b$
$x \in \mathbb{R}^Q$

where C is the matrix of the criteria coefficients of dimension $(K \times Q)$, A the matrix of the constraint coefficients of dimension $(M \times Q)$ and b is the vector of right-hand values dimension M, where M is the number of constraints.

3.3 Definition of optimality

Let $\mathcal{S} \subset \mathbb{R}^Q$ be the set of solutions and $\mathcal{Z} \subset \mathbb{R}^K$ the image in the criteria space of $\mathcal{S}$ by K criteria Z_i. We consider that the order structure associated with $\mathbb{R}^K$ is, $\forall x, y \in \mathbb{R}^K$:

$$x \leq y \Leftrightarrow x_i \leq y_i, \ \forall i = 1, ..., K$$
$$x = y \Leftrightarrow x_i = y_i, \ \forall i = 1, ..., K$$

This order defines a partial preorder, valid for $K \geq 2$. We may note that for single criterion optimisation problems ($K = 1$), the structure associated with $\mathbb{R}$ is a total preorder, *i.e.* there is no incomparability between two solutions. Thus in the single criterion case, the definition of an optimal solution is straightforward. In the multicriteria case this definition is no longer trivial because a solution minimising simultaneously all the criteria rarely occurs. We then use a more general definition of optimality: that of the Pareto optima.

Definition 29
$x \in \mathcal{S}$ is a weak Pareto optimum, also called a weakly efficient solution, if and only if $\nexists y \in \mathcal{S}$ such that $\forall i = 1, ..., K,\ Z_i(y) < Z_i(x)$. We note WE the set of weak Pareto optima of $\mathcal{S}$. The set WE defines in the criteria space the trade-off curve, also called the efficiency curve.

This definition introduces a general class of Pareto optima, but other kinds of Pareto optima exist. Definitions 30 and 31 concern subsets of WE.

Definition 30
$x \in \mathcal{S}$ is a strict Pareto optimum, also called an efficient solution or a strict efficient solution, if and only if $\nexists y \in \mathcal{S}$ such that $\forall i = 1, ..., K,\ Z_i(y) \leq Z_i(x)$ with at least one strict inequality. We note E the set of strict Pareto optima of $\mathcal{S}$ and we have $E \subseteq WE$.

Notice that [Ehrgott, 2000b] introduces a slightly different definition of strict Pareto optimality. Definitions 29 and 30 are illustrated in figure 3.3 where the extreme Pareto optima correspond to extreme points of the polyhedron.

Very often, we prefer to be interested in the set E rather than in the set WE, as the latter may contain solutions which are of little interest to the decision maker.

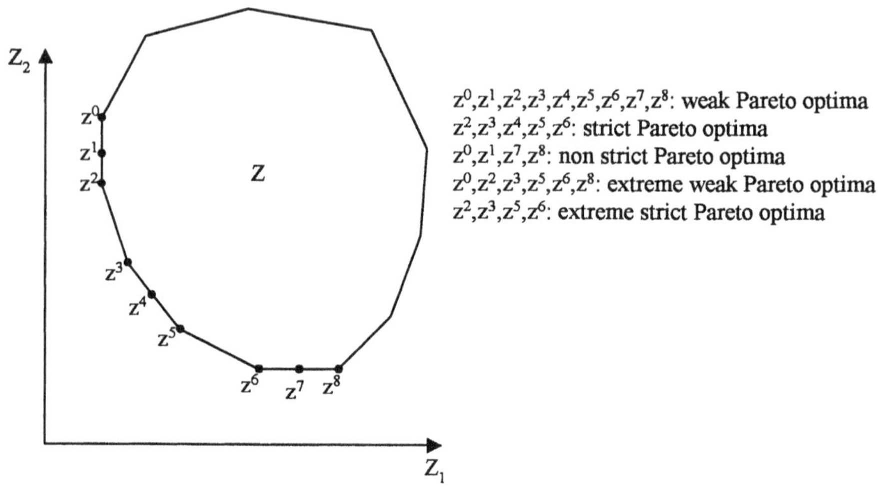

Fig. 3.3. Illustration of weak and strict Pareto optima in the case where $\mathcal{Z}$ defines a polyhedron

Definition 31 *[Geoffrion, 1968]*
Let $x, y \in \mathcal{S}, y \neq x$ and $I_y = \{i \in [1; K]/Z_i(y) < Z_i(x)\}$. $x \in \mathcal{S}$ is a proper Pareto optimum , also called a proper efficient solution if and only if x is a strict Pareto optimum and $\exists M > 0$ such that
$\forall y \in \mathcal{S}, y \neq x, I_y \neq \emptyset \Rightarrow$
$\forall\ i \in I_y, (\exists j, 1 \leq j \leq K$ *with* $Z_j(x) < Z_j(y))$ *such that* $\dfrac{Z_i(x) - Z_i(y)}{Z_j(y) - Z_j(x)} \leq M$.
We note PRE the set of the proper Pareto optima of $\mathcal{S}$ and we have $PRE \subseteq E$.

These definitions are only valid if each criterion Z_i can reach its minimal value. We suppose that it is thus in the remainder of this book. We notice that the wording of definition 31, which is illustrated in figure 3.4 in the bicriteria case, is redundant. Indeed, if there exists a value $M > 0$ as introduced in this definition, then x^0 is a strict Pareto optimum. In the particular case of Multicriteria Linear Programming (MLP) and of Multicriteria Mixed Integer Programming (MMIP) and if the number of constraints is finite, then we have $E = PRE$ ([Steuer, 1986]).

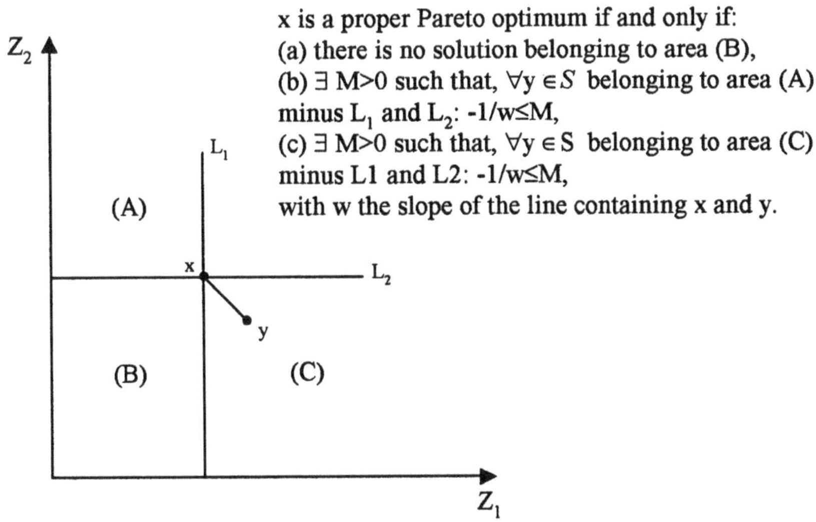

Fig. 3.4. Illustration of the definition of proper Pareto optima

An interesting result concerning the connectedness of the sets WE and E is presented in [Warburton, 1983] in the general case of vectors optimisation problems. We recollect at once some basic definitions.

Definition 32
A function $f : \mathbb{R}^n \rightarrow \mathbb{R}$ *is convex if and only if* $\forall z^1, z^2 \in \mathbb{R}^n$, $\forall \lambda \in [0; 1]$ $f(\lambda z^1 + (1-\lambda)z^2) \leq \lambda f(z^1) + (1-\lambda)f(z^2)$.

Definition 33
A function $f : \mathbb{R}^n \rightarrow \mathbb{R}$ *is quasi-convex if and only if* $\forall z^1, z^2 \in \mathbb{R}^n$, $\forall \lambda \in]0; 1[$ $f(\lambda z^1 + (1-\lambda)z^2) \leq \max(f(z^1); f(z^2))$. *It is strictly quasi-convex if* $f(\lambda z^1 + (1-\lambda)z^2) < \max(f(z^1); f(z^2))$.

Definition 34
A set $\mathcal{S} \subset \mathbb{R}^n$ *is convex if and only if* $\forall z^1, z^2 \in \mathcal{S}$, $\forall \lambda \in [0; 1]$, $\lambda z^1 + (1-\lambda)z^2 \in \mathcal{S}$.

Definition 35
A set $\mathcal{S} \subset \mathbb{R}^n$ *is compact if and only if it is closed and bounded.*

Theorem 2 *[Warburton, 1983]*
Let $a \in \mathcal{Z}$ *and* $C(a) = \cap_{i=1}^{Q} L_{\leq}^{i}(a_i)$ *with* $L_{\leq}^{i}(a_i) = \{x \in \mathcal{S}/Z_i(x) \leq a_i\}$. *If* $\mathcal{S}$ *is a convex and compact set we have the following results:*

- *If* $\forall i = 1, ..., K$, Z_i *is a quasi-convex function, then the set* WE *is connected. If moreover* $\forall a \in Z_1(\mathcal{S}) \times \ldots \times Z_K(\mathcal{S})$, $C(a)$ *is compact then* WE *is not empty.*

- *If* $\forall i = 1, ..., K$, Z_i *is a strictly quasi-convex function then the set* E *is connected. If moreover* $\forall a \in Z_1(\mathcal{S}) \times \ldots \times Z_K(\mathcal{S})$, $\mathcal{C}(a)$ *is compact then* E *is not empty.*

Some similar results in the framework of Multicriteria Linear Programming are presented in [Yu and Zeleny, 1975].

3.4 Geometric interpretation using dominance cones

We give here a brief idea of a geometric interpretation of the definitions of Pareto optima in the case where the criteria are linear functions of the form $Z_i(x) = c^i x$, $\forall i = 1, ..., K$. This interpretation is based on the use of dominance cones.

Definition 36
A set $\mathcal{C} \subset \mathbb{R}^n$ *is a cone if and only if* $\forall x \in \mathcal{C}$, $\forall \alpha \in \mathbb{R}^+$, $\alpha x \in \mathcal{C}$. *If moreover* $\mathcal{C} \cap -\mathcal{C} = \{0\}$ *with* $-\mathcal{C} = \{-x/x \in \mathcal{C}\}$, *then* $\mathcal{C}$ *is pointed.*

Definition 37
Let p *vectors* $v^i \in \mathbb{R}^n$ *and* $\mathcal{C} = \{v \in \mathbb{R}^n / v = \sum_{i=1}^{p} \lambda_i v^i, \lambda_i \geq 0\}$:

- *The vectors* v^i *are the generators of the cone* $\mathcal{C}$.
- *Let* $i \in [1; p]$. *If there exists* $[\lambda_1; ...; \lambda_{i-1}; \lambda_{i+1}; \lambda_K]^T \geq 0$ *such that* $v^i = \sum_{k=1, k\neq i}^{p} \lambda_k v^k$ *then* v^i *is a non essential generator (*$\mathcal{C}$ *can be generated without the vector* v^i*). Otherwise,* v^i *is an essential generator.*
- *The dimension of the cone* $\mathcal{C}$ *is equal to the number of linearly independent vectors* v^i.

We note in the remainder $\mathcal{C}_Z$ the convex criteria cone generated by the gradients c^i of the criteria Z_i. To introduce the notion of dominance set, it is convenient to define the notion of semi-positive polar cone.

Definition 38
We note $\mathcal{C}_Z^{\geq}$ *the semi-positive polar cone generated by the generator vectors of* $\mathcal{C}_Z$ *and we have:*

$$\mathcal{C}_Z^{\geq} = \{y \in \mathbb{R}^n / c^i y \geq 0, \forall\ i = 1, ..., K, [c^1 y; \ldots; c^K y] \neq 0\} \cup \{0\}.$$

$\mathcal{C}_Z^{\geq}$ *contains all the vectors of* $\mathbb{R}^n$ *making an angle lower than or equal to 90 degrees with the generators of* $\mathcal{C}_Z$. *The dominance set at a point* $\overline{x} \in \mathcal{S}$ *is then defined by* $D_{\overline{x}} = \{\overline{x}\} - \mathcal{C}_Z^{\geq} = \{x \in \mathbb{R}^n / x = \overline{x} - y$ *with* $y \in \mathbb{R}^n, [c^1 y; \ldots; c^K y] \neq 0$ *and* $c^i y \geq 0, \forall\ i = 1, ..., K\} \cup \{\overline{x}\}$.

A geometric representation is given in figure 3.5. In this figure, $-\mathcal{C}_Z^{\geq}$ is represented at the point $\overline{x}$.

Theorem 3 *See for example [Steuer, 1986]*
$x^0 \in \mathcal{S}$ *is a strict Pareto optimum if and only if* $D_{x^0} \cap \mathcal{S} = \{x^0\}$.

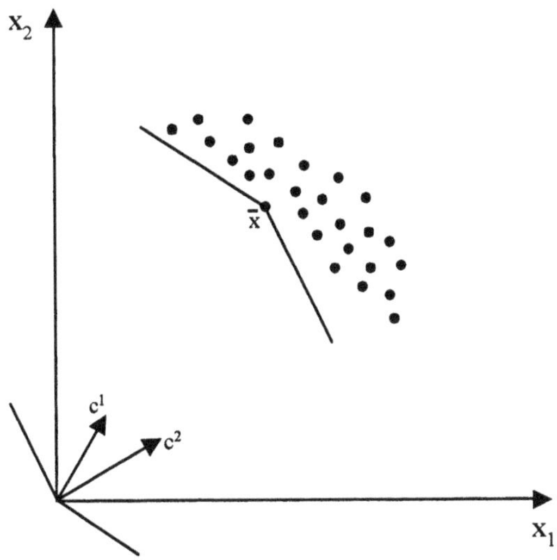

Fig. 3.5. A dominance set

It is also possible to present a similar result for weak Pareto optima by considering $D_{x^0} = x^0 - \mathcal{C}_Z^{>}$ with $\mathcal{C}_Z^{>} = \{y \in \mathbb{R}^n / c^i y > 0, \forall\, i = 1, ..., K\} \cup \{0\}$.

The more the angles between the different gradients c^i are important the more $\mathcal{C}_Z^{\geq}$ is reduced, which has a tendency to increase the number of strict Pareto optima for a given problem. Let us consider a bicriteria problem. Let c^1 and c^2, the two gradients of Z_1 and Z_2, be the generators of the cone $\mathcal{C}_Z^{\geq}$. Figure 3.6 presents three cases. In case 1, the dominance set at the point $\overline{x}$ is the open half-space below the line passing this point. This line is excluded from $D_{\overline{x}}$. In case 2, the dominance set at the point $\overline{x}$ is demarcated by a quadrant whereas in case 3 this set is itself reduced to point $\overline{x}$. We note thus that in case 1, a point $\overline{x}$ has "little chance" of being a strict Pareto optimum whereas in case 3 they all are. We note that the dominance cones constitute not only a tool to geometrically interpret the notion of Pareto optimum in the decision space, but equally they provide information on the number of potential Pareto optima.

In criteria space, geometric interpretation is simplified given that the image of the dominance set is the quadrant defined by the half-lines emerging from $Z(\overline{x})$ and parallel to the reference axes (figure 3.7).

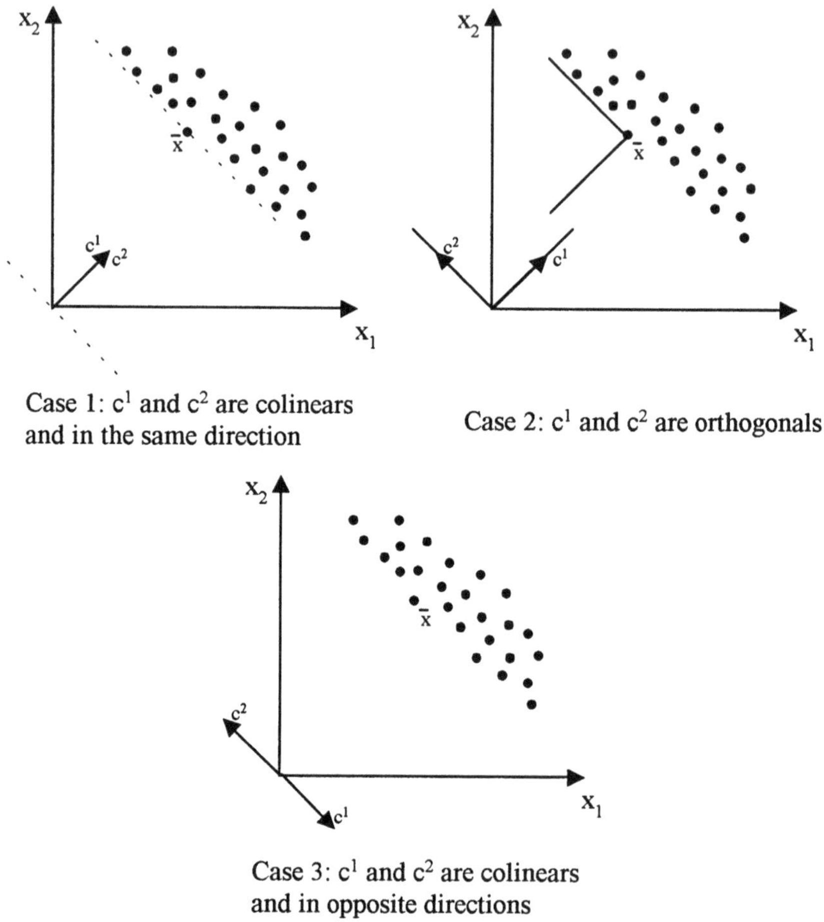

Fig. 3.6. Three cases for a bicriteria problem

3.5 Classes of resolution methods

Pareto optima correspond to "best trade-off" solutions between different conflicting criteria. Clearly it appears that only the decision maker can choose the most satisfactory solution for his problem, among the set E (or WE). Traditionally, multicriteria optimisation problems are part of the MCDM approach and with this heading we assume that when the decision maker chooses his solution, he optimises a utility function, *i.e.* an aggregation function of the criteria. This function is not known with certainty, but we assume that the solution it optimises is a Pareto optimum. Among the solutions which we are going to seek we can distinguish:

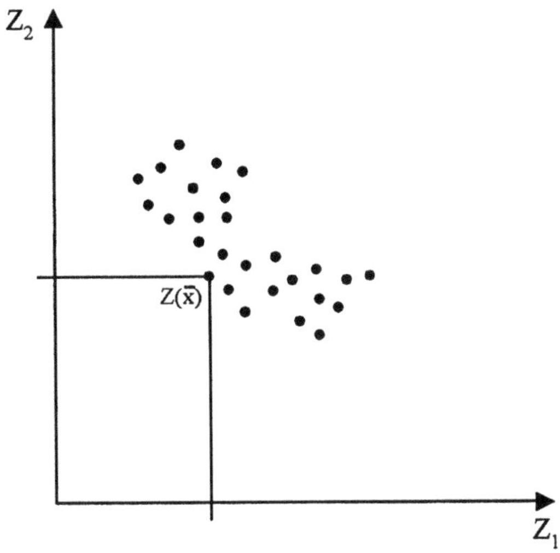

Fig. 3.7. Interpretation in criteria space

1. Solutions which are proper, strict or weak Pareto optima.
2. Among the Pareto optima, those which best satisfy the requirements of the decision maker.

The analyst must propose a resolution algorithm for the multicriteria optimisation problem, *i.e.* an algorithm which will enable the decision maker to choose his solution. For this he must take account of all the information at his disposal: the decision maker may provide the weights of the criteria to the resolution algorithm or he may give the goals to be attained, *etc.* Moreover, the analyst knows that the resolution of a multicriteria optimisation problem cannot be done without the intervention of the decision maker. A resolution algorithm which does not enable the decision maker to intervene, can only determine the whole Pareto optima set.
[Evans, 1984] presents three occasions where the decision maker can intervene: before, during or after the resolution process. A general category of methods can be associated to each of these occasions:

1. The methods enabling the decision maker to intervene before the resolution process are called *a priori*.
2. The methods enabling the decision maker to intervene during the course of the resolution process are called *interactive*.
3. The methods enabling the decision maker to intervene after the resolution process are called *a posteriori*.

In the *a priori* methods, the resolution process cannot be performed without the decision maker having provided a set of information, as for example the value of the weights of the criteria for the minimisation of a linear combination of criteria. Determination of the value of these parameters constitutes a problem itself, which requires the use of a decision aid method. The interested reader is referred particularly to [Roy, 1985], [Vincke, 1989] and [Roy and Bouyssou, 1993].

In the *interactive* methods, the resolution process is iterative. Each iteration provides the decision maker a solution, which is not necessarily a Pareto optimum. He then orients the process by providing, directly or indirectly, new values for the parameters of the problem. For example, it may concern new weightings for the linear combination, or improvement/damaging of certain values of criteria in relation to the current solution. The process is then capable of calculating a new solution and the following iteration can begin. This category of methods has been the object of numerous studies in the field of multicriteria optimisation and more generally in the field of decision aid ([Vanderpooten, 1990]).

Finally, *a posteriori* methods aim to provide the decision maker with an exhaustive set of Pareto optima, among which belongs the most satisfactory solution. The set of Pareto optima suggested to the decision maker depends on the properties of the solved problem.

3.6 Determination of Pareto optima

The solution adopted to the problem of taking into account the conflicting criteria depends on the information which the decision maker can provide. From the point of view of the analyst it is possible to classify the different methods of determining Pareto optima by means of this information (figure 3.8).

The results presented in this section lead to an aggregation of criteria in one or several more general criteria, by adding new parameters (weights, goals, *etc.*) to the problem. Generally, the more interesting the results for these new criteria are, the more difficult is their application (tuning of the parameters, algorithmic complexity, *etc.*). The choice of a method necessitates therefore a trade-off between the quality of the calculable solutions and the ease of its application.

3.6.1 Determination by convex combination of criteria

A traditional result is proposed by [Geoffrion, 1968]. It concerns the minimisation of a convex combination of criteria, for which the basic result is pre-

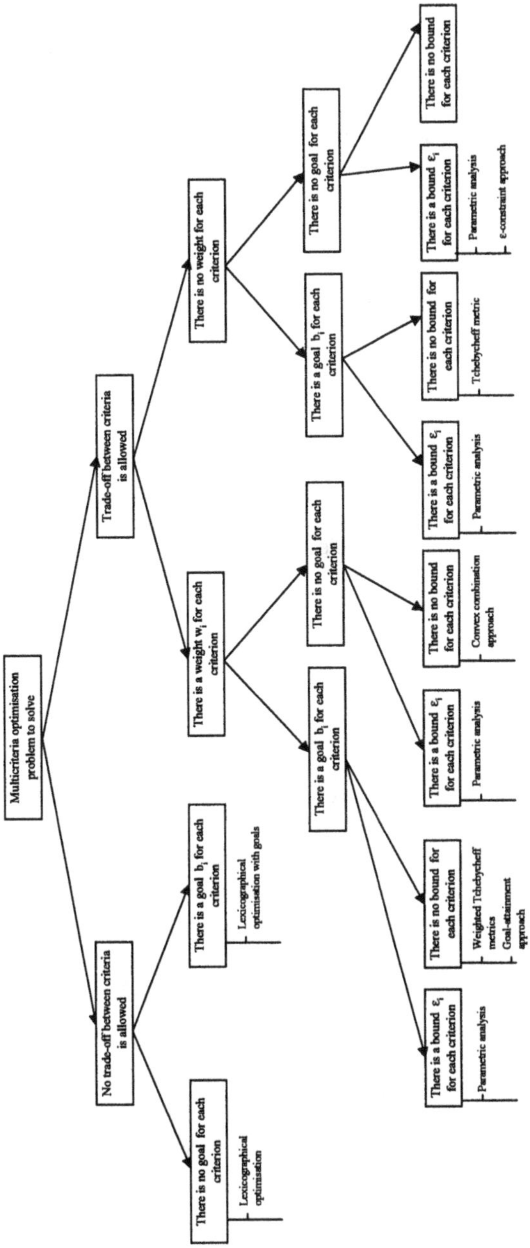

Fig. 3.8. A general typology of multicriteria optimisation problems

sented in theorem 4, also called "Geoffrion's theorem" in the remainder. It concerns a necessary and sufficient condition for the determination of proper Pareto optima.

Theorem 4 *[Geoffrion, 1968]*
Let $\mathcal{S}$ be the convex set of the solutions and K criteria Z_i convex on $\mathcal{S}$. x^0 is a proper Pareto optimum if and only if $\exists \alpha \in \mathbb{R}^K$, with $\alpha_i \in]0;1[$ and $\sum_{i=1}^{K} \alpha_i = 1$, such that x^0 is an optimal solution of the problem (P_α):

$$\mathit{Min}\ g(Z(x))\ \mathit{with}\ g(Z(x)) = \sum_{i=1}^{K} \alpha_i Z_i(x)$$
$$\mathit{subject\ to}$$
$$x \in \mathcal{S}$$

Proof.
$\boxed{\Leftarrow}$ Let us show that if x^0 is an optimal solution of (P_α) with α fixed, then x^0 is a proper Pareto optimum. For this, it is sufficient to show the existence of $M > 0$ such as it is presented in definition 31. Let us proceed by contradiction, *i.e.* suppose that x^0 is an optimal solution of (P_α) with α fixed, and that x^0 is not a proper Pareto optimum.
Then, $\forall M > 0, \exists x^1 \neq x^0, x^1 \in \mathcal{S}$ and $\exists i \in I_{x^1}$, where $I_{x^1} = \{i \in [1;K]/Z_i(x^1) < Z_i(x^0)\}$, such that:
$\forall j, 1 \leq j \leq K$, with $Z_j(x^0) < Z_j(x^1)$, we have $\dfrac{Z_i(x^0) - Z_i(x^1)}{Z_j(x^1) - Z_j(x^0)} > M$.
Let us write $M = K \times \max_{a,b=1,\dots,K} \left(\dfrac{\alpha_a}{\alpha_b}\right)$ and x^1 a solution verifying the hypothese.
Note $J_1 = \{j \in [1;K]/Z_j(x^0) < Z_j(x^1)\}$.
$\forall j \in J_1, Z_i(x^0) - Z_i(x^1) > M \times (Z_j(x^1) - Z_j(x^0))$
$\Rightarrow Z_i(x^0) - Z_i(x^1) > K \times \max_{a,b}(\dfrac{\alpha_a}{\alpha_b}) \times (Z_j(x^1) - Z_j(x^0)), \forall j \in J_1$
$\Rightarrow Z_i(x^0) - Z_i(x^1) > K \times \dfrac{\alpha_j}{\alpha_i} \times (Z_j(x^1) - Z_j(x^0)), \forall j \in J_1$
$\Rightarrow Z_i(x^0) - Z_i(x^1) > |J_1| \times \dfrac{\alpha_j}{\alpha_i} \times (Z_j(x^1) - Z_j(x^0)), \forall j \in J_1$, since $K > |J_1|$
$\Rightarrow \dfrac{\alpha_i}{|J_1|}(Z_i(x^0) - Z_i(x^1)) > \alpha_j(Z_j(x^1) - Z_j(x^0)), \forall j \in J_1$
$\Rightarrow \dfrac{\alpha_i}{|J_1|} Z_i(x^0) + \alpha_j Z_j(x^0) > \dfrac{\alpha_i}{|J_1|} Z_i(x^1) + \alpha_j Z_j(x^1), \forall j \in J_1$
$\Rightarrow \sum_{j \in J_1} \dfrac{\alpha_i}{|J_1|} Z_i(x^0) + \sum_{j \in J_1} \alpha_j Z_j(x^0) > \sum_{j \in J_1} \dfrac{\alpha_i}{|J_1|} Z_i(x^1) + \sum_{j \in J_1} \alpha_j Z_j(x^1)$
$\Rightarrow \sum_{j \in J_1 \cup \{i\}} \alpha_j Z_j(x^0) > \sum_{j \in J_1 \cup \{i\}} \alpha_j Z_j(x^1) \quad$ **(A)**
Note $J_2 = \{j \in [1;K]/Z_j(x^0) \geq Z_j(x^1)\}$.
We have $J_1 \cap J_2 = \emptyset$ and $J_1 \cup J_2 = [1;K]$. $\forall \ell \in J_2$, we have $\alpha_\ell Z_\ell(x^0) \geq \alpha_\ell Z_\ell(x^1)$ **(B)**.
(A) and **(B)** $\Rightarrow \sum_{i=1}^{K} \alpha_i Z_i(x^0) > \sum_{i=1}^{K} \alpha_i Z_i(x^1)$, which contradicts the fact that x^0 is an optimal solution of (P_α). x^0 is therefore a proper Pareto optimum.

$\boxed{\Rightarrow}$ Let us suppose that x^0 is a proper Pareto optimum and let us show that $\exists \alpha \in]0;1[^K$ such that x^0 is an optimal solution of (P_α).
$x^0 \in PRE \Leftrightarrow \exists M > 0$ such that $\forall i = 1, ..., K$ the system (S^i) should not have a solution $y \in \mathcal{S}$.

$$(S^i) \begin{cases} Z_i(y) < Z_i(x^0) \\ Z_i(x^0) - Z_i(y) > M \times (Z_j(y) - Z_j(x^0)) \quad \forall j = 1, ..., K, j \neq i \end{cases}$$

$$\Leftrightarrow (S^i) \begin{cases} Z_i(y) < Z_i(x^0) \\ Z_i(x^0) + M \times Z_j(x^0) > Z_i(y) + M \times Z_j(y) \; \forall j = 1, ..., K, j \neq i \end{cases}$$

Given that the criteria Z_i are convex functions, we have the following result ([Berge and Gouila-Houri, 1965]): $\exists \; \lambda_j^i \geq 0, \forall i = 1, ..., K, \sum_{j=1}^{K} \lambda_j^i = 1$, such that we deduce from the system $(S^i), \forall i = 1, ..., K$, the following system (S'^i):

$$(S'^i) \begin{cases} \lambda_i^i Z_i(y) \leq \lambda_i^i Z_i(x^0) \\ \lambda_j^i (Z_i(x^0) + M \times Z_j(x^0)) \geq \lambda_j^i (Z_i(y) + M \times Z_j(y)), \; \forall j = 1, ..., K, j \neq i \end{cases}$$

with at least one strict inequality.

$\Rightarrow \forall i = 1, ..., K, \nexists y \in \mathcal{S}$ such that $\lambda_i^i Z_i(y) + \sum_{j=1, j\neq i}^{K} \lambda_j^i (Z_i(y) + M Z_j(y)) \leq \lambda_i^i Z_i(x^0) + \sum_{j=1, j\neq i}^{K} \lambda_j^i (Z_i(x^0) + M Z_j(x^0))$

$$\Rightarrow \forall i = 1, ..., K, \nexists y \in \mathcal{S} \; / \; Z_i(y) + M \sum_{j=1, j\neq i}^{K} \lambda_j^i Z_j(y) \leq Z_i(x^0) + M \sum_{j=1, j\neq i}^{K} \lambda_j^i Z_j(x^0)$$

$$\Rightarrow \nexists y \in \mathcal{S} \; / \; \sum_{i=1}^{K} \left(Z_i(y) + M \sum_{j=1, j\neq i}^{K} \lambda_j^i Z_j(y) \right) \leq \sum_{i=1}^{K} \left(Z_i(x^0) + M \sum_{j=1, j\neq i}^{K} \lambda_j^i Z_j(x^0) \right)$$

$$\Rightarrow \nexists y \in \mathcal{S} \; / \sum_{j=1}^{n} Z_j(y) + M \sum_{i=1, i\neq j}^{K} \sum_{j=1}^{K} \lambda_j^i Z_j(y) \leq \sum_{j=1}^{n} Z_j(x^0) + M \sum_{i=1, i\neq j}^{K} \sum_{j=1}^{K} \lambda_j^i Z_j(x^0)$$

$$\Rightarrow \nexists y \in \mathcal{S} \; / \sum_{j=1}^{K} (1 + M \sum_{i=1, i\neq j}^{K} \lambda_j^i) Z_j(y) \leq \sum_{j=1}^{K} (1 + M \sum_{i=1, i\neq j}^{K} \lambda_j^i) Z_j(x^0)$$

$\Rightarrow \exists \alpha_j \; / \; \alpha_j = \dfrac{1+M \sum_{i=1, i\neq j}^{K} \lambda_j^i}{K+M \sum_{j=1}^{K} \sum_{i=1, i\neq j}^{K} \lambda_j^i}$, $\forall j = 1, ..., K$, verifying that $\sum_{j=1}^{K} \alpha_j = 1$, and such that $\sum_{j=1}^{K} \alpha_j Z_j(y) \leq \sum_{j=1}^{K} \alpha_j Z_j(x^0)$ have no solution $y \in \mathcal{S}$. Therefore x^0 is an optimal solution of (P_α).□

In theorem 4, the parameters α_i cannot be equal to zero because in the opposite case, the generated solutions would not all be proper Pareto optima. More precisely, we would obtain a necessary and sufficient condition for the determination of weak Pareto optima.

Lemma 2

Let $\mathcal{S}$ be the convex set of solutions and K criteria Z_i convexes on $\mathcal{S}$. x^0 is a weak Pareto optimum if and only if $\exists\alpha \in \mathbb{R}^K$, with $\alpha_i \in [0;1]$ and $\sum_{i=1}^K \alpha_i = 1$, such that x^0 is an optimal solution of the problem (P_α).

Proof.

$\boxed{\Leftarrow}$ Let us suppose that x^0 is an optimal solution of (P_α) with $\alpha \in [0;1]^K$ fixed and let us show that x^0 is a weak Pareto optimum. Let us proceed by contradiction, *i.e.* we suppose that x^0 is not a weak Pareto optimum.

Let us suppose that $\exists x^1$ such that $\forall i = 1, ..., K, Z_i(x^1) < Z_i(x^0)$. We have:

$\alpha_i(Z_i(x^1) - Z_i(x^0)) \leq 0$ because $\alpha_i \geq 0,\ \forall i = 1, ..., K$

but as $\sum_{i=1}^{K}\alpha_i = 1, \exists j$ such that $\alpha_j > 0 \Rightarrow \alpha_j(Z_j(x^1) - Z_j(x^0)) < 0$

$$\Rightarrow \sum_{i=1}^{K}\alpha_i(Z_i(x^1) - Z_i(x^0)) < 0$$

$$\Rightarrow \sum_{i=1}^{K}\alpha_i Z_i(x^1) < \sum_{i=1}^{K}\alpha_i Z_i(x^0),$$

which contradicts the fact that x^0 is an optimal solution of (P_α). x^0 is therefore a weak Pareto optimum.

$\boxed{\Rightarrow}$ Let us suppose that x^0 is a weak Pareto optimum and let us show that $\exists\alpha \in [0;1]^K$ such that x^0 is an optimal solution of (P_α).

$x^0 \in WE \Leftrightarrow \nexists x^1 \in \mathcal{S}$ such that $Z_i(x^1) < Z_i(x^0),\ \forall i = 1, ..., K$, by definition.

Given that the criteria Z_i are convex functions, we have the following result ([Berge and Gouila-Houri, 1965]): $\exists\alpha \in \mathbb{R}^K$ with $\alpha_j \geq 0, \forall j = 1, ..., K$ and $\sum_{j=1}^{K}\alpha_j = 1$, such that we deduce from the previous inequalities that $\nexists x^1 \in \mathcal{S}$ such that $\forall i = 1, ..., K, \alpha_i Z_i(x^1) < \alpha_i Z_i(x^0)$

$$\Rightarrow \nexists x^1 \in \mathcal{S} \text{ such that } \sum_{i=1}^{K}\alpha_i Z_i(x^1) < \sum_{i=1}^{K}\alpha_i Z_i(x^0)$$

$\Rightarrow x^0$ is an optimal solution of (P_α).□

The level curves are a practical tool to geometrically illustrate different optimisation problems. Concerning the minimisation of a convex combination of criteria, problem (P_α) can be interpreted in the following manner: let $X_=(a) = \{x \in \mathcal{S} / \sum_{i=1}^K \alpha_i Z_i(x) = a$ with $\alpha_i \in]0;1[$ and $\sum_{i=1}^K \alpha_i = 1\}$ be the set of level curves in the decision space. We write $L_=(a) = Z(X_=(a))$. To solve (P_α) is equivalent to determining the level curve of minimal value g^* such that $L_=(g^*)$ is tangential to $\mathcal{Z}$ in the criteria space (figure 3.9). $L_=(g^*) \cap \mathcal{Z}$ defines in the decision space a set of Pareto optima for the multicriteria problem.

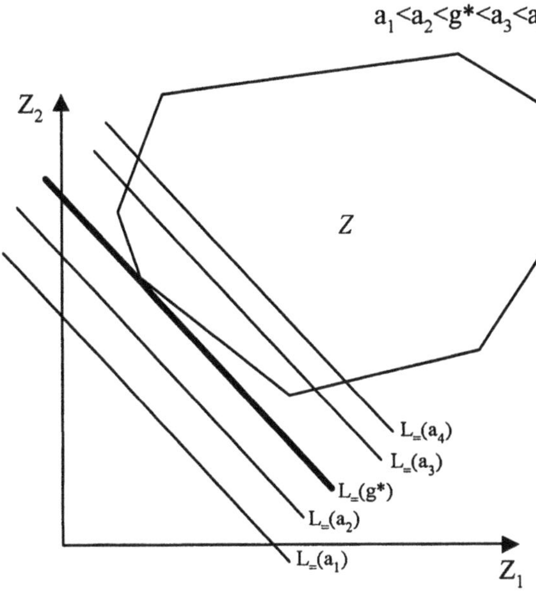

Fig. 3.9. Geometric interpretation of a problem (P_α)

In the case of a priori methods, we must define a way to obtain the weights of the criteria to use in the objective function. Within the field of a posteriori methods, we must conduct a parametric analysis by means of α. We note $\Lambda = \{\alpha = (\alpha_1; \ldots; \alpha_K)/\forall i, \alpha_i \in]0;1[\text{ and } \sum_{i=1}^{K} \alpha_i = 1\}$. The basic idea consists of dividing Λ into v parts Λ_i such that $\Lambda = \cup_{i=1}^{v} \Lambda_i$. Each part Λ_i is allocated a division OPT_i of the set of Pareto optima such that $\forall \alpha^1, \alpha^2 \in \Lambda_i$, if we note $OPT_i(\alpha^1)$ the set of the optimal solutions of (P_{α^1}) and $OPT_i(\alpha^2)$ the set of optimal solutions of (P_{α^2}) then $OPT_i(\alpha^1) = OPT_i(\alpha^2) = OPT_i$. Within the field of interactive methods, we can iteratively vary, according to the instructions of the decision maker, the value of the weights α_i. These instructions can be, according to the algorithm under consideration, new weights, desired improvements, *etc.*

Theorem 4 and lemma 2 are only valid if the set $\mathcal{S}$ and the criteria Z_i are convex. If we suppose that the criteria are not convex functions, then only the necessary condition remains valid: the optimal solutions of a problem (P_α) are (proper or weak) Pareto optima. Moreover, as we shall see in section 3.8 for Multicriteria Mixed Integer Programming, these results no longer allow the full determination of the set of Pareto optima.

3.6.2 Determination by parametric analysis

An interesting result is proposed by [Soland, 1979], since it allows the calculation of all the strict Pareto optima, while being simple to use. Before presenting this result we recall the definition of a strictly increasing function.

Definition 39 *See for example [Schwartz, 1967]*
A function $f : \mathbb{R}^K \to \mathbb{R}$ is strictly increasing if and only if $\forall x, y \in \mathbb{R}^K$, $x \neq y$, $x \leq y \Rightarrow f(x) < f(y)$.

Theorem 5 *[Soland, 1979]*
Let G_Y be the set of strictly increasing functions from $\mathbb{R}^K$ to $\mathbb{R}$ which are lower bounded on $\mathcal{Z}$, and $g \in G_Y$. $x^0 \in \mathcal{S}$ is a strict Pareto optimum if and only if $\exists b \in \mathbb{R}^K$ such that x^0 is an optimal solution of the following problem $(P_{(g,b)})$:

$$\begin{aligned} &Min\ g(Z(x)) \\ &subject\ to \\ &\quad x \in \mathcal{S} \\ &\quad Z(x) \leq b \end{aligned}$$

Proof.
$\boxed{\Leftarrow}$ Let us show that if x^0 is an optimal solution of $(P_{(g,b)})$ with $g \in G_y$ and $b \in \mathbb{R}^K$ fixed, then x^0 is a strict Pareto optimum. Let us proceed by contradiction, *i.e.* we suppose that x^0 is not a strict Pareto optimum with this same vector b.
Then $x^1 \in \mathcal{S}$ exists such that $Z(x^1) \leq Z(x^0)$ with $Z(x^1) \neq Z(x^0)$. As g is a strictly increasing function on $\mathcal{Z}$, we have $g(Z(x^1)) < g(Z(x^0))$. Moreover, as x^0 is a solution of $(P_{(g,b)})$, we have $Z(x^0) \leq b$, and therefore $Z(x^1) \leq b$, which guarantees that x^1 equally satisfies the constraints of $(P_{(g,b)})$. x^1 is therefore also a solution of $(P_{(g,b)})$ and we thus arrive at a contradiction with the optimality hypothesis of x^0 for $(P_{(g,b)})$. x^0 is therefore a strict Pareto optimum.
$\boxed{\Rightarrow}$ Let $g \in G_Y$ be fixed. Let us show that if x^0 is a strict Pareto optimum then $b \in \mathbb{R}^K$ exists such that x^0 is an optimal solution of $(P_{(g,b)})$. We take $b = Z(x^0)$. Let us proceed by contradiction to show that x^0 is an optimal solution of the problem $(P_{(g,b)})$, *i.e.* we suppose that $\exists x^1 \in \mathcal{S}$ satisfying the constraints of $(P_{(g,b)})$ with $g(Z(x^1)) < g(Z(x^0))$. We have:

$$\begin{cases} g(Z(x^1)) < g(Z(x^0)) \\ Z(x^1) \leq Z(x^0) = b \end{cases}$$

As g is a strictly increasing function on $\mathcal{Z}$, this system implies that $Z(x^1) \leq Z(x^0)$ with at least one criterion Z_k such that $Z_k(x^1) < Z_k(x^0)$, which contradicts the fact that x^0 is a strict Pareto optimum. x^0 is therefore an optimal solution of problem $(P_{(g,b)})$□

The problem $(P_{(g,b)})$ is generic and simple to use since the function g is chosen by the analyst. For example, we can choose to minimise a convex combination of criteria, which enables us to set a necessary and sufficient condition for the calculation of strict Pareto optima, even for non convex problems.

Geometrically, the problem $(P_{(g,b)})$ can be interpreted by means of level curves. Let $\mathcal{S}' = \{x \in \mathcal{S}/Z(x) \leq b\}$, $X_=(a) = \{x \in \mathcal{S}'/g(Z(x)) = a\}$ and $L_=(a) = Z(X_=(a))$. Solving $(P_{(g,b)})$ corresponds to determining the level curve of minimal value g^* such that $L_=(g^*)$ is tangential to $\mathcal{Z}'$ in criteria space (figure 3.10). $L_=(g^*) \cap \mathcal{Z}'$ defines in decision space a set of strict Pareto optima for the multicriteria problem.

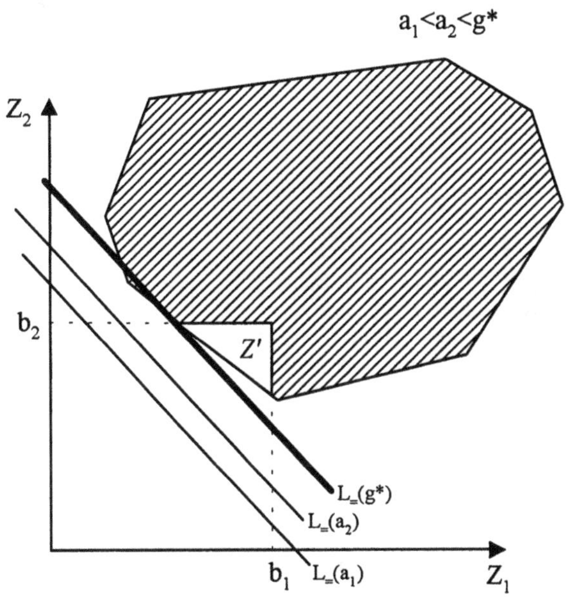

Fig. 3.10. Geometric interpretation of a problem $(P_{(g,b)})$

Use of this result in the resolution of multicriteria problems depends on the determination of the vector b when the function g is fixed. In an interactive procedure or in an a posteriori procedure, we must iteratively vary the vector b to obtain several Pareto optima. For example, we can start with an initial vector which is composed of high values and next reduce these values either according to the analyst's instructions (interactive algorithm) or according to a reduction procedure which enables us to enumerate the set E. In an a priori method, it is sufficient to ask the decision maker for the bound values b_i.

3.6.3 Determination by means of the ϵ-constraint approach

The ϵ-constraint approach is often used in the literature. It minimises a criterion knowing that the others $K-1$ are upper bounded ([Haimes et al., 1971] and [Haimes et al., 1975]). Theorem 6, presented in [Soland, 1979], comes from the results proposed in [Yu, 1974], and enable us to calculate strict Pareto optima.

Theorem 6 *[Yu, 1974]*
$x^0 \in \mathcal{S}$ is a strict Pareto optimum if and only if $\forall k \in [1;K]$ $\exists \epsilon^k = (\epsilon_1^k;\ldots;\epsilon_{k-1}^k;\epsilon_{k+1}^k;\ldots;\epsilon_K^k) \in \mathbb{R}^{K-1}$ such that $Z(x^0)$ is the unique criteria vector corresponding to the optimal solution of the following problem (P_{ϵ^k}):

$$\begin{aligned}&Min\ Z_k(x)\\&subject\ to\\&\quad x \in \mathcal{S}\\&\quad Z_i(x) \leq \epsilon_i^k,\ \forall i \in [1;K], i \neq k\end{aligned}$$

Proof.
$\boxed{\Rightarrow}$ Let us suppose that x^0 is a strict Pareto optimum and let us show that $\forall k \in [1;K]$, $\exists \epsilon^k = (\epsilon_1^k;\ldots;\epsilon_{k-1}^k;\epsilon_{k+1}^k;\ldots;\epsilon_K^k) \in \mathbb{R}^{K-1}$ such that $Z(x^0)$ is the unique criteria vector corresponding to the optimal solutions of the problem (P_{ϵ^k}). We take $\epsilon^k = (Z_1(x^0);\ldots;Z_{k-1}(x^0);Z_{k+1}(x^0);\ \ldots;Z_K(x^0))$, $\forall k = 1,\ldots,K$. Let us proceed by contradiction, to show that, $\forall k = 1,\ldots,K$, $Z(x^0)$ is the unique criteria vector corresponding to the optimal solutions of problem (P_{ϵ^k}).
Let us suppose that $\exists k \in [1;K]$ such that $\exists x^1 \in \mathcal{S}$ optimal solution of (P_{ϵ^k}), with $Z(x^0) \neq Z(x^1)$. We have:

$$\begin{cases} Z_k(x^1) \leq Z_k(x^0) \\ Z_i(x^1) \leq \epsilon_i^k = Z_i(x^0)\ \forall i = 1,\ldots,K, i \neq k \\ Z(x^0) \neq Z(x^1) \end{cases}$$

This system contradicts the fact that x^0 is a strict Pareto optimum.
$\boxed{\Leftarrow}$ Let us suppose that $\forall k \in [1;K], \exists \epsilon^k = (\epsilon_1^k;\ldots;\epsilon_{k-1}^k;\epsilon_{k+1}^k;\ldots;\epsilon_K^k) \in \mathbb{R}^{K-1}$ such that $Z(x^0)$, $x^0 \in \mathcal{S}$, is the unique criteria vector corresponding to the optimal solutions of the problem (P_{ϵ^k}) and we show that x^0 is a strict Pareto optimum. Let us proceed by contradiction, *i.e.* let us suppose that x^0 is not a strict Pareto optimum. Then, $x^1 \in \mathcal{S}$ exists such that $Z(x^1) \leq Z(x^0)$ with $Z(x^1) \neq Z(x^0)$. Let us consider $k \in [1;K]$. For all $\epsilon^k \in \mathbb{R}^{K-1}$ such that $Z_i(x^0) \leq \epsilon_i^k \times k_i$, $\forall i = 1,\ldots,K$, $i \neq k$, x^1 is a solution of (P_{ϵ^k}) for $Z_i(x^1) \leq Z_i(x^0) \leq \epsilon_i^k$. Moreover, $Z_k(x^1) \leq Z_k(x^0)$ implies that either $Z_k(x^1) = Z_k(x^0)$, or $Z_k(x^1) < Z_k(x^0)$ which contradicts in every case the fact that $Z(x^0)$ is the unique criteria vector solution of (P_{ϵ^k}).□

The result shown in theorem 6 is quite difficult to implement, notably because of the constraint of uniqueness. In the case where this is not taken into account, we have the following theorem.

Theorem 7 *[Miettinen, 1994]*
Let $x^0 \in \mathcal{S}$. If $\exists k \in [1;K]$, and if $\exists \epsilon^k = (\epsilon_1^k;\ldots;\epsilon_{k-1}^k;\epsilon_{k+1}^k;\ldots;\epsilon_K^k) \in \mathbb{R}^{K-1}$, such that x^0 is an optimal solution of the following problem (P_{ϵ^k}):

$$\begin{array}{l} Min\ Z_k(x) \\ subject\ to \\ \quad x \in \mathcal{S} \\ \quad Z_i(x) \leq \epsilon_i^k,\ \forall i \in [1;K], i \neq k \end{array}$$

then x^0 *is a weak Pareto optimum.*

Proof.
Let us consider $x^0 \in \mathcal{S}$, $k \in [1;K]$, and $\epsilon^k = (\epsilon_1^k;\ldots;\epsilon_{k-1}^k;\epsilon_{k+1}^k;\ldots;\epsilon_K^k) \in \mathbb{R}^{K-1}$, such that x^0 is an optimal solution of problem (P_{ϵ^k}). Let us proceed by contradiction to show that x^0 is a weak Pareto optimum.
Let us suppose that $\exists x^1 \in \mathcal{S}$ such that $Z(x^1) < Z(x^0)$. We have therefore $\forall i \in [1;K], i \neq k, Z_i(x^1) < Z_i(x^0) \leq \epsilon_i^k$, and x^1 satisfies the constraints of (P_{ϵ^k}). As $Z_k(x^1) < Z_k(x^0)$, the optimality hypothesis of x^0 for (P_{ϵ^k}) is no longer verified which is a contradiction. x^0 is therefore a weak Pareto optimum.□

The reciprocal of theorem 7 is false. Let us consider a problem with three criteria where the set $\mathcal{Z}$ contains the following criteria vectors:

$$\begin{array}{l} Z^1 = [3;5;5]^T \text{ (non dominated)} \\ Z^2 = [4;4;6]^T \text{ (non dominated)} \\ Z^3 = [3;5;6]^T \text{ (weakly non dominated)} \\ Z^4 = [4;5;7]^T \text{ (weakly non dominated)} \end{array}$$

It appears then that for all criteria Z_k and all vectors ϵ^k, Z^4 will never be a solution to problem (P_{ϵ^k}). To realise this it is sufficient to construct the three possible problems (P_{ϵ^k}) and to verify that Z^4 is never an optimal solution. Nevertheless, when the convexity of the set $\mathcal{S}$ and of the criteria Z_i is imposed, it is possible to show that the condition of theorem 7 becomes a necessary and sufficient condition.

Lemma 3
Let $\mathcal{S}$ *be a convex set and* K *criteria* Z_i *convex on* $\mathcal{S}$. $x^0 \in \mathcal{S}$ *is a weak Pareto optimum if and only if* $\exists k \in [1;K]$ *and* $\exists \epsilon^k = (\epsilon_1^k;\ldots;\epsilon_{k-1}^k;\epsilon_{k+1}^k;\ldots;\epsilon_K^k) \in \mathbb{R}^{K-1}$ *such that* x^0 *is an optimal solution of problem* (P_{ϵ^k}).

Proof.
$\boxed{\Leftarrow}$ The proof is identical to that of theorem 7.
$\boxed{\Rightarrow}$ Let us suppose that x^0 is a weak Pareto optimum and let us show that $\exists\ k \in [1;K]$ and $\exists \epsilon^k \in \mathbb{R}^{K-1}$ such that x^0 is an optimal solution of the problem (P_{ϵ^k}). We proceed by contradiction by considering that $\forall k$, $\forall \epsilon^k$, $\exists x^k$ such that x^k satisfies the constraints of (P_{ϵ^k}) and $Z_k(x^k) < Z_k(x^0)$.
A solution x^k always exists which verifies the following system $(S_{\epsilon^k}^k)$, $\forall k$, $\forall \epsilon^k \geq [Z_1(x^0);\ldots;Z_{k-1}(x^0);Z_{k+1}(x^0);\ldots;Z_K(x^0)]^T$:

$$\begin{cases} Z_k(x^k) < Z_k(x^0) & \\ Z_i(x^k) \leq \epsilon_i^k & \forall i = 1,\ldots,K, i \neq k \\ Z_i(x^0) \leq \epsilon_i^k & \forall i = 1,\ldots,K, i \neq k \end{cases}$$

Let us take for example, $\epsilon_i^k = Z_i(x^0)$, $\forall i = 1, ..., K, i \neq k$, because thus x^0 remains a solution of the corresponding problem (P_{ϵ^k}). As $\mathcal{S}$ is a convex set and Z_i are convex functions on $\mathcal{S}$, we have: $\forall \alpha \in [0;1]^K$, with $\sum_{j=1}^{K} \alpha_j = 1$, $\exists x^\alpha \in \mathcal{S}$ such that $Z(x^\alpha) = \sum_{j=1}^{K} \alpha_j Z(x^j)$. We have therefore, $\forall \alpha \in [0;1]^K$:
$Z_i(x^\alpha) = \sum_{j=1}^{K} \alpha_j Z_i(x^j) < Z_i(x^0), \forall i = 1, ..., K$.
Therefore $Z(x^\alpha) < Z(x^0)$ and x^0 is dominated which is a contradiction.□

The above results do not assume that the criterion to be minimised is fixed, which is not necessarily practical from the point of view of their use in an algorithm. A result similar to theorem 7, but more simple by assuming that the criterion to be minimised is fixed, is proposed in the following lemma.

Lemma 4
Let a criterion Z_k, with $k \in [1;K]$, be fixed. If $\exists \epsilon^k = (\epsilon_1^k; \ldots; \epsilon_{k-1}^k; \epsilon_{k+1}^k; \ldots; \epsilon_K^k) \in \mathbb{R}^{K-1}$ such that $x^0 \in \mathcal{S}$ is an optimal solution of the problem (P_{ϵ^k}), then x^0 is a weak Pareto optimum.

Proof.
We suppose that k is fixed. Let $\epsilon^k = (\epsilon_1^k; \ldots; \epsilon_{k-1}^k; \epsilon_{k+1}^k; \ldots; \epsilon_K^k) \in \mathbb{R}^{K-1}$ such that $x^0 \in \mathcal{S}$ is an optimal solution of the problem (P_{ϵ^k}). Let us proceed by contradiction to show that x^0 is a weak Pareto optimum. Pursuit of the proof is similar to that of theorem 7.
Let us suppose that $\exists x^1 \in \mathcal{S}$ such that $Z(x^1) < Z(x^0)$. We have therefore on one hand $\forall i \in [1;K], i \neq k, Z_i(x^1) < Z_i(x^0) \leq \epsilon_i^k$, which guarantees that x^1 satisfies the constraints of (P_{ϵ^k}), and on the other hand $Z_k(x^1) < Z_k(x^0)$, which contradicts the optimality hypothesis of x^0 for (P_{ϵ^k}). x^0 is therefore a weak Pareto optimum.□

Lemma 4 shows, that when the criterion is fixed, the set of the calculable Pareto optima is a subset of the set of the weak Pareto optima. By contrast to theorem 7, the addition of convexity hypothesis to the set $\mathcal{S}$ and the functions Z_i does not guarantee that all the set WE is calculable. A counter example is given in figure 3.11. Nevertheless, we can show that the subset of WE which is calculable by lemma 4 contains the set E.

Lemma 5
Let a criterion Z_k, with $k \in [1;K]$, be fixed. If x^0 is a strict Pareto optimum, then $\exists \epsilon^k = (\epsilon_1^k; \ldots; \epsilon_{k-1}^k; \epsilon_{k+1}^k; \ldots; \epsilon_K^k) \in \mathbb{R}^{K-1}$ such that $x^0 \in \mathcal{S}$ is an optimal solution of problem (P_{ϵ^k}).

Proof.
We suppose that k is fixed. Let x^0 be a strict Pareto optimum and let us show that $\exists\ \epsilon^k$ such that x^0 is an optimal solution of the problem (P_{ϵ^k}). We take

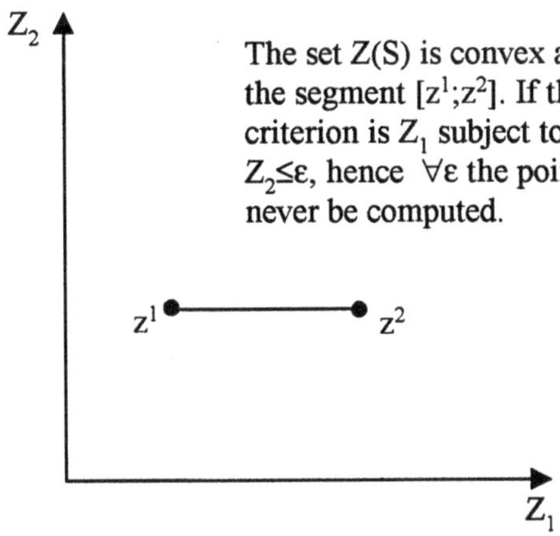

Fig. 3.11. Counter example of the reciprocal of lemma 4 under convexity hypothesis

$\epsilon^k = [Z_1(x^0);\ldots;Z_{k-1}(x^0);\, Z_{k+1}(x^0);\ldots;Z_K(x^0)]^T$. We proceed by contradiction to show that x^0 is an optimal solution of the defined problem (P_{ϵ^k}), *i.e.* we suppose that $\exists x^1$ such that $Z_k(x^1) < Z_k(x^0)$ and $Z_i(x^1) < \epsilon_i^k$, $\forall i = 1,...,K, i \neq k$.
We have the following system:

$$\begin{cases} Z_k(x^1) < Z_k(x^0) \\ Z_i(x^1) \leq Z_i(x^0) \quad \forall i = 1,...,K, i \neq k \end{cases}$$

$\Rightarrow Z(x^1) < Z(x^0)$
We arrive at a contradiction with the fact that x^0 is a strict Pareto optimum. x^0 is therefore an optimal solution of the problem (P_{ϵ^k}) previously defined.□

Geometrically, the problem (P_{ϵ^k}) can be interpreted by means of level curves. Let $k \in [1;K]$ and $\epsilon^k = (\epsilon_1^k;\ldots;\epsilon_{k-1}^k;\epsilon_{k+1}^k;\ldots;\epsilon_K^k) \in \mathbb{R}^{K-1}$. Let us define $S^k = \{x \in S/Z_i(x) \leq \epsilon_i^k \ \forall i \in [1;K], i \neq k\}$, $X_=(a)^k = \{x \in S^k/Z_k(x) = a\}$ and $L_=(a)^k = Z(X_=(a)^k)$. To solve (P_{ϵ^k}) is equivalent to determining the level curve with the minimal level curve value a^* such that $L_=(a^*)^k$ is tangential to $Z(S^k)$ in the criteria space (figure 3.12). If $\forall\ k, \exists\ S^k$ such that $L_=(a^*)^k \cap Z(S^k) = \{Z(x^*)\}$ then x^* is a strict Pareto optimum for the multicriteria problem.

The ϵ-constraint approach has been used widely in the literature (see for example [Steuer, 1986]) because it is easy to use in an interactive algorithm: the decision maker can interactively specify and modify the bounds and analyse the influence of these modifications on the final solution. In the context of an algorithm which determines the set of strict Pareto optima, one of the re-

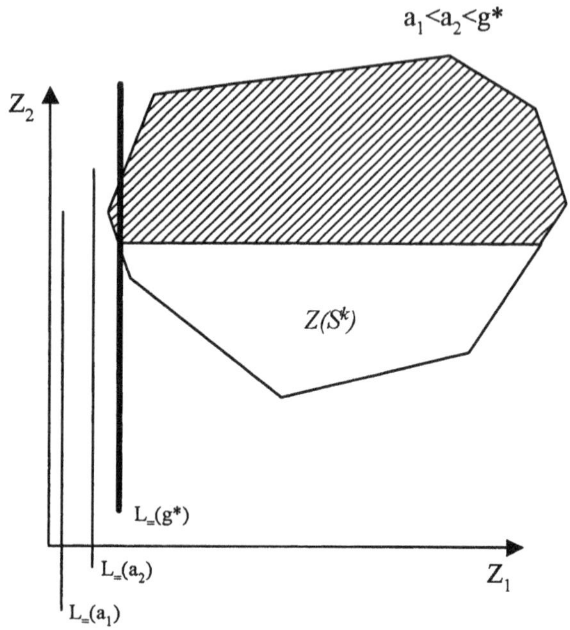

Fig. 3.12. Geometric interpretation of a problem (P_{ϵ^k})

sults presented can be used to vary the upper bounds. For each fixed bound, a weak Pareto optimum is calculated by solving a problem (P_{ϵ^k}). [Steuer, 1986] presents a result for the estimation of the local trade-offs between two criteria, useable in the context of such an algorithm to vary these bounds. Another advantage of the ϵ-constraint approach lies in the fact that at each iteration, we retrieve a single criterion problem for which we can already know an efficient resolution algorithm.

3.6.4 Use of the Tchebycheff metric

To determine the Pareto optima it is possible to use a metric and to search for "the closest possible" solution to a reference criteria vector. In this section, we are interested in a particular metric: the Tchebycheff metric ([Bowman, 1976]). Before presenting this metric, as well as the related theorem, we recall some definitions linked to the reference points, or reference criteria vectors. The following definition assumes that each criterion can reach its minimal value.

Definition 40
$z^{id} = [z_1^{id}; \ldots; z_K^{id}]^T$ *is* **the ideal point**, *or* **ideal criteria vector** *if and only*

if $z_i^{id} = \min_{x \in \mathcal{S}}(Z_i(x)), \forall i = 1, ..., K$*. Generally, this vector does not correspond to any feasible solution.*

Definition 41
Let K *vectors* $z^i = [z_1^i; \ldots; z_K^i]^T$ *verifying* $z_i^i = z_i^{id}, \forall i = 1, ..., K$*. The* **gains matrix**, *noted* G*, is defined by* $G_{j,i} = z_j^i, \forall i = 1, ..., K, \forall j = 1, ..., K$*. This matrix is not necessarily unique.*

Definition 42
Let G *be the gains matrix.* **The nadir** *is a criteria vector, noted* z^{na}*, defined by* $z_j^{na} = \max_{i=1,\ldots,K}(G_{j,i}), \forall j = 1, ..., K$*. We note that this point depends on the gains matrix considered (when there are several of these).*

Definition 43
z^{ut} *is a* **utopian point**, *or* **utopian criteria vector** *if and only if* z^{ut} *dominates* z^{id}*, i.e.* $z^{ut} \leq z^{id}$ *with at least one strict inequality. This point does not correspond to any feasible solution.*

Definition 44
Generally speaking we call **reference point**, *or* **reference criteria vector** *every vector* z^{ref} *which is considered as an objective to reach. The objective is to find the closest possible solution to this point, in the sense of a function to be optimised. The points* z^{id}*,* z^{na} *and* z^{ut} *are reference points.*

The previous definitions are traditional and are often used in interactive methods. To measure the distance of a solution from a reference point, we use a metric, as for example that of Tchebycheff.

Definition 45 *[Bowman, 1976]*
Let z^1 *and* $z^2 \in \mathbb{R}^K$*. The Tchebycheff metric is a measure of the distance in* $\mathbb{R}^K$ *between* z^1 *and* z^2*, defined by:*

$$\|z^1 - z^2\|_T = \max_{i=1,\ldots,K}(|z_i^1 - z_i^2|).$$

To use this metric in the area of the determination of Pareto optima ([Bowman, 1976]), we use a special reference point which we call the *Tchebycheff point*. Let $z^* \in \mathbb{R}^K$ such that z^* is an optimal solution of the minimisation problem of K criteria according to the lexicographical order $Z_1 \to Z_2 \to \ldots \to Z_K$. This means that the vector z^* is such that $z_i^* = \min_{x \in \mathcal{S}^{i-1}}(Z_i(x))$ with $\mathcal{S}^i = \{x \in \mathcal{S}^{i-1} / Z_i(x) = \min_{x' \in \mathcal{S}^{i-1}}(Z_i(x'))\}$ and $\mathcal{S}^0 = \mathcal{S}$. $\forall \theta = (0, \theta_2, \ldots, \theta_K) \in \mathbb{R}^K$, $(z^* - \theta)$ is called a Tchebycheff point.

Theorem 8 *[Bowman, 1976]*
If $x^0 \in \mathcal{S}$ *is a strict Pareto optimum then* $\exists \theta^* = (0, \theta_2^*, \ldots, \theta_K^*) \in \mathbb{R}^K$ *such that* x^0 *is an optimal solution of the following problem* (P_θ)*:*

$$\begin{aligned}&Min\ \|Z(x)-(z^*-\theta^*)\|_T\\&subject\ to\\&\qquad x\in\mathcal{S}\end{aligned}$$

Proof.
For all $x^1 \in \mathcal{S}, \nexists u \geq 0,\ u \neq 0$, such that $Z(x^0) = Z(x^1) + u$ because x^0 is a strict Pareto optimum. Let us take $\theta_1^* = 0$ and $\theta_i^* = -Z_i(x^0) + z_i^* - z_1^* + Z_1(x^0),\ \forall i = 2, ..., K$.
We deduce from this that $\forall i = 2, ..., K,\ Z_i(x^0) - (z_i^* - \theta_i^*) = Z_i(x^0) - z_i^* - Z_i(x^0) + z_i^* - z_1^* + Z_1(x^0)$
$\Leftrightarrow \forall i = 1, ..., K, Z_i(x^0) - (z_i^* - \theta_i^*) = Z_1(x^0) - z_1^*$.
Thus, we have:
$\|Z(x^0) - (z^* - \theta^*)\|_T = \max\left(|Z_1(x^0) - z_1^*|; |Z_1(x^0) - z_1^*|; \ldots; |Z_1(x^0) - z_1^*|\right)$
i.e. $\|Z(x^0) - (z^* - \theta^*)\|_T = |Z_1(x^0) - z_1^*|$, and
$\|Z(x^1) - (z^* - \theta^*)\|_T = \max_{i=1,\ldots,K}(|Z_i(x^1) - z_i^* + \theta_i^*|)$
$= \max(|Z_1(x^1) - z_1^*|; |Z_2(x^1) - Z_2(x^0) - z_1^* + Z_1(x^0)|; \ldots; |Z_K(x^1) - Z_K(x^0) - z_1^* + Z_1(x^0)|)$
now, as $\forall x^1 \in \mathcal{S}, \nexists u \geq 0, u \neq 0$, such that $Z(x^0) = Z(x^1) + u$, we have necessarily $u < 0$
$\Rightarrow |Z_i(x^1) - Z_i(x^0) - z_1^* + Z_1(x^0)| = |-u_i - z_1^* + Z_1(x^0)| > |-z_1^* + Z_1(x^0)|$
We obtain thus:
$\|Z(x^1) - (z^* - \theta^*)\|_T = \max(|Z_1(x^1) - z_1^*|; \max_{i=2,\ldots,K}(|-u_i - z_1^* + Z_1(x^0)|)) > |Z_1(x^0) - z_1^*| = \|Z(x^0) - (z^* - \theta^*)\|_T$.
Therefore, θ^*exists such that x^0 is an optimal solution of (P_θ).□

In theorem 8, the determination of a strict Pareto optimum is made by using a Tchebycheff point $(z^* - \theta)$. It is obvious that this point must not correspond to any feasible solution of $\mathcal{S}$ otherwise the optimal solution of (P_θ) would be the point $(z^* - \theta)$ which is not necessarily a Pareto optimum. Geometrically, the problem (P_θ) can be interpreted by means of level curves (figure 3.13). Let z^* and θ be fixed, $X_=(a) = \{x \in \mathcal{S}/\|Z(x) - (z^* - \theta^*)\|_T = a\}$ and $L_=(a) = Z(X_=(a))$. Solving (P_θ) is equivalent to determining the level curve of minimal value a^* such that $L_=(a^*) \neq \emptyset$. The solutions of $X_=(a^*)$ are then solutions of (P_θ).

The use of this metric in a resolution algorithm is related to the position of the Tchebycheff point $(z^* - \theta)$. In an interactive algorithm, we may suggest to the decision maker a first solution corresponding to an initial Tchebycheff point. The instructions he gives enable us next to vary this point and to repeat the process, until a satisfactory solution is obtained. In an a posteriori algorithm we must get a procedure enabling us to vary $(z^* - \theta)$ and eliminate all the dominated solutions of the set of obtained solutions.

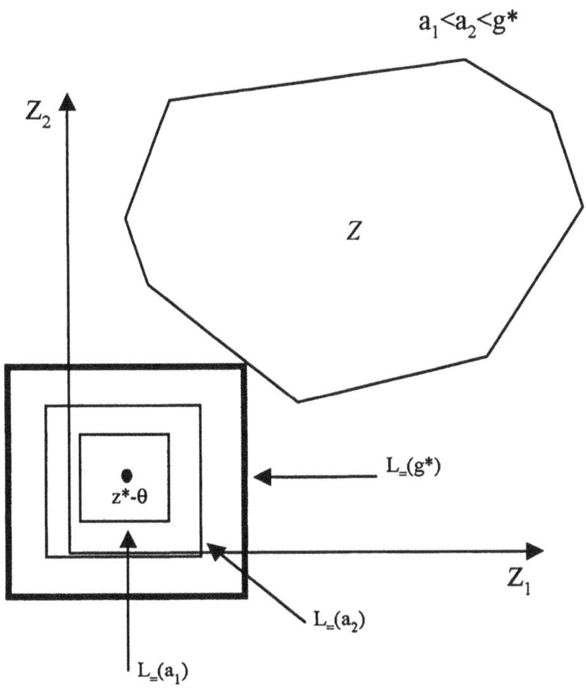

Fig. 3.13. Geometric interpretation of a problem (P_θ)

3.6.5 Use of the weighted Tchebycheff metric

When we consider that weights λ_i are associated with criteria, it is possible to use a generalisation of the Tchebycheff metric. In this case, we make use of several results which are more interesting than that presented in the previous section. We begin with the definition of the weighted Tchebycheff metric.

Definition 46
Let z^1 and $z^2 \in \mathbb{R}^K$. The weighted Tchebycheff metric is a weighted measure of the distance in $\mathbb{R}^K$ between z^1 and z^2, defined by:

$$\|z^1 - z^2\|_{Tp} = \max_{i=1,\dots,K} (\lambda_i |z_i^1 - z_i^2|) \text{ with } \lambda \in \mathbb{R}_+^K.$$

The principal result tied to the determination of Pareto optima is displayed in theorem 9.

Theorem 9 *[Bowman, 1976]*
If $x^0 \in \mathcal{S}$ is a strict Pareto optimum then $\exists \lambda \in \mathbb{R}_{+*}^K$ such that x^0 is an optimal solution of the following problem (P_λ):

$$\begin{array}{l} Min\ \|Z(x) - z^{ut}\|_{Tp} \\ subject\ to \\ \quad x \in \mathcal{S} \end{array}$$

with $z^{ut} \in \mathbb{R}^K$ a utopian point.

Proof.
Let x^0 be a strict Pareto optimum and $\lambda \in \mathbb{R}^K_{+*}$ defined by:

$$\begin{cases} \lambda_i = \dfrac{1}{Z_i(x^0) - z_i^{ut}} & \text{if } Z_i(x^0) \neq z_i^{ut} \\ \lambda_i = 1 & \text{otherwise} \end{cases}$$

with $z^{ut} \in \mathbb{R}^K$ a fixed utopian point. We have $z^{ut} \leq Z(x)$, $\forall x \in \mathcal{S}$ with at least one strict inequality, therefore $|Z_i(x^0) - z_i^{ut}| = Z_i(x^0) - z_i^{ut}$, $\forall i = 1, ..., K$, from where $\lambda_i|Z_i(x^0) - z_i^{ut}| = 1$ if $Z_i(x^0) \neq z_i^{ut}$, and 0 otherwise.
We deduce from this that $\|Z(x^0) - z^{ut}\|_{Tp} = \max_{i=1,\dots,K}(\lambda_i(Z_i(x^0) - z_i^{ut})) \leq 1$.
Let $x^1 \in \mathcal{S}$, we have $\|Z(x^1) - z^{ut}\|_{Tp} = \max_{i=1,\dots,K}(\lambda_i(Z_i(x^1) - z^{ut}))$
$= \max\left(\max_{i/Z_i(x^0)\neq z_i^{ut}} \dfrac{Z_i(x^1) - z^{ut}}{Z_i(x^0) - z^{ut}}; \max_{i/Z_i(x^0)=z_i^{ut}} (Z_i(x^1) - z^{ut})\right)$. As x^0 is a strict Pareto optimum, $\nexists x^1 \in \mathcal{S}$ such that $Z_i(x^1) \leq Z_i(x^0)$, $\forall i = 1, ..., K$, with $Z(x^1) \neq Z(x^0)$, and we deduce from this that $\exists i / Z_i(x^1) - z_i^{ut} > Z_i(x^0) - z_i^{ut}$.
Whence $\|Z(x^1) - z^{ut}\|_{Tp} > 1$, and x^0 is an optimal solution of (P_λ).□

Theorem 9 remains valid if we consider that x^0 is a weak Pareto optimum. Besides, the result shown in this theorem is a sufficient condition and if we are interested in its opposite, we can simply show that the calculable solutions are weak Pareto optima.

Lemma 6
Let $\lambda \in \mathbb{R}^K_{+*}$ and $z^{ut} \in \mathbb{R}^K$ be a utopian point. If $x^0 \in \mathcal{S}$ is an optimal solution of the problem (P_λ), then x^0 is a weak Pareto optimum.

Proof.
Let us proceed by contradiction and suppose that x^0 is an optimal solution of (P_λ) and that it is not a weak Pareto optimum. Then, $\exists x^1 \in \mathcal{S}$ such that $Z_i(x^1) < Z_i(x^0)$, $\forall i = 1, ..., K$.
$\Rightarrow \lambda_i|Z_i(x^1) - z_i^{ut}| < \lambda_i|Z_i(x^0) - z_i^{ut}|$ for $\lambda_i > 0$ and $z_i^{ut} \leq Z_i(x)$, $\forall i = 1, ..., K$, $\forall x \in \mathcal{S}$
$\Rightarrow \max_{i=1,\dots,K}(\lambda_i|Z_i(x^1) - z_i^{ut}|) < \max_{i=1,\dots,K}(\lambda_i|Z_i(x^0) - z_i^{ut}|)$,
which contradicts the fact that x^0 is an optimal solution of (P_λ).□

Corollary 2 makes a synthesis of the results presented in lemma 6 and in theorem 9 for the calculation of weak Pareto optima.

Corollary 2
$x^0 \in \mathcal{S}$ is a weak Pareto optimum if and only if $\exists \lambda \in \mathbb{R}^K_{+*}$ and $z^{ut} \in \mathbb{R}^K$ a utopian point, such that x^0 is an optimal solution of the problem (P_λ).

If we are only interested in the determination of strict Pareto optima, we can then use the result presented in theorem 10.

Theorem 10 *See [Teghem, 1996] in the case of MLP*
$x^0 \in \mathcal{S}$ is a strict Pareto optimum if and only if $\exists \lambda \in \mathbb{R}^K_{+*}$ and $z^{ut} \in \mathbb{R}^K$ a utopian point, such that x^0 is an optimal solution of problem (P_λ) and $Z(x^0)$ is the unique optimal criteria vector.

Proof.
$\boxed{\Rightarrow}$ The proof is identical to that of theorem 9 in which $Z(x^0)$ is also the unique optimal criteria vector.
$\boxed{\Leftarrow}$ Let us suppose that $\exists \lambda \in \mathbb{R}^K_{+*}$ and $z^{ut} \in \mathbb{R}^K$ a utopian point, such that $x^0 \in \mathcal{S}$ is an optimal solution of (P_λ) with $Z(x^0)$ the unique optimal criteria vector. Let us show by contradiction that x^0 is a strict Pareto optimum.
Let $x^1 \in \mathcal{S}$ such that $Z(x^1) \leq Z(x^0)$ with $Z(x^1) \neq Z(x^0)$
$\Leftrightarrow \lambda_i(Z_i(x^1) - z_i^{ut}) \leq \lambda_i(Z_i(x^0) - z_i^{ut})$, $\forall i = 1, ..., K$, with at least one strict inequality
$\Leftrightarrow \max_{i=1,...,K}(\lambda_i(Z_i(x^1) - z_i^{ut})) \leq \max_{i=1,...,K}(\lambda_i(Z_i(x^0) - z_i^{ut}))$
Two cases can appear:

- $\max_{i=1,...,K}(\lambda_i(Z_i(x^1) - z_i^{ut})) = \max_{i=1,...,K}(\lambda_i(Z_i(x^0) - z_i^{ut}))$ and that contradicts the uniqueness hypothesis of $Z(x^0)$,
- $\max_{i=1,...,K}(\lambda_i(Z_i(x^1) - z_i^{ut})) < \max_{i=1,...,K}(\lambda_i(Z_i(x^0) - z_i^{ut}))$ and that contradicts the fact that x^0 is an optimal solution of (P_λ).

In every case we end up with a contradiction, which leads to the conclusion that x^0 is a strict Pareto optimum.□

Geometrically, the problem (P_λ) can be interpreted by means of level curves (figure 3.14). Let z^{ut} and λ be fixed, $X_=(a) = \{x \in \mathcal{S} / \|Z(x) - z^{ut}\|_{Tp} = a\}$ and $L_=(a) = Z(X_=(a))$. To solve (P_λ) is equivalent to determining the level curve of minimal value a^* such that $L_=(a^*) \neq \emptyset$. The solutions of $X_=(a^*)$ are then the solutions of (P_λ).

This approach depends on the utopian vector z^{ut} and the weights λ_i. An example of its use in an a posteriori algorithm is of making z^{ut} vary. For each vector obtained, it is then necessary to conduct a parametric analysis of λ_i in order to obtain all the Pareto optima. In an interactive algorithm we use the instructions of the decision maker to make z^{ut} and λ vary.

3.6.6 Use of the augmented weighted Tchebycheff metric

It is possible to use a still more general form of the Tchebycheff metric than that presented in the previous section. The basic result yielded is interesting

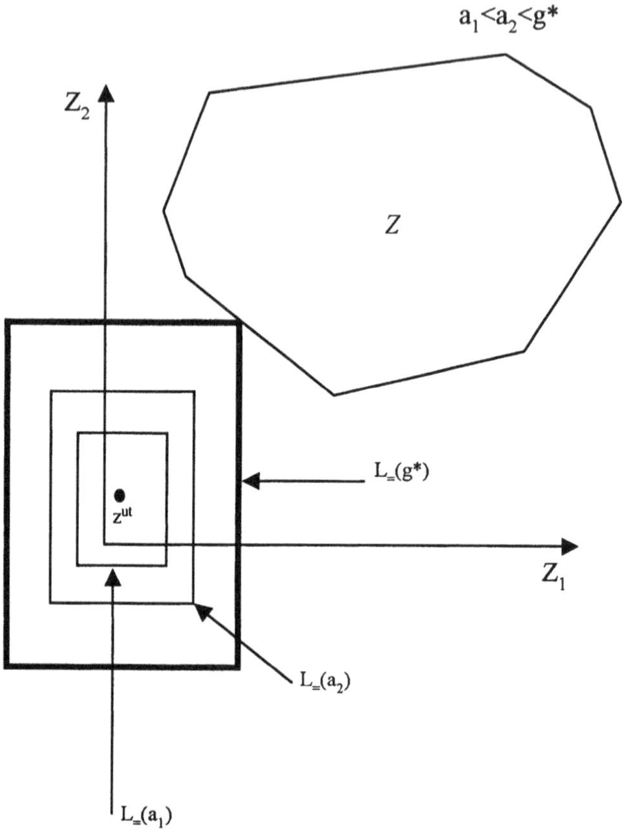

Fig. 3.14. Geometric interpretation of a problem (P_λ)

but difficult to apply in practice. Thus, we present at the end of this section a more convenient result. At the outset we define the considered metric.

Definition 47
Let z^1 and $z^2 \in \mathbb{R}^K$. The augmented weighted Tchebycheff metric is a weighted measure of the distance in $\mathbb{R}^K$ between z^1 and z^2, defined by:

$$\|z^1 - z^2\|_{Tpa} = \max_{i=1,\dots,K}(\lambda_i|z_i^1 - z_i^2|) + \rho\sum_{i=1}^{K}|z_i^1 - z_i^2|$$

with $\lambda \in \mathbb{R}_+^K$ and $\rho \in \mathbb{R}_+^*$ a low value.

The use of the augmented weighted Tchebycheff metric to calculate Pareto optima leads us to the following theorem.

Theorem 11 *See [Teghem, 1996] in the case of MLP*
$x^0 \in \mathcal{S}$ is a strict Pareto optimum if and only if $\exists \lambda \in \mathbb{R}^K_{+*}$, $z^{ut} \in \mathbb{R}^K$ a utopian point and $\exists \rho \in \mathbb{R}^*_+$ a low value, such that x^0 is an optimal solution of the following problem $(P_{(\lambda,\rho)})$:

$$\begin{array}{l} Min\ \|Z(x) - z^{ut}\|_{Tpa} \\ subject\ to \\ \quad x \in \mathcal{S} \end{array}$$

Proof.
$\boxed{\Rightarrow}$ Let us suppose that x^0 is a strict Pareto optimum and let us show that $\exists \lambda \in \mathbb{R}^K_{+*}$, $z^{ut} \in \mathbb{R}^K$ a utopian point and $\exists \rho \in \mathbb{R}^*_+$ such that x^0 is an optimal solution of $(P_{(\lambda,\rho)})$.
Let z^{ut} be fixed and such that $z^{ut} < z^{id}$, *i.e.* $\forall x \in \mathcal{S}$, $z_i^{ut} < Z_i(x)$. We define $\lambda \in \mathbb{R}^K_{+*}$ by $\lambda_i = \dfrac{1}{Z_i(x^0) - z_i^{ut}}$ for $Z_i(x^0) \neq z_i^{ut}, \forall i = 1, ..., K$.
We have then $\lambda_i(Z_i(x^0) - z_i^{ut}) = 1$, whence $\max\limits_{i=1,\dots,K}(\lambda_i(Z_i(x^0) - z_i^{ut})) = 1$.
As x^0 is a strict Pareto optimum, $\nexists x^1 \in \mathcal{S}$ such that $Z_i(x^1) \leq Z_i(x^0)$, $\forall i = 1, ..., K$ with $Z(x^1) \neq Z(x^0)$.
$\Leftrightarrow \forall x^1 \in \mathcal{S}$, $Z(x^1) \neq Z(x^0)$, $\exists j \in \{1, ..., K\}$ such that $Z_j(x^1) > Z_j(x^0)$, whence $\lambda_j(Z_j(x^1) - z_j^{ut}) > \lambda_j(Z_j(x^0) - z_j^{ut})$.
$\Rightarrow \lambda_j(Z_j(x^1) - z_j^{ut}) > 1$
$\Rightarrow \max\limits_{i=1,\dots,K}(\lambda_i(Z_i(x^1) - z_i^{ut})) > 1 = \max\limits_{i=1,\dots,K}(\lambda_i(Z_i(x^0) - z_i^{ut}))$.
Let the value ρ defined by:

$$\begin{cases} \rho < \dfrac{\min\limits_{x\in\mathcal{S}, Z(x)\neq Z(x^0)}\left(\max\limits_{i=1,\dots,K}(\lambda_i(Z_i(x) - z_i^{ut})) - \max\limits_{i=1,\dots,K}(\lambda_i(Z_i(x^0) - z_i^{ut}))\right)}{\max\limits_{x\in\mathcal{S}, Z(x)\neq Z(x^0)}\left(\sum\limits_{i=1}^{K}(Z_i(x^0) - Z_i(x))\right)} \\ \qquad\qquad \text{if } \max\limits_{x\in\mathcal{S}, Z(x)\neq Z(x^0)}\left(\sum\limits_{i=1}^{K}(Z_i(x^0) - Z_i(x))\right) > 0 \\ \rho \in \mathbb{R}^+_* \text{ and ordinary, otherwise.} \end{cases}$$

$\forall x^1 \in \mathcal{S}$, we distinguish two cases:

1. $\max\limits_{x\in\mathcal{S}, Z(x)\neq Z(x^0)}\left(\sum\limits_{i=1}^{K}(Z_i(x^0) - Z_i(x))\right) > 0$, and then
$\rho \times \max\limits_{x\in\mathcal{S}, Z(x)\neq Z(x^0)}\left(\sum\limits_{i=1}^{K}(Z_i(x^0) - Z_i(x))\right) <$
$\min\limits_{x\in\mathcal{S}, Z(x)\neq Z(x^0)}\left(\max\limits_{i=1,\dots,K}(\lambda_i(Z_i(x) - z_i^{ut})) - \max\limits_{i=1,\dots,K}(\lambda_i(Z_i(x^0) - z_i^{ut}))\right)$
$\Rightarrow \rho \times \sum\limits_{i=1}^{K}(Z_i(x^0) - Z_i(x^1) - z_i^{ut} + z_i^{ut}) <$
$\min\limits_{x\in\mathcal{S}, Z(x)\neq Z(x^0)}\left(\max\limits_{i=1,\dots,K}(\lambda_i(Z_i(x) - z_i^{ut})) - \max\limits_{i=1,\dots,K}(\lambda_i(Z_i(x^0) - z_i^{ut}))\right)$
$\Rightarrow \rho\sum\limits_{i=1}^{K}(Z_i(x^0) - z_i^{ut}) - \rho\sum\limits_{i=1}^{K}(Z_i(x^1) - z_i^{ut}) < \max\limits_{i=1,\dots,K}(\lambda_i(Z_i(x^1) - z_i^{ut})) -$

$\max_{i=1,\dots,K}(\lambda_i(Z_i(x^0) - z_i^{ut}))$

$\Rightarrow \max_{i=1,\dots,K}(\lambda_i(Z_i(x^0) - z_i^{ut})) + \rho \times \sum_{i=1}^{K}(Z_i(x^0) - z_i^{ut}) < \max_{i=1,\dots,K}(\lambda_i(Z_i(x^1) - z_i^{ut})) + \rho \times \sum_{i=1}^{K}(Z_i(x^1) - z_i^{ut})$

$\Rightarrow \|Z(x^0) - z^{ut}\|_{Tpa} < \|Z(x^1) - z^{ut}\|_{Tpa}$.

2. $\max_{x\in\mathcal{S},Z(x)\neq Z(x^0)}(\sum_{i=1}^{K}(Z_i(x^0) - Z_i(x))) \leq 0$, and in this case $\rho \in \mathbb{R}_*^+$ ordinary and then:

$\rho \times \max_{x\in\mathcal{S},Z(x)\neq Z(x^0)}(\sum_{i=1}^{K}(Z_i(x^0) - Z_i(x))) \leq 0$

$\Rightarrow \rho \times \sum_{i=1}^{K}(Z_i(x^0) - Z_i(x^1) + z_i^{ut} - z_i^{ut}) \leq 0$

$\Rightarrow \rho \times \sum_{i=1}^{K}(Z_i(x^0) - z_i^{ut}) \leq \rho \times \sum_{i=1}^{K}(Z_i(x^1) - z_i^{ut})$

We have therefore $\max_{i=1,\dots,K}(\lambda_i(Z_i(x^0) - z_i^{ut})) - \max_{i=1,\dots,K}(\lambda_i(Z_i(x^1) - z_i^{ut}))$
$+\rho \max_{x\in\mathcal{S},Z(x)\neq Z(x^0)}(\sum_{i=1}^{K}(Z_i(x^0) - Z_i(x))) < 0$

$\Rightarrow \|Z(x^0) - z^{ut}\|_{Tpa} < \|Z(x^1) - z^{ut}\|_{Tpa}$

Whence $\exists\rho, \lambda$, and z^{ut} such that x^0 is an optimal solution of $(P_{(\lambda,\rho)})$.

[$\Leftarrow$] Let us suppose that $\exists\lambda \in \mathbb{R}_{+*}^K$, $z^{ut} \in \mathbb{R}^K$ is a utopian point and $\exists\rho \in \mathbb{R}_+^*$ such that x^0 is an optimal solution of $(P_{(\lambda,\rho)})$ and let us show that x^0 is a strict Pareto optimum. We proceed by contradiction.

Let $x^1 \in \mathcal{S}, x^1 \neq x^0$, such that $Z(x^1) \leq Z(x^0)$ with $Z(x^1) \neq Z(x^0)$.

$\forall i = 1, ..., K, Z_i(x^1) - z_i^{ut} \leq Z_i(x^0) - z_i^{ut}$ with at least one strict inequality.

$$\Rightarrow \begin{cases} \max_{i=1,\dots,K}(\lambda_i(Z_i(x^1) - z_i^{ut}) \leq \max_{i=1,\dots,K}(\lambda_i(Z_i(x^0) - z_i^{ut}) \\ \rho\sum_{i=1}^{K}(Z_i(x^1) - z_i^{ut}) < \rho\sum_{i=1}^{K}(Z_i(x^0) - z_i^{ut}) \end{cases}$$

Whence $\|Z(x^1) - z^{ut}\|_{Tpa} < \|Z(x^0) - z^{ut}\|_{Tpa}$, which contradicts the fact that x^0 is an optimal solution of $(P_{(\lambda,\rho)})$. x^0 is therefore a strict Pareto optimum.□

The principal inconvenience of this metric is linked to the determination of the parameter ρ. In the proof of the necessary condition of theorem 11, we propose a method of regulating this parameter. Nevertheless, this method is not usable in practice given that it requires the evaluation of an upper bound which depends on the set $\mathcal{S}$. [Steuer, 1986] notices that a numeric method does not exist to deduce a value of ρ when z^{ut} and λ are fixed. In practice, we have to consider the values between 10^{-4} and 10^{-2}. The problem $(P_{(\lambda,\rho)})$ can be interpreted by means of level curves (figure 3.15). Let z^*, λ and ρ be fixed, $X_=(a) = \{x \in \mathcal{S}/\|Z(x) - z^{ut}\|_{Tpa} = a\}$ and $L_=(a) = Z(X_=(a))$.

Solving $(P_{(\lambda,\rho)})$ is equivalent to determining the level curve of minimal value a^* such that $L_=(a^*) \neq \emptyset$. The solutions of $X_=(a^*)$ are then the solutions of $(P_{(\lambda,\rho)})$.

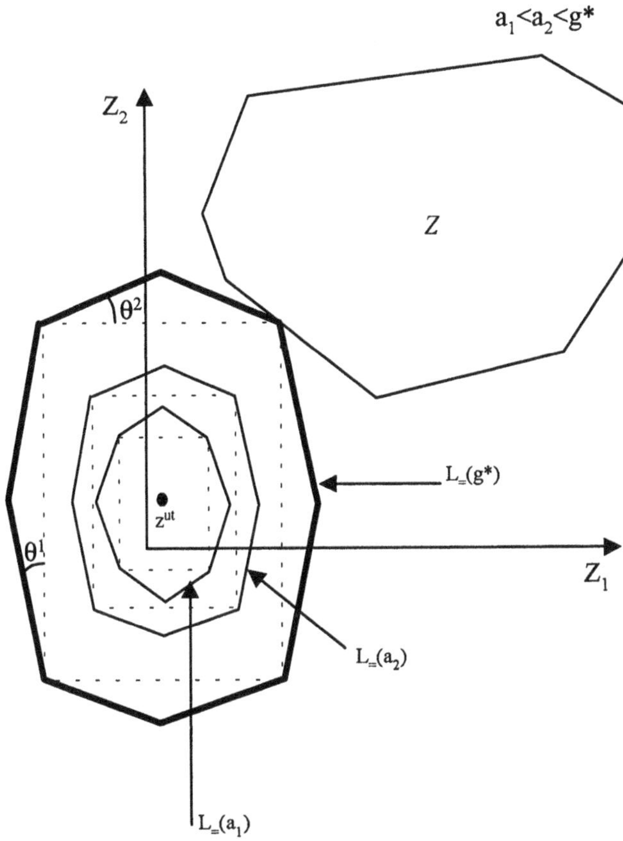

Fig. 3.15. Geometric interpretation of a problem $(P_{(\lambda,\rho)})$

In figure 3.15 we have represented by means of broken lines the contour generated by the weighted Tchebycheff metric. This enables us to visualise the influence of the term $\rho \sum_{i=1}^{K} |Z_i(x) - z_i^{ut}|$ on the search for a strict Pareto optimum in the case of a linear problem. The angles θ_1 and θ_2 are functions of the value ρ and in the example we have ([Steuer, 1986]):

$$\theta_1 = tan^{-1}(\frac{\rho}{1-\lambda_2+\rho}), \text{ and } \theta_2 = tan^{-1}(\frac{\rho}{1-\lambda_1+\rho})$$

We thus notice that the greater the value ρ becomes the more important the angles become. As we have seen in section 3.6.5, The use of the weighted Tchebycheff metric can generate weak Pareto optima (several solutions belong to a line of a broken rectangle). The presence of the term $\rho \sum_{i=1}^{K} |Z_i(x) - z_i^{ut}|$ in the augmented metric will only lead to retaining, among the solutions obtained by the weighted Tchebycheff metric, those which are strict Pareto.

A similar approach to that presented in this section consists of breaking down the augmented weighted Tchebycheff metric into two criteria and defining a lexicographical order. Let $T_1 = \max_{i=1,\ldots,K} (\lambda_i |Z_i(x) - z_i^{ut}|)$, and $T_2 = \sum_{i=1}^{K} |Z_i(x) - z_i^{ut}|$ and the lexicographical order $T_1 \rightarrow T_2$: among the solutions having an optimal value of the criterion T_1, we choose the one having the lowest value of T_2. We note T_1^* the optimal value of the criterion T_1.

Theorem 12 *See for example [Steuer, 1986]*
$x^0 \in S$ is a strict Pareto optimum if and only if $\exists \lambda \in \mathbb{R}_{+*}^K$ and $z^{ut} \in \mathbb{R}^K$ a utopian point such that x^0 is an optimal solution of the following problem (P_λ^{Lex}):

$$\begin{aligned} &Min\ T_2 \\ &subject\ to \\ &\quad x \in S \\ &\quad T_1 = T_1^* \end{aligned}$$

The advantage of theorem 12 lies in the fact that we no longer have to empirically fix a value ρ. Moreover, this approach only generates strict Pareto optima. Using it is equivalent, in theory, to minimising initially a weighted Tchebycheff metric (see corollary 2 and theorem 10). If several solutions are then obtained we apply for a second time minimisation of the term $\sum_{i=1}^{K} |Z_i(x) - z_i^{ut}|$ to obtain a strict Pareto optimum and to remove the non strict weak Pareto optima. In practice, we realise the minimisation of the functions T_1 and T_2, according to a lexicographical order, at one go.

3.6.7 Determination by the goal-attainment approach

An approach which is similar to those using the Tchebycheff metrics is the goal-attainment approach ([Gembicki, 1973] and [Wierzbicki, 1990]). This requires the definition of a goal, for the criteria, and we search for the solution which best approaches this. The difference to the approaches based on Tchebycheff metrics is in the way in which this solution is sought.

Theorem 13 *[Gembicki, 1973], [Wierzbicki, 1990]*
$x^0 \in S$ is a weak Pareto optimum if and only if $\exists\ z^{ref} \in \mathbb{R}^K$ a reference

point and $w \in \mathbb{R}^K_{+*}$ a weights vector such that x^0 is an optimal solution of the following problem $(P_{(z^{ref},w)})$:

$$\textit{Max } g(Z(x)) \textit{ with } g(Z(x)) = \min_{i=1,\dots,K}\left(\frac{1}{w_i}(z_i^{ref} - Z_i(x))\right)$$
$$\textit{subject to}$$
$$x \in \mathcal{S}$$

Proof.
$\boxed{\Rightarrow}$ Let us suppose that x^0 is a weak Pareto optimum and let us show that $\exists z^{ref}$ and $\exists w$ such that x^0 is an optimal solution of the problem $(P_{(z^{ref},w)})$. We take $z^{ref} = Z(x^0)$ and ordinary $w > 0$. Let us proceed by contradiction to show that x^0 is an optimal solution of the problem $(P_{(z^{ref},w)})$. Let $z^0 \in \mathbb{R}$ be the value of the objective function obtained for x^0. We have $z^0 = \min_{i=1,\dots,K}\left(\frac{1}{w_i}(z_i^{ref} - Z_i(x^0))\right)$. Let us suppose that $\exists x^1 \neq x^0 \in \mathcal{S}$ and $\exists z^1 \in \mathbb{R}$ such that:

$$\begin{cases} Z(x^1) + z^1 w \leq z^{ref} \\ z^1 > z^0 \end{cases}$$

Which is equivalent to:

$$\begin{cases} Z(x^0) + z^0 w \leq Z(x^0) & \text{(A)} \\ Z(x^1) + z^1 w \leq Z(x^0) & \text{(B)} \\ z^1 > z^0 & \text{(C)} \end{cases}$$

The inequality (A) implies that $z^0 = 0$. The inequality (C) implies then that $z^1 > 0$. Finally, the inequality (B) implies that $Z(x^1) < Z(x^0)$ which contradicts the fact that x^0 is a weak Pareto optimum. x^0 is therefore an optimal solution of the problem $(P_{(z^{ref},w)})$.
$\boxed{\Leftarrow}$ Let us suppose that $\exists z^{ref0} \in \mathbb{R}^K$ and $w^0 \in \mathbb{R}^K_{+*}$ such that $x^0 \in \mathcal{S}$ is the optimal solution of $(P_{(z^{ref0},w^0)})$. Let us proceed by contradiction and suppose that x^0 is an optimal solution of $(P_{(z^{ref0},w^0)})$, and x^0 is not a weak Pareto optimum. Note $z^0 = \min_{i=1\dots K}\left(\frac{1}{w_i^0}(z_i^{ref0} - Z_i(x^0))\right)$. Then, $\exists x^1 \in \mathcal{S}$ such that $Z_i(x^1) < Z_i(x^0)$, $\forall i = 1,\dots,K$. Then, $\forall i = 1,\dots,K$, $Z_i(x^1) + z^0 w_i^0 < Z_i(x^0) + z^0 w_i^0$ and as $z^0 \leq \frac{1}{w_i^0}(z_i^{ref0} - Z_i(x^0))$ we have $Z_i(x^1) + z^0 w_i^0 \leq z_i^{ref0}$, and therefore x^1 is a solution of $(P_{(z^{ref0},w^0)})$.
$\forall i,\ Z_i(x^1) < Z_i(x^0)$
$\Rightarrow \frac{1}{w_i^0}(z_i^{ref0} - Z_i(x^1)) > \frac{1}{w_i^0}(z_i^{ref0} - Z_i(x^0))$ for $w > 0$
$\Rightarrow \frac{1}{w_i^0}(z_i^{ref0} - Z_i(x^1)) > z^0$,
which contradicts the fact that x^0 is an optimal solution of $(P_{(z^{ref},w)})$.□

In section 3.6.6 we have seen that the consideration of two criteria T_1 (of maximum type) and T_2 (of sum type) enables us to determine only strict

Pareto optima. We were then concerned with a lexicographical problem. In the goal-attainment approach area, we can show that the addition of a sub-criterion of the sum type allows us to return to the problem $(P_{(g,b)})$ presented in the section 3.6.2.

Theorem 14
Let $z^{ref} \in \mathbb{R}^K$ be a reference vector, $w \in \mathbb{R}^K_{+*}$ a weights vector and $(P^s_{(z^{ref},w)})$ the problem defined by:

$$\begin{aligned} &Max\ h(Z(x))\ with\ h(x) = \sum_{i=1}^{K}(\frac{1}{w_i}(z_i^{ref} - Z_i(x))) \\ &subject\ to \\ &\qquad \min_{i=1,...,K}(\frac{1}{w_i}(z_i^{ref} - Z_i(x))) = z^* \\ &\qquad x \in \mathcal{S} \end{aligned}$$

with $z^* = \max_{x\in\mathcal{S}}(\min_{i=1,...,K}(\frac{1}{w_i}(z_i^{ref} - Z_i(x))))$.
Problem $(P^s_{(z^{ref},w)})$ is equivalent to a parametric problem $(P_{(g,b)})$ where $g(Z(x)) = \sum_{i=1}^{K}\alpha_i Z_i(x)$, $\alpha_i > 0, \forall i = 1,...,K$, with $\alpha_i = \frac{1}{w_i}$ and $b_i = z_i^{ref} - w_i z^*$, $\forall i = 1,...,K$.

Proof.
(i) We know that $\min_{i=1,...,K}(\frac{1}{w_i}(z_i^{ref} - Z_i(x))) = z^*$
$\Leftrightarrow \frac{1}{w_i}(z_i^{ref} - Z_i(x)) \geq z^*, \forall i = 1,...,n$
$\Leftrightarrow Z_i(x) \leq z_i^{ref} - w_i z^*, \forall i = 1,...,n.$
We note $b_i = z_i^{ref} - w_i z^*, \forall i = 1,...,n.$
(ii) Maximising $\sum_{i=1}^{K}(\frac{1}{w_i}(z_i^{ref} - Z_i(x)))$ is equivalent to minimising $\sum_{i=1}^{K}\frac{1}{w_i}Z_i(x)$.
Knowing that $w_i > 0$, $\forall i = 1,...,n$, the new objective function is strictly increasing. From the points (i) and (ii) we deduce that the problem $(P^s_{(z^{ref},w)})$ is equivalent to a problem $(P_{(g,b)})$ with $g(Z(x)) = \sum_{i=1}^{K}\frac{1}{w_i}Z_i(x)$ and $b_i = z_i^{ref} - w_i z^*$, $\forall i = 1,...,K.$□

Theorem 14 allows us to apply the results which are valid for the parametric approach to the problem $(P^s_{(z^{ref},w)})$. Thus we deduce from this that the solution of this problem allows us to obtain a strict Pareto optimum and that all these optima may be calculated by solving a problem $(P^s_{(z^{ref},w)})$. The proof theorem 14 shows equally that the maximisation of the criterion of type sum is equivalent to a problem (P_α) (see section 3.6.1).

Lemma 7
Let $z^{ref} \in \mathbb{R}^K$ a reference vector, $w \in \mathbb{R}^K_{+*}$ a weights vector and $(P^p_{(z^{ref},w)})$ the problem defined by:

$$Max \sum_{i=1}^{K} (\frac{1}{w_i}(z_i^{ref} - Z_i(x)))$$
subject to
$$x \in \mathcal{S}$$

The problem $(P^p_{(z^{ref},w)})$ *is equivalent to the problem* (P_α) *with* $\alpha_i = \frac{1}{w_i \overline{w}}$, $\forall i = 1, ..., K$, *and* $\overline{w} = \sum_{i=1}^{K} \frac{1}{w_i}$.

Proof.
Following from point (ii) of the proof of theorem 14.□

Lemma 7 leads to the conclusion that the solutions calculated are proper Pareto optima and that it is not wise to solve $(P^p_{(z^{ref},w)})$ to calculate Pareto optima when the convexity hypotheses have not been verified. A geometric interpretation of the problem $(P_{(z^{ref},w)})$ is proposed in figure 3.16. Two cases concerning the position of the point z^{ref} can occur. In the first case, z^{ref} does not correspond to any feasible solution. The solution of $(P_{(z^{ref},w)})$ is equivalent to projecting the point z^{ref} onto the trade-off curve in a direction specified by the weights value w_i. In the second case, the result is identical despite the fact that z^{ref} corresponds to one or more feasible solutions.

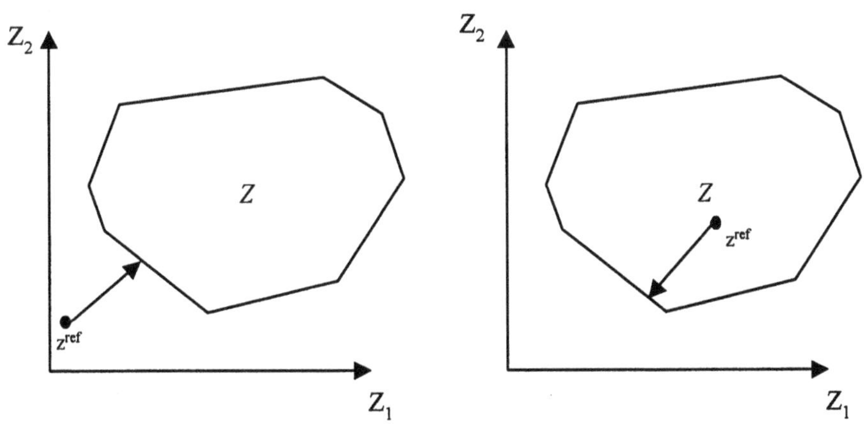

Fig. 3.16. Geometric interpretation of a problem $(P_{(z^{ref},w)})$

If we go to a more detailed analysis of the functioning of theorem 13, we realise that the solution of the problem $(P_{(z^{ref},w)})$ does not solely depend on the values z^{ref} and w. In fact, the significance of the weights w and of the reference vector z^{ref} depends on the relative position of this vector with respect to the set $\mathcal{Z}$. A simple example is presented in figure 3.17. The set $\mathcal{Z}$ is made up of the vectors z^1 and z^2, and the weights given by the decision maker are $\frac{1}{w} = [100; 10]^T$. In the first step, we suppose that the reference point given by the decision maker is the point z^{ref1}. The optimal solution of the problem $(P_{(z^{ref},w)})$ then corresponds to the vector z^1, since we have $\min(100\times(5-20); 10\times(5-40)) > \min(100\times(5-40); 10\times(5-20))$. Therefore, we notice that this optimal solution minimises the distance to z^{ref1} for the criterion Z_1. Thus, the greater the weight w_i is the more we search for a solution minimising the criterion Z_i. Let us now consider in the second step that the decision maker gives the vector z^{ref2} as the reference point. The optimal solution of the problem $(P_{(z^{ref},w)})$ corresponds now to the vector z^2 since we have $\min(100\times(60-20); 10\times(60-40)) < \min(100\times(60-40); 10\times(60-20))$. Interpretation in weight terms of w_i is thus inverted: the lower the weight w_i is the more we go in search of a solution minimising the criterion Z_i. Thus, it is difficult to tell the decision maker if an important value for w_i means that Z_i is an important criterion or of little importance, since this depends on the position of the vector z^{ref} in relation to the set of solutions.

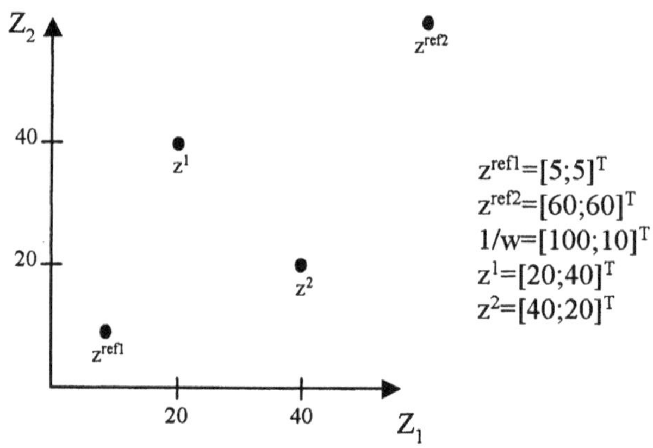

Fig. 3.17. Meaning of the weights w_i regarding the position of z^{ref}

This example shows well that following the position of the reference point with respect to the set $\mathcal{Z}$, the meaning of the weights can be radically different. This implies that for the decision maker who will fix the weights, the importance of a criterion is difficult to control. Use of the goal-attainment approach therefore makes the role of the analyst a particular factor of this problem. To overcome this it is possible for example to stipulate that the reference point should be a utopian point.

3.6.8 Other methods for determining Pareto optima

Other methods for determining Pareto optima exist in the literature. For example, it is possible to derive results using a different metric than the ones presented in the previous sections. Principally, we present in this section the approaches without any trade-off allowed where a lexicographical order between the criteria is defined. Other methods enable us to determine existing Pareto optima. We refer to [Ehrgott, 2000b] for a presentation of different approaches such as the *"max-ordering"* approach or the global lexicographical approach.

Use of a lexicographical order

A technique frequently used to minimise several criteria consists of defining an optimisation order. This type of problem occurs when no trade-off between the criteria is authorised. It concerns an optimisation problem according to a lexicographical order, defined without any loss of generality by the criteria indices, $Z_1 \rightarrow Z_2 \rightarrow \ldots \rightarrow Z_K$, and noted $min_{Lex}(Z)$.
To determine an optimal solution x^0 of $min_{Lex}(Z)$ is equivalent to finding a solution $x^0 \in \mathcal{S}^K$ with

$$\mathcal{S}^1 = \{x^0 \in \mathcal{S}/Z_1(x^0) = \min_{x \in \mathcal{S}}(Z_1(x))\},$$
$$\mathcal{S}^2 = \{x^0 \in \mathcal{S}^1/Z_2(x^0) = \min_{x \in \mathcal{S}^1}(Z_2(x))\}, \ldots,$$
$$\mathcal{S}^K = \{x^0 \in \mathcal{S}^{K-1}/Z_K(x^0) = \min_{x \in \mathcal{S}^{K-1}}(Z_K(x))\}.$$

A necessary and sufficient condition for the existence of a solution of the problem $min_{Lex}(Z)$ is that each criterion Z_i is lower bounded on each subset $\mathcal{S}^{i-1}$ and that $\mathcal{S} \neq \emptyset$ ([Steuer, 1986]).

Property 4
1) $\forall x^0 \in \mathcal{S}^k, 1 \leq k \leq K, x^0$ *is a weak Pareto optimum,*
2) $\forall x^0 \in \mathcal{S}^K, x^0$ *is a strict Pareto optimum.*

Proof.
1) Let us proceed by contradiction. We suppose that $\exists x^1 \in \mathcal{S}$ such that $Z_j(x^1) < Z_j(x^0), \forall j = 1, ..., K$. It is obvious that for $j = 1$ there is a contradiction with the fact that $x^0 \in \mathcal{S}^k \subseteq \mathcal{S}^1$. x^0 is therefore a weak Pareto optimum.
2) We must show that $\nexists\, x^1 \in \mathcal{S}, x^1 \neq x^0$, such that $Z_i(x^1) \leq Z_i(x^0), \forall i = 1, ..., K$, with at least one strict inequality. Two cases can arise:

- $x^1 \in \mathcal{S} - \mathcal{S}^1$: Given that $Z_1(x^0) = \min_{x \in \mathcal{S}}(Z_1(x)) < Z_1(x^1)$, x^1 does not dominate x^0 therefore $\nexists x^1 \in \mathcal{S} - \mathcal{S}^1$ which dominates x^0.
- $\exists\, i \in \{1, ..., K\}$ such that $x^1 \in \mathcal{S}^i$: $\forall j = 1, ..., i$, $Z_j(x^1) = Z_j(x^0)$ and $\forall j = i +$

$1, ..., K$, $Z_j(x^0) \leq Z_j(x^1)$ which implies that we cannot have $Z_i(x^1) \leq Z_i(x^0)$, $\forall i = 1, ..., K$, with at least one strict inequality.

Therefore x^0 is a strict Pareto optimum.□

Use of a lexicographical order with goals

An approach derived from the problem min_{Lex} is to consider that the criteria are sorted according to the order $Z_1 \rightarrow Z_2 \rightarrow \ldots \rightarrow Z_K$, and that for every criterion there is a goal to reach. Thus, we no longer search for the minimal value for every criterion in the set $\mathcal{S}^i$, but we search for a solution which is the closest to the goal we wish to reach. This problem, noted min_{Lexobj} takes shape as follows: let z^{ref} be a reference vector. Determination of an optimal solution x^0 of $min_{Lexobj}(Z)$ is equivalent to finding a solution $x^0 \in \mathcal{S}^K$ with:

$$\begin{aligned} S^1 &= \{x^0 \in \mathcal{S}/|Z_1(x^0) - z_1^{ref}| = \min_{x\in\mathcal{S}}(|Z_1(x) - z_1^{ref}|)\}, \\ S^2 &= \{x^0 \in \mathcal{S}^1/|Z_2(x^0) - z_2^{ref}| = \min_{x\in\mathcal{S}^1}(|Z_2(x) - z_2^{ref}|))\}, \ldots \\ S^K &= \{x^0 \in \mathcal{S}^{K-1}/|Z_K(x^0) - z_K^{ref}| = \min_{x\in\mathcal{S}^{K-1}}(|Z_K(x) - z_K^{ref}|))\}. \end{aligned}$$

The definition of the above problem $min_{Lexobj}(Z)$ assumes that the distance between the reference point z^{ref} and the set of vectors of $\mathcal{Z}$ is measured by a metric L_∞ in $\mathbb{R}$.

Property 5
If z^{ref} is either the ideal point z^{id}, or a utopian point z^{ut}, then the problems $min_{Lex}(Z)$ and $min_{Lexobj}(Z)$ are equivalents.

Proof.
It is sufficient to show that for a set $\mathcal{S}^i$ minimisation of the term $|Z_j(x) - z_j^{ref}|$ is equivalent to minimisation of the criterion $Z_j(x)$. We have $z^{ref} = z^{id}$ or $z^{ref} = z^{ut}$ $\Rightarrow |Z_j(x) - z_j^{ref}| = Z_j(x) - z_j^{ref}$. Thus, minimising $Z_j(x) - z_j^{ref}$ is equivalent to minimising $Z_j(x)$ since z_j^{ref} is a constant.□

By contrast to the problem $min_{Lex}(Z)$, membership to the set E of a solution of the problem min_{Lexobj} cannot be guaranteed. Similarly, a solution $x^0 \in \mathcal{S}^i$, $\forall i = 1, ..., K-1$, can be a dominated solution.

3.7 Multicriteria Linear Programming (MLP)

The methods presented in the previous sections are valid without having to suppose strong hypotheses on the structure of the criteria and on the structure of the set of solutions. Nevertheless, some of the results presented are simplified in the case of Multicriteria Linear Programming (MLP).

3.7.1 Initial results

We define an MLP model as follows:

$$\text{Min } Z_1, \text{ with } Z_1 = \sum_{j=1}^{Q} c_j^1 x_j = c^1 x$$

$$\vdots$$

$$\text{Min } Z_K, \text{ with } Z_K = \sum_{j=1}^{Q} c_j^K x_j = c^K x$$

subject to

$$Ax = b$$
$$x \in \mathbb{R}^Q$$

with A the coefficients matrix $(M \times Q)$ and b the constants vector of size M. The set of solutions $\mathcal{S}$ is a polyhedron defined by the constraints of the problem: it is therefore by definition convex. Moreover, each criterion Z_i is a linear function and therefore convex and $\mathcal{Z}$ is thus a convex polyhedron. Before considering the application of the theorems addressed in section 3.6, we shall present a few results on the connectedness of the sets E and WE.

Lemma 8
The set WE is connected.

Proof.
Direct application of theorem 2.□

Lemma 9 *[Yu and Zeleny, 1975]*
Let E_{ex} be the set of the extreme points of the polyhedron $\mathcal{S}$ which are strict Pareto optima. The set E_{ex} is connected.

Given that each point $x^0 \in E$ can be expressed by a convex combination of points $x^i \in E_{ex}$, we can deduce from lemma 9 that the set E is connected.

3.7.2 Application of the previous results

Theorem 4, presented in section 3.6.1, enables us to determine proper Pareto optima in the general case by minimisation of a convex combination of criteria. In the context of problems with real variables we shall see that this theorem is slightly different. Let us return firstly to the definition of a proper Pareto optimum. We have seen in section 3.3 that a proper Pareto optimum was a strict Pareto optimum verifying the following condition:

Properness condition: $\exists M > 0$ *such that*
$\forall y \neq x, y \in \mathcal{S},\ I_y(x) \neq \emptyset \Rightarrow$
$\forall\ i \in I_y, \exists j, 1 \leq j \leq K$ *with* $Z_j(x) < Z_j(y)$ *such that* $\frac{Z_i(x)-Z_i(y)}{Z_j(y)-Z_j(x)} \leq M$
with $I_y(x) = \{i \in [1; K]/Z_i(y) < Z_i(x)\}$.

We can show that for every linear problem, every strict Pareto optimum is proper (see [Steuer, 1986]). In other words, every strict Pareto optimum verifies the above properness condition and theorem 4 enables us to determine the set E. By authorising weights α_i being equal to 0 in this theorem, we obtain lemma 2. Given the paucity of parameters to regulate in the approach, this is easier to use for the resolution of problems which can be modeled by MLP. An obvious interest in theorem 4 (and in the results derived from it) is to enable the design of a simple interactive algorithm causing only variations on the weights.

Concerning the ϵ-constraint approach the result presented in lemma 3 holds since in the context of problems which can be modeled by MLP, the set of solutions and the set of criteria vectors are convex sets. This result implies therefore that the set WE can be determined by varying the value of k and of the bounds ϵ^k. By contrast, even with the convexity hypotheses of $\mathcal{S}$ and the criteria Z_i, the reciprocals of lemmas 4 and 5 are not valid. In other words, even for problems which can be modeled by MLP, the use of the ϵ-constraint approach, when the criterion to minimise is fixed, only enables us to reach a subset W of WE. We have $E \subseteq W$.

Concerning the results related to the parametric analysis (theorem 5), to the Tchebycheff metrics (theorems 8, 10 and 11), to the goal-attainment approach (theorem 13) and to the lexicographical approach (section 3.6.8), their application does not raise any problem in the context of linear problems with real variables.

3.8 Multicriteria Mixed Integer Programming (MMIP)

3.8.1 Initial results

The absence of convexity hypotheses on $\mathcal{Z}$ implies that non supported solutions appear. We thus distinguish for the problems which can only be modeled by Multicriteria Mixed Integer Programming (MMIP) the *supported* Pareto optima and the *non supported* Pareto optima. Figure 3.18 presents this distinction through an example. Set $\mathcal{Z}$ is the set of points represented and $co(\mathcal{Z})$ is the convex hull defined by $\mathcal{Z}$. We have $co(\mathcal{Z}) = \{z \in \mathbb{R}^K/\forall \alpha_i \in [0;1], \sum_{i=1}^K \alpha_i = 1$, and $\forall z^i \in \mathcal{Z}, z = \sum_{i=1}^K \alpha_i z^i\}$. The point z^0 corresponds to one or several non supported strict Pareto optima since z^0 does not belong to the border of $co(\mathcal{Z})$. The point z^4 represents non supported weak Pareto optima.

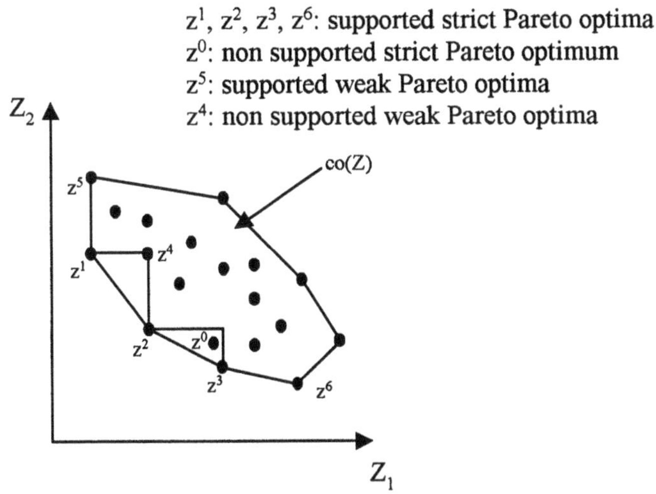

Fig. 3.18. Supported and non supported Pareto optima

We denote by WE_s and E_s the weak supported Pareto and the strict supported Pareto optima, respectively. WE_{ns} and E_{ns} denote the set of non supported weak Pareto and the set of non supported strict Pareto optima, respectively.

3.8.2 Application of the previous results

Geoffrion's theorem (theorem 4) proposes a result based on the minimisation of a convex combination of criteria. This theorem is not suitable in the domain of MMIP given that the set $\mathcal{S}$ is not convex. In this case we make use of a degraded version of Geoffrion's theorem.

Theorem 15

Let $\alpha \in [0;1]^K$ *such that* $\sum_{i=1}^{K} \alpha_i = 1$. *If* $x^0 \in \mathcal{S}$ *is an optimal solution of the problem* (P_α) *then* x^0 *is a weak Pareto optimum.* (P_α) *is defined by:*

$$Min\ g(Z(x)),\ with\ g(Z(x)) = \sum_{i=1}^{K} \alpha_i Z_i(x)$$

subject to

$$x \in \mathcal{S}$$

Proof.
Identical to the proof of the sufficient condition of lemma 2.□

If we consider in theorem 15 non null weights, *i.e.* $\alpha \in]0;1[^K$, then the solutions of (P_α) are strict Pareto optima. Theorem 15 shows that certain Pareto optima cannot be calculated by minimising a convex combination of criteria. In other words, whatever the chosen weights, certain Pareto optima will never be solutions of (P_α). These are the non supported Pareto optima. An illustration is proposed in figure 3.19. The vectors z^1 and z^2 correspond to the supported strict Pareto optima whereas z^0 corresponds to a non supported Pareto optimum.

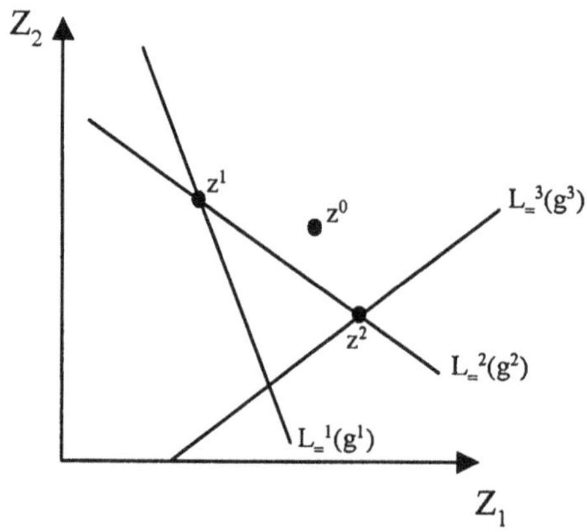

Fig. 3.19. Geoffrion's theorem and non supported Pareto optima

To understand the notion of non supported Pareto optima we define a set of level curves. We set $X^i_{=}(g^i) = \{x \in S / \sum_{i=1}^{K} \alpha^i_j Z_j(x) = g^i\}$ and $L^i_{=}(g^i) = Z(X^i_{=}(g^i))$ with $g^i \in \mathbb{R}$ the minimal value such that $X^i_{=} \cap S \neq \emptyset$. Therefore, we note that $\forall \alpha^i \in [0;1]^K$, the criteria vector z^0 does not correspond to any solution of (P_{α^i}). A direct consequence of this result is that the resolution of non convex problems by convex combination of criteria does not enable us to propose all the solutions $x^0 \in WE$ to the decision maker. In other words, solutions of potential interest cannot be proposed to him.

Concerning the ϵ-constraint approach only lemma 3 cannot be applied since the set S is not convex. Thus, the set of calculable solutions, even if the criterion to minimise is not fixed is only a subset, denoted by W, of the set WE. We still have $E \subseteq W$.

Concerning the results related to the parametric analysis (theorem 5), to the Tchebycheff metrics (theorems 8, 10 and 11) and to the goal-attainment approach (theorem 13), their application does not raise any problem in the context of linear programs having integer variables. These approaches enable us to determine the supported as well as the non supported Pareto optima. Concerning the lexicographical approach (section 3.6.8), we have $S^K \subseteq E_s$ whatever be the defined order of the criteria.

3.8.3 Some classical algorithms

Numerous algorithms, based on either an interactive method, or an a posteriori method, have been proposed in the literature. As a general rule, these algorithms tend to separate the search for Pareto optima into two steps. In the first step, we are interested in the supported Pareto optima and in the second step in the non supported Pareto optima.

The algorithm of [Klein and Hannan, 1982] is among the most classical algorithms. It enumerates the image of the set E in the criteria space. The principle of the algorithm lies in the resolution of q single criterion problems. The problem noted (P_1), of the minimisation of criterion Z_1 is solved at the first step. We denote by s^1 the solution which is obtained. The problem (P_2) is then constructed by adding to the problem (P_1) the disjunctive constraint "$Z_1(x) \leq Z_1(s^1) - \epsilon$ *or* $Z_2(x) \leq Z_2(s^1) - \epsilon$ *or* ... *or* $Z_K(x) \leq Z_K(s^1) - \epsilon$" where $\epsilon > 0$, for example $\epsilon = 1$. The implementation of this constraint in a mathematical model necessitates of course the addition of boolean variables. Klein and Hannan also propose an implementation of this algorithm. An inconvenience of this approach lies in the fact that the criteria vectors corresponding to weak Pareto optima can be generated as well.

Other algorithms, of a heuristic nature, have been proposed in the literature. [Ulungu et al., 1995] propose a generic *simulated annealing* algorithm to approximate the set E. The characteristic of this algorithm lies in the acceptance test of a solution y belonging to the neighbourhood of the solution x. Since the problem is multicriteria the authors use a convex combination F_ℓ of the criteria to get an evaluation of the solutions. Knowing $F_\ell(x)$ and $F_\ell(y)$ the solution y is kept according to the classic scheme of simulated annealing algorithms. The solutions of each iteration are stored as *potential Pareto optima*. This heuristic is iterated several times for the different values of the weights of the convex combination. The sets of solutions which are obtained are then aggregated to obtain an approximation of the set E. Another heuristic is proposed in which the evaluation function is the weighted Tchebycheff metric. Other similar heuristics have been proposed by [Ulungu et al., 1999]. Equally, we can refer to the works of [Czyzak and Jaszkiewicz, 1997] who also propose a generic simulated annealing algorithm.

Besides, [Gandibleux et al., 1997] propose a *tabu search* algorithm which approximates the set E. At each iteration of the algorithm, the solutions y in the neighbourhood of the current solution are evaluated by a metric L_p and L_p^λ. Upon reaching a single criterion evaluation of the solutions it is then possible to apply the scheme of a classic tabu algorithm. At each iteration among the best M solutions y of the neighbourhood of x, we can add the solutions which are not dominated to the set E under construction. The solutions of this set can become dominated, and are therefore eliminated. The weights of the metric L_p^λ are updated at each iteration by a procedure described by the authors. An application of this algorithm to a particular problem is also presented.

A panorama of resolution algorithms for linear and non linear multicriteria problems is addressed by [Climaco et al., 1997]. Besides, a state-of-the-art of resolution algorithms and of Operational Research problems is presented by [Ulungu and Teghem, 1994]. They address for instance the multicriteria assignment problem, the multicriteria travelling salesman problem or still yet the multicriteria knapsack problem. More recently, we find in [Ehrgott and Gandibleux, 2000] a study of the multiciteria problems most addressed in the literature of Operational Research. They tackle notably the principal resolution algorithms.

[Tuyttens et al., 1999] address a bicriteria assignment problem. This problem, noted BAP, is $\mathcal{NP}$-hard ([Serafini, 1987]) and is defined by:

$$\text{Min } z_k(x), \text{ with } z_k(x) = \sum_{i=1}^{n}\sum_{j=1}^{n} c_{i,j}^{K} x_{i,j},\ \forall k = 1, ..., 2$$

subject to

$$\sum_{j=1}^{n} x_{i,j} = 1,\ \forall i = 1, ..., n$$

$$\sum_{i=1}^{n} x_{i,j} = 1,\ \forall j = 1, ..., n$$

$$x_{i,j} \in \{0; 1\}$$

The costs $c_{i,j}^k$ are assumed to be positive. Firstly, an improvement of an exact algorithm described by [Ulungu and Teghem, 1995] to determine the set E is proposed. This algorithm proceeds in two phases. In the first one, the set of strict supported Pareto optima is calculated and in the second one, the non supported strict Pareto optima are addressed. Besides, an improvement of the simulated annealing procedure described by [Ulungu et al., 1999] is proposed. Some experimental results show that the heuristic determines few strict Pareto optima when $n \geq 25$. By contrast, these results show that the improved version gives, on average, better results than the basic version.

[Ulungu and Teghem, 1997] address a bicriteria knapsack problem. This problem, noted BKSP, is defined by:

$$\text{Max } z_k(x), \text{ with } z_k(x) = \sum_{j=1}^{n} c_j^K x_j, \ \forall k = 1, ..., 2$$

subject to

$$\sum_{j=1}^{n} w_j x_j \leq W$$

$$x_j \in \{0; 1\}$$

The costs c_j^k, the weights w_j and W are assumed to be positive. This problem is $\mathcal{NP}$-hard and a branch-and-bound procedure is proposed to enumerate the set E. The search tree constructed is a binary tree where at each node we decide whether an object takes part or not in the contents of the knapsack. This algorithm was inspired by the procedure of [Martello and Toth, 1990] for the single criterion problem. Ulungu and Teghem also study the generalisation of their algorithm in the tricriteria case. The problem BKSP is similarly addressed in [Visée et al., 1998] who propose two exact enumeration algorithms of the set E. These two algorithms proceed in two phases. In the first, the set of supported strict Pareto optima is calculated by solving iteratively the single criterion knapsack problems where the objective function is a convex combination of two criteria. These problems are solved using Martello and Toth's algorithm. The difference between the two algorithms lies in the second phase where the set of non supported strict Pareto optima is generated. The first algorithm uses an adaptation of a procedure proposed by [Ulungu and Teghem, 1995] whereas the second uses an adaptation of the Branch-and-Bound procedure proposed by [Ulungu and Teghem, 1997]. Several experimental results show that the number of strict Pareto optima is a function of the weights w_j and the capacity W and that the number of non supported Pareto optima is largely greater than the number of supported Pareto optima. Comparisons show that the first algorithm can tackle problems with up to 120 objects whereas the second is capable of tackling problems with up to 500 objects. The problem BKSP is similarly solved by [Gandibleux and Fréville, 1998]. Initially, they propose dominance conditions to reduce the search space. A tabu search algorithm to approximate the set E is proposed next. This heuristic integrates the dominance conditions mentioned and is issued from the heuristic presented by [Gandibleux et al., 1997].

Among the methods for solving multicriteria optimisation problems we can similarly refer to the evolutionary algorithms. [Bentley and Wakefield, 1996], [Cvetkovic and Parmee, 1998] and [Coello Coello, 1999] show that the proposed algorithms are generally of type a posteriori, and that they optimise:

- a linear combination of criteria,
- the criteria according to a lexicographical order,

- an objective function linked to the goal-attainment approach,
- one of the criteria using the ϵ-constraint approach.

3.9 The complexity of multicriteria problems

In this section we are interested in the complexity of certain types of multicriteria optimisation problems. Then, just as there are well known reduction trees for the classic scheduling criteria (see chapter 2), we present some reduction results among different objective functions. These results are independent of the structure of the problem. In the remainder of this section we note $\mathcal{S}$ the set of solutions.

3.9.1 Complexity results related to the solutions

Firstly we define several basic multicriteria optimisation problems.

Let O_w^1 be the problem of determining one weak Pareto optimum. We set:
O_w^1: Data: Let $\mathcal{S}$ be the set of solutions,
Objective: Find one solution $x^0 \in \mathcal{S}$ such that $\nexists x^1 \in \mathcal{S} \setminus \{x^0\}$ such that $Z(x^1) < Z(x^0)$.

Let O_w^a be the problem of determining all the weak Pareto optima. We set:
O_w^a: Data: Let $\mathcal{S}$ be the set of solutions,
Objective: Find all the solutions $x^0 \in \mathcal{S}$ such that $\nexists x^1 \in \mathcal{S} \setminus \{x^0\}$ such that $Z(x^1) < Z(x^0)$.

In the same way, we define O_s^1 the problem of determining one strict Pareto optimum and O_s^a the problem of determining all the strict Pareto optima.

Some works in the literature are interested in generating all the solutions of a problem. These are called generation problems. Particular classes of complexity have been defined for these problems. The interested reader is referred to [?]. In the remaining discussion we do not consider these complexity classes but only the classical ones ([Garey and Johnson, 1979]).

We first show two simple results.

Lemma 10
A polynomial Turing reduction $\propto_T$ exists such that $O_w^1 \propto_T O_s^1$. A polynomial Turing reduction $\propto_T$ exists such that $O_w^a \propto_T O_s^a$.

Proof.
Straightforward.□

Lemma 11 concerns the relationship between the complexity of single criterion and multicriteria problems. It shows that determination of any weak Pareto optimum is a problem which is simpler than the simplest of its single criterion problems.

Lemma 11
Let there be K criteria Z_i and the K associated single criterion problems O_i. For all criterion Z_i, $\forall i = 1, ..., K$, a polynomial Turing reduction exists α_T such that $O_w^1 \propto_T O_i$.

Proof.
Straightforward.□

Notice that for all the reductions presented in this section, the four conditions of definition 12 hold. This means that all these reductions are pseudopolynomial reductions.

3.9.2 Complexity results related to objective functions

It is interesting to study the links, in terms of complexity, between the different kind of objective functions introduced in this chapter.

• In lemma 12 we are interested in the case where a lexicographical order among the criteria is stated. We define the optimisation problem O_{Lex} for the order $Lex(Z_1, \ldots Z_K)$ as follows:

O_{Lex}: Data: Let $\mathcal{S}$ be the set of solutions,
Objective: Find a solution $x^0 \in \mathcal{S}$ such that, $\forall i = 1, ..., K$, $Z_i(x^0) = \min_{x' \in \mathcal{S}^{i-1}} (Z_i(x'))$ with $\mathcal{S}^i = \{x \in \mathcal{S}^{i-1} / Z_{i-1}(x) = \min_{x' \in \mathcal{S}^{i-1}} (Z_{i-1}(x'))\}$ and $\mathcal{S}^0 = \mathcal{S}$.

Lemma 12
Let there be K criteria Z_i and the associated optimisation problem O_{Lex}. We have $O_1 \propto_T O_{Lex}$ and $O_s^1 \propto_T O_{Lex}$ whatever the order of criteria.

Proof.
O_1 is the optimisation problem of the criterion Z_1. Demonstration of $O_1 \propto_T O_{Lex}$ for the order $Z_1 \rightarrow \ldots \rightarrow Z_K$ follows immediately from the property 1. It is the same for the proof of $O_s^1 \propto_T O_{Lex}$ whatever the order of criteria.□

• We are now interested in the optimisation problem in which we look for the minimisation of a convex combination of the criteria. We define the optimisation problem O_ℓ as follows:

O_ℓ: Data: Let $\mathcal{S}$ be the set of solutions and $\alpha \in [0;1]^K$, such that $\sum_{i=1}^{K} \alpha_i = 1$,

Objective: Find a solution $s^0 \in \mathcal{S}$ such that $\sum_{i=1}^{K} \alpha_i Z_i(s^0) = \min_{s' \in \mathcal{S}} (\sum_{i=1}^{K} \alpha_i Z_i(s'))$.

Lemma 13
Let there be K criteria Z_i and the associated optimisation problem O_ℓ. We have:

1. $O_i \propto_T O_\ell$, $\forall i = 1, ..., K$,
2. $O_{Lex} \propto_T O_\ell$, *whatever the order among the criteria,*
3. $O_\ell \propto_T O_w^a$.

Proof.
1) The algorithm A used to solve the problem O_i is defined by:

Algorithm A:
$\alpha_i = 1$;
$\alpha_j = 0$, $\forall j = 1, ..., K, j \neq i$;
Call $S[\alpha_1; \ldots; \alpha_K; s^0]$;

In this algorithm, the procedure S solves the problem O_ℓ and returns the calculated solution s^0.
We note that if this procedure has a polynomial time complexity, then the algorithm A is equally so, which proves that $O_i \propto_T O_\ell$, $\forall i = 1, ..., K$.

2) We suppose that the order is that defined by the indices, *i.e.* $Lex(Z_1, \ldots, Z_K)$. The algorithm A which we propose to solve O_{Lex}, is close to that presented previously:

Algorithm A:
$\beta_1 = 1$;
$\beta_j = 0$, $\forall j = 2, ..., K$;
Call $S[\beta_1; \ldots; \beta_K; s^1]$;
For $i = 2$ to K Do
  $\alpha_i = 1$;
  $\alpha_j = 0$, $\forall j = 1, ..., K, i \neq j$;
  Call $S[\alpha_1; \ldots; \alpha_K; s^2]$;
  $\delta = Z_i(s^1) - Z_i(s^2)$;
  $\beta_i = 1$;
  $\beta_j = \beta_j \times \delta$, $\forall j = 1, ..., i-1$;
  Call $S[\beta_1; \ldots; \beta_K; s^1]$;
End for;

In this algorithm the procedure S solves a version of the problem O_ℓ where the weights are positive but not normalised to 1. If we know how to solve this problem, then we also know how to solve the problem O_ℓ. Algorithm A solves the problem O_{Lex} given that at each iteration we calculate the weights in such a way that the value of the previously minimised criterion is not increased. The value δ represents the largest improvement of the criterion in hand and modification of the weights β_i guarantee that we are not enabling trade-offs with the previous criteria. We notice that if the procedure S has a polynomial time complexity, then the algorithm A is equally so, which proves $O_{Lex} \propto_T O_\ell$.

3)The algorithm A presented below solves the problem O_ℓ.

Algorithm A:
Call $F = S[\alpha_1, \alpha_2, \ldots, \alpha_K]$;
/* F contains the set of weak Pareto optima sorted in ascending order of values $\sum_{i=1}^{K} \alpha_i Z_i$ */
Return $F(1)$;

S is a procedure which solves the problem O_w^a and sorts the weak Pareto optima found by increasing order of values $\sum_{i=1}^{K} \alpha_i Z_i$.□

• Concerning the parametric approach, few results exist due to the generic form of theorem 5. We define the optimisation problem O_p as follows:

O_p: Data: Let $\mathcal{S}$ be the set of solutions, $k = [k_1; ...; k_K]^T$ a vector of K constants and a strictly increasing function $g : \mathbb{R}^k \to \mathbb{R}$,
Objective: Find a solution $x^0 \in \mathcal{S}$ such that $g(Z(x^0)) = \min_{x' \in \mathcal{S}}(g(Z(x')))$ subject to $Z(x^0) \leq [k_1; \ldots; k_K]^T$.

Lemma 14
Let there be K criteria Z_i and the associated optimisation problem O_p. We have $O_s^1 \propto_T O_p$.

Proof.
Deduced from property 1 and theorem 5.□

• In the next lemma we are interested in the ϵ-contraint approach. We suppose that the criterion Z_1 is minimised and we define the problem O_ϵ as follows:

O_ϵ : Data: Let $\mathcal{S}$ be the set of solutions and $K-1$ constants ϵ_j, $\forall j = 2, ..., K$,
Objective: Find a solution $x^0 \in \mathcal{S}$ such that $Z_1(x^0) = \min_{x' \in \mathcal{S}}(Z_1(x'))$ subject to $Z_j(x^0) \leq \epsilon_j$, $\forall j = 2, ..., K$.

Lemma 15
Let there be K criteria Z_i and the associated optimisation problem O_ϵ. We have:

1. $O_1 \propto_T O_\epsilon$,
2. $O_\epsilon \propto_T O_f^t$.

Proof.
1) We introduce a resolution algorithm A for the problem O_1.

Algorithm A:

$k_j = \infty,\ \forall j = 1, ..., K;$
Call $S[k_2; \ldots; k_K; s^0];$

The procedure S used in this algorithm solves the problem O_ϵ. We therefore have $O_1 \propto_T O_\epsilon$. The value k_j can be initiated eventually with an upper bound on the criterion Z_j, $\forall j = 2, ..., K$.

2) Let the resolution algorithm A for the problem O_ϵ be defined as follows:

Algorithm A:

```
Call S[σ];
Min = ∞;
For (all s ∈ σ) do
|  If (Z_j(s) ≤ ε_j, ∀j = 2,...,K and Z_1(s) < Min) Then
|  |  s* = s;
|  |  Min = Z_1(s);
|  End If;
End For;
```

Procedure S solves the problem O_f^t. We note that if procedure S has a polynomial time complexity, then the number of elements in σ is bounded by a polynomial of *Long* which is the length of the instance. In this case, the algorithm A is equally polynomial.□

A special link also exists between the problem O_{Lex} and the problems O_ϵ^i, where O_ϵ^i refers to the problem O_ϵ in which we minimise the criterion Z_i instead of the criterion Z_1.

Lemma 16
If all the problems O_ϵ^i, $\forall i = 1, ..., K$, are polynomially solvable, then the problem O_{Lex} is equally so whatever the order of the criteria under consideration. Conversely, if a problem O_{Lex}, for a fixed order, is $\mathcal{NP}$-hard then at least one of the problems O_ϵ^i is $\mathcal{NP}$-hard.

Proof.
The proof is based on the existence of a polynomial Turing reduction. Let us suppose, without loss of generality, that the lexicographical order is that defined by the indices, *i.e.* $Lex(Z_1, \ldots, Z_K)$. We introduce an algorithm A which solves the corresponding problem O_{Lex} and which is defined as follows:

Algorithm A:

```
k_j = ∞, ∀j = 1,...,K;
For i = 1,...,K Do
|  Call S[k_1; ...; k_{i-1}; k_{i+1}; ...; k_K; i; s^0];
|  k_i = Z_i(s^0);
End For;
```

The procedure S used in this algorithm solves the problem O_ϵ^i. We notice that if all the problems O_ϵ^i are polynomially solvable, running of the procedure S can be

realised in polynomial time and the algorithm A is polynomially solvable. Conversely, if the problem O_{Lex} is $\mathcal{NP}$-hard then at least one running of the procedure S cannot be done in polynomial time.
Besides, we deduce that this reasoning is valid whatever the order among the criteria in the lexicographical order.□

We denote by D_i the decision problem associated with the criterion Z_i, defined as follows:

D_i : Data: Let $\mathcal{S}$ be the set of solutions and D a value,
Question: Does a solution $x^0 \in \mathcal{S}$ exist such that $Z_i(x^0) \leq D$?

If it appears to be difficult to establish a general reduction of the problems O_i, for $i \neq 1$, towards the problem O_ϵ, we can show that such reductions exist if we consider the decision problems D_i.

Lemma 17
Let there be K criteria Z_i and the associated optimisation problem O_ϵ. We have $D_i \propto_T O_\epsilon$, $\forall i = 2, ..., K$.

Proof.
To solve a problem D_i, for a fixed index i, *i.e.* to provide an answer *True* or *False*, it is sufficient to consider the following algorithm A:

Algorithm A:
$\epsilon_j = \infty$, $\forall j = 2, ..., K$, $j \neq i$;
$\epsilon_i = D$;
Call $S[\epsilon_2; \ldots; \epsilon_K; s^0; answer]$;

S is a procedure which solves O_ϵ and which returns a solution s^0 if $answer = True$.□

• Concerning the Tchebycheff metric approaches and the goal-attainment approach, it appears to be difficult to propose polynomial Turing reductions given the parameters used in these approaches. If we denote the minimisation problems of the Tchebycheff metrics by O_T, O_{Tp} and O_{Tpa}, we can simply show that polynomial Turing reductions exist such that $O_f^1 \propto_T O_T$, $O_f^1 \propto_T O_{Tp}$ and $O_f^1 \propto_T O_{Tpa}$. The same is true for the goal-attainment approach, the problem of which is denoted by O_g.
All the reductions stated in this section are polynomial Turing reductions which are not sufficient to show strong $\mathcal{NP}$-hardness reducibility, since we need pseudo-polynomial reductions. However, we can easily prove the following result.

Corollary 3
The polynomial Turing reductions introduced in lemma 12, 13, 14, 15, 16 and 17 are also pseudo-polynomial reductions.

Proof.
The result can be shown by simply applying the definition 12. As the reductions

considered are polynomial Turing reductions, the conditions 1 and 2 are verified. Besides, notice that for all these reductions $Length'[I'] = Length[\propto_T (I')]$ and $Max[I'] = Max[\propto_T (I')]$, $\forall I'$. Therefore, the conditions 3 and 4 are also verified.□

3.9.3 Summary

The set of reductions shown in the previous section is summarised in figure 3.20.

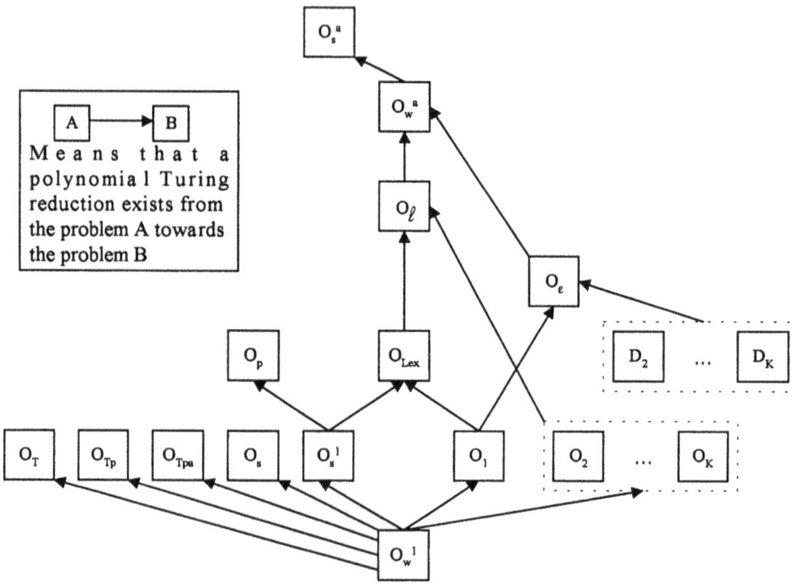

Fig. 3.20. Polynomial reductions tree

These results are especially interesting to study the complexity of multicriteria problems when we know this of single criterion problems. Moreover, they show that the multicriteria problems are likely to be $\mathcal{NP}$-hard given that they are at least as difficult as the single criterion problems. For example, the decision problem associated with the bicriteria shortest path problem in a graph ([Serafini, 1987]), is $\mathcal{NP}$-complete whilst the single criterion problems are not. The same is true for the decision problem associated with the bicriteria assignment problem.

Concerning the study of theoretical results for the complexity of multicriteria problems, we can refer to [Ehrgott, 2000b] who studies certain problems for which the set of solutions $\mathcal{S}$ is defined in the following way: let

$E = \{e_1; \ldots; e_N\}$ be a set of elements and $\mathcal{S} = \{s/s \subseteq E\}$. The complexity of bicriteria problems where the criteria are functions of form "max" or "$\sum$" is studied using the ϵ-constraint approach. It is shown that the problems composed of one or two criteria of the form "$\sum$" are the most difficult to solve.

3.10 Interactive methods

Interactive methods have been the object of numerous works since the 1970s. Their interest is in allowing the decision maker to lead the resolution process. This avoids the problems connected to the incomparability of Pareto optima. An interactive method proceeds by iterations. Each iteration comprises two phases ([Steuer, 1986] and [Gardiner and Vanderpooten, 1997]):

1. A *dialogue* phase where a solution is presented to the decision maker.
2. A *calculation* phase where the method uses the instructions of the decision maker to calculate a new solution.

The final solution held by the decision maker must be a Pareto optimum. When we perfect an interactive algorithm, we must pay attention to its convergence towards a final solution. Two cases can occur: the convergence of the algorithm can be shown mathematically or the convergence depends on the behaviour of the decision maker. In the first case we can show that the algorithm will run no more than k iterations. Then, the decision maker must have retained a solution before the end of the process. For the second type of algorithm it is not possible to restrict the number of iterations since the convergence depends on the behaviour of the decision maker. For example, he may reject a solution initially and accept it several iterations later ([Vincke, 1989]). A typology of interactive methods is proposed in [Vanderpooten, 1992]. This typology reflects the different types of convergence. We can distinguish:

1. The *search* oriented methods which depend on the hypothesis which the decision maker cannot change his mind about during the resolution process. The objective is to converge towards the solution which the decision maker wants. This convergence then depends uniquely on the method used to obtain this solution and may be limited.
2. The *learning* oriented methods which depend on the hypothesis which the wishes of the decision maker can evolve during the resolution process. At one given iteration, these methods must, beginning with the information provided by the decision maker at the time of the previous iterations, try to determine the solution of the current iteration. We can classify these methods as "one shot methods".
3. The *mixed* methods which combine the *search* and *learning* phases.

[Gardiner and Vanderpooten, 1997] show that historically the learning oriented methods are more recent than the search oriented methods. They similarly propose a panorama of the principal existing interactive methods.

Another typology is proposed by [Steuer, 1986] in the case of problems which can be modeled by linear programming. By contrast to the typology proposed by [Vanderpooten, 1992], the one presented by Steuer classifies the interactive methods according to the implemented techniques. We distinguish:

1. The methods which proceed by *reducing the solutions set.* With each iteration, constraints on the values of the criteria are added. The set of solutions to consider with the following iteration is thus reduced.
2. The methods which proceed by *reducing the set of possible weights for the criteria.* In these methods we assume that a weight is assigned to each criterion. With each iteration the set of possible values of these weights is reduced according to decision maker's instructions.
3. The methods which proceed by *reducing the criteria cone.* This cone is reduced with each iteration. If the number of iterations is not limited then the cone converges towards a unique vector c. That brings us back to transforming the multicriteria problem into a single criterion problem for which the optimal solution is the Pareto optimum acceptable by the decision maker.
4. The methods which proceed by *navigating in the set of solutions.* With each iteration a solution is retained by the decision maker who next indicates the new search direction to calculate the next solution. For example, this research direction may be calculated by improvements on the criteria which the decision maker wishes, related to the current solution.

We do not aim to presente a complete state-of-the-art of interactive methods. We simply present in table 3.1 a summary of the most classical methods. Equally, we mention the existence of interactive software, as for example the NIMBUS software ([Miettinen, 1999]).

3.11 Goal programming

The origins of goal programming return us to [Charnes et al., 1955] and [Charnes and Cooper, 1961]. The special feature of this programming is in the statement of goals for each criterion to best satisfy. Thus, we do not seek to optimise directly the criteria as in traditional mathematical programming. To illustrate the principle of goal programming we introduce the problem (P_{obj}) defined by:

Table 3.1. Summary of some interactive methods

Reference	A	B	C	D	I	II	III	Context
[Benayoun et al., 1971]	X				X			MLP
[Geoffrion et al., 1972]				X	X			MLP
[Roy, 1976]				X		X		
[Zionts and Wallenius, 1976] and [Zionts and Wallenius, 1983]		X			X			MLP
[Vincke, 1976]				X		X		MLP uniquely
[Steuer, 1977]			X		X			MLP uniquely
[Steuer and Wood, 1986]		X			X			
[Wierzbicki, 1990] and [Wierzbicki, 1982]				X	X			
[Steuer and Choo, 1983]		X			X			
[Korhonen and Laakso, 1986]				X		X		
[Lévine and Pomerol, 1986]	X				X			Discrete problems
[Jacquet-Lagrèze et al., 1987]			X		X			
[Vanderpooten, 1988]	X					X		
[Lofti and Zionts, 1990] and [Lofti et al., 1992]	X			X			X	Discrete problems
[Jaszkiewicz and Slowinski, 1997]	X		X		X			Discrete problems
[Ulungu et al., 1998]	X					X		MMIP
[Alves and Climaco, 2000]	X					X		MMIP
[Kaliszewski, 2000]				X	X			

A: Method by reduction of the set of solutions
B: Method by reduction of the set of weights
C: Method by reduction of the criteria cone
D: Method by navigation
I: Search oriented method
II: Learning oriented method
III: Mixed method

Criterion I: $Z_1(x)$ Objective: $Z_1(x) \leq b_1$
Criterion II: $Z_2(x)$ Objective: $Z_2(x) = b_2$
Criterion III: $Z_3(x)$ Objective: $Z_3(x) \in [b_3^{\ell b}; b_3^{ub}]$
subject to
$x \in \mathcal{S}$

where the three objectives of (P_{obj}) represent three categories of objective which can be encountered. In the problem (P_{obj}), the objective of criterion I shows that a solution with a low value Z_1 is searched, if possible a value which is smaller than b_1. The objective of criterion II forces calculation of a solution which the value of the criterion Z_2 is equal to b_2 while in the case of criterion III the value of the criterion Z_3 has to belong to the interval $[b_3^{\ell b}; b_3^{ub}]$. The criteria objectives define in the criteria space the *utopian set*, noted $\mathcal{U}$. If $\mathcal{Z} \cap \mathcal{U} \neq \emptyset$ then $\forall x$ such that $Z(x) \in \mathcal{Z} \cap \mathcal{U}$, x is a solution of the problem, and in this case dominated solutions can exist which are solutions of the problem (P_{obj}). But we can have $\mathcal{Z} \cap \mathcal{U} = \emptyset$ and in this case, we must determine a solution for which the criteria vector is "as close as possible", in the sense of a function which remains to be defined, of the utopian set. For that, we transform the problem (P_{obj}) into a problem (P_{slack}) by introducing positive slack variables d_i^+ and/or d_i^- and supplementary constraints to translate the objectives of each criterion.

For the objective imposed on the criterion Z_1, we will introduce a slack variable d_1^+ and the constraint $Z_1(x) - d_1^+ \leq b_1$.

For the objective imposed on the criterion Z_2, we will introduce the slack variables d_2^- and d_2^+ and the constraint $Z_2(x) - d_2^+ + d_2^- = b_2$.

For the objective imposed on the criterion Z_3, we will introduce the slack variables d_3^+ and d_3^- and the two following constraints: $Z_3(x) + d_3^- \geq b_3^{\ell b}$ and $Z_3(x) - d_3^+ \leq b_3^{ub}$.

In the problem (P_{slack}), these are then the slack variables which are optimised. There exist several types of problems (P_{slack}) which distinguish themselves by the way in which the slack variables are optimised. Traditionally we find:

1. *Archimedian* problems. We speak similarly of *archimedian goal programming.*
2. *Preemptive* or *lexicographical* problems. We speak similarly of *preemptive or lexicographical programming.*
3. *Interactive* problems, which are a mixture of archimedian and lexicographical problems. Similarly, we speak of *interactive goal programming.*
4. *Reference point* problems, which are particular lexicographical problems. Similarly, we speak of *goal programming by reference.*
5. Problems *with multiple functions.* Similarly, we speak of *multicriteria goal programming.*

In goal programming, the notion of Pareto optima is not defined for the problem (P_{obj}) but for the problem (P_{slack}) ([Steuer, 1986]). A solution to the problem (P_{slack}) is a couple (x, d) where $x \in S$ and d is the vector of the p slack variables, each component of which can be noted d_i.

Definition 48
Let (x, d^x) be a solution of the problem (P_{slack}). $x \in S$ is a strict Pareto-slack optimum, called also an efficient-slack or a strict efficient-slack solution, if and only if $\nexists (y, d^y), y \in S$, such that $\forall i = 1, ..., p$, $d_i^y \leq d_i^x$ with at least one strict inequality. We note E_{slack} the set of strict Pareto-slack optima.

It is possible to state a similar definition for the notion of weak Pareto-slack optimum. The set of weak Pareto-slack optima is noted WE_{slack}. The solutions of the problems (P_{slack}) presented in the following sections, are generally Pareto-slack optima. They are not necessarily Pareto optima for the criteria of the problem (P_{obj}). That is equivalent to saying that a solution of a problem modeled in the form of a goal program can be dominated by another solution. To avoid this problem, different works study the possibilty of reconstructing a Pareto optimum for the criteria under consideration from the optimal solution of the problem (P_{obj}). The interested reader may refer notably to [Tamiz et al., 1999]. We shall now present different types of goal programming.

3.11.1 Archimedian goal programming

When trade-offs between different objectives are allowed and when the weights can be defined by the decision maker, then we can use archimedian goal programming. In this case, the problem (P_{slack}) is written in the form:

$$\text{Min } \alpha_1^+ d_1^+ + \alpha_2^+ d_2^+ + \alpha_2^- d_2^- + \alpha_3^+ d_3^+ + \alpha_3^- d_3^-$$

subject to

$$(C) \begin{cases} x \in \mathcal{S} \\ Z_1(x) - d_1^+ \leq b_1 \\ Z_2(x) - d_2^+ + d_2^- = b_2 \\ Z_3(x) + d_3^- \geq b_3^{lb} \\ Z_3(x) - d_3^+ \leq b_3^{ub} \\ d_i^+ \geq 0, \ \forall i = 1, ..., 3 \\ d_i^- \geq 0, \ \forall i = 2, ..., 3 \end{cases}$$

In general, we suppose that the weights $\alpha_i^{+/-}$ are positive. For this problem, it is possible to apply Geoffrion's theorem to show that the resolution of the problem (P_{slack}) enables to calculate a weak or a strict Pareto-slack optimum following the value of the weights. If the set $\mathcal{S}$ is not convex, then the solution of the problem (P_{slack}) does not enable us to determine non supported Pareto-slack optima.

3.11.2 Lexicographical goal programming

When it is not possible to compensate between different objectives, we can use lexicographical goal programming. We then define a lexicographical order between the objectives. Let us suppose in our example that this order is that of the criteria indices. The problem (P_{slack}) is written then in the form:

$$min_{Lex}(d_1^+, d_2^+ + d_2^-, d_3^+ + d_3^-)$$

subject to

$$(C)$$

The solution of the problem (P_{slack}) is a strict Pareto-slack optimum.

3.11.3 Interactive goal programming

Interactive goal programming intervenes when we can define classes of objectives such that it is possible to define a strict order between these classes and such that only trade-offs are allowed between criteria of the same class.

For example, for the problem (P_{obj}) introduced previously we can define two classes. The first groups the slack variables associated to objectives I and II. We note f_1 the convex combination of the slack variables associated with this class. The second class groups the slack variables associated to objective III and we note f_2 the convex combination of these slack variables. We consider the lexicographical order given by the indices of the classes. The problem (P_{slack}) is written then in the form:

$$\begin{array}{c} min_{Lex}(f_1, f_2) \\ \text{subject to} \\ (C) \end{array}$$

The problem (P_{slack}) is solved traditionally by an interactive algorithm. At the first step, the decision maker provides the classes, the order of the classes and the weights. The problem (P_{slack}) is therefore solved and the solution obtained is presented to the decision maker who can modify the weights and/or the classes and/or the order between the classes. A new solution is calculated and the process is repeated until the desired solution is reached. Besides, if the set $\mathcal{S}$ is bounded, then each optimal solution of the problem (P_{slack}) is a weak or strict Pareto-slack optimum (see for example [Steuer, 1986]).

3.11.4 Reference goal programming

This type of goal programming, is inspired by the methods using reference points, and was proposed by [Ogryczak, 1994]. More exactly, the objective function of the problem (P_{slack}) is broken down in the same way as in the problem of the minimisation of an augmented weighted Tchebycheff metric according to a lexicographical order (see theorem 12). The problem (P_{slack}) is then written in the form:

$$\begin{array}{c} min_{Lex}(T_1, T_2) \\ \text{subject to} \\ (C) \end{array}$$

Ogryczak shows that every solution of this problem is a strict Pareto optimum for the criteria of the problem (P_{obj}). The extension of this model to a problem by lexicographical reference is presented in [Ogryczak, 1997].

3.11.5 Multicriteria goal programming

As for interactive goal programming problems the decision maker defines classes of objectives and provides the weights for each objective. Convex combinations f_i for each class are also constructed. The solution of the problem (P_{slack}) returns us to determining the set of the strict Pareto-slack optima.

4. An approach to multicriteria scheduling problems

4.1 Justification of the study

4.1.1 Motivations

In the context of production, the planning phase is broken down hierarchically into different levels: strategic, tactical and operational. The production plan at the tactical level determines the quantities of products to make by time period. Its objectives are:

- to satisfy the customers' requirements, that is to say to supply the customer with the product he wants, in the desired quantity and at the desired date,
- to balance continuously the existing resources and the resources necessary for production, by avoiding underloading as well as overloading,
- to ensure production at lowest cost or at least with maximum profitability.

Next, at the operational level, the established plan must be followed as best as it can. This is not without bringing up some coherence problems, allied to the fact that the first module handles aggregated information, and the second detailled information. Scheduling has as principal objectives:

- to minimise work-in-process in the shop,
- to have high respect for the planned and promised delivery dates given to the customers,
- and to optimise the shop resources.

By its very nature therefore, a scheduling problem in the context of production is very often multicriteria. RCPSP may also involve several criteria of time and cost type ([Herroelen et al., 1998a] and [Hapke et al., 1998]) as for example:

- the respect of delivery dates,
- the cost related to the duration of an activity when this duration belongs to an interval and has to be fixed.

Examples of such problems are time/cost trade-off problems. As a general rule, and as [Roy, 1985] points out, taking several criteria into account enables us to provide the decision maker with a more realistic solution. Some concrete examples are presented in section 4.1.2.

Different states-of-the-art of multicriteria scheduling can be found in the literature (see [Dileepan and Sen, 1988], [Fry et al., 1989], [Hoogeveen, 1992a], [Nagar et al., 1995a] and [Hoogeveen, 2005]). Analysis of these works underlines:

- the necessity of knowing the results of the domain of multicriteria optimisation to understand well the difficulties related to taking into account conflicting criteria,
- the need for a typology enables us to formalise the different types of problems and to unify the notation of these problems,
- the need for a knowledge of the results on single criterion scheduling problems.

Application of multicriteria optimisation constitutes a field of activity which has been little explored until today.

4.1.2 Some examples

Many scheduling problems in the production domain involve several criteria. We find in the literature numerous works dealing with a category of problems which correspond well to a situation: the need to produce "Just-in-Time". This need translates into two wishes, one is not to deliver to the client late, the other is not to store the finished products. To produce "Just-in-Time" is therefore a trade-off between producing slightly late and not too early. Numerous definitions of "Just-in-Time" scheduling exist in the literature. These works are presented in chapter 5.

We now present some scheduling problems corresponding to practical situations, whatever their application field.

Manufacture of bottles
A factory manufactures glass bottles the colours of which are selected in advance at the planning phase ([T'kindt et al., 2001]). A furnace containing the molten glass of a given colour, serves several different forming machines. These machines are fitted with several moulds, allowing several types of bottles to be made, which correspond to several orders. Changing a mould on a machine takes a negligible time compared to the production time, thus allowing the changeover from one product to another in hidden time. The manufacture of a product by a machine creates a profit which can be measured. One of the objectives is therefore, given the production horizon, to assign the jobs to the machines, in order to maximise the total profit. On the other hand, change of colour in the furnace affects the set of machines which it serves, and this change can only occur when all the machines have

completed their current production. In order not to allow the machines to be inactive for a too long time, which creates a prohibitive cost, we desire that the machines should cease production within a limited timeframe. A second criterion aims therefore to assign the jobs in order to minimise the greatest difference of workload between two machines. The decision maker wishes to find the better trade-off between the total profit and the greatest idle time of the machines.

Electroplating and chemical industry
This category of problems returns us to the Hoist Scheduling Problem in the literature. A certain number of tanks containing chemicals are available for the galvanisation treatment of items. Arrival of the items in the shop is cyclic. These items pass from one tank to another by means of a transportation robot (or a pool of robots) usually suspended above the tanks. The processing time, or soaking time, of the items in the tanks is a variable of the problem. Indeed, the chemical engineers give a minimum and maximum duration for each soaking, thus leaving complete freedom for the analyst to calculate the best durations. The basic problem is to seek a minimum cycle time, *i.e.* a minimum value of the makespan criterion. Nevertheless, two factors force us to consider this problem from the multicriteria point of view. Firstly, practicalities show that scheduling of the movement of the tranportation robots (handling and placing of the items into the tanks) is the most difficult part to determine to efficiently minimise the cycle time. Next, for most of the tanks (therefore the chemicals baths) respecting the minimum soaking time is the only vital consideration. In practice we can sometimes exceed the maximum soaking time if it enables us to better manage movements of the robots. Thus, the problem becomes bicriteria when we want to minimise the cycle time and, for example, a weighted sum of overtaking the soaking times compared to the authorised maximum soaking times ([Fargier and Lamothe, 2001]).

Steel hot rolling mill industry
The steel hot rolling mill problem consists in producing steel coils starting from steel slabs ([Cowling, 2003]). In this problem the shop can be decomposed into two parts: a huge slabyard in which the steel slabs are stored waiting to be processed by the rolling mill, and the rolling mill in itself. Each slab has particular characteristics and can be used to process several kinds of steel coils. When a slab has been selected to be processed, it is transported by cranes up to the rolling mill and introduced into a furnace in which it is subjected to a high temperature. After the furnace, the hot steel slab passes into a series of rolls that submit it to high pressures in order to achieve the desired width, thickness and hardness for the steel coil. Notice that to each shift of processed orders is associated an ideal sequencing shape which take account of additional constraints related, for instance, to the furnace and the fact that we cannot make varying its temperature has we want. One of the

desire of the planner is to reduce the changes of pressure settings between two consecutive produced coils because this can severely alters their quality. Besides, has the rolls are in contact with hot steel they are quickly worn and must be replaced by new rolls. Accordingly the production of coils is planned by shifts of a few hours. There are also a certain number of additional constraints. The aim is to sequence the steel coils in order to maximise the value of the coils rolled in the sequence, to minimise the changes in characteristics between two consecutive coils, to minimise the number of non-essential crane movements and to minimise the deviation from the ideal sequencing shape.

Car assembly
Car production lines create multicriteria scheduling problems for the subcontractors. This is especially true for car seats. The manufacturer and the assembler of cars are synchronised and the sequencing of a vehicle on the production line automatically instructs the manufacturer to produce seats. This stipulates a limited time for their delivery. This problem is a Just-in-Time scheduling problem since early production of a seat creates for the assembler additional storage costs (higher than storage costs of an engine). Conversely, late delivery of seats causes the assembly line to halt. The vehicle in question must then be repositioned to the front of the line, which causes additional production costs.

Processing of cheques
The organisation of a processing centre, dedicated to perform operations on cheques (debit, credit, printing, *etc.*) is similar to a production centre. More precisely, it can be represented as a three-stage hybrid flowshop problem, where the jobs pass several times through the same stage (recirculation). We can associate two due dates to each job. The first relates to the completion time of an operation of the routing which transfers data to customers. The second relates to the completion time of the last operation of the jobs. If this date is not respected, delivery of the cheques is delayed by a whole day, which creates a cost proportional to the amount of money delayed. Two different criteria are associated with these due dates. The first is that of the maximum tardiness, to be minimised in order to limit upsetting the customers, and the second is the weighted number of late jobs where the associated weight is the cost incurred by the delay ([Bertel and Billaut, 2004]). These two criteria do not have the same importance for the firm, which wants above all to minimise the second and only then the first.

Scheduling problems related to transport
Numerous planning and scheduling problems occur when dealing with transportation of goods or passengers. Among others, the aircrew rostering problem can be seen as a multicriteria problem ([Lucic and Teodorovic, 1999]). This problem arises when dealing with the scheduling of crews to flights in

air transport. Assume there is a set of flights to do and a set of predefined rotations, a rotation being a sequence of flights. Knowing a set of pilots we have to assign them to rotations without violating constraints related to the air security and the skill of the pilot. For example, a pilot only flies one type of aircraft, his monthly flying time is limited to 85 hours, the number of takeoffs per month is limited to 90, *etc.* Besides, each day a pilot stays in a foreign country, he has a foreign per diem allowance. The aim is to minimise two criteria. The first one is the average relative deviation per pilot between the real and ideal monthly flight time and the second one is the average absolute deviation per pilot between the real and ideal number of foreign per diem allowances during the month.
Another application in transport scheduling is related to passenger train services planning in high-speed rail lines ([Chang et al., 2000]). This problem occurs when dealing with inter-city transportation, where we have a lot of train stations and a possibly huge quantity of passengers. Given a set of stations the aim is to determine stop-schedules in order to satisfy the constraints of the problem and to minimise the criteria. A stop-schedule is a sequence of stations at which a train must stop. We also have to determine the minimal number of trains required to satisfy the stop-schedules. Two criteria are minimised: the total operating cost for the planning horizon and the passenger's total travel time loss for the planning horizon.

Timetabling problems

In academic administration, the resources usually are students, faculties, staff, facilities, equipment, finances and time. Resource allocation problems refers to the determination of the levels of certain resources to be allocated among a number of competing activities. For the allocation of certain resources, specific names are given such as, for instance, scheduling or timetabling, when dealing with the allocation of courses, timeslot, examinations and classrooms. The research addressing these problems (see [Mustafa and Goh, 1996]) propose the use of goal programming, heuristics and interactive methods.

Sports scheduling

Sports scheduling is a particular area of scheduling theory which is closely related to timetabling problems: the aim in sports scheduling is usually to set a timetable of matches in a tournament or a championship. This kind of problem being hardly constrained it can be sometimes interesting to relax constraints into objectives, by the way leading to a multicriteria scheduling problem. [Wright, 2005] presents the particular case of the National Basketball League (NBL) of New Zealand. Ten basket teams meet twice in home and away matches, leading for each team to eighteen matches in a season. As only fifteen week-ends are available to play the matches, all teams have at least one week-end with two matches, which does not simplify the problem because additional constraints exist on these "doubling up" week-ends (the two teams that meet in a doubling up week-end must meet away and must not be located too far from each other). Other constraints are also described. Due to the complexity of the problem and the way a timetable is built by the NBL, most of the hard constraints are relaxed into objectives which are equal to 0 when the original related constraint is met. This leads to a total of twenty criteria minimised in a convex combination reflecting the total cost of constraint violation.

Satellite scheduling
Satellites are rare and costly resources that must accomplish defined tasks. One example of a multicriteria satellite scheduling problem is provided by [Gabrel and Vanderpooten, 2002] who focus on the scheduling of an earth observing satellite. Such a satellite has to daily process a series of photos of the earth according to a daily plan. This plan has to be calculated in order to fullfil a set of contraints: each photo must be taken in a given time window due to the satellite track, set-up times exist between two photos, the satellite can only take photos in the daylight, *etc.* Besides, the problem is so much constrained that, often, some photos cannot be done. Henceforth, the scheduling problem also concerns the choice of the photos to process. Three criteria are to be considered: (i) maximise the demand satisfaction, (ii) maximise the sum of the priorities of the scheduled photos, (iii) minimise the number of used camera. Gabrel and Vanderpooten solve this problem by enumerating all strict Pareto optimal paths in a tricriteria graph. This cannot be done in polynomial time. It is also interesting to notice that this problem can be modelled as a single machine problem (the satellite) with n jobs (the photos), time windows, set-up times and with a rejection cost (see for instance [Bartal et al., 2000]).

4.2 Presentation of the approach

4.2.1 Definitions

We now present a breakdown of the multicriteria scheduling problems by setting out the different phases which are more linked to Multicriteria Decision Aid, Multicriteria Optimisation, or Scheduling.

Definition 49
We call a **multicriteria scheduling problem** *the problem which consists of computing a Pareto optimal schedule for several conflicting criteria. This problem can be broken down into three sub-problems:*

1. **modelling of the problem**, *whose resolution leads to the determination of the nature of the scheduling problem under consideration as well as the definition of the criteria to be taken into account,*

2. **taking into account of criteria**, *whose resolution leads to indication of the resolution context and the way in which we want to take into account the criteria. The analyst finalises a decision aid module for the multicriteria problem, also called a module for taking account of criteria,*
3. **scheduling**, *whose resolution leads us to find a solution of the problem. The analyst finalises an algorithm for solving the scheduling problem, also called a resolution module for the scheduling problem.*

Modelling of the problem ([Roy, 1985]) is done with the decision maker, and consists on one hand of defining what are the relevant criteria which have to be taken into account. We assume that these criteria are conflicting that is to say that minimising one criterion is not equivalent to minimising another. On the other hand, we define at this phase the environment where the scheduling problem occurs, that is to say the set of resources available to carry out these jobs (it may concern machines and personel in the case of a shop, or another kind of resource), and the manner in which the shop is organised. We identify in some way the nature of the scheduling problem. Finally, we define the particular constraints of the problem: authorised preemption or not, release dates, *etc.* All this interactive process is done when a company wants to solve a scheduling problem. The analyst and the decision maker work together to define the problem, so that the analyst can draw up a model.

A large part of the difficulty in solving a multicriteria problem lies in the **taking account of the criteria**. During this phase, the decision maker provides the information concerning his perception of the criteria: firstly he states whether or not he authorises trade-offs between the criteria. If this is not so, he indicates the order in which the criteria should be optimised. On the other hand, if trade-offs are allowed, he indicates whether it is possible to associate a weight to the criteria if this has any sense, and he gives the weights eventually; he indicates the objectives to achieve for each criterion if he knows them; *etc.* Next, he arranges the choice of the method indicating whether he wants an algorithm which will give him a unique solution, taking into account the supplied information, or whether he prefers to intervene in the resolution procedure. The latter case occurs when he is not sure how to answer the questions. Finally, he might wish to see all the possible solutions in order to retain the one which interests him. These choices will automatically direct the respective method to an *a priori*, *interactive* or *a posteriori* algorithm. The information gathered on the problem at this phase and the way in which the decision maker is able and wishes to tackle it will allow the analyst to choose an appropriate resolution approach, whatever should be his choice: a linear combination of criteria, a parametric approach or another method. The result is the form of the objective function of the scheduling problem for which a resolution algorithm must be proposed. This phase will usually lead the analyst to finalise a module to take account of the criteria, that is to say an algorithm which will perform the interactions asked for by the decision maker (launching an interactive procedure, a posteriori procedure, *etc.*).

Scheduling has as objective to provide a schedule which optimises the objective function which was defined at the previous stage. The obtained solution is a Pareto optimum for the multicriteria scheduling problem. The analyst has therefore to finalise a scheduling module that will solve the scheduling problem resulting from the previous stages.

It is important to emphasise that [Faure, 1979] already advised the thorough breaking down of the tasks. He stated what was and what was not the competence of the operational researcher. He eventually advised that the problems should be tackled from a multicriteria point of view, by means of multicriteria analysis. Therefore, the approach which we present is not new: it simply proposes to effect these concepts by means of Decision Aid for the resolution of multicriteria scheduling problems.

Figure 4.1 presents the breakdown of *multicriteria scheduling problems* as it was developed in definition 49.

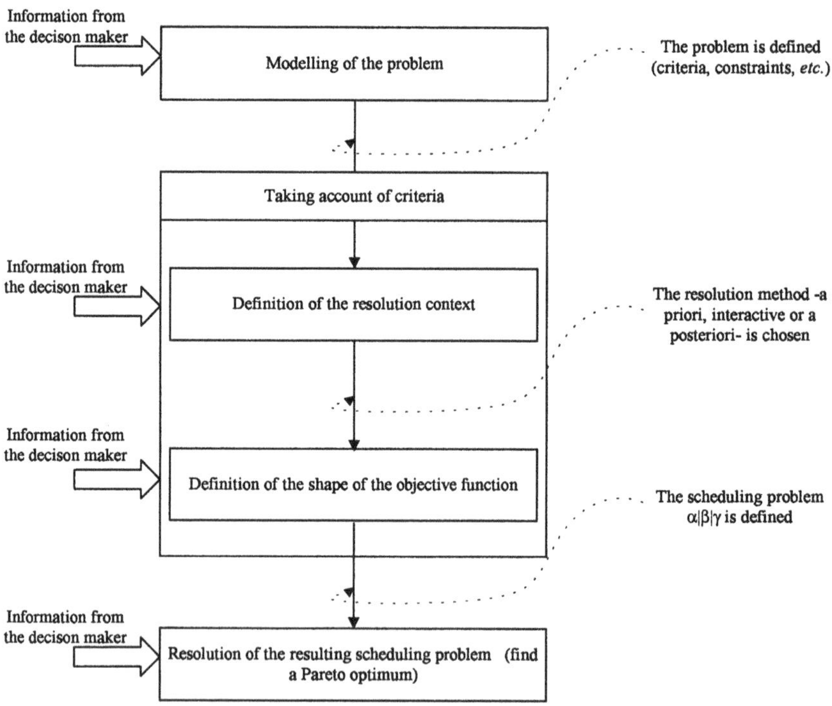

Fig. 4.1. A framework for solving multicriteria scheduling problems

4.2.2 Notation of multicriteria scheduling problems

At the phase of *taking account of criteria*, and following the information which it sets out, the analyst chooses a resolution approach for the scheduling problem and thus defines a scheduling problem. Taking account of the diversity of the methods of determining Pareto optima (see chapter 3), the functions to optimise for the scheduling problem can take different forms. Each one translates a method of determining a Pareto optimum. The criteria do not change and they correspond to those defined during the phase of *modelling of the problem.*

A multicriteria scheduling problem, after the modelling phase, can be noted in a general way by using the three-field notation, where the field γ contains the list of criteria: $\alpha|\beta|Z_1, Z_2, \ldots, Z_K$. The scheduling problem produced by the phase of taking account of the criteria may equally be noted by means of the three fields, where only field γ is spread. We define the following new functions for this field:

- Z if the objective is to minimise the unique criterion Z (single criterion problem). It concerns the well known case, *i.e.* Z may be C_{max}, T_{max}, *etc.*
- $F_\ell(Z_1, \ldots, Z_K)$ if the objective is to minimise a linear convex combination of the K criteria. For example, this case can agree if the decision maker can allocate a weight to each criterion.
- $\epsilon(Z_u/Z_1, \ldots, Z_{u-1}, Z_{u+1}, \ldots, Z_K)$, indicates that only the criterion Z_u is minimised, subject to all the other criteria being upper bounded by known values. This case is distinguished from the the previous case because the function to be minimised is Z_u and this criterion is not subject to any bound constraint. The analyst is in the area of the ϵ-constraint approach.
- $P(Z_1, \ldots, Z_K)$ indicates a non decreasing function of the criteria to minimise, if we suppose that all the criteria are upper bounded by known values. In this case, the analyst is in the area of parametric analysis.
- $F_T(Z_1, \ldots, Z_K)$ indicates an objective function which is the expression of a distance to a known ideal solution. The distance is calculated by using the Tchebycheff metric. This ideal solution must not be reachable.
- $F_{Tp}(Z_1, \ldots, Z_K)$ indicates an objective function which is the expression of a distance to a known ideal solution. The distance is calculated by using the weighted Tchebycheff metric. This ideal solution must not be reachable.
- $F_{Tpa}(Z_1, \ldots, Z_K)$ indicates an objective function which is the expression of a distance to a known ideal solution. The distance is calculated by using the augmented weighted Tchebycheff metric. This ideal solution must not be reachable.
- $F_s(Z_1, \ldots, Z_K)$ indicates a very particular function which takes into account a known ideal solution to find the sought solution. The analyst is in the area of the goal-attainment approach.
- $GP(Z_1, Z_2, \ldots, Z_K)$, if there are goals to reach for each criterion in the scheduling problem (goal programming). The problem is not to optimise

the criteria, but to find a solution which satisfies the goals, even if this solution does not correspond to a Pareto optimum.

- $Lex(Z_1, Z_2, \ldots, Z_K)$ indicates that the decision maker does not authorise trade-offs between the criteria. The order in which the criteria are given is related to their importance, the most important being in first place. The analyst uses the lexicographical order and optimises the criteria one after the other.
- $\#(Z_1, Z_2, \ldots, Z_K)$ indicates the enumeration problem of all the Pareto optima. Therefore we associate uniquely to this problem an a posteriori resolution algorithm which does not use any of the aggregation methods presented in chapter 3.

Among these approaches the most encountered in the literature are the F_ℓ, *Lex*, *GP* and # approaches.

4.3 Classes of resolution methods

We have seen (figure 4.1) that the analyst has to solve three problems in order to propose a resolution algorithm to the decision maker. According to the answers he receives he will create one resolution algorithm rather than another. We can distinguish three cases:

1. The decision maker desires a unique solution from the tool provided for him. In other words he chooses an *a priori* method. In this case the algorithm which the analyst produces is composed of a module which selects the value of the parameters, which enables to obtain an instance of a scheduling problem. The parameters are the input of the second module, which is responsible for the resolution of the scheduling problem. The solution obtained is returned to the decision maker.
2. The decision maker would like to intervene in the resolution of the scheduling problem. In other words he chooses an *interactive* method. In this case, the first module of the algorithm will discuss with him to determine and at each iteration the new search direction, and next the second module will solve the scheduling problem and return the calculated solution. If he wishes to pursue the search, a new search direction is pointed out and the process is repeated.
3. Finally, if the decision maker prefers to choose the solution within a set of Pareto optima, he positions himself in the *a posteriori* area. The first module will cause the parameters of the objective function to vary in order that the second should be able to calculate the whole set of Pareto optima. This set is returned to the decision maker.

Figure 4.2 represents the three methods of searching for a solution, with the two phases which constitute them.

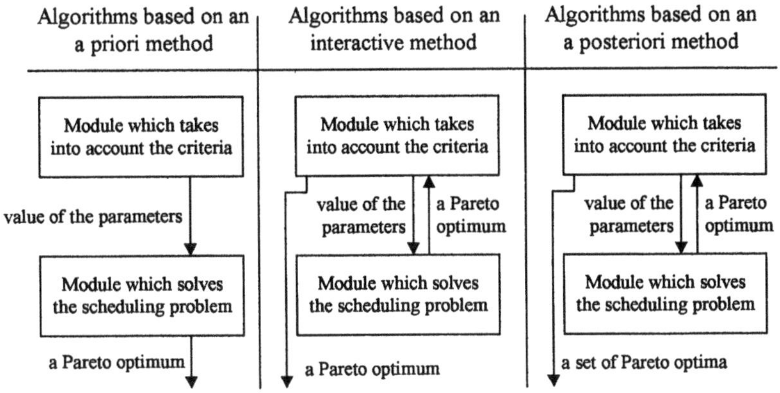

Fig. 4.2. Breakdown of the resolution methods for multicriteria problems

4.4 Application of the process - an example

Let us suppose that when modelling the problem, the decision maker brings up a three-stage hybrid flowshop problem, each stage having identical machines (see for instance "Processing of cheques", section 4.1.2). The jobs have different release dates and different due dates. The first objective to be identified is the criterion $\overline{U}^w$ and the second is the criterion T_{max}. The multicriteria scheduling problem addressed can be denoted by $HF3, (PM^{(\ell)})_{\ell=1}^3|r_i, d_i|\overline{U}^w$, T_{max}. Next, we can find several possible situations.

First situation:
The decision maker wishes to see all the strict Pareto optima of the problem, in order to choose the one which best suits him. The analyst is therefore directed to an a posteriori method.
For this he can solve, for example, the problem:

$$HF3, (PM^{(\ell)})_{\ell=1}^3|r_i, d_i|\epsilon(\overline{U}^w/T_{max})$$

with a large value for ϵ at the start, then smaller and smaller values. This leads finally to the enumeration of all the weak Pareto optima.
The analyst can also solve the problem:

$$HF3, (PM^{(\ell)})_{\ell=1}^3|r_i, d_i|F_\ell(\overline{U}^w, T_{max})$$

By making the weights of the linear combination vary, he can enumerate all the supported strict Pareto optima. Next, he can look for the non supported optima using another method.
He can also propose an enumeration method of type branch-and-bound or of type dynamic programming. He then solves the problem:

$$HF3, (PM^{(\ell)})_{\ell=1}^3|r_i, d_i|\#(\overline{U}^w, T_{max})$$

Second situation:
The analyst has convinced the decision maker that the enuneration of all the strict Pareto optima would be long and of little interest, because of the huge number of solutions.
The decision maker would like therefore that the cost of the proposed solution is the closest possible to a cost $(\overline{U}^{w0}, T^0_{max})$ that he manages to fix empirically. The analyst goes therefore for an a priori method and the problem to solve is the problem:

$$HF3, (PM^{(\ell)})_{\ell=1}^3 | r_i, d_i | F_T(\overline{U}^w, T_{max})$$

or else of the type $F_{Tp}(\ldots)$ or $F_{Tpa}(\ldots)$ if the intended solution is not reachable. Otherwise, he may solve the problem:

$$HF3, (PM^{(\ell)})_{\ell=1}^3 | r_i, d_i | F_s(\overline{U}^w, T_{max})$$

Third situation:
The decision maker not knowing how to tackle his problem, wishes to be helped to identify the Pareto optimum which best suits him. The analyst therefore sets up an interactive algorithm.
At the start he solves, for example, the problem:

$$HF3, (PM^{(\ell)})_{\ell=1}^3 | r_i, d_i | F_\ell(\overline{U}^w, T_{max})$$

then he modifies the weights using the new search direction given by the decision maker at each iteration. Remember that by this method, only the supported Pareto optima are able to be proposed.
The analyst can equally solve the problem:

$$HF3, (PM^{(\ell)})_{\ell=1}^3 | r_i, d_i | P(\overline{U}^w, T_{max})$$

by making vary the bounds fixed for the criteria, depending on the orientations of the decision maker.

4.5 Some complexity results for multicriteria scheduling problems

In this section we go back to the complexity theory but applied to multicriteria scheduling problems. We consider these problems in the light of the complexity classes presented in chapter 2 and the reductions provided in chapter 3. We first consider the complexity of multicriteria scheduling problems in terms of $\mathcal{NP}$-hardness before turning our attention to the complexity of the counting and enumeration of Pareto optima.

We have seen that a multicriteria problem is $\mathcal{NP}$-hard if the calculation of a weak Pareto optimum is an $\mathcal{NP}$-hard problem. Moreover, for a problem with K criteria, it is sufficient that the optimisation of a single criterion is $\mathcal{NP}$-hard for the multicriteria problem to be so. [Chen and Bulfin, 1993] are equally interested in such results since they set the rules which enable us to deduce the complexity of bicriteria scheduling problems beginning with the corresponding single criterion problems. The multicriteria problems under consideration by this study are the problems:

- where a lexicographical order among the criteria is defined,
- where the criteria are aggregated by a linear combination,
- where all the Pareto optima are generated.

In section 3.9 we have demontrated several reductions among the general problems. It is possible to consider new reductions in the framework of certain classic criteria in scheduling.

Lemma 18
For all $Z_1 \in \{C_{max}, L_{max}, \overline{C}, \overline{C}^v, \overline{U}, \overline{U}^v, \overline{T}, \overline{T}^v\}$ *there exist a polynomial Turing reduction such that:*

1. $\alpha|\beta|Lex(Z_1, \overline{C}) \propto_T \alpha|\beta|Lex(Z_1, \overline{C}^w)$,
2. $\alpha|\beta|Lex(Z_1, \overline{T}) \propto_T \alpha|\beta|Lex(Z_1, \overline{T}^w)$,
3. $\alpha|\beta|Lex(Z_1, \overline{U}) \propto_T \alpha|\beta|Lex(Z_1, \overline{U}^w)$.

Proof.
It is possible to solve an $\alpha|\beta|Lex(Z_1, \overline{C})$ problem by using an algorithm for the corresponding $\alpha|\beta|Lex(Z_1, \overline{C}^w)$ problem, by setting $v_i = 1$, $\forall i = 1, ..., n$. The solution returned is optimal for criterion Z_1 and minimises criterion $\overline{C}$. We can use similar reasoning to prove the two other reductions.□

Other more interesting reductions can be considered among certain criteria.

Lemma 19
For all $Z_1 \in \{C_{max}, \overline{C}, \overline{C}^w\}$ *there exist a polynomial Turing reduction such that:*

1. $\alpha|\beta|Lex(Z_1, \overline{C}) \propto_T \alpha|\beta|Lex(Z_1, \overline{T})$,
2. $\alpha|\beta|Lex(Z_1, \overline{C}^w) \propto_T \alpha|\beta|Lex(Z_1, \overline{T}^w)$,
3. $\alpha|\beta|Lex(Z_1, C_{max}) \propto_T \alpha|\beta|Lex(Z_1, L_{max})$.

Proof.
It is possible to solve an $\alpha|\beta|Lex(Z_1, \overline{C})$ problem by using an algorithm for the corresponding $\alpha|\beta|Lex(Z_1, \overline{T})$ problem, by setting $d_i = 0$, $\forall i = 1, ..., n$ because criterion Z_1 does not take the due dates into account. Similar reasoning is useable to prove the two other reductions.□

Lemma 20
For all $Z_1 \in \{C_{max}, \overline{C}, \overline{C}^w\}$ *there exist a polynomial Turing reduction such that:*

1. $\alpha|\beta|Lex(Z_1, L_{max}) \propto_T \alpha|\beta|Lex(Z_1, \overline{T})$,
2. $\alpha|\beta|Lex(Z_1, L_{max}) \propto_T \alpha|\beta|Lex(Z_1, \overline{U})$.

Proof.
The two reduction proofs being similar we can show the first uniquely.
If we only consider the criteria L_{max} and $\overline{T}$ we can show (see for example [Brucker, 2004]) the existence of a polynomial Turing reduction of the criterion L_{max} towards the criterion $\overline{T}$. This reduction rests on the fact a schedule s exists such that $L_{max}(s) \leq k$ if and only if an optimal schedule s' exists for the criterion $\overline{T}$ (by considering $d'_i = d_i + k$) in which no job is late. We use this result to show the existence of a reduction of the $\alpha|\beta|Lex(Z_1, L_{max})$ problem towards the $\alpha|\beta|Lex(Z_1, \overline{T})$ problem.
We consider the resolution algorithm of a $\alpha|\beta|Lex(Z_1, L_{max})$ problem as follows:

Algorithm A:
$k = \max_{j=1,\ldots,n}(d_j);$
$d'_i = d_i - k, \ \forall i = 1, \ldots, n;$
Call $S[d'_1; \ldots; d'_n; s^0];$
While $(\overline{T}(s^0) > 0)$ Do
 $k = \min_{T_i(s^0)>0}(T_i(s^0));$
 $d'_i = d_i - k, \ \forall i = 1, \ldots, n;$
 Call $S[d'_1; \ldots; d'_n; s^0];$
End While;

The procedure S solves the $\alpha|\beta|Lex(Z_1, \overline{T})$ problem and returns the calculated solution s^0. This solution satisfies the optimality constraint for the criterion Z_1, since it is not based on the due dates. Therefore, it is also a solution which satisfies the constraints of the $\alpha|\beta|Lex(Z_1, L_{max})$ problem.
The number of iterations produced by the algorithm A is a unique function of the number of jobs given that: (i) the value k is at each iteration a lower bound on the minimal value of the criterion L_{max}, (ii) at each iteration the number of late jobs decreases, (iii) the maximal number of late jobs is equal to n. If the procedure S is polynomial, then the algorithm A is also.□

The results of lemma 18, 19 and 20 are summarised in the reduction trees presented in figures 4.3 and 4.4.

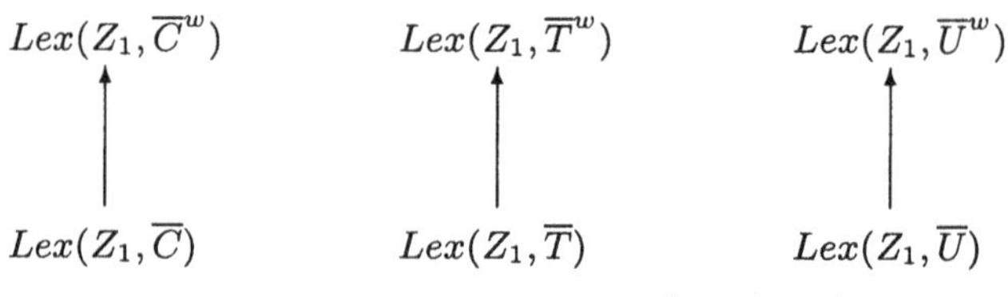

$\forall Z_1 \in \{C_{max}, L_{max}, T_{max}, \overline{C}, \overline{T}, \overline{U}, \overline{C}^{w'}, \overline{U}^{w'}, \overline{T}^{w'}\}$

Fig. 4.3. Reductions for a lexicographical minimization (1)

The complexity of bicriteria scheduling problems on a single machine has been considered by [Hoogeveen, 1992a], [Chen and Bulfin, 1993] and next

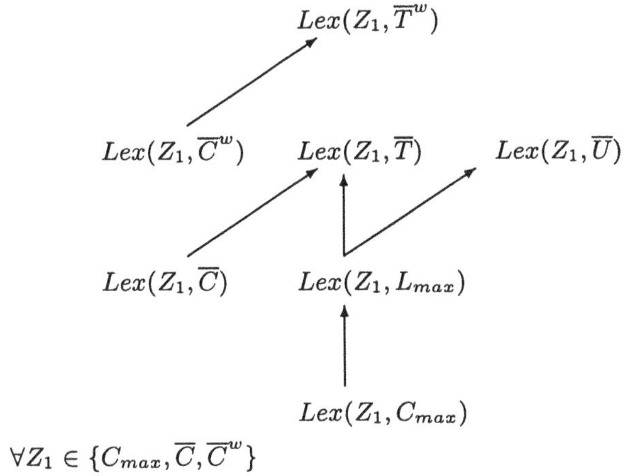

Fig. 4.4. Reductions for a lexicographical minimization (2)

[Lee and Vairaktarakis, 1996] who draw up state-of-the-art surveys. The complexity of bicriteria problems on multiple machines is addressed by [Chen and Bulfin, 1994]. The polynomial reductions presented in section 3.9 show that knowledge of the complexity of lexicographical multicriteria problems is as important as that of single criterion problems, when we want to study the complexity of a multicriteria problem. By way of illustration, we give in tables 4.1, 4.2 and 4.3 some complexity results for bicriteria scheduling problems on a single machine of the type Lex, F_ℓ, and ϵ-contraint.

Table 4.1. Complexity of scheduling problems of type $1||Lex(Z_1, Z_2)$

		Z_2								
		L_{max}	T_{max}	g_{max}	$\overline{C}$	$\overline{C}^w$	$\overline{T}$	$\overline{T}^w$	$\overline{U}$	$\overline{U}^w$
Z_1	L_{max}	—	—	*	*	**+	O	O	O	**
	T_{max}	—	—	*	*	**	**	**	O	**
	f_{max}	*	*	*	*	**+	**	**+	**−	**
	$\overline{C}$	*	*	*	—	—	*	*	*	*
	$\overline{C}^w$	*	*	*	—	—	**	**	*	**
	$\overline{T}$	**	**	**	**	**	—	—	**	**
	$\overline{T}^w$	**+	**+	**+	**+	**+	—	—	**+	**+
	$\overline{U}$	O	O	**	**	**+	**	**+	—	—
	$\overline{U}^w$	**	**	**	**	**+	**	**+	—	—

*: $\mathcal{P}$ / **: $\mathcal{NP}$-hard / **−: weakly $\mathcal{NP}$-hard / **+: strongly $\mathcal{NP}$-hard / O: open

A glance at the literature shows that when solving multicriteria scheduling problems we are often interested in enumerating or counting the number of

Table 4.2. Complexity of scheduling problems of type $1||\epsilon(Z_1/Z_2)$

		Z_2							
		L_{max}	T_{max}	$\bar{C}$	$\bar{C}^w$	$\bar{T}$	$\bar{T}^w$	$\bar{U}$	$\bar{U}^w$
Z_1	L_{max}	—	—	*	O	**	**+	O	**
	T_{max}	—	—	*	O	**	**+	O	**
	$\bar{C}$	*	*	—	—	**	**+	**	**+
	$\bar{C}^w$	**+	O	—	—	**	**+	**	**+
	$\bar{T}$	**	**	**	**	—	—	**	**
	$\bar{T}^w$	**+	**+	**+	**+	—	—	**+	**+
	$\bar{U}$	O	O	O	O	**	**+	—	—
	$\bar{U}^w$	**	**	**	**	**	**+	—	—

*: $\mathcal{P}$ / **: $\mathcal{NP}$-hard / ** −: weakly $\mathcal{NP}$-hard
/ ** +: strongly $\mathcal{NP}$-hard / O: open

Table 4.3. Complexity of scheduling problems of type $1||F_\ell(Z_1, Z_2)$

		Z_2							
		L_{max}	T_{max}	$\bar{C}$	$\bar{C}^w$	$\bar{T}$	$\bar{T}^w$	$\bar{U}$	$\bar{U}^w$
Z_1	L_{max}	—	—	*	**+	**	**+	O	**
	T_{max}	—	—	*	**	**	**+	O	**
	$\bar{C}$	—	—	—	—	**	**+	**	**
	$\bar{C}^w$	—	—	—	—	**	**+	**+	**
	$\bar{T}$	—	—	—	—	—	—	**	**
	$\bar{T}^w$	—	—	—	—	—	—	**+	**+

*: $\mathcal{P}$ / **: $\mathcal{NP}$-hard / ** −: weakly $\mathcal{NP}$-hard
/ ** +: strongly $\mathcal{NP}$-hard / O: open

strict Pareto optima. Thus, it becomes necessary to consider the complexity classes provided in section 2.2.3 to evaluate the complexity of solving multicriteria scheduling problems ([T'kindt et al., 2005]). We first provide general results and next give tables which summarize the complexity of multicriteria scheduling problems tackled in the literature. But first of all, we define the problems under consideration, which is a key point for the remainder of this section.

Basically, we can either solve a multicriteria scheduling problem in criteria space or in solution space. The first solution approach, namely the *descriptive approach*, consists in counting or enumerating the set of non dominated criteria vectors whilst the second one, namely the *constructive approach*, consists in counting or enumerating the Pareto optima. Intuitively, we guess that the second version of a multicriteria scheduling problem is harder than the first one since more "solutions" are involved. Often in the literature we are interested in solving the descriptive version of a multicriteria scheduling problem by enumerating one strict Pareto optimum per non dominated criteria vector. Let us first introduce instrumental definitions.

The optimisation problem O associated to a multicriteria scheduling problem consists in calculating a single strict Pareto optimal schedule with respect to the criteria (and it is any strict Pareto optimal schedule). The counting problem C associated to the above problem O consists in counting the number of strict Pareto optimal schedules. At last, the enumeration problem E associated to problem O consists in enumerating all the strict Pareto optima. All these problems are constructive problems. Whenever necessary we will consider their descriptive version, using the same notation if this raises no ambiguity.

Let us first consider a simple bicriteria problem, referred to as $F2|d_i = d, \textit{unknown } d|\bar{U}, d$. Calculating a single strict Pareto optimal schedule can be done in polynomial time, or equivalently problem O belongs to class $\mathcal{P}$. This is a direct consequence of the fact that the strict Pareto optimal schedule associated to the non dominated criteria vector with $\bar{U} = 0$ can be calculated in polynomial time since in this case problem O is equivalent to solving the $F2||C_{max}$ problem, which is polynomial ([Johnson, 1954]), and setting $d = C^*_{max}$. Besides, it is clear that the descriptive counting version of this bicriteria problem belongs to class $\mathcal{FP}$ since the number of non dominated criteria vectors is exactly equal to $(n+1)$. The complexity of the constructive enumeration of this set is stated in the following lemma.

Lemma 21 *The constructive enumeration problem associated to the* $F2|d_i = d, \textit{unknown } d|\bar{U}, d$ *problem is* $\mathcal{ENP}$*-complete.*

Proof.
Jozefowska et al. ([Jozefowska et al., 1994]) exhibited a polynomial reduction from the PARTITION problem towards the $F2|d_i = d, \textit{unknown } d, d = D, \bar{U} = \epsilon|-$ problem with particular values of D and ϵ and such that the $(n-\epsilon)$th job completes at time D on machine 2. Let us refer to this particular problem as $F2_p$. The proposed reduction is parsimonious and as the counting version of PARTITION is $\#P$-complete ([Garey and Johnson, 1979]) we deduce that counting the number of feasible solutions to the $F2_p$ problem is $\#P$-complete. According to property 3 (see section 2.2.3) we deduce that the enumeration of those feasible solutions is $\mathcal{ENP}$-complete.
It is remarkable that the set of solutions of $F2_p$ is a subset of the set of strict Pareto optima for criteria d and $\bar{U}$ which leads to the result that the enumeration of all the strict Pareto optima is also $\mathcal{ENP}$-complete.□

Starting from this example problem several remarks can be derived. First, the descriptive counting problem is in $\mathcal{FP}$ due to the property that the number of distinct values for criteria $\bar{U}$ is equal to $(n+1)$ and that to each of these values there exists a non dominated criteria vector. Even if this property is quite strong, a weaker one can be stated for classic scheduling criteria.

Property 6 *For any discrete bicriteria scheduling problem involving two criteria among C_{max}, T_{max}, L_{max}, $\bar{C}$, $\bar{C}^w$, $\bar{T}$ and $\bar{T}^w$, the number of non dominated criteria vectors is upper bounded by $f(Length, Max)$, where f is a polynomial function of Length and Max.*

Proof.
We separate the proof into two parts.
1) Assume that among the two criteria at least one is the C_{max}, T_{max} or L_{max} criterion. Remind that $C_{max} = \max_{1 \leq i \leq n}(C_i)$, $L_{max} = \max_{1 \leq i \leq n}(C_i - d_i)$ and $T_{max} = \max_{1 \leq i \leq n}(\max(0; C_i - d_i))$. An upper bound on the worst value of such a criterion for a strict Pareto optimum is given by $\sum_{i=1}^{n}\sum_{j=1}^{m} p_{i,j}$, which is the sum of the processing times of the n jobs on the m machines. Conversely, a lower bound on the best value for a strict Pareto optimum is given by $-\sum_{i=1}^{n}\sum_{j=1}^{m} p_{i,j}$. Henceforth for a given criterion the range of values that it can take is comprised in $[-\sum_{i=1}^{n}\sum_{j=1}^{m} p_{i,j}; \sum_{i=1}^{n}\sum_{j=1}^{m} p_{i,j}]$ and as these three criteria can only take discrete values inside this interval, it follows that the number of non dominated criteria vectors is upper bounded by $2 \times \sum_{i=1}^{n}\sum_{j=1}^{m} p_{i,j} = f(Length, Max)$.
2) Now assume that the two criteria are sum criteria, *i.e.* $\bar{C}$, $\bar{C}^w$, $\bar{T}$ and $\bar{T}^w$. Remind that $\bar{C} = \sum_{i=1}^{n} C_i$, $\bar{C}^w = \sum_{i=1}^{n} w_i C_i$, $\bar{T} = \sum_{i=1}^{n} \max(0; C_i - d_i)$ and $\bar{T}^w = \sum_{i=1}^{n} w_i \max(0; C_i - d_i)$. Based on the same reasonning than in the first part of the proof we can derive that for a given criterion the range of values it can take is comprised in $[0; n \times \sum_{k=1}^{n} w_k \sum_{i=1}^{n}\sum_{j=1}^{m} p_{i,j}]$, with $w_k = \frac{1}{n}$ in case of criteria $\bar{C}$ and $\bar{T}$. As all these four criteria can only take discrete values inside this interval, it follows that the number of non dominated criteria vectors is upper bounded by $n * \sum_{k=1}^{n} w_k \sum_{i=1}^{n}\sum_{j=1}^{m} p_{i,j} = f(Length, Max)$.□

A similar straigthforward property can be established in the particular case of the number of tardy jobs criterion.

Property 7 *For any discrete bicriteria scheduling problem involving criterion $\bar{U}$, the number of non dominated criteria vectors is upper bounded by $(n+1) = f(Length)$, where f is a polynomial function of Length. In case of the weighted number of tardy jobs criterion, denoted by $\bar{U}^w$, the number of non dominated criteria vectors is upper bounded by $(n+1)\max_{1 \leq i \leq n} w_i = g(Length, Max)$ where g is a polynomial function of Length and Max.*

Proof.
Similar to that of property 6.□

Let us consider again the example problem, for which the calculation of a single strict Pareto optimum is achieved by solving an ϵ-constrained problem, namely the $F2|d_i = d$, *unknown* $d|\epsilon(d/\bar{U})$, which consists in imposing the desired value of criterion $\bar{U}$ and calculating the minimal value of the common due date d. As this problem is $\mathcal{NPO}$-complete, the constructive enumeration

problem cannot be solved in polynomial time. But it is clear that, for a bicriteria scheduling problem, if the calculation of each non dominated criteria vector can be done in polynomial time, for instance by solving an ϵ-constrained problem, and if the number of such vectors is upper bounded by $f(n)$ with f a polynomial function, then counting the number of non dominated criteria vectors is in class $\mathcal{FP}$ and the associated descriptive enumeration problem is in $\mathcal{P}$. Moreover, if the number of non dominated criteria vectors cannot be shown to be upper bounded by $f(n)$ then we can conclude that the descriptive enumeration problem belongs to class $\mathcal{EP}$. Caution must be taken when showing that the calculation of each strict Pareto optimum can be achieved in polynomial time: some well-known approaches do not enable us to calculate all these optima. For instance, minimising a convex combination of multiple criteria on a non convex problem leads only to the calculation of the subset of *supported* strict Pareto optima. Henceforth, even if this problem can be polynomially solved we cannot conclude that the descriptive enumeration of all strict Pareto optima is in class $\mathcal{EP}$.
It is remarkable that in the literature on multicriteria scheduling involving enumeration problems, always the descriptive enumeration problem is considered. And it is usually solved by calculating to each non dominated criteria vector a strict Pareto optimum. It means that we solve a problem potentially harder than the descriptive enumeration problem since we not only output a set of criteria vectors but a set of criteria vectors and a set of schedules. To complete this section we provide in Tables 4.4 and 4.5 synthesizes of complexity results for some descriptive multicriteria scheduling problems tackled in the literature. In both tables the first column contains the problem notation and the three following columns contain the complexity of the problem of calculating a single Pareto optimum, the counting problem and the enumeration problem respectively. In column O the method used to calculate a single Pareto optimum is indicated in parenthesis. *Lex* refers to the lexicographic method, ϵ to the ϵ-constrained method, F_ℓ to the convex combination method, GP to the goal programming method, F_T to the Tchebycheff method and # to a basic enumerative method. The fifth column presents some additional information about the cardinality of the set of strictly non dominated criteria vectors and the sixth column gives references dealing with the problem.

Table 4.4. The complexity of some easy optimisation, counting and enumeration multicriteria scheduling problems

Problem	O	C	E	Remarks	References
$1 \mid s_i, d_i, 0 \leq d_i - s_i \leq p_i, nmit \mid L_{max}, P_{max}$	$\mathcal{P}_{(\epsilon)}$	$\mathcal{FP}$	$\mathcal{P}$	$\lvert Z_E \rvert \leq n$	[Hoogeveen, 1996]
$1 \mid p_i = 1, d_i, nmit \mid \overline{E}, \overline{U}$	$\mathcal{P}_{(\epsilon)}$	$\mathcal{FP}$	$\mathcal{P}$	$\lvert Z_E \rvert \leq n+1$	[Kondakci et al., 1997]
$1 \mid p_i = 1, d_i, nmit \mid E_{max}, \overline{U}$	$\mathcal{P}_{(\epsilon)}$	$\mathcal{FP}$	$\mathcal{P}$	$\lvert Z_E \rvert \leq n+1$	[Kondakci et al., 1997]
$1 \mid p_i = 1, d_i, nmit \mid \overline{E}, \overline{T}, \overline{U}$	$\mathcal{P}_{(\epsilon \text{ o } F_\ell)}$	$\mathcal{FP}$	$\mathcal{P}$	$\lvert Z_E \rvert \leq n+1$	[Kondakci et al., 1997]
$1 \mid \mid f^1_{max}, f^2_{max}, \ldots, f^K_{max}$	$\mathcal{P}_{(\epsilon)}$	$\mathcal{FP}$	$\mathcal{P}$	$\lvert Z_E \rvert \leq \left(\frac{n(n-1)}{2}+1\right)^{K-1}$	[Hoogeveen, 1992b]
$1 \mid \mid \overline{C}, f_{max}$	$\mathcal{P}_{(\epsilon)}$	$\mathcal{FP}$	$\mathcal{P}$	$\lvert Z_E \rvert \leq \frac{n(n-1)}{2}+1$	[John, 1984], [Hoogeveen and VandeVelde, 1995]
$1 \mid p_i = 1, d_i \mid overlineC^w, T_{max}$	$\mathcal{P}_{(\epsilon)}$	$\mathcal{FP}$	$\mathcal{P}$	$\lvert Z_E \rvert \leq n+1$	[Chen and Bulfin, 1990]
$1 \mid p_i = 1, d_i \mid \overline{U}, T_{max}$	$\mathcal{P}_{(\epsilon)}$	$\mathcal{FP}$	$\mathcal{P}$	$\lvert Z_E \rvert \leq n+1$	[Chen and Bulfin, 1990]
$1 \mid p_i = 1, d_i \mid \overline{U}^w, T_{max}$	$\mathcal{P}_{(\epsilon)}$	$\mathcal{FP}$	$\mathcal{P}$	$\lvert Z_E \rvert \leq n+1$	[Chen and Bulfin, 1990]
$1 \mid p_i = 1, d_i \mid \overline{T}^w, T_{max}$	$\mathcal{P}_{(\epsilon)}$	$\mathcal{FP}$	$\mathcal{P}$	$\lvert Z_E \rvert \leq n+1$	[Chen and Bulfin, 1990]
$P2 \mid pmtn, d_i \mid L_{max}, C_{max}$	$\mathcal{P}_{(\epsilon)}$	$\mathcal{FP}$	$\mathcal{P}$	At most 2 extreme points on the Pareto curve	[Mohri et al., 1999]
$P3 \mid pmtn, d_i \mid L_{max}, C_{max}$	$\mathcal{P}_{(\epsilon)}$	$\mathcal{FP}$	$\mathcal{P}$	At most 3 extreme points on the Pareto curve	[Mohri et al., 1999]
$Q \mid p_i = p \mid f_{max}, g_{max}$	$\mathcal{P}_{(\epsilon)}$	$\mathcal{FP}$	$\mathcal{P}$	$\lvert Z_E \rvert \leq O(n^2)$	[Tuzikov et al., 1998]
$Q \mid p_i = p \mid \overline{g}, f_{max}$	$\mathcal{P}_{(\epsilon)}$	$\mathcal{FP}$	$\mathcal{P}$	$\lvert Z_E \rvert \leq O(n^2)$	[Tuzikov et al., 1998]
$Q \mid pmtn \mid \overline{C}, C_{max}$	$\mathcal{P}_{(\epsilon)}$	$\mathcal{FP}$	$\mathcal{P}$	At most $O(m \times n)$ extreme points on the Pareto curve	[Mc Cormick and Pinedo, 1995]

Table 4.5. The complexity of some hard optimisation, counting and enumeration multicriteria scheduling problems

Problem	O	C	E	Remarks	References
$1 \mid d_i \mid \overline{E}, \overline{T}$	$\mathcal{NPOC}_{(F_\ell)}$	#P	$\mathcal{ENP}\backslash\mathcal{P}$		[Szwarc, 1993], [Kim and Yano, 1994],[Fry et al., 1996]
$1 \mid d_i, nmit \mid \overline{E}, \overline{T}$	$\mathcal{NPOC}_{(F_\ell)}$	#P	$\mathcal{ENP}\backslash\mathcal{P}$		[Fry and Leong, 1986], [Azizoglu et al., 1991]
$1 \mid d_i = d, nmit \mid \overline{E}, \overline{T}$	$\mathcal{NPOC}_{(F_\ell)}$	#P	$\mathcal{ENP}\backslash\mathcal{P}$		[Sundararaghavan and Ahmed, 1984]
$1 \mid s_i, d_i \mid \overline{P}, \overline{T}$	$\mathcal{NPOC}_{(F_\ell)}$	#P	$\mathcal{ENP}\backslash\mathcal{P}$		[Koulamas, 1996]
$1 \mid d_i, nmit \mid \overline{E}^w, \overline{U}$	$\mathcal{NPOC}_{(\epsilon)}$	#P	$\mathcal{ENP}\backslash\mathcal{EP}$	$\lvert Z_E \rvert \leq n+1$	[Chand and Schneeberger, 1988]
$1 \mid d_i \mid \overline{E}^\alpha, \overline{T}^\beta$	$\mathcal{NPOC}_{(F_\ell)}$	#P	$\mathcal{ENP}\backslash\mathcal{P}$		[Fry et al., 1987a], [Fry and Blackstone, 1988], [James and Buchanan, 1997], [James and Buchanan, 1998]
$1 \mid r_i, d_i \mid \overline{E}^\alpha, \overline{T}^\beta$	$\mathcal{NPOC}_{(F_\ell)}$	#P	$\mathcal{ENP}\backslash\mathcal{P}$		[Yano and Kim, 1991], [Mazzini and Armentano, 2001]
$1 \mid d_i, nmit \mid \overline{E}^\alpha, \overline{T}^\beta$	$\mathcal{NPOC}_{(F_\ell)}$	#P	$\mathcal{ENP}\backslash\mathcal{P}$		[Ow and Morton, 1988], [Ow and Morton, 1989], [Li, 1997], [Almeida and Centeno, 1998], [Liaw, 1999]
$1 \mid d_i = d \geq \sum p_i, nmit \mid \overline{E}^\alpha, \overline{T}^\beta$	$\mathcal{NPOC}_{(F_\ell)}$	#P	$\mathcal{ENP}\backslash\mathcal{P}$		[VandenAkker et al., 1998a]
$1 \mid d_i = d \geq \sum p_i, S_{sd}, nmit, classes \mid \overline{E}^\alpha, \overline{T}^\beta$	$\mathcal{NPOC}_{(F_\ell)}$	#P	$\mathcal{ENP}\backslash\mathcal{P}$		[Azizoglu and Webster, 1997]
$1 \mid d_i = d\ unknown, S_{sd}, nmit \mid \overline{E}^\alpha, \overline{T}^\beta$	$\mathcal{NPOC}_{(F_\ell)}$	#P	$\mathcal{ENP}\backslash\mathcal{P}$		[Webster et al., 1998]
$1 \mid d_i, nmit \mid \overline{E}, \overline{T}, \overline{C}$	$\mathcal{NPOC}_{(F_\ell)}$	#P	$\mathcal{ENP}\backslash\mathcal{P}$		[Dileepan and Sen, 1991]
$1 \mid d_i \mid \overline{E}, \overline{T}, \overline{C}$	$\mathcal{NPOC}_{(F_\ell)}$	#P	$\mathcal{ENP}\backslash\mathcal{P}$		[Fry et al., 1987b]
$1 \mid d_i, nmit \mid E_{max}, \overline{C}$	$\mathcal{NPOC}_{(Lex)}$	#P	$\mathcal{ENP}\backslash\mathcal{P}$		[Azizoglu et al., 1997]
$1 \mid d_i \mid \overline{U}, \overline{C}$	$\mathcal{NPOC}_{(Lex)}$	#P	$\mathcal{ENP}\backslash\mathcal{EP}$	$\lvert Z_E \rvert \leq n+1$	[Emmons, 1975b]
$1 \mid d_i \mid \overline{T}, \overline{C}$	$\mathcal{NPOC}_{(Lex)}$	#P	$\mathcal{ENP}\backslash\mathcal{P}$		[Lin, 1983]
$1 \mid d_i \mid \overline{C}, \overline{U}, T_{max}$	$\mathcal{NPOC}_{(\epsilon)}$	#P	$\mathcal{ENP}\backslash\mathcal{P}$		[Nelson et al., 1986]
$1 \mid d_i \mid L_{max}, \overline{C}^w$	$\mathcal{NPOC}_{(Lex)}$	#P	$\mathcal{ENP}\backslash\mathcal{P}$		[Chand and Schneeberger, 1984], [Hoogeveen, 1992a],[Smith, 1956], [Bansal, 1980], [Chand and Schneeberger, 1986], [Heck and Roberts, 1972], [Burns, 1976], [Miyazaki, 1981]
$1 \mid d_i \mid \overline{C}^w, \overline{T}^w$	$\mathcal{NPOC}_{(F_\ell)}$	#P	$\mathcal{ENP}\backslash\mathcal{P}$		[VanWassenhove and Gelders, 1978]
$P2 \mid d_i \mid T_{max}, \overline{U}$	$\mathcal{NPOC}_{(Lex)}$	#P	$\mathcal{ENP}\backslash\mathcal{EP}$	$\lvert Z_E \rvert \leq n+1$	[Sarin and Hariharan, 2000]
$P \mid d_i \mid \overline{C}, \overline{U}$	$\mathcal{NPOC}_{(\#)}$	#P	$\mathcal{ENP}\backslash\mathcal{EP}$	$\lvert Z_E \rvert \leq n+1$	[Ruiz-Torres et al., 1997]
$F2 \mid prmu \mid C_{max}, \overline{C}$	$\mathcal{NPOC}_{(Lex)}$	#P	$\mathcal{ENP}\backslash\mathcal{P}$		[Rajendran, 1992], [Neppalli et al., 1996], [Gupta et al., 2001], [Gupta et al., 2002], [Gupta et al., 1999b], [T'kindt et al., 2003], [Nagar et al., 1995b], [Serifoglu and Ulusoy, 1998], [Yeh, 1999]
$F2 \mid r_i, prmu \mid C_{max}, \overline{C}$	$\mathcal{NPOC}_{(F_\ell)}$	#P	$\mathcal{ENP}\backslash\mathcal{P}$		[Chou and Lee, 1999]
$F2 \mid prmu, d_i \mid T_{max}, C_{max}$	$\mathcal{NPOC}_{(Lex)}$	#P	$\mathcal{ENP}\backslash\mathcal{P}$		[Daniels and Chambers, 1990]
$F2 \mid prmu, d_i \mid C_{max}, \overline{U}$	$\mathcal{NPOC}_{(\#)}$	#P	$\mathcal{ENP}\backslash\mathcal{EP}$	$\lvert Z_E \rvert \leq n+1$	[Liao et al., 1997]
$F2 \mid prmu, d_i \mid C_{max}, \overline{T}$	$\mathcal{NPOC}_{(\#)}$	#P	$\mathcal{ENP}\backslash\mathcal{P}$		[Liao et al., 1997]
$F \mid prmu, d_i, nmit \mid \overline{E}^w, \overline{T}^w$	$\mathcal{NPOC}_{(F_\ell)}$	#P	$\mathcal{ENP}\backslash\mathcal{P}$		[Zegordi et al., 1995]
$J \mid d_i \mid C_{max}, \overline{C}, \overline{I}, T_{max}, \overline{U}$	$\mathcal{NPOC}_{(F_T)}$	#P	–		[Huckert et al., 1980]
$J \mid d_i \mid C_{max}, \overline{C}, \overline{E} + \overline{T}$	$\mathcal{NPOC}_{(GP)}$	#P	$\mathcal{ENP}\backslash\mathcal{P}$		[Deckro et al., 1982]
$O2 \mid \mid C_{max}, \overline{C}$	$\mathcal{NPOC}_{(Lex)}$	#P	$\mathcal{ENP}\backslash\mathcal{P}$		[Gupta and Werner, 1999], [Kyparisis and Koulamas, 2000]

Table 4.4 presents results for problems in which computing a single strictly non dominated criteria vector can be achieved in polynomial time. All the problems presented are polynomial in their optimisation, counting and enumeration versions. Notice that for $P\{2,3\}|pmtn, d_i|\ L_{max}, C_{max}$ and $Q|pmtn|\bar{C}, C_{max}$ problems, the set of strictly non dominated criteria vectors is continuous and piecewise linear, thus either reduced to the empty set, to a single element set or to an infinite set. Accordingly the considered optimisation, counting and enumeration problems are related to the calculation of the strictly non dominated criteria vectors that are extreme points of the tradeoff curve.

Table 4.5 presents results for problems in which calculating a single strict Pareto optimum is a $\mathcal{NPO}$-complete problem (referred to as $\mathcal{NPOC}$ in the first column). Concerning the counting problems we were not able to establish either their completeness or to prove that they are polynomially solvable. Besides, notice that even though the enumeration problems cannot be solved in polynomial time, we do not state that they are $\mathcal{ENP}$-complete since no formal proofs are provided. For some of the problems mentioned, the calculation of a single strict Pareto optimum is achieved by minimising a convex combination of criteria (referred to as F_ℓ in the first column). As previously noted in this section, this approach does not allow calculating all strict Pareto optima since some are not minima of the convex combination whatever the weights. However, it is clear that if minimising a convex combination of criteria is not a polynomial problem, then there is no opportunity for the enumeration problem to be solvable in polynomial time.

5. Just-in-Time scheduling problems

5.1 Presentation of Just-in-Time (JiT) scheduling problems

One of the classical objectives in shop scheduling is linked to the respect of the due dates which attend, for example, the meetings with customers on the delivery dates of the manufactured products. For numerous problems, the criterion used in this case is a measure of the tardiness of the finished products, as for example the *average tardiness*, the *maximum tardiness* or yet *the number of late jobs*. Nevertheless, even though for example, storage of products means a non negligible cost, it is necessary to optimise, at least, just as well a criterion linked to the earliness of jobs.
Historically, interest in JiT for manufacturing appeared after the second world war in the Toyota company factories (described in [Pinedo and Chao, 1999]). In the context of vehicles production, a certain number of components are produced by subcontractors. The JiT scheduling problem appears for the latter since the subcontracted parts must be delivered at the moment of the vehicle assembly. A late delivery leads to the halt of the assembly line because it is necessary to withdraw the vehicle concerned in order to be able to reposition it at the head of the line. This means a penalty for the customer. Conversely, manufacture of the subcontracted parts in advance means a storage charge for the subcontractor which may not be negligible. This is notably the case, nowadays, for car seats for which storage costs are very high. More generally, we note that a JiT scheduling problem appears when the due dates have to be respected and when parts do not have a negligible storage cost.

Contrary to mass production, where a stock of finished products is built up, JiT production consists of regulating manufacture. In terms of stocks, the objective is to plan the regular arrival of the materials which are necessary for the manufacture of the products. We wish to reduce not only the intermediate stocks but equally the stock of finished products. In this situation, we want to calculate a plan such that all these products are manufactured just at the moment when they have to be used. In scheduling terms the objective is therefore to calculate a schedule such that the finished products (or jobs) should be available "Just-in-Time". We must therefore optimise, at least, a measure of the tardiness of the jobs as well as a measure of their earliness. For the latter we distinguish two categories of criteria: those which measure the earliness of a job in relation to a desired start time and those which measure this earliness in relation to a due date. In the first case, we only consider that processing a job earlier than necessary will disrupt the supply chain of raw materials, which leads to disruption of stock levels and which therefore must be penalised. For the second category of criteria we only consider that stocks of finished product generate a cost which we want to reduce. When the difference between the due date and the desired start time for each job is equal to the total processing time of the job, we can then show that these two categories of criteria are equivalent.

Literature on JiT scheduling problems addresses essentially single machine and parallel machines problems. The objective of this chapter is to present a set of significant works in the domain.
We first present a typology of such problems as dealt with in the literature, and next provide a general model of Just-in-Time shop scheduling problems. We conclude this chapter by providing a literature review of major works.

5.2 Typology of JiT scheduling problems

The literature contains numerous works on JiT scheduling problems and several states-of-the-art surveys have been published (see among others [Baker and Scudder, 1990], [Hall and Posner, 1991], [Gordon et al., 2002a], [Gordon et al., 2002b] and more recently [Kaminsky and Hochbaum, 2004] and [Gordon et al., 2004]). The JiT scheduling problems can be separated according to the definition of *their due dates* and the *optimised criteria.*

5.2.1 Definition of the due dates

The *due dates* often result from a choice made by the decision maker and constitute a data for the analyst. In this case, we consider that *these dates are fixed.* Conversely, problems occur for which the due date of a job or an order result in negotiations between the decision maker and his customer. In this case, the decision maker must set up an algorithm which returns a schedule and a due date taking account of other jobs already scheduled. We consider then that *the due date is unknown.* If the date which is calculated is far from that desired by the customer, then a reduction of the order price may be suggested, and therefore a compromise solution is looked for. On the other hand, the more the due dates are spaced the greater is the probability that the order will be delivered on time. Thus, for the decision maker, the problem is to find a trade-off between the cost created by a potential delay and a non negligible storage cost. Besides, we encounter problems for which

each job has its own due date. We speak of a problem with *arbitrary due dates.* Conversely, we speak of a problem with *common due date.* We distinguish between two cases. A common due date is said to be non restrictive if increasing it does not enable us to compute a schedule with a lower value of the objective function. Otherwise, the common due date is said to be restrictive. For single machine problems if $d \geq \sum_{i=1}^{n} p_i$ then the due date d is clearly non restrictive.
We notice that the problems with an unknown common due date are equivalent to the problems with a fixed and non restrictive common due date. In other words, the optimal solutions of these two problems are the same schedule and same objective value, the sole difference being the value of the common due date.

Determination of due dates is a crucial point in JiT production. In fact, fixing too many close dates can lead to disturbance of product stocks since few jobs can be completed at their due date. Conversely, fixing the dates too far apart can lead to a reduction in production of the factory. Determination of these due dates is generally done by the decision maker, alone or during the course of negotiations with his customers, before solving the scheduling problem. The analyst must then just calculate a schedule of jobs so that they are completed JiT. For the definition of due dates, we encounter different models ([Ragatz and Mabert, 1984]). Amongst the most classic, can be found the model CON (*CONstant flow allowance model*) in which we consider that all the jobs have a common due date. When all the due dates are different, we encounter in the literature the model SLK (*SLacK*) which considers that all the jobs J_i are such that $d_i = r_i + p_i + q$ where p_i represents the sum of the processing times of the operations of job J_i and q a common tail. This case can occur when the due dates are fixed by the decision maker who then proceeds to use the value of criterion $\overline{C}$ as an estimation of the value q. In the model TWK (*Total WorK content*) the due dates are defined by $d_i = r_i + kp_i$, $\forall i = 1, ..., n$, where k is a positive integer. In the model NOP (*Number of OPerations*) these dates are defined by $d_i = r_i + kn_i$, $\forall i = 1, ..., n$, where k is a positive integer and n_i the number of operations of job J_i. Finally, the model PPW (*Processing-Plus-Wait*) combines models SLK and TWK since $d_i = r_i + kp_i + q$, $\forall i = 1, ..., n$, where k is a positive integer and q a common tail which can be negative. Very often, the dates d_i are considered as unknown because k and q are variables to be determined.

5.2.2 Definition of the JiT criteria

Solving a JiT scheduling problem necessitates at least the optimisation of a criterion related to the tardiness of jobs and a criterion related to their earliness. As we have previously commented, two categories of problems are encountered. In the first, the earliness of jobs is defined *by relation to the due dates*. We consider then that the earliness of job J_i is defined by $E_i = \max(0; d_i - C_i)$. The maximum earliness is denoted by E_{max}. In the second type of problem, the earliness of jobs is defined by relation to a desired start time s_i. We speak then of the promptness of job J_i, which is defined by $P_i = \max(0; s_i - t_i)$. The maximum promptness is denoted by P_{max}. Basically, these problems are encountered when the start time of a job can induce costly disturbances of stocks of raw materials. For problems for which $d_i = s_i + p_i$, $\forall i = 1, ..., n$, we have $P_i = E_i$.

For the majority of problems which are considered in the literature, *only criteria linked to earliness and tardiness* of jobs are optimised. Very often, the objective function does not constitute a regular criterion, and thus we are led to consider schedules with insertion of voluntary idle times before the operations. This means that we can delay the processing of jobs so that they complete on time, to the detriment of the storage costs of semi-finished products. Thus, for certain problems we also consider the *minimisation of a criterion reflecting these storage costs*. It mainly concerns the criterion $\overline{C}$ minimisation of which leads to minimising the inventory costs.

The diversity of problems leads to a large number of objective functions. Furthermore, a precise definition of a Just-in-Time schedule does not exist. These two reasons have favoured the appearance of numerous models with different objective functions. Table 5.1 presents a summary of the principal objective functions considered in the literature. The first column of the table shows the objective function and the second states whether this function corresponds to a regular criterion. If this is not the case, it means that it is necessary to consider the class of schedules with idle time insertion when solving the problem in order to compute an optimal solution. Nevertheless, in certain works the constraint *"no-machine idle time"* (nmit) is imposed in spite of the fact that the objective function is not regular. Justification of this hypothesis is connected with prohibitive costs occuring when a machine becomes inactive.

Certain equivalences exist between different objective functions. For example, we have $\overline{E} + \overline{T} = \sum |L_i|$ because $E_i + T_i = |L_i|$. Similarly, we have $L_i^2 = E_i^2 + T_i^2$ which enables us to deduce that the objective functions $\alpha \sum L_i^2$ and $\alpha \sum (E_i^2 + T_i^2)$ are the same. For some problems, each job J_i has a unit earliness penalty, denoted by α_i, and a unit tardiness penalty, denoted by β_i. These penalties are the weights in the objective function. We distinguish the following cases:

1. The weights are asymetrical, *i.e.* $\exists i, i = 1, ..., n, \alpha_i \neq \beta_i$.
2. The weights are symetrical, *i.e.* $\forall i = 1, ..., n, \alpha_i = \beta_i$.

3. The weights do not depend on the jobs, *i.e.* $\forall i = 1, ..., n, \alpha_i = \alpha$ and $\beta_i = \beta$.
4. The weights depend on the jobs, *i.e.* $\exists i, j, i \neq j, i, j = 1, ..., n, \alpha_i \neq \alpha_j$ or $\beta_i \neq \beta_j$.

Table 5.1. Summary of the principal types of JiT objective functions

Objective function	Regular criterion
$\overline{E} + \overline{T}$	No
$\alpha\overline{E} + \beta\overline{T}$	No
$\overline{E}^{\alpha} + \overline{T}^{\beta}$	No
$(\overline{E} + \overline{T})^2$	No
$\sum_{i=1}^{n} \sum_{j=i+1}^{n} \lvert C_i - C_j \rvert$	No
$\sum_{i=1}^{n} \sum_{j=i+1}^{n} (C_i - C_j)^2$	No
$\sum_{i=1}^{n} (C_i - \overline{C})^2$	No
$\alpha \sum_{i=1}^{n} E_i^2 + \beta \sum_{i=1}^{n} T_i^2$	No
$\sum_{i=1}^{n} \alpha_i E_i^2 + \sum_{i=1}^{n} \beta_i T_i^2$	No
$\max_{i=1,\ldots,n} (\alpha_i \lvert L_i \rvert)$	No
$\max(g(E_{max}), h(T_{max}))$ with g and h two increasing functions	No
$\max_{i=1,\ldots,n} (g(E_i), h(T_i))$ with g and h two convex functions	No
$\alpha\overline{E} + \beta\overline{T} + \gamma d$	No
$\alpha\overline{E} + \beta\overline{T} + \gamma\overline{C}$	No
$\alpha\overline{E} + \beta\overline{T} + \gamma \max(0, d_i - A)$ with A a due date	No
$\overline{U}^{\alpha} + \overline{E}^{\beta}$	No
$\overline{U}^{\alpha} + \gamma d$	Yes
$\overline{U}^{\alpha} + \gamma \max(0, d_i - A)$ with A a due date	Yes

5.3 A new approach for JiT scheduling

JiT scheduling problems occur in the context of JiT production. This evident fact implies that the roots of JiT scheduling have to be searched in the abundant literature on JiT production which has been the subject of a lot of studies and is now well defined. Among others, [Nollet et al., 1994] describe a JiT production system as a system which "processes and delivers finish goods *just-in-time* to be sold, components *just-in-time* to be assembled into finished goods and materials bought *just-in-time* to be converted into components". In a JiT production system quality and productivity have to be improved at all stages of the industrial system. This implies reducing wastings and taking account of human factors ([Nollet et al., 1994]). Under the term "wasting", Nollet et al. gather a series of elements:

1. Wasting due to overproduction which induces useless storage costs, increased human requirements, *etc.* This can be reduced by producing just what is needed and by satisfying the lead times.
2. Wasting due to waitings caused by machine breakdowns for instance.
3. Wasting due to useless transportation and material handling, for instance, when two resources are too far from each other.
4. Wasting due to a failing or badly prepared production process.
5. Wasting due to the storage of in-process or finished goods. This is a crucial point of a JiT policy.
6. Wasting due to production flaws, which can be limited by increasing the efficiency of the production process (this is related to the concept of total quality in JiT philosophy).

Another way to define briefly the JiT philosophy, complementary to that of Nollet et al., is given by [Baglin et al., 2001]: each product must ideally be processed on a "chain of machines". This means that when a job enters the shop it has to be processed ideally by the machines without waiting time, as if they were available for it alone. This is the *smoothing* of the job flow. Clearly, each machine must also have a smooth flow of jobs to process in order to be made cost-effective.

All the above elements are production based, but in this book we only focus on the scheduling component of the production system. Henceforth, only a subset of these elements concerns scheduling. Firstly, the notion of "chain of machines" can be easily translated into the "no-wait" constraint of classic scheduling theory. However, in the case of "sufficiently closed" due dates, imposing the no-wait constraint may result in increasing the tardiness of products, *i.e.* customer dissatisfaction. Consequently, we may be allowed to violate this constraint and thus have increased in-process storage costs in order to limit the tardiness in producing orders. This means strictly processing products on a "chain of machines" is a concept that may conflict with that of limiting wastes due to the storage of in-process products. Limiting wasting caused by the storage of materials is, as quoted by Nollet et al., a key point in JiT production system. Storage is related to three distinct elements of production: the raw materials, the in-process and subcontracted components, and the finished products. The aim is, henceforth, to improve the quality and productivity at each level where we encounter these elements in order to reduce the induced storage costs and answering as much as possible the lead times ([Schonberger, 1982]).

Firstly, consider the case of raw materials. The need in raw materials is often evaluated at a mid-term planning level, *i.e.* far away from the scheduling phase. Starting from the routings and the decomposition of a product, the required raw materials and components are often ordered independently of the scheduling phase. Hence, during the Material Requirements Planning phase in a MRP system, we decide of which materials will be made available in the shop, in which quantity and at which time. As in this phase we do not have an accurate view of what will be the real operations schedule, materials are usually made available in the shop before the start of such a schedule (or sufficiently early before an operation, requiring materials, starts). Thus, the calculation of a schedule in a JiT environment can be achieved without having to accurately take account of the need in raw materials.
The situation for in-process and subcontracted components is different, notably for work in-process components because they induce storage constraints and costs which are directly related to the operations schedule. This is also the case for finished products. It follows that, when calculating a JiT schedule, the limitation of work in-process and finished products storage must be taken into account. As a consequence lead times are reduced and the products tend to be produced on a "chain of machines".

In the remainder of this section we develop a mathematical formulation of the costs to be minimised when calculating a JiT schedule and show how this formulation includes the different costs functions optimised in the literature on JiT scheduling (see section 5.2).

5.3.1 Modelling of production costs in JiT scheduling for shop problems

Consider a job J_i that has be processed on a set of m machines, following a sequence $\pi_i = (\pi_i(1); \pi_i(2); ...; \pi_i(m))$ with $\pi_i(k)$ the number of the k-th machine which processes J_i. Whenever sequences π_i, $\forall i = 1, ..., n$, are fixed we face a jobshop or flowshop problem whilst if determining these sequences is a part of the problem, then we face an openshop problem.
We assume that J_i can be decomposed into, at most, q_i equal-size sublots. This assumption enables us to be more general than in classic scheduling where jobs are often *indivisible*, *i.e.* $q_i = 1$, $\forall i = 1, ..., n$. Besides, in the case of *divisible* jobs, *i.e.* $q_i > 1$, $\forall i = 1, ..., n$, the lead times can be reduced by enabling lot-streaming. This consists in tranferring any sublot of an operation to the next machine without waiting for the completion of the whole operation (see figure 5.1). All sublots of the same job must be sequentially processed on any given machine, and between two of these sublots voluntary

idle times can be inserted if this helps in reducing the costs. For simplicity purpose we assume that all operations are decomposed into δ equal-size sublots, where δ has to be calculated in order to minimise the costs. We also make use of the following additional notations:

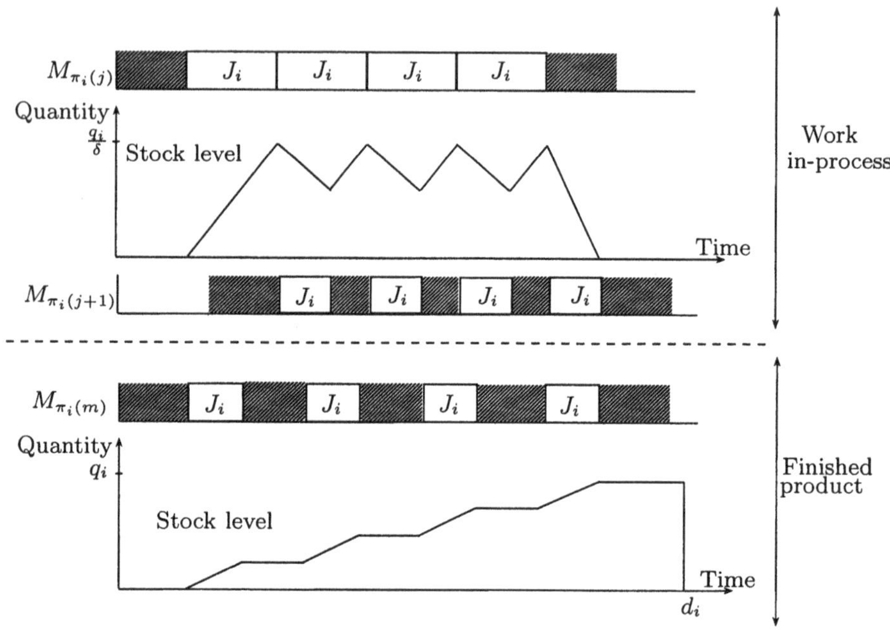

Fig. 5.1. Evolution of stock levels for a given job J_i with 4 equal-size sublots

Data:

$\gamma_i^{\pi_i(j)}$: unit storage cost of work in-processes between machines $M_{\pi_i(j)}$ and $M_{\pi_i(j+1)}$,

κ_i : unit storage cost of finish products,

λ_i : the cost, per sublot, for the decomposition of job J_i into sublots,

β_i : unit cost for completing job J_i tardy (penalty costs),

Variables:

$f_{i,j}^p(t)$: number of elements of job J_i produced by $M_{\pi_i(j)}$ from time 0 to t in the work in-process storage area which follows $M_{\pi_i(j)}$,

$f^c_{i,j}(t)$: number of elements of job J_i consumed by $M_{\pi_i(j)}$ from time 0 to t in the work in-process storage area which precedes $M_{\pi_i(j)}$,
$t_{i,j,k}$: starting time of the k-th sublot of job J_i on machine $M_{\pi_i(j)}$.

The total cost induced by a job J_i comprises the cost for the storage of work in-processes, the storage of finished products, the cost for the decomposition into sublots and the cost for delivering J_i tardy.

Lemma 22
The total cost of job J_i when produced Just-in-Time is defined by:

$$\begin{aligned} Z_i = \;& \beta_i T_i + \delta\lambda_i - \kappa_i q_i T + \kappa_i q_i t_{i,\pi_i(m),\delta} + \kappa_i q_i \frac{p_{i,\pi_i(m)}}{\delta} + \kappa_i q_i E_i \\ & + \sum_{j=1}^{m} (\gamma_i^{\pi_i(j)} - \gamma_i^{\pi_i(j-1)}) \sum_{t=0}^{T} f^p_{i,\pi_i(j)}(t) \end{aligned}$$

with T a high value, $\gamma_i^{\pi_i(0)} = 0$ and $\gamma_i^{\pi_i(m)} = \kappa_i$.

Proof.
The cost Z_i is defined as the sum of three costs: the cost for delivering job J_i tardy, defined by $\beta_i T_i$, the cost for decomposing job J_i into sublots, defined by $\delta\lambda_i$, and the cost for storing J_i. For the latter, we refer to figure 5.1 to have an illustration of the evolution of stock levels, even though on this figure these evolutions are assumed to be continuous. We now focus on the calculation of the storage costs. We have

$$\begin{aligned} Z_i = \;& \beta_i T_i + \delta\lambda_i + \kappa_i \sum_{t=0}^{T} \left(f^p_{i,\pi_i(m)}(t) - f^c_{i,\pi_i(m+1)}(t)\right) \\ & + \sum_{j=1}^{m-1} \gamma_i^{\pi_i(j)} \left(\sum_{t=0}^{T} \left(f^p_{i,\pi_i(j)}(t) - f^c_{i,\pi_i(j+1)}(t)\right)\right) \end{aligned}$$

with $f^c_{i,\pi_i(m+1)}(t)$ the number of finished products of J_i consumed from time 0 to t. Here we assume that the stock of finished products is emptied instantaneously on the last machine either at the due date d_i, or at the completion time of J_i if J_i is tardy. As $\sum_{t=0}^{T} f^c_{i,\pi_i(j)}(t) = \sum_{t=0}^{T} f^p_{i,\pi_i(j)}(t)$, by rearranging the sums in the previous formulae and setting $\gamma_i^{\pi_i(0)} = 0$ and $\gamma_i^{\pi_i(m)} = \kappa_i$, we have

$$\begin{aligned} Z_i = \;& \beta_i T_i + \delta\lambda_i - \kappa_i \sum_{t=0}^{T} f^c_{i,\pi_i(m+1)}(t) \\ & + \sum_{j=1}^{m} (\gamma_i^{\pi_i(j)} - \gamma_i^{\pi_i(j-1)}) \sum_{t=0}^{T} f^p_{i,\pi_i(j)}(t). \end{aligned}$$

By replacing $\sum_{t=0}^{T} f^c_{i,\pi_i(m+1)}(t)$ by its formulation, *i.e.* $q_i(T - t_{i,\pi_i(m),\delta} - \frac{p_{i,\pi_i(m)}}{\delta} - E_i)$ we obtain the formulation given in the lemma.□

It is interesting to notice that the cost function Z_i is independent from the consumption of elements in the storage areas. In the following lemma we define accurately the functions $f^p_{i,\pi_i(j)}$.

Lemma 23
We have $\sum_{t=0}^{T} f^p_{i,\pi_i(j)}(t) = -\frac{q_i p_{i,\pi_i(j)}}{2\delta} - \frac{q_i}{\delta} \sum_{k=1}^{\delta} t_{i,\pi_i(j),k} + q_i T$.

Proof.
Calculating the mathematical expression of the term $\sum_{t=0}^{T} f^p_{i,\pi_i(j)}(t)$ is equivalent

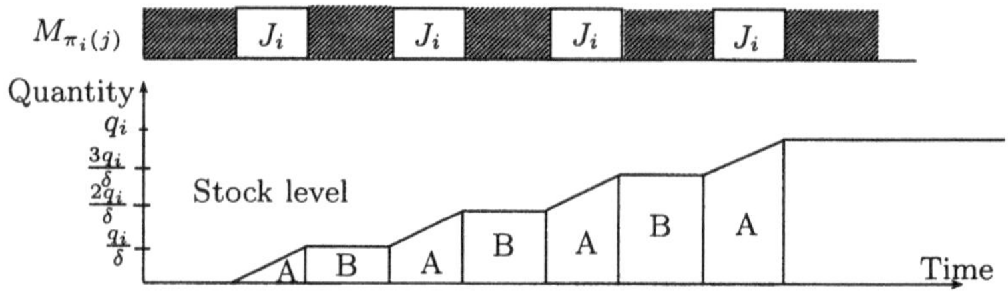

Fig. 5.2. The production function $f^p_{i,\pi_i(j)}$ of a given job J_i with 4 equal-size sublots

to calculate the area below the stock level curve if we only consider the stock supplying and not the consumption of elements by machine $M_{\pi_i(j+1)}$ (see figure 5.2 for an example). This area can be decomposed into two kinds of areas: areas A and areas B. The sum of areas A is exactly equal to $\frac{q_i p_{i,\pi_i(j)}}{2}$. The sum of areas B is dependent on the starting times of each sublots and we have

$$\begin{aligned}
\sum_{t=0}^{T} f^p_{i,\pi_i(j)}(t) &= \frac{q_i p_{i,\pi_i(j)}}{2} \\
&\quad + \frac{q_i}{\delta}\left(t_{i,\pi_i(j),2} - t_{i,\pi_i(j),1} - \frac{p_{i,\pi_i(j)}}{\delta}\right) \\
&\quad + \frac{2q_i}{\delta}\left(t_{i,\pi_i(j),3} - t_{i,\pi_i(j),2} - \frac{p_{i,\pi_i(j)}}{\delta}\right) \\
&\quad + \ldots \\
&\quad + \frac{(\delta-1)q_i}{\delta}\left(t_{i,\pi_i(j),\delta} - t_{i,\pi_i(j),\delta-1} - \frac{p_{i,\pi_i(j)}}{\delta}\right) \\
&\quad + q_i(T - t_{i,\pi_i(j),\delta} - \frac{p_{i,\pi_i(j)}}{\delta}) \\
&= \frac{q_i p_{i,\pi_i(j)}}{2} \\
&\quad - \frac{q_i p_{i,\pi_i(j)}}{\delta^2}(1 + 2 + \ldots + \delta) \\
&\quad - \frac{q_i}{\delta}\sum_{k=1}^{\delta} t_{i,\pi_i(j),k} \\
&\quad + q_i T \\
&= \frac{q_i p_{i,\pi_i(j)}}{2} - \frac{q_i p_{i,\pi_i(j)}}{\delta^2} \times \frac{(\delta+1)\delta}{2} \\
&\quad - \frac{q_i}{\delta}\sum_{k=1}^{\delta} t_{i,\pi_i(j),k} + q_i T \\
&= -\frac{q_i p_{i,\pi_i(j)}}{2\delta} - \frac{q_i}{\delta}\sum_{k=1}^{\delta} t_{i,\pi_i(j),k} + q_i T.
\end{aligned}$$

□

By putting Lemma 23 into Lemma 22 we can to state the total scheduling cost of job J_i.

Corollary 4
The total scheduling cost of job J_i when produced Just-in-Time is defined by

$$\begin{aligned}
Z_i = \ & \beta_i T_i + \delta\lambda_i + \kappa_i q_i E_i + \kappa_i q_i \frac{p_{i,\pi_i(m)}}{\delta} + \kappa_i q_i t_{i,\pi_i(m),\delta} \\
& - \frac{q_i}{\delta}\sum_{j=1}^{m}(\gamma_i^{\pi_i(j)} - \gamma_i^{\pi_i(j-1)})\sum_{k=1}^{\delta} t_{i,\pi_i(j),k} \\
& - \frac{q_i}{2\delta}\sum_{j=1}^{m}(\gamma_i^{\pi_i(j)} - \gamma_i^{\pi_i(j-1)})p_{i,\pi_i(j)}.
\end{aligned}$$

In the next section we study the particularization, of the production cost given in the above corollary, to several shop configurations. We also show the links with existing objective functions in classic Just-in-Time scheduling literature.

5.3.2 Links with objective functions of classic JiT scheduling

In the previous section the scheduling cost of a job J_i in a workshop has been stated. Table 5.2 provides particularizations of this cost to given shop environments. Whenever necessary simplifications of notation have been made in this table. The first column contains the shop environment and the indication of lot-streaming. The second column contains the mathematical formulation of the cost Z_i stated in Corollary 4 and the third column contains a function which minimisation is equivalent to the minimisation of Z_i. Notice that the configurations without lot-streaming are equivalent to lot-streaming with $q_i = \delta = 1$. It is remarkable that once the lot-streaming is possible the mathematical formulation of the scheduling cost Z_i of job J_i is not a linear function, since the term δ is a variable to calculate. Besides, the formulations for the single machine environment can be straightly adapted to some parallel machines environments.

Table 5.2. Particularizations of the scheduling cost of a job J_i

Shop environment	Mathematical formulation	Optimisation equivalence
2-machine flowshop (lot-streaming)	$\beta_i T_i + \lambda_i \delta + \kappa_i q_i E_i$ $+\frac{\gamma_i q_i}{\delta}\left(\sum_{k=1}^{\delta} t_{i,2,k} - \sum_{k=1}^{\delta} t_{i,1,k}\right)$ $-\frac{\kappa_i q_i}{\delta}\sum_{k=1}^{\delta} t_{i,2,k} + \frac{\kappa_i q_i p_{i,2}}{2\delta}$ $+\frac{\gamma_i q_i}{2\delta}(p_{i,2} - p_{i,1}) + \kappa_i q_i t_{i,2,\delta}$	
2-machine flowshop (no lot-streaming)	$\beta_i T_i + \lambda_i + \kappa_i q_i E_i$ $+\gamma_i(C_{i,2} - C_{i,1}) + \frac{\kappa_i p_{i,2}}{2}$ $+\frac{\gamma_i}{2}(p_{i,1} - p_{i,2})$	$\beta_i T_i + \kappa_i q_i E_i + \gamma_i(C_{i,2} - C_{i,1})$
Single machine (lot-streaming)	$\beta_i T_i + \lambda_i \delta + \kappa_i q_i E_i$ $-\frac{\kappa_i q_i}{\delta}\sum_{k=1}^{\delta} t_{i,k} + \frac{\kappa_i q_i p_i}{2\delta}$ $+\kappa_i q_i t_{i,\delta}$	
Single machine (no lot-streaming)	$\beta_i T_i + \lambda_i + \kappa_i E_i + \frac{\kappa_i p_i}{2}$	$\beta_i T_i + \kappa_i E_i$

We are now ready to study the links between the modelling provided in section 5.3.1 and the objective function encountered in the literature on JiT scheduling (see table 5.1, page 139).
The objective functions $\bar{\mathbf{E}} + \bar{\mathbf{T}}$, $\alpha\bar{\mathbf{E}} + \beta\bar{\mathbf{T}}$ and $\bar{\mathbf{E}}^{\alpha} + \bar{\mathbf{T}}^{\beta}$ of table 5.1 are obtained by linear combination of the Z_i's in the case of single machine environments without lot-streaming. The two first functions are particular cases

of the last one. For shop problems, or even the single machine problem with lot-streaming, these three functions do not completely fit with the objective of scheduling the jobs Just-in-Time. For instance, the objective function obtained by linear combination of the Z_i's in the case of the 2-machine flowshop problem without lot-streaming is $\bar{E}^\alpha + \bar{T}^\beta + \bar{C}^\gamma - \sum_{i=1}^n \gamma_i C_{i,1}$. As indicated in table 5.1 the objective function $\mathbf{\bar{E}^\alpha + \bar{T}^\beta + \bar{C}^\gamma}$, or special cases, is sometimes minimised in a single machine environment without lot-streaming. The main argument, found in the literature, for minimising the weighted sum of completion times criteria is that it reduces the average presence time in the shop of a job, which in turns tends to reduce the average storage time. This is partially true when the lot-streaming is enabled for the single machine problem and for the flowshop problem. Even when lot-streaming is disabled for the flowshop problem the sum of the Z_i's is not exactly equivalent to minimise the sum of weighted earliness, tardiness and completion times. Similar comments hold for the objective functions $\alpha\mathbf{\bar{E}} + \beta\mathbf{\bar{T}} + \gamma\mathbf{d}$ and $\alpha\mathbf{\bar{E}} + \beta\mathbf{\bar{T}} + \gamma\max(\mathbf{0}, \mathbf{d_i} - \mathbf{A})$ of table 5.1 in the case of an unknown common due date d or in the case of unknown due dates d_i which have to be as close as possible to a desired common due date A.
Similarly, the objective functions $\alpha\sum_{\mathbf{i=1}}^{\mathbf{n}} \mathbf{E_i^2} + \beta\sum_{\mathbf{i=1}}^{\mathbf{n}} \mathbf{T_i^2}$ and $\sum_{\mathbf{i=1}}^{\mathbf{n}} \alpha_\mathbf{i}\mathbf{E_i^2} + \sum_{\mathbf{i=1}}^{\mathbf{n}} \beta_\mathbf{1}\mathbf{T_i^2}$ of table 5.1 are obtained by linear combination of the Z_i's power 2, only in the case of single machine environments without lot-streaming. But for other shop environment or when lot-streaming is allowed, minimising these two functions does not completely reflects the objective of JiT scheduling. Similar comments can be done for the $(\mathbf{\bar{E}} + \mathbf{\bar{T}})^\mathbf{2}$ objective function of table 5.1.
Another important class of objective functions of table 5.1 are those related to the difference between completion times. For instance the problem of minimising the Completion Time Variance (CTV) consists in minimising the objective function $\sum_{\mathbf{i=1}}^{\mathbf{n}}(\mathbf{C_i} - \mathbf{\bar{C}})^\mathbf{2}$ of table 5.1. [Merten and Muller, 1972] have introduced this problem in the context of computing systems with large data files for which often the response time to a user's request is strongly dependent on the time required to access or retrieve the file referenced by the user. But it is also recognized that the CTV problem has application to JiT scheduling since it leads to make the jobs staying approximately the same time in the shop. So, the production is smoothed (see for instance [Viswanathkumar and Srinivasan, 2003]). But this intuitive argument seems not to clearly link this objective function to JiT philosophy. Another, more convincing, argument lies to the fact that the CTV objective function can be seen as a special case of $\sum_{i=1}^n Z_i^2$ with an unknown common due date $d = \bar{C}$ in the case of a single machine problem without lot-streaming. But for the objective functions $\sum_{\mathbf{i=1}}^{\mathbf{n}}\sum_{\mathbf{j=i+1}}^{\mathbf{n}} |\mathbf{C_i} - \mathbf{C_j}|$ and $\sum_{\mathbf{i=1}}^{\mathbf{n}}\sum_{\mathbf{j=i+1}}^{\mathbf{n}}(\mathbf{C_i} - \mathbf{C_j})^\mathbf{2}$ of table 5.1 the links with JiT philosophy are less clear.
To conclude this analyse, we only point out that the objective function $\max_{\mathbf{i=1,\ldots,n}}(\beta_\mathbf{i}|\mathbf{L_i}|)$ of table 5.1 is exactly equal to $\max_{i=1,\ldots,n}(Z_i)$ for a sin-

gle machine problem without lot-streaming but with symetric weights, *i.e.* $\beta_i = \kappa_i, \forall i = 1, ..., n$. Again, for other shop configurations this objective function does not fully apply the JiT philosophy.
The links between the remaining objective functions of table 5.1 and JiT philosophy are not straightforward.

5.4 Optimal timing problems

The objective functions minimised in JiT scheduling are interesting because they have a direct practical meaning, but also they are often non *regular functions* (see chapter 1 for a formal definition of a regular function). Consequently, the set of *active schedules*, or even *semi-active schedules*, is not dominant. This implies that sometimes it is interesting, from the viewpoint of the objective function, to insert voluntary idle times before the starting of a job on a machine. Along the years, several authors have thus focused on the *optimal timing problem*, *i.e.* on the problem of determining the optimal start time of each job, when the sequences of jobs on the machines are known. Often, when the sequencing problem on each machine is solved, the optimal timing problem can be solved in polynomial time. We review in this section some of the major optimal timing problems. These problems are referred in the three-field notation of scheduling problems by adding the constraint *seq* in field β.

5.4.1 The $1|d_i, seq|F_\ell(\bar{T}^\alpha, \bar{E}^\beta)$ problem

The works of [Garey et al., 1988] concern several JiT problems. The authors show that the $1|d_i|F_\ell(\overline{T}, \overline{E})$ problem with $F_\ell(\overline{T}, \overline{E}) = \overline{T} + \overline{E} = \sum_{i=1}^{n} |C_i - d_i|$ is $\mathcal{NP}$-hard. They are then interested in solving this problem when the sequence of jobs is imposed, denoted by $1|d_i, seq|F_\ell(\overline{T}, \overline{E})$, and proposing an optimal algorithm with an average complexity in $O(n \log(n))$.
The jobs are placed iteratively in order of the imposed sequence. We note σ_{i-1} the partial sequence obtained at the iteration $i-1$. Let J_i be the job to be inserted in the iteration i. If $C_{max}(\sigma_{i-1}) + p_i \leq d_i$ then the job J_i starts at the date $d_i - p_i$ and an idle time is inserted before J_i. Otherwise, if $C_{max}(\sigma_{i-1}) + p_i > d_i$ then the job J_i is processed just after the sequence σ_{i-1}. We then try to timeshift part of the sequence $\sigma_i = \sigma_{i-1}//\{J_i\}$. We define a block by a maximum set of consecutive jobs, and we denote by B_k the last block of σ_i (figure 5.3). If most of the jobs in B_k are late then it is interesting to shift B_k to the left until this is no longer the case or until B_k could no longer be timeshifted.

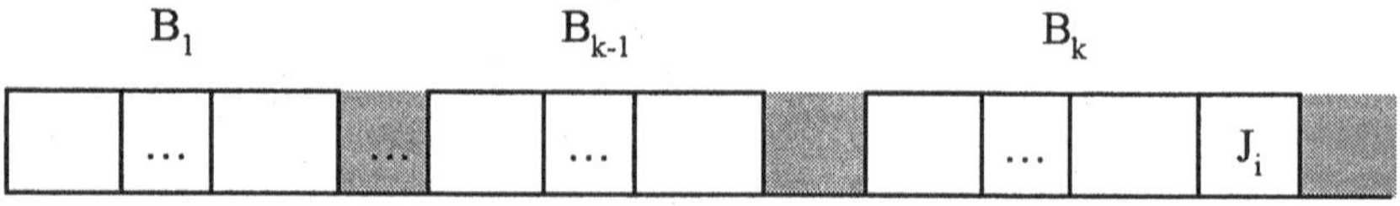

Fig. 5.3. Definition of a block

ALGORITHM EGTW1

/* σ: the schedule under construction */
/* We assume that the jobs sequence is $(J_1, J_2, J_3, \ldots, J_n)$ */
$\sigma = \emptyset$;
For $i = 1$ to n do
  If $(d_i - p_i > C_{max}(\sigma))$ Then
    Schedule the job J_i at time $t_i = d_i - p_i$;
    $\sigma = \sigma // \{J_i\}$;
  Else
    Schedule the job J_i at time $t_i = C_{max}(\sigma)$;
    $\sigma = \sigma // \{J_i\}$;
    Let B_k be the last block of σ;
    Let r be the number of jobs $J_i \in B_k \ / \ C_i - d_i > 0$;
    If $(r > (|B_k| - r))$ Then
      Let $\delta = \min_{J_i \in B_k / C_i > d_i} (C_i - d_i)$;
      Let ω bet the starting time of the first job of B_k;
      Let π be the completion time of the last job of B_{k-1} (0 if $k = 1$);
      $\forall j \in B_k$, $t_j = t_j - \min(\delta; \omega - \pi)$;
    End If;
  End If;
End For;

[Garey et al., 1988]

Fig. 5.4. An optimal algorithm to calculate start times of jobs

The principle of this algorithm, denoted by EGTW1, is presented in figure 5.4.

Example.
We consider a scheduling problem for which $n = 5$. The job sequence is that of the indices.

i	1	2	3	4	5
p_i	2	4	3	5	2
d_i	8	10	14	18	19

(i) $\sigma = \emptyset$, $d_1 - p_1 = 6 > 0$ and the job J_1 is scheduled at time $t_1 = 6$.
(ii) $\sigma = (J_1)$, $C_{max}(\sigma) = 8$, $d_2 - p_2 = 6 < 8$ and the job J_2 is scheduled at the date $t_2 = 8$. $r = 1 = |B_k| - r$ and we perform a timeshift with $\sigma = (J_1, J_2)$, $\delta = 2$, $\omega = 6$ and $\pi = 0$. We have $t_1 = 4$ and $t_2 = 6$.
(iii) $\sigma = (J_1, J_2)$, $C_{max}(\sigma) = 10$, $d_3 - p_3 = 11 > 10$ and the job J_3 is scheduled at time $t_3 = 11$.
(iv) $\sigma = (J_1, J_2, J_3)$, $C_{max}(\sigma) = 14$, $d_4 - p_4 = 13 < 14$ and the job J_4 is scheduled at time $t_4 = 14$. $r = 1 = |B_k| - r$ and we perform a timeshift with $\sigma = (J_1, J_2, J_3, J_4)$,

$\delta = 1$, $\omega = 11$ and $\pi = 10$. We have $t_3 = 10$ and $t_4 = 13$.
(v) $\sigma = (J_1, J_2, J_3, J_4)$, $C_{max}(\sigma) = 18$, $d_5 - p_5 = 17 < 19$ and the job J_5 is scheduled at time $t_5 = 18$. $r = 1 < |B_k| - r = 4$ and we do not perform a timeshift.

We obtain the schedule presented in figure 5.5, and $\sum_{i=1}^{n} |L_i| = 4$.

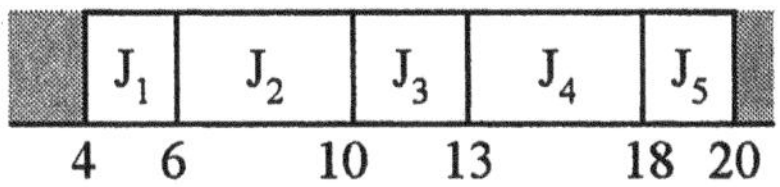

$$\sum_{i=1}^{n} |L_i| = 4$$

Fig. 5.5. The schedule calculated by the algorithm EGTW1

Next, Garey, Tarjan and Wilfong show that the $1|p_i = 1, d_i|\overline{T} + \overline{E}$ problem can be solved by this algorithm. Finally, they are interested in adding constraints to the $1|d_i|\overline{T} + \overline{E}$ problem like time windows for each job or *chain* precedence constraints. In these two configurations they propose generalisations of the algorithm EGTW1.

For the $1|d_i|F_\ell(\overline{E}^\alpha, \overline{T}^\beta)$ problem, the calculation of the start times of jobs when the sequence is fixed is addressed by [Szwarc and Mukhopadhyay, 1995]. This problem is polynomially solvable and the authors propose an algorithm based on a breakdown of the sequence into blocks. When $d_{i+1} - d_i \leq p_i$ then jobs J_i and J_{i+1} belong to the same block. Besides, it is only necessary to insert idle time between two blocks. The algorithm starts by building an active schedule, *i.e.* all the jobs are processed without idle time. Using the inequality mentioned above jobs are grouped into blocks. Then the blocks are timeshifted from the left to the right, starting with the first block. The proposed algorithm is in $O(cn)$ where c is the number of blocks and experimental results show that for problems up to 500 jobs the average calculation time is lower than 2 seconds. Besides, for this size of problem, this algorithm is almost 30 times faster than that proposed by [Davis and Kanet, 1993].

5.4.2 The $P\infty|prec, f_i\ convex|\sum_i f_i$ problem

This scheduling problem has been considered by [Chrétienne and Sourd, 2003] which naively does not looks like an optimal timing problem. However, as we will see, by particularizing suitably the cost functions and the precedence constraints we get an optimal timing problem for a class of Just-in-Time scheduling problems. Chrétienne and Sourd provide first theoretical insights

and a general algorithm which we briefly present here. First, notice that each job J_i is defined by a desired start time s_i, a processing time p_i and a cost function $f_i(t)$.
The general algorithm follows the same line than algorithm EGTW1. Jobs are sorted according to their rank in the graph of precedence constraints and scheduled in this order. Again, the notion of *block* is considered here and defined as a set of jobs in which for each job, either its start time coincides with the completion time of another job in this set, or its completion time coincides with the start time of another job in this set. When a new job is added in a partial schedule it is either scheduled at its desired start time if possible, or scheduled at the end of the block B with which it conflicts. Henceforth, block B is enlarged and next the question becomes to left timeshift or not the new block B. Let t_B be the start time of that block, *i.e.* the lowest start time of the jobs in B. First, if there does exist $t < t_B$ such that $\sum_{J_i \in B} f_i(t) < \sum_{J_i \in B} f_i(t_B)$ the block is not left timeshifted. Otherwise, let t_B^* be the ideal start time at which the contribution of block B is minimal. B is left timeshifted until either we met t_B^* or, as in the algorithm EGTW1, we met another block B'. In that case the new block B is defined by $B = B \cup B'$. Then we try to left timeshift the new block B if necessary to minimise the total cost. But there is also a third case that can occur when shifting a block: it can be split into several blocks. This occurs when a sub-block b of block B is on-time whilst the remaining block $B - b$ still needs to be left timeshifted in order to decrease its total cost. It is due to the fact that in the problem, jobs can be processed in parallel and clearly this event cannot occur in the problem tackled by Garey, Tarjan and Wilfong.
Notice that this algorithm is polynomial as far as we are capable of computing in polynomial time the ideal start times t_B^*. This is implied by the fact that the cost functions f_i are convex functions.

This general algorithm is particularized to various special cases as the scheduling problem with the cost functions f_i being linear earliness-tardiness costs. The problems with particular precedence constraints like tree and chains are also investigated. We focus on the problem with linear earliness-tardiness costs since the corresponding problem, referred to as $P\infty|s_i|F_\ell(\bar{E}^\alpha, \bar{T}^\beta)$, enables to solve a class of optimal timing problems depending on how the precedence constraints are set.
For this problem we assume that each job J_i is defined by a desired start time s_i, a processing time p_i, a unitary earliness cost α_i and a unitary tardiness cost β_i. The cost induced by job J_i in the schedule is defined by $f_i = \alpha_i \max(0, s_i - t_i) + \beta_i \max(0, t_i - s_i)$. As each job has only one operation, this cost is equivalent to $\alpha_i E_i + \beta_i T_i$. We first introduce theoretical notions useful for the algorithm.
To each block B, let G be the associated graph of precedence constraints with processing times on the arcs. We denote by $\Gamma(B)$ the *spanning active*

equality tree associated to B, *i.e.* the spanning tree on G in which all arcs are *active*, *i.e.* if we delete an arc the two created sub-blocks B^1 and B^2 are conflicting: one must be timeshifted in order to decrease its contribution to the objective function, by the way increasing the contribution of the other block. Notice that the spanning active equality tree of a block does not need to be computed at each iteration of the algorithm since it is only updated when merging two blocks: for two merged blocks B and B' the spanning tree of the new block $B = B \cup B'$ is equal to $\Gamma(B) \cup \Gamma(B')$. We now must describe how are calculated the ideal start times t_B^* for the particular earliness-tardiness cost functions. First notice that the cost functions f_i are piecewise linear functions, each one admitting a single breakpoint. Thus, we define to each block B a set of *singular points* t_j^B defined by $t_j^B = s_j + t_B - t_j$, $\forall J_j \in B$, and each singular point corresponds to a change in the slope of at least one job of block B. By the way in each spanning active equality tree $\Gamma(B)$ we maintain on the arcs slopes: for a given arc (i, j) the slope $\ell_{i,j}$ corresponds to the unit time contribution to the total cost of the jobs associated to nodes that follows node j in $\Gamma(B)$. We also denote by $\ell(B)$ the slope of block B which can be interpreted as the unit time contribution to the total cost of the jobs in B. For instance if B is made up of one early job J_i and one tardy job J_j, we have $\ell(B) = \alpha_i + \beta_j$. A consequence is that all the singular points of a block are the breakpoints of the cost function of the block, *i.e.* its contribution to the total cost. The ideal start time t_B of a block B is then the breakpoint which leads to the minimum cost and the left timeshift of the block is done from one breakpoint to the next one unless we meet the ideal start time of the block or we meet another block. In the latter case we merge the two blocks and left timeshift the new block if it is not at its ideal start time (its slope is negative). Another case may occur when meeting a breakpoint: the current block must be split into two sub-blocks since one sub-block is on-time (the slope of an arc in the graph $\Gamma(B)$ is negative). Among the two blocks, the one with the positive slope is next left timeshifted. The details of the algorithm, denoted by ECS1, are given in figures 5.6 and 5.7.
Chrétienne and Sourd show that it can be implemented in $O(n \max(n, M))$-time with M the number of precedence constraints. When the graph of the precedence constraints is a tree graph the complexity of the algorithm ECS1 becomes $O(n^2)$-time. The time complexity can again be reduced to $O(n \log(n))$ in case the precedence graph is of type chain.

The algorithm $ECS1$ is of a very high importance for solving optimal timing problems in Just-in-Time scheduling problems. It can be applied to a large number of problems as far as all jobs are made up of a single operation. Besides, the presence of release dates and deadlines can be easily taken into account by introducing appropriate dummy jobs in the graph of precedence constraints (see [Estève et al., 2004] for an application).

ALGORITHM ECS1 (1)

```
/* A: the set of precedence constraints */
/* S: the set of jobs ranked according to their rank in the graph of the
    precedence constraints */
b = 0; // b is the number of blocks
t_i = +∞, ∀i = 1, ..., n;
While S ≠ ∅ do
|  // We create a new block with only job J_S[1]
|  b = b + 1;
|  B_b = {J_S[1]};
|  If (∀(i, S[1]) ∈ A, s_S[1] ≥ t_i + p_i)) Then
|  |  // Job J_S[1] is on-time
|  |  Schedule the job J_S[1] at time t_S[1] = s_S[1];
|  |  ℓ_B_b = αS[1];
|  |  S = S − {S[1]};
|  Else
|  |  // Job J_S[1] is not on-time
|  |  ℓ_B_b = βS[1];
|  |  S = S − {S[1]};
|  |  While (∃B such that ℓ(B) < 0) Do
|  |  |  Let B be a block with ℓ(B) < 0; // B is not on-time
|  |  |  Left timeshift block B until one the following event occurs:
|  |  |  |  1) ∃J_i ∈ B, such that J_i starts at time s_i.
|  |  |  |     // We change the slopes in the current block
|  |  |  |     Set ℓ(B) = ℓ(B) − α_i − β_i;
|  |  |  |     Call update_tree(B, i, −α_i − β_i);
|  |  |  |  2) ∃B', J_j ∈ BandJ_i ∈ B' such that t_j = t_i + p_i.
|  |  |  |     // We merge blocks B and B'
|  |  |  |     Let J_j ∈ BandJ_i ∈ B' be such that t_j = t_i + p_i;
|  |  |  |     Call update_tree(B,j,ℓ(B'));
|  |  |  |     Call update_tree(B',i,ℓ(B));
|  |  |  |     G = G ∪ G' ∪ {(i, j)};
|  |  |  |     B = B ∪ B'; ℓ(B) = ℓ(B) + ℓ(B');
|  |  |  |     Γ(B) = Γ(B) ∪ Γ(B') ∪ {(i, j)};
|  |  |  |     b = b − 1; Renumber the blocks consecutively;
|  |  |  |  3) ∃(i, j) ∈ Γ(B) such that ℓ_i,j < 0.
|  |  |  |     // We split block B between jobs J_i and J_j
|  |  |  |     Let B = B' ∪ B'' where B'' is the block defined by the
|  |  |  |       jobs following J_j in G;
|  |  |  |     Separate Γ(B) and G accordingly in sub-graphes;
|  |  |  |     ℓ(B'') = ℓ_i,j; ℓ(B') = ℓ(B) − ℓ_i,j;
|  |  |  |     Call update_tree(B',i,−ℓ(B''));
|  |  |  |     Call update_tree(B'',j,−ℓ(B'));
|  |  |  |     b = b + 1; Renumber the blocks consecutively;
|  |  End While;
|  End If;
End While;
```

[Chrétienne and Sourd, 2003]

Fig. 5.6. An optimal algorithm to calculate start times of jobs for the $P\infty|s_i|F_\ell(\bar{E}^\alpha, \bar{T}^\beta)$ problem

ALGORITHM ECS1 (2)

Procedure update_tree(B,i,δ);
Set i visited;
For (j unvisited such that $\ell_{i,j} < 0$ or $\ell_{j,i} < 0$ in $\Gamma(B)$) Do
| If $(j,i) \in A$ Then $\ell_{j,i} = \ell_{j,i} + \delta$;
| Call update_tree(B,i,δ);
End For;

[Chrétienne and Sourd, 2003]

Fig. 5.7. The procedure update_tree of algorithme ECS1

5.4.3 The $1|f_i$ *piecewise linear*$|F_\ell(\sum_i f_i, \sum_j I_j)$ problem

[Sourd, 2005] considers the problem in which all jobs are already sequenced on a single machine, without loss of generality, in the order $(J_1, J_2, ..., J_n)$. Each job J_i is defined by a processing time p_i and a cost function f_i which is piecewise linear with a number of segments that may be greater than two. Therefore, this problem generalises the earliness-tardiness problem for which the cost functions have only two segments. Besides, we assume that each inserted idle times j induces a cost mesured by a cost function I_j. The aim is to solve the optimal timing problem by minimising $\sum_i f_i + \sum_j I_j$. As outlined by Sourd, functions f_i enable to model a certain number of real situations as for instance the presence of time windows in which jobs must be processed: if a job cannot be processed in a certain time period then the corresponding cost f_i is set to $+\infty$ during this period.

Unfortunately the problem is shown to be $\mathcal{NP}$-hard in the weak sense. Sourd proposes a dynamic programming algorithm to solve the problem which complexity is $O(n^2 UB)$ time, with UB an upper bound on the makespan value of the optimal schedule. The algorithm also works when the problem is no more defined as a single machine problem but as a general scheduling problem without resource constraint and with a tree precedence graph. Next, more particular problems are considered as for instance the earliness-tardiness problem around a common due date or the problem with convex cost functions.

5.5 Polynomially solvable problems

5.5.1 The $1|d_i = d \geq \sum p_i|F_\ell(\bar{E}, \bar{T})$ problem

[Kanet, 1981a] is interested in a JiT problem where the objective is to determine a schedule which minimises the *deviation of the completion times of jobs in relation to a due date*. This problem is noted $1|d_i = d \geq \sum p_i|F_\ell(\overline{E}, \overline{T})$ with $F_\ell(\overline{E}, \overline{T}) = \overline{E} + \overline{T}$. The common due date is non restrictive. This problem is solvable in polynomial time and Kanet proposes the algorithm, denoted by EJK1 and presented in figure 5.8. The maximum complexity of this algorithm is in $O(n^2)$.

ALGORITHM EJK1

/* T: the set of n jobs to schedule */
/* A: the sequence of jobs scheduled early or on-time */
/* R: the sequence of jobs scheduled tardy */
$A = R = \emptyset$;
$setA = 1$;
<u>For</u> $i = 1$ <u>to</u> n <u>Do</u>
  Let J_k be such that $p_k = \max_{J_l \in T}(p_l)$;
  <u>If</u> $(setA = 1)$ <u>Then</u>
    $A = A//\{J_k\}$;
  <u>Else</u>
    $R = \{J_k\}//R$;
  <u>End If</u>;
  $T = T - \{J_k\}$;
  $setA = 1 - setA$;
<u>End For</u>;
$S = A//R$;
Compute the start time of jobs in S in such a way that the last job of A completes at time d and that the first job of R starts at time d;

[Kanet, 1981a]

Fig. 5.8. An optimal algorithm for the $1|d_i = d \geq \sum p_i|F_\ell(\overline{E}, \overline{T})$ problem

The resolution of this problem is based on the fact that the set of V-shaped schedules is dominant. We say that a schedule is V-shaped if the set of jobs J_i such that $C_i \leq d$ are ordered according to the rule LPT and if the set of jobs J_i such that $C_i > d$ are ordered according to the rule SPT. Kanet also shows that it is sufficient to consider the schedules without the addition of voluntary idle time after processing of the first job, the latter being able to start at a date greater than 0. In the example of figure 5.9 we note that no permutation of jobs can reduce the value of the criterion $\overline{E}+\overline{T}$. It is sufficient to consider the permutation of the jobs J_i and J_j and to deduce that it does not decrease the value of the objective function.

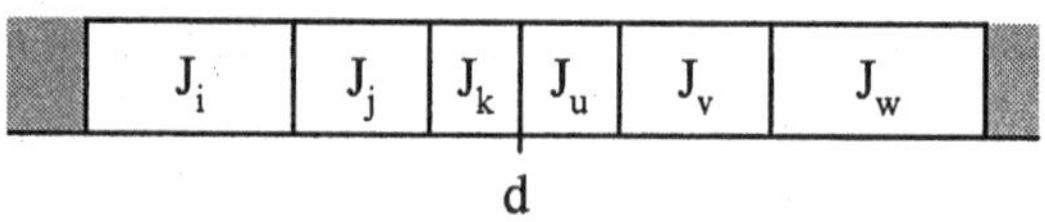

Fig. 5.9. An example of a V-shaped schedule

Example.
We consider a scheduling problem for which $n = 5$ and $d = 18$. We apply the algorithm EJK1.

i	1	2	3	4	5
p_i	2	4	3	5	2

(i) $A = R = \emptyset$, $setA = 1$,
(ii) $k = 4$, $A = (J_4)$, $R = \emptyset$, $setA = 0$,
(iii) $k = 2$, $A = (J_4)$, $R = (J_2)$, $setA = 1$,
(iv) $k = 3$, $A = (J_4, J_3)$, $R = (J_2)$, $setA = 0$,
(v) $k = 1$, $A = (J_4, J_3)$, $R = (J_1, J_2)$, $setA = 1$,
(vi) $k = 5$, $A = (J_4, J_3, J_5)$, $R = (J_1, J_2)$, $setA = 0$.
We obtain the schedule presented in figure 5.10.

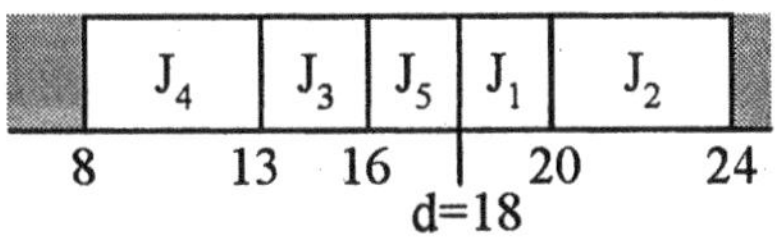

$$\sum_{i=1}^{n} |L_i| = 15$$

Fig. 5.10. The schedule calculated by the algorithm EJK1

A similar problem is tackled by [Bagchi et al., 1986] who are interested in the $1|d_i = d \geq \delta|F_\ell(\overline{T}, \overline{E})$ problem with $F_\ell(\overline{T}, \overline{E}) = \overline{T} + \overline{E}$. We suppose that the jobs are such that $p_1 \geq p_2 \geq \ldots \geq p_n$ and we define $\delta = p_1 + p_3 + \ldots + p_n$ if n is odd and $\delta = p_2 + p_4 + \ldots + p_n$ otherwise. This is the limit value of d so that it should not be restrictive. To solve this problem we can use a polynomial enumeration algorithm based on a branch-and-bound algorithm. Besides, Bagchi, Sullivan and Chang show through two examples that this problem is equivalent to a $P2||\overline{C}$ problem, which is solvable in polynomial time.

5.5.2 The $1|d_i = d\ unknown, nmit|F_\ell(\overline{E}, \overline{T}, d)$ problem

[Panwalker et al., 1982] study a JiT problem where all the jobs have the same unknown due date d which is also to be minimised. This problem is denoted by $1|d_i = d\ unknown, nmit|F_\ell(\overline{E}, \overline{T}, d)$, with $F_\ell(\overline{E}, \overline{T}, d) = \alpha\overline{E} + \beta\overline{T} + \gamma nd$. Given that the common due date d is to be determined, an optimal solution for this problem exists which contains no voluntary idle time. When $\gamma \geq \beta$ the problem is very simple to solve since the reduction of one time unit of d enables us to modify the value of the objective function from at least $n\beta - n\gamma \leq 0$. An optimal solution is obtained therefore by setting $d^* = 0$ and by classifying the jobs according to the rule SPT. When $\gamma < \beta$, an optimal solution exists in which the date d coincides with the completion time of a job in position k. More precisely, we have $k = \lceil \frac{n(\beta-\gamma)}{(\beta+\alpha)} \rceil$. An optimal algorithm in $O(n\log(n))$ time, denoted by EPSS1, is proposed by Panwalker, Smith and Seidmann to solve the whole problem (figure 5.12).

Example.
We consider a problem for which $n = 5$, $\alpha = 4$, $\beta = 5$ and $\gamma = 3$.

i	1	2	3	4	5
p_i	2	4	3	5	2

(i) $k = 2$,
(ii) $\pi_i = n\gamma + (i-1)\alpha$, $\forall i = 1, 2$ and $\pi_i = (n+1-i)\beta$, $\forall i = 3, ..., 5$,

position i	1	2	3	4	5
π_i	15	19	15	10	5

$I = (2, 1, 3, 4, 5)$ and $J = (J_1, J_5, J_3, J_2, J_4)$.
(iii) $d^* = 4$ and we obtain the schedule presented in figure 5.11.

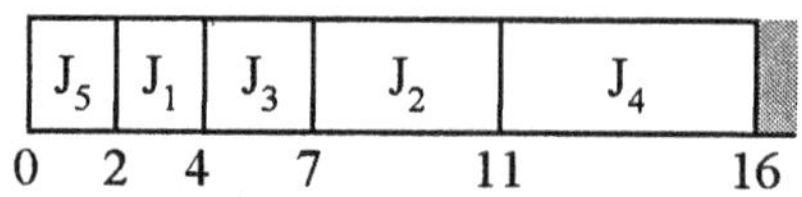

$$F_\ell(\overline{E}, \overline{T}, d) = 178$$

Fig. 5.11. The schedule calculated by the algorithm EPSS1

ALGORITHM EPSS1

Step 1: $k = \max(0; \lceil \frac{n(\beta-\gamma)}{(\beta+\alpha)} \rceil)$;
Step 2: $\forall i = 1, ..., k$, $\pi_i = n\gamma + (i-1)\alpha$;
$\forall i = k+1, ..., n$, $\pi_i = (n+1-i)\beta$;
/* π_i is the weight of the job scheduled in position i */
I is the list of positions sorted by decreasing value of π_i;
J is the list of jobs sorted using the rule SPT;
Step 3: Build the optimal schedule S^* such that the job $J[i]$ is assigned in position $I[i]$, $\forall i = 1, ..., n$;
$d^* = C_{[k]}$; /* $C_{[0]} = 0$ */

[Panwalker et al., 1982]

Fig. 5.12. An optimal algorithm for the $1|d_i = d\ unknown, nmit|F_\ell(\overline{E}, \overline{T}, d)$ problem

Extension to other connected problems is also studied. For example, addition of the term $\delta\overline{C}$ to the objective function leads to a problem which is solvable in polynomial time. Panwalker, Smith and Seidmann also study the case with distinct due dates d_i. An extension in the case where the jobs can be grouped into classes is studied by [Chen, 1996]. The treated problem is noted $1|d_i = d\ unknown, nmit, classes|F_\ell(\overline{E}, \overline{T}, \overline{B}, d)$. All the jobs have a common due date d to be determined, and are delivered in batches after being processed on the machine. The delivery date of the job J_i is noted D_i. All the early jobs are delivered in a single batch to the date d, *i.e.* are such that $D_i = d$. The criterion $\overline{B}$ represents the number of batches which are delivered after this date. Chen proposes for this problem an optimal dynamic programming algorithm, of which time complexity is in $O(n^5)$.

5.5.3 The $1|p_i \subseteq [\underline{p}_i; \overline{p}_i] \cap \mathbb{N}, d_i = d\ non\ restrictive|F_\ell(\overline{E}, \overline{T}, \overline{CC}^w)$ problem

This problem, with $F_\ell(\overline{E}, \overline{T}, \overline{CC}^w) = \alpha\overline{E} + \beta\overline{T} + \overline{CC}^w$, is tackled by [Chen et al., 1997]. The processing time p_i of each job J_i is a variable to determine. Additional assumptions are made:

1. $\forall j = 1, ..., n, \forall i = 1, ..., n, \overline{p}_i - \underline{p}_i = \overline{p}_j - \underline{p}_j$,
2. the crashing time cost criterion is defined by $\overline{CC}^w = \sum_{i=1}^{n} c_i(\overline{p}_i - p_i)$ where c_i is an increasing penalty function.

Chen, Lu and Tang first show that there exist an optimal schedule in which the hth job completes at time d, with $h = \lceil \frac{n\beta}{\alpha+\beta} \rceil$. Next they propose to reduce the problem to an assignment problem, by introducing costs $v_{i,k}$ of scheduling the job J_i to the position k. We have:

$$v_{i,k} = \begin{cases} \min\limits_{j=0,\ldots,(\overline{p}_i - \underline{p}_i)} \{(k-1)\alpha(\underline{p}_i + j) + c_i(\overline{p}_i - \underline{p}_i - j)\} \\ \qquad \text{If } k \leq h, \text{ i.e. job } J_i \text{ is early or on-time,} \\ \min\limits_{j=0,\ldots,(\overline{p}_i - \underline{p}_i)} \{(n-k+1)\beta(\underline{p}_i + j) + c_i(\overline{p}_i - \underline{p}_i - j)\} \\ \qquad \text{If } k > h, \text{ i.e. job } J_i \text{ is tardy.} \end{cases}$$

Notice that in both cases we can deduce, from the value of j which gives the minimum, the value of the exact processing time p_i if job J_i is scheduled in position k: $p_i = \underline{p}_i + j$. When the costs $v_{i,k}$ are computed the problem can be reduced to an assignment problem, that can be solved in $O(n^3)$ time. A model of this problem, denoted by ECLT1, is introduced in figure 5.13.

5.5.4 The $P|d_i = d\ non\ restrictive, nmit|F_\ell(\overline{E}, \overline{T})$ problem

[Sundararaghavan and Ahmed, 1984] study a scheduling problem for which the jobs have the same due date, denoted by d, which is *non restrictive*. The

Mathematical formulation ECLT1	
/* $h = \lceil \frac{n\beta}{\alpha+\beta} \rceil$ */	
/* $\forall k = 1, ..., h, \forall i = 1, ..., n,$ */	
/* $v_{i,k} = \min_{j=0,...,(\overline{p}_i - \underline{p}_i)} \{(k-1)\alpha(\underline{p}_i + j) + c_i(\overline{p}_i - \underline{p}_i - j)\}$ */	
/* $\forall k = h+1, ..., n, \forall i = 1, ..., n,$ */	
/* $v_{i,k} = \min_{j=0,...,(\overline{p}_i - \underline{p}_i)} \{(n-k+1)\beta(\underline{p}_i + j) + c_i(\overline{p}_i - \underline{p}_i - j)\}$ */	
Data:	n, the number of jobs, $v_{i,k}$, $i = 1, ..., n$, $k = 1, ..., n$, the cost of assigning the job J_i to position k.
Variables:	$y_{i,k}$, $i = 1, ..., n$, $m = 1, ..., n$, boolean variable, equal to 1 if job J_i is assigned in position k and 0 otherwise.
Objective:	Minimise $\sum_{i=1}^{n}\sum_{k=1}^{n} v_{i,k}y_{i,k}$
Constraints:	$\sum_{k=1}^{n} y_{i,k} = 1, \forall i = 1, ..., n$ $\sum_{i=1}^{n} y_{i,k} = 1, \forall k = 1, ..., n$ $y_{i,k} \in \{0; 1\}, \forall i = 1, ..., n, \forall k = 1, ..., n$

Fig. 5.13. An MIP model for the $1|p_i \in [\underline{p}_i; \overline{p}_i] \cap \mathbb{N}, d_i = d$ *non restrictive*$|F_\ell(\overline{E}, \overline{T}, \overline{CC}^w)$ problem

aim is to minimise the criteria $\overline{E}$ and $\overline{T}$ via a convex combination $F_\ell(\overline{E}, \overline{T})$ with $F_\ell(\overline{E}, \overline{T}) = \overline{E} + \overline{T}$. Insertion of voluntary idle time before each job is forbidden when the machines have started to process the jobs. This problem is solvable in polynomial time.

If S is an optimal solution for the non restrictive problem, then $|n_i - n_k| \leq 1, \forall i, k = 1, ..., m$, with n_j the number of jobs processed by machine M_j and $\sum_{j=1}^{m} n_j = n$. In the case where $m = 1$, the hypothesis *d non restrictive* can be verified easily ([Bagchi et al., 1986]). In the general case $m \geq 2$, we can verify a posteriori that the due date d is restrictive if $\forall j = 1, ..., m, d - \sum_{i=1}^{v_j} p_{A_j[i]} \geq 0$ with A_j the list of the v_j early or on-time jobs on M_j in an optimal schedule. The proposed algorithm, denoted by ESA1, is presented in figure 5.15. It generalises that proposed for the single machine problem, denoted by $1|d_i = d, nmit|F_\ell(\overline{E}, \overline{T})$. A V-shaped schedule is constructed by assigning and sequencing the jobs iteratively on the machines.

Example.
We consider a problem for which $n = 10$, $m = 2$ and $d_i = d = 37$, $\forall i = 1, ..., 10$.

i	1	2	3	4	5	6	7	8	9	10
p_i	20	18	16	14	12	10	8	6	4	2

(i) We place the m first jobs early on the machines, *i.e.*
$A_1 = (J_1),\ A_2 = (J_2)$,
$R_1 = \emptyset,\ R_2 = \emptyset$.
(ii) J_3 is tardy on M_1 and J_4 is tardy on M_2.
$A_1 = (J_1),\ A_2 = (J_2)$,
$R_1 = (J_3),\ R_2 = (J_4)$.
(iii) We repeat the process until we obtain
$A_1 = (J_1, J_5, J_9),\ A_2 = (J_2, J_6, J_{10})$,
$R_1 = (J_7, J_3),\ R_2 = (J_8, J_4)$.
(iv) The due date d is non restrictive because $d = 37 > \max(36; 30)$. We obtain the schedule shown in figure 5.14.

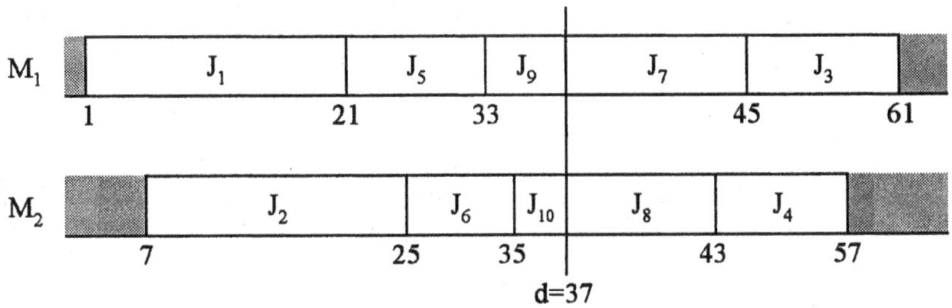

$F_\ell(\overline{E}, \overline{T}) = 92$

Fig. 5.14. The schedule calculated by the algorithm ESA1

5.5.5 The $P|d_i = d\ unknown, nmit|F_\ell(\overline{E}, \overline{T})$ problem

[Emmons, 1987] is interested in a more general problem than the one tackled by [Sundararaghavan and Ahmed, 1984] where $F_\ell(\overline{E}, \overline{T}) = \alpha\overline{E} + \beta\overline{T}$. This problem is solvable in polynomial time ([De et al., 1991]).

When $m = 1$, [Kanet, 1981a] proposes an optimal polynomial algorithm for an equivalent problem. Besides, [Hall, 1986] shows that in the cases $m = 1$ and $\alpha = \beta = 1$, we have:

$$\overline{E} + \overline{T} = \sum_{i=1}^{n} |C_i - d| = \sum_{j=1}^{v} (j-1) \times p_{[j]} + \sum_{j=1}^{u} j \times p_{[n-j+1]}$$

with $d = C_{[v]}$, v the number of early or on-time jobs, u the number of tardy jobs and $p_{[j]}$ the processing time of the job in position j. The previous formula is valid when the set of early jobs and the set of tardy jobs have been

ALGORITHM ESA1

```
/* We assume that p_1 ≥ ... ≥ p_n */
/* A_j is the list of early or on-time jobs on M_j */
/* R_j is the list of tardy jobs on M_j */
Step 1: /* We determine the lists A_j and R_j */
        k = 1;
        For i = 1 to n Do
            If (i ≤ m) Then
                /* The job J_i is the first scheduled job on M_i */
                A_i = {J_i}; R_i = ∅;
            Else
                If (|A_k| - 1 < |R_k|) Then
                    /* The job J_i is scheduled early on M_k */
                    A_k = A_k//{J_i}; k = k + 1;
                Else
                    /* The job J_i is scheduled tardy on M_k */
                    R_k = {J_i}//R_k; k = k + 1;
                End If;
            End If;
            If (k > m) Then
                k = 1;
            End If;
        End For;
Step 2: /* We check that the due date d is non restrictive */
        /* and we locate in time the jobs */
        All the sequences R_j start at t = d;
        For j = 1 to m Do
            If (d ≤ Σ_{k=1}^{|A_j|} p_{A_j[k]}) Then
                Print "The due date is restrictive";
                END;
            Else
                A_j starts at time t = d - Σ_{k=1}^{|A_j|} p_{A_j[k]};
            End If;
        End For;
Step 3: Print the resulting schedule and Ē + T̄;
```

[Sundararaghavan and Ahmed, 1984]

Fig. 5.15. An optimal algorithm for the $P|d_i = d$ *non restrictive, nmit*$|\ F_\ell(\overline{E}, \overline{T})$ problem

determined. In the case of parallel machines, Hall shows that:

$$\overline{E}+\overline{T}=\sum_{k=1}^{m}(\sum_{j=1}^{v_k}(j-1)\times p_{[j]}^{k}+\sum_{j=1}^{u_k}j\times p_{[n-j+1]}^{k})$$

with v_k the number of early and on-time jobs assigned to M_k, u_k the number of tardy jobs assigned to M_k and $p_{[j]}^{k}$ the processing time of the job in position j on M_k. Besides, we have $d = C_{[v_1]}^{1} = C_{[v_2]}^{2} = \ldots = C_{[v_m]}^{m}$ with $C_{[v_j]}^{j}$ the completion time of the job in position v_j on M_j, $\forall j = 1, ..., m$. [Emmons, 1987] shows that when the weights α and β are different we have:

$$\alpha\overline{E}+\beta\overline{T}=\sum_{k=1}^{m}\left(\sum_{j=1}^{v_k}\alpha\times(j-1)\times p_{[j]}^{k}+\sum_{j=1}^{u_k}\beta\times j\times p_{[n-j+1]}^{k}\right)$$

Thus, when the sets of tardy and early jobs on each machine are fixed, the optimal schedule is a V-shaped one on each machine.

In order to solve the problem when $\alpha \neq \beta$, [Emmons, 1987] proposes an algorithm, denoted by EEM1 (figure 5.16), based on that of [Hall, 1986]. The principal difference between the former algorithm and algorithm ESA1 lies in the choice of the assignment in a set A_j or R_j. In algorithm EEM1 this choice is made by taking account of the weights α and β.

Example.
We consider a problem for which $n = 10$, $m = 2$, $\alpha = 4$ and $\beta = 1$.

i	1	2	3	4	5	6	7	8	9	10
p_i	20	18	16	14	12	10	8	6	4	2

(i) We place the m first jobs early on the machines, *i.e.*
$A_1 = (J_1)$, $A_2 = (J_2)$,
$R_1 = \emptyset$, $R_2 = \emptyset$.
(ii) Job J_3 is tardy on M_1 and job J_4 is tardy on M_2. We obtain:
$A_1 = (J_1)$, $A_2 = (J_2)$,
$R_1 = (J_3)$, $R_2 = (J_4)$.
(iii) Job J_5 is early on M_1 and job J_6 is early on M_2. We obtain:
$A_1 = (J_1, J_5)$, $A_2 = (J_2, J_6)$,
$R_1 = (J_3)$, $R_2 = (J_4)$.
(iv) Job J_7 is tardy on M_1 and job J_8 is tardy on M_2. We obtain:
$A_1 = (J_1, J_5)$, $A_2 = (J_2, J_6)$,
$R_1 = (J_7, J_3)$, $R_2 = (J_8, J_4)$.
(v) Job J_9 is tardy on M_1 and job J_{10} is tardy on M_2. We obtain:
$A_1 = (J_1, J_5)$, $A_2 = (J_2, J_6)$,
$R_1 = (J_9, J_7, J_3)$, $R_2 = (J_{10}, J_8, J_4)$.

```
                        ALGORITHM EEM1
/* We assume that p_1 ≥ ... ≥ p_n */
/* A_j is the list of early or on-time jobs on M_j */
/* R_j is the list of tardy jobs on M_j */
Step 1:  /* We compute the lists A_j and R_j */
         k = 1;
         For i = 1 to n Do
           If (i ≤ m) Then
             /* The job J_i is the first scheduled job on M_i */
             A_i = {J_i}; R_i = ∅;
           Else
             If ((|A_k| - 1) × α < |R_k| × β) Then
               /* The job J_i is scheduled early on M_k */
               A_k = A_k//{J_i}; k = k + 1;
             Elsc
               /* The job J_i is scheduled tardy on M_k */
               R_k = {J_i}//R_k; k = k + 1;
             End If;
           End If;
           If (k > m) Then
             k = 1;
           End If;
         Enf For;
Step 2:  /* We locate in time the lists */
         d = max_{i=1,...,m} ( Σ_{j=1}^{|A_i|} p_{A_i[j]} );
         All the sequences R_j start at t = d;
         For j = 1 to m Do
           A_j starts at time t = d - Σ_{k=1}^{|A_j|} p_{A_j[k]};
         End For;
Step 3:  Print the resulting schedule, αĒ + βT̄ and d;
                        [Emmons, 1987]
```

Fig. 5.16. An optimal algorithm for the $P|d_i = d$ *unknown*, *nmit*$|$ $F_\ell(\overline{E}, \overline{T})$ problem

(vi) The due date d is given by $d = \max(32; 28) = 32$. We obtain the schedule presented in figure 5.17.

Emmons is also interested in the $P|d_i = d$ *unknown*, *nmit*$|$ $Lex(F_\ell(\overline{E}, \overline{T}), C_{max})$ problem with $F_\ell(\overline{E}, \overline{T}) = \alpha\overline{E} + \beta\overline{T}$. He justifies taking account of the criterion C_{max} at the second level by the fact that several optimal schedules for the objective function $F_\ell(\overline{E}, \overline{T})$ but with different makespan values exist. Once the lists A_j and R_j have been calculated, other optimal schedules obtained by producing permutations of jobs between sets A_j and R_j can exist. In order to solve the tricriteria problem, Emmons proposes an al-

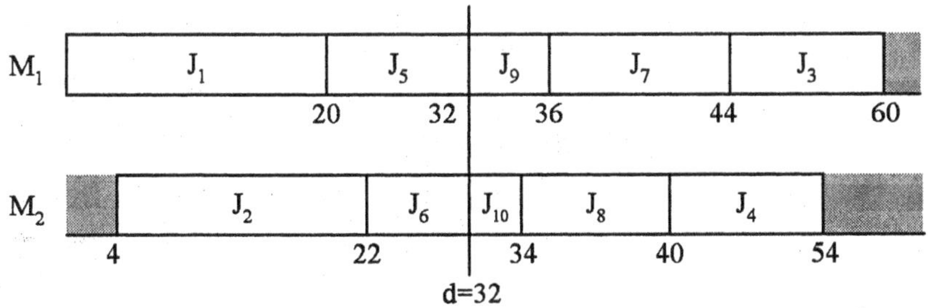

$F_\ell(\overline{E},\overline{T}) = 164$

Fig. 5.17. The schedule calculated by the algorithm EEM1

gorithm which improves the schedule obtained by the algorithm EEM1. It is based on a particular aggregation operator. Let us consider two lists L_1 and L_2 of m jobs. The aim is to aggregate L_1 and L_2 in order to create a third list, denoted by L_3, composed of m fictitious jobs. The aggregation process consists of taking from L_1 the job with the largest processing time and from L_2 the job with the smallest processing time. These two jobs are aggregated in L_3 and are deleted from the lists L_1 and L_2. This process is repeated until the initial lists are empty. An example is presented in figure 5.18.

J_i	p_i
J_1	4
J_2	7
J_3	9
J_4	15
J_5	12
J_6	8
J'_1	19
J'_2	17
J'_3	19

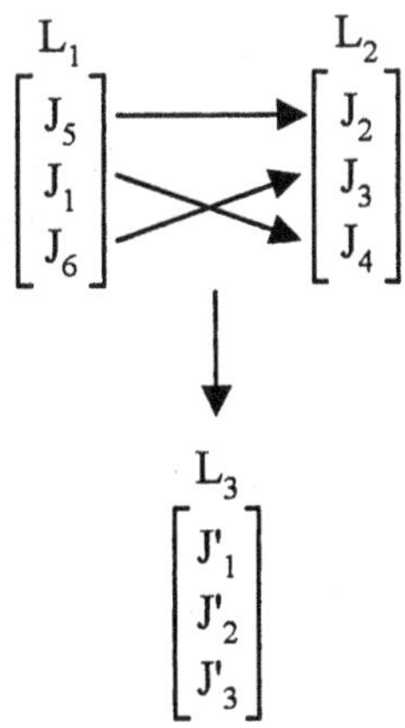

Fig. 5.18. An example of aggregation of jobs

The algorithm proposed by Emmons, denoted by EEM2, is presented in figure 5.19.

ALGORITHM EEM2

Step 1: Apply the algorithm EEM1. Let S^0 be the obtained schedule;
/* We now reduce to a fictitious problem such that $n = rm$. */
/* A_i and R_i are the lists calculated in algorithm EEM1 */
$k_1 = \max_{i=1,...,m}(|A_i|)$; $k_2 = \max_{i=1,...,m}(|R_i|)$;
Add, if necessary, fictitious jobs J_{n+j}, with $p_{n+j} = 0$,
in the lists A_i in such a way that $|A_i| = k_1$, $\forall i = 1, ..., m$;
Add, if necessary, fictitious jobs J_{n+j}, with $p_{n+j} = 0$,
in the lists R_i in such a way that $|R_i| = k_2$, $\forall i = 1, ..., m$;

Step 2: /* We build the lists to aggregate */
Let $A = (a_{i,j})$ be the matrix of dimension $m \times (k_1 + k_2)$
such that $a_{i,j}$ is the number of the jobs assigned in position j
on the machine M_i;
$\forall i = 1, ..., k_1, E_i = [a_{1,i}; a_{2,i}; \ldots; a_{m,i}]^T$;
$\forall i = 1, ..., k_2, F_i = [a_{1,k_1+i}; a_{2,k_1+i}; \ldots; a_{m,k_1+i}]^T$;

Step 3: /* We aggregate the lists F_i */
$F'_0 = [0; \ldots; 0]^T$;
For $i = 1$ to k_2 Do
  | Aggregate F'_{i-1} and F_i to obtain F'_i;
End For;

Step 4: /* We aggregate the lists E_i */
$E'_0 = [0; \ldots; 0]^T$;
For $i = 1$ to k_1 Do
  | Aggregate E'_{i-1} and E_i to obtain E'_i;
End For;

Step 5: /* Building of the schedule S^1 */
For $i = 1$ to m Do
  | The jobs aggregated to compute $E'_{k_1}[i]$ are scheduled
  | on M_i in the order of their fusion;
  | The jobs considered to compute $F'_{k_2}[i]$ are next
  | scheduled on M_i, following their aggregation order;
End For;
/* The obtained schedule is denoted S^1 */

Step 6: Print S^1, $\alpha\overline{E} + \beta\overline{T}$ and the value d;

[Emmons, 1987]

Fig. 5.19. An optimal algorithm for the $P|d_i = d$ *unknown*, $nmit|Lex(F_\ell(\overline{E},\overline{T}), C_{max})$ problem

Example.
We consider a problem for which $n = 10$, $m = 2$, $\alpha = 4$ and $\beta = 1$.

i	1	2	3	4	5	6	7	8	9	10
p_i	20	18	16	14	12	10	8	6	4	2

(i) The schedule obtained by the algorithm EEM1 is the one presented in the previous example. The criterion C_{max} has a value of 60 for this schedule, $k_1 = |A_1| = |A_2| = 2$ and $k_2 = |R_1| = |R_2| = 3$. So, we do not add a dummy job.
(ii) The matrix A is defined by:

$$A = \begin{bmatrix} 1 & 5 & 9 & 7 & 3 \\ 2 & 6 & 10 & 8 & 4 \end{bmatrix}$$

$E_1 = [1,2]^T$, $E_2 = [5,6]^T$
$F_1 = [9,10]^T$, $F_2 = [7,8]^T$, $F_3 = [3,4]^T$.
(iii) We aggregate the lists F_i and we obtain:
$F_1' = [11,12]^T$, $F_2' = [13,14]^T$ and $F_3' = [15,16]^T$ with:

i	11	12	13	14	15	16
p_i	2	4	10	10	24	26

(iv) We aggregate the lists E_i and we obtain:
$E_1' = [17,18]^T$ and $E_2' = [19,20]^T$ with:

i	17	18	19	20
p_i	18	20	30	30

(v) In order to calculate E_2', J_1 is aggregated with J_6 and J_2 is aggregated with J_5. We therefore find on M_1 J_2 then J_5 and on M_2, J_1 then J_6. Next, by doing the same thing with F_3', we go backwards and we find J_9, J_8 then J_3 on M_1, and J_{10}, J_7 and J_4 on M_2. The obtained schedule is presented in figure 5.20.

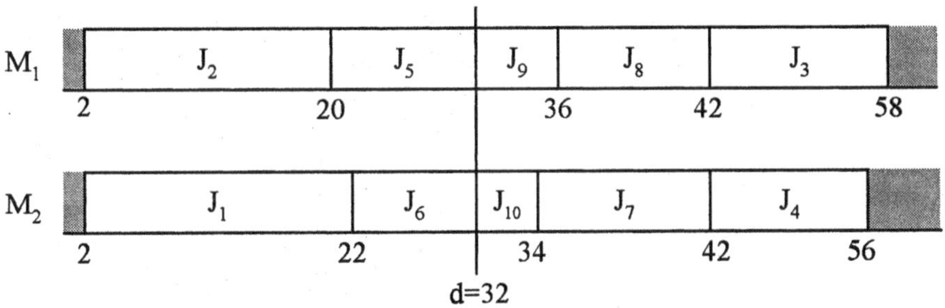

$C_{max} = 58$, $F_\ell(\overline{E}, \overline{T}) = 164$

Fig. 5.20. Schedule calculated by the algorithm EEM2

5.5.6 The $P|d_i = d\ unknown, p_i = p, nmit|F_\ell(\overline{E}, \overline{T}, d)$ problem

[Cheng and Chen, 1994] study a scheduling problem where the jobs have a common due date which is to be determined. Besides, the processing times are all supposed to be equal to a value p. The aim is to compute a schedule which minimises the objective function $F_\ell(\overline{E}, \overline{T}, d) = \alpha\overline{E} + \beta\overline{T} + \gamma nd$. This problem is solvable in polynomial time.

We recall that when $m = 1$, the problem with ordinary processing times is solved by an optimal polynomial algorithm ([Panwalker et al., 1982]). The single machine problem addressed by Panwalker, Smith and Seidmann is broadened to m machines by [Cheng, 1989], who proposes an heuristic to solve it. The latter is $\mathcal{NP}$-hard (see [Cheng and Kahlbacher, 1992]). For the problem with equal processing times, and when $\gamma \geq \beta$, we reduce to the minimisation of criterion $\overline{C}$.

Lemma 24
If $\gamma \geq \beta$, then the optimal value of the due date d, denoted by d^*, is $d^* = 0$. The $P|d_i = d$ unknown$, p_i = p|F_\ell(\overline{E}, \overline{T}, d)$ problem is then reduced to the $P|p_i = p|\overline{C}$ problem.

Proof.
Let S^* be the optimal solution and d^* be the corresponding due date. Let us suppose that $d^* > 0$ and consider another solution defined by $S' = S^*$ and $d' = d^* - 1$. Then we have: $F_\ell(\overline{E}, \overline{T}, d)(S^*, d^*) - F_\ell(\overline{E}, \overline{T}, d)(S', d')$
$= \alpha\overline{E}(S^*, d^*) + \beta\overline{T}(S^*, d^*) + \gamma nd^* - \alpha\overline{E}(S^*, d') - \beta\overline{T}(S^*, d') - \gamma nd'$
Because $d' < d^*$, we have $\alpha\overline{E}(S^*, d^*) \geq \alpha\overline{E}(S^*, d')$. On the other hand, $\gamma nd^* - \gamma nd' = \gamma n$. We have similarly $\beta\overline{T}(S^*, d^*) \leq \beta\overline{T}(S^*, d')$, but $\beta(\overline{T}(S^*, d') - \overline{T}(S^*, d^*)) \leq \beta n \leq \gamma n$. Thus, $F_\ell(\overline{E}, \overline{T}, d)(S^*, d^*) - F_\ell(\overline{E}, \overline{T}, d)(S', d') \geq 0$. Then, the solution defined by $S' = S^*$ and $d' = d^* - 1$ is not worse than that defined by S^* and d^*. Therefore an optimal solution exists for which $d^* = 0$.
In this case $\overline{E} = 0$ and the criterion $\overline{T}$ is equivalent to the criterion $\overline{C}$. The problem reduces to the $P|p_i = p|\overline{C}$ problem, which is polynomially solvable.□

To solve the $P|d_i = d$ *unknown*$, p_i = p|F_\ell(\overline{E}, \overline{T}, d)$ problem in the case where $\gamma < \beta$, Cheng and Chen use the results for the $1|d_i = d, p_i = p, nmit|F_\ell(\overline{E}, \overline{T})$ problem. For the single machine problem, a schedule is defined completely by the starting time S_0 of the sequence of jobs. The starting time which corresponds to an optimal schedule is given by:

$$S_0^* = max(0; d - u \times p) \text{ with } u = \lceil \frac{n\beta}{\alpha + \beta} \rceil$$

Lemma 25 *[Cheng and Chen, 1994]*
For the $1|d_i = d$ unknown$, p_i = p, nmit|F_\ell(\overline{E}, \overline{T}, d)$ problem we have:

1. *$F_\ell(\overline{E}, \overline{T}, d)$ is a decreasing function on d when $d \in [0; r \times p]$,*
2. *$F_\ell(\overline{E}, \overline{T}, d)$ is an increasing function on d when $d \in]r \times p; +\infty[$,*

with $r = \lceil \frac{n(\beta - \gamma)}{\alpha + \beta} \rceil$.

Regarding the parallel machines problem, an optimal schedule which verifies $|n_i - n_j| \leq 1, \forall i, j = 1, ..., m$, with n_ℓ the number of jobs assigned on machine M_ℓ exists. This implies that two groups of machines exist. The group A gathers together the $(m - h)$ first machines (M_1 to M_{m-h}) which process k jobs each. The group B gathers together the h last machines (M_{m-h+1} to M_m) which process $(k + 1)$ jobs each. We have $k = \lfloor \frac{n}{m} \rfloor$ and $n = km + h$. Knowing that all the jobs have the same characteristics, they can be split indifferently into two sets N_A and N_B. The first contains the jobs processed on machines of group A and the second those processed on machines of group B. Let ST_A and ST_B be the start times of the first jobs on each machine of the group A and of the group B respectively. If S_0^j is the start time of the sequence of jobs on machine M_j, we have $S_0^j = ST_A$, $\forall j \in A$, and $S_0^j = ST_B$, $\forall j \in B$.

Theorem 16 *[Cheng and Chen, 1994]*
Let $r_A = \lceil \frac{k(\beta-\gamma)}{\alpha+\beta} \rceil$, $r_B = \lceil \frac{(k+1)(\beta-\gamma)}{\alpha+\beta} \rceil$, $d_A = r_A \times p$ *and* $d_B = r_B \times p$. d_A *(respectively* d_B*) is the optimal due date obtained by considering only jobs scheduled on machines of group A (respectively B). We set similarly* $d'_A = u_A \times p$ *and* $d'_B = u_B \times p$ *with* $u_A = \lceil \frac{k\beta}{\alpha+\beta} \rceil$ *and* $u_B = \lceil \frac{(k+1)\beta}{\alpha+\beta} \rceil$. *If* $d_B = d_A + p$ *then two cases occur:*

- *First case:* $d'_A > d_A$. *If* $r_A \leq \frac{n(\beta-\gamma)}{m(\alpha+\beta)}$, *then there is an optimal schedule for which* $d^* = d_B$ *and* $ST_A = ST_B = 0$. *Otherwise* $d^* = d_A$ *and* $ST_A = ST_B = 0$.
- *Second case:* $d'_A = d_A$. *If* $r_A \leq \frac{h(k+1)\beta - n\gamma}{h(\alpha+\beta)}$, *then an optimal schedule exists for which* $d^* = d_B$, $ST_A = p$ *and* $ST_B = 0$. *Otherwise* $d^* = d_A$ *and* $ST_A = ST_B = 0$.

If $d_A = d_B$, *then there is an optimal schedule in which* $d^* = d_A$ *and* $ST_A = ST_B = 0$.

The algorithm proposed by Cheng and Chen, denoted by ECC1, is presented in figure 5.23.

Example.
We consider a problem for which $m = 5$, $n = 21$, and $p_i = 1, \forall i = 1, ..., n$. We study two instances.

- Let us consider in the first instance $\alpha = 20$, $\beta = 30$ and $\gamma = 2$. We obtain then $k = 4$, $h = 1$, $A = \{M_1, \dots, M_4\}$, $B = \{M_5\}$, $r_A = 3$, $r_B = 3$, $u_A = 3$, $u_B = 3$, $d_A = 3$, $d_B = 3$, $d'_A = 3$ and $d'_B = 3$. The case $d_A = d_B$ of theorem 16 is verified (figure 5.21), therefore $d^* = 3$.

- Let us now suppose that $\alpha = 20$, $\beta = 60$ and $\gamma = 2$. We have then $r_A = 3$, $r_B = 4$, $u_A = 3$, $u_B = 4$, $d_A = 3$, $d_B = 4$, $d'_A = 3$ and $d'_B = 4$. Case $d_A + p = d_B$ of theorem 16 is verified. Moreover $d'_A = d_A$ and $r_A \leq 3.225$. We deduce from this that an optimal schedule exists such that $d^* = d_B = 4$, $ST_A = 1$ and $ST_B = 0$ (figure 5.22).

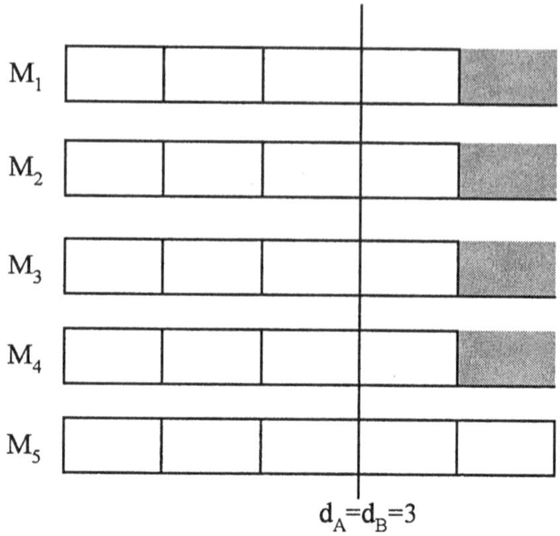

$F_\ell(\overline{E}, \overline{T}, d) = 636$

Fig. 5.21. Case where $d_A = d_B$

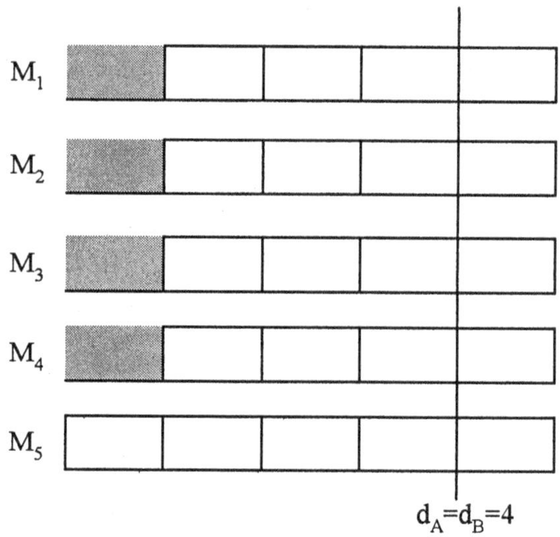

$F_\ell(\overline{E}, \overline{T}, d) = 828$

Fig. 5.22. Case where $d_A + p = d_B$

ALGORITHM ECC1

Step 1: /* Initialisation of the algorithm */
$k = \lfloor \frac{n}{m} \rfloor$; $h = n - km$;
$A = \{M_1, \ldots, M_{m-h}\}$; $B = \{M_{m-h+1}, \ldots, M_m\}$;
$r_A = \lceil \frac{k(\beta - \gamma)}{\alpha + \beta} \rceil$; $r_B = \lceil \frac{(k+1)(\beta - \gamma)}{\alpha + \beta} \rceil$;
$u_A = \lceil \frac{k\beta}{\alpha + \beta} \rceil$; $u_B = \lceil \frac{(k+1)\beta}{\alpha + \beta} \rceil$;
$d_A = r_A \times p$; $d_B = r_B \times p$;
$d'_A = u_A \times p$; $d'_B = u_B \times p$;

Step 2: /* Assignment of jobs on machines */
Partition the set J in m sub-sets $N_1, \ldots, N_m$ such that:
$|N_j| = k$, $\forall j \in [1, m-h]$, and $|N_j| = k+1$, $\forall j \in [m-h+1, m]$;
The jobs of set N_j are assigned on machine M_j, $\forall j = 1, ..., m$;

Step 3: /* Computation of the start times and of the due date d^* */
If $((h = 0)$ or $(d_B = d_A))$ Then
| $d^* = d_A$; $ST_A^* = ST_B^* = 0$; END;
End If;
If $(d'_A > d_A)$ Then
  If $(r_A \leq \frac{n(\beta - \gamma)}{m(\alpha + \beta)})$ Then
  | $d^* = d_B$; $ST_A^* = ST_B^* = 0$; END;
  Else
  | $d^* = d_A$; $ST_A^* = ST_B^* = 0$; END;
  End If;
Else
  If $(r_A \leq \frac{h(k+1)\beta - n\gamma}{h(\alpha + \beta)})$ Then
  | $d^* = d_B$;
  | $ST_A^* = p$; $ST_B^* = 0$; END;
  Else
  | $d^* = d_A$; $ST_A^* = ST_B^* = 0$; END;
  End If;
End If;

Step 4: Print the resulting schedule, d^* and the value of the objective function;

[Cheng and Chen, 1994]

Fig. 5.23. An optimal algorithm for the $P|d_i = d$ *unknown*$, p_i = p|F_\ell(\overline{E}, \overline{T}, d)$ problem

5.5.7 The $R|p_{i,j} \in [\underline{p}_{i,j}; \overline{p}_{i,j}], d_i = d$ *unknown*$|F_\ell(\overline{T}, \overline{E}, \overline{CC}^w)$ problem

[Alidaee and Ahmadian, 1993] are interested in a Just-in-Time scheduling problem where the processing times are not data of the problem, and where we have $p_{i,j} \in [\underline{p}_{i,j}; \overline{p}_{i,j}]$, $\forall i = 1, ..., n, \forall j = 1, ..., m$. Besides, all the jobs have the same due date d which has to be determined. The aim is to minimise the function $F_\ell(\overline{T}, \overline{E}, \overline{CC}^w) = \alpha\overline{T} + \overline{E} + \overline{CC}^w$. This problem is solvable in polynomial time.

For the single machine problem ([Panwalker and Rajagopalan, 1982]) we know that:

- the optimal due date d^* coincides with the completion time of a job,
- the set of V-shaped schedules is dominant,
- an optimum sequence of jobs exist such that, $\forall i = 1, ..., n$, $p_i = \underline{p}_i$ or $\overline{p}_i$.

These results can be extended to the case where m is ordinary. Moreover, an optimal due date d^* exists which coincides with the completion time of a job on each machine. The parallel machines problem can be reduced to a transportation problem solvable in $O(n^3)$. This problem is obtained by considering the set of possible assignments of jobs on machines and for all positions. Moreover, when the sequences of jobs on machines are known, the determination of the optimal processing times is done according to the following rule:
If J_i is scheduled on M_j and is tardy then:

$$x_{i,j} = \begin{cases} \overline{p}_{i,j} - \underline{p}_{i,j} & \text{if } w_{i,j} < \beta k, \\ 0 & \text{if } w_{i,j} \geq \beta k. \end{cases}$$

If J_i is scheduled on M_j and is early or on-time then:

$$x_{i,j} = \begin{cases} \overline{p}_{i,j} - \underline{p}_{i,j} & \text{if } w_{i,j} < \alpha(k-1), \\ 0 & \text{if } w_{i,j} \geq \alpha(k-1). \end{cases}$$

with k the number of jobs processed after J_i if this is scheduled on M_j.

5.5.8 Other problems

• [Hoogeveen, 1996] is interested in two problems where the earliness of the jobs is expressed in relation to desired start times. These problems are denoted by $1|s_i, d_i, s_i \in [d_i - p_i; d_i], nmit|\epsilon(L_{max}/P_{max})$ and $1|s_i, d_i, s_i \in [d_i - p_i; d_i]|\epsilon(L_{max}/P_{max})$. Hoogeveen shows that these two problems are solvable in polynomial time whereas in the case where the data s_i and d_i are arbitrary (with $s_i \leq d_i$) these problems become $\mathcal{NP}$-hard in the strong sense. The difference between the two problems is that in the first one insertion of voluntary idle time before each job is forbidden. In both cases, minimisation of the criterion P_{max} brings us back to maximising the real start times. Thus, Hoogeveen shows that the constraint $P_{max} \leq \epsilon$ brings us back to imposing release dates defined by $r_i = s_i - \epsilon, \forall i = 1, ..., n$. We obtain then a problem that can be denoted by $1|r_i, d_i, r_i \in [d_i - p_i - \epsilon; d_i - \epsilon], \beta|L_{max}$ with $\beta \in \{\emptyset, nmit\}$. To solve these two problems, two optimal algorithms based on greedy methods are proposed. The algorithm which solves the $1|s_i, d_i, s_i \in [d_i - p_i; d_i], nmit|\epsilon(L_{max}/P_{max})$ problem with ϵ fixed is of time complexity

$O(n\log(n))$ whereas that without the constraint $nmit$ is in $O(n^2\log(n))$. Following this, Hoogeveen proposes a determination algorithm of the set E when the insertion of voluntary idle time is forbidden. This algorithm iteratively modifies the parameter ϵ of the $1|s_i, d_i, s_i \in [d_i - p_i; d_i], nmit|\epsilon(L_{max}/P_{max})$ problem and each iteration calls the algorithm which solves it. The latter only determines strict Pareto optima. Thus the set E can be calculated completely. Moreover, Hoogeveen shows that the number of strict Pareto optima is at most equal to n.

• [Bector et al., 1988] are interested in the $1|d_i = d, d\ unknown|\ F_\ell(\overline{E},\overline{T})$ problem, with $F_\ell(\overline{E},\overline{T}) = \overline{E}+\overline{T}$ and restrict their study to the set of schedules with no insertion of voluntary idle time after the start of processing of the first job. Remember that a classical result ([Webster et al., 1998], see section 5.2.1) states that solving problems with an unknown common due date is equivalent to solving problems with a fixed and non restrictive common due date. The distinction between these two types of problems is important for the decision maker because of the difference in the value of the date d. [Bector et al., 1988] propose a goal programming model of the problem with unknown date d and deduce some properties for an optimal schedule. Notably, they show that in such a schedule, the common due date d is equal to the completion time of the job in position r in the sequence with $\frac{n}{2} \le r < \frac{n}{2}+1$. This result has been shown in part by [Francis and White, 1974] and Bector, Gupta and Gupta propose a more complete proof. Moreover, they show that the set of V-shaped schedules is dominant for this problem and then propose an optimal algorithm which starting from an initial V-shaped sequence, proceeds by permutations of jobs to obtain an optimal V-shaped sequence.

• [Kondakci et al., 1997] consider the $1|p_i = 1, d_i,\ nmit|\epsilon(\overline{E}/\overline{U})$, $1|p_i = 1, d_i, nmit|\epsilon(E_{max}/\overline{U})$ and $1|p_i = 1, d_i, nmit|\epsilon(F_\ell(\overline{E},\overline{T})/\overline{U})$ problems with $F_\ell(\overline{E},\overline{T}) = \overline{E}+\overline{T}$, and for which the insertion of voluntary idle time before each job is forbidden. To solve these problems, they propose a mixed integer program which is that of the assignment problem, with the criterion $\overline{U}$ inserted as a constraint. Enumeration of the set of weak Pareto optima is solved by considering firstly that the value of the criterion $\overline{U}$ corresponds to an optimal solution of a single criterion problem with $\overline{E}$, E_{max} or $\overline{E}+\overline{T}$, depending on the considered problem. The bicriteria problem is then solved and at each iteration the value of the upper bound of the criterion $\overline{U}$ is reduced by one and the bicriteria problem is solved once again.

• [Ahmed and Sundararaghavan, 1990] study the minimisation problem of the weighted earliness and tardiness when the weights are *symetrical*, dependent on the jobs and are equal to the processing times. We also assume that all the jobs have the same non restrictive due date. The problem addressed is denoted by $1|d_i = d \geq \sum p_i|F_\ell(\overline{E}^w, \overline{T}^w)$ with $F_\ell(\overline{E}^w, \overline{T}^w) = \sum_{i=1}^{n} p_i(E_i + T_i)$. We can show that the set of schedules without insertion of voluntary idle time except before the first job is dominant. To solve this problem a greedy algorithm is proposed which sorts at the first step jobs according to the rule LPT. n schedules S_i are next obtained by timeshifting the sequence of jobs so that the ith job of the schedule S_i completes at time d. The optimal schedule is the one having the minimal objective function value.

• [Garey et al., 1988] study a particular JiT problem in which the jobs have unit processing times. This problem is denoted by $1|p_i = 1, d_i|F(E_i, T_i)$ with $F(E_i, T_i) = \max_{i=1,\ldots,n}(E_i+T_i)$. To solve this problem Garey, Tarjan and Wilfong propose an optimal algorithm in $O(n \log(n))$ time which uses an algorithm for the $1|p_i = 1, d_i, F(E_i, T_i) \leq D|-$ problem. To determine the optimal value D^* of the objective function, for the original problem, the algorithm proceeds by binary search on an interval $[D_{lb}; D_{ub}]$. This algorithm can be used to solve the problem with arbitrary processing times. In this case, its time complexity is in $O(n^2)$.

• When the earliness of the jobs is defined in relation to a desired start time, [Sidney, 1977] is interested in a problem where the start times and the due dates are *agreeable*. The problem addressed is noted $1|s_i, d_i, s_i \leq s_j \Leftrightarrow d_i \leq d_j|F(f(T_{max}), g(P_{max}))$ with $F(f(T_{max}), g(P_{max})) = \max(f(T_{max}), g(P_{max}))$. The functions f and g are taken to be continuous and increasing on $\mathbb{R}$ and P_{max} refers to the maximum promptness of jobs. The treated problem is thus analogous to that tackled by [Hoogeveen, 1996]. According to Sidney, this approach can be used in project scheduling problems in the chemical industry. Sidney moreover supposes that the dates s_i and d_i are *agreeable*, *i.e.* $\forall i, j = 1, ..., n$, $s_i \leq s_j \Leftrightarrow d_i \leq d_j$. To solve this problem, he proposes an optimal algorithm which proceeds in two steps. An optimal sequence of jobs is obtained by sorting them in increasing order of start times s_i. Next, an algorithm is applied to determine the real start times from the sequence. This problem is taken up by [Lakshminarayan et al., 1978] who show that it is possible to improve the algorithm which determines the real start times when the sequence is fixed. They then show that the complexity of the general algorithm is in $O(n \log(n))$ time whereas for Sidney it is in $O(n^2)$.

• Few JiT scheduling problems with more than two criteria have been addressed in the literature. [Seidmann et al., 1981] consider a tricriteria problem in which the due dates are unknown but must be as close as possible to a common due date. The problem is noted $1|d_i\ unknown, nmit, A|F_\ell(\overline{E}, \overline{T}, \overline{A})$ with $F_\ell(\overline{E}, \overline{T}, \overline{A}) = \alpha\overline{E} + \beta\overline{T} + \gamma\overline{A}$. The criterion $\overline{A}$ is defined by $\overline{A} =$

$\sum_{i=1}^{n} \max(0; d_i - A)$, where A is a due date which we do not wish to pass by. We suppose besides that insertion of voluntary idle time on the machine is forbidden. To solve this problem Seidmann, Panwalker and Smith propose an optimal algorithm in $O(n \log(n))$. The jobs are numbered according to the rule SPT. The optimal due dates d_i are then calculated in the following manner, $\forall i = 1, ..., n$:

$$d_i = \begin{cases} \sum_{j=1}^{i} p_j & \text{if } \gamma \leq \beta \\ \min(A; \sum_{j=1}^{i} p_j) & \text{otherwise} \end{cases}$$

A similar problem, but with a common known due date and criteria $\overline{U}^w$ and $\overline{A}$, is tackled by [De et al., 1991]. The problem is denoted by $1|d_i = d, A|F_\ell(\overline{U}^w, \overline{A})$ with $F_\ell(\overline{U}^w, \overline{A}) = \overline{U}^w + \gamma\overline{A}$. We define $M = \sum_{j/\frac{w_j}{p_j} > \gamma} p_j$ the threshold value A such that the problem is restricted or not. If $A < M$ then the problem is so and $\mathcal{NP}$-hard. In this case, De, Ghosh and Wells propose an heuristic based on a relaxation of a model of the problem. If $A \geq M$ then the problem is not restricted and solvable in polynomial time. An optimal algorithm is proposed by the authors.

5.6 $\mathcal{NP}$-hard problems

5.6.1 The $1|d_i, nmit|F_\ell(\overline{E}^\alpha, \overline{T}^\beta)$ problem

[Ow and Morton, 1988] and [Ow and Morton, 1989] consider the weighted early/tardy problem with no voluntary idle times insertion. They propose sequencing rules to solve the problem. Ow and Morton show that any adjacent pair of jobs (J_i, J_j) such that J_i immediately precedes J_j in the optimal sequence, must satisfy the following condition: $\mathcal{P}_{i,j}(s_i) \geq \mathcal{P}_{j,i}(s_j)$ with $s_i = d_i - t - p_i$ the slack of job J_i, t being the earliest time the machine is available for processing this job, and

$$\mathcal{P}_{i,j}(s_i) = \begin{cases} \dfrac{\beta_i}{p_i} & \text{if } s_i \leq 0, \\ \dfrac{\beta_i}{p_i} - s_i\left(\dfrac{\alpha_i + \beta_i}{p_i p_j}\right) & \text{if } 0 \leq s_i \leq p_j, \\ -\dfrac{\alpha_i}{p_i} & \text{otherwise.} \end{cases}$$

Then, a priority can be associated to each job J_i by comparison with a dummy job with average processing time $\overline{p} = \sum_{i=1}^{n} p_i$. The linear priority rule, denoted by LIN-ET, for job J_i is defined by:

$$\mathcal{P}_i(s_i) = \begin{cases} \dfrac{\beta_i}{p_i} & \text{if } s_i \leq 0, \\ \dfrac{\beta_i}{p_i} - s_i\left(\dfrac{\alpha_i + \beta_i}{p_i k \overline{p}}\right) & \text{if } 0 \leq s_i \leq k\overline{p}, \\ -\dfrac{\alpha_i}{p_i} & \text{otherwise.} \end{cases}$$

with k a given parameter, that should reflect the average number of jobs that may conflict at each time a sequencing decision is to be made. The priority rule depends on the slack of job J_i. The first extreme situation occur when job J_i is tardy, i.e. $s_i \leq 0$, and the priority rule is then WSPT. The second extreme situation occurs when job J_i is early, with $s_i \geq k\overline{p}$, and the priority rule is then WLPT. The piecewise linear function $\mathcal{P}_i(s_i)$ corresponding to LIN-ET is shown in figure 5.24.

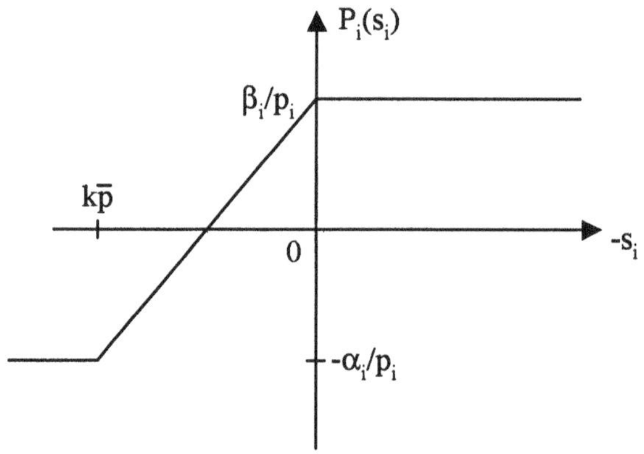

Fig. 5.24. LIN-ET priority rule

We can notice that $\mathcal{P}_i(s_i) = 0 \Leftrightarrow s_i = \dfrac{\beta_i}{\alpha_i + \beta_i} k\overline{p}$. However, using this rule, the problem of jobs conflicting can make the obtained sequence far from the optimal solution. To avoid this problem, Ow and Morton propose another priority rule, denoted by EXP-ET, defined as follows:

$$\mathcal{P}_i(s_i) = \begin{cases} \frac{\beta_i}{p_i} exp\left[-\frac{s_i(\alpha_i+\beta_i)}{\alpha_i\overline{p}}\right] & \text{if } 0 \leq s_i \leq \frac{\beta_i}{\alpha_i+\beta_i}k\overline{p}, \\ h_i^{-2} \times \left(\frac{\beta_i}{p_i} - s_i\left(\frac{\alpha_i+\beta_i}{p_ik\overline{p}}\right)\right)^3 & \text{if } \frac{\beta_i}{\alpha_i+\beta_i}k\overline{p} < s_i \leq k\overline{p}. \end{cases}$$

The parameter k controls the time at which the priority of a job increases. The algorithm that implements the priority rules is presented in figure 5.25.

ALGORITHM HOM1

```
/* k is a given parameter, for instance k = 3 if n = 8 or 15, k = 5 if n = 25 */
T = {J_1, J_2, ..., J_n};
p̄ = (1/n) Σ_{i=1}^{n} p_i;
t = 0;
S = ∅;
While T ≠ ∅ Do
  | For J_i ∈ T Do
  |   | s_i = d_i − t − p_i;
  |   | Compute P_i(s_i); /* depending on LIN-ET or EXP-ET priority rule */
  | End For;
  | Let J_k ∈ T/P_k(s_k) = max_{J_i ∈ T} P_i(s_i);
  | S = S//{J_k};
  | T = T − {J_k};
  | t = t + p_k;
End While;
```

[Ow and Morton, 1988] and [Ow and Morton, 1989]

Fig. 5.25. An heuristic algorithm for the $1|d_i, nmit|F_\ell(\overline{E}^\alpha, \overline{T}^\beta)$ problem.

Then, Ow and Morton propose several versions of a filtered beam search procedure to solve the problem. This method is a truncated branch-and-bound algorithm, because only a certain number of branches of the search tree are explored. Experimental results show that the average deviation between the best solution and the best lower bound comprises between 5% and 10%. [Li, 1997] proposes for this problem a neighbouring heuristic which uses a set of n operators k-NAPI ($k = 0, ..., n-1$) where k-NAPI refers to the operator realising the permutations of two jobs separated by k jobs. Starting with an initial sequence calculated by means of an heuristic based on the rule EXP-ET , the operator 0-NAPI is applied until no further improvement can be achieved. The operator 1-NAPI is applied next, then the operator 2-NAPI, *etc.* Li also proposes a branch-and-bound procedure for which the lower bound is the sum of two bounds LB_1 and LB_2, valid for the single criterion problems $\overline{T}^\beta$ and $\overline{E}^\alpha$. Each of these boundaries is obtained by solving a lagrangean relaxation model (relaxation of constraints defining the variables T_i and E_i). The primal problem for each bound is solved either using the rule

WSPT or the rule WLPT. The corresponding dual problem is next solved by applying a perturbation algorithm of the langrangean coefficients which does not modify the sequence calculated for the primal problem. Experimental results show that the branch-and-bound procedure solves all the problems with up to 25 jobs in less than 100 seconds. Besides, the proposed heuristic is compared with that presented by [Ow and Morton, 1989] and the results show that the first mentioned is the most successful (in time and quality).
[Liaw, 1999] proposes algorithms which are very close to those of [Li, 1997]. Firstly, he provides a neighbouring heuristic in $O(n^4)$ time, which improves the schedule calculated using the rule EXP-ET. The neighbouring operators considered differ from k-NAPI and no comparison with Li's heuristic is presented. Liaw also proposes a lower bound calculated according to an identical step to that used by Li. The principal difference lies in the two sub-problems considered to calculate LB_1 and LB_2. Experimental results show that the lower bound proposed by Liaw is better than that proposed by Li. Nevertheless, concerning the branch-and-bound procedure the experimental results show that it is appreciably equivalent to that of Li.
[Almeida and Centeno, 1998] are similarly interested in the $1|d_i, nmit|F_\ell(\overline{E}^\alpha, \overline{T}^\beta)$ problem and propose an heuristic which iteratively uses tabu search, simulated annealing and local search heuristics. These ones use three neighbouring operators: API, k-NAPI and a particular operator. Starting with an initial solution obtained by applying the rule EXP-ET, the heuristics are successively applied according to a particular scheme. Diversification is introduced by means of a random selection step of a solution in the neighbourhood of the current solution. Experimental results only show that the proposed heuristic produces better results than the meta-heuristics used alone.

5.6.2 The $F|prmu, d_i, nmit|F_\ell(\overline{E}^w, \overline{T}^w)$ problem

[Zegordi et al., 1995] study a Just-in-Time flowshop scheduling problem and consider that the insertion of voluntary idle time before each job is forbidden. This problem is strongly $\mathcal{NP}$-hard because the corresponding single machine problem is also.

Zegordi, Itoh and Enkawa propose a simulated annealing heuristic, denoted by HZIE1, the peculiarity of which lies in the neighbourhood operator. They use the definition of a priority function ([Ow and Morton, 1989]) for a single machine problem and they extend it to a m-machine problem. Let S be a permutation schedule. We define a lower bound for the earliest start time of the job in ith position on the machine M_m in S by:

$$t_{S[i],m} = \max_{j=1,\dots,i} \left(\sum_{k=1}^{m-1} p_{S[j],k} \right) + \sum_{j=1}^{i-1} p_{S[j],m}, \forall i = 1, ..., n$$

An upper bound on the algebraic earliness is then $s_{S[i]} = d_{S[i]} - (t_{S[i],m} + p_{S[i],m})$, $\forall i = 1, ..., n$. Generalisation of the priority functions of Ow and Morton, denoted by $P^B_{S[i]}$ and $P^F_{S[i]}$, can be stated as follows:

$$\forall i = 2, ..., n, \ P^F_{S[i]} = w_{S[i]} - \frac{s_{S[i]}(w_{S[i]} + h_{S[i]})}{p_{S[i-1],m}}$$

$$\forall i = 1, ..., n-1, \ P^B_{S[i]} = \frac{s_{S[i]}(w_{S[i]} + h_{S[i]})}{p_{S[i+1],m}} - w_{S[i]}$$

The more $P^F_{S[i]}$ is important, the more it is interesting to permutate jobs in ith and $(i-1)$th position in S. Conversely, the more $P^B_{S[i]}$ is important the more it can be interesting to permutate jobs in ith and $(i+1)$th position. For example, if the bound on the algebraic earliness for position i is positive, then we estimate that the job in this position is late. We have then $P^F_{S[i]} > P^B_{S[i]}$ and we prefer to permutate jobs in position i and $(i-1)$.
At a given iteration of the algorithm, we get a solution S from which we search for the best neighbour S'. For this, it is sufficient to calculate the values of the priority functions. Amongst all the values of the priorities $P^F_{S[i]}$ and $P^B_{S[i]}$ we search for the greatest value. The corresponding permutation to this is then done and we obtain the schedule S'. Zegordi, Itho and Enkawa state that it is possible to consider the exact values of the algebraic earliness by setting $s_{S[i]} = d_{S[i]} - C_{S[i]}$, $\forall i = 1, ..., n$. The priority functions will be thus more realistic but more costly in terms of the calculation time necessary to obtain the values $C_{S[i]}$. The heuristic HZIE1 is presented in figure 5.26.

Concerning regulation of the temperature, Zegordi, Itoh and Enkawa refer to [Connolly, 1990]. An initial schedule S is randomly generated. A random permutation of jobs is performed in S and the variation Δ of the objective function is memorised. The initial schedule is then restored and a new permutation is performed. This process is repeated 50 times. The minimal value Δ_{min}, and the maximal value Δ_{max} which result from these permutations are then obtained. The initial temperature T_0 and the final temperature T_f are defined by:
$T_0 = \Delta_{min} + \frac{1}{10}(\Delta_{max} - \Delta_{min})$,
$T_f = \Delta_{min}$.

At a given temperature, Zegordi, Itho and Enkawa consider that no permutation is able to improve the current solution if all the values of the priority functions are negative. A new value of the temperature is then calculated by the formula $T_{i+1} = \dfrac{T_i}{1+\beta T_i}$ with $\beta = \dfrac{T_0 - T_f}{MT_0T_f}$ and $M = 50\dfrac{n(n-1)}{2}$. Two stopping conditions are presented:

- There are two temperature changes without modification of the current solution.

```
ALGORITHM HZIE1
Step 1:  /* Initialisation of the algorithm */
         Generate randomly a schedule S;
         Compute T_0 and T_f;
         T = T_0;
         M = 50 n(n-1)/2; β = (T_0 - T_f)/(M T_0 T_f);
         S* = S;
         Compute the priorities P^F_S[i] and P^B_S[i];
Step 2:  /* Main part */
         While (a stopping criterion is not verified) Do
           While (there exists a positive priority value) Do
             Search the best neighbour S';
             Δ_f = Ē^α(S) + T̄^β(S) - Ē^α(S') - T̄^β(S');
             If (Δ_f > 0) Then
               S = S';
               Compute the priorities P^F_S[i] and P^B_S[i];
             Else
               p = e^(Δ_f / T);
               Choose randomly a number x in the interval [0; 1];
               If (x ≤ p) Then
                 S = S';
                 Compute the priorities P^F_S[i] and P^B_S[i];
               End If;
             End If;
             If (Ē^α(S*) + T̄^β(S*) - Ē^α(S) - T̄^β(S) > 0) Then
               S* = S;
             End If;
           End While;
           T = T / (1 + βT);
         End While;
Step 3:  Print S*, Ē^α and T̄^β;
[Zegordi et al., 1995]
```

Fig. 5.26. An heuristic algorithm for the $F|prmu, d_i, nmit|F_\ell(\overline{T}^w, \overline{E}^h)$ problem

- The number of permutations performed is greater than M.

Experimental results show that the heuristic HZIE1 is more efficient than simulated annealing algorithms proposed by [Wilhelm and Ward, 1987] and [Connolly, 1990]. However, the latter are not adapted to resolution of the Just-in-Time problem.

5.6.3 The $P|d_i = d$ *non restrictive*, $nmit|f_{max}(\overline{E}^w, \overline{T}^w)$ problem

[Li and Cheng, 1994] are interested in a Just-in-Time scheduling problem where all the jobs have the same due date which is not restrictive. The

aim is to determine a schedule which minimises an objective function defined by $f_{max}(\overline{E}^w, \overline{T}^w) = \max_{i=1,\ldots,n}(w_i(E_i+T_i)) = \max_{i=1,\ldots,n}(w_i|L_i|)$. We are only interested in the set of schedules without insertion of voluntary idle times, except before the first job assigned on each machine.
Li and Cheng show that the problem is strongly $\mathcal{NP}$-hard and present a greedy heuristic, denoted by HLC1. The jobs are grouped by decreasing order of their weights w_i and are placed iteratively on machine M_j which minimises $|L_i|$. The algorithm is presented in figure 5.29. The worst case ratio of this heuristic is given by $f_{max}^{HLC1}/f_{max}^* \leq 2m$.

Example.
We consider a problem for which $n = 10$, $m = 2$ and $d = 40$.

i	1	2	3	4	5	6	7	8	9	10
p_i	2	4	6	8	10	12	14	16	18	20
w_i	20	19	18	17	16	15	14	13	12	11

(i) $L = \{J_1, \ldots, J_{10}\}$,
(ii) We schedule the m first jobs on the machines and we obtain the partial schedule presented in figure 5.27.

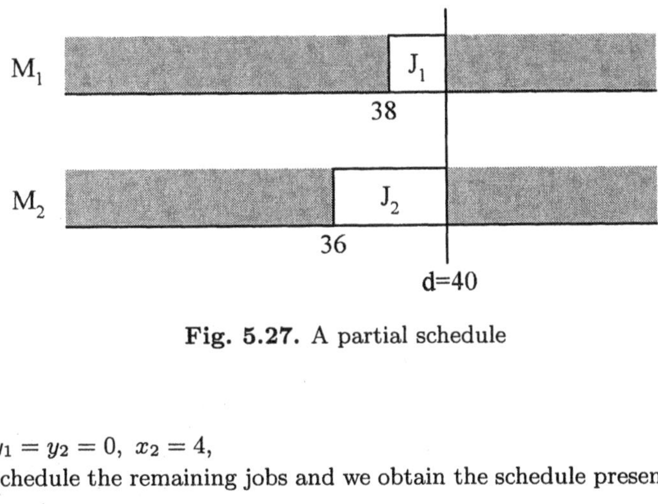

Fig. 5.27. A partial schedule

$x_1 = 2,\ y_1 = y_2 = 0,\ x_2 = 4,$
(iii) We schedule the remaining jobs and we obtain the schedule presented in figure 5.28.

An improvement of this heuristic can be obtained by recalculating the start time of the first job on each machine. For this an ideal common due date d_j for all jobs scheduled on machine M_j, is calculated by considering that the sequence of jobs is fixed. Let S_j be the sequence of jobs processed on M_j. The due date d_j is such that $\exists J_i \in S_j / C_i < d_j, \exists J_{i'} \in S_j / C_{i'} > d_j$ and $w_i(d_j - C_i) = w_{i'}(C_{i'} - d_j) = \max_{J_k \in S_j}(w_k|C_k - d_j|)$. The new start time of the first job on machine M_j is then increased by $d - d_j$, *i.e.* the sequence S_j is

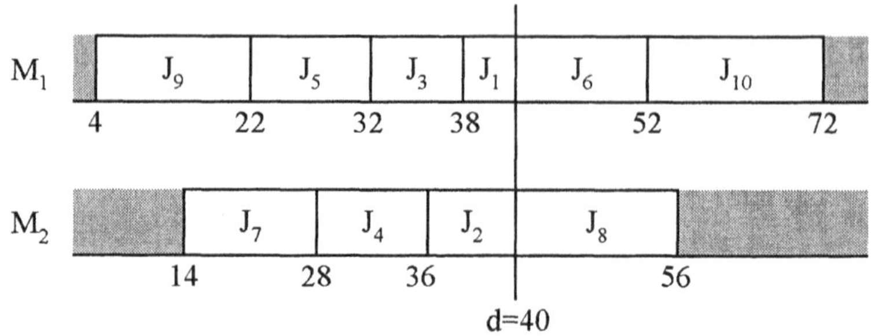

$f_{max} = 352$

Fig. 5.28. The schedule calculated by the heuristic HLC1

ALGORITHM HLC1

/* $d - x_j$ is the time at which machine M_j starts to process */
/* the jobs assigned on it */
/* $d + y_j$ is the time at which machine M_j completes to process */
/* the jobs assigned on it */

Step 1: /* Initialisation of the algorithm */
 $L = \{J_i$ sorted by decreasing value of $w_i\}$;
 For $i = 1$ to m Do
  $J_k = L[1]$;
  Assign job J_k on machine M_i such that $C_k = d$;
  $x_i = p_k$; $y_i = 0$;
  $L = L - \{J_k\}$;
 End For;

Step 2: /* Scheduling of the $n - m$ remaining jobs */
 For $i = 1$ to $(n - m)$ Do
  $J_k = L[1]$;
  Let machine M_j be such that x_j is minimum;
  Let machine $M_{j'}$ be such that $y_{j'}$ is minimum;
  If $((y_{j'} + p_k \leq x_j)$ or $(d - x_j < p_k))$ Then
   Job J_k is scheduled last on machine $M_{j'}$;
   $y_{j'} = y_{j'} + p_k$;
  Else
   Job J_k is scheduled first on machine M_j ;
   $x_j = x_j + p_k$;
  End If;
  $L = L - \{J_k\}$;
 End For;

Step 3: Print the resulting schedule and $f_{max}(\overline{E}^w, \overline{T}^w)$;

[Li and Cheng, 1994]

Fig. 5.29. An heuristic algorithm for the $P|d_i = d$ *non restrictive*, $nmit|f_{max}(\overline{E}^w, \overline{T}^w)$ problem

timeshifted. The heuristic, denoted by HLC2, is presented in figure 5.30. Its complexity is in $O(mn^2)$ time.

```
                         ALGORITHM HLC2
/* S_j is the sequence of jobs processed on machine M_j */
/* t_j is the start time of the first job on machine M_j */
Step 1:  Compute a schedule s using the heuristic HLC1;
Step 2:  For j = 1 to m Do
           | Sequence again the jobs J_i processed on M_j and
           | such that C_i < d, by decreasing value of w_i;
         End For;
Step 3:  /* We compute the new start times of machines */
         For j = 1 to m Do
           | /* We compute the ideal due date for this machine */
           | Z = ∞;
           | For i = 1 to |S_j| Do
           |   | For k = i + 1 to |S_j| Do
           |   |   | d' = (w_{S_j[i]} C_{S_j[i]} + w_{S_j[k]} C_{S_j[k]}) / (w_{S_j[i]} + w_{S_j[k]});
           |   |   | If (w_{S_j[i]} |C_{S_j[i]} - d'| < Z) Then
           |   |   |   | d_j = d'; Z = w_{S_j[i]} × |C_{S_j[i]} - d'|;
           |   |   | End If;
           |   | End For;
           | End For;
           | /* The jobs processed on M_j are timeshifted */
           | t_j = t_j + d - d_j;
         End For;
Step 4:  Print the resulting schedule and the value of the objective function;
                      [Li and Cheng, 1994]
```

Fig. 5.30. An heuristic algorithm for the $P|d_i = d$ *non restrictive*, *nmit*$|f_{max}(\overline{E}^w, \overline{T}^w)$ problem

Li and Cheng propose next a lower bound on the value of the objective function, which is used to measure the performance of the heuristic HLC2. Experimental results show that with m fixed, the average ratio f_{max}^{HLC2}/LB decreases when the number of jobs increases. Conversely, when n is fixed the average ratio increases proportionally with the number of machines.

Regarding the multicriteria approach used by Li and Cheng to tackle the Just-in-Time scheduling problem, we notice that the objective function considered is a particular case of an objective function produced from the goal-attainment approach (see chapter 3). In fact, it is sufficient to consider the objective function $\min_{i=1,\dots,n}(\frac{1}{v_i}(b_i - |L_i|))$ with $w_i = \frac{1}{v_i}$ and $b_i = 0$, $\forall i = 1, \dots, n$.

This implies that for each job, we associate a criterion defined by $|L_i|$ and that one or several weak Pareto optima for these n criteria are determined.

5.6.4 Other problems

• The problem which is considered in the literature as the basis of JiT scheduling problems is denoted by $1|d_i|F_\ell(\overline{T}, \overline{E})$. It is $\mathcal{NP}$-hard because the $1|d_i|\overline{T}$ problem is so. [Szwarc, 1993] studies the sequencing of two jobs if they have to be performed consecutively and with no idle time between the two processings. The original problem may break down into blocks where the jobs of a block are scheduled consecutively and two successive blocks are separated by an idle time. The sufficient conditions proposed are then used to sequence the jobs within the blocks. Szwarc proposes a branching scheme, useable in a branch-and-bound procedure, which does not consider schedules dominated by the previous conditions. He considers similarly the particular case where $d_i = d, \forall i = 1, ..., n$. Besides, [Azizoglu et al., 1991] propose for the $1|d_i, nmit|F_\ell(\overline{T}, \overline{E})$ problem, an adaptation of the heuristic presented by [Ow and Morton, 1989] for the $1|d_i, nmit|F_\ell(\overline{E}^\alpha, \overline{T}^\beta)$ problem. A branch-and-bound procedure is similarly proposed and experimental results show that in the more favourable configurations problems with up to 20 jobs can be solved.
[Kim and Yano, 1994] tackle the $1|d_i|F_\ell(\overline{E}, \overline{T})$ problem, with $F_\ell(\overline{E}, \overline{T}) = \overline{E} + \overline{T}$, and propose heuristics and an exact algorithm to solve it. We recall that when the sequence of jobs is known, calculation of start times can be realised in $O(n \log(n))$ by an algorithm proposed by [Garey et al., 1988] (see algorithm EGTW1). In the case where only two jobs J_i and J_j have to be sequenced, with $d_i \leq d_j$, Kim and Yano show that if they conflict (*i.e.* $d_j - d_i < p_j$) then:

1. J_i is scheduled before J_j if $d_i + p_j - d_j < d_j + p_i - d_i$ and J_j is scheduled before J_i otherwise (figure 5.31, case a).
2. If the jobs are scheduled before d_i then J_i preceeds J_j if $p_i > p_j$ and J_j preceeds J_i otherwise (figure 5.31, case b).
3. If the jobs are scheduled after $\max(d_i - p_i, d_j - p_j)$ then J_i preceeds J_j if $p_i < p_j$ and J_j preceeds J_i otherwise (figure 5.31, case c).

These results can be used as dominance conditions in a branch-and-bound procedure even if they are particular cases of earlier results presented by [Szwarc, 1993]. Kim and Yano propose next two lower bounds and a branch-and-bound algorithm. To calculate an upper bound they apply the algorithm for the calculation of start times EGTW1 beginning with the sequences obtained by several priority rules. Experimental results show that the exact algorithm is limited to problems containing around 20 jobs.
This problem is taken up again by [Fry et al., 1996] who propose a branch-and-bound procedure based on a breakdown of the problem into blocks. Ex-

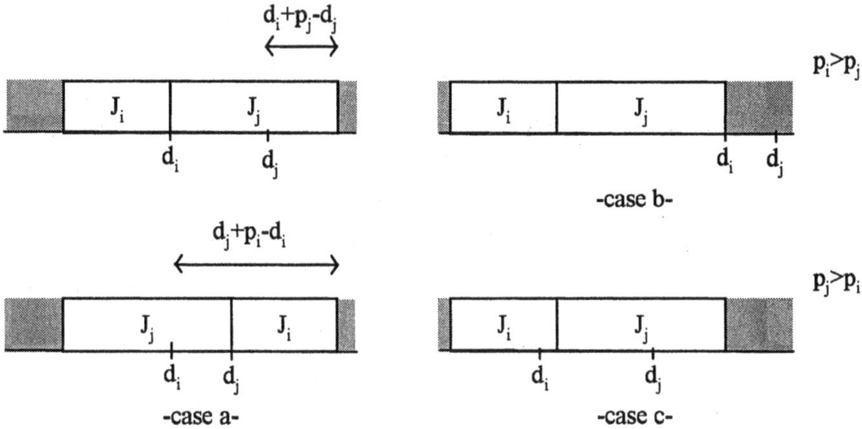

Fig. 5.31. Different configurations for sequencing two jobs

perimental results show that this algorithm solves problems with up to 25 jobs.
When the insertion of voluntary idle times before every job is forbidden (constraint $nmit$), [Fry and Leong, 1986] propose an integer linear program to solve the problem.

• The common due date problem, denoted by $1|d_i = d, nmit|F_\ell(\overline{T}, \overline{E})$, has been studied by [Sundararaghavan and Ahmed, 1984]. The due date d may be restrictive which implies that the problem addressed is $\mathcal{NP}$-hard, because the $1|d_i = d < \sum p_i, nmit|\ F_\ell(\overline{T}, \overline{E})$ problem is also. The set of weakly V-shaped schedules is dominant. A schedule is said to be weakly V-shaped if all the jobs J_i such that $C_i \leq d$, are sorted according to the rule LPT and if all the jobs J_i such that $t_i \geq d$, are sorted according to the rule SPT (see figure 5.32). All the V-shaped schedules are also weakly V-shaped. Notice that if the common due date concides with the completion time of a job then weakly V-shaped schedules are also V-shaped schedules.

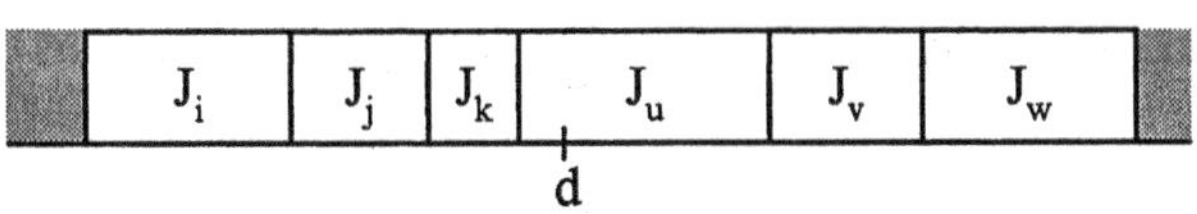

Fig. 5.32. An example of a weakly V-shaped schedule

Sundararaghavan and Ahmed propose an heuristic based on a greedy method, inspired by the algorithm proposed by [Kanet, 1981b] for the case $d \geq \sum_{i=1}^{n} p_i$.
For the problem with a restrictive common due date denoted by $1|d_i = d < \sum p_i, nmit|F_\ell(\overline{T}, \overline{E})$, [Bagchi et al., 1987a] propose a branch-and-bound procedure. Notice that the notion of restrictive common due date is stated in [Bagchi et al., 1986] who are interested in the $1|d_i = d < \delta, nmit|F_\ell(\overline{T}, \overline{E})$ problem with $F_\ell(\overline{T}, \overline{E}) = \overline{T} + \overline{E}$. The bound δ is defined by $\delta = p_1 + p_3 + \ldots + p_n$ if n is odd and $\delta = p_2 + p_4 + \ldots + p_n$ if not (by supposing that $p_1 \geq \ldots \geq p_n$). This quantity represents the value of the date d below which the problem is restrictive. Clearly, we have $\delta < \sum_{i=1}^{n} p_i$.
We suppose that all optimal schedules are such that the start time of the sequence, noted t_0, is equal to 0. To solve this problem, Sundararaghavan and Ahmed propose a branch-and-bound procedure. [Szwarc, 1989] takes up this problem again and studies the case where the date t_0 is fixed in advance and equal to 0. He is interested in properties of this problem and proposes necessary conditions for a schedule to be optimal. He provides next a branch-and-bound procedure which makes use of the conditions previously shown to prune nodes in the search tree. The value of the initial upper bound is calculated by the heuristic of [Sundararaghavan and Ahmed, 1984]. Experimental results show that the algorithm can solve problems with at least 25 jobs. Finally, Szwarc is interested in the case where the start time of the sequence is not fixed. He shows, with the help of an example, that contrary to the claims of [Bagchi et al., 1986], optimal schedules exist for which t_0 is not equal 0.

• When the earliness is measured in comparison with desired start times, [Koulamas, 1996] studies the $1|s_i, d_i|F_\ell(\overline{T}, \overline{P})$ problem for which $F_\ell(\overline{T}, \overline{P}) = \overline{T} + \overline{P}$. Koulamas shows that this problem is $\mathcal{NP}$-hard and proposes seven heuristics to solve it as well as an optimal algorithm based on an enumeration method. Dominance conditions allowing the enumeration algorithm to be more efficient are also described. Experimental results show that two of the heuristics produce results which are close to the optimal solution.

• [Chand and Schneeberger, 1988] deal with a particular case of the $1|d_i, nmit|\epsilon(\overline{E}^w/\overline{U})$ problem where the objective is to minimise the criterion $\overline{E}^w$ under the constraint $\overline{U} \leq 0$, *i.e.* $\overline{U} = 0$. Chand and Schneeberger show that for this problem, minimisation of the criterion $\overline{E}^w$ is equivalent to minimisation of the criterion $\overline{C}^w$. They deduce that the problem addressed is $\mathcal{NP}$-hard and propose an heuristic based on the algorithm of [Smith, 1956] for the $1|d_i, L_{max} = 0|\overline{C}^w$ problem. A dynamic programming algorithm to calculate an optimal solution is presented and the experimental results show the efficiency of these algorithms.

• The $1|d_i|F_\ell(\overline{E}^\alpha, \overline{T}^\beta)$ problem is the generalisation of the basic JiT scheduling problem. This problem is strongly $\mathcal{NP}$-hard given that the $1|d_i|\overline{T}^w$ problem is also. To calculate an optimal solution, [Fry et al., 1987a] consider the class of schedules with insertion of voluntary idle times, which is dominant for this problem. An heuristic based on an improvement algorithm of an initial sequence by permutation of jobs is proposed. It enables only the calculation of a jobs sequence. Insertion of idle times before each job is next realised by solving a mathematical program. [Fry and Blackstone, 1988] take up this problem again in the context of the method of production organisation *"Optimised Production Technology"* (see for example [Goldratt and Cox, 1984]). They propose a mixed integer linear program for the single machine scheduling problem. The design of tabu search algorithms for this problem is studied by [James and Buchanan, 1997] and [James and Buchanan, 1998]. They propose different implementations of two different approaches. In the first the algorithm calculates a sequence then solves the mathematical model proposed by [Fry et al., 1987a] to obtain a schedule. The second approach considers a particular coding of sequences. For each calculated solution an heuristic is used to deduce a feasible schedule.

• When jobs have distinct release times the problem is noted $1|r_i, d_i|F_\ell(\overline{E}^\alpha, \overline{T}^\beta)$ and is strongly $\mathcal{NP}$-hard. [Yano and Kim, 1991] consider a special case where the objective function is defined by $F_\ell(\overline{E}^\alpha, \overline{T}^\beta) = \sum_{i=1}^{n}(\alpha_i E_i + \beta_i T_i)$ where α_i and β_i are functions of the processing times. They propose five heuristics and a branch-and-bound algorithm.
[Mazzini and Armentano, 2001] deal with the general problem with ordinary weights and propose a greedy heuristic and a local search heuristic. The former computes a schedule by assigning to each job J_i a priority which is equal to $d_i - p_i$ if $r_i + p_i \leq d_i$ and r_i otherwise. At each iteration the unscheduled job with the lowest priority value is inserted in the partial schedule under construction. This insertion is done in order to minimize the cost generated in the objective function. Conflicts with already scheduled jobs are solved according to the rules presented by Mazzini and Armentano. After having scheduled all the jobs, a procedure to compute optimal idle times between jobs is used. The greedy heuristic requires $O(n^3)$ time. The local search heuristic uses as an initial schedule the solution of the greedy heuristic. The neighbourhood operator applied during the search is the *Adjacent Pairwise Interchange* operator (API): at each iteration the heuristic permutates two adjacent jobs and then recomputes the optimal idle times for the new sequence obtained. To decide if a swap of two jobs can lead to a decrease in the value of the objective function, Mazzini and Armentano propose a generalisation of a result presented by [Ow and Morton, 1988]. This one states a necessary condition to have precedences between jobs in an optimal schedule. Some computational experiments show that the local search heuristic does not improve so much

the schedule computed by the greedy heuristic. The average improvement is around 0.3%.

• [VandenAkker et al., 1998a] and [VandenAkker et al., 1998b] are interested in the previous problem when we have $d_i = d \geq \sum p_j$, $\forall i = 1, ..., n$. The problem addressed is therefore denoted by $1|d_i = d \geq \sum p_j, nmit|F_\ell(\overline{E}^\alpha, \overline{T}^\beta)$. This problem is $\mathcal{NP}$-hard because the problem with symetrical weights is so (see [Hall and Posner, 1991]). Van den Akker, Hoogeveen and Van de Velde notice that in some optimal schedules, the common due date d coincides with the completion time of a job. The jobs completing before the date d must be sorted by decreasing order of the values $\frac{p_i}{\alpha_i}$ whereas those completing after the date d must be sorted by increasing order of the values $\frac{p_i}{\beta_i}$. To solve this problem an exact algorithm combining the lagrangean relaxation and a method of columns generation is proposed. Experimental results show that problems with up to 125 jobs are solved in less than 8 minutes.
[Azizoglu and Webster, 1997] consider this problem when families of jobs are defined. When two jobs belonging to two different families are processed consecutively, a setup time must be considered. Thus, we attribute to each family a setup time supposed to be independent of the other families. The problem addressed by the authors can be denoted by $1|d_i = d \geq \sum p_i, S_{sd}, nmit, classes|F_\ell(\overline{E}^\alpha, \overline{T}^\beta)$. Azizoglu and Webster present some properties which enable the determination of an optimal schedule. These properties are generalisations of results presented in [Hall and Posner, 1991] in the case where the weights of the criteria are symetrical (*i.e.* $\alpha_i = \beta_i$, $\forall i = 1, ..., n$) and if there is only a single jobs class. As for the the problem without setup times ([VandenAkker et al., 1998a]), Azizoglu and Webster show notably that an optimal schedule exists such that the due date d coincides with the completion time of a job. Moreover, they show that an optimal schedule exists in which the jobs completed before the date d must be sorted by decreasing order of the values $\frac{p_i}{\alpha_i}$ whereas those completing after the date d must be sorted by increasing order of values $\frac{p_i}{\beta_i}$. A branch-and-bound procedure using the properties introduced, to reduce the size of the search tree, is then presented. An heuristic based on a filtered beam search is also proposed. Experimental results show that the exact algorithm can solve problems with 20 jobs in less than 15 minutes.
[Webster et al., 1998] tackle a similar problem where the due date d is unknown, *i.e.* is a variable to be determined. This problem is denoted by $1|d_i = d\ unknown, S_{sd}, nmit|F_\ell(\overline{E}^\alpha, \overline{T}^\beta)$ and is $\mathcal{NP}$-hard because the $1|d_i = d \geq \sum p_i|\sum w_i(T_i + E_i)$ problem is also (see [Hall and Posner, 1991]). Webster, Job and Gupta remind us that for this problem, insertion of voluntary idle times before execution of the jobs is not necessary in order to calculate an optimal solution. To solve it they propose a genetic algorithm which they compare to the branch-and-bound procedure presented by [Azizoglu and Webster, 1997]. The computation time allocated to the exact

algorithm is one hour maximum. The experimental results show that the genetic algorithm produces better results than the truncated branch-and-bound procedure.

- [Gupta and Sen, 1983] are interested in the $1|d_i, nmit|F(E_i, T_i)$ problem with $F(E_i, T_i) = \sum_{i=1}^{n}(E_i + T_i)^2$. To solve it they propose a branch-and-bound procedure where each node is evaluated by a lower bound which is calculated using the SPT rule and a neighbouring algorithm. Secondly, an heuristic is presented. This heuristic is the branch-and-bound algorithm in which certain nodes are not explored. The choice of non explored nodes is made according to the following step: consider a constant $Y \geq 0$ and x_k the number of nodes generated to obtain the kth complete sequence (corresponding to a leaf of the tree). The heuristic terminates the exploration of the tree when $x_{k+1} \geq Yx_k$. Some experimental results show that the heuristic is very successful (in both quality and time).
[Bagchi et al., 1987b] are interested in this problem when all the jobs have the same due date which has to be determined. The problem obtained is denoted by $1|d_i = d, nmit|F(E_i,\ T_i)$. Two cases can be distinguished, *i.e.* the problem with $d \geq \sum_{i=1}^{n} p_i$ (non restrictive case) and the problem with $d < \sum_{i=1}^{n} p_i$ (restrictive case). For each case a branch-and-bound procedure which calculates the optimal schedule and due date is proposed. Dominance conditions are also presented and they allow the second problem to be solved efficiently. Gupta and Sen show that in the case where $d = \frac{1}{n}\sum_{i=1}^{n} p_i$ their algorithm is faster than that proposed by [Eilon and Chowdhury, 1977].

- [Dileepan and Sen, 1991] consider in the $1|d_i, nmit|F(\overline{E}, \overline{T},\ \overline{C})$ problem with $F(\overline{E}, \overline{T}, \overline{C}) = (1-\alpha)\sum_{i=1}^{n}(L_i^2) + \alpha\overline{C}$ and propose a branch-and-bound procedure. Experimental results show that their algorithm is faster than that of [Gupta and Sen, 1983] who solve the $1|d_i|\sum_{i=1}^{n}(L_i^2)$ problem.
- [Bagchi et al., 1987a] study the $1|d_i = d, nmit|F_\ell(\sum E_i^2,\ \sum T_i^2)$ problem and distinguish restrictive and non restrictive problems, *i.e.* problems for which $d \geq \sum_{i=1}^{n} p_i$ and $d < \sum_{i=1}^{n} p_i$. In the case of each problem they propose a branch-and-bound procedure which takes into account dominance conditions

to prune nodes in the search tree. Some experimental results are also presented.

• Accounting for a criterion linked to the storage costs of semi-finished products is studied by [Fry et al., 1987b] who are interested in the $1|d_i|F_\ell(\overline{C},\overline{T},\overline{E})$ problem. This problem is $\mathcal{NP}$-hard because the $1|d_i|\overline{T}$ problem is also. They propose a branch-and-bound procedure which uses dominance conditions at each node of the search tree. Besides, the insertion of idle times between each job is realised by solving a linear program. This model, denoted by EFLR1, is presented in figure 5.33. It is solved at each node of the tree by considering only jobs which have already been sequenced. Experimental results show that the branch-and-bound procedure solves problems with up to 15 jobs.

Mathematical formulation EFLR1	
Data:	n, the number of jobs, α, β, γ, the criteria weights, $s(i)$, $i = 1, ..., n$, the number of the job in position i, p_i, $i = 1, ..., n$, the processing time of job J_i, d_i, $i = 1, ..., n$, the due date of job J_i.
Variables:	δ_i, i=1,...,n, length of the idle time inserted before job J_i , C_i, $i = 1, ..., n$, the completion time of job J_i, E_i, $i = 1, ..., n$, the earliness of job J_i, T_i, $i = 1, ..., n$, the tardiness of job J_i.
Objective:	Minimise $\sum_{i=1}^{n}(\alpha E_{s(i)} + \beta T_{s(i)} + \gamma C_{s(i)})$
Constraints:	$C_{s(i)} - T_{(s(i-1)} + E_{s(i-1)} - \delta_{s(i)} = d_{s(i-1)} + p_{s(i)}, \forall i = 1, ..., n$ $-C_{s(i)} + T_{s(i)} - E_{s(i)} = -d_{s(i)}, \forall i = 1, ..., n$ $T_{s(0)} = E_{s(0)} = \delta_{s(0)} = 0$ $E_{s(i)} \geq 0, \forall i = 1, ..., n$ $T_{s(i)} \geq 0, \forall i = 1, ..., n$ $\delta_{s(i)} \geq 0, \forall i = 1, ..., n$

Fig. 5.33. A mathematical model for the calculation of start times for the $1|d_i|F_\ell(\overline{C},\overline{T},\overline{E})$ problem

5.7 Open problems

Few JiT scheduling problems have an open complexity and often we are concerned with very particular problems.

5.7.1 The $Q|d_i = d\ unknown, nmit|F_\ell(\overline{E},\overline{T})$ problem

[Emmons, 1987] is interested in a Just-in-Time scheduling problem where the machines M_j have different processing speeds denoted by k_j. The time necessary to process job J_i on M_j is $\frac{p_i}{k_j}$. The complexity of this problem is open.

The objective function $F_\ell(\overline{E},\overline{T}) = \alpha\overline{E} + \beta\overline{T}$ can be rewritten in the form $\sum_{j=1}^{m}(\sum_{e=1}^{v_j}\alpha \times (e-1)\frac{p_{[e],j}}{k_j} + \sum_{e=1}^{u_j}\beta \times e\frac{p_{[n-e+1],j}}{k_j})$ with v_j the number of early and on-time jobs assigned to M_j, u_j the number of tardy jobs assigned to M_j and $p_{[e],j}$ the processing time of the job assigned to position e on M_j. The common due date d is then defined by $d = \max_{j=1,\ldots,m}(\sum_{e=1}^{v_j}\frac{p_{[e],j}}{k_j})$. The algorithm proposed by Emmons, denoted by HEM3, solves the problem by considering the jobs in decreasing order of their processing time and by assigning them to the machines, in such a way as to load them in proportion to their processing speed. This algorithm is a generalisation of the algorithm EEM1 which solves the problem on identical machines. The algorithm HEM3 is presented in figure 5.35.

Example.
We consider a problem for which $n = 10$, $m = 2$, $\alpha = 4$ and $\beta = 1$.

i	1	2	3	4	5	6	7	8	9	10
p_i	20	18	16	14	12	10	8	6	4	2

j	1	2
k_j	3	1

(i) $A_1 = (J_1),\ A_2 = (J_2),\ R_1 = \emptyset,\ R_2 = \emptyset$.
(ii) $\ell_1 = 1,\ \ell_2 = 1$
$A_1 = (J_1, J_3),\ A_2 = (J_2),\ R_1 = \emptyset,\ R_2 = \emptyset$.
(iii) $\ell_1 = 2,\ \ell_2 = 1$
$A_1 = (J_1, J_3),\ A_2 = (J_2, J_4),\ R_1 = \emptyset,\ R_2 = \emptyset$.
(iv) $\ell_1 = 1,\ \ell_2 = 1$
$A_1 = (J_1, J_3),\ A_2 = (J_2, J_4),\ R_1 = (J_5),\ R_2 = \emptyset$.
(v) $\ell_1 = 1,\ \ell_2 = 2$
$A_1 = (J_1, J_3),\ A_2 = (J_2, J_4),\ R_1 = (J_5),\ R_2 = (J_6)$.
(vi) After the last iteration of the algorithm we obtain:
$A_1 = (J_1, J_3),\ A_2 = (J_2, J_4),\ R_1 = (J_9, J_7, J_5),\ R_2 = (J_{10}, J_8, J_6)$.
(vii) $d = \max(36/3; 32/1) = 32$. We obtain the schedule presented in figure 5.34.

5.7.2 Other problems

• [Adamopoulos and Pappis, 1996] tackle the $1|d_i\ unknown, nmit|F_\ell(\overline{E}^\alpha,\overline{T}^\beta)$ problem. They consider moreover that the weights of earliness and tardiness are functions of job processing times. To solve this problem, they propose four branch-and-bound procedures. Each of these is adapted to a particular definition of the weights. The due dates d_i are calculated according to the model SLK.

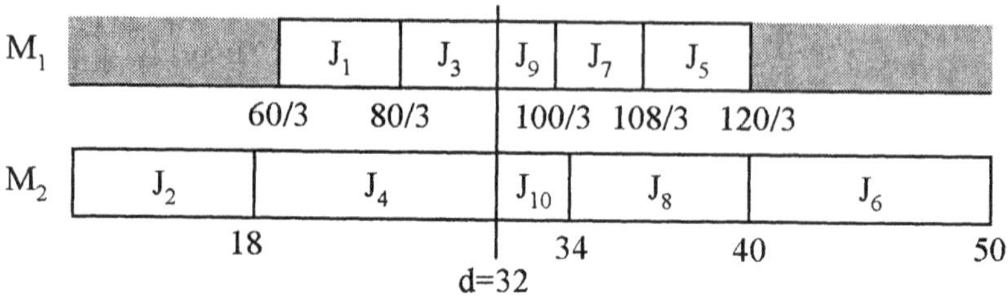

$F_\ell(\overline{E}, \overline{T}) = 344/3$

Fig. 5.34. The schedule calculated by the algorithm HEM3

ALGORITHM HEM3

/* We assume that $p_1 \geq \ldots \geq p_n$ */
/* A_j is the list of early jobs on M_j */
/* R_j is the list of tardy jobs on M_j */
<u>Step 1:</u> /* We compute the lists A_j and R_j */
<u>For</u> $i = 1$ <u>to</u> n <u>Do</u>
  <u>If</u> $(i \leq m)$ <u>Then</u>
    /* Job J_i the first one scheduled on M_i */
    $A_i = \{J_i\}$; $R_i = \emptyset$;
  <u>Else</u>
    Let ℓ_1 be such that $\alpha(|A_{\ell_1}| - 1)/k_{\ell_1} = \min_{\ell=1,\ldots,m}(\alpha(|A_\ell| - 1)/k_\ell)$;
    Let ℓ_2 be such that $\beta|R_{\ell_2}|/k_{\ell_2} = \min_{\ell=1,\ldots,m}(\beta|R_\ell|/k_\ell)$;
    <u>If</u> $(\alpha(|A_{\ell_1}| - 1)/k_{\ell_1} \leq \beta|R_{\ell_2}|/k_{\ell_2})$ <u>Then</u>
      /* Job J_i is scheduled early on M_{ℓ_1} */
      $A_{\ell_1} = A_{\ell_1}//\{J_i\}$;
    <u>Else</u>
      /* Job J_i is scheduled tardy on M_{ℓ_2} */
      $R_{\ell_2} = \{J_i\}//R_{\ell_2}$;
    <u>End If</u>
  <u>End If</u>
<u>End For</u>
<u>Step 2:</u> /* We schedule the lists */
$d = \max_{j=1,\ldots,m}(\sum_{e=1}^{v_j} \frac{p_{[e],j}}{k_j})$;
All the sequences R_j start at time $t = d$;
<u>For</u> $j = 1$ <u>to</u> m <u>Do</u>
  A_j starts at time $t = d - \sum_{k=1}^{|A_j|} p_{A_j[k]}/k_j$;
<u>End For</u>
<u>Step 3:</u> <u>Print</u> the resulting schedule, $\alpha\overline{E} + \beta\overline{T}$ and d;

[Emmons, 1987]

Fig. 5.35. An heuristic algorithm for the $Q|d_i = d$ *unknown*, $nmit|F_\ell(\overline{E}, \overline{T})$ problem

• Minimisation of the largest deviation between the algebraic lateness leads to the determination of a JiT schedule. The $1|d_i, nmit|\ F_\ell(L_{max}, L_{min})$ problem with $F_\ell(L_{max}, L_{min}) = L_{max} - L_{min}$ and $L_{min} = \min_{i=1,\ldots,n}(L_i)$ is treated by [Gupta and Sen, 1984]. They only consider the set of semi-active schedules which is not dominant for this problem and propose a branch-and-bound procedure to solve it. An improvement of the bounds used in this problem is proposed by [Tegze and Vlach, 1988].
[Liao and Huang, 1991] propose for this problem an algorithm in $O(n^2\overline{p}\log(n))$ time where $\overline{p} = \sum_{i=1}^{n} p_i$. The special feature of this algorithm is in the fact that it concerns an a posteriori algorithm for the $1|d_i, nmit|\epsilon(-L_{min}/L_{max})$ problem which chooses among the calculated solutions the strict Pareto optimum which minimises $L_{max} - L_{min}$.
Accounting for a criterion linked to the the work-in-process minimisation is studied by [Sen et al., 1988] who are interested in the $1|d_i, nmit|F_\ell(\overline{C}, L_{max} - L_{min})$ problem. They propose a branch-and-bound procedure to enumerate the set of strict Pareto optima. Given that a convex combination is minimised, this algorithm only determines the set of supported strict Pareto optima. Experimental results which are presented show that for a problem with 9 jobs the average number of supported strict Pareto optima is between 5.2 and 8.3 for an average computation time between 2.4 and 38.1 seconds.

6. Robustness considerations

6.1 Introduction to flexibility and robustness in scheduling

Scheduling is generally seen as a function with known inputs. For instance, the set of available machines is supposed to be known and the processing times of operations are supposed to be fixed. The model used for solving the problem is supposed to be the most suitable model – even if it is often a model corresponding to a simplified version of the problem ([McKay et al., 1998]). However, it is well known that *real-word scheduling problems usually are very different from the mathematical models studied by researchers in academia* ([Pinedo, 1995]).
Sometimes, the scheduler does not take care of the real application of its schedule, because this schedule is only used for simulating reasons. But in a real-world context, jobs arrive continuously, machines can break down, operators may be absent, critical tools may already been used, raw materials deliveries can be delayed, preferences of operators are not taken into account, processing times are not perfectly known, etc. When the schedule has to be applied the probability to process this schedule exactly as planned is very low.
In such a context, it is clear that decision makers have to react in real time to modify the proposed schedule, in order to always have a feasible solution and the notion of "quality" of a schedule can be discussed. The quality of a schedule is valid before the schedule becomes on line, but on line, the problem is to maintain a feasible solution, without blocking problems and if possible with a good quality. We can notice that an optimal schedule can be modified very quickly in a real time context, and can lead finally to a very bad solution, if this apparently optimal schedule was very sensitive to the perturbations that occur. On the other hand, a schedule with a "not so bad" value of the objective function may lead to a "not so bad" solution even after some unexpected events, if it was not too sensitive to the perturbations. This is the reason why searching for a compromise between the quality and the robustness of a schedule takes all the sense.

When the scheduler does not take uncertainty into account when building a solution, the proposed solution is called a *predictive* schedule and the solution approach a *predictive* approach. In order to deal with uncertainty, [Davenport and Beck, 2000] separate solution approaches into two categories: *proactive* approaches that take account of some knowledge of uncertainty, and *reactive* approaches for which the schedule is revised in real time, each time an unexpected event occurs. [Herroelen and Leus, 2005] distinguish five approaches in project scheduling, considering also stochastic scheduling, scheduling under fuziness and sensitivity analysis as possible approaches.
The aim of proactive scheduling is to make the schedule more *robust*. Several definitions ([Davenport and Beck, 2000]) have been proposed for robustness in the literature. Among others, [Billaut et al., 2005] state that *a schedule is robust if its quality is little sensitive to data uncertainties and to unexpected events*, and for [Leon et al., 1994] *a robust schedule is one that is likely valid under a wide variety of disturbances.* [Davenport and Beck, 2000] conclude that when dealing with uncertainty, *it is very likely to employ both proactive and reactive techniques.*
Robustness is related to *flexibility*, that can be seen as a freedom given in real time to the decision maker, allowing him to repair the schedule if an unexpected event or a non modeled constraint makes it infeasible. Flexibility can take several aspects ([Billaut et al., 2005]). The *temporal flexibility* allows a decision maker to start an operation earlier or latter, the *sequencing flexibility* allows the decision maker to modify or to define its own sequence of operations on a machine, the *assignment flexibility* allows to modify the assignment of an operation to another resource and finally the *mode flexibility* allows to modify the execution mode of an operation (overlapping, preemption, setup considerations, etc.) in real time.

When considering robust scheduling problems, one difficulty is to define a measure of the robustness or of the flexibility that is proposed in real time. Some approaches in the literature associate two measures to a schedule: a measure for the robustness or the flexibility, that has to be maximized and a measure for the quality of a schedule. The measure of the quality is generally a classical objective function in scheduling like makespan or maximum lateness. We focus in this chapter on the approaches in the literature dealing with robustness and consider more than one criterion. Other approaches dealing with a single criterion concerning robustness, flexibility, or stability are not presented here. The interested reader can refer to the more recent surveys of [Aytug et al., 2005] and [Herroelen and Leus, 2005].

Some of the approaches presented in this chapter propose sequential flexibility by characterizing a set of solutions. Since these approaches does not explicitly make any assumption on which uncertainties are considered and how, they are not really "proactive methods". But since the aim of these methods is to propose to the decision maker some possible decisions related to the sequence of operations, respecting a given quality of the final solution, and with the concern to provide robustness, these methods are not only "predictive" ones. Section 6.2 presents approaches that aim at characterizing a set of solutions for some scheduling problems. Section 6.3 presents approaches that deal with single machine problems. Section 6.4 focuses on flowshop and jobshop problems whilst Section 6.5 deals with resource constrained project scheduling problems.

6.2 Approaches that introduce sequential flexibility

6.2.1 Groups of permutable operations

[Artigues et al., 2005] consider a general shop scheduling problem where n operations have to be scheduled on m machines, m_i denotes the machine allocated to the processing of operation O_i. Each operation O_i has a release date r_i and a due date d_i and there are precedence relations between some pairs of operations. Instead of a sequence of operations, the authors associate to each machine a sequence of groups of operations where the operations within a group are totally permutable ([Erschler and Roubellat, 1989]). Hence, the problem is to assign each operation to mutually exclusive ordered groups, so-called the ordered group assignment problem. An ordered group assignment, denoted by Π, defines on each machine M_k, a sequence $g_{k,1},\ldots,g_{k,\nu_k}$ of ν_k groups where $\nu_k \leq n_k$, the number of operations processed on M_k verifying $\bigcup_{\tau=1}^{\nu_k} g_{k,\tau} = \{O_i | m_i = M_k\}$ and $\bigcap_{\tau=1}^{\nu_k} g_{k,\tau} = \emptyset$.
Let $g(i)$ denote the group that contains operation O_i. We have $|g(i)| \geq 1$. We assume that on each machine M_k, any operation belonging to a group $g_{k,\tau}$ has to start after the completion of any operation belonging to group $g_{k,\tau-1}$. In terms of the disjunctive graph, this means that all disjunctive arcs are oriented from $g_{k,\tau-1}$ to $g_{k,\tau}$.
Let us consider an example with 8 operations: $1 \prec 2$, $3 \prec 4$, $5 \prec 6$ and $7 \prec 8$; operations 1, 3, 6 and 8 are processed on machine M_1, operations 2, 4, 5 and 7 are processed on machine M_2; all the processing times are unitary, all the release dates are equal to 0 and all the due dates are equal to 4.
The sequence of groups that is represented in figure 6.1 enables to characterize 16 schedules, without enumerating them: for any order of the operations inside each group, the precedence constraints and the due dates are answered.

To evaluate a given ordered group assigment Π, a worst-case earliest completion time is associated to each operation. The worst-case earliest completion time $\underline{C}_i^{\Pi}$ is the maximum earliest completion time of operation O_i among all the semi-active schedules characterized by Π. Artigues et al. show that all the worst case earliest completion times can be determined by longest path

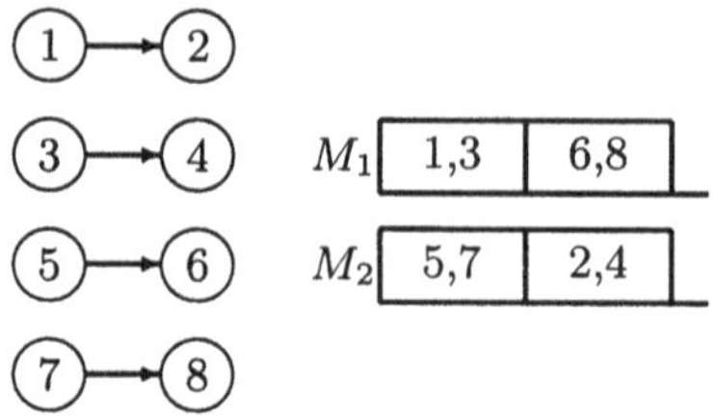

Fig. 6.1. Example of a sequence of groups

computations in a graph associated with an ordered group assignment. They provide the steps to build this graph.

The flexibility of an ordered group assignment is intuitively related to the total number of groups, denoted by $\#Gps$. They also propose, as a measure of flexibility, the number of characterized sequences, denoted by $\#Seq$. The quality of an ordered group assignment is given by the quality of the worst characterized schedule. Thus, if the flexibility increases (the number of groups decreases), the number of characterized sequences increases and the quality of the worst characterized schedule decreases. In practice, it is necessary to reach a compromise between the proposed flexibility and the quality of the worst characterized solution. To tackle this multicriteria scheduling problem, the authors use the ϵ-constraint approach assuming that the objective is to maximize the flexibility, respecting a threshold value on the quality.

The authors propose some algorithms for single machine problems. For solving jobshop problems, a branch-and-bound algorithm is used to optimally solve the classical $J||C_{max}$ problem. Then, a heuristic algorithm is proposed to build groups on machines, starting from the known optimal solution, *i.e.* given the optimal sequence of jobs on each machine. A maximum deviation Δ on the makespan value is given, which leads to the definition of deadlines for all jobs and then algorithms for single machine problems are used iteratively. Artigues et al. notice that for problems with $n > m$, a high level of flexibility can be reached for an acceptable increase of the worst case makespan.

[Esswein et al., 2005] tackle three classical two-machine shop problems: the $F2||C_{max}$, the $J2||C_{max}$ and the $O2||C_{max}$ problems. A measure for the flexibility is proposed:

$$\phi = \frac{2n - \#Gps}{2n - 2}$$

so that if all the operations are assigned to the same group, the flexibility is equal to 100% (one group per machine), and if there is only one operation per group (no flexibility), ϕ is equal to 0%. The authors search for a compromise between the flexibility and the worst characterized schedule.

Heuristic algorithms with interesting worst-case performance ratio are proposed to solve these problems. For the flowshop problem, one interesting result is that a heuristic algorithm enables to provide high flexibility even if the upper bound on the quality is set to the optimal makespan value.

The presented concept of ordered group assignment is equivalent to the concept of ordered assignment introduced by [Wu et al., 1999].
It can be noticed that this concept of groups of permutable operations has been implemented in a real time workshop scheduling software package ORDO^R, used now in more than 60 companies ([Billaut and Roubellat, 1996]).

6.2.2 Partial order between operations

[Aloulou, 2002] considers a single machine environment where release times are associated to the operations. In order to propose not only a single solution to the decision maker, but a set of solutions, Aloulou proposes to characterize a set of solutions S by a partial order between operations. Two criteria are associated to measure the quality of a partial order. Since it is not possible to enumerate all the characterized solutions, only the quality of the best characterized solution and of the worst characterized solution for both criteria are determined ([Aloulou et al., 2004]). We denote by $Z_k^{\min}(S)$ and $Z_k^{\max}(S)$ the value of the best and the worst characterized solution for criterion Z_k, $1 \leq k \leq 2$.
Finally, the performance of a partial order between operations is a function of these four parameters plus the coordinates of the utopian point (minimimum of each criterion when considered separately, denoted by Z_1^* and Z_2^*). Figure 6.2 illustrates the definition of the quality of a set of solutions.

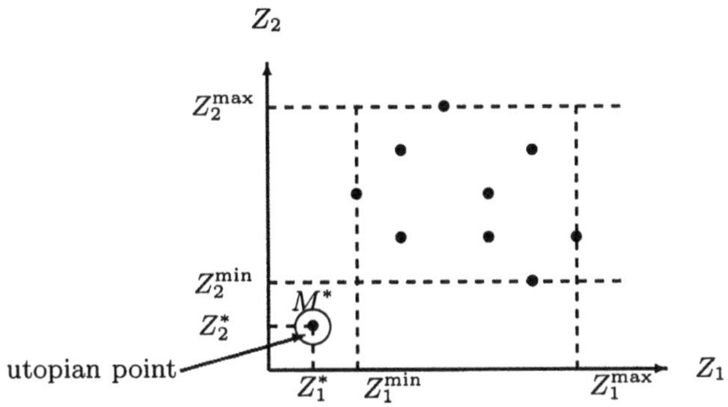

Fig. 6.2. Quality of a set of solutions characterized by a partial order of operations

A measure of the performance of a solution S is given by the following relations.

$$D(S) = \alpha D_1(S) + (1-\alpha)D_2(S)$$

$$D_k(S) = \beta_k \frac{Z_k^{\min}(S)}{Z_k^*} + (1-\beta_k)\frac{Z_k^{\max}(S)}{Z_k^*}, \forall k, 1 \leq k \leq 2$$

with α and β_k real parameters belonging to the interval $[0,1]$.
The smaller the value $D(S)$ the best the solution S.

The ideal measure of the sequential flexibility is the number of characterized solutions, *i.e.* the number of "linear extensions of a partially ordered set", but this problem is #P-complete as shown by [Brightwell and Winkler, 1991]. Thus, Aloulou measures the sequential flexibility by the number of non-oriented edges in the transitive graph representing the partial order, i.e. the number of non fixed precedences. This measure is denoted by $Z_{seqflex}$. As a measure for the temporal flexibility, Aloulou proposes to compute the mean slack, where the slack is determined with the worst possible starting time for each operation. This measure is denoted by $Z_{tempflex}$.
[Aloulou, 2002] provides a genetic algorithm to find solutions that minimize a linear combination of $D(S)$, $Z_{seqflex}$ and $Z_{tempflex}$.

[Policella, 2005a, Policella, 2005b] considers a resource constrained project scheduling problem with minimum and maximum time lags. The aim is to propose a set of solutions with an implicit and compact representation of this set. The author introduces a partial order schedule ($\mathcal{POS}$), *i.e.* a set of feasible solutions to a scheduling problem that can be represented by a graph with the activity on nodes and with arcs to represent the constraints between activities, such that any "time feasible" schedule defined by the graph is also a "feasible" schedule. The makespan of a $\mathcal{POS}$ is defined as the makespan of its earliest start schedule, where each activity is scheduled to start at its earliest start time.

Some metrics are proposed to compare $\mathcal{POS}$ [Policella et al., 2004]. Two metrics give an evaluation of the flexibility and one measure gives an evaluation of the stability of the solutions found.
The first measure for evaluating the flexibility is $Z_{seqflex}$ (as defined in [Aloulou and Portmann, 2003]). The second metric is based on the slacks associated to the activities:

$$Z_{slackflex} = 100 \times \sum_{i \neq j} \frac{|d(C_j, t_i) - d(C_i, t_j)|}{H \times n \times (n-1)}$$

with t_i and C_i the starting time and the completion time of activity i, H the horizon time and n the number of activities. $d(t1, t2)$ is the distance between the two time points t_1 and t_2. This metric characterizes the fluidity of a

solution, i.e. its availability to absord temporal variation in the execution of activities. The higher the value of $Z_{slackflex}$ the higher the probability of localized changes.
To measure the stability, [Policella et al., 2004] introduce a third measure, called disruptibility, denoted by Z_{disrup} and defined by:

$$Z_{disrup} = \frac{1}{n}\sum_{i=1}^{n} \frac{sl_i}{num(i, \Delta_i)}$$

with sl_i the slack of activity i (difference between latest and earliest starting times) and $num(i, \Delta_i)$ a function that returns the number of activities that are shifted in the process if activity i is shifted to the right for Δ_i time units. For solving the problem, [Policella et al., 2004] propose several heuristic algorithms. The more efficient is called the two-step ESTA^C procedure (for Earliest Start Time Algorithm with a post processing phase), that first computes a solution and then translates it into a flexible $\mathcal{POS}$.

6.2.3 Interval structures

[La, 2005] considers the $1|r_i, d_i|L_{max}$ problem and aims at proposing a set of solutions to the decision maker. An interval $[r_i, d_i]$ is associated to each operation O_i and an interval structure is defined based on [Allen, 1981]'s relations. Let us consider two intervals A and B, *during(A,B)* is true if and only if $r_B < r_A \leq d_A < d_B$. A top of an interval structure is an interval T such that for all A, Allens' relation *during(A,T)* never holds. Given a top T_α, a T-pyramid P_α is a set of intervals A such that *during(T,A)* holds.
[Erschler et al., 1983] show that a set of dominant sequences is composed by sequences such that:

- the tops of intervals are sequenced in the r_i increasing order (d_i in case of equality),
- before the first top of interval, are sequenced the operations that belong to the first T-pyramid in the r_i non decreasing order,
- after the last top of interval, are sequenced the operations that belong to the last T-pyramid in the d_i non decreasing order,
- between two tops T_k and T_{k+1} are sequenced first the operations that belong to P_k and not to P_{k+1} in the d_i non decreasing order ; then the operations that belong to $P_k \cap P_{k+1}$ in an arbitrary order ; and finally the operations that belong to P_{k+1} but not to P_k, in the r_i non decreasing order.

Figure 6.3 illustrates an interval structure for the following example: $n = 6$ operations, release dates $r = (2, 1, 0, 6, 4, 8)$, due dates $d = (3, 5, 10, 7, 9, 11)$. The tops of this interval structure are operations $T_1 = 1$, $T_2 = 4$ and $T_3 = 6$, and the T-pyramids are $P_1 = \{2, 3\}$, $P_2 = \{3, 5\}$ and $P_3 = \emptyset$. This interval structure characterizes the following sequences: (3,2,1,5,4,6), (3,2,1,4,5,6),

(3,1,2,5,4,6), (3,1,2,4,5,6), (2,1,3,5,4,6), (2,1,3,4,5,6), (1,2,3,5,4,6), (1,2,3,4,5,6), (2,1,5,4,3,6), (2,1,4,5,3,6), (1,2,5,4,3,6), and (1,2,4,5,3,6).

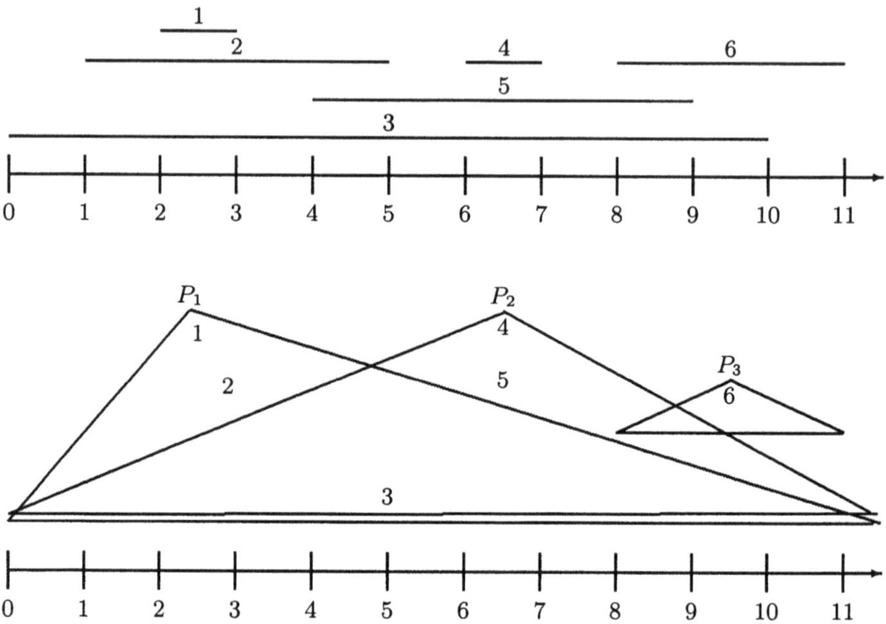

Fig. 6.3. Illustration of an interval structure

La proposes one measure for the flexibility and two measures for the quality. The flexibility is equal to the number of characterized sequences, which is equal to $\prod_{q=1}^{P}(q+1)^{n_q}$ with P the number of pyramids and n_q the number of operations different from a top, that belong exactly to q pyramids. For the example, $\prod_{q=1}^{P}(q+1)^{n_q} = (1+1)^2 \times (2+1)^1 \times (3+1)^0 = 4 \times 3 \times 1 = 12$ sequences.

Two measures are associated to each operation: its best possible lateness and its worst possible lateness, both computed in $O(n \log n)$. The quality of a set of solutions is measured by the maximum of the best possible lateness for all the operations, denoted by $\max(L_j^{\min})$ and by the worst possible lateness, denoted by $\max(L_j^{\max})$.

A branch-and-bound algorithm is proposed to characterize a set of solutions. Problems with 100 operations are solved in less than two seconds on the average, and enable to characterize up to 10^{12} sequences.

A base of an interval structure is an interval B such that for all A, Allen's relation *during(B,A)* never holds. Given a base B_α, a b-pyramid P_α related to B_α is the set of intervals A such that *during(A,B)*$_\alpha$ holds. [Briand et al., 2005] use the concept of b-pyramid to characterize a subset of optimal sequences for the $F2||C_{max}$ problem. Two interval structures are defined: an interval structure with the jobs such that $p_{i,1} \leq p_{i,2}$: an interval $[p_{i,1}, p_{i,2}]$ is associated to these jobs; and an interval structure with the jobs such that $p_{i,1} \geq p_{i,2}$: an interval $[p_{i,2}, p_{i,1}]$ is associated to these jobs. A huge number of solutions are characterized in polynomial time, including all the Johnson's sequences.

This characterization can be considered as robust since the interval structures do not change if the relative order of the processing times $p_{i,1}$, $p_{i,2}$ remains unchanged.

6.3 Single machine problems

6.3.1 Stability *vs* makespan

[Wu et al., 1993] address the problem of rescheduling jobs after a disruption has occurred on the single machine of the system. Heads and tails are associated to each operation. As a consequence of this disruption, a particular operation has an additional and unforeseen processing time. Two conflicting scheduling objectives are considered: (1) to minimize the makespan and (2) at the same time to minimize the system impact due to the disruption.
The authors assume that the machine returns to service at time t_0. A subset of jobs denoted by N' have to be rescheduled. The original schedule is denoted by S_0.

The makespan criterion is obtained by totally rescheduling the jobs of N', after an updating of ready times: $r_i = \max(r_i, t_0)$, for any operation i of N'. A new schedule S_m is computed by using the algorithm of [Carlier, 1982].
Two measures are proposed for the system impact criterion. In order to minimize the deviation from the original sequence, operations of N' are right-shifted, using up idle times each time it is possible. We denote by S_r the right-shift schedule.
The first measure for the system impact criterion is the average absolute start time differences from the original schedule S_0. We denote by t_i the starting time of operation i in the first schedule and t_i'' in the new schedule S. The total start-time deviation is given by:

$$D_0(S) = \sum_{i \in N'} |t_i'' - t_i|$$

The second measure is based on the right-shift schedule S_r. The total start-time deviation is given by:

$$D_r(S) = \sum_{i \in N'} |t_i'' - t_i'|$$

The authors search for the set of efficient schedules and use a linear combination of criteria to explore the frontier. They propose two sets of local search heuristics: pairwise swapping methods and local search based on genetic algorithms. All these methods are comparable in terms of quality, but one pairwise swapping method requires the least computation time. Results show that the stability can be improved significantly with little sacrifice in efficiency (measured by the makespan).

6.3.2 Robust evaluation *vs* distance to a baseline solution

[Sevaux and Sorensen, 2004] study a single machine problem in which the objective is to minimize the total weighted number of late jobs, denoted by $1|r_j|\overline{U}$. They propose a genetic algorithm to solve this problem in its standard version, thus using a fitness value $f(S)$ equal to the sum of the weights of the late jobs in solution S. This evaluation is called "the quality of a solution":

$$f(S) = \sum_{j=1}^{n} w_j U_j$$

Then, they propose to obtain robust schedules. Assuming that the solution S has been obtained with problem data P, that represents the characteristics of the jobs, the fitness can be denoted by $f(S, P)$. The solution S is implemented on a modified set of data, denoted by P_i, and evaluated by $f(S, P_i)$. A weight c_i is associated to the set of data P_i according to its importance and m denotes the number of derived data sets to evaluate.
The fitness function is replaced by a "robust evaluation function" denoted by $f^*(S)$ and defined by:

$$f^*(S) = \frac{1}{m} \sum_{i=1}^{m} c_i f(S, P_i)$$

This function measures the quality robustness. The robustness of a solution is defined by the authors as "a property of a solution that is similar to a given baseline solution x^0, *i.e.* for which the distance to the baseline solution is small". The distance between two schedules can be interpreted as the number of changes that have to be made to the first schedule to turn it into the second one, a change being an insertion of a job into the schedule, a deletion of a job or the substitution of a job by another one.
The robustness of a solution is measured by two objectives: the quality robustness and a small distance to the initial solution. The decision maker searches for a compromise solution for these two measures. The genetic algorithm proposed by Sevaux and Sorensen generates non dominated solutions that improve both criteria iteratively.

6.4 Flowshop and jobshop problems

6.4.1 Average makespan of a neighbourhood

[Jensen and Hansen, 1999] consider a jobshop environment with makespan minimization. They define the neighbourhood of a jobshop schedule s, denoted by $\mathcal{N}(s)$, as the set of all the feasible schedules that can be created from s by interchanging two consecutive operations on the same machine. Notice that $s \in \mathcal{N}(s)$. The robustness of a schedule s, denoted by $R(s)$, is defined by a weighted average makespan of the schedules in the neighbourhood of s. The weight function $w(s, s')$ reflects the expected probabilities of encountering schedule s' in $\mathcal{N}(s)$. The robustness of schedule s is defined by

$$R(s) = \sum_{s' \in \mathcal{N}(s)} w(s, s') C_{max}(s')$$

This objective function can be seen as the agregation of the criteria of the makespan of neighbour schedules, including the makespan of s, that is also to minimize.
Jensen and Hansen propose a genetic algorithm to solve the problem. When the fitness is evaluated, the makespan is calculated for the original schedule s, and for a number of its neighbours. The objective value on which the fitness is based is set to the mean of these calculated makespans. The acceptance of new individuals is defined as follows. Individual s is replaced by its offspring o if $C_{max}(o) < C_{max}(s) + (C_{max}(s) - LB)\delta$, with LB a trivial lower bound and $\delta < 1$ a given value.
Tests are conducted on classical instances of the jobshop literature: some instances of [Lawrence, 1984] and the well-known instance FT10 of [Fischer and Thompson, 1963]. Jensen and Hansen show that it is possible to limit the number of makespan evaluations by choosing a random subset of neighbours in $\mathcal{N}(s)$, and to obtain robust solutions in a more reasonable computation time.

6.4.2 Sensitivity of operations *vs* makespan

[Kawata et al., 2003] consider the classical jobshop problem referred to as $J||C_{max}$. They notice that in general, many minimum makespan schedules exist and they propose to select the best solution among the optimal ones. They assume that the optimal makespan value is known and they consider only active schedules. The authors denote by E_j the sensitivity of operation j, and by W_j the set of operations which start time will be delayed if the completion time of operation O_j is delayed by one time unit. The sensitivity is defined by $E_j = |W_j|$.

The robustness of a schedule is defined by $R = \max_{\forall O_j} E_j$. This definition implies that the smaller the value of R the more robust the associated schedule. The authors propose a branch-and-bound algorithm to find a schedule with an optimal makespan value and then with an optimal robustness value, *i.e.* they solve the $J||Lex(C_{max}, R)$ problem. The proposed method can only solve problems with up to 10 jobs and 5 machines.

6.5 Resource Constrained Project Scheduling Problems (RCPSP)

Concerning robust and reactive resource constrained project scheduling problems, [Herroelen and Leus, 2004] propose a review and a classification of the procedures. Two types of robustness measures are presented: the *solution robustness*, related to the insensitivity of the activity start times to changes in the input data; and the *quality robustness*, related to the insensitivity of the schedule performance. However, most of the described approaches focus on a single criterion.

6.5.1 Quality in project scheduling *vs* makespan

[Icmeli-Tukel and Rom, 1997] explain that most of the studies in RCPSP literature consider as an objective function the makespan minimization or the Net Present Value maximization. They notice that *the problems decision makers are facing are more complicated than those studied in the project scheduling literature.* They indicate that generally, the objective is to maximize the quality, where the quality is measured by the degree to which a project's outcome conforms to the customer's requirements and the degree to which the project completes within budget and on schedule. Their objective is then to eliminate the reworking associated with incorrectly completed activities.

Icmeli-Tukel and Rom explain that many activities of a project need to be totally or partially reworked to achieve the full customer satisfaction. This rework requires additional resources, usually in the form of overtime, that is more expensive than regular time. This creates an additional cost called the reworked cost. Of course, the rework can also have some impacts on the project duration. They consider that the total amount of reworked time and of reworked cost are bounded. They propose two mixed integer linear programs, that are solved by using OSL software. The objective function is defined by $Z = Q_1 + Q_2$, where Q_1 and Q_2 represent the proportion of the total reworked time used and of the total reworked cost used, respectively. These variables cannot really be considered as criteria, gathered into a linear combination since they are not conflicting. The computational experiments conducted by the authors show that one model performs better than the other.

[Haouari and Fawzan, 2002] tackle the same problem. They define the quality of a schedule by three factors: the performance, the conformance to specifications and the robustness of the design. They consider that the performance is indicated in the makespan measure of the schedule. The conformance to specifications consists in respecting activities requirements, resource capacities and precedence constraints. The robustness of the design is *the degree to which the planned schedule could be achieved as intended even if undesirable conditions occur.*
Haouari and Al-Fawzan define the robustness of a schedule as its ability to cope with small increases in the duration of some activities. The problem is modeled as a bi-objective problem. They define sl_i as the slack of activity O_i, *i.e.* the amount of time an activity can slip without causing a project duration increase. A weight w_i is associated to each activity and the robustness of a schedule is given by $R = \sum_{O_i \in \Omega} w_i sl_i$, with Ω the set of activities. The γ-field of the problem notation is (R, C_{max}) with R to maximize and C_{max} to minimize. The authors propose several versions of a Tabu search algorithm to approximate the set of efficient solutions.

6.5.2 Stability *vs* makespan

[Van de Vonder et al., 2005] propose a heuristic to generate stable solutions to the RCPSP. A weight w_i is associated to each activity O_i. This weight denotes a relative cost of starting the activity one time unit earlier or later. Stability is measured as the weighted sum of deviations between planned and actual activity start times. Instead of building a semi-active schedule, generating stable schedules consists in introducing idle times between activities, in order to absord uncertainty during the process, like a duration increase.
The proposed solution procedure works as follows. The problem is solved to optimality for makespan minimization, using the branch-and-bound presented by [Demeulemeester and Herroelen, 2002]. The project due date is fixed to $\frac{3}{2}C^*_{max}$ and the float $float_i$ of each activity O_i is computed. Let $t_i(BB)$ denotes the start time of activity O_i in the optimal solution and $t_i(S)$ the starting time of activity O_i in the solution under construction. We have $t_i(S) = t_i(BB) + \alpha_i \times float_i$, and α_i is called a float factor. In order to build feasible solutions, *i.e.* without resource conflicts, the insertion procedure presented by [Artigues and Roubellat, 2000] is used to determine interesting float factors. This heuristic is called RFDFF by the authors.
Then, Demeulemeester and Herroelen consider the critical chain approach of [Goldratt, 1997] who introduces some buffers in order to protect the project due date from variability in the critical chain activities. This method is denoted by CC/BM in the paper.

The authors propose computational experiments to investigate whether it is advantageous to protect a schedule only for makespan performance or also for stability. They study the impact of a lot of parameters (number of activities, weighting parameters, ...) and conclude that the advantage of the two scheduling approaches depends on the project characteristics.

7. Single machine problems

7.1 Polynomially solvable problems

7.1.1 Some $1|d_i|\overline{C}, f_{\max}$ problems

In this section we provide various results for single machine problems involving criteria $\overline{C}$ and f_{max}, where f_{max} refers to a maximum increasing function of completion times. We first focus on the $1|d_i|\epsilon(\overline{C}/L_{\max})$ problem since criterion L_{max} is a particular case of the function f_{max}. Next we briefly review the results available for the general $1|d_i|\epsilon(\overline{C}/f_{\max})$ problem.

The $1|d_i|\overline{C}, L_{\max}$ problem

The early paper met in the literature is due to [Smith, 1956], and deals with a particular case of the $1|d_i|\epsilon(\overline{C}/L_{\max})$ problem where $L_{max} = 0$ is imposed. The algorithm of [Smith, 1956] is extended to the $1|d_i|\epsilon(\overline{C}/L_{\max})$ problem by [Heck and Roberts, 1972], who propose an *a priori* algorithm. An *a posteriori* algorithm for this problem is provided by [VanWassenhove and Gelders, 1980]. This algorithm represents a major step in multicriteria scheduling and it has led to numerous similar, exact or heuristic, algorithms. Its principle is as follows. For a fixed value ϵ, a strict Pareto optimum is determined using a greedy algorithm which combines the rules SPT and EDD. The constraint $L_{max} \leq \epsilon$ is equivalent to imposing deadlines on jobs, and so, the algorithm proceeds backward, starting from the last position. At each position, a list of eligible jobs is calculated and among this one the SPT/EDD priority rule is applied to select the job to schedule. The next value ϵ is deduced from the built schedule. The *a posteriori* algorithm, denoted by EWG1, is presented in figure 7.1 and requires, as shown by Van Wassenhove and Gelders, $O(n^2 \log(n)\overline{p})$ time with $\overline{p} = \sum_{i=1}^{n} p_i$.

Example.
We consider a problem for which $n = 5$.

i	1	2	3	4	5
p_i	3	5	6	7	9
d_i	23	22	24	22	18

```
                         ALGORITHM EWG1
/* T is the set of jobs to schedule */
/* We assume that p_1 <= p_2 <= ... <= p_n */
Step 1:  /* Initialisation of the algorithm */
         ε = Σ_{i=1}^{n} p_i;
         /* Initialisation of the deadlines */
         ~d_i = d_i + ε, ∀i = 1, ..., n;
         End=FALSE; E = ∅;
Step 2:  /* Computation of the set E */
         While (End=FALSE) Do
             L = T; S = ∅;
             /* We use a modified version of the rule SPT */
             While ((End=FALSE) and (L ≠ ∅)) Do
                 F = {J_i ∈ L / ~d_i >= Σ_{J_k ∈ L} p_k};
                 If (F = ∅) Then End=TRUE;
                 Else
                     Let J_i ∈ F be such that p_i = max_{J_k ∈ F}(p_k);
                     /* Break ties by choosing the job */
                     /* with the greatest due date */
                     S = {J_i}//S;
                     L = L - {J_i};
                 End if;
             End While;
             If (L = ∅) Then
                 E = E + {S};
                 ε = L_max(S) - 1;
                 ~d_i = d_i + ε, ∀i = 1, ..., n;
                 End=FALSE;
             End If;
         End While;
Step 3:  Print E;
                [VanWassenhove and Gelders, 1980]
```

Fig. 7.1. An a posteriori algorithm for the $1|d_i|\epsilon(\overline{C}/L_{max})$ problem

(i) $\epsilon = 30$, $\widetilde{d_i} = [53; 52; 54; 52; 48]^T$, End=FALSE and $E = \emptyset$.
(ii) $L = \{J_1, J_2, J_3, J_4, J_5\}$, $S_1 = \emptyset$.
$F = \{J_1, J_2, J_3, J_4, J_5\}$, $i = 5$, $S_1 = (J_5)$.
$F = \{J_1, J_2, J_3, J_4\}$, $i = 4$, $S_1 = (J_4, J_5)$.
$F = \{J_1, J_2, J_3\}$, $i = 3$, $S_1 = (J_3, J_4, J_5)$.
$F = \{J_1, J_2\}$, $i = 2$, $S_1 = (J_2, J_3, J_4, J_5)$.
$F = \{J_1\}$, $i = 1$, $S_1 = (J_1, J_2, J_3, J_4, J_5)$, End=TRUE, $L_{max}(S) = 12$ and $\overline{C}(S_1) = 76$.
$E = \{(J_1, J_2, J_3, J_4, J_5)\}$.
End=FALSE, $\epsilon = 11$, $\widetilde{d_i} = [34; 33; 35; 33; 29]^T$.

(iii) $L = \{J_1, J_2, J_3, J_4, J_5\}$, $S_2 = \emptyset$.
$F = \{J_1, J_2, J_3, J_4\}$, $i = 4$, $S_2 = (J_4)$.
$F = \{J_1, J_2, J_3, J_5\}$, $i = 5$, $S_2 = (J_5, J_4)$.
$F = \{J_1, J_2, J_3\}$, $i = 3$, $S_2 = (J_3, J_5, J_4)$.
$F = \{J_1, J_2\}$, $i = 2$, $S_2 = (J_2, J_3, J_5, J_4)$.
$F = \{J_1\}$, $i = 1$, $S_2 = (J_1, J_2, J_3, J_5, J_4)$, End=TRUE, $L_{max}(S_2) = 8$ and $\overline{C}(S_2) = 78$.
$E = \{(J_1, J_2, J_3, J_4, J_5); (J_1, J_2, J_3, J_5, J_4)\}$.
End=FALSE,$\epsilon = 7$, $\widetilde{d}_i = [30; 29; 31; 29; 25]^T$.
(iv) $L = \{J_1, J_2, J_3, J_4, J_5\}$, $S_3 = \emptyset$.
$F = \{J_1, J_3\}$, $i = 3$, $S_3 = (J_3)$.
$F = \{J_1, J_2, J_4, J_5\}$, $i = 5$, $S_3 = (J_5, J_3)$.
$F = \{J_1, J_2, J_4\}$, $i = 4$, $S_3 = (J_4, J_5, J_3)$.
$F = \{J_1, J_2\}$, $i = 2$, $S_3 = (J_2, J_4, J_5, J_3)$.
$F = \{J_1\}$, $i = 1$, $S_3 = (J_1, J_2, J_4, J_5, J_3)$, End=TRUE, $L_{max}(S_3) = 6$ and $\overline{C}(S_3) = 80$.
$E = \{(J_1, J_2, J_3, J_4, J_5); (J_1, J_2, J_3, J_5, J_4); (J_1, J_2, J_4, J_5, J_3)\}$.
End=FALSE,$\epsilon = 5$, $\widetilde{d}_i = [28; 27; 29; 27; 22]^T$.
(v) $L = \{J_1, J_2, J_3, J_4, J_5\}$, $S_4 = \emptyset$.
End=TRUE, $L \neq \emptyset$.

Experimental results show that for a problem having 50 jobs there may be up to 29 strict Pareto optima.
From step (iv) of the above example, it appears that schedules of set E are quite similar from one Pareto optimum to the next one. Let's take the two first ones, namely sequences $(J_1, J_2, J_3, J_4, J_5)$ and $(J_1, J_2, J_3, J_5, J_4)$. They only differ by job J_5 which, giving the L_{max} value in the first schedule, is scheduled earlier in the second one. The same remark holds for job J_4 between the second and third schedules. This yields the conclusion that, in the EWG1 algorithm, when calculating one strict Pareto optimum few changes must been done from the one calculated at the previous iteration. [John, 1984] provides results in this vein, however we present here more accurate results. They provide mathematical insights on the enumeration problem.
We first define an instrumental notation: we write $J_i \succ J_j$ iff $(p_i > p_j)$ or $(p_i = p_j$ and $d_i \geq d_j)$. Besides, we denote by $\sigma^{(k)}$ the schedule builds by the EWG1 algorithm at the kth iteration of Step 2, and $N_j^{(k)}$ refers to the set of unscheduled jobs when choosing a job for position j of $\sigma^{(k)}$ (it is exactly the set L in figure 7.1), whilst $R_j^{(k)} = \sum_{i \in N_j^{(k)}} p_i$. Consider that we are building a sequence $\sigma^{(k)}$ in the EWG1 algorithm. Then, we define the slack of job J_i if scheduled in position j as the gap before meeting its deadline:

$$G_j^{(k)}(i) = \begin{cases} \tilde{d}_i^{(k)} - R_j^{(k)} & \text{if } J_i \in N_j^{(k)} \\ -\infty & \text{otherwise} \end{cases}$$

the value $\tilde{d}_i^{(k)}$ is the value of the deadline of job J_i at the kth iteration of

Step 2 in the EWG1 algorithm. A negative slack $G_j^{(k)}(i)$ indicates that job J_i cannot be scheduled in position j in $\sigma^{(k)}$. Let us define $S_j^{(k)}$ as the set of jobs J_i with a positive gap $G_j^{(k)}(i)$ and it is clear that $S_j^{(k)}$ is the set of candidate jobs for position j in schedule $\sigma^{(k)}$ in the EWG1 algorithm (it is exactly the set F in figure 7.1). We now define the slack of schedule $\sigma^{(k)}$ as follows: first, we define $\lambda_j^{(k)}$ as the slack of the job scheduled in position j in $\sigma^{(k)}$, *i.e.* $\lambda_j^{(k)} = G_j^{(k)}(\sigma^{(k)}(j))$. Accordingly, the slack $\lambda^{(k)}$ of schedule $\sigma^{(k)}$ is defined by $\lambda^{(k)} = \min_{1 \le j \le n}(\lambda_j^{(k)})$. It is clear that jobs giving the slack of a given schedule are those which yield the maximum lateness value, equal to $(\epsilon - \lambda^{(k)})$.
In the EWG1 algorithm, schedule $\sigma^{(k+1)}$ is built from schedule $\sigma^{(k)}$ by decreasing the job slacks, hence yielding to a change in the positions in $\sigma^{(k)}$ with a slack value of $\lambda^{(k)}$. Assume that different positions in sequence $\sigma^{(k)}$, noted $q_u^{(k)}$ and called *critical positions*, are such that $\lambda_{q_u^{(k)}}^{(k)} = \lambda^{(k)}$. All jobs in a critical position in $\sigma^{(k)}$ are scheduled earlier in $\sigma^{(k+1)}$. Let us refer to $Q^{(k)}$ as the set of these critical positions and we refer to $q_*^{(k)}$ as the maximal critical position in $Q^{(k)}$. We now define the *target position* associated to a critical position, the former corresponding in $\sigma^{(k)}$ to the best candidate for being scheduled in $\sigma^{(k+1)}$ in the critical position.

Definition 50 *The target position, denoted by $l_u^{(k)}$, associated to the critical position $q_u^{(k)}$ is the index that satisfies the three conditions:*

1. $\sigma^{(k)}(l_u^{(k)}) \in S_{q_u^{(k)}}^{(k)}$
2. $G_{q_u^{(k)}}^{(k)}(\sigma^{(k)}(l_u^{(k)})) > \lambda^{(k)}$
3. $\forall i \in \{l_u^{(k)}+1; ...; q_u^{(k)}-1\}$, $\sigma^{(k)}(i) \notin S_{q_u^{(k)}}^{(k)}$ *or* $\left(\sigma^{(k)}(i) \in S_{q_u^{(k)}}^{(k)}, \sigma^{(k)}(l_u^{(k)}) \prec \sigma^{(k)}(i) \text{ and } G_{q_u^{(k)}}^{(k)}(\sigma^{(k)}(i)) = \lambda^{(k)}\right)$

Condition 1 of the above definition states that the job in a target position can be scheduled in the corresponding critical position. Condition 2 implies that the target position is not itself a critical position and condition 3 implies that if there is another candidate job for a critical position it cannot be scheduled in the critical position in $\sigma^{(k+1)}$.

We denote by $l_*^{(k)}$ the minimal target position in $\sigma^{(k)}$. Notice that each position $q_u^{(k)}$ has at most one associated $l_u^{(k)}$ and if there exists one position $q_u^{(k)}$ with no associated target position, then schedule $\sigma^{(k)}$ is the last strict Pareto optimum calculated by the EWG1 algorithm.

Property 8 *In $\sigma^{(k)}$, $\forall q_u^{(k)} \in Q^{(k)}$, $\forall i \in \{l_u^{(k)} + 1; ...; q_u^{(k)}\}$, $\sigma^{(k)}(i) \succ \sigma^{(k)}(l_u^{(k)})$.*

Proof.
We show the result exhibiting a contradiction. Assume that there exists a position $j_0 \in \{l_u^{(k)} + 1; ...; q_u^{(k)}\}$ such that job $\sigma^{(k)}(l_u^{(k)}) \succ \sigma^{(k)}(j_0)$. Using definition 50, we know that $\sigma^{(k)}(l_u^{(k)})$ can be scheduled in position $q_u^{(k)}$ in $\sigma^{(k)}$. Since we have $\tilde{d}_i^{(k)} - R_j^{(k)} < \tilde{d}_i^{(k)} - R_{j-1}^{(k)}$, $\forall i = 1, ..., n$, $\forall j = 1, ..., n$, we know that $\sigma^{(k)}(l_u^{(k)})$ can be scheduled in all positions $u < q_u^{(k)}$, including j_0. But job j_0 has been assigned to this position, which means that either $(p_{\sigma^{(k)}(j_0)} > p_{\sigma^{(k)}(l_u^{(k)})})$ or $(p_{\sigma^{(k)}(j_0)} = p_{\sigma^{(k)}(l_u^{(k)})}$ and $\tilde{d}_{\sigma^{(k)}(j_0)}^{(k)} > \tilde{d}_{\sigma^{(k)}(l_u^{(k)})}^{(k)})$. This contradicts the assumption that $\sigma^{(k)}(l_u^{(k)}) \succ \sigma^{(k)}(j_0)$.□

Property 9 *Let j be a position which is not critical in $\sigma^{(k)}$. If $N_j^{(k+1)} = N_j^{(k)}$ then, $\sigma^{(k+1)}(j) = \sigma^{(k)}(j)$.*

Proof.
Straightforward.□

We are now ready to state how to build the strict Pareto optimum $\sigma^{(k+1)}$ making rearrangements on $\sigma^{(k)}$.

Theorem 17 *Schedule $\sigma^{(k+1)}$ is obtained from schedule $\sigma^{(k)}$ only by exchanging in $\sigma^{(k)}$ jobs in positions $[\chi, ..., q_*^{(k)}]$ where χ is the minimal position of the jobs scheduled in a higher position in $\sigma^{(k+1)}$ than in $\sigma^{(k)}$. We have $\chi \leq l_*^{(k)}$.*

Proof.
We prove the result by showing how can be built $\sigma^{(k+1)}$ by using $\sigma^{(k)}$ and starting from the last position. Remember that $\forall i = 1, ..., n$, $\tilde{d}_i^{(k+1)} = \tilde{d}_i^{(k)} - \lambda^{(k)} - 1$.
Consider the last position, and assume without loss of generality that $q_*^{(k)} < n$. We have $N_n^{(k+1)} = N_n^{(k)} = \{1, ..., n\}$. Hence, as position n is not a critical position and thanks to property 9, the same job is scheduled in position n both in schedules $\sigma^{(k)}$ and $\sigma^{(k+1)}$, and we have $N_{(n-1)}^{(k+1)} = N_{(n-1)}^{(k)}$. Using the same argument for positions $(n-1)$ to $q_*^{(k)} + 1$, we prove that $\sigma^{(k+1)}(i) = \sigma^{(k)}(i)$, $\forall i \in \{q_*^{(k)} + 1, ..., n\}$.
In the second part of the proof, we consider jobs scheduled in positions $\chi, ..., q_*^{(k)}$. First consider that $\chi = l_*^{(k)}$. We start with position $q_*^{(k)}$ and assume that the critical position corresponding to that position is $q_v^{(k)}$. Due to definition 50 and since $q_v^{(k)} = q_*^{(k)}$, job $\sigma^{(k)}(l_v^{(k)})$ is scheduled in position $q_v^{(k)}$ in $\sigma^{(k+1)}$. Remember that $\sigma^{(k)}(q_v^{(k)}) \succ \sigma^{(k)}(l_v^{(k)})$, which yields $R_{(q_v^{(k)}-1)}^{(k+1)} \geq R_{(q_v^{(k)}-1)}^{(k)}$. Therefore, set $S_{(q_v^{(k)}-1)}^{(k+1)}$ contains a subset of $S_{(q_v^{(k)}-1)}^{(k)}$ plus job $\sigma^{(k)}(q_v^{(k)})$. Without loss of generality, assume that either position $(q_v^{(k)} - 1)$ is not a critical position either $(q_v^{(k)} - 1) = l_v^{(k)}$ (otherwise apply the same reasoning and consider position $(q_v^{(k)} - 2)$). We have two different possible configurations: either $\sigma^{(k)}(q_v^{(k)} - 1) \in S_{(q_v^{(k)}-1)}^{(k)}$ or not. In the latter case, assume that there exists a job J_π, scheduled in $\sigma^{(k)}$ in a position in $\{1, ..., l_*^{(k)}\}$,

such that J_π is the greatest job in $S^{(k+1)}_{(q_v^{(k)}-1)}$. Therefore it is scheduled in $\sigma^{(k+1)}$ in position $(q_v^{(k)}-1)$. Hence, we can update χ and set $\chi = \min(\tau^{(k)}(\pi);\chi)$, with $\tau^{(k)}(\pi)$ the position of job J_π in $\sigma^{(k)}$. That process can be iterated until position χ and it is straightforward that schedule $\sigma^{(k+1)}$ may be different from $\sigma^{(k)}$ between positions χ and $q_*^{(k)}$. When considering a critical position $q_w^{(k)}$ in $\{\chi, ..., q_*^{(k)}\}$ two situations can occur. Either job $\sigma^{(k)}(l_w^{(k)})$ has not already been scheduled in $\sigma^{(k+1)}$ in a position greater than $q_w^{(k)}$, either it was also the target position of another critical position $q_x^{(k)} > q_w^{(k)}$. In the former case, exactly the same reasoning than previously can be applied for position $q_w^{(k)}$ (*i.e.* job $\sigma^{(k)}(l_w^{(k)})$ is scheduled in $\sigma^{(k+1)}$ in this position). In the latter case, another job J_μ such that $J_\mu \prec \sigma^{(k)}(l_w^{(k)}) \prec \sigma^{(k)}(q_w^{(k)})$ is scheduled in position $q_w^{(k)}$ in $\sigma^{(k+1)}$, and $\chi = \min(\tau^{(k)}(\mu);\chi)$, with $\tau^{(k)}(\mu)$ the position of job J_μ in $\sigma^{(k)}$.
For the third part of the proof, we only need to consider positions from $(\chi-1)$ down to 1. We can easily check that no job scheduled in $\sigma^{(k)}$ in a position greater than or equal to χ is scheduled in $\sigma^{(k+1)}$ in a position lower than χ, since otherwise we would violate the previous definition of χ as a job scheduled in a smallest position than χ in $\sigma^{(k)}$ would need to be scheduled after position χ in $\sigma^{(k+1)}$. Hence, it follows that $N^{(k+1)}_{(\chi-1)} = N^{(k)}_{(\chi-1)}$. Property 9 yields the conclusion that $\forall j = 1, ..., (\chi-1)$, $\sigma^{(k+1)}(j) = \sigma^{(k)}(j)$ which gives the last part of the proof.□

It is interesting to notice that the proof of the above theorem gives a way to compute the value χ when building schedule $\sigma^{(k+1)}$. We can also derive that each job in a critical position in a strict Pareto optimum $\sigma^{(k)}$, is scheduled earlier in any other strict Pareto optimum $\sigma^{(k')}$ with $k' > k$. Henceforth, from theorem 17 it appears that starting from $\sigma^{(k)}$ we can build the next strict Pareto optimum $\sigma^{(k+1)}$ by applying Step 2 of the algorithm $EWG1$ only between positions χ and $q_*^{(k)}$. A modified version of this algorithm is proposed by [Esswein et al., 2001].

Example.
Let us consider the previous example in which we applied algorithm EWG1 algorithm. Three strict Pareto optima have been found: $\sigma^{(1)} = (J_1, J_2, J_3, J_4, J_5)$, $\sigma^{(2)} = (J_1, J_2, J_3, J_5, J_4)$ and $\sigma^{(3)} = (J_1, J_2, J_4, J_5, J_3)$. Notice that $J_1 \prec J_2 \prec J_3 \prec J_4 \prec J_5$.
Assume that we have already calculated $\sigma^{(1)}$ and we want to build $\sigma^{(2)}$. The slacks are given in the following table.

$G_j^{(1)}(i) \rightarrow$ $\downarrow$	1	2	3	4	5	$\lambda_j^{(1)}$
5	23	22	24	22	18	18
4	32	31	33	31	$-\infty$	31
3	39	38	40	$-\infty$	$-\infty$	40
2	45	44	$-\infty$	$-\infty$	$-\infty$	44
1	50	$-\infty$	$-\infty$	$-\infty$	$-\infty$	50

The slack of $\sigma^{(1)}$ is equal to $\lambda^{(1)} = 18 = \epsilon - L_{max}(\sigma^{(1)})$.

There is only one critical position $q_1^{(1)}$ since there is only one position with a slack equal to 18, *i.e.* $q_1^{(1)} = q_*^{(1)} = 5$ and $Q^{(1)} = \{q_1^{(1)}\}$. Notice that $S^{(1)}_{q_1^{(1)}} = \{J_1, J_2, J_3, J_4, J_5\}$. By applying definition 50 the target position associated to $q_1^{(1)}$ is equal to $l_1^{(1)} = l_*^{(1)} = 4$ since job $J_{l_1^{(1)}} = J_4 \in S^{(1)}_{q_1^{(1)}}$ has the largest processing time. The interested reader can check property 8. The examination of the proof of theorem 17 shows that $\chi = l_*^{(1)} = l_1^{(1)}$. As $l_*^{(1)} + 1 = q_*^{(1)}$ sequence $\sigma^{(2)}$ is built from $\sigma^{(1)}$ by swapping jobs in positions $l_*^{(1)}$ and $q_*^{(1)}$ in $\sigma^{(1)}$.
The same reasoning can next be applied on $\sigma^(2)$ to deduce $\sigma^{(3)}$.

From the previous results we can derive a result, differently proved by [Hoogeveen and VandeVelde, 1995].

Theorem 18 *The number of strictly non dominated criteria vectors is at most equal to* $\frac{n(n-1)}{2} + 1$*, and the bound is tight.*

Proof.
For a given schedule $\sigma^{(k)}$, we define for each job J_i a maximal position $\tau_{max}^{(k)}(i)$ at which it can be scheduled, *i.e.* $\forall j > \tau_{max}^{(k)}(i)$, $G_j^{(k)}(i) < 0$. Besides, $\forall i = 1, ..., n$, $\forall k' > k$, $\tau_{max}^{(k')}(i) \leq \tau_{max}^{(k)}(i)$.
Notice that if there exists more than one critical position equal to 1, $\sigma^{(k+1)}$ does not exist and $\sigma^{(k)}$ is the schedule with the smallest $\bar{C}$ value among all feasible schedules. It can be generalized in the following way: if there exists a position $j \in \{1, ..., n\}$ such that there is more than j maximal positions $\tau_{max}^{(k)}(i)$ lower than or equal to j, schedule $\sigma^{(k+1)}$ does not exist. Hence to guarantee that $\sigma^{(k+1)}$ exists we have to check that $\sum_{i=1}^n \tau_{max}^{(k)}(i) \geq (1+2+...+n) = \frac{n(n-1)}{2}$.
To determine the maximum number of strictly non dominated criteria vectors, we need to compute the greatest value of k such that $\sigma^{(k)}$ exists but not $\sigma^{(k+1)}$. Let us start with $\tau_{max}^{(1)}(i) = n$, $\forall i = 1, ..., n$, which means that $\sum_{i=1}^n \tau_{max}^{(1)}(i) = n^2$. As at least one job, which is in a critical position, has a maximal position that is decreased while building $\sigma^{(k+1)}$ from $\sigma^{(k)}$. Assume that in the worst case exactly one maximal position is decreased by one unit. We have $\frac{n(n-1)}{2} \leq \sum_{i=1}^n \tau_{max}^{(k)}(i) \leq \sum_{i=1}^n \tau_{max}^{(1)}(i) - k + 1 = n^2 - k + 1$ and the maximal k value is achieved for $\frac{n(n-1)}{2} + 1$.
To prove that this bound is tight, consider any instance with two jobs where $p_1 < p_2$ and $d_1 > d_2$. The only two sequences correspond to strictly non dominated criteria vectors and we have $2(1)/2 + 1 = 2$.

The above theorem leads to the conclusion that the algorithm $EWG1$ has not a pseudo-polynomial time complexity, since the numuber of strict Pareto optima calculated by this algorithm is bounded by $\frac{n(n-1)}{2} + 1$. Consequently, the algorithm $EWG1$ requires $O(n^3 \log(n))$ time.□

[Nelson et al., 1986] also study this enumeration problem for which they propose a branch-and-bound algorithm which determines a subset of the set of weak Pareto optima. Dominance conditions are used to improve the efficiency of the algorithm.

[Sen and Gupta, 1983] study a similar problem which involves the minimisation of criteria $\overline{C}$ and T_{max}. They are implicitly interested in the determination of weak Pareto optima, because they seek to determine the optimal solutions for the $1|d_i|F_\ell(T_{\max}, \overline{C})$ problem with $F_\ell(T_{\max}, \overline{C}) = \alpha T_{\max} + (1-\alpha)\overline{C}$ and $\alpha \in [0; 1]$. In order to solve it, Sen and Gupta propose a branch-and-bound algorithm which enumerates the set of solutions minimising all the possible convex combinations of the criteria. Following the results presented in chapter 3, we deduce that the calculated solutions belong to the set WE_s.

The $1|d_i|\overline{C}, f_{\max}$ problem

[Emmons, 1975a] is interested in the minimisation of the criteria $\overline{C}$ and $f_{\max}$ via the $1||Lex(f_{\max}, \overline{C})$ problem. To solve this, Emmons proposes a greedy algorithm based on the algorithm of [Lawler, 1973] for the $1|prec|f_{max}$ problem.
[John, 1984] studies the $1||\epsilon(\overline{C}/f_{\max})$ problem for which he proposes an algorithm which determines the set E. This algorithm starts with an optimal sequence for the $1||Lex(\overline{C}, f_{\max})$ problem. Initially, we set ϵ to the value of the f_{max} criterion of this solution minus 1. To compute one strict Pareto optimum, a $1||\epsilon(\overline{C}/f_{max})$ problem with ϵ fixed is solved. Under the assumption that f_{max} is a reversible function, this problem can be reduced to a $1|\tilde{d}_i|\overline{C}$ problem, which is polynomially solved by Smith's backward algorithm (see [VanWassenhove and Gelders, 1980]). After the current solution has been computed, the value ϵ is updated to the value of the f_{max} criterion found and the procedure is iterated. John provides results to improve the computation of the current strict Pareto optima, knowing the one computed at the previous iteration. From one strict Pareto optima to the other, only parts of the sequences are changed by permutations of jobs. This may reduce the practical average complexity. John shows that the complexity of this algorithm is in $O(n^2X)$ with X being the number of strict Pareto optima. He also shows that $X < \frac{1}{4}(n^2-1)(p_{max} - p_{min})$ if n is even and that $X < \frac{1}{4}n^2(p_{max} - p_{min})$ otherwise, with $p_{max} = \max_{i=1,\dots,n}(p_i)$ and $p_{min} = \min_{i=1,\dots,n}(p_i)$.
[Hoogeveen and VandeVelde, 1995] are also interested in this problem. They propose an algorithm based on a greedy method to determine a strict Pareto optimum when ϵ is fixed and they next describe an *a posteriori* algorithm which determines the set E by making ϵ vary. Classically, this approach enables us to determine a subset of the set WE. Nevertheless, Hoogeveen and Van de Velde show that the *a posteriori* algorithm does not generate the weak Pareto optima which are not strict. Similarly, they show that the cardinality

of the set E is at most $n(n-1)/2+1$. This upper bound is clearly more precise than that proposed by [John, 1984].

7.1.2 The $1|s_i, pmtn, nmit|F_\ell(\overline{C}, P_{\max})$ problem

In the previous section regular maximum criteria have been investigated together with the total completion time criterion. The case of a particular non regular criterion is considered by [Hoogeveen and van de Velde, 2001]: the maximum promptness. To any job J_i let s_i be the associated desired starting time, which can merely seen as a release date that can be violate at a certain cost. Let $P_i(\sigma) = s_i - t_i(\sigma)$ be the promptness of job J_i in a given schedule σ, and $P_{max} = \max_{1\leq i\leq n}(P_i)$ is the maximum promptness. This criterion is minimised simultaneously with criterion $\bar{C}$ via a convex combination $\alpha\bar{C}+(1-\alpha)P_{max}$. Preemption of jobs is allowed but not the insertion of voluntary idle times between jobs except before the first job of the exchange.

Hoogeveen and van de Velde study the enumeration of the optimal solutions of the above objective function for all values of α (in fact only one optimal solution per α value is calculated). This corresponds to the enumeration of the supported strict Pareto optima. In fact, this enumeration is achieved by an algorithm which iteratively solves $1|s_i, pmtn, nmit|\epsilon(\overline{C}/P_{\max})$ problems and obtains a set of strict Pareto optima which comprises the supported ones. This algorithm works in a way similar to algorithm EWG1. First, the $1|s_i, nmit|P_{max}$ problem is solved by the MTST rule: "*schedule at each time t the job with the smallest desired starting time*". Let P^*_{max} and $\bar{C}^{sup}$ be the obtained criteria values which constitute the first Pareto optimum calculated. For any value $\epsilon > P^*_{max}$, the corresponding ϵ-constraint problem is equivalent to the $1|r_i = s_i - \epsilon, pmtn|\bar{C}$ problem which can be polynomially solved by applying the SRPT rule: "*schedule at any time t the job with the smallest remaining processing time among those available*". This leads to a new Pareto optimum. The main question is how to obtain the set of ϵ values such that the solution of the corresponding ϵ-contraint problems are the supported strict Pareto optima. The solution algorithm proposed by Hoogeveen and van de Velde calculates a bigger set of ϵ values, *i.e.* for some ϵ value in this set the corresponding optimal solution is a non supported optimum. However, they do not provide information on the fact that their algorithm enumerates or not the whole set of strict Pareto optima. The basic idea on which is based the algorithm is that, starting from a previously calculated strict Pareto optimum σ, it is necessary to increase ϵ of such a quantity that there is an interchange of two jobs in σ. If this does not occur the optimal solution of the ϵ-constraint problem cannot be a supported strict Pareto optimum. The detailled algorithm, denoted by EHV1, is presented in figure 7.2.
Hoogeveen and van de Velde show that there is at most $n(n-1)+1$ supported strict Pareto optima. As the SRPT rule requires $O(n^2)$ time, the EHV1 al-

```
ALGORITHM EHV1
/* T is the set of jobs to schedule */
Step 1:  /* Initialisation of the algorithm */
         Apply rule MTST to solve the 1|pmtn|P_max problem and let
            P*_max be the optimal solution value;
         Apply rule SPT to solve the 1||C̄ problem and let P^sup_max be the P_max
            value of the calculated solution;
         ε = P*_max;
         π = 0; a_i = +∞, ∀i = 1, ..., n;
         End=FALSE; E_s = ∅;
Step 2:  /* Computation of the set E_s */
         While (End=FALSE) Do
           | Apply rule SRPT to solve the 1|pmtn, r_i = max(0, s_i − ε)|C̄
           |    problem and let σ be the optimal schedule;
           | E_s = E_s ∪ {σ};
           | Let J_k be the job that starts at time π in σ;
           | /* We compute the minimal increase in ε to get the next
           |    strict Pareto optimum */
           | If (J_k is a preempted job) Then
           |   | a_k = p'_k(π) where p'_k(π) is the length of the portion of
           |   |    job J_k that starts at time π;
           |   | π = C_k(σ);
           | Else
           |   | Ψ_k = {J_j/s_j − ε > t_k(σ) and p_j > p_k};
           |   | a_k = min_{J_j∈Ψ_k}(s_j − ε − t_k(σ));
           |   | π = C_k(σ);
           | End If;
           | If (π < Σ_{i=1}^n p_i) Then Goto Step 2;
           | ε = min_{j=1,...,n}(a_j) + ε;
           | If (ε = P^sup_max) Then End=TRUE;
         End While;
Step 3:  Remove from E_s the non supported solutions;
         Print E_s;
[Hoogeveen and van de Velde, 2001]
```

Fig. 7.2. An a posteriori algorithm for the $1|s_i, pmtn, nmit|F_\ell(\overline{C}, P_{max})$ problem

gorithm requires $O(n^4)$ time. They also show that the problem without preemption but with $\alpha > 0.5$ can be solved in $O(n^4)$ time.

7.1.3 The $1|p_i \in [\underline{p}_i; \overline{p}_i], d_i|F_\ell(T_{max}, \overline{CC}^w)$ problem

[Vickson, 1980b] is interested in a bicriteria scheduling problem where the processing times of jobs are decision variables. This problem is denoted by $1|p_i \in [\underline{p}_i; \overline{p}_i], d_i|F_\ell(T_{max}, \overline{CC}^w)$. The criterion $\overline{CC}^w$ is called the crashing time costs criterion and represents the weighted sum of the slack of processing times in relation to the maximum allowed times, *i.e.* $\overline{CC}^w = \sum_{i=1}^{n} w_i x_i$ with

$x_i \in [0; \overline{p}_i - \underline{p}_i]$. The variable x_i represents the amount of compression of job J_i for which the processing time is equal to $p_i = \overline{p}_i - x_i$. Notice that the expression $\alpha T_{max} + \beta \overline{CC}^w$ is equivalent to the expression $T_{max} + \overline{CC}^{w'}$. We consider here therefore that $F_\ell(T_{max}, \overline{CC}^w) = T_{max} + \overline{CC}^w$. This type of criterion has an application, for example, in hoist scheduling problems where the soaking times of the items, assimilated with the processing times, are not determined in advance. In project scheduling problems we also find an application of such a criterion. The second criterion studied by Vickson is the criterion T_{max} which is formulated for these problems by:

$$T_{max}(S) = \max_{i=1,\dots,n} \left(\max(0; \sum_{j=1}^{i} (\overline{p}_{S[j]} - x_{S[j]}) - d_{S[i]}) \right).$$

where $S[i]$ refers to the ith job in schedule S. To solve the bicriteria problem, Vickson proposes a mixed integer program and a polynomial algorithm, denoted by ERV1 (figure 7.4), which requires $O(n^2)$ time. A sequence of jobs is initially obtained by applying the rule EDD and by considering that $p_i = \overline{p}_i$, $\forall i = 1, ..., n$. We have therefore $\overline{CC}^w = 0$ and a compression enabling us to reduce the value of the criterion T_{max}, increases the value of the criterion $\overline{CC}^w$. The algorithm ERV1 initiates therefore a series of compressions such that the reduction of T_{max} from one time unit compensates the increase of the criterion $\overline{CC}^w$.

Example.
We consider a problem for which $n = 4$.

i	1	2	3	4
$\underline{p}_i$	1	2	3	1
$\overline{p}_i$	3	4	5	3
w_i	1	0	4	2
d_i	3	4	10	12

(i) $S = (J_1, J_2, J_3, J_4)$ and $p_i = [3; 4; 5; 3]^T$.
$T_{max} = 3$, $\overline{CC}^w = 0$ and $F_\ell(T_{max}, \overline{CC}^w) = 3$.
$k = 2$.
(ii) The solution S is not optimal.
(iii) $j = 2$, $\delta_j = 2$, $T^j_{max} = 0$ and $\delta_j < (T_{max} - T^j_{max})$.
$p_i = [3; 2; 5; 3]^T$, $T_{max} = 1$, $\overline{CC}^w = 0$ and $F_\ell(T_{max}, \overline{CC}^w) = 1$.
(iv) The solution S is optimal because $\forall j \leq k / p_j > \underline{p}_j$, $w_j \geq 1$. The schedule S is presented in figure 7.3 and $T_{max} + \overline{CC}^w = 1$.

[VanWassenhove and Baker, 1982] are interested in the $1|p_i \in [\underline{p}_i; \overline{p}_i], d_i| \epsilon(T_{max}/\overline{CC}^w)$ problem for which they propose a greedy algorithm which determines the set of strict Pareto optima. The complexity of this algorithm is in $O(n^2)$ time. It is then extended to the more general case of a criterion f_{max} defined by $f_{max} = \max_{i=1,\dots,n} (g_i(C_i))$. The functions $g_i(t)$ are

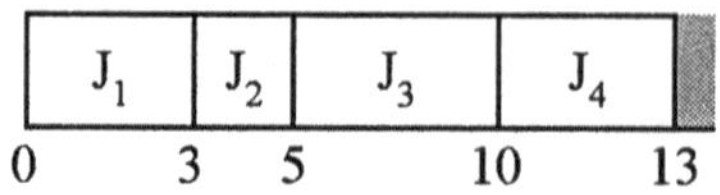

Fig. 7.3. The schedule calculated by the algorithm ERV1

ALGORITHM ERV1

/* T is the set of jobs to schedule */
/* We assume that $d_1 \leq d_2 \leq \ldots \leq d_n$ */
/* $\underline{p}_i$, minimum processing time of job J_i, $\forall i = 1, ..., n$ */
/* $\overline{p}_i$, maximum processing time of job J_i, $\forall i = 1, ..., n$ */

Step 1: /* Initialisation of the algorithm */
$p_i = \overline{p}_i$, $\forall i = 1, ..., n$;
$S = (J_1, J_2, \ldots, J_n)$; $T_{max} = \max_{i=1,\ldots,n}(0; C_i - d_i)$; $\overline{CC}^w = 0$;
Let J_k be such that $\max(0; C_k - d_k) = T_{max}$;
/* Break ties by choosing the job with the smallest value C_i */

Step 2: /* We check if the current solution is optimal */
If $((T_{max} = 0)$ or $(p_i = \underline{p}_i, \forall i = 1, ..., k))$ Then
  Goto Step 4;
End If;
If $((T_{max} > 0)$ and $(w_i \geq 1, \forall i = 1, ..., k$ such that $p_i > \underline{p}_i))$ Then
  /* The decrease of T_{max} from one time unit does not */
  /* compensate the increase of $\overline{CC}^w$ */
  Goto Step 4;
End If;

Step 3: /* Improvement of the schedule */
Let J_j be such that $j \leq k$, $p_j > \underline{p}_j$, $w_j = \min_{i=1,\ldots,k, p_i > \underline{p}_i}(w_i)$;
$\delta_j = p_j - \underline{p}_j$; /* Maximum compression */
$T^j_{max} = \max_{i=1,\ldots,(j-1)}(\max(0; C_i - d_i))$;
If $(\delta_j < (T_{max} - T^j_{max}))$ Then
  /* We do a maximum compression of job J_j */
  $p_j = \underline{p}_j$; $T_{max} = T_{max} - \delta_j$; $\overline{CC}^w = \overline{CC}^w + w_j\delta_j$;
Else
  /* We reduce criterion T_{max} until T^j_{max} */
  $p_j = p_j - (T_{max} - T^j_{max})$; $T_{max} = T^j_{max}$;
  $\overline{CC}^w = \overline{CC}^w + w_j(T_{max} - T^j_{max})$;
  Let J_k be such that $\max(0; C_k - d_k) = T_{max}$;
  /* Break ties by choosing the job with the smallest value C_i */
End If;
Goto Step 2;

Step 4: Print S, T_{max}, $\overline{CC}^w$;

[Vickson, 1980b]

Fig. 7.4. An optimal algorithm for the $1|p_i \in [\underline{p}_i; \overline{p}_i], d_i|F_\ell(T_{max}, \overline{CC}^w)$ problem

assumed to be non decreasing and such that an order of jobs verifying $g_1(t) \geq g_2(t) \geq \ldots \geq g_n(t),\ \forall t \geq 0$ exists.

7.1.4 The $1|p_i \in [\underline{p}_i; \overline{p}_i], d_i|F_\ell(\overline{C}, \overline{CC}^w)$ problem

[Vickson, 1980b] studies the minimisation problem of criteria $\overline{C}$ and $\overline{CC}^w$ via the $1|p_i \in [\underline{p}_i; \overline{p}_i]|F_\ell(\overline{C}, \overline{CC}^w)$ problem and shows that this problem can be reduced to an assignment problem solvable in $O(n^3)$ time.
[Chen et al., 1997] consider the problem with integer processing times, denoted by $1|p_i \in [\underline{p}_i; \overline{p}_i] \cap \mathbb{N}|F_\ell(\overline{C}, \overline{CC}^w)$. The criterion $\overline{CC}^w$ is defined by $\overline{CC}^w = \sum_{i=1}^{n} c_i(\overline{p}_i - p_i)$ where c_i is an increasing cost function. Chen, Lu and Tang also assume that $\forall i,j, 1 \leq i,j \leq n, \overline{p}_i - \underline{p}_i = \overline{p}_j - \underline{p}_j$. They propose to reduce the problem to an assignment problem by introducing costs $v_{i,k}$ of scheduling job J_i in position k in the schedule. More precisely, $v_{i,k}$ is the contribution to the objective function of job J_i if it is scheduled in position k. We have:

$$v_{i,k} = \min_{j=0,\ldots,(\overline{p}_i - \underline{p}_i)} \{(n-k+1)(\underline{p}_i + j) + c_i(\overline{p}_i - \underline{p}_i - j)\}.$$

Notice that we can deduce, from the value of j which gives the minimum, the value of the exact processing time p_i if job J_i is scheduled in position k: $p_i = \underline{p}_i + j$. When the costs $v_{i,k}$ are computed the problem can be reduced to an assignment problem that can be solved in $O(n^3)$ time. A integer program, denoted by ECLT2, of this problem is introduced in figure 7.5.

7.1.5 Other problems

Minimisation of K increasing functions of the completion times

[Hoogeveen, 1992b] studies the general problem of the minimisation of K functions of the completion times, denoted by f^i_{max} and assumed to be increasing. We have $f^i_{\max}(S) = \max_{j=1,\ldots,n} f^i_j(C_j(S))$ with f^i_j being also increasing functions. Hoogeveen proposes an a posteriori algorithm for the $1||\epsilon(f^1_{\max}/f^2_{\max}, \ldots, f^K_{\max})$ problem and distinguishes both bicriteria and multicriteria cases.
First case: $K = 2$. Hoogeveen shows that a modification of the algorithm of [Lawler, 1973] enables us to solve the problem optimally when the bound ϵ is fixed. The complexity of the algorithm is in $O(n^2)$ time and the number of strict Pareto optima is at most $n(n-1)/2+1$. He then proposes an algorithm which determines the set E in $O(n^4)$ time.

Mathematical formulation ECLT2	
/* $\forall k = 1, ..., n, \forall i = 1, ..., n,$ */	
/* $v_{i,k} = \min_{j=0,...,(\overline{p}_i - \underline{p}_i)} \{(n-k+1)(\underline{p}_i + j) + c_i(\overline{p}_i - \underline{p}_i - j)\}$ */	
Data:	n, the number of jobs, $v_{i,k}$, $i = 1, ..., n$, $k = 1, ..., n$, the cost of assigning the job J_i to position k.
Variables:	$y_{i,k}$, $i = 1, ..., n$, $k = 1, ..., n$, boolean variable, equal to 1 if job J_i is assigned to position k, and 0 otherwise.
Objective:	Minimise $\sum_{i=1}^{n}\sum_{k=1}^{n} v_{i,k}y_{i,k}$
Constraints:	$\sum_{k=1}^{n} y_{i,k} = 1, \forall i = 1, ..., n$
	$\sum_{i=1}^{n} y_{i,k} = 1, \forall k = 1, ..., n$
	$y_{i,k} \in \{0; 1\}, \forall i = 1, ..., n, \forall k = 1, ..., n$

Fig. 7.5. An MIP model for the $1|p_i \in [\underline{p}_i; \overline{p}_i] \cap \mathbb{N}|F_\ell(\overline{C}, \overline{CC}^w)$ problem

Second case: $K > 2$. In the general case with K criteria, the cardinality of the set E is at most $(n(n-1)/2+1)^{K-1}$. The algorithm proposed by Hoogeveen to determine this set is an extension of the one proposed for the case $K = 2$. Its algorithmic complexity is in $O(n^{K(K+1)-6})$ time when $K \geq 3$.

Minimisation of the average weighted completion time

[Chen and Bulfin, 1990] study some bicriteria scheduling problems with unit processing times. This kind of study sometimes enables us to find complexity results for some problems. Sometimes, it is possible to find an application of such problems in computing systems, or even more according to Chen and Bulfin, in car production shops as for example with Toyota (see [Monden, 1998]). Chen and Bulfin are interested in the $1|p_i = 1, d_i|Lex(\overline{C}^w, Z_2)$ problems with $Z_2 \in \{\overline{T}, \overline{T}^w, \overline{U}, \overline{U}^w, T_{\max}\}$, for which they propose greedy algorithms, in $O(n\log(n))$ time, based on the rule $WSPT$.

Moreover, Chen and Bulfin study the $1|p_i = 1, d_i|\epsilon(\overline{C}^w / T_{\max})$ problem for which they propose an algorithm which enumerates the set E. The $1|p_i = 1, d_i|F_\ell(\overline{C}^w, Z_2)$ problems with $Z_2 \in \{\overline{T}, \overline{T}^w, \overline{U}, \overline{U}^w\}$ are similarly addressed. Chen and Bulfin state that the algorithm of [Aneja and Nair, 1979], which enables us to solve a bicriteria assignment problem, can be easily modified to solve these problems. Thus, they propose to determine the set E whereas the approach F_ℓ only enables us to compute solutions of the set E_s in the case where the solutions set is not convex. Chen and Bulfin also tackle the $1|p_i = 1, d_i|Lex(Z_1, \overline{C}^w)$ problems with $Z_1 \in \{\overline{T}^w, \overline{U}, \overline{U}^w, T_{\max}\}$, and show how to reduce these problems to an assignment problem solvable in $O(n^3)$ time. For the $1|p_i = 1, d_i|Lex(\overline{T}, \overline{C}^w)$ problem they propose a greedy algorithm in $O(n\log(n))$ time.

Minimisation of tool changing costs

• [Gupta et al., 1997] study a problem in which $\mathcal{M}$ customer orders are taken into account. Each one of these orders, denoted by $\mathcal{O}_j$, $\forall j = 1, ..., \mathcal{M}$, is composed of n_j jobs. The number of jobs to schedule is equal to $n = \sum_{j=1}^{\mathcal{M}} n_j$. Moreover, we suppose that k predefined classes of jobs B_ℓ exist and that $|\mathcal{O}_j \cap B_\ell| = 1$, $\forall j = 1, ..., \mathcal{M}, \forall \ell = 1, ..., k$. Each order contains exactly one job of each class. Moreover, the processing of two jobs $J_{[i]}$ and $J_{[i+1]}$ ($J_{[i]}$ refers to the job in position i) belonging to different classes induces a setup cost, denoted by $SC_{[i],[i+1]}$, depending on the class of $J_{[i+1]}$ and which is equal to the corresponding setup time. The aim is to minimise two criteria:

- The cost of changing tools which is defined by $\overline{SC} = \sum_{i=2}^{n} SC_{[i-1],[i]}$. We notice that the minimisation of this criterion leads to the minimisation of criterion C_{max},
- The carrying cost, which is defined by $\overline{AC} = \sum_{j=1}^{\mathcal{M}} \max_{J_\ell, J_i \in \mathcal{O}_j} (0; C_i - C_\ell)$. Such a cost may appear, for example, when partial processing of an order implies that it is stored waiting for the complete processing of the order.

Gupta, Ho and Vanderveen consider that trade-offs between the criteria $\overline{AC}$ and $\overline{SC}$ are forbidden, because a lexicographical order $Lex(\overline{SC}, \overline{AC})$ is defined between these criteria. The problem addressed is denoted by $1|classes, orders, S_{sd}|Lex(\overline{SC}, \overline{AC})$. An optimal schedule for the criterion $\overline{SC}$ is such that all the jobs in the same class are processed consecutively and the minimisation of the criterion $\overline{AC}$ leads then to schedule classes on one hand, and the jobs within these classes on the other hand. An optimal algorithm in $O(n\log(\mathcal{M}))$ time is proposed.

• [Gupta et al., 1997] are next interested in the opposite lexicographical problem, that is to say in the $1|classes, orders, S_{sd}|Lex(\overline{AC}, \overline{SC})$ problem. Gupta, Ho and Vanderveen show that an optimal schedule for the criterion $\overline{AC}$ is such that all the jobs belonging to the same order are processed consecutively. Among all these jobs the first to be carried out is the one having the greatest sum of processing and setup times. The aim becomes therefore the determination of a sequence of orders as well as the jobs completing these orders, in a way that the criterion $\overline{SC}$ is minimised. This problem can be reduced to a particular case of the travelling salesman problem for which they propose an optimal algorithm in $O(n)$ time.

Minimisation of due date based criteria

[Chen and Bulfin, 1990] are interested in problems where the jobs have unit processing times. They consider the $1|p_i = 1, d_i|Lex(\overline{T}^w, Z_2^1)$ problems, with $Z_2^1 \in \{\overline{U}, \overline{U}^w\}$ and the $1|p_i = 1, d_i|Lex(\overline{U}, Z_2^2)$ and $1|p_i = 1, d_i|Lex(\overline{U}^w, Z_2^2)$ problems with $Z_2^2 = \{\overline{T}, \overline{T}^w\}$ which they model as an assignment problem solvable in $O(n^3)$ time. Chen and Bulfin also study the $1|p_i = 1, d_i|Lex(\overline{T}, Z_2^1)$ problems for which they propose an optimal greedy algorithm. Besides, they state that for the $1|p_i = 1, d_i|F_\ell(\overline{U}, Z_2^2)$ and $1|p_i = 1, d_i|F_\ell(\overline{U}^w, Z_2^2)$ problems, the algorithm of [Aneja and Nair, 1979] can be modified easily to determine the set E. In fact, only the solutions of the set E_s can be determined. Chen and Bulfin are also interested in the minimisation of the criterion $T_{\max}$ via the $1|p_i = 1, d_i|Lex(T_{\max}, Z_2^3)$ problems, with $Z_2^3 = \{\overline{U}, \overline{U}^w, \overline{T}^w\}$, which they reduce to an assignment problem. Likewise for $1|p_i = 1, d_i|\epsilon(Z_2^3/T_{\max})$ problems.

7.2 $\mathcal{NP}$-hard problems

7.2.1 The $1|d_i|\overline{T}, \overline{C}$ problem

This problem has been tackled by [Lin, 1983] who proposes an *a posteriori* algorithm. This problem is $\mathcal{NP}$-hard because the $1|d_i|\overline{T}$ is also. Lin proposes dominance conditions between jobs, which are valid in all strict Pareto schedules. To determine the set E, a dynamic programming algorithm which integrates these dominance conditions is described. This algorithm is based on the multicriteria dynamic programming algorithm introduced by [Yu, 1978] and [Yu and Seiford, 1981]. At each phase j, $\forall j = 1, ..., n$, we deal with the set, or state e_j, of the considered j jobs. Therefore, there are at each phase j, j possibilities or decisions x_j, to schedule a job in the first position in the set e_j. We note T the set of the n jobs to be scheduled and we define for each decision $x_j \in e_j$ a criteria vector $\widetilde{r}_j(e_j, x_j)$ by:

$$\widetilde{r}_j(e_j, x_j) = [\max\big(\sum_{J_k \in T - e_j} p_k + p_j - d_j, 0\big); \sum_{J_k \in T - e_j} p_k + p_j]^T.$$

We can therefore define the recurrence function by:

$$\widetilde{F}_j(e_j, x_j) = \min_{x_k \in e_j - \{x_j\}} (\widetilde{F}_{j-1}(e_j - \{x_j\}, x_k)) + \widetilde{r}_j(e_j, x_j).$$

This function is therefore a vector which is composed of the values of the criteria $\overline{T}$ and $\overline{C}$ of the best schedule having the job x_j in the first position of the set e_j. We set $\widetilde{F}_0(\emptyset, \emptyset) = [0; 0]^T$ and we search the criteria vectors which are not dominated among the vectors $\widetilde{F}_n(T, J_k)$, $\forall J_k \in T$.

Example.
We consider a problem for which $n = 4$.

i	1	2	3	4
p_i	1	2	3	4
d_i	2	7	5	6

(i) At phase 1, we consider all the possibilities of scheduling a job in last position. We have therefore:

e_1	$\{J_1\}$	$\{J_2\}$	$\{J_3\}$	$\{J_4\}$
$\sum_{J_k \in T - e_1} p_k$	9	8	7	6
x_1	J_1	J_2	J_3	J_4
$\widetilde{r}_1(e_1, x_1)$	$[8; 10]^T$	$[3; 10]^T$	$[5; 10]^T$	$[4; 10]^T$
$\widetilde{F}_1(e_1, x_1)$	$[8; 10]^T$	$[3; 10]^T$	$[5; 10]^T$	$[4; 10]^T$

(ii) After having calculated phases 2, 3 and 4 we obtain strictly non dominated solutions $[5; 20]^T$ and $[4; 21]^T$. Each result corresponds to a sequence:

- (J_1, J_2, J_3, J_4) for which $\overline{T} = 5$ and $\overline{C} = 20$. We notice that it is also an optimal solution for the $1||\overline{C}$ problem,
- (J_1, J_3, J_2, J_4) for which $\overline{T} = 4$ and $\overline{C} = 21$. It is also an optimal solution for the $1||\overline{T}$ problem.

The set of solutions in criteria space is represented in figure 7.6. The non dominated criteria vectors are indicate in the figure using small circles.

Experimental results presented by Lin show that for a problem with 12 jobs the maximum computational time is under 5 seconds and the maximum number of strict Pareto optima is about 96.

7.2.2 The $1|r_i, p_i \in [\underline{p}_i; \overline{p}_i] \cap \mathbb{N}|F_\ell(C_{max}, \overline{CC}^w)$ problem

This problem with integer controllable processing times has been tackled by [Chen et al., 1997]. The processing times are defined as follows: (i) $p_i \in [\underline{p}_i; \overline{p}_i] \cap \mathbb{N}$, and (ii) $\forall i, j\ \overline{p}_i - \underline{p}_i = \overline{p}_j - \underline{p}_j = k$.
This problem is shown to be $\mathcal{NP}$-hard by reduction from the knapsack problem. The criterion $\overline{CC}^w$ is defined by $\overline{CC}^w = \sum_{i=1}^{n} c_i(\overline{p}_i - p_i)$. When the processing times are known the problem is polynomially solvable by using the rule *Shortest Ready Time first.* Thus the major difficulty lies in computing the optimal values of the processing times. To this purpose, Chen, Lu and Tang provide a dynamic programming algorithm of which the time complexity is in $O(knt_{max})$ where t_{max} is an upper bound on the optimal C_{max} value,

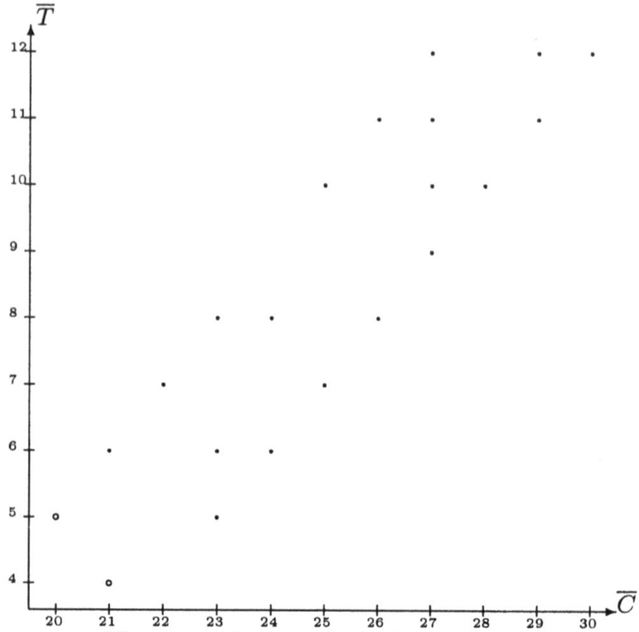

Fig. 7.6. The set of criteria vectors

defined by $t_{max} = \max_{i=1,\dots,n}(r_i) + \sum_{i=1}^{n} \overline{p}_i$. Without loss of generality assume that $r_1 \le r_2 \le ... \le r_n$. $\widetilde{F}(j,t)$ is the value of the objective function when considering only the sub-sequence $(1,...,j)$ with a makespan value equal to t. We have $\widetilde{F}(j,t) = \min_{i=1,\dots,(k+1)} \{g_i(j,t)\}$, $\forall j = 2,...,n$, $\forall t = 0,...,t_{max}$. The function $g_i(j,t)$ is the value of the objective function for the sub-sequence $(1,...,j)$, with a makespan equal to t and if the job J_j has a processing time equal to $p_j = (\underline{p}_j + i - 1)$. Therefore we have:

$$g_i(j,t) = \begin{cases} \widetilde{F}(j-1, t-(\underline{p}_j + i - 1)) & \\ \qquad +c_j(\underline{p}_j + i - 1) & \text{if } t \ge r_j + \underline{p}_j + i - 1 \\ \infty & \text{otherwise} \end{cases}$$

Notice that from the value of i which gives the minimum value of $\widetilde{F}(j,t)$ we can deduce the value of p_j. The initial conditions of the recurrence relation are as follows, $\forall t = 0,...,t_{max}$:

$$\widetilde{F}(1,t) = \begin{cases} c_1(\overline{p}_1) & \text{if } t \ge r_1 + \overline{p}_1 \\ c_1(\underline{p}_1 + i - 1) & \text{if } r_1 + \underline{p}_1 + i - 1 = t \\ & \text{and } i = 1,...,k \\ \infty & \text{if } t < r_1 + \underline{p}_1 \end{cases}$$

Besides, $p_1 = \underline{p}_1 + i - 1$ if $\widetilde{F}(1,t) = c_1(\underline{p}_1 + i - 1)$, $\forall i = 1, ..., k+1$. The optimal solution is obtained by computing $\min_{t=0,\dots,t_{max}} (\widetilde{F}(n,t) + t)$.

7.2.3 The $1|r_i, p_i \in [\underline{p}_i; \overline{p}_i] \cap \mathbb{N}|F_\ell(\overline{U}^w, \overline{CC}^w)$ problem

This problem with integer controllable processing times has been tackled by [Chen et al., 1997]. The processing times are defined as follows: (i) $p_i \in [\underline{p}_i; \overline{p}_i] \cap \mathbb{N}$, and (ii) $\forall i, j\ \overline{p}_i - \underline{p}_i = \overline{p}_j - \underline{p}_j = k$.
First the special case with a common due date is shown to be $\mathcal{NP}$-hard. Chen, Lu and Tang propose a dynamic programming algorithm which requires $O(nkd_{max})$ time, where $d_{max} = \max_{i=1,\dots,n} (d_i)$. Before presenting this algorithm, they show that an optimal schedule exists such that: (i) each tardy job is scheduled after all the early and on-time jobs, (ii) all early or on-time jobs are ordered according to the rule EDD, and (iii) For each tardy job J_i we have $p_i = \overline{p}_i$. At each phase we decide to schedule a job early (or on-time), or tardy. All the early and on-time jobs are scheduled according to the rule EDD. So, without loss of generality, we assume that $d_1 \leq ... \leq d_n$. $\widetilde{F}(j,t)$ is the value of the objective function when considering only the sub-sequence $(1, ..., j)$ and when the jobs J_i such that $C_i \leq d_i$ do not complete after time t. We have, $\forall j = 2, ..., n$, $\forall t = 0, ..., d_{max}$:

$$\widetilde{F}(j,t) = \begin{cases} \min\{\min_{i=1,\dots,(k+1)} (\widetilde{F}(j-1, t-(\underline{p}_j + i - 1)) & \\ \qquad +c_j(\underline{p}_j + i - 1)); & \\ \qquad \widetilde{F}(j-1,t) + c_j(\overline{p}_j) + w_j\} & \text{if } t \leq d_j \\ \infty & \text{otherwise} \end{cases}$$

To deduce the value of the processing time p_j, $\forall j = 2, ..., n$, from the previous recurrence relation, we have to distinguish different cases:

$$p_j = \begin{cases} \overline{p}_j & \text{if } t \leq d_j \text{ and } \widetilde{F}(j,t) = \widetilde{F}(j-1,t) + c_j(\overline{p}_j) + w_j \\ \underline{p}_j + i - 1 & \text{if } t \leq d_j \text{ and } \widetilde{F}(j,t) = \widetilde{F}(j-1, t-(\underline{p}_j + i - 1)) \\ & \qquad +c_j(\underline{p}_j + i - 1), \text{ and } i = 1, ..., (k+1) \\ \overline{p}_j & \text{otherwise} \end{cases}$$

The initial conditions are the following, $\forall t = 0, ..., d_{max}$:

$$\widetilde{F}(1,t) = \begin{cases} w_1 + c_1(\overline{p}_1) & \text{if } t = 0 \\ c_1(\underline{p}_1 + i - 1) & \text{if } d_1 \geq t = \underline{p}_1 + i - 1 \text{ and } i = 1, ..., k+1 \\ \infty & \text{otherwise} \end{cases}$$

Besides, the value of p_1 is given by:

$$p_1 = \begin{cases} \overline{p}_1 & \text{if } \widetilde{F}(1,t) = w_1 + c_1(\overline{p}_1) \\ & \text{or } \widetilde{F}(1,t) = c_1(\overline{p}_1) \\ & \text{or } \widetilde{F}(1,t) = \infty \\ \underline{p}_1 + i - 1 & \text{if } \widetilde{F}(1,t) = c_1(\underline{p}_1 + i - 1) \text{ and } i = 1, ..., k \end{cases}$$

The optimal solution is obtained by computing $\min_{t=0,\ldots,d_{max}} (\widetilde{F}(n,t) + t)$.

Chen, Lu and Tang also tackle the $1|d_i, p_i \in [\underline{p}_i; \overline{p}_i] \cap \mathbb{N}|F_\ell(T_{max}, \overline{CC}^w)$ problem that they show to be $\mathcal{NP}$-hard. They provide a pseudo-polynomial time algorithm based on the dynamic programming algorithm for the problem with the $\overline{U}^w$ criterion. Firstly, we compute T^*_{max} the optimal value of criterion T_{max} computed by the rule EDD with $p_i = \overline{p}_i$, $\forall i = 1, ..., n$. By setting $w_i = \infty$, $\forall i = 1, ..., n$ and performing a binary search in the interval $[0; T^*_{max}]$ it is possible to solve optimally the problem with the T_{max} criterion. For each value $z \in [0; T^*_{max}]$, fictitious due dates $d'_i = d_i + z$, $\forall i = 1, ..., n$, are computed and the corresponding $\overline{U}^w$ problem is solved. If its optimal solution has no tardy jobs, then an optimal solution exists, for the T_{max} problem, such that $T_{max} \leq z$.

7.2.4 Other problems

Minimisation of the average completion time

- [Azizoglu et al., 1997] study the $1|d_i, nmit|\epsilon(\overline{C}/E_{\max})$ problem which is strongly $\mathcal{NP}$-hard since the $1|d_i, nmit|Lex(E_{\max}, \overline{C})$ problem is also (see [Hoogeveen, 1992a]). Azizoglu, Kondakci and Koksalan propose an a priori algorithm and restrict the search for a Pareto optimum to the class of schedules with insertion of machine idle times. Dominance conditions are presented and used in an heuristic which approximates the set WE.

Notice that when the $nmit$ constraint is disabled the bicriteria problem, referred to as $1|d_i|\epsilon(\overline{C}/E_{\max})$, remains strongly $\mathcal{NP}$-hard and reduces to the $1|r_i|\overline{C}$ problem with $r_i = d_i - \epsilon - p_i$, $\forall i = 1, ..., n$, and ϵ is the bound on the E_{max} criterion. It is possible to design an a posteriori algorithm which main line is similar to that of algorithm $EWG1$, except that changing the ϵ value results in shifting all the release dates and no more the deadlines. Besides, to enumerate all strict Pareto optima it is necessary to consider all integer values of ϵ within the time interval $[0; E_{max}(SPT)]$ where $E_{max}(SPT)$ refers to the value of the maximum earliness criterion in the schedule computed using the SPT rule. The $1|r_i|\overline{C}$ problem has been extensively studied in the literature. Recently, [Della Croce and T'kindt, 2002] proposed a *recovering beam search* algorithm which is, to the best of our knowledge, the most efficient heuristic for this problem. Reported computational results show that this heuristic is close to the lower bound calculated by using the rule SRPT (*Shortest Remaining Processing Time first*). Notice that this bound has been seriously

improved by [Della Croce and T'kindt, 2003]. By using the improved lower bound and the heuristic it is, henceforth, possible to calculate a tight time interval containing the optimal $\overline{C}$ value. This latter can be calculated using the efficient branch-and-bound algorithm proposed by [Chu, 1992].
A lower approximation of the trade-off curve can be obtained by iteratively calculating the SRPT lower bound (or its improved version), denoted by LB^ϵ, for all integer values $\epsilon \in [0; E_{max}(SPT)]$. Similarly, it is possible to obtain an upper approximation by using the above quoted recovering beam search algorithm to calculate upper bounds UB^ϵ. It is interesting to notice that, $\forall \epsilon, \epsilon' \geq \min_{1 \leq i \leq n}(d_i - p_i)$, we have $LB^\epsilon = LB^{\epsilon'} + n(\epsilon' - \epsilon)$ and $UB^\epsilon = UB^{\epsilon'} + n(\epsilon' - \epsilon)$.

• [Emmons, 1975b] studies the $1|d_i|Lex(\overline{U}, \overline{C})$ problem which has been shown to be $\mathcal{NP}$-hard by [Chen and Bulfin, 1993]. Emmons considers firstly the algorithm of [Moore, 1968] for the $1|d_i|\overline{U}$ problem and shows that this algorithm is not optimal for the bicriteria problem. He proposes then a branch-and-bound algorithm and shows that the dominance conditions enable us to prune nodes in the search tree.

• The enumeration of the Pareto optima for the criteria $\overline{C}$ and $\overline{U}$ is studied by [Nelson et al., 1986] who propose an *a posteriori* algorithm for the $1|d_i|\epsilon(\overline{C}/\overline{U})$ problem. This algorithm is a branch-and-bound algorithm which determines a subset of the set of weak Pareto optima. This algorithm proceeds by determining iteratively a value ϵ, and then by minimising the criterion $\overline{C}$ under the constraint $\overline{U} \leq \epsilon$. Every level of the search tree contains solutions such that this constraint is verified for the same value ϵ. Besides, they present dominance conditions which they use to reduce the search space. Nelson, Sarin and Daniels propose similarly two heuristics based on the previous optimal algorithm, *i.e.* truncated branch-and-bound algorithms, which approximate a subset of WE. The problem of enumerating the Pareto optima is taken up again by [Kiran and Unal, 1991] who propose general conditions for calculating these optima. These conditions are notably related to properties of the sequence obtained by applying the SPT rule and Smith's algorithm for the $1|d_i|\epsilon(\bar{C}/L_{max})$ problem.

• [Nelson et al., 1986] study the $1|d_i|\epsilon(\overline{C}/\overline{U}, T_{\max})$ problem for which they propose a branch-and-bound algorithm which determines a subset of the set of weak Pareto optima. To increase the efficiency of this algorithm and to reduce the search space, Nelson, Sarin and Daniels use dominance conditions.

Minimisation of the average weighted completion time

• [Chand and Schneeberger, 1984] propose a dynamic programming algorithm to solve the $1|d_i|Lex(L_{\max}, \overline{C}^w)$ problem. They show similarly that this problem is $\mathcal{NP}$-hard. Its complexity is also studied by [Hoogeveen, 1992a] who shows its strongly $\mathcal{NP}$-hardness.

• [Smith, 1956] studies a particular case of the $1|d_i|\epsilon(\overline{C}^w/L_{\max})$ problem because he is interested in the minimisation of the criterion $\overline{C}^w$ under the constraint $L_{\max} = 0$. This problem is strongly $\mathcal{NP}$-hard since the $1|d_i|Lex(L_{\max}, \overline{C}^w)$ problem is also. Smith proposes an algorithm based on the rules EDD and WSPT, which he conjectures as being optimal. [Emmons, 1975a] shows by a counter example that this conjecture is false. This problem is taken up again by [Bansal, 1980] who proposes a branch-and-bound algorithm to determine the optimal solution, if it exists.
[Chand and Schneeberger, 1986] show that for a certain number of problems and if a solution with $L_{\max} = 0$ exists, the algorithm proposed by Smith is optimal. This is the case notably for problems where the weights w_i are defined by $w_i = f(p_i)$, with a decreasing function f.
[Heck and Roberts, 1972] study the general problem of the minimisation of criterion $\overline{C}^w$ under the constraint $L_{max} \leq \epsilon$. This problem is strongly $\mathcal{NP}$-hard due to the fact that: (i) when ϵ is fixed it reduces to the $1|\tilde{d}_i|\overline{C}^w$ problem, and (ii) the $1|\tilde{d}_i|\overline{C}^w$ problem is strongly $\mathcal{NP}$-hard ([Lenstra et al., 1977]). To solve this problem they propose an heuristic based on a result presented in [Smith, 1956]. [Burns, 1976] also proposes an heuristic based on a neighbourhood method. Following this [Miyazaki, 1981] returns to this problem and shows that it exists a polynomial reduction from the $1|d_i, L_{max} \leq \epsilon|-$ problem towards the $1|\tilde{d}_i|-$ (or $1|d'_i, L_{max} = 0|-$) problem. Thus, we are led back to the problem which was studied by [Smith, 1956]. Miyazaki proposes then conditions to improve a sequence by permutation of adjacent jobs. A neighbourhood heuristic, which uses the heuristic of [Smith, 1956] to obtain an initial sequence is presented. The complexity of the proposed heuristic is in $O(n^3)$ time. The experimental results demonstrate its efficiency in comparison with the heuristics proposed by [Smith, 1956] and [Burns, 1976]. No comparison is made with either the heuristic of [Heck and Roberts, 1972] or the branch-and-bound algorithm of [Bansal, 1980].

• [VanWassenhove and Gelders, 1978] are interested in the minimisation of the criteria $\overline{C}^w$ and $\overline{T}^w$ via the $1|d_i|\ F_\ell(\overline{C}^w, \overline{T}^w)$ problem which is strongly $\mathcal{NP}$-hard given that the $1|d_i|\overline{T}^w$ is also. They propose dominance conditions based on a result demonstrated by [Lawler et al., 1975] and four resolution algorithms. The first three are branch-and-bound algorithms which only differ by the lower bound used at each node. In the first algorithm the lower bound of a node is calculated by solving a transportation problem applied to unscheduled jobs at this node. Van Wassenhove and Gelders show how to construct the transportation cost matrix. In the second proposed branch-and-bound algorithm, the lower bound of each node is calculated by solving an assignment problem applied to the unscheduled jobs at the current node. If the unscheduled job J_i is placed in the non occupied position j then it is possible to get a lower bound $c_{i,j}$ of the contribution to the objective function of the job J_i. These bounds are used as costs $c_{i,j}$ when solving the assignment problem. Dominance conditions shown by Van Wassenhove and Gelders are also used. For the third algorithm a method proposed by [Fisher, 1976] to calculate the lower bounds is used. These bounds are calculated by a dynamic programming algorithm. Finally, Van Wassenhove and Gelders propose a dynamic programming algorithm, which solves the initial problem and uses the dominance condition presented. Experimental results show that this algorithm is faster but requires more memory space than the branch-and-bound algorithms. They speculate that for problems with more than 40 jobs the algorithm which combines a branch-and-bound algorithm and a dynamic programming algorithm is more efficient than the others.

Minimisation of tool changing costs

• [Bourgade et al., 1995] are interested in an industrial scheduling problem related to the production of glass packaging. The aim of this problem is to determine a schedule which minimises the maximum tardiness $T_{\max}$ and the total tool changing costs on the machine. These costs, denoted by $SC_{[i-1],[i]}$ with $[i]$ the job in the ith position, are assumed to be dependent on the sequence. The problem tackled is denoted by $1|d_i, S_{sd}|F(\overline{SC}, T_{\max})$. Bourgade, Aguilera, Penz and Binder propose a mixed integer program and two possible definitions of the objective function F are considered:

$$F(\overline{SC}, T_{\max}) = \frac{\overline{SC}}{\delta} + \alpha \sum_{i=1}^{n} exp^{\max(0;T_i - T^*_{\max})},$$

$$\text{and } F(\overline{SC}, T_{\max}) = \frac{\overline{SC}}{\delta} + \max\left(0; (T_{\max} - T^*_{\max}) \times (1+\alpha)\right),$$

with $T^*_{\max}$ the optimal value of the criterion $T_{\max}$ for the $1|d_i|T_{\max}$ problem. The $1|S_{sd}|\overline{SC}$ problem is $\mathcal{NP}$-hard, since it reduces to the travelling salesman problem and then the bicriteria problem is also: it is sufficient to consider $\alpha = 0$ in the first function and $\alpha = -1$ in the second. In order to solve these two problems Bourgade, Aguilera, Penz and Binder propose a branch-and-bound algorithm. Experimental results show that the solutions obtained by minimisation of the first objective function F can be dominated solutions.

• [Barnes and Vanston, 1981] tackle a similar problem, which is denoted by $1|S_{sd}|F_\ell(\overline{SC}, \overline{C}^w)$. This one is $\mathcal{NP}$-hard. Barnes and Vanston show that it can reduce to the travelling salesman problem and they propose an heuristic which uses the rule "choice of the closest unvisited town" to calculate a schedule. They also propose two optimal algorithms. The first is a branch-and-bound algorithm and the second is a dynamic programming algorithm. The latter uses a lower bound for each decision to reduce the search space.

Experimental results show that the dynamic programming algorithm is faster than the branch-and-bound algorithm. These results show moreover that the relative deviation between the heuristic and the optimal solution is on average 0.66%.

7.3 Open problems

7.3.1 The $1|d_i|\bar{U}, T_{max}$ problem

[Shantikumar, 1983] is the first who tackled the minimisation of criteria $\bar{U}$ and T_{max} while solving the $1|d_i|Lex(\bar{U}, T_{max})$ problem. He proposes a heuristic and a branch-and-bound algorithm in which dominance conditions are used to prune nodes in the search tree. Each node is evaluated by a lower bound, the calculation of which depends on the algorithm presented by [Moore, 1968] for the $1|d_i|\overline{U}$ problem. No experimental result is presented by Shantikumar, however later works done by [Gupta et al., 1999a] show that this exact algorithm is not capable of solving problems with more than 30 jobs in size. Later on, [Gupta and Ramnarayanan, 1996] propose a heuristic algorithm based on Moore's algorithm for the $1|d_i|\bar{U}$ problem, and an interchange improving procedure.

Up to now the complexity of the $1|d_i|Lex(\bar{U}, T_{max})$ problem is open but assumed to be non polynomial by [Gupta et al., 1999a] who propose a branch-and-bound algorithm to solve it. It is based on several results given below. The first theorem is trivial and states that once the sets of on-time and tardy jobs have been fixed (so the value of criterion $\bar{U}$ is determined), the T_{max} criterion is minimised by applying twice the EDD rule.

Theorem 19 *[Gupta et al., 1999a]*
There exists an optimal schedule in which on-time jobs are sequenced in EDD order, and tardy jobs are sequenced in EDD order.

The next theorem states a result that can be used to fix a job in the last position of the sequence. Notice that this result is close to the one used by Shanthikumar to build his constructive heuristic.

Theorem 20 *[Gupta et al., 1999a]*
For a given partition of the jobs into a set E of on-time jobs and a set T of tardy jobs, let $J_i \in E$ and $J_j \in T$ be two jobs such that $d_i = \max_{J_k \in E}(d_k)$ and $d_j = \max_{J_k \in T}(d_k)$. If $d_i \geq \sum_{k=1}^{n} p_k$ then there exists an optimal schedule in which job J_i is sequenced last. Otherwise, there exists an optimal schedule in which job J_j is sequenced last.

In the remainder we assume, without loss of generality, that jobs are numbered according to the EDD order, *i.e.* $d_1 \leq d_2 \leq ... \leq d_n$. From theorem 20 it follows that if $d_n \geq \sum_{k=1}^{n} p_k$ then there exists an optimal schedule in which job J_n is scheduled last. By applying this remark repeatedly we can reduce the set of jobs to be scheduled. This procedure is applied in a *preprocessing phase* which also reduces the size of the instance by trying to determine jobs which necessarily early of tardy. Let E (resp. T) be the set of early (resp. tardy) jobs in the schedule, denoted by S, given by Moore's algorithm for the $1|d_i|\bar{U}$ problem. The two following results are applied:

1. Let $J_j \in E$ and S' be the schedule obtained by applying theorem 19 on sets $E//\{J_j\}$ and $T \cup \{J_j\}$. If $\bar{U}(S) \neq \bar{U}(S')$ then job J_j is necessarily on-time.
2. Let $J_j \in T$ and S' be the schedule obtained by applying theorem 19 on sets $E \cup \{J_j\}$ and $T//\{J_j\}$. If $\bar{U}(S) \neq \bar{U}(S')$ then job J_j is necessarily late.

Henceforth, by applying the whole preprocessing phase we can reduce the problem size by deriving the set of jobs L^0 that are scheduled last, the set of jobs E^0 that are necessarily early and the set of jobs T^0 that are necessarily late. The set of remaining jobs is denoted by N^0.

Starting from this partitioning of the initial set of jobs, a branch-and-bound process is applied. Each node of the search tree represents a partition of the set of jobs since, thanks to theorem 19, it is possible to derive the sequencing of jobs inside each set of early or tardy jobs. Henceforth, from a node s two child nodes are created by selecting a job $J_h \in N^s$ and assigning it either in E^s or in T^s. The root node s is defined by $E^s = E^0$, $T^s = T^0$ and $N^s = N^0$. The choice of the job J_h to branch from depends on the calculation of the lower and upper bounds provided by the authors.

The lower bound proposed by Gupta, Hariri and Potts is based on a relaxation, at a node s, of the subproblem defined by set N^s. The idea is to partition N^s, and eventually change the due dates of some jobs, into two sets E' and T' such that we can prove this partition is optimal for the modified instance. The relaxation is based on an unproved result provided by the authors.

Property 10 *[Gupta et al., 1999a]*
Let n' be the smallest index, where $0 \leq n' \leq |N^s|$ such that

$$d_{n'} + \sum_{k=n'+1}^{j} p_k \leq d_j, \ \forall j = n'+1, ..., |N^s|, \text{ with } d_0 = 0.$$

In any schedule with the minimum number of tardy jobs, jobs $J_{n'+1}, ..., J_{|N^s|}$ must be on-time.

The details of the lower bound, denoted by HGHP1, are given in figure 7.7. This bound requires $O(n\log(n))$ time. At each node an upper bound is also calculated in $O(n^2)$ time by applying algorithm HGHP2 (figure 7.8). Notice that for a given node, HGHP1 is run before HGHP2.

```
ALGORITHM HGHP1
/* N^s is the set of unscheduled jobs, numbered from 1 to |N^s| */
/* We assume that d_1 <= d_2 <= ... <= d_|N^s| */
Step 1:  /* Initialisation of the algorithm */
         Find n' according to property 10 on N^s;
         Ē = {J_{n'+1}, ..., J_|N^s|};
         E = T = ∅; t = 0;
         d'_i = ∞, ∀i = 1, ..., n;
Step 2:  /* Computation of the sets E and T */
         For (j = 1 to n') Do
         |   t = t + p_j; E = E ∪ {J_j};
         |   If (t > d_j) Then
         |   |   Let J_i ∈ E such that p_i = max_{J_k ∈ E}(p_k);
         |   |   d'_i = d_j; t = t − p_i; E = E − {J_i}; T = T ∪ {J_i};
         |   End If;
         End For;
Step 3:  /* Computation of the sets E' and T' */
         d'_i = d_i, ∀J_i ∈ T^s;
         T = T ∪ T^s;
         Order T = {J_j1, ..., J_jℓ} such that d_j1 <= ... <= d_jℓ;
         Let the index 1 <= i <= ℓ be such that t + Σ_{k=1}^{i} p_jk <= d_n';
         T' = {J_j(i+1), ..., J_jℓ}; E' = Ē;
Step 4:  /* Calculation of the lower bound on the T_max */
         /* using the modified due dates d'_i */
         LB = T_max(EDD(T')/t); /* EDD(T') starts at time t */
         Return LB
[Gupta et al., 1999a]
```

Fig. 7.7. A lower bound for the $1|d_i|Lex(\bar{U}, T_{max})$ problem

Gupta, Hariri and Potts also present four dominance conditions, used to prune nodes of the search tree, one of which being due to [Shantikumar, 1983]. These four conditions are given below.

Theorem 21

A node s is dominated and thus pruned if one on the following condition holds:

1. *([Shantikumar, 1983])* $\exists J_j \in T^s$, $\exists J_k \in E^s$ *such that* $p_j \leq p_k$, $d_j \leq d_k$, *and* $d_j - p_j \geq d_k - p_k$.
2. $\exists J_j \in T^s$, $\exists J_k \in E^s$ *such that* $p_j \leq p_k$, $d_j \leq d_k$, *and* $\sum_{i=1}^{h} p_i \geq d_h$, $\forall h = 1, ..., k$.
3. $\exists J_i, J_k \in T^s$, $\exists J_j \in E^s$ *such that* $p_i \leq p_j$, $d_j \leq d_i \leq d_k$ *and* $d_j \geq d_k - p_k$.
4. $\exists J_i \in T^s$, $\exists J_j, J_k \in E^s$ *such that* $p_i \leq p_k$, $d_i \leq d_k \leq d_j$ *and* $d_i \geq d_j - p_j$.

When applying these conditions special care must be taken to jobs have the same values of processing times or due dates. Besides, at each node obtained

ALGORITHM HGHP2

Step 1: /* Initialisation */
Retreive from HGHP1 T, E, $\bar{E}$ and the d_i''s;
Apply iteratively theorem 20 on $E \cup \bar{E}$ and T
to build sequence S;
$UB = T_{max}(S)$;

Step 2: /* Improvement of the current seed sequence */
Let J_h be such that $T_h = T_{max}(S)$
(break ties by choosing the job with the smallest rank in S);
<u>If</u> ($d_h' \neq +\infty$ <u>and</u> $d_h' > d_h$) <u>Then</u>
| Let $J_k \in E$ be the job such that $d_k = d_h'$;
| $E = E \cup \{J_h\} \backslash \{J_k\}$; $T = T \cup \{J_k\} \backslash \{J_h\}$;
| Apply iteratively theorem 20 on $E \cup \bar{E}$ and T to obtain S;
| <u>If</u> (all jobs of $\bar{E} \cup E$ cannot be scheduled on-time) <u>Then</u>
| | $UB' = +\infty$;
| <u>End If</u>;
| <u>If</u> ($UB' < UB$) <u>Then</u>
| | $UB = UB'$;
| <u>Go to</u> Step 2;
| <u>End If</u>;
<u>End If</u>;

Step 3: <u>Return</u> UB;

[Gupta et al., 1999a]

Fig. 7.8. An upper bound for the $1|d_i|Lex(\bar{U}, T_{max})$ problem

by assigning job J_h to set E^s or T^s they are applied with jobs in N^s assuming that they will be assumed in T^s or E^s, respectively.

Gupta, Hariri and Potts conduct intensive testings to evaluate the efficiency of their branch-and-bound algorithm. They also compare it to their implementation of the branch-and-bound algorithm of [Shantikumar, 1983].

The obtained results show that the latter is limited to problems with up to 30 jobs whilst the proposed branch-and-bound algorithm is capable of solving to optimality problems with up 100 jobs. From the results it appears that, for most values of n, between one third and one half of the problems are solved after the preprocessing at the root node. Additional testings show that the second dominance condition presented previously is the most efficient one and gives very good results.

[Nelson et al., 1986] study the more general problem which is denoted by $1|d_i|\epsilon(\overline{U}/T_{\max})$ for which they propose a branch-and-bound algorithm to determine a subset of the set of weak Pareto optima. An heuristic is proposed which enables us to determine a subset of the set of weak Pareto optima.

7.3.2 Other problems

Minimisation of the average completion time

[Fry and Leong, 1987] study the $1|d_i|F_\ell(\overline{E},\overline{C})$ problem for which they propose a mixed integer program. Experimental results show that the optimal solution can be determined in less than 100 seconds for problems with 10 jobs.

Minimisation of crashing time costs

[Vickson, 1980a] studies the $1|p_i \in [\underline{p}_i;\overline{p}_i]|F_\ell(\overline{C}^w,\overline{CC}^w)$ problem. Vickson does not present a study of its complexity but he speculates that this is $\mathcal{NP}$-hard, in contrast to the $1|p_i \in [\underline{p}_i;\overline{p}_i]|\ F_\ell(\overline{C},\overline{CC}^w)$ and $1|p_i \in [\underline{p}_i;\overline{p}_i], d_i|F_\ell(T_{\max},\overline{CC}^w)$ problems. Vickson proposes a branch-and-bound algorithm and a greedy heuristic based on the rule WSPT. One case study shows that the heuristic is capable of sequencing and calculating the optimal processing time of certain jobs. For other jobs, we have to use the branch-and-bound algorithm.

8. Shop problems

8.1 Two-machine flowshop problems

In this section we are interested in multicriteria flowshop scheduling problems with two machines. Each job J_i is processed on the machine M_1 for a duration $p_{i,1}$, then on the machine M_2 for a duration $p_{i,2}$. In this context, the multicriteria scheduling problem which is addressed the most in the literature involves the minimisation of the criteria $\overline{C}$ and C_{max}. Different scheduling problems are derived according to the form of the considered objective function.

8.1.1 The $F2|prmu|Lex(C_{max}, \overline{C})$ problem

[Rajendran, 1992]

This problem is strongly $\mathcal{NP}$-hard ([Chen and Bulfin, 1994]) and Rajendran proposes two heuristics and one exact algorithm to solve it. These two heuristics, denoted by HCR1 and HCR2, use the algorithm ESJ1 of [Johnson, 1954] to obtain an optimal initial sequence for the criterion C_{max}. Next they perform adjacent job permutations which are chosen by two indicators D_i and D'_i, generally defined for a sequence S and a position r by:

$$D_{S[r]} = p_{S[r],1} + p_{S[r],2} - p_{S[r+1],1} - p_{S[r+1],2}$$
$$D'_{S[r]} = 2p_{S[r],1} + p_{S[r],2} - 2p_{S[r+1],1} - p_{S[r+1],2}$$

The aim of these permutations is to reduce the value of the criterion $\overline{C}$ of the schedule S. The next job to be permutated is determined according to these indicators. The heuristic HCR1 uses the indicator D_i and ties between several jobs are broken using D'_i. The heuristic HCR2 uses the indicator D'_i and ties between several jobs are broken using D_i. The heuristic HCR1 is presented in figure 8.1 and the heuristic HCR2 is similar. We frequently refer in the literature to the best schedule calculated by HCR1 and HCR2.

Example.
We consider a problem for which $n = 10$ and we apply the heuristic HCR1.

ALGORITHM HCR1

/* T is the set of the n jobs to schedule */
/* ESJ1 is the algorithm of [Johnson, 1954] for the $F2|prmu|C_{max}$ problem */
Step 1: Apply algorithm ESJ1 to obtain the schedule S;
Step 2: Let k be the index in S such that

$$\sum_{r=1}^{k} p_{S[r],1} - \sum_{r=1}^{k-1} p_{S[r],2} = \max_{u=1,\dots,n} \left(\sum_{r=1}^{u} p_{S[r],1} - \sum_{r=1}^{u-1} p_{S[r],2}\right);$$

For $r = 1$ to n Do
  If $(r = k-1)$ or $(r = k)$ or $(r = n)$ Then
    $D_{S[r]} = -1$;
    $D'_{S[r]} = -1$;
  Else
    $D_{S[r]} = p_{S[r],1} + p_{S[r],2} - p_{S[r+1],1} - p_{S[r+1],2}$;
    $D'_{S[r]} = 2p_{S[r],1} + p_{S[r],2} - 2p_{S[r+1],1} - p_{S[r+1],2}$;
  End If;
End For;
$L = \{r / D_{S[r]} \geq 0\}$;
Sort L by decreasing order of values D_i (break ties by choosing the job with the greatest value D'_i);
Step 3: While $(L \neq \emptyset)$ Do
  $r = L[1]$;
  $S' = S$ after permutation of jobs in positions r and $(r+1)$;
  If $((C_{max}(S') = C_{max}(S))$ and $(\overline{C}(S') < \overline{C}(S)))$ Then
    $S = S'$;
    Goto Step 2;
  End If;
  $L = L - \{r\}$;
End While;
Step 4: Print $S, C_{max}(S)$ and $\overline{C}(S)$;

[Rajendran, 1992]

Fig. 8.1. An heuristic algorithm for the $F2|prmu|Lex(C_{max}, \overline{C})$ problem

i	1	2	3	4	5	6	7	8	9	10
$p_{i,1}$	5	6	7	10	10	8	13	7	10	2
$p_{i,2}$	10	8	11	10	9	7	5	4	2	1

(i) The schedule obtained by the algorithm $ESJ1$ is $S = (J_1, J_2, J_3, J_4, J_5, J_6, J_7, J_8, J_9, J_{10})$ and we have $C^*_{max} = C_{max}(S) = 79$ and $\overline{C}(S) = 521$.
$k = 10$.
(ii) Calculation of the initial indicators

r	1	2	3	4	5	6	7	8	9	10
$D_{S[r]}$	1	−4	−2	1	4	−3	7	−1	−1	−1
$D'_{S[r]}$	0	−5	−5	1	6	−8	13	−4	−1	−1

$L = \{J_7, J_5, J_4, J_1\}$.
(iii) $S' = (J_1, J_2, J_3, J_4, J_5, J_6, J_8, J_7, J_9, J_{10})$, $C_{max}(S') = 79 = C^*_{max}$ and $\overline{C}(S') = 521$.
$L = \{J_5, J_4, J_1\}$.

(iv) $S' = (J_1, J_2, J_3, J_4, J_6, J_5, J_7, J_8, J_9, J_{10})$, $C_{max}(S') = 79 = C^*_{max}$ and $\overline{C}(S') = 519 < \overline{C}(S)$.
We set therefore $S = S'$ and we still have $k = 10$.
(v) Calculation of the indicators

r	1	2	3	4	5	6	7	8	9	10
$D_{S[r]}$	1	−4	−2	5	−4	1	7	−1	−1	−1
$D'_{S[r]}$	0	−5	−5	7	−6	−2	13	−4	−1	−1

$L = \{J_7, J_4, J_1, J_6\}$
We apply the heuristic HCR1 until it halts and we obtain the schedule S which is presented in figure 8.2.

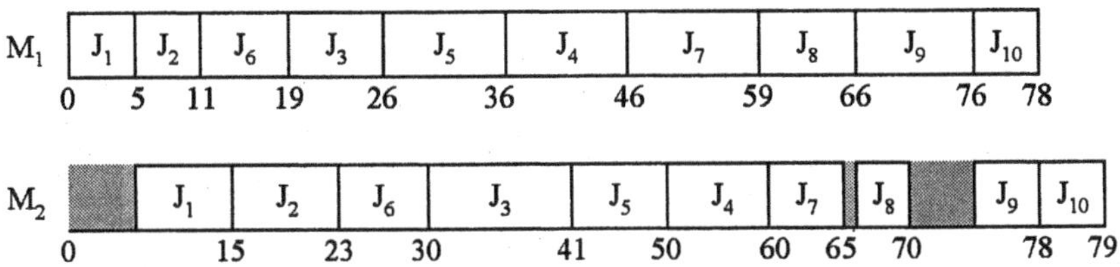

$C_{max}(S) = 79 = C^*_{max}$ and $\overline{C}(S) = 511$

Fig. 8.2. The schedule calculated by the heuristic HCR1

Rajendran also proposes a branch-and-bound algorithm to determine an optimal solution. Every node includes a list σ of n' scheduled jobs, a set Ω of $n - n'$ unscheduled jobs and two lower bounds. The first bound is an evaluation of the value of the criterion C_{max} knowing that jobs in σ are already scheduled. The second bound is an evaluation of the value of the criterion $\overline{C}$. Rajendran uses the bounds of [Ignall and Schrage, 1965] to calculate this lower bound.
The lower bound on the criterion C_{max} is calculated by sorting on each machine the jobs in Ω by increasing order of their processing times. With these two independent orders we can thus define dummy jobs such that the dummy job number k the kth processing time on both machines. The sequence obtained is concatenated at the end of sequence σ and the lower bound of the criterion C_{max} is obtained by calculating the value of the criterion C_{max} of this schedule. This evaluation is obviously a lower bound whereas it is possible to obtain an exact evaluation in polynomial time of the value of the criterion C_{max} at each node. It is sufficient to concatenate σ with the sequence obtained by applying the algorithm $ESJ1$ on the set Ω and to calculate the value of the criterion C_{max} of this new schedule.
This implies that the branch-and-bound algorithm, denoted by ECR1, proposed by Rajendran (figure 8.3) can preserve a node after evaluation whereas

this does not enable us afterwards to obtain a schedule with an optimal makespan. The search strategy used is the best first strategy.

```
                              ALGORITHM ECR1
/* T is the set of n jobs to schedule */
Step 1:  /* Initialisation of the algorithm */
         Apply heuristic HCR1 to obtain the schedule S';
         Apply heuristic HCR2 to obtain the schedule S'';
         /* Initialisation of the upper bound */
         If (C̄(S') < C̄(S'')) Then
           | S_ref = S';
         Else
           | S_ref = S'';
         End If;
         Cmax_ref = Cmax(S_ref); C̄_ref = C̄(S_ref);
         Create the root node s0: σ0 = ∅ ; Ω0 = T; Q = {s0};
Step 2:  /* Main part of the branch-and-bound */
         While (Q ≠ ∅) Do
           Choose the node s_i with the lowest value of LB_C̄ in Q;
           Q = Q − {s_i}; Ω = Ω_i;
           For k = 1 to |Ω_i| Do
             Select a job J_j in Ω: Ω = Ω − {J_j};
             Create a child node s_{i+1}^(k): σ_{i+1}^(k) = σ_i//{J_j}; Ω_{i+1}^(k) = Ω_i − {J_j};
             Compute LB_Cmax(s_{i+1}^(k)) and LB_C̄(s_{i+1}^(k));
             If ( (LB_Cmax(s_{i+1}^(k)) ≤ Cmax_ref) and (LB_C̄(s_{i+1}^(k)) < C̄_ref) )
             Then
               If (Ω_{i+1}^(k) ≠ ∅) Then Q = Q + {s_{i+1}^(k)};
               Else
                 | S_ref = σ_{i+1}^(k);
                 | C̄_ref = C̄(S_ref);
               End If;
             End If;
           End For;
         End While;
Step 3:  Print S_ref, Cmax_ref and C̄_ref;
                              [Rajendran, 1992]
```

Fig. 8.3. An optimal algorithm for the $F2|prmu|Lex(C_{max}, \overline{C})$ problem

The heuristic HCR1 has the advantage of being optimal if $\min_{i=1,\dots,n}(p_{i,1}) > \max_{i=1,\dots,n}(p_{i,2})$. This configuration corresponds to the case where *the machine* M_1 *dominates the machine* M_2. Before proving the optimality of the algorithm HCR1 in this case we introduce preliminary results in lemma 26, 27 and 28 .

Lemma 26
Let T be a set of n jobs J_i such that $\min_{i=1,...,n}(p_{i,1}) > \max_{i=1,...,n}(p_{i,2})$. A schedule S is optimal for the criterion C_{max} if and only if S is such that $p_{S[n],2} = \min_{i=1,...,n}(p_{i,2})$.

Proof.
Under the hypothesis $\min_{i=1,...,n}(p_{i,1}) > \max_{i=1,...,n}(p_{i,2})$ we have $C_{max}(S) = \sum_{i=1}^{n} p_{i,1} + p_{S[n],2}$. Thus a schedule S is optimal for the criterion C_{max} if and only if $p_{S[n],2} = \min_{i=1,...,n}(p_{i,2})$.□

Proof of lemma 26 also shows that there are at least $(n-1)!$ equivalent optimal solutions for the criterion C_{max}.

Lemma 27
Under the hypothesis $\min_{i=1,...,n}(p_{i,1}) > \max_{i=1,...,n}(p_{i,2})$, every permutation done by the heuristics HCR1 and HCR2 leads to an optimal schedule for the criterion C_{max}.

Proof.
After having obtained an optimal schedule S for the criterion C_{max} by using the algorithm ESJ1, the heuristics HCR1 and HCR2 search for the value k such that $\sum_{i=1}^{k} p_{S[i],1} - \sum_{i=1}^{k-1} p_{S[i],2}$ be a maximum. Given that, $\forall i = 1, ..., n, p_{S[i],1} - p_{S[i],2} > 0$, we have $k = n$. Because these heuristics forbid permutations with the kth job – Rajendran shows that this can only lead to increase the criterion C_{max} – we therefore deduce the result.□

Lemma 28
Under the hypothesis $\min_{i=1,...,n}(p_{i,1}) > \max_{i=1,...,n}(p_{i,2})$, an optimal schedule for the single criterion $\overline{C}$ is obtained by scheduling the jobs in increasing order of $p_{i,1}$.

Proof.
In every schedule S we necessarily have $C_{S[i],2} = C_{S[i],1} + p_{S[i],2}$, $\forall i = 1, ..., n$. We deduce immediately from this that minimisation of the criterion $\overline{C}$ is equivalent to minimisation of $\sum_{i=1}^{n} C_{S[i],1}$. This sum is minimised by applying the rule SPT on machine M_1, which leads to the result.□

Lemma 29
Under the hypothesis $\min_{i=1,...,n}(p_{i,1}) > \max_{i=1,...,n}(p_{i,2})$, the heuristic HCR1 computes the optimal solution of the problem $F2|prmu|Lex(C_{max}, \overline{C})$.

Proof.
Initially, the heuristic HCR1 uses the algorithm ESJ1 to obtain an optimal sequence S for the criterion C_{max}. From lemma 27, we know that all the permutations performed on the sequence S will not modify its optimality for the criterion C_{max}. These permutations are based on the indicator $D_{S[r]}$. If $D_{S[r]} \geq 0$ then we must permutate the jobs in position r and $r+1$ to try to get a schedule having a lower value of the criterion $\overline{C}$. When a better sequence is found, all the coefficients D_i are recalculated and we examine whether new permutations are needed. The sequence calculated by the algorithm ESJ1 can be broken down into two sub-sequences u and v (see different implementations of ESJ1 recalled in [Proust, 1992]) such that $u = \{J_i/p_{i,1} < p_{i,2}\}$ and $v = \{J_i/p_{i,2} \leq p_{i,1}\}$. At the beginning, u is sorted by increasing order of values $p_{i,1}$ and v by decreasing order of values $p_{i,2}$. From lemma 28, we can deduce that the list u must not be modified if we wish to minimise the criterion $\overline{C}$. Therefore, no permutation that could do HCR1 on the list u will be retained, and HCR1 can only do permutations on the list v.
At an arbitrary iteration, let there be two consecutive jobs J_i and J_j in the list v. We recall that $D_i = p_{i,1} + p_{i,2} - p_{j,1} - p_{j,2}$. If $p_{i,2} \geq p_{j,2}$, then two cases can occur:

- $p_{i,1} \geq p_{j,1}$ then $D_i \geq 0$ and these two jobs are permutated. We then find a lower value of the criterion $\overline{C}$ (lemma 28),
- $p_{i,1} < p_{j,1}$ and $D_i \geq 0$ the permutation of J_i and J_j does not lead to a lower value of the criterion $\overline{C}$ (lemma 28) and therefore the sequence is not retained.

Besides, if $p_{i,2} < p_{j,2}$, then we have already performed a permutation of J_i and J_j which has allowed the criterion $\overline{C}$ to be minimised: therefore it is not of interest to permutate these two jobs again. With lemma 27, we deduce that HCR1 will reorder the list v in increasing order of the values $p_{i,1}$, without modifying the last job of v. The heuristic respects lemma 26 and 28 and therefore solves the $F2|prmu|Lex(C_{max}, \overline{C})$ problem optimally.□

Experimental results show that the algorithm ECR1 is limited to problems with up to 15 jobs.

[Gupta et al., 2001]

Gupta, Neppali and Werner propose nine heuristics and one optimal algorithm to solve the $F2|prmu|Lex(C_{max}, \overline{C})$ problem. They study two particular cases for which an optimal schedule can be constructed in polynomial time:

1. We suppose that $\forall i = 1, ..., n$, $p_{i,1} \leq p_{i,2}$ and $\forall i, j = 1, ..., n$, $i \neq j$, $p_{i,1} \leq p_{j,1} \Rightarrow p_{i,2} \leq p_{j,2}$. Then an optimal schedule can be obtained by sorting the jobs in increasing order of the values $p_{i,2}$.
2. If $\min_{i=1,...,n}(p_{i,1}) \geq \max_{j=1,...,n}(p_{j,2})$, then an optimal schedule can be obtained by sorting the jobs in increasing order of the values $p_{i,1}$ and by sequencing the job with the smallest $p_{i,2}$ in the last position.

With regard to the first case, the proof is deduced from the fact that the rule SPT which is applied to the processing times on the second machine

independently minimises the criteria $\overline{C}$ and C_{max}. With regard to the second case, we find a similar result to that shown in lemma 29.
The optimal algorithm, denoted by EGNW1, proposed by Gupta, Neppalli and Werner proceeds by enumeration. The dominated sequences are eliminated by using a result derived from the following theorem.

Theorem 22 *[Gupta, 1972]*
We denote by ω, δ and π three partial sequences. Let us consider two sequences $\omega\pi$ and $\delta\pi$. If $C_{max}(\omega) \leq C_{max}(\delta)$ and $\overline{C}(\omega) \leq \overline{C}(\delta)$, then we have $C_{max}(\omega\pi) \leq C_{max}(\delta\pi)$ and $\overline{C}(\omega\pi) \leq \overline{C}(\delta\pi)$.

This result can be particularised and used as a dominance condition in a branch-and-bound algorithm. In this case we make use of the following theorem.

Theorem 23 *[Gupta, 1972]*
We denote by ω and π two partial sequences and J_i and J_i two jobs. Let us consider two sequences $\omega J_i J_j \pi$ and $\omega J_j J_i \pi$. If $C_{max}(\omega J_i J_j) \leq C_{max}(\omega J_j J_i)$ and $C_{max}(\omega J_i) + C_{max}(\omega J_i J_j) \leq C_{max}(\omega J_j) + C_{max}(\omega J_j J_i)$, then we have $C_{max}(\omega J_i J_j \pi) \leq C_{max}(\omega J_j J_i \pi)$ and $\overline{C}(\omega J_i J_j \pi) \leq \overline{C}(\omega J_j J_i \pi)$.

The algorithm EGNW1 proceeds by enumerating for every position of the sequence the jobs which can be placed in it. Certain jobs are eliminated if, at a given position, they cannot lead to an optimal schedule for the criterion C_{max}. If a partial sequence is dominated using theorem 23 then the corresponding node is pruned. The algorithm is presented in figure 8.4.

The nine heuristics also presented by Gupta, Neppalli and Werner are greedy algorithms and neighbourhood algorithms. Experimental results show that on average one of these heuristics, denoted by HGNW1, dominates the others. This heuristic proceeds by inserting a job into a partial sequence at each iteration. All possible insertion positions are tested, leading thus to several new sequences. The best sequence is retained for the next iteration. The heuristic HGNW1 is presented in figure 8.5. Its complexity is in $O(n^4)$ time.

Example.
We consider the earlier example, *i.e.* for which $n = 10$.

i	1	2	3	4	5	6	7	8	9	10
$p_{i,1}$	5	6	7	10	10	8	13	7	10	2
$p_{i,2}$	10	8	11	10	9	7	5	4	2	1

(i) The schedule calculated by algorithm J is $S^* = (J_1, J_2, \ldots, J_{10})$ with $C^*_{max} = 79$ and $\overline{C}(S^*) = 521$. We set $S = (J_1)$ and $position = 1$.
(ii) For J_2 we construct the sequences $S^{2,0} = (J_2, J_1)$ and $S^{2,1} = (J_1, J_2)$.
For J_3 we construct the sequences $S^{3,0} = (J_3, J_1)$ and $S^{3,1} = (J_1, J_3)$.
For J_4 we construct the sequences $S^{4,0} = (J_4, J_1)$ and $S^{4,1} = (J_1, J_4)$,...
For J_{10} we construct the sequences $S^{10,0} = (J_{10}, J_1)$ and $S^{10,1} = (J_1, J_{10})$.
$L = \{S^{2,0}, S^{2,1}, S^{3,0}, S^{3,1}, S^{4,0}, S^{4,1}, S^{5,0}, S^{5,1}, S^{6,0}, S^{6,1}, S^{7,1}, S^{8,0}, S^{8,1}\}$.

```
ALGORITHM EGNW1
/* T is the set of n jobs to schedule */
/* ESJ1 is the algorithm of [Johnson, 1954] */
/* C*_max is the optimal value of criterion C_max */
Step 1: /* Initialisation of the algorithm */
        G = {(J1); (J2); ...; (Jn)};
        Level = 1;
Step 2: /* Enumeration of the set of possible schedules */
        While (Level ≠ n) Do
            /* We check if we can eliminate sequences using
            theorem 23 */
            If (∄σ ∈ G such that |σ| = Level) Then
                Among the sequences of length Level + 1 of G apply
                theorem 23 to eliminate dominated sequences;
                Level = Level + 1;
            End If;
            Let σ be a sequence of G such that |σ| = Level;
            G = G − {σ};
            Ω = T − σ;
            For i = 1 to |Ω| Do
                σ_i = σ//{Ω[i]};
                /* We test the value of the criterion C_max */
                If (max( Σ_{J_j ∈ σ_i} p_{j,1} + C_max(ESJ1(Ω − {Ω[i]}));
                    C_{σ_i,2} + Σ_{j ∈ Ω−{Ω[i]}} p_{i,2}) ≤ C*_max) Then
                    | G = G + {σ_i};
                End If;
            End For;
        End While;
Step 3: Apply theorem 23;
        Print G[1], C_max(G[1]) and C̄(G[1]);
[Gupta et al., 2001]
```

Fig. 8.4. An optimal algorithm for the $F2|prmu|Lex(C_{max}, \overline{C})$ problem

We have $S^{u,v} = S^{8,1}$ and $\overline{C}(S^{8,1}//J(J_2, J_3, \ldots, J_7, J_9, J_{10})) = 500 < \overline{C}^*$. We update S^*.
We take $S = S^{8,0}$ because $\overline{C}(S^{8,0})$ is minimum.
(iii) We iterate and we obtain the schedule S^* presented in figure 8.6.

Experimental results show similarly that HGNW1 is better than HCR1 and HCR2. Comparisons with the optimal algorithm EGNW1 are presented for problems with up to 10 jobs, and show that the heuristic HGNW1 is on average 0.6% of the optimal solution for the criterion $\overline{C}$.

ALGORITHM HGNW1

/* T is the set of n jobs to schedule */
/* $ESJ1$ is the algorithm of [Johnson, 1954] */
/* $S_{[j)}$ is a sub-sequence of S containing the j first jobs */
/* $S_{(position-j]}$ is a sub-sequence of S containing the $(position - j)$ last jobs */
<u>Step 1:</u> /* Initialisation of the algorithm */
  $S^* = ESJ1(T)$;
  $C^*_{max} = C_{max}(S^*)$;
  $S = S^*[1]$;
  $position = 1$;
<u>Step 2:</u> /* We build a schedule */
  <u>While</u> ($position \leq n$) <u>Do</u>
    <u>For</u> $J_i \in (T - S)$ <u>Do</u>
      <u>For</u> $j = 0$ <u>to</u> $position$ <u>Do</u>
        $S^{i,j} = S_{[j)}//\{J_i\}//S_{(position-j]}$;
      <u>End For</u>;
    <u>End For</u>;
    $L = \{S^{i,j} / C_{max}(S^{i,j}//ESJ1(T - S^{i,j})) = C^*_{max}\}$;
    Let $S^{u,v}$ be such that $\overline{C}(S^{u,v}//ESJ1(T - S^{u,v})) = \min_{S^{k,l} \in L} \overline{C}(S^{k,l}//ESJ1(T - S^{k,l}))$;
    <u>If</u> ($\overline{C}(S^{u,v}//ESJ1(T - S^{u,v})) < \overline{C}(S^*)$) <u>Then</u>
      $S^* = S^{u,v}//ESJ1(T - S^{u,v})$;
    <u>End If</u>;
    Let $S^{p,q}$ be such that $\overline{C}(S^{p,q}) = \min_{S^{k,l} \in L} \overline{C}(S^{k,l})$;
    $S = S^{p,q}$;
    $position = position + 1$;
  <u>End while</u>;
<u>Step 3:</u> <u>Print</u> $S^*, C_{max}(S^*)$ and $\overline{C}(S^*)$;

[Gupta et al., 2001]

Fig. 8.5. An heuristic algorithm for the $F2|prmu|Lex(C_{max}, \overline{C})$ problem

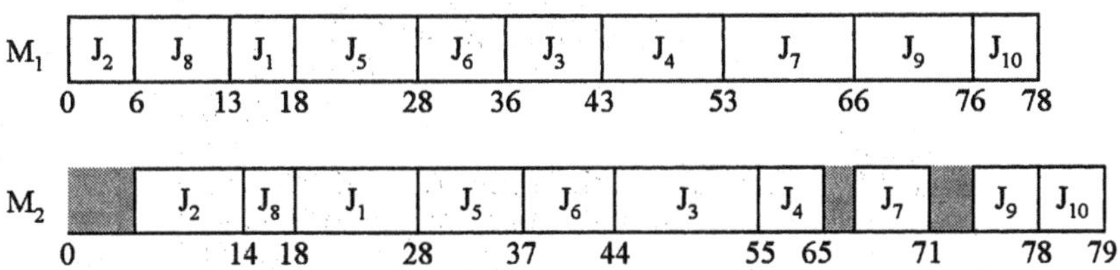

$C_{max}(S^*) = 79$ and $\overline{C}(S^*) = 489$

Fig. 8.6. The schedule calculated by the heuristic HGNW1

[T'kindt et al., 2003]

T'kindt, Gupta and Billaut propose an heuristic, denoted by HTGB1, to solve the $F2|prmu|Lex(C_{max}, \overline{C})$ problem, which is an extension of that presented by [Nagar et al., 1995b] and next by [Billaut et al., 1998]. The heuristic HTGB1 proceeds in two steps: in the first step a schedule is constructed by a greedy algorithm while in the second this schedule is improved by a local search. The greedy step adapts the functionning of the rule SPT to the flowshop problem, by placing at each iteration the job having the lowest completion time on machine M_2, and such that at least one optimal schedule exists for the criterion C_{max} starting with the sequence of jobs already scheduled. The complexity of this phase is in $O(n^3)$ time. The second phase of the heuristic proceeds by permutating the jobs by the operator k-NAPI. For a given position i in the sequence, the permutation with the job in position $k+i$ is carried out. The heuristic HTGB1 is presented in figure 8.8.

Example.
We consider the earlier example, *i.e.* for which $n = 10$.

i	1	2	3	4	5	6	7	8	9	10
$p_{i,1}$	5	6	7	10	10	8	13	7	10	2
$p_{i,2}$	10	8	11	10	9	7	5	4	2	1

We uniquely apply the greedy step of the heuristic HTGB1.
(i) $t = 0$, $S = \emptyset$ and $L = (J_{10}, J_8, J_9, J_2, J_1, J_6, J_3, J_7, J_5, J_4)$.
The job J_{10} cannot be put in the first position because an optimal schedule for the criterion C_{max}, which starts with this job, does not exist.
$S = (J_8)$.
(ii) $t = 4$ and $L = (J_{10}, J_9, J_2, J_1, J_6, J_3, J_7, J_5, J_4)$.
The jobs J_{10} and J_9 cannot be put in the second position.
$S = (J_8, J_2)$.
(iii) $t = 8$ and $L = (J_{10}, J_9, J_6, J_1, J_7, J_3, J_5, J_4)$.
The jobs J_{10} and J_9 cannot be put in the third position.
$S = (J_8, J_2, J_6)$.
(iv) $t = 7$ and $L = (J_{10}, J_9, J_1, J_3, J_7, J_5, J_4)$.
The jobs J_{10} and J_9 cannot be put in the fourth position.
$S = (J_8, J_2, J_6, J_1)$.
(v) $t = 12$ and $L = (J_{10}, J_9, J_7, J_5, J_4, J_3)$.
The jobs J_{10} and J_9 cannot be put in the fifth position.
$S = (J_8, J_2, J_6, J_1, J_7)$.
(vi) $t = 5$ and $L = (J_{10}, J_9, J_3, J_5, J_4)$.
The jobs J_{10} and J_9 cannot be put in the sixth position.
$S = (J_8, J_2, J_6, J_1, J_7, J_3)$.
(vii) $t = 11$ and $L = (J_{10}, J_9, J_5, J_4)$.
The jobs J_{10} and J_9 cannot be put in the seventh position.
$S = (J_8, J_2, J_6, J_1, J_7, J_3, J_5)$.
(viii) $t = 10$ and $L = (J_{10}, J_9, J_4)$.
The jobs J_{10} and J_9 cannot be put in the eighth position.
$S = (J_8, J_2, J_6, J_1, J_7, J_3, J_5, J_4)$.
(ix) $t = 10$ and $L = (J_{10}, J_9)$.

The job J_{10} cannot be put in the ninth position.
$S = (J_8, J_2, J_6, J_1, J_7, J_3, J_5, J_4, J_9)$.
(x) We obtain the schedule S presented in figure 8.7.

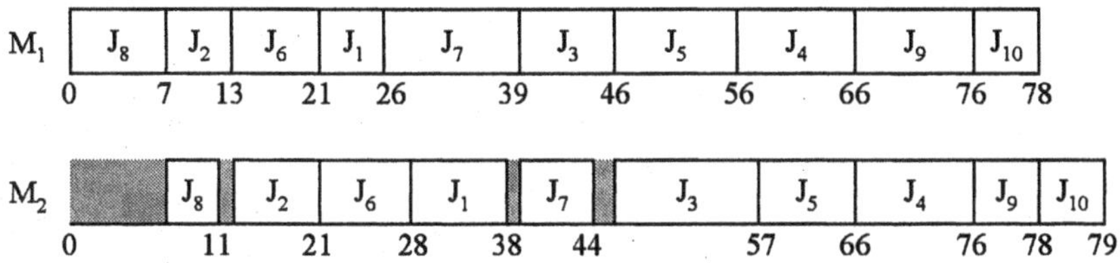

$C_{max}(S) = 79$ and $\overline{C}(S) = 498$

Fig. 8.7. The schedule calculated by the heuristic HTGB1

The local search phase does not improve the solution S.

T'kindt, Gupta and Billaut also study several exact methods and propose a mixed integer programming model, a dynamic programming algorithm and a branch-and-bound algorithm. The latter is the most successful. For each node, an exact evaluation of the criterion C_{max} is carried out. The lower bounds for the criterion $\overline{C}$ are based on a lagrangean relaxation and the linear relaxation of the program. These bounds are adapted to the bicriteria problem because they integrate the optimality constraint of the criterion C_{max}. Besides which, the authors show that the dominance conditions for the $F2|prmu|\overline{C}$ problem are not necessarily valid for the bicriteria problem. Therefore, they adapt certain existing conditions and propose a new generic condition.

In the following lemma, we denote by T the set of jobs to be scheduled, $\overline{C}^{\pi}(\omega)$ the sum of the completion times of the jobs of sequence ω, if they are scheduled after sequence π.

Lemma 30 *[T'kindt et al., 2003]*
Let us consider two partial sequences π and σ. We denote by $\omega = T - \sigma$ and $\omega' = T - \pi$. Let Δ be a value such that $\Delta \leq \overline{C}^{\pi}(\omega') - \overline{C}^{\sigma}(\omega)$.
If $C_{max}(\sigma//J(\omega)) = C^*_{max}$ and $C_{max}(\pi//J(\omega')) = C^*_{max}$ and $\overline{C}(\sigma) - \overline{C}(\pi) \leq \Delta$, then σ dominates π.

To obtain the value Δ of lemma 30 we can calculate a lower bound LB of the term $\overline{C}^{\pi}(\omega')$ and an upper bound UB of the term $\overline{C}^{\sigma}(\omega)$. We note then $\Delta = LB - UB$. T'kindt, Gupta and Billaut use the heuristics SPT on M_1,

ALGORITHM HTGB1

```
/* T is the set of jobs to schedule */
/* ESJ1 is the algorithm of [Johnson, 1954] */
/* C*_max is the optimal value of criterion C_max */
Step 1:  /* Initialisation of the algorithm */
         t = 0; S = ∅; C*_max = C_max(ESJ1(T)); L = T;
Step 2:  /* Greedy step */
         While (L ≠ ∅) Do
           | Sort L by increasing values of max(t; p_{i,1}) + p_{i,2} (break ties
           | by choosing the job with the lowest value p_{i,1});
           | /* [i] is the ith job in the list L */
           | bool = FALSE; i = 1;
           | While ((bool = FALSE) and (i ≤ |L|)) Do
           |   | t(i) = max(t − p_{[i],1}, 0) + p_{[i],2};
           |   | /* C_max(S|t): makespan of the schedule S if M_2 is only */
           |   | /* available at time t */
           |   | If (C_max(ESJ1(L − {J_[i]})|t(i))+
           |   |            Σ_{J_j ∈ S} p_{j,1} + p_{[i],1} = C*_max) Then
           |   |   | bool=TRUE; k = i;
           |   | Else
           |   |   | i = i + 1;
           |   | End If;
           | End While;
           | S = S//{J_[k]}; L = L − {J_[k]}; t = t(k);
         End While;
Step 3:  /* Improvement step */
         i = 1;
         While (i ≤ n) Do
           | j = i + 1;
           | While (j ≤ n) Do
           |   | S' is obtained by permutating S[i] and S[j] in S;
           |   | If ((C_max(S') = C*_max) and (C̄(S') < C̄(S))) Then
           |   |   | S = S'; i = 1; j = i + 1;
           |   | Else
           |   |   | j = j + 1;
           |   | End If;
           | End While;
           | i = i + 1;
         End While;
Step 4:  Print S, C*_max and C̄(S);
```

[T'kindt et al., 2003]

Fig. 8.8. An heuristic algorithm for the $F2|prmu|Lex(C_{max}, \overline{C})$ problem

SPT on M_2 and the greedy phase of the heuristic HTGB1 to construct partial sequences.

Experimental results show that the heuristic HTGB1 is better than the heuristic HGNW1 both in quality and time. Besides, the proposed branch-and-bound algorithm solves problems containing up to 35 jobs in the most difficult cases.

[T'kindt et al., 2002]

T'kindt, Monmarché, Tercinet and Laugt investigate the effectiveness of Ant Colony Optimisation algorithms (ACO) on this problem. The basic idea of these algorithms comes from the ability of ants to find shortest paths from their nest to food locations. Considering a combinatorial optimisation problem, an ant iteratively builds a solution of the problem. This constructive procedure is conducted using at each step a probability distribution that corresponds to the pheromone trails in real ants. Once a complete solution has been computed, pheromone trails are updated according to the quality of the best solution built ([Dorigo et al., 1999]).
Hence, cooperation between ants is performed with the common structure that is the shared pheromone matrix. Due to the simple structure of a solution to the lexicographical problem, which reduces to a sequence of jobs, the pheromone matrix is a job-position matrix defined as follows: Let τ be this matrix and $\tau_{i,j}$ the probability of having job J_i at position j in a good schedule for the $\bar{C}$ criterion. $\tau_{i,j}$ is referred to as the *pheromone trail*, and higher is this value higher is the probability to have job J_i in position j in a good solution for the bicriteria problem. Each ant of the nest builds a feasible solution starting from position 1 and going onwards. For a given position, the most suitable job for position j is chosen according to either the *intensification* mode or the *diversification* mode. We note p_0 the selection probability of being in one of these two modes. Let σ be the subsequence of the $j-1$ first scheduled jobs. In the intensification mode, an ant chooses as the most suitable job for position j, the one with the highest value of $\tau_{i,j}$ such that it exists at least one optimal schedule for the makespan beginning with $\sigma//\{J_i\}$. This *makespan check* can be done using Johnson's algorithm for the $F2||C_{max}$ problem. Let S be the schedule obtained by applying this algorithm on the set of jobs not in $\sigma//\{J_i\}$. If the value of the makespan for the schedule $\sigma//\{J_i\}//S$ is equal to the optimal value, then it exists at least one optimal schedule for the makespan that begins with subsequence $\sigma//\{J_i\}$. In the diversification mode, an ant uses a wheel process to select the most suitable job. This procedure is the same than in classic genetic algorithms except that only a job satisfying the makespan check described before, can be chosen.

When an ant has built a complete schedule, a local search is applied. This one is performed as follows. For each position j of the schedule, compute $n-j$ schedules by applying the 1-API, 2-API, ..., $(n-j)$-API operators, where the k-API operator is defined as follows: consider a fixed value k, a schedule S and a position $i < n-k$ in this schedule. After applying the k-API operation on S at position i we obtain a schedule S' where the jobs in position i and $i+k$ in S have been exchanged. Among the calculated schedules plus the starting one, keep the schedule that has an optimal value of the makespan and the lowest value for the total completion time criterion. Therefore, consider position $j+1$. This local search has an overall $O(n^3)$ time complexity. After all the schedules have been built by the ants, the best one is kept and the pheromone matrix is updated using the evaporation and enforcement processes. The former decreases the pheromone trails by setting them to ρ% of their previous value whilst the latter increases the pheromone trails that correspond to the schedule kept at the current iteration. The heuristic terminates if the number of iterations exceeds the total number of iterations allowed.

Using a local search algorithm within the ACO heuristic reinforces the convergence of the algorithm since few different schedules may be considered at the end of each iteration. To regulate the use of diversification and intensification processes the scheme of classic ACO heuristics is modified by the authors which consider that diversification is preferred at the beginning of the solution process whilst intensification is preferred at the end. That principle is equivalent to the acceptance probability controlling in Simulated Annealing search. In the proposed heuristic, it means that the selection probability p_0 is no longer fixed along the solution process. Let N be the total number of iterations before stopping. At an iteration k, the selection probability is defined by $p_0 = \frac{\log(k)}{\log(N)}$. Hence, for an ant lower is the value p_0 and higher is the chance to choose a job at position j using the diversification mode. A straight consequence is that it is no longer necessary to initially generate randomly the pheromone trails: as diversification is enforced at the beginning of the resolution, it is sufficient to consider equal initial values for the $\tau_{i,j}$'s. As in the ACO heuristic proposed by Stutzle ([Stuztle, 1998]), the values $\tau_{i,j}$ belong to an interval $[\tau_{min}; \tau_{max}]$ to avoid pheromone trails from being negligible. The heuristic, denoted by HTMTL1 (figure 8.9), requires $O(n^3)$ time. Computational experiments show that heuristic HTMTL1 strongly outperforms heuristic HTGB1 in quality but requires more calculation time.
T'kindt, Monmarché, Tercinet and Laugt also experimentally study the *stability* of their heuristic, *i.e.* when run several times on the same instance what is the distribution of the $\bar{C}$ criterion ? Is the set of the obtained values narrowed ? A statistical analysis is conducted and Fischer's coefficient, which is a measure of the degree of flattening of a frequency curve near its mode, is calculated on the values of the $\bar{C}$ criterion calculated by the heuristic run

ALGORITHM HTMTL1

/* Let T be the set of jobs to schedule */
/* Let N be the number of iterations and M the number of ants */
Step 1: $\rho = 0.9$; $\tau_{max} = \frac{1}{1-\rho}$;
$\tau_{min} = \tau_{max}/5$; $\tau_{i,j} = \tau_{max}$, $\forall i,j = 1..n$;$S_{best} = (J_1; J_2; \ldots; J_n)$;
Step 2: For *Iteration*=1 to N Do
  $p_0 = \frac{\log(Iteration)}{\log(N)}$;
  For *Ant*=1 to M Do
    $L = T$; $S_{ant} = \emptyset$;
    For *Position*=1 to n Do
      Generate a random number $0 \le p \le 1$;
      If ($p \ge p_0$) Then
        /* Diversification mode */
        Using the values $\tau_{i,Position}$, $J_i \in L$, apply a wheel and the *makespan check* to select the job J_k to schedule at current *Position*;
      Else
        /* Intensification mode */
        Choose the job J_k with the highest value $\tau_{i,Position}$, $J_i \in L$, that satisfies the *makespan check*, to schedule at current *Position*;
      End If
      $S_{ant}[Position] = J_k$; $L = L - \{J_k\}$;
    End For
    Start the local search on S_{ant} to improve it;
  End For
  Let S be the best schedule for the $\sum C_i$ criterion computed by the ants;
  $\tau_{i,j} = \rho\tau_{i,j}$, $\forall i,j = 1..n$; $\tau_{S[j],j} = \tau_{S[j],j} + \frac{1}{\sum C_i(S)}$, $\forall j = 1..n$;
  If S improves S_{best} for the $\sum C_i$ criterion, set $S_{best} = S$;
End For
Step 3: Display S_{best}, $C_{max}(S_{best})$ and $\sum C_i(S_{best})$;

[T'kindt et al., 2002]

Fig. 8.9. An ACO algorithm for the $F2|prmu|Lex(C_{max}, \overline{C})$ problem

several times on a set of instances. This yields to the conclusion that the distribution of these values follows a normal distribution with a standard deviation lower than 0.22%, *i.e.* 95% of the values generated by the heuristic on the same instance are within 0.22% of the average value.

Other results

Numerous neighbourhood or population based heuristics have also been presented in the literature. [Neppalli et al., 1996] propose genetic algorithms for this problem. The most successful algorithm is obtained by considering that each chromosome of the population is evaluated by a convex combination of the criteria C_{max} and $\overline{C}$ with a weight equal to n for the first and equal to 1 for the second.

[Gupta et al., 2002] implement several neighbourhood heuristics: tabu search, simulated annealing and a two-level local search. Experimental results show that the genetic algorithm of [Neppalli et al., 1996] is dominated both in time and quality by the better proposed heuristic, which is the two-level local search. This algorithm takes as input data the solution calculated by the heuristic HGNW1 and proceeds as follows. Starting with the current solution the operator NAPI (*Non Adjacent Pairwise Interchange*) is used to generate the *high level* neighbourhood, denoted by V_1. We actually only keep a fixed number h of solutions of this neighbourhood, which are chosen randomly. In the second step, we use for each retained solution of V_1, the operator API (*Adjacent Pairwise Interchange*) to calculate the *low level* neighbourhood, denoted by V_2. We eliminate from each neighbourhood V_2 the solutions dominated using a dominance condition and those which do not have an optimal makespan. Among the h solutions obtained (at most), we consider the best solution for the criterion $\overline{C}$. Choice of the next current solution between the calculated one and the previous current solution, is made using a procedure which is similar to that obtained in the simulated annealing algorithms (probabilistic choice). Regarding the computational time, this heuristic is relatively slow compared to the heuristic HTGB1 since it requires the running of the heuristic HGNW1. Gupta, Hennig and Werner do not present experimental results to compare in terms of quality the two-level local search with HGNW1. [Gupta et al., 1999b] propose a tabu search algorithm and are mainly interested in a framework which enables us to determine the values of the parameters best adapted for this algorithm. Only comparisons with heuristics HCR1 and HCR2 are presented.

8.1.2 The $F2|prmu|F_\ell(C_{max}, \overline{C})$ problem

[Nagar et al., 1995b]

Nagar, Heragu and Haddock are interested in the problem where the criteria C_{max} and $\overline{C}$ are minimised using a convex combination. This problem is strongly $\mathcal{NP}$-hard because the lexicographical problem $F2|prmu|Lex(C_{max}, \overline{C})$ is also.

Nagar, Heragu and Haddock propose a greedy heuristic, denoted by HNHH1 (figure 8.11). In the particular case where the job processing times are the same on the two machines, *i.e.* $p_{i,1} = p_{i,2}$, $\forall i = 1, ..., n$, this heuristic determines the optimal schedule.

Example.
We consider a problem for which $n = 10$.

i	1	2	3	4	5	6	7	8	9	10
$p_{i,1}$	5	6	7	10	10	8	13	7	10	2
$p_{i,2}$	10	8	11	10	9	7	5	4	2	1

(i) $C_1 = C_2 = 0$ and $S = \emptyset$.
(ii) $T = (J_{10}, J_8, J_9, J_2, J_1, J_6, J_3, J_7, J_5, J_4)$.
$S = (J_{10})$, $C_1 = 2$ and $C_2 = 3$,
(iii) $T = (J_8, J_9, J_2, J_1, J_6, J_3, J_7, J_5, J_4)$.
$S = (J_{10}, J_8)$, $C_1 = 9$ and $C_2 = 13$,
(iv) $T = (J_9, J_2, J_1, J_6, J_3, J_7, J_5, J_4)$.
$S = (J_{10}, J_8, J_9)$, $C_1 = 19$ and $C_2 = 21$,
(v) $T = (J_2, J_1, J_6, J_3, J_7, J_5, J_4)$.
$S = (J_{10}, J_8, J_9, J_2)$, $C_1 = 25$ and $C_2 = 33$,
(vi) $T = (J_6, J_1, J_7, J_3, J_5, J_4)$.
$S = (J_{10}, J_8, J_9, J_2, J_6)$, $C_1 = 33$ and $C_2 = 40$,
(vii) $T = (J_1, J_3, J_7, J_5, J_4)$.
$S = (J_{10}, J_8, J_9, J_2, J_6, J_1)$, $C_1 = 38$ and $C_2 = 50$,
(viii) $T = (J_7, J_5, J_4, J_3)$.
$S = (J_{10}, J_8, J_9, J_2, J_6, J_1, J_7)$, $C_1 = 51$ and $C_2 = 56$,
(ix) $T = (J_3, J_5, J_4)$.
$S = (J_{10}, J_8, J_9, J_2, J_6, J_1, J_7, J_3)$, $C_1 = 58$ and $C_2 = 69$,
(x) $T = (J_5, J_4)$. We obtain the schedule S presented in figure 8.10.

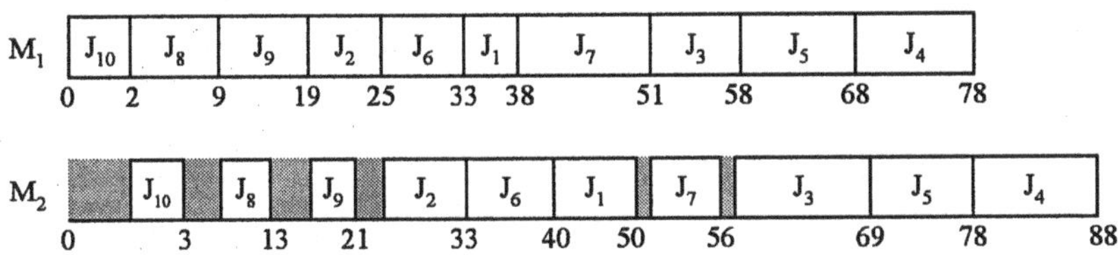

$C_{max}(S) = 88$ and $\overline{C}(S) = 451$

Fig. 8.10. The schedule calculated by the heuristic HNHH1

We notice that this solution is calculated independently from the weights of the criteria in the objective function.

A branch-and-bound algorithm is also proposed by Nagar, Heragu and Haddock. At each node a job is scheduled after the jobs already sequenced. A lower bound is calculated by using the linear combination of a lower bound on criterion C_{max} and a lower bound on criterion $\overline{C}$.

[Sivrikaya-Serifoglu and Ulusoy, 1998]

Sivrikaya-Serifoglu and Ulusoy are similarly interested in the $F2|prmu|F_\ell(C_{max}, \overline{C})$ problem for which they propose an heuristic, denoted by HSU1.

ALGORITHM HNHH1
/* T is the set of jobs to schedule */
Step 1: /* Initialisation of the algorithm */
$C_1 = C_2 = 0$; $S = \emptyset$;
Step 2: /* Greedy phase */
While ($T \neq \emptyset$) Do
Sort T by increasing value of $\max(C_1 + p_{i,1}; C_2) + p_{i,2}$;
$C_1 = C_1 + p_{T[1],1}$; $C_2 = \max(C_1; C_2) + p_{T[1],2}$;
$S = S//\{T[1]\}$; $T = T - \{T[1]\}$;
End While;
Step 3: Print S, C^*_{max} and $\overline{C}(S)$;
[Nagar et al., 1995b]

Fig. 8.11. An heuristic algorithm for the $F2|prmu|F_\ell(C_{max}, \overline{C})$ problem

This attempts to sequence the jobs by a method which is close to the rule SPT applied on machine M_1, and on machine M_2 in the case of ties. As a second objective it tries to minimise the sum of the idle times on the second machine. The heuristic HSU1 is presented in figure 8.13. In order to improve the result obtained by the heuristic HSU1, the algorithms 2-opt and 3-opt are used on the calculated schedule.

Example.
We consider the previous example with $n = 10$.

i	1	2	3	4	5	6	7	8	9	10
$p_{i,1}$	5	6	7	10	10	8	13	7	10	2
$p_{i,2}$	10	8	11	10	9	7	5	4	2	1

(i) $S = (J_{10})$, $C_{S,1} = 2$, $C_{S,2} = 3$,
(ii) $CS = \emptyset$, $k = 1$, $S = (J_{10}, J_1)$, $C_{S,1} = 7$ and $C_{S,2} = 17$,
(iii) $CS = \{J_2, J_3, J_6, J_8\}$, $k = 8$, $S = (J_{10}, J_1, J_8)$, $C_{S,1} = 14$ and $C_{S,2} = 21$,
(iv) $CS = \{J_2\}$, $k = 2$, $S = (J_{10}, J_1, J_8, J_2)$, $C_{S,1} = 20$ and $C_{S,2} = 29$,
(v) $CS = \{J_3, J_6\}$, $k = 6$, $S = (J_{10}, J_1, J_8, J_2, J_6)$, $C_{S,1} = 28$ and $C_{S,2} = 36$,
(vi) $CS = \{J_3\}$, $k = 3$, $S = (J_{10}, J_1, J_8, J_2, J_6, J_3)$, $C_{S,1} = 35$ and $C_{S,2} = 47$,
(vii) $CS = \{J_4, J_5, J_9\}$, $k = 9$, $S = (J_{10}, J_1, J_8, J_2, J_6, J_3, J_9)$, $C_{S,1} = 45$ and $C_{S,2} = 49$,
(viii) $CS = \emptyset$, $k = 5$, $S = (J_{10}, J_1, J_8, J_2, J_6, J_3, J_9, J_5)$, $C_{S,1} = 55$ and $C_{S,2} = 64$,
(ix) $CS = \emptyset$, $k = 4$, $S = (J_{10}, J_1, J_8, J_2, J_6, J_3, J_9, J_5, J_4)$, $C_{S,1} = 65$ and $C_{S,2} = 75$,
(x) $CS = \emptyset$ and $k = 7$. We obtain the schedule S presented in figure 8.12.

We notice that this solution is calculated independently of the weights of the criteria in the objective function.

Sivrikaya-Serifoglu and Ulusoy also propose three branch-and-bound algorithms. The only difference between these three algorithms is the branching scheme. The first branch-and-bound algorithm, denoted by ESU1 and presented in figure 8.14, constructs the schedules by placing, at each node, a job at the end of the partial sequence of jobs already scheduled. The second

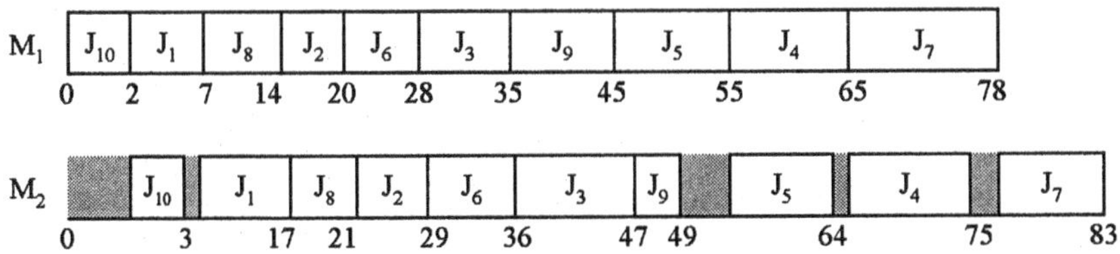

$\overline{C}(S) = 424$ and $C_{max}(S) = 83$

Fig. 8.12. The schedule calculated by the heuristic HSU1

ALGORITHM HSU1

/* T is the set of n jobs to schedule */
/* $C_{S,1}$ is the completion time of the last job of S on M_1 */
/* $C_{S,2}$ is the completion time of the last job of S on M_2 */
Step 1: Let J_k be such that $p_{k,1} = \min_{J_i \in T}(p_{i,1})$;
  /* Break ties by choosing the job with the smallest value $p_{i,2}$ */
  $T = T - \{J_k\}$; $S = (J_k)$;
  $C_{S,1} = p_{k,1}$; $C_{S,2} = p_{k,1} + p_{k,2}$;
Step 2: While ($T \neq \emptyset$) Do
    $CS = \{J_i \in T / p_{i,1} < (C_{S,2} - C_{S,1})\}$;
    If ($CS = \emptyset$) Then
      Let J_k be such that $p_{k,1} = \min_{J_i \in T}(p_{i,1})$;
      /* Break ties by choosing the job with the smallest */
      /* value $p_{i,2}$ */
    Else
      Let J_k be such that $p_{k,2} = \min_{J_i \in CS}(p_{i,2})$;
      /* Break ties by choosing the job with the smallest */
      /* value $p_{i,1}$ */
    End If;
    $S = S//\{J_k\}; T = T - \{J_k\}$;
    $C_{S,1} = C_{S,1} + p_{k,1}$;
    $C_{S,2} = \max(C_{S,1}; C_{S,2}) + p_{k,2}$;
  End While;
Step 3: Print S and $F_\ell(C_{max}(S), \overline{C}(S))$;

[Sivrikaya-Serifoglu and Ulusoy, 1998]

Fig. 8.13. An heuristic algorithm for the $F2|prmu|F_\ell(C_{max}, \overline{C})$ problem

branch-and-bound algorithm constructs the schedules by placing, at each node, a job at the beginning of the partial sequence. The third branch-and-bound algorithm uses a mixed approach. At each node we associate a partial schedule of the form $(\sigma^F, *, \ldots, *, \sigma^D)$. σ^F is the list of the jobs sequenced at the beginning whereas σ^D is the list of jobs sequenced at the end. At an odd depth node, we place a job at the end of the sequence σ^F. At an even

depth node, we place a job at the beginning of the sequence σ^D. The search strategy is the depth-first strategy.
The lower bound for a node, in the algorithm ESU1, is given by: $LB = \alpha LB_{C_{max}} + \beta LB_{\overline{C}}$ where α and β are the weights of the criteria in the objective function. The lower bound of the criterion C_{max}, denoted by $LB_{C_{max}}$, is obtained by applying algorithm ESJ1 ([Johnson, 1954]) on the set of unscheduled jobs and by concatenating this sequence with the set of jobs already scheduled. The value of the criterion C_{max} for this sequence is the value of the lower bound. Calculation of the lower bound of the criterion $\overline{C}$, denoted by $LB_{\overline{C}}$, is a function of the index $D_a = \sum_{i=1}^{n} p_{i,1} - \sum_{i=1}^{n} p_{i,2}$ presented by [Nagar et al., 1995b] and which indicates which is the most loaded machine. For a given problem, when $D_a < 0$ we use the bound $LB_{\overline{C}}^-$ and in the opposite case, we use the bound $LB_{\overline{C}}^+$. We note σ the sequence of jobs already scheduled and Ω the set of unscheduled jobs. k is the number of jobs in σ. We have:

$$LB_{\overline{C}}^+ = \overline{C}(\sigma) + \sum_{j=1}^{n-k} \max\left(\sum_{i=1}^{j} p_{\tau[i],1} + \sum_{i=1}^{k} p_{\sigma[i],1}; C_{\sigma,2}\right) + \sum_{i=1}^{n-k} p_{\tau[i],2}$$

with τ the list of jobs of Ω sorted according to the rule SPT on machine M_1. The second bound is defined by:

$$LB_{\overline{C}}^- = \overline{C}(\sigma) + \sum_{j=1}^{n-k-1} \left(C_{\sigma,2} + \sum_{i=1}^{j} p_{\tau'[i],2}\right)$$
$$+ \max\left(C_{\sigma,2} + \sum_{i=1}^{n-k-1} p_{\tau'[i],2}; \sum_{i=1}^{n} p_{i,1}\right) + p_{\tau'[n-k],2}$$

with τ' the list of jobs of Ω sorted according to the rule SPT on machine M_2. These bounds are extensions of those proposed by [Ignall and Schrage, 1965]. The branch-and-bound algorithms proposed by Sivrikaya-Serifoglu and Ulusoy are compared through experimental results. They show that the algorithm ESU1 is the most efficient and that it solves problems with up to 18 jobs but no computational time is given. They are similarly interested in the efficiency of the heuristic HSU1 with regard to the heuristic HNHH1 and they show that HSU1 improves the results of HNHH1 by at least 6%. Besides, the heuristic appears to calculate solutions which are closer to the optimum in spite of not taking account of the weights of the objective function. This can only be explained by a weak dispersion of the set of non dominated criteria vectors.

```
ALGORITHM ESU1
/* T is the set of n jobs to schedule */
/* α and β are the weights of criteria */
Step 1:  /* Initialisation of the algorithm */
         Apply the heuristic HSU1 on T to get the schedule S_ref;
         F_ref = αC_max(S_ref) + βC̄(S_ref);
         D_a = Σ_{i=1}^{n} p_{i,1} − Σ_{i=1}^{n} p_{i,2};
         Create the root node s_0: σ_0 = ∅ ; Ω_0 = T; Q = {s_0};
Step 2:  /* Main part of the branch-and-bound */
         While (Q ≠ ∅) Do
             Choose a node s_i in Q: Q = Q − {s_i};
             /* Choice done according to the search strategy */
             Ω = Ω_i;
             For k = 1 to |Ω_i| Do
                 Select a job J_j in Ω: Ω = Ω − {J_j};
                 Create a child node s_{i+1}^{(k)}: σ_{i+1}^{(k)} = σ_i//{J_j} and
                 Ω_{i+1}^{(k)} = Ω_i − {J_j};
                 If (D_a < 0) Then
                     LB(s_{i+1}^{(k)}) = αLB_{C_max}(s_{i+1}^{(k)}) + βLB_{C̄}^{−}(s_{i+1}^{(k)});
                 Else
                     LB(s_{i+1}^{(k)}) = αLB_{C_max}(s_{i+1}^{(k)}) + βLB_{C̄}^{+}(s_{i+1}^{(k)});
                 End If;
                 If (LB(s_{i+1}^{(k)}) < F_ref) Then
                     If (Ω_{i+1}^{(k)} ≠ ∅) Then Q = Q + {s_{i+1}^{(k)}};
                     Else
                         S_ref = σ_{i+1}^{(k)};
                         F_ref = αC_max(S_ref) + βC̄(S_ref);
                     End If;
                 End If;
             End For;
         End While;
Step 3:  Print S_ref and F_ref;
[Sivrikaya-Serifoglu and Ulusoy, 1998]
```

Fig. 8.14. An optimal algorithm for the $F2|prmu|F_\ell(C_{max}, \overline{C})$ problem

[Yeh, 1999]

Yeh is interested in the $F2|prmu|F_\ell(C_{max}, \overline{C})$ problem for which he proposes an improvement of the heuristic HNHH1 and a branch-and-bound algorithm. The latter constructs progressively a schedule at each node by adding a job after the last scheduled job. A lower bound of the objective function is calculated from the linear combination of a bound for the criterion C_{max} and a bound for the criterion $\overline{C}$. The first is calculated in the same way as in the algorithm ESU1 whilst the second is an improvement of a bound of [Ignall and Schrage, 1965]. It is calculated by considering only the second machine and by sorting the jobs according to the rule SPT. A lower bound of the criterion $\overline{C}$ is then deduced to which is added the sum of the idle times obtained by applying Johnson's algorithm to these jobs. Experimental results show that the proposed branch-and-bound algorithm is limited to problems with up to 14 jobs.

8.1.3 The $F2|prmu, r_i|F_\ell(C_{max}, \overline{C})$ problem

[Chou and Lee, 1999] consider that jobs have release dates and propose a mixed integer program. They also present an heuristic, denoted by HCL1, which is similar to a filtered beam search procedure. The heuristic explores a tree where each node contains the schedule under construction and the set of unscheduled jobs. The branching scheme consists of scheduling a job after those already scheduled. For a given node, a filter is applied to keep only the interesting nodes. We note σ the list of jobs scheduled at node s and Ω the set of unscheduled jobs. For each job $J_i \in \Omega$, the contribution to the objective function is given by Q_i:

$$Q_i = \big(\max[\max(C_1(\sigma); r_i) + p_{i,1} - C_2(\sigma); 0] + p_{i,2}\big) \times \big(\alpha|\Omega| + \beta\big)$$

with α the weight of the criterion $\overline{C}$ and β the weight of the criterion C_{max}. Likewise, we define the smallest contribution of the job scheduled after J_i by:

$$R_i = \min_{J_j \in \Omega - \{J_i\}} \Big(p_{j,2} + \max\big(\max[\max(C_1(\sigma); r_i) + p_{i,1}; r_j] + p_{j,2} - [\max(\max(C_1(\sigma); r_i) + p_{i,1}; C_2(\sigma)) + p_{i,2}]; 0\big)\Big) \times \Big(\alpha|\Omega| - 1 + \beta\Big)$$

Chou and Lee use a weight f_i for the filter defined by $f_i = Q_i + R_i$. The nodes created from node s are those for which the scheduled job $J_i \in \Omega$ is of minimum weight f_i. The heuristic HCL1 is presented in figure 8.15. Experimental results on small instances show the efficiency of the heuristic.

8.1.4 The $F2|prmu|\epsilon(\overline{C}/C_{max})$ problem

[Sayin and Karabati, 1999] are interested in the determination of the set of strict Pareto optima for the criteria C_{max} and $\overline{C}$. This problem is shown to be $\mathcal{NP}$-hard in the strong sense. To determine these solutions they use a result of the ϵ-constraint approach.

Lemma 31 *[Sayin and Karabati, 1999]*
A schedule $S^0 \in S$ is a strict Pareto optimum if and only if:

ALGORITHM HCL1

/* T is the set of n jobs to schedule */
/* f_i is the weight of job J_i */
Step 1: /* Initialisation of the algorithm */
  Create the root node s_0: $\sigma_0 = \emptyset$; $\Omega_0 = T$; $Q = \{s_0\}$;
  $F_{ref} = \infty$;
Step 2: /* Main part of the search */
  While ($Q \neq \emptyset$) Do
    s_i is the last node in Q;
    $Q = Q - \{s_i\}$;
    $L = \{J_j \in \Omega_i / f_j = \min_{J_k \in \Omega_i} (f_k)\}$;
    For $k = 1$ to $|L|$ Do
      Create a child node s_i^k: $\sigma_i^k = \sigma_i // \{L[k]\}$ and
      $\Omega_i^k = \Omega_i - \{L[k]\}$;
      If ($\Omega_i^k \neq \emptyset$) Then
        $Q = Q + \{s_i^k\}$;
      Else
        If ($\alpha\overline{C}(\sigma_i^k) + \beta C_{max}(\sigma_i^k) < F_{ref}$) Then
          $S_{ref} = \sigma_i^k$;
          $F_{ref} = \alpha\overline{C}(\sigma_i^k) + \beta C_{max}(\sigma_i^k)$;
        End If;
      End If;
    End For;
  End While;
Step 3: Print S_ref and F_ref;

[Chou and Lee, 1999]

Fig. 8.15. An heuristic algorithm for the $F2|prmu, r_i|F_\ell(C_{max}, \overline{C})$ problem

1. *$\exists \epsilon \in \mathbb{R}^+$ such that S^0 is an optimal solution of the problem (P_ϵ):*
   Min $C_{max}(S)$
   subject to
   $\overline{C}(S) \leq \epsilon$
   $S \in \mathcal{S}$
2. *$\nexists S^1 \in \mathcal{S}$ such that $C_{max}(S^1) = C_{max}(S^0)$ and $\overline{C}(S^1) < \epsilon$.*

This lemma can easily be demonstrated by lemma 4 and 5 (chapter 3). Lemma 31 is used in a general algorithm, denoted by ESK1 (figure 8.16), for the determination of the set E.
In order to solve the problems (P_{ϵ_i}) and (Q_{s^0}) presented in figure 8.16, Sayin and Karabati propose two branch-and-bound algorithms which are iteratively called. The algorithm ESK1 is then implemented according to a scheme proposed by [Klein and Hannan, 1982] by integrating these two procedures. This implementation implies that one node is not explored several times. The resulting algorithm is denoted by ESK2 (figure 8.17). A node s of the search tree is defined by a partial schedule σ of the jobs scheduled

ALGORITHM ESK1

Step 1: /* Initialisation of the algorithm */
$i = 1$; $E = \emptyset$; $\epsilon_i = \infty$;
End=FALSE;
Step 2: /* Computation of the set E */
While (End=FALSE) Do
  Let S^0 be a solution of the problem (P_{ϵ_i}):
    Min $C_{max}(S)$
    subject to
      $\overline{C}(S) \leq \epsilon_i$
      $S \in \mathcal{S}$
  If (S^0 does not exist) Then
    End=TRUE;
  Else
    Let S^i be a solution of the problem (Q_{S^0}):
      Min $\overline{C}(S)$
      subject to
        $C_{max}(S) = C_{max}(S^0)$
        $S \in \mathcal{S}$
    $E = E + \{S^i\}$;
    $i = i + 1$;
    $\epsilon_i = \overline{C}(S^i) - 1$;
  End If;
End While;
Step 2: Print E;

[Sayin and Karabati, 1999]

Fig. 8.16. An optimal algorithm for the $F2|prmu|\epsilon(\overline{C}/C_{max})$ problem

first and a set Ω of the unscheduled jobs. Starting with s, a node is created by adding at the end of σ a job of Ω. We also associate with the node s a lower bound $LB_{C_{max}}(s)$ of the criterion C_{max}, a lower bound $LB_{\overline{C}}(s)$ of the criterion $\overline{C}$ and an upper bound $C_{max}^{sup}(s)$ of the criterion C_{max}. The latter bound is the largest value of the criterion C_{max} of an active schedule when σ is fixed. It is defined by $C_{max}^{sup}(s) = C_{max}(\sigma//J_r(\Omega))$ with $J_r(\Omega)$ the reverse sequence of Johnson's one on set Ω. The lower bound $LB_{C_{max}}(s)$ is calculated using the algorithm $ESJ1$ on the set Ω. It is defined by $LB_{C_{max}}(s) = C_{max}(\sigma//J(\Omega))$. Concerning the lower bound of the criterion $\overline{C}$, Sayin and Karabati use three existing bounds which are: the first bound proposed by [Della Croce et al., 1996], that proposed by [VandeVelde, 1990] and that proposed by [Karabati and Kouvelis, 1993]. Besides, the branch-and-bound algorithm updates a list, denoted by E, of schedules which correspond to potentially non dominated criteria vectors. At each terminal node s_t of the tree, the algorithm adds to E the schedule σ_t if this is not dominated by a schedule belonging to E. Likewise, all the schedules of E dominated by σ_t are deleted from the list. Besides, Sayin and Karabati use the dominance condition proposed by [Della Croce et al., 1996] for the $F2|prmu|\overline{C}$ problem which remains valid for the bicriteria problem. They similarly propose dominance conditions based on theorem 22. At a node s, the sequence δ of theorem 22 is defined by $\delta = \sigma$. The sequence δ is then compared to sequences ω defined by:

- $\omega = \pi J_i J_j$ if $\delta = \pi J_j J_i$, with π a sub-sequence and J_i and J_j two jobs,
- $\omega = ESJ1(\delta)$ with $ESJ1$ the algorithm of [Johnson, 1954],
- $\omega = SPT1(\delta)$ with SPT1 the rule SPT applied to machine M_1,
- $\omega = SPT2(\delta)$ with SPT2 the rule SPT applied to machine M_2.

Two computational experiments are presented by Sayin and Karabati. In the first, the processing times are generated between 1 and 10 according to a uniform law. The results obtained show that the algorithm ESK2 can solve every problem with up to 22 jobs. The average number of non dominated criteria vectors lies between 1.5 and 2.1, which means that the criteria for these problems do not conflict. The second type of experiment concerns problems for which the processing times are generated between 1 and 100. These problems appear to be more difficult to solve because the algorithm ESK2 cannot solve some problems comprising 20 jobs.

ALGORITHM ESK2

/* T is the set of n jobs to schedule */
/* $ESJ1$ is the algorithm of [Johnson, 1954] */
/* L_i^P is the list of nodes used to solve the problem $(P_{\epsilon_{i+1}})$ */
/* L_i^Q is the list of nodes used to solve the problem (Q_{s_i}) */

Step 1: /* Resolution of the problem (P_{ϵ_1}) */
    $S_1 = ESJ1(T)$; $UB_{\overline{C}} = \overline{C}(S_1)$; $C_{max}^{P_{\epsilon_1}} = C_{max}(S_1)$; $i = 1$; $E = \emptyset$;
    Build the node s_0: $\sigma_0 = \emptyset$, $\Omega_0 = T$;
    $L_1^P = \emptyset$; $L_1^Q = \{s_0\}$;

Step 2: /* Resolution of the problem (Q_{s_i}) */
    While $(L_i^Q \neq \emptyset)$
        Let s_k be the last node in L_i^Q;
        If $((LB_{\overline{C}}(s_k) \geq UB_{\overline{C}})$ or $(C_{max}^{sup}(s_k) < C_{max}^{P_{\epsilon_i}}))$ Then
            /* The node s_k cannot lead to an optimal schedule for */
            /* (P_{ϵ_j}) and (Q_{s_j}) with $j > i$ */
            $L_i^Q = L_i^Q - \{s_k\}$;
        Else
            If $((LB_{C_{max}}(s_k) > C_{max}^{P_{\epsilon_i}})$ or $(LB_{\overline{C}}(s_k) \geq UB_{\overline{C}}))$ Then
                /* The node s_k cannot lead to an optimal schedule */
                /* for (Q_{s_i}) but may be a solution of a problem */
                /* (P_{ϵ_j}) for $j > i$ */
                $L_i^Q = L_i^Q - \{s_k\}$; $L_i^P = L_i^P + \{s_k\}$;
            Else
                /* We create child nodes */
                Create the child nodes of s_k and on each of these nodes apply dominance conditions;
                /* $P(s_k)$ is the set of remaining child nodes */
                $L_i^Q = L_i^Q - \{s_k\} + P(s_k)$;
            End If;
        End If;
        If $((s_k$ is a leaf) and $(C_{max}(s_k) = C_{max}^{\epsilon_i})$
                and $(\overline{C}(s_k) < UB_{\overline{C}}))$ Then
            $UB_{\overline{C}} = \overline{C}(\sigma_k)$;
        End If;
    End While;

to follow on the next page

Fig. 8.17. An optimal algorithm for the $F2|prmu|\epsilon(\overline{C}/C_{max})$ problem - (1)

ALGORITHM ESK2 (remainder)

```
Step 3:  /* Resolution of problem (P_{ε_{i+1}}) */
         While (L_i^P ≠ ∅) Do
            Let s_k be the last node in L_i^P;
            If (LB_{C̄}(s_k) ≥ UB_{C̄}) Then
               /* The node s_k can not lead to an optimal */
               /* schedule for (P_{ε_j}) and (Q_{s_j}) with j > i */
               L_i^P = L_i^P − {s_k};
            Else
               If (LB_{C_max}(s_k) ≥ UB_{C_max}) Then
                  /* The node s_k cannot lead to an optimal solution for (P_{ε_{i+1}}) */
                  /* but may be a solution of a problem (Q_{s_j}) for j > i */
                  L_i^P = L_i^P − {s_k}; L_{i+1}^Q = L_{i+1}^Q − {s_k};
               Else
                  /* We create child nodes */
                  Create all the child nodes of s_k and for each of those
                  apply dominance conditions;
                  /* P(s_k) is the set of remaining child nodes */
                  L_i^P = L_i^P − {s_k} + P(s_k);
               End If;
            End If;
            If (s_k a leaf ) Then E = E + {σ_k};
         End While;
         If (L_{i+1}^Q ≠ ∅) Then
            i = i + 1; Goto Step 2;
         End If;
Step 4:  Print E and Z(E);
```

[Sayin and Karabati, 1999]

Fig. 8.17. An optimal algorithm for the $F2|prmu|\epsilon(\overline{C}/C_{max})$ problem - (2)

8.1.5 The $F2|prmu, d_i|\#(C_{max}, T_{max})$ problem

[Daniels and Chambers, 1990] are interested in the determination of the set of strict Pareto optima which is a $\mathcal{NP}$-hard problem because the $F2|prmu, d_i|T_{max}$ problem is also.

Daniels and Chambers propose a branch-and-bound algorithm, denoted by EDC1 (figure 8.18), to determine the set E. Each node s of the tree consists of a list σ of the jobs scheduled last, of a set Ω of unscheduled jobs, of a lower bound $LB_{C_{max}}(s)$ of the criterion C_{max} and of a lower bound $LB_{T_{max}}(s)$ of the criterion T_{max}. The lower bound $LB_{C_{max}}(s)$ is obtained by applying Johnson's algorithm on the set Ω and we have $LB_{C_{max}}(s) = C_{max}(J(\Omega)//\sigma)$. $LB_{C_{max}}(s)$ is the minimal value of the criterion C_{max} for all schedules completing with the sequence σ. The lower bound $LB_{T_{max}}(s)$ is broken down into three bounds:

$$LB_{T_{max}}(s) = \max\left(LB^1_{T_{max}}(\sigma); LB^2_{T_{max}}(\Omega); LB^3_{T_{max}}(\Omega)\right).$$

The *first lower bound* is defined by:

$$LB^1_{T_{max}}(\sigma) = \max_{J_i \in \sigma}(0; C_i(J(\Omega)//\sigma) - d_i)$$

The *second lower bound* is obtained by sorting the jobs of Ω according to the rule EDD. We thus obtain the list L. $LB^2_{T_{max}}(\Omega)$ is calculated by considering only the machine M_2:

$$LB^2_{T_{max}}(\Omega) = \max\left(0; \min_{J_i \in \Omega}(p_{i,1}) + \max_{i=1,\dots,|L|}(\sum_{j=1}^{i} p_{L[j],2} - d_{L[i]})\right)$$

The bound $LB^3_{T_{max}}(\Omega)$ is calculated by relaxing the disjunctive constraints on the machine M_2. With L the list of jobs of Ω sorted by increasing order of the values $(d_i - p_{i,2})$, we have:

$$LB^3_{T_{max}}(\Omega) = \max\left(0; \max_{i=1,\dots,|L|}(\sum_{j=1}^{i} p_{L[j],1} + p_{L[i],2} - d_{L[i]})\right)$$

Daniels and Chambers similarly present some rules to prune nodes in the search tree. We denote by E_{part} the set of the strict Pareto optima already obtained. A node s is pruned if:

- $\exists x \in E_{part}$ such that $LB_{C_{max}}(s) \geq C_{max}(x)$ and $LB_{T_{max}}(s) \geq T_{max}(x)$, *i.e.* if an element of E_{part} dominates s,
- $LB_{T_{max}}(s) = T_{max}(J(\Omega)//\sigma)$ because in this case among all of the schedules ending with σ, the schedule $J(\Omega)//\sigma$ minimises simultaneously the criteria C_{max} and T_{max}.

Dominance conditions are also proposed.

Theorem 24 *[Daniels and Chambers, 1990]*
If $p_{j,2} \leq \min(p_{j,1}; p_{i,2})$ and $d_i \leq d_j$, then a schedule $S \in E$ in which J_j precedes J_i does not exist.

Theorem 25 *[Daniels and Chambers, 1990]*
If $p_{i,1} \leq \min(p_{j,1}; p_{i,2})$ and $d_i \leq d_j$, then a schedule $S \in E$ in which J_j precedes immediately J_i does not exist.

Theorem 26 *[Daniels and Chambers, 1990]*
Let P be a partial sequence containing at least three jobs. We denote by J_i and J_j, with J_j preceding J_i, the last two jobs added to P. P' is the sequence obtained after permutation of J_i and J_j. We note $L_k = \sum_{l=1}^{k} p_{P'[l],2} - d_{P'[k]}$. If $\min(p_{i,1}; p_{j,2}) \leq \min(p_{j,1}; p_{i,2})$ and if $\exists k \in P', k \neq j$, such that $L_k > L_j$, then a schedule $S \in E$ containing P as a sub-sequence does not exist.

The child nodes of s are constructed by taking a job of Ω and by putting it at the beginning of the sequence σ. The next node to consider is the node with the smallest bound $LB_{C_{max}}$. Experimental results show that the average number of calculated criteria vectors is between 1.4 and 2.7. Problems with 20 jobs are solved on average in less than 70 seconds. The total number of optima calculated is low which means that, from a theoretical point of view the criteria do not conflict.
Daniels and Chambers also propose an heuristic which approximates the set E. This heuristic, denoted by HDC3, was inspired by the algorithm of [VanWassenhove and Gelders, 1980] which solves the $1|d_i|\epsilon(\overline{C}/L_{max})$ problem. This heuristic is composed of two modules. The first module causes a constant ϵ to vary in a certain interval. For each value, the second module calculates a schedule which minimises the criterion C_{max} under the constraint $T_{max} \leq \epsilon$. The heuristic HDC3 is presented in figure 8.19.

Example.
We apply the heuristic HDC3. We consider a problem for which $n = 10$ and $\delta = 0.5$.

i	1	2	3	4	5
$p_{i,1}$	1	3	8	10	8
$p_{i,2}$	4	7	9	6	2
d_i	18	11	27	25	20

(i) $T = \{J_1, J_2, J_3, J_4, J_5\}$, $\delta = 0.5$, $T_{max}(ESJ1(T)) = 10$, $\epsilon = 9.5$, $E = \emptyset$ and $I_j = \emptyset$, $\forall j = 1, ..., 10$.
(ii) $\ell = 5$, $L = \{J_3, J_4, J_5\}$, $k = 5$, $S = (J_5)$, $T = \{J_1, J_2, J_3, J_4\}$.
(iii) $\ell = 4$, $L = \{J_1, J_3, J_4\}$, $k = 4$, $S = (J_4, J_5)$, $T = \{J_1, J_2, J_3\}$.
(iv) $\ell = 3$, $L = \{J_1, J_2, J_3\}$, $k = 3$, $S = (J_3, J_4, J_5)$, $T = \{J_1, J_2\}$.
(v) $\ell = 2$, $L = \{J_1, J_2\}$, $k = 2$, $S = (J_2, J_3, J_4, J_5)$, $T = \{J_1\}$.
(vi) $\ell = 1$, $L = \{J_1\}$, $k = 1$, $S = (J_1, J_2, J_3, J_4, J_5)$, $T = \emptyset$.
(vii) We obtain the schedule $S = (J_1, J_2, J_3, J_4, J_5)$ and $T_{max}(S) = 10 > \epsilon$.

ALGORITHM EDC1

/* T is the set of n jobs to schedule */
/* E is the set of strict Pareto optima */
/* $ESJ1$ is the algorithm of [Johnson, 1954] */
Step 1: /* Initialisation of the algorithm */
 $E = \emptyset$;
 Create the root node: $\sigma_0 = \emptyset$; $\Omega_0 = T$; $Q = \{s_0\}$;
Step 2: /* Main part of the branch-and-bound */
 While ($Q \neq \emptyset$) Do
  Select in Q the node s_i with the lowest value $LB_{C_{max}}$:
   $Q = Q - \{s_i\}$;
  $\Omega = \Omega_i$;
  For $k = 1$ to $|\Omega_i|$ Do
   Choose a job J_j in Ω such that $\{J_j\}//\sigma_i$ is not dominated: $\Omega = \Omega - \{J_j\}$;
   Create a child node $s_{i+1}^{(k)}$: $\sigma_{i+1}^{(k)} = \{J_j\}//\sigma_i$; $\Omega_{i+1}^{(k)} = \Omega_i - \{J_j\}$;
   Compute $LB_{C_{max}}(s_{i+1}^{(k)})$;
   Compute $LB_{T_{max}}(s_{i+1}^{(k)})$;
   If ($\nexists x \in E$ such that $(LB_{C_{max}}(s_{i+1}^{(k)}) \geq C_{max}(x)$ and $LB_{T_{max}}(s_{i+1}^{(k)}) \geq T_{max}(x)))$ Then
    If $(LB_{T_{max}}(s_{i+1}^{(k)}) = T_{max}(ESJ1(\Omega_{i+1}^{(k)})//\sigma_{i+1}^{(k)}))$
    Then $E = E + \{ESJ1(\Omega_{i+1}^{(k)})//\sigma_{i+1}^{(k)}\}$;
    Else $Q = Q + \{s_{i+1}^{(k)}\}$;
    End If;
   End If;
  End For;
 End While;
Step 3: Print E;

[Daniels and Chambers, 1990]

Fig. 8.18. An optimal algorithm for the $F2|prmu, d_i|\#(C_{max}, T_{max})$ problem

$k = 5$ and $I_5 = \{J_5\}$.
(viii) By reapplying the previous steps up to iteration (vi) we obtain $S = (J_1, J_2, J_3, J_5, J_4)$ and
$T_{max}(S) = 8 \leq \epsilon$.
(ix) We set $\epsilon = 7.5$, and $T = \{J_1, J_2, J_3, J_4, J_5\}$. For $\ell = 5$, $L = \emptyset$. So, there is no solution with $T_{max} < 7.5$ for HDC3. The two non dominated solutions are $(J_1, J_2, J_3, J_4, J_5)$ and $(J_1, J_2, J_3, J_5, J_4)$.

Experimental results concerning the number of sequences evaluated by the heuristic HDC3 and the number of Pareto optima obtained, are presented.

```
ALGORITHM HDC3
/* T is the set of n jobs to schedule */
/* E is the set of strict Pareto optima */
/* I_ℓ, ℓ = 1,...,n, is the set of jobs that cannot be put in position ℓ */
/* ESJ1 is the algorithm of [Johnson, 1954] */
/* δ ∈]0;1[ is an ordinary value */
Step 1:  /* Initialisation of the algorithm */
         ε = T_max(ESJ1(T)) − δ;
         E = ∅;
         I_j = ∅, ∀j = 1,...,n;
Step 2:  /* Building a schedule */
         For ℓ = n downto 1 Do
         |  L = {J_i ∈ T, J_i ∉ I_ℓ / Σ_{j∈T} p_{j,1} + p_{i,2} − d_i ≤ ε};
         |  /* L is the set of jobs that can be put in position ℓ */
         |  If (L = ∅) Then
         |  |  /* The solutions found are in E */
         |  |  Print E;
         |  |  END;
         |  End If;
         |  Let J_k ∈ L be such that C_{k,2}(J(T)) = max_{J_i∈L}(C_{i,2}(J(T)));
         |  S[ℓ] = J_k;
         |  T = T − {J_k};
         End for;
Step 3:  /* We evaluate the obtained schedule */
         If (T_max(S) > ε) Then
         |  Let J_k be such that T_k(S) > ε and C_{k,2}(S) = max_{J_j/T_j(S)>ε}(C_{j,2});
         |  Let q be the position in S of J_k;
         |  I_q = I_q + {J_k};
         Else
         |  E = E + {S};
         |  ε = T_max(S) − δ;
         End If;
         T = {J_1;...;J_n};
         Goto Step 2;
[Daniels and Chambers, 1990]
```

Fig. 8.19. An heuristic algorithm for the $F2|prmu, d_i|\epsilon(C_{max}/T_{max})$ problem

8.1.6 The $F2|prmu, d_i|\#(C_{max}, \overline{U})$ problem

[Liao et al., 1997] are interested in the determination of the set of strict Pareto optima for the criteria C_{max} and $\overline{U}$. They do not show the complexity of this problem. Nevertheless, it is possible to show knowing the complexity of the $F2|prmu, d_i|L_{max}$ problem, that the bicriteria problem is strongly $\mathcal{NP}$-hard.

The algorithm proposed by Liao, Yu and Joe is a branch-and-bound algorithm, denoted by ELYJ1. Each node s of the search tree is composed of a list σ of the jobs which are scheduled last, of a set Ω of unscheduled jobs, of a lower bound $LB_{C_{max}}(s)$ of the criterion C_{max} and a lower bound $LB_{\overline{U}}(s)$ of the criterion $\overline{U}$. The lower bound $LB_{C_{max}}(s)$ is obtained by applying algorithm ESJ1 of [Johnson, 1954] on the set Ω and we have $LB_{C_{max}}(s) = C_{max}(J(\Omega)//\sigma)$. $LB_{C_{max}}(s)$ is the minimal value of the criterion C_{max} for all schedules ending with the sequence σ. The calculation of the lower bound $LB_{\overline{U}}(s)$ breaks down as follows. We have $LB_{\overline{U}}(s) = LB^1_{\overline{U}}(\sigma) + LB^2_{\overline{U}}(\Omega)$ with:

$$LB^1_{\overline{U}}(\sigma) = \sum_{J_i \in \sigma} U_i(J(\Omega)//\sigma)$$

The lower bound $LB^2_{\overline{U}}$ related to the unscheduled jobs is defined by:

$$LB^2_{\overline{U}}(\Omega) = \max(LB^3_{\overline{U}}(\Omega); LB^4_{\overline{U}}(\Omega))$$

To calculate the bound $LB^3_{\overline{U}}(\Omega)$, Liao, Yu and Joe breakdown the flowshop problem into a single machine problem which is denoted by $1|p_i = p_{i,1}, d_i = d_i - p_{i,2}|\overline{U}$. Moore's algorithm ([Moore, 1968]) is then applied to solve this problem. $LB^3_{\overline{U}}(\Omega)$ is the value of the criterion $\overline{U}$ obtained for the reduced problem.

The bound $LB^4_{\overline{U}}(\Omega)$ is calculated by solving the $1|r_i = r = \min_{j \in \Omega}(p_{j,1}), p_i = p_{i,2}, d_i|\overline{U}$ problem. A modified version of Moore's algorithm can be used, by considering that the machines M_1 and M_2 are free sooner than the date r. The bounds which are presented are similar to those presented by [Daniels and Chambers, 1990].

Liao, Yu and Joe also present some rules to prune the search tree. We note E_{part} the set of strict Pareto optima already obtained during the exploration of the tree. A node s is pruned if:

- $\exists x \in E_{part}$ such that $LB_{C_{max}}(s) \geq C_{max}(x)$ and $LB_{\overline{U}}(s) \geq \overline{U}(x)$.
- $LB_{\overline{U}}(s) = \overline{U}(ESJ1(\Omega)//\sigma)$, because the schedule $ESJ1(\Omega)//\sigma$ among all the schedules that end with σ, minimises simultaneously the criteria C_{max} and $\overline{U}$.

The dominance conditions presented in the following theorems are used in the algorithm ELYJ1.

Theorem 27 *[Liao et al., 1997]*
Let $\sigma' = J_j J_i \sigma$ and $\sigma'' = J_i J_j \sigma$, with σ a sequence and J_i and J_j two jobs. The sequence σ'' dominates the sequence σ' if the following three conditions

are verified:
(i) $U_i = 0$ *in the schedule* $ESJ1(\Omega - \{J_j\} - \{J_i\})//\sigma'$,
(ii) $\min(p_{i,1}, p_{j,2}) \leq \min(p_{i,2}, p_{j,1})$,
(iii) $d_i \leq d_j$.

Theorem 28 *[Liao et al., 1997]*
Let $\sigma' = J_j J_i \sigma$ *and* $\sigma'' = J_i J_j \sigma$, *with* σ *a sequence and* J_i *and* J_j *two jobs. The sequence* σ'' *dominates the sequence* σ' *if the two following conditions are verified:*
(i) *in the schedule* $ESJ1(\Omega - \{J_j\} - \{J_i\})//\sigma'$, $U_i = 0$ *and* $U_j = 1$,
(ii) $\min(p_{i,1}, p_{j,2}) \leq \min(p_{i,2}, p_{j,1})$.

Theorem 29 *[Liao et al., 1997]*
Let $\sigma' = J_j J_i \sigma$ *and* $\sigma'' = J_i J_j \sigma$, *with* σ *a sequence and* J_i *and* J_j *two jobs. The sequence* σ'' *dominates the sequence* σ' *if the following five conditions are verified:*
(i) $U_i = 0$ *in the schedule* $ESJ1(\Omega - \{J_j\} - \{J_i\})//\sigma'$,
(ii) $p_{i,1} \leq p_{i,2}$,
(iii) $p_{i,1} \leq p_{j,1}$,
(iv) $p_{i,2} \leq p_{j,2}$,
(v) $d_i \leq d_j$.

The child nodes of s are constructed by taking a job of Ω and adding it to the beginning of the sequence σ. The next node to be processed is the node with the smallest value of the bound $LB_{C_{max}}$. The algorithm ELYJ1 is presented in figure 8.20.

Experimental results show that the proposed algorithm enables us to process problems with up to 30 jobs. Besides, the lower are the due dates d_i the more difficult are the problems to solve. Finally, the average number of non dominated criteria vectors is between 1.1 and 1.8. This means that the criteria C_{max} and $\overline{U}$ are not conflicting.

8.1.7 The $F2|prmu, d_i|\#(C_{max}, \overline{T})$ problem

When the criteria considered are C_{max} and $\overline{T}$, the determination of the set of strict Pareto optima is proposed by [Liao et al., 1997]. This problem can be shown to be strongly $\mathcal{NP}$-hard.

The algorithm proposed by Liao, Yu and Joe is a branch-and-bound algorithm, denoted by ELYJ2, which is very close to the algorithm ELYJ1 (figure 8.20) for the $F2|prmu, d_i|\#(C_{max}, \overline{U})$ problem. Each node s of the search tree comprises a list σ of jobs scheduled last, a set Ω of unscheduled jobs, a lower bound $LB_{C_{max}}(s)$ of the criterion C_{max} and a lower bound $LB_{\overline{T}}(s)$ of the criterion $\overline{T}$. The lower bound $LB_{C_{max}}(s)$ is obtained by applying the algorithm J of [Johnson, 1954] on the set Ω, and we have:

ALGORITHM ELYJ1

```
/* T is the set of n jobs to schedule */
/* E is the set of strict Pareto optima */
/* J is the algorithm of [Johnson, 1954] */
Step 1:  /* Initialisation of the algorithm */
         E = ∅;
         Create the root node s_0: σ_0 = ∅ ; Ω_0 = T; Q = {s_0};
Step 2:  /* Main part of the branch-and-bound */
         While (Q ≠ ∅) Do
           Choose a node s_i with the lowest value of LB_{C_max} in Q;
           Q = Q − {s_i};
           Ω = Ω_i;
           For k = 1 to |Ω_i| Do
             Select a job J_j in Ω such that J_j σ_i is not
             dominated: Ω = Ω − {J_j};
             Create a child node s_{i+1}^{(k)}:
                 σ_{i+1}^{(k)} = J_j σ_i; Ω_{i+1}^{(k)} = Ω_i − {J_j};
             Compute LB_{C_max}(s_{i+1}^{(k)});
             Compute LB_{\bar{U}}(s_{i+1}^{(k)});
             If (∄x ∈ E such that (LB_{C_max}(s_{i+1}^{(k)}) ≥ C_max(x)
             and LB_{\bar{U}}(s_{i+1}^{(k)}) ≥ \bar{U}(x)) ) Then
               If (LB_{\bar{U}}(s_{i+1}^{(k)}) = \bar{U}(J(Ω_{i+1}^{(k)})//σ_{i+1}^{(k)}))
               Then E = E + {J(Ω_{i+1}^{(k)})//σ_{i+1}^{(k)}};
               Else Q = Q + {s_{i+1}^{(k)}};
               End If;
             End If;
           End For;
         End While;
Step 3:  Print E;
```

[Liao et al., 1997]

Fig. 8.20. An optimal algorithm for the $F2|prmu, d_i|\#(C_{max}, \overline{U})$ problem

$$LB_{C_{max}}(s) = C_{max}(J(\Omega)//\sigma)$$

$LB_{C_{max}}(s)$ is the minimal value of criterion C_{max} for all schedules ending with the sequence σ. Calculation of the lower bound $LB_{\overline{T}}(s)$ is as follows:

$$LB_{\overline{T}}(s) = LB^1_{\overline{T}}(\sigma) + LB^2_{\overline{T}}(\Omega)$$

with:

$$LB^1_{\overline{T}}(\sigma) = \sum_{J_i \in \sigma} T_i(J(\Omega)//\sigma)$$

To calculate the bound $LB^2_{\overline{T}}(\Omega)$ we construct a dummy problem from the jobs of Ω. The algorithm used is denoted by HLYJ1, and is presented in figure 8.21.

The bounds presented are similar to those proposed for the $F2|prmu, d_i|$ $\#(T_{max}, C_{max})$ problem by [Daniels and Chambers, 1990]. Liao, Yu and Joe

ALGORITHM HLYJ1

```
/* Ω' is the set of unscheduled jobs */
/* L1 is the list of processing times p_{i,1}, of jobs in Ω', sorted by */
/* increasing value */
/* L2 is the list of processing times p_{i,2}, of jobs in Ω', sorted by */
/* increasing value */
/* D is the list of due dates d_i, of jobs in Ω', sorted by increasing value */
Let J_ℓ ∈ Ω be such that p_{ℓ,1} + p_{ℓ,2} = min_{J_i∈Ω} (p_{i,1} + p_{i,2});
Ω' = Ω − {J_ℓ};
p'_{1,1} = p_{ℓ,1}; p'_{1,2} = p_{ℓ,2}; d'_1 = d_ℓ;
C'_{1,2} = p'_{1,1} + p'_{1,2};
LB^2_T(Ω) = max(0; C'_{1,2} − d'_1);
For i = 2 to |Ω| Do
  | p'_{i,1} = L1[i − 1]; p'_{i,2} = L2[i − 1]; d'_i = D[i − 1];
  | C'_{i,2} = max(Σ_{j=1}^{i} p'_{j,1} + p'_{i,2}; Σ_{j=1}^{i} p'_{j,2} + p'_{1,1});
  | LB^2_T(Ω) = LB^2_T(Ω) + max(0; C'_{i,2} − d'_i);
End For;
```

[Liao et al., 1997]

Fig. 8.21. Calculation of the lower bound $LB^2_{\overline{T}}(\Omega)$

also use a dominance condition on the criterion $\overline{T}$ to prune nodes in the search tree.

Theorem 30 *[Sen et al., 1989]*
Let $S = \pi_1 J_i J_j \pi_2$ and $S' = \pi_1 J_j J_i \pi_2$ be two schedules with π_1 and π_2 two sequences and J_i and J_j two jobs. S dominates S' if the following three conditions are verified:
(i) $d_i \leq d_j$,
(ii) $p_{i,2} - d_i \leq p_{j,2} - d_j$,
(iii) $p_{i,1} \leq \min(p_{i,2}; p_{j1})$.

The child nodes of s are built by taking a job of Ω and adding it to the beginning of the sequence σ. The next node to be processed is the node with the smallest value of the bound $LB_{C_{max}}$. The algorithm ELYJ2 is presented in figure 8.22.

Experimental results show that the algorithm ELYJ2 solves problems with up to 30 jobs. Besides, the lower are the due dates d_i the more difficult are the problems to solve. Finally, the average number of non dominated criteria vectors is between 1.2 and 3.1, which means that the criteria C_{max} and $\overline{T}$ do not conflict so much.

ALGORITHM ELYJ2

/* T is the set of n jobs to schedule */
/* E is the set of strict Pareto optima */
/* $ESJ1$ is the algorithm of [Johnson, 1954] */
Step 1: /* Initialisation of the algorithm */
  $E = \emptyset$;
  Create the root node s_0: $\sigma_0 = \emptyset$; $\Omega_0 = T$; $Q = \{s_0\}$;
Step 2: /* Main part of the branch-and-bound */
  While ($Q \neq \emptyset$) Do
    Select the node s_i with the lowest value $LB_{C_{max}}$ in Q: $Q = Q - \{s_i\}$;
    $\Omega = \Omega_i$;
    For $k = 1$ to $|\Omega_i|$ Do
      Choose a job J_j in Ω such that $J_j\sigma_i$ is not dominated: $\Omega = \Omega - \{J_j\}$;
      Create a child node $s_{i+1}^{(k)}$: $\sigma_{i+1}^{(k)} = \{J_j\}//\sigma_i$ and $\Omega_{i+1}^{(k)} = \Omega_i - \{J_j\}$;
      Compute $LB_{C_{max}}(s_{i+1}^{(k)})$;
      Compute $LB_{\overline{T}}(s_{i+1}^{(k)})$;
      If ($\nexists x \in E$ such that ($LB_{C_{max}}(s_{i+1}^{(k)}) \geq C_{max}(x)$ and $LB_{\overline{T}}(s_{i+1}^{(k)}) \geq \overline{T}(x)$)) Then
        If ($LB_{\overline{T}}(s_{i+1}^{(k)}) = \overline{T}(ESJ1(\Omega_{i+1}^{(k)})//\sigma_{i+1}^{(k)})$)
        Then $E = E + \{J(\Omega_{i+1}^{(k)})//\sigma_{i+1}^{(k)}\}$;
        Else $Q = Q + \{s_{i+1}^{(k)}\}$;
        End If;
      End If;
    End For;
  End While;
Step 3: Print E;

[Liao et al., 1997]

Fig. 8.22. An optimal algorithm for the $F2|prmu, d_i|\#(C_{max}, \overline{T})$ problem

8.2 m-machine flowshop problems

In this section we consider flowshop problems where m machines are necessary to process the jobs. The latter use the machines in order of their index, *i.e.* M_1 then M_2, *etc.*, up to M_m.

8.2.1 The $F|prmu|Lex(C_{max}, \overline{C})$ problem

[Selen and Hott, 1986] and [Wilson, 1989] solve this problem by using mixed integer programming. It is strongly $\mathcal{NP}$-hard because the particular case where $m = 2$ is also.

The model presented by [Selen and Hott, 1986] is based on the fact that for two jobs in jth and $(j+1)$th positions in a schedule S, we have the following relation:

$$X^k_{[j+1]} + p_{[j+1],k} + W^{k+1}_{[j+1]} = X^{k+1}_{[j+1]} + p_{[j],k+1} + W^{k+1}_{[j]}$$
$$\forall k = 1, ..., m-1 \text{ and } \forall j = 1, ..., n-1$$

with $X^k_{[j]}$ the idle time on machine M_k before the processing of the jth job of S, $p_{[j],k}$ the processing time on machine M_k of the jth job of S, and $W^k_{[j]}$ the waiting time before machine M_k of the jth job of S (figure 8.23).

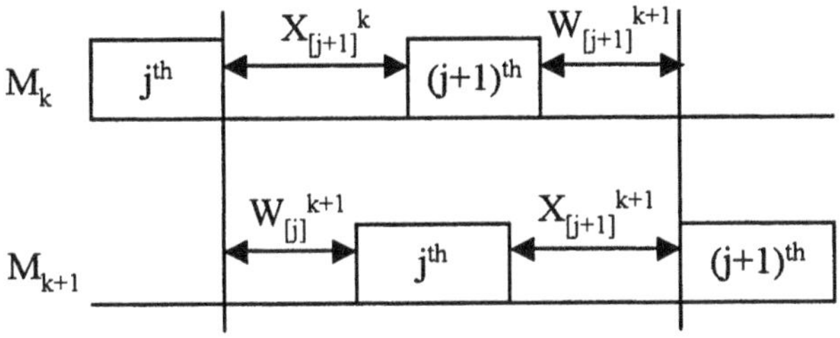

Fig. 8.23. Illustration of the variables

This model, denoted by ESH1 (figure 8.24) requires $mn + n - m + 3$ constraints, n^2 0-1 variables and $2mn + 1$ integer variables. This model can be partially found in [Baker, 1974]. Firstly Selen and Hott calculate the optimal value of the criterion C_{max} by using the mathematical model ESH1 but with the makespan as the objective function. Next, they solve the bicriteria problem using with the model ESH1.

The model proposed by [Wilson, 1989] requires less variables but more constraints. It is based on the fact that for a schedule S we have the following relation:

$$s_{[j+1],k+1} \geq C_{[j+1],k} \text{ and } s_{[j+1],k+1} \geq C_{[j],k+1}$$
$$\forall k = 1, ..., m-1 \text{ and } j = 1, ..., n-1$$

with $s_{[j],k}$ the start time on machine M_k of the job in jth position in S and $C_{[j],k}$ the completion time on machine M_k of the jth job of S.

This model, denoted by EJW1 (figure 8.25) requires: $2mn + n - m + 2$ constraints, n^2 0-1 variables and $mn+1$ integer variables. As for the model ESH1 we must in a first step solve the mathematical problem that minimises the makespan, to know its optimal value. Next, they solve the bicriteria problem using the model EJW1.

Mathematical formulation ESH1	
Data:	n, the number of jobs, m, the number of machines, $p_{i,j}$, $i = 1, ..., n$, $j = 1, ..., m$, the processing times of jobs, C^*_{max}, the optimal value of criterion C_{max}.
Variables:	$z_{i,j}$, boolean variable, equal to 1 if J_i is in position j and 0 otherwise, $X^k_{[j]}$, idle time on machine M_k before the start time of the job in position j, $W^k_{[j]}$, waiting time before machine M_k of the job in position j, $\overline{C}$, value of the criterion.
Objective:	Minimise $\overline{C}$
Constraints:	$\sum_{i=1}^{n} z_{i,j} = 1, \quad \forall j = 1, ..., n,$ $\sum_{j=1}^{n} z_{i,j} = 1, \quad \forall i = 1, ..., n,$ $X^k_{[j+1]} + \sum_{i=1}^{n} z_{i,j+1} p_{i,k} + W^{k+1}_{[j+1]} = X^{k+1}_{[j+1]} + \sum_{i=1}^{n} z_{i,j} p_{i,k+1} + W^{k+1}_{[j]}, \quad \forall k = 1, ..., m-1, \ j = 1, ..., n-1,$ $\sum_{i=1}^{n} X^m_{[i]} + \sum_{i=1}^{n} p_{i,m} = C^*_{max}$ $C^*_{max} = \sum_{k=1}^{n} X^m_{[k]} + \sum_{j=1}^{n} p_{j,m}$ $\overline{C} = \sum_{i=1}^{n} (\sum_{k=1}^{i} X^m_{[k]} + \sum_{k=1}^{i} \sum_{j=1}^{n} z_{j,k} p_{j,m})$
[Selen and Hott, 1986]	

Fig. 8.24. An MIP model for the $F|prmu|Lex(C_{max}, \overline{C})$ problem

8.2.2 The $F|prmu|\#(C_{max}, \overline{C})$ problem

[Gangadharan and Rajendran, 1994]

Gangadharan and Rajendran are interested in minimising the criteria C_{max} and $\overline{C}$, and they restrict their study to the set of permutation schedules. No objective function is explicitly defined and the problem is to find a solution belonging to the set O defined by:

$$O = \{S / \forall S' \neq S, \frac{C_{max}(S) - C_{max}(S')}{min\left(C_{max}(S); C_{max}(S')\right)} + \frac{\overline{C}(S) - \overline{C}(S')}{min\left(\overline{C}(S); \overline{C}(S')\right)} \leq 0\}$$

The heuristic proposed is based on a simulated annealing method which is executed with two different initial sequences. The best solution calculated is retained. The general heuristic algorithm, denoted by HGR1, is presented in

Mathematical formulation EJW1	
Data:	n, the number of jobs, m, the number of machines, $p_{i,j}$, $i = 1, ..., n, j = 1, ..., m$, the processing times of jobs, C^*_{max}, the optimal value of criterion C_{max}.
Variables:	$z_{i,j}$, boolean variable, equal to 1 if J_i is in position j and 0 otherwise, $s^k_{[j]}$, start time on machine M_k of the job in position j, $\overline{C}$, value of the criterion.
Objective:	Minimise $\overline{C}$
Constraints:	$\sum_{i=1}^{n} z_{i,j} = 1, \forall j = 1, ..., n,$ $\sum_{j=1}^{n} z_{i,j} = 1, \forall i = 1, ..., n,$ $s^1_{[1]} = 0,$ $s^1_{[j+1]} = s^1_{[j]} + \sum_{i=1}^{n} z_{i,j} p_{i,1}, \forall j = 1, ..., n-1,$ $s^{k+1}_{[1]} = s^k_{[1]} + \sum_{i=1}^{n} z_{i,1} p_{i,k}, \forall k = 1, ..., m-1,$ $s^{k+1}_{[j]} \geq s^k_{[j]} + \sum_{i=1}^{n} z_{i,j} p_{i,k}, \forall j = 2, ..., n \text{ and } \forall k = 1, ..., m-1,$ $s^k_{[j+1]} \geq s^k_{[j]} + \sum_{i=1}^{n} z_{i,j} p_{i,k}, \forall j = 1, ..., n-1 \text{ and } \forall k = 2, ..., m,$ $s^m_{[n]} + \sum_{i=1}^{n} z_{i,n} p_{i,m} = C^*_{max},$ $\overline{C} = \sum_{j=1}^{n} s^m_{[j]} + \sum_{i=1}^{n} p_{i,m}.$
[Wilson, 1989]	

Fig. 8.25. An MIP model for the $F|prmu|Lex(C_{max}, \overline{C})$ problem

figure 8.26. The initial sequences are obtained by the heuristics HGR2 and HGR3, detailed below.
The heuristic HGR2 only minimises the criterion C_{max} (figure 8.27). It is based on a sorting procedure which uses the following indices:

$$T_i = \frac{\sum_{j=1}^{m} j \times p_{i,j}}{\sum_{j=1}^{m} p_{i,j}}, \forall i = 1, ..., n, \text{ and } \theta_i = \sum_{j=1}^{m} p_{i,j}, \forall i = 1, ..., n$$

ALGORITHM HGR1
/* HGR2: the heuristic for the $F\|prmu\|C_{max}$ problem */
/* HGR3: the heuristic for the $F\|prmu\|\overline{C}$ problem */
/* RS: the simulated annealing heuristic used by the authors */
Step 1: Apply HGR2 to obtain the schedule S;
Apply RS to obtain the schedule R with S as the initial schedule;
Step 2: Apply HGR3 to obtain the schedule S';
Apply RS to obtain the schedule R' with S' as the initial schedule;
Step 3: /* We keep the best schedule */
If $\left(\frac{C_{max}(R) - C_{max}(R')}{min(C_{max}(R); C_{max}(R'))} + \frac{\overline{C}(R) - \overline{C}(R')}{min(\overline{C}(R); \overline{C}(R'))} \leq 0\right)$ Then
Print $R, C_{max}(R)$ and $\overline{C}(R)$;
Else
Print $R', C_{max}(R')$ and $\overline{C}(R')$;
End If;
[Gangadharan and Rajendran, 1994]

Fig. 8.26. An heuristic algorithm for the $F|prmu|\#(C_{max}, \overline{C})$ problem

If $T_i \geq (m+1)/2$ then the processing time $p_{i,j}$ of job J_i increases globally when j increases.

The jobs having a low value of the index T_i, therefore lower values $p_{i,j}$ when j is closer to 1 than to m, will be placed at the beginning of the resulting schedule. Jobs having larger $p_{i,j}$ on the last machines than on the first will be placed at the end of the schedule. We notice here a characteristic of the algorithm which is similar to that of [Johnson, 1954] for the $F2|prmu|C_{max}$ problem (see also [Bonney and Gundry, 1976]).

ALGORITHM HGR2
Step 1: $T_i = \sum_{j=1}^{m} j \times p_{i,j} / \sum_{j=1}^{m} p_{i,j}, \forall i = 1, ..., n;$
$\theta_i = \sum_{j=1}^{m} p_{i,j}, \forall i = 1, ..., n;$
Step 2: $Q' = \{J_i/T_i \geq (m+1)/2\};$
$Q'' = \{J_i/T_i < (m+1)/2\};$
Step 3: Sort the jobs in Q' by increasing value of θ_i;
Sort the jobs in Q'' by decreasing value of θ_i;
Step 4: $S = Q'//Q''$;
Step 5: Print S and $C_{max}(S)$;
[Gangadharan and Rajendran, 1994]

Fig. 8.27. An heuristic algorithm for the $F|prmu|C_{max}$ problem

The heuristic HGR3 considers only the minimisation of criterion $\overline{C}$. It is based on the results of [Rajendran and Chaudhuri, 1991]. Let a weight ω_i be defined by $\omega_i = \sum_{j=1}^{m}(m-j+1) \times p_{i,j}$, $\forall i = 1, ..., n$. Rajendran and Chaudhuri show that by sorting the jobs by increasing order of weights ω_i, we obtain a schedule which minimises the criterion $\overline{C}$ in an heuristic manner. This index is similar to the one defined by [Page, 1961].

Experimental results show that the heuristic HGR1 is better than those proposed for the $F|prmu|C_{max}$ problem by [Ogbu and Smith, 1990] and [Ho and Chang, 1991]. From a theoretical point of view the definition of the set O may seem to be surprising regarding the bicriteria minimisation problem. We can show that this set is a subset of the set of strict Pareto optima.

Lemma 32
We have $O \subseteq E$.

Proof.
We shall proceed by contradiction. Let us suppose that $\exists S \in O$ such that $S \notin E$. $S \notin E \Leftrightarrow \exists S'$ such that $C_{max}(S') \leq C_{max}(S)$ and $\overline{C}(S') \leq \overline{C}(S)$ with at least one strict inequality.
$\Rightarrow \frac{C_{max}(S) - C_{max}(S')}{min(C_{max}(S); C_{max}(S'))} + \frac{\overline{C}(S) - \overline{C}(S')}{min(\overline{C}(S); \overline{C}(S'))} > 0$, which contradicts the fact that $S \in O$.□

Notice that the reciprocal is false. Let us consider an example where the set of solutions is reduced to two schedules S and S' such that $C_{max}(S) = 15$, $\overline{C}(S) = 23$, $C_{max}(S') = 14$ and $\overline{C}(S') = 24$. We then have $O = \{S'\}$ and $E = \{S, S'\}$.

The problem addressed by [Gangadharan and Rajendran, 1994] is equivalent to the determination of a solution belonging to the subset O of E. The heuristic HGR1 gives an arbitrary solution belonging to the set O.

[Rajendran, 1994] and [Rajendran, 1995]

[Rajendran, 1995] proposes an heuristic which calculates a solution belonging to the set O of sequences defined by:

$$O = \{S/\forall S' \neq S, \frac{C_{max}(S)-C_{max}(S')}{min\left(C_{max}(S);C_{max}(S')\right)} + \frac{\overline{C}(S)-\overline{C}(S')}{min\left(\overline{C}(S);\overline{C}(S')\right)} < 0\}$$

This heuristic, denoted by HCR3, is based on a neighbourhood method having the same scheme as the heuristics HCR1 and HCR2 presented by

[Rajendran, 1992] to solve the $F2|prmu|Lex(C_{max}, \overline{C})$ problem. The heuristic HCR3 is presented in figure 8.28.

```
ALGORITHM HCR3
/* T is the set of n jobs to schedule */
/* HCDS1 is the algorithm of [Campbell et al., 1970] */
Step 1:  Apply HCDS1 to obtain the schedule S*;
         For i = 1 to (n - 1) Do
           | Swap the jobs S*[i] and S*[i+1] in S* to obtain S';
           | If (C_max(S') < C_max(S*)) Then S* = S';
         End For;
Step 2:  For r = 1 to |S*| Do
           | D_{S*[r]} = sum_{j=1}^{m} p_{S*[r],j} - sum_{j=1}^{m} p_{S*[r+1],j};
           | D'_{S*[r]} = sum_{j=1}^{m} (m - j + 1) x p_{S*[r],j} - sum_{j=1}^{m} (m - j + 1) x p_{S*[r+1],j};
         End For;
         L = {i/D_{S*[i]} >= 0};
         Sort L by decreasing value of D_i (break ties by choosing the job
         with the greatest value D'_i);
Step 3:  While (L != Ø) Do
           | i = L[1];
           | S = S* with the jobs in ith and (i+1)th position swapped;
           | If ((C_max(S) - C_max(S*))/min(C_max(S); C_max(S*))
           |     + (C̄(S) - C̄(S*))/min(C̄(S); C̄(S*)) < 0) Then
           |   | S* = S;
           |   | Goto Step 2;
           | End If;
           | L = L - {i};
         End While;
Step 4:  Print S*, C_max(S*) and C̄(S*);
[Rajendran, 1995]
```

where

$$D_{S^*[r]} = \sum_{j=1}^{m} p_{S^*[r],j} - \sum_{j=1}^{m} p_{S^*[r+1],j};$$

$$D'_{S^*[r]} = \sum_{j=1}^{m} (m-j+1) \times p_{S^*[r],j} - \sum_{j=1}^{m} (m-j+1) \times p_{S^*[r+1],j};$$

$$\text{If } \left(\frac{C_{max}(S) - C_{max}(S^*)}{min(C_{max}(S); C_{max}(S^*))} + \frac{\overline{C}(S) - \overline{C}(S^*)}{min(\overline{C}(S); \overline{C}(S^*))} < 0\right) \text{ Then}$$

Fig. 8.28. An heuristic algorithm for the $F|prmu|\#(C_{max}, \overline{C})$ problem

Experimental results are presented and the heuristic HCR3 is compared with an heuristic proposed by [Ho and Chang, 1991] and which solves the $F|prmu|C_{max}$ problem.

Rajendran broadens the heuristic HCR3 similarly to the problem with three criteria $F|prmu|C_{max}, \overline{C}, \overline{I}$, where $\overline{I}$ is the sum of the idle times on all the machines, *i.e.* $\overline{I} = \sum_{k=1}^{m} I_k$ with I_k the sum of idle times on machine M_k. The heuristic obtained, denoted by HCR4, is identical to HCR3 except in the test of step 3 where we must read for HCR4:

"If $\left(\frac{C_{max}(S)-C_{max}(S^*)}{min\left(C_{max}(S);C_{max}(S^*)\right)} + \frac{\overline{C}(S)-\overline{C}(S^*)}{min\left(\overline{C}(S);\overline{C}(S^*)\right)} + \frac{\overline{I}(S)-\overline{I}(S^*)}{min\left(\overline{I}(S);\overline{I}(S^*)\right)} < 0\right)$ Then..."

Comparisons with the heuristic of [Ho and Chang, 1991] are also presented and they show that HCR4 gives better results for the three criteria.

[Rajendran, 1994] studies this problem when the processing times can be equal to zero. This constraint is not generally taken into account because it modifies calculation of the completion times of jobs on machines.

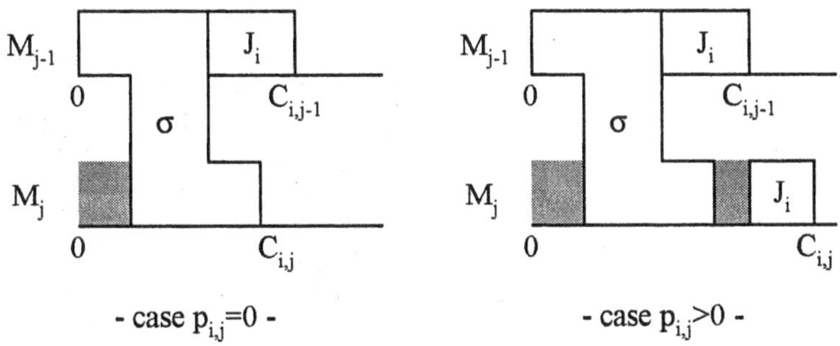

Fig. 8.29. The influence of zero processing times

Thus, to avoid idle times which are of no use, Rajendran authorises cases where $C_{i,j} < C_{i,j-1}$ (see figure 8.29). This implies on the other hand that the completion time of a job J_i is defined by $C_i = \max_{j=1,\dots,m}(C_{i,j})$, to be able to take account of the case where the last operations have zero duration. In order to solve this problem a modified version of the heuristic HCR3, denoted by HCR5, is presented in figure 8.30. The differences between these two heuristics are in the initialisation phase, where in HCR5 a variant of the heuristic HNEH1 is used instead of the heuristic HCDS1, and in the calculation of the indices D_i and D'_i.

Rajendran presents experimental results in which HCR5 is compared to the heuristic of [Ho and Chang, 1991]. This comparison is made on the criteria C_{max}, $\overline{C}$ and $\overline{I}$. As in the case where the processing times are strictly positive, heuristic HCR5 gives better results than the heuristic presented by [Ho and Chang, 1991].

8.2.3 The $F|prmu, d_i|\epsilon(C_{max}/T_{max})$ problem

[Daniels and Chambers, 1990] propose an *a posteriori* algorithm which is a generalisation of the heuristic HDC3. Knowing a value ϵ the heuristic, denoted

ALGORITHM HCR5

/* T is the set of n jobs to schedule */
/* HNEH1b is a modified version of HNEH1: in the first phase jobs are */
/* sorted by decreasing value of $\sum_{j=1}^{m} p_{i,j}/n_i$, with */
/* n_i the number of operations of job J_i which have not a zero */
/* processing time */

<u>Step 1:</u> Apply HNEH1b to obtain the schedule S^*;
<u>For</u> $i = 1$ <u>to</u> $(n-1)$ <u>Do</u>
  Swap the jobs $S^*[i]$ and $S^*[i+1]$ in S^* to obtain S';
  <u>If</u> $(C_{max}(S') < C_{max}(S^*))$ <u>Then</u> $S^* = S'$;
<u>End For</u>;

<u>Step 2:</u> <u>For</u> $r = 1$ <u>to</u> $|S^*|$ <u>Do</u>

$$D_{S^*[r]} = \frac{\sum_{j=1}^{m} p_{S^*[r],j}}{m_{S^*[r]}} - \frac{\sum_{j=1}^{m} p_{S^*[r+1],j}}{m_{S^*[r+1]}};$$

$$D'_{S^*[r]} = \frac{\sum_{j=1}^{m} (m-j+1) p_{S^*[r],j}}{m_{S^*[r]}} - \frac{\sum_{j=1}^{m} (m-j+1) p_{S^*[r+1],j}}{m_{S^*[r+1]}};$$

<u>End For</u>;
$L = \{i / D_{S^*[i]} \geq 0\}$;
Sort L by decreasing value of D_i (break ties by choosing the job with the greatest value D'_i);

<u>Step 3:</u> <u>While</u> $(L \neq \emptyset)$ <u>Do</u>
  $i = L[1]$;
  $S = S^*$ with the jobs in ith and $(i+1)$th position swapped;
  <u>If</u> $\left(\frac{C_{max}(S) - C_{max}(S^*)}{min(C_{max}(S); C_{max}(S^*))} + \frac{\overline{C}(S) - \overline{C}(S^*)}{min(\overline{C}(S); \overline{C}(S^*))} < 0\right)$ <u>Then</u>
    $S^* = S$;
    <u>Goto</u> Step 2;
  <u>End If</u>;
  $L = L - \{i\}$;
<u>End While</u>;

<u>Step 4:</u> <u>Print</u> $S^*, C_{max}(S^*)$ and $\overline{C}(S^*)$;

[Rajendran, 1994]

Fig. 8.30. An heuristic algorithm for the $F|prmu|\#(C_{max}, \overline{C})$ problem

by HDC4, searches the jobs J_i which can be scheduled in the last position, *i.e.* such that:

$$\sum_{\ell=1}^{n} p_{\ell,1} + \sum_{j=2}^{m} p_{i,j} - d_i \leq \epsilon$$

For each candidate for the last position, the heuristic HNEH1 is applied to the $n-1$ remaining jobs. Thus a complete schedule is obtained for each candidate. Amongst all these schedules, we retain the one which maximises the criterion C_{max}. The corresponding candidate job is placed in the last position of the schedule and the process is repeated until all the jobs are scheduled. If the final solution does not respect the constraint $T_{max} \leq \epsilon$ then the algorithm returns to the last sequenced job and attempts to place another candidate job. This back-tracking process is repeated until a feasible schedule is obtained or until all the candidate jobs have been tried in all the positions. The heuristic HDC4 is presented in figure 8.31.

```
ALGORITHM HDC4
/* T is the set of n jobs to schedule */
/* E is the set of strict Pareto optima */
/* I_ℓ, 1 ≤ ℓ ≤ n, is the set of jobs which cannot be placed in position ℓ */
/* HNEH1 is the algorithm of [Nawaz et al., 1983] */
/* δ ∈]0; 1[ is an ordinary value */
Step 1:  /* Initialisation of the algorithm */
         ε = T_max(HNEH1(T)) − δ;
         E = ∅;
         I_j = ∅, ∀j = 1, ..., n;
Step 2:  /* Building of a schedule */
         For ℓ = n to 1 Do
           L = {J_i ∈ T, J_i ∉ I_ℓ / Σ_{j∈T} p_{j,1} + Σ_{j=2}^{m} p_{i,j} − d_i ≤ ε};
           /* L is the set of jobs that can be placed in position ℓ */
           If (L = ∅) Then
             /* The solutions found are in E */
             Return E;
             END;
           End If;
           Let J_k ∈ L be such that:
             C_{k,m}(HNEH1(T) − {J_k}) = max_{J_i∈T}(C_{i,m}(HNEH1(T) − {J_i}));
           S[ℓ] = J_k;
           T = T − {J_k};
         End For;
Step 3:  /* We evaluate the built schedule */
         If (T_max(S) > ε) Then
           Let J_k be such that T_k(S) > ε and C_{k,m}(S) = max_{J_j/T_j(S)>ε}(C_{j,m});
           Let q be the position in S of J_k;
           I_q = I_q + {J_k};
         Else
           E = E + {S};
           ε = T_max(S) − δ;
         End If;
         T = {J_1; ...; J_n};
         Goto Step 2;
[Daniels and Chambers, 1990]
```

Fig. 8.31. An heuristic algorithm for the $F|prmu, d_i|\epsilon(C_{max}/T_{max})$ problem

Daniels and Chambers present experimental results in which they compare the heuristic HDC4 to an enumeration method. The results show that the cardinality of the set of strictly non dominated criteria vectors increases in proportion to the number of machines. Moreover, they show that on average 50% of the strict Pareto optima are calculated by HDC4. Nevertheless, as for the heuristic HDC3, the non strict but weak Pareto optima can be generated.

8.2.4 The $F|p_{i,j} \in [\underline{p}_{i,j}; \overline{p}_{i,j}], prmu|F_\ell(C_{max}, \overline{CC}^w)$ problem

[Nowicki, 1993] is interested in a problem where the processing time of jobs have to be determined. Crashing time costs are measured by the criterion $\overline{CC}^w$ which is defined by:

$$\overline{CC}^w = \sum_{i=1}^{n}\sum_{j=1}^{m} w_{i,j}x_{i,j}$$

where $x_{i,j}$ represents the compression of the operation $O_{i,j}$ defined by $p_{i,j} = \overline{p}_{i,j} - x_{i,j}$. [Nowicki and Zdrzalka, 1990] present a state-of-the-art survey of such problems. The problem addressed by Nowicki is $\mathcal{NP}$-hard.

For the particular two-machine problem, Nowicki proposes an approximation algorithm with the guaranteed performance of $\frac{4}{3}$. This algorithm is similar to the one presented by [Nowicki and Zdrzalka, 1988]. We consider an initial compression vector x^0 such that, $\forall i = 1, ..., n, \forall j = 1, ..., m, x^0_{i,j} \in [0; \overline{p}_{i,j} - \underline{p}_{i,j}]$. Processing times being fixed, Johnson's algorithm gives an initial sequence of jobs. The second phase of this algorithm considers that this sequence is fixed and searches for a vector x which minimises the objective function $F_\ell(C_{max}, \overline{CC}^w)$. This can be done by solving a linear program. Guaranteed performance of $\frac{3}{2}$ is obtained ([Nowicki and Zdrzalka, 1988]) by considering $x^0_{i,j} = (1 - c_{i,j}) \times (\overline{p}_{i,j} - \underline{p}_{i,j})$ where $c_{i,j}$ is the normalisation to 1 of the weight $w_{i,j}$. The worst case performance is reduced to $\frac{4}{3}$ by considering $x^0_{i,j} = \mu_{i,j} \times (\overline{p}_{i,j} - \underline{p}_{i,j})$ where $\mu_{i,j} = \max\big(\min(\dfrac{1+\alpha(m-1)}{\alpha m} - \dfrac{c_{i,j}}{\alpha}; 1); 0\big)$ and $\alpha = 1 - \rho m/[\rho + \sqrt{\rho(m-1)}]^2$ with ρ being the guaranteed performance of the sequencing algorithm. Nowicki shows that the bound of $\frac{4}{3}$ is the lowest which we can possibly find. In the case $m = 2$, we have $\rho = 1$ because algorithm ESJ1 is an optimal algorithm.
When the number of machines is not equal to two, algorithm ESJ1 can no longer be used to calculate a sequence. We suppose in the following that an heuristic, with a guaranteed performance of ρ is used. When the vector x^0 is defined as previously for the performance $\frac{4}{3}$, Nowicki shows that the guaranteed performance of the algorithm is equal to $\rho + (m-\rho)/(2\rho + 2\sqrt{\rho(m-1)} - 1)$.

8.2.5 The $F|p_{i,j} = p_i \in [\underline{p}_i; \overline{p}_i], prmu|\#(C_{max}, \overline{CC}^w)$ problem

[Cheng and Shakhlevich, 1999] address a particular flowshop problem where all the operations of a job have the same processing time, *i.e.* $p_{i,j} = p_i$, $\forall i = 1, ..., n$. We speak of a proportionated flowshop problem. Besides, the processing times are variables to be determined, and we have $p_i \in [\underline{p}_i; \overline{p}_i]$, $\forall i = 1, ..., n$. The crashing time costs are measured by the criterion $\overline{CC}^w$ which is defined by $\overline{CC}^w = \sum_{i=1}^{n} w_i x_i$ where $x_i \in [0; \overline{p}_i - \underline{p}_i]$ and it represents compression of the job J_i, *i.e.* $p_i = \overline{p}_i - x_i$. Cheng and Shakhlevich are interested in the determination of the strict Pareto optima, which is a polynomially solvable problem.

When processing times are fixed any permutation schedule minimises the criterion C_{max}. Then, the optimal value of the criterion C_{max} is given by:

$$C^*_{max} = (m-1) \max_{i=1,\ldots,n}(p_i) + \sum_{i=1}^{n} p_i$$

Similarly, when compressions x_i are fixed, the optimal value of the criterion C_{max} does not depend on the schedule.

Cheng and Shakhlevich propose an a posteriori algorithm which is based on the enumeration of the extreme Pareto points of the polyhedron of the solutions in criteria space. We can model the problem with a linear program because the variables x_i take real values and because every schedule minimises the criterion C_{max}. The principle of the algorithm, denoted by ECS1, is the following. Knowing an extreme point of the trade-off curve, it is possible to obtain the next extreme Pareto point by reducing the processing time of one or several jobs. Let s^0 be a solution defined by the processing times, *i.e.* $s^0 = [p_1; p_2; \ldots; p_n]^T$ and let $(C^{(0)}_{max}; \overline{CC}^{w(0)})$ be the associated criteria vector. In s^0, J_i is a job such that either $p_i < \max_{j=1,\ldots,n}(p_j)$, or $p_i = \max_{j=1,\ldots,n}(p_j)$ and $\exists J_k$ such that $p_k = p_i$. Reduction by one unit of the processing time of J_i leads to a reduction by one unit of the value of the criterion C_{max} of s^0. The ratio δ_i, which is the trade-off between the two criteria, is defined by $\delta_i = w_i$. It corresponds to an increase in criterion $\overline{CC}^w$ when the processing time p_i is decreased by one time unit. Let us now consider compression of all the longest jobs of s^0. Let z be the maximum decrease of the longest processing times so that they remain the longest. We define $L = \{J_i / p_i = \max_{j=1,\ldots,n}(p_j)\}$ and $\delta_L = \sum_{J_j \in L} w_j / (m + |L| - 1)$. From an extremity of the trade-off curve, obtained by solving the $F|p_{i,j} = p_i \in [\underline{p}_i; \overline{p}_i], prmu|Lex(C_{max}, \overline{CC}^w)$ problem, a series of compressions is performed to arrive at the other extremity of the curve. For a given extreme Pareto point, the next extreme point is calculated by choosing the lowest ratio δ_i or δ_L and by maximum compressing the corresponding job(s). This smaller ratio corresponds to the slope of the facet of the polyhedron which is between the current extreme point and the next point calculated. Algorithm ECS1 is presented in figure 8.32. Its time complexity is in $O(n\log(n))$.

Example.
We consider a scheduling problem for which $n = 5$ and $m = 2$.

i	1	2	3	4	5
$\underline{p}_i$	3	5	4	2	3
$\overline{p}_i$	7	7	5	4	4
w_i	1	1	3	4	5

(i) $p = [7;7;5;4;4]^T$ and $\delta = [1;1;3;4;5]^T$.
$p' = 7$, $L = \{J_1, J_2\}$, $Z = 2$ and $p'' = 5$.
$\delta_L = 2/3$, $i = 1$, $g = 0$ and $E = \{(34;0)\}$.
(ii) $g = 1$, $\delta_1 \geq \delta_L$.
$z = \min(2;2) = 2$, $p' = 5$.
$E = E + \{(28;4)\}$, $p = [5;5;5;4;4]^T$, $L' = \{J_3\}$, $Z' = 1$ and $Z = \min(0;1) = 0$.
$L = \{J_1, J_2, J_3\}$, $\delta_L = 5/4$, $p'' = 4$, $\delta_L = \infty$.
(iii) $g = 2$, $\delta_1 < \delta_L$.
$z_1 = 2$, $p = [3;5;5;4;4]^T$ and $E = E + \{(26;6)\}$.
$J_1 \in L \Rightarrow L = \{J_2, J_3\}$, $\delta_L = 4/3$ and $Z = 0$.
$p'' = 4$ and $i = 2$.
(iv) $g = 3$, $\delta_2 < \delta_L$.
$z_2 = 0$, $L = \{J_3\}$, $\delta_L = 3/2$ and $Z = 1$.
$i = 3$.
(v) $g = 4$, $\delta_3 \geq \delta_L$.
$z = 1$, $p' = 4$.
$E = E + \{(24;9)\}$, $p = [3;5;4;4;4]^T$, $L' = \{J_4, J_5\}$, $Z' = 1$ and $Z = 0$.
$L = \{J_4, J_5, J_3\}$, $\delta_L = 3$, $p'' = 0$ and $\delta_L = \infty$.
(vi) $g = 5$, $\delta_3 < \delta_L$.
$z_3 = 0$, $L = \{J_4, J_5\}$, $\delta_L = 3$ and $Z = 1$.
$i = 4$.
(vii) $g = 6$, $\delta_4 \geq \delta_L$.
$z = 1$, $p' = 3$.
$E = E + \{(21;18)\}$, $p = [3;5;4;3;3]^T$, $L' = \emptyset$, $Z' = 0$ and $Z = 0$.
$L = \{J_4, J_5\}$, $\delta_L = 3$, $p'' = 0$ and $\delta_L = \infty$.
(viii) $g = 7$, $\delta_4 < \delta_L$.
$z_4 = 1$, $p = [3;5;4;2;3]^T$ and $E = E + \{(20;22)\}$.
$J_4 \in L \Rightarrow L = \{J_5\}$, $\delta_L = 5/2$ and $Z = 0$.
$p'' = 0$ and $i = 5 = n$.
(ix) We obtain therefore $E = \{(34;0); (28;4); (26;6); (24;9); (21;18); (20;22)\}$.

ALGORITHM ECS1

/* We assume that $w_1 \leq w_2 \leq \ldots \leq w_n$ */
/* We consider the solution of the $Lex(C_{max}, \overline{CC}^w)$ problem */
$p_i = \overline{p}_i, \ \forall i = 1, ..., n;$
$\delta_i = w_i, \ \forall i = 1, ..., n; \ p' = \max_{j=1,...,n}(p_j);$ /* individual ratio */
$L = \{J_i / p_i = p'\}; \ Z = \min_{J_i \in L}(p' - \underline{p}_i);$
$p'' = \max_{J_j \notin L}(p_j);$
$\delta_L = \sum_{J_i \in L} w_i/(m + |L| - 1);$ /* Ratio of the longest jobs */
$i = 1; \ g = 0; \ C_{max}^{(g)} = (m-1)p' + \sum_{i=1}^{n} \overline{p}_i; \ \overline{CC}^{w(g)} = 0;$
$E = \{(C_{max}^{(g)}; \overline{CC}^{w(g)})\};$
<u>While</u> $(i \leq n)$ <u>Do</u>
  $g = g + 1;$
  <u>If</u> $(\delta_i < \delta_L)$ <u>Then</u> /* We compress a single job */
    $z_i = p_i - \underline{p}_i; \ p_i = p_i - z_i;$
    $C_{max}^{(g)} = C_{max}^{(g-1)} - z_i; \ \overline{CC}^{w(g)} = \overline{CC}^{w(g-1)} + w_i z_i;$
    $E = E + \{(C_{max}^{(g)}; \overline{CC}^{w(g)})\};$
    <u>If</u> $(J_i \in L)$ <u>Then</u>
      $L = L - \{J_i\}; \ \delta_L = \sum_{J_j \in L} w_j/(m + |L| - 1); \ Z = \min_{J_j \in L}(p' - p_j);$
    <u>End If</u>;
    $p'' = \max_{J_j \notin L}(p_j); \ i = i + 1;$
  <u>Else</u> /* We compress all the longest jobs */
    $z = \min(Z, p' - p''); \ p' = p' - z;$
    $C_{max}^{(g)} = C_{max}^{(g-1)} - (m + |L| - 1)z; \ \overline{CC}^{w(g)} = \overline{CC}^{w(g-1)} + z \sum_{J_j \in L} w_j;$
    $E = E + \{(C_{max}^{(g)}; \overline{CC}^{w(g)})\};$
    /* We update the information */
    $p_j = p_j - z, \ \forall J_j \in L;$
    $L' = \{J_j \notin L / p_j = p'\}; \ Z' = \min_{J_j \in L'}(p' - \underline{p}_j);$
    $Z = \min(Z - z; Z'); \ L = L \cup L'; \ \delta_L = \sum_{J_j \in L} w_j/(m + |L| - 1);$
    $p'' = \max_{J_j \notin L}(p_j);$
    <u>If</u> $(Z = 0)$ <u>Then</u> $\delta_L = \infty;$
  <u>End If</u>;
<u>End While</u>;
<u>Print</u> E;

[Cheng and Shakhlevich, 1999]

Fig. 8.32. An optimal algorithm for the $F|p_{i,j} = p_i \in [\underline{p}_i; \overline{p}_i], prmu|\#(C_{max}, \overline{CC}^w)$ problem

Cheng and Shakhlevich extend the algorithm ECS1 to cases where the criterion $\overline{CC}^w$ is defined as a convex or concave function.

8.3 Jobshop and Openshop problems

8.3.1 Jobshop problems

Few multicriteria jobshop scheduling problems have been addressed in the literature. [Huckert et al., 1980] study the $J|d_i|F_T(C_{max}, \overline{C}, \overline{I}, T_{max}, \overline{U})$ problem which is strongly $\mathcal{NP}$-hard. They propose an interactive algorithm which is inspired by the STEM method ([Benayoun et al., 1971]). This algorithm is clearly split into two modules as indicated in chapter 4. The first interacts with the decision maker by deducing a new Tchebycheff point z^{ref}. The greedy heuristics are then carried out for the new scheduling problem obtained and the solution which is calculated is presented to the Decision maker. The interactive procedure stops at his command.

[Deckro et al., 1982] study the $J|d_i|GP(C_{max}, \overline{C}, \overline{E} + \overline{T})$ problem and they propose a mixed integer program to solve it. Regarding the multicriteria optimisation aspect they consider goal programming. The proposed model applies equally to the case where the operations require a certain number of machines on which they must be processed.

8.3.2 The $O2||Lex(C_{max}, \overline{C})$ problem

When only the criterion C_{max} is minimised the problem is solvable in polynomial time ([Gonzalez and Sahni, 1976]). We recall that the optimal value of the criterion C_{max} is given by:

$$C^*_{max} = \max(\sum_{i=1}^{n} p_{i,1}; \max_{i=1,\ldots,n}(p_{i,1} + p_{i,2}); \sum_{i=1}^{n} p_{i,2})$$

The minimisation problem of criterion $\overline{C}$ is strongly $\mathcal{NP}$-hard and from the complexity proof proposed by [Achugbue and Chin, 1982] it can be deduced that the $O2||Lex(C_{max}, \overline{C})$ problem is equally so.

[Gupta and Werner, 1999]

Gupta and Werner show that if the optimal value of the criterion C_{max} is equal to $\max_{i=1,\ldots,n}(p_{i,1} + p_{i,2})$, then an optimal schedule for the bicriteria problem can be obtained in polynomial time as follows.
Let the job J_r be such that $p_{r,1} + p_{r,2} = \max_{i=1,\ldots,n}(p_{i,1} + p_{i,2})$. Two schedules are

constructed by assigning, in the first one, the first operation of J_r on machine M_1 and by assigning, in the second one, the first operation of J_r on machine M_2. In the first case the jobs remaining to be scheduled are sequenced on machine M_1 according to the rule SPT and the jobs are arbitrarily sequenced on machine M_2. In the second case, we proceed in the same way but by considering the second machine.

The most difficult problems to solve are those for which $C^*_{max} = \max(\sum_{i=1}^{n} p_{i,1}; \sum_{i=1}^{n} p_{i,2})$. Gupta and Werner propose in this case an extension of the heuristic HGNW1 for the $F2|prmu|Lex(C_{max}, \overline{C})$ problem. They differentiate between two symmetrical cases for which $C^*_{max} = \sum_{i=1}^{n} p_{i,1}$ and $C^*_{max} = \sum_{i=1}^{n} p_{i,2}$. The extension of HGNW1 in the first case considers the initial sequence of the jobs given by [Gonzalez and Sahni, 1976]'s algorithm for machine M_1. The first job of this sequence is assigned on the first machine. All the other first operations of the jobs are assigned on the second machine. The insertion principle of the heuristic HGNW1 is applied next. As for the flowshop problem the optimality test of the criterion C_{max} for a partial sequence is carried out by scheduling the remaining jobs using the algorithm of [Johnson, 1954]. The sequence obtained is then concatenated on the two machines to the partial schedule and the makespan value obtained is compared to the value C^*_{max}.

[Kyparisis and Koulamas, 2000]

Kyparisis and Koulamas study several particular cases for which the lexicographical problem is solvable in polynomial time.

Lemma 33 *[Kyparisis and Koulamas, 2000]*
The $O2||Lex(C_{max}, \overline{C})$ problem is polynomially solvable with a complexity in $O(n^2)$ time if $\min_{i=1,\ldots,n}(p_{i,1}) \geq 2 \times \max_{i=1,\ldots,n}(p_{i,2})$.

Lemma 34 *[Kyparisis and Koulamas, 2000]*
The $O2||Lex(C_{max}, \overline{C})$ problem is polynomially solvable with a complexity in $O(n\log(n))$ time if

$$\max_{i=1,\ldots,n}(p_{i,1} + p_{i,2}) \geq \max(\sum_{i=1}^{n} p_{i,2}; \sum_{i=1}^{n} p_{i,1}).$$

Lemma 35 *[Kyparisis and Koulamas, 2000]*
The $O2||Lex(C_{max}, \overline{C})$ problem is polynomially solvable with a complexity in $O(n\log(n))$ time if
(i) the number of jobs n is even,

(ii) $\forall i = 1, ..., \frac{n}{2}$, $p_{2i,1} = p_{2i-1,2}$ *and* $p_{2i-1,1} = p_{2i,2}$ *with* $p_{n+1,1} + p_{n+1,2} = \max_{i=1,\dots,n}(p_{i,1} + p_{i,2})$.

Kyparisis and Koulamas propose several heuristics for the bicriteria problem for different configurations.
When $\min_{i=1,\dots,n}(p_{i,1}) \geq \max_{i=1,\dots,n}(p_{i,2})$, *i.e.* machine M_1 dominates machine M_2, an algorithm in $O(n\log(n))$ time with a worst case performance guarantee of $1 + \frac{1}{n}$ is presented.

8.3.3 The $O3||Lex(C_{max}, \overline{C})$ problem

[Kyparisis and Koulamas, 2000] study a polynomial sub-problem of the three-machine problem. The latter is strongly $\mathcal{NP} - hard$ problem.

Lemma 36 *[Kyparisis and Koulamas, 2000]*
The $O3||Lex(C_{max}, \overline{C})$ problem is polynomially solvable with a complexity in $O(n^2)$ time if $\min_{i=1,\dots,n}(p_{i,1}) \geq 2 \times \max_{i=1,\dots,n}(p_{i,2}, p_{i,3})$.

Kyparisis and Koulamas also propose an heuristic in $O(n\log(n))$ time for the case where $\min_{i=1,\dots,n}(p_{i,1}) \geq \max_{i=1,\dots,n}(p_{i,2}, p_{i,3})$, *i.e.* the machine M_1 dominates the machines M_2 and M_3. This heuristic is similar to that presented for the two-machine problem. Its worst case performance guarantee is equal to $1 + \frac{2(n+2)}{(n(n+1))}$.

9. Parallel machines problems

9.1 Problems with identical parallel machines

9.1.1 The $P2|pmtn, d_i|\epsilon(L_{max}/C_{max})$ problem

[Mohri et al., 1999] are interested in a bicriteria scheduling problem where two machines are available to process n independent jobs that can be preempted at any (real) time. Each job J_i is defined by a processing time p_i and a due date d_i. Without loss of generality we assume that $d_1 \leq d_2 \leq ... \leq d_n$. The aim is to schedule the jobs in such a way that the makespan C_{max} and the maximum lateness L_{max} are minimised. By considering the ϵ constraint approach they provide a characterisation of strictly non dominated criteria vectors. This problem is solvable in polynomial time.

Firstly, Mohri, Masuda and Ishii tackle the $P2|pmtn, d_i|L_{max}$ problem which can be solved by iteratively solving $P2|pmtn, \widetilde{d_i}|-$ problems using the procedure of [Sahni, 1979]. At each iteration, a $P2|pmtn, \widetilde{d_i} = d_i + L|-$ problem is solved: if a feasible solution to this problem exists, then a schedule for which the value of the maximum lateness criterion is equal to L exists. Otherwise, no such schedule exists. Starting with Sahni's procedure they show the following result.

Lemma 37 *[Mohri et al., 1999]*
The optimal value of the L_{max} criterion for the $P2|pmtn, d_i|L_{max}$ problem is given by:

$$L^*_{max} = \frac{1}{2} \max_{i=1,...,n} \Big(\sum_{j=1}^{i} p_j - \min_{k=1,...,i}(d_k + \sum_{j=k+1}^{i} p_j) - \min_{k=1,...,i-1}(d_k + \sum_{j=k+1}^{i-1} p_j)\Big),$$

under the assumption that $p_i \leq d_i$, $\forall i = 1, ..., n$.

This result is extended to the $P2|pmtn, d_i|\epsilon(L_{max}/C_{max})$ problem when the constraint on the makespan is fixed, *i.e.* when we have $C_{max} \leq \epsilon$. In this case we have the following result.

Lemma 38 *[Mohri et al., 1999]*
The optimal value of the L_{max} criterion for the $P2|pmtn, d_i, C_{max} \leq \epsilon|L_{max}$ problem is denoted by L^{ϵ}_{max}. We have:

$$L^{\epsilon}_{max} = \max\{L^*_{max}; \max_{i=1,...,n}(\sum_{j=1}^{i} p_j - \epsilon - \min_{k=1,...,i-1}(d_k + \sum_{j=k+1}^{i-1} p_j))\},$$

under the assumption that $p_i \leq d_i$, $\forall i = 1, ..., n$.

The resolution of the $P2|pmtn, d_i|\epsilon(L_{max}/C_{max})$ problem with a fixed value ϵ is similar to the resolution of the $P2|pmtn, d_i|L_{max}$ problem. The only difference lies in the construction of the deadlines at each iteration. For the bicriteria problem we have $\widetilde{d}_i = \min(d_i + L; \epsilon)$, $\forall i = 1, ..., n$. Therefore, using Sahni's procedure, if we found a feasible schedule for these deadlines then a schedule exists for which the makespan is lower than ϵ and the value of the maximum lateness is equal to L.

Mohri, Masuda and Ishii propose a characterisation of the set E. They identify a sufficient condition for the existence of a single strictly non dominated criteria vector. This condition can be seen as a consequence of the mathematical expression of L^{ϵ}_{max}.

Theorem 31 *[Mohri et al., 1999]*
Let $F = \max_{i=1,...,n}(\sum_{j=1}^{i} p_j - \min_{k=1,...,i-1}(d_k + \sum_{j=k+1}^{i-1} p_j))$. If $L^*_{max} \geq F - C^*_{max}$ then there exists a single strictly non dominated criteria vector defined by $[C^*_{max}; L^*_{max}]^T$. C^*_{max} is the optimal value of the makespan for the $P2|pmtn|C_{max}$ problem can be stated as follows ([McNaughton, 1959]):

$$C^*_{max} = \max(\max_{i=1,...,n} p_i; \frac{1}{2}\sum_{i=1}^{n} p_i).$$

If the condition of theorem 31 does not hold the set E is contained, in the criteria space, in a line segment limited by the criteria vectors $[C^*_{max}; F - C^*_{max}]^T$ and $[C^+_{max}; L^*_{max}]^T$, where C^+_{max} is the minimal value of the makespan of an optimal schedule for the L_{max} criterion. The value C^+_{max} can be obtained from the feasible schedule returned by Sahni's procedure for the $P2|pmtn, \widetilde{d}_i = d_i + L^*_{max}|-$ problem. Besides, for any given criteria vector $[C; L]^T$ on the line segment a corresponding schedule is obtained using Sahni's procedure with $\widetilde{d}_i = \min(d_i + L; C)$, $\forall i = 1, ..., n$.

Example.
We consider a problem for which $n = 5$.

i	1	2	3	4	5
p_i	3	7	4	8	10
d_i	5	10	12	13	15

(i) We have:
$C^*_{max} = \max\{\max(3;7;4;8;10); \frac{1}{2}(3+7+4+8+10)\} = \max\{10;16\} = 16$ and,
$L^*_{max} = \frac{1}{2}\max\{3-5; 10-\min(5+7;10)-5; 14-\min(5+7+4;10+4;12)-\min(5+7;10); 22-\min(5+7+4+8;10+4+8;12+8;13)-\min(5+7+4;10+4;12); 32-\min(5+7+4+8+10;10+4+8+10;12+8+10;13+10;15)-\min(5+7+4+8;10+4+8;12+8;13)\}$
$= \frac{1}{2}\max\{-2;-5;-8;-3;4\} = 2.$
(ii) $F = \max\{3; 10-5; 14-\min(5+7;10); 22-\min(5+7+4;10+4;12); 32-\min(5+7+4+8;10+4+8;12+8;13)\}$
$= \max\{3;5;4;10;19\} = 19.$
We do not have $L^*_{max} = 2 \geq F - C^*_{max} = 19 - 16 = 3$ and thus the set E is defined in the criteria space by a line segment. The first extremity of this line segment is $[C^*_{max}; F - C^*_{max}]^T = [16;3]^T$. To get the second extremity we need to compute C^+_{max}, which is done by applying Sahni's algorithm with $\widetilde{d}_i = d_i + 2, \forall i = 1, ..., 5$. The obtained schedule is presented in figure 9.1 and we have $C^+_{max} = 17$.

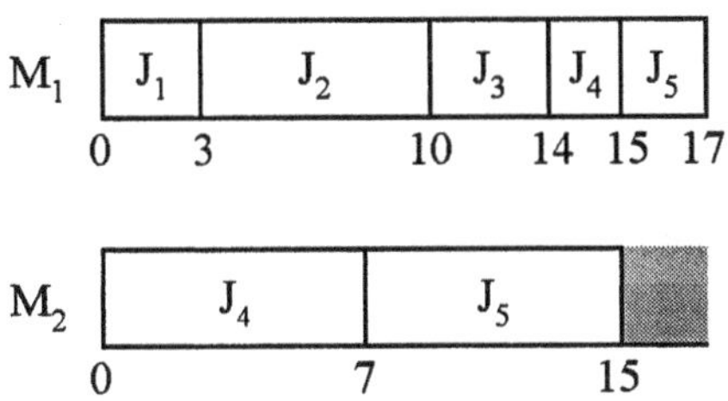

Fig. 9.1. The schedule computed to obtain C^+_{max}

The second extremity is therefore $[17;2]^T$ and the line segment is shown in figure 9.2.

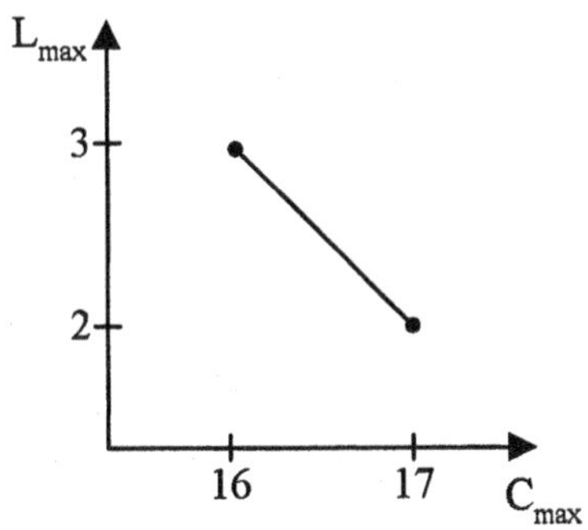

Fig. 9.2. The set E in criteria space

This scheduling problem has a strong particularity when $|E| > 1$, which is to concentrate the strictly non dominated criteria vectors on a single line segment. Generally, the trade-off curve is piecewise linear, *i.e.* it is made up of several line segments. For the problem under consideration, the property can be established from lemma 38 where the mathematical expression of L_{max}^{ϵ} is a maximum of two terms. The first one is a constant, the optimal value L_{max}^*, whilst the second one is the equation of a hyperplan in $\mathbb{R}^2$ of the form $a - \epsilon$ where a is a constant.

9.1.2 The $P3|pmtn, d_i|\epsilon(L_{max}/C_{max})$ problem

[Mohri et al., 1999] consider the extension to the three-machine case of the problem tackled in section 9.1.1. n independent jobs have to be processed and can be preempted at any (real) time. Each job J_i is defined by a processing time p_i and a due date d_i. Without loss of generality we assume that $d_1 \leq d_2 \leq ... \leq d_n$. As for the two-machine problem they provide a characterisation of the set of strict Pareto optima, by considering the problem $\epsilon(L_{max}/C_{max})$. This problem is solvable in polynomial time.

Firstly, Mohri, Masuda and Ishii tackle the $P3|pmtn, d_i|L_{max}$ problem which can be solved by iteratively solving $P3|pmtn, \tilde{d}_i|-$ problems using the procedure of [Sahni, 1979]. Starting with Sahni's procedure they show the following result.

Lemma 39 *[Mohri et al., 1999]*
Under the assumption that $p_i \leq d_i$, $\forall i = 1, ..., n$, the optimal value of the L_{max} criterion for the $P3|pmtn, d_i|L_{max}$ problem is given by:

$$L_{max}^* = \frac{1}{3} \max_{i=1,...,n} \Big(\sum_{j=1}^{i} p_j - E_i - \min_{k=1,...,i-1} (E_k + E_{k-1} + \sum_{j=k+1}^{i-1} p_j)\Big), \text{ where}$$

$$E_i = \min_{k=1,...,i} (d_k + \sum_{j=k+1}^{i} p_j).$$

Next, this result is extended to the $P3|pmtn, d_i|\epsilon(L_{max}/C_{max})$ problem when the constraint on the makespan is fixed, *i.e.* when we have $C_{max} \leq \epsilon$. In this case we have the following result.

Lemma 40 *[Mohri et al., 1999]*

Let $F_1 = \max_{i=1,...,n} \Big(\sum_{j=1}^{i} p_j - \min_{k=1,...,i-1} (E_k + E_{k-1} + \sum_{j=k+1}^{i-1} p_j)\Big)$

and $F_2 = \max_{i=1,...,n} \Big(\sum_{j=1}^{i} p_j - \min_{k=1,...,i-1} (E_{k-1} + \sum_{j=k+1}^{i-1} p_j)\Big)$,

where $E_i = \min_{k=1,...,i} (d_k + \sum_{j=k+1}^{i} p_j)$. *The optimal value of the L_{max} criterion* *for the $P3|pmtn, d_i, C_{max} \leq \epsilon|L_{max}$ problem is denoted by L^{ϵ}_{max}. Under the assumption that $p_i \leq d_i$, $\forall i = 1, ..., n$, we have:*

$$L^{\epsilon}_{max} = \max\left(L^*_{max}; F_1 - \epsilon; F_2 - 2\epsilon\right).$$

The resolution of the $P3|pmtn, d_i|\epsilon(L_{max}/C_{max})$ problem with a fixed value ϵ is similar to the resolution of the $P3|pmtn, d_i|L_{max}$ problem. The only difference lies in the construction of the deadlines at each iteration. For the bicriteria problem we have $\widetilde{d_i} = \min(d_i + L; \epsilon)$, $\forall i = 1, ..., n$. Therefore, using Sahni's procedure, if we found a feasible schedule for these deadlines then a schedule for which the makespan is lower than ϵ and the value of the maximum tardiness is equal to L exists.

Mohri, Masuda and Ishii propose a characterisation of the set E. As for the two-machine case, they identify a sufficient condition for having $|E| = 1$. However, this condition is more complicated for the three-machine problem.

Theorem 32 *[Mohri et al., 1999]*
If $L^*_{max} \geq F_2 - 2C^*_{max}$ and $L^*_{max} \geq F_1 - C^*_{max}$ then there exists a single strictly non dominated criteria vector defined by $[C^*_{max}; L^*_{max}]^T$. C^*_{max} is the optimal value of the makespan for the $P3|pmtn|C_{max}$ problem given by ([McNaughton, 1959]):

$$C^*_{max} = \max(\max_{i=1,\ldots,n} p_i; \frac{1}{3}\sum_{i=1}^{n} p_i).$$

Mohri, Masuda and Ishii claim that if the condition of theorem 32 does not hold, the set E is contained in the criteria space in a piecewise linear part made up of two line segments. Unfortunately, this is not always true. In some situations, one of these two line segments corresponds to a set of criteria vectors with a L_{max} value equal to L^*_{max}. In this case, the concerned line segment corresponds to solutions which belong to the set WE and not E. We prove the following result.

Theorem 33
Let F_1 and F_2 be defined as in lemma 40. We have the four following cases:

1. *If $L^*_{max} < F_2 - 2C^*_{max}$ and $L^*_{max} \geq F_1 - C^*_{max}$ then the set E defines in criteria space a single line segment with extreme points $[C^*_{max}; F_2 - 2C^*_{max}]^T$ and $[\frac{1}{2}(F_2 - L^*_{max}); L^*_{max}]^T$.*
2. *If $L^*_{max} \geq F_2 - 2C^*_{max}$ and $L^*_{max} < F_1 - C^*_{max}$ then the set E defines in criteria space a single line segment with extreme points $[C^*_{max}; F_1 - C^*_{max}]^T$ and $[F_1 - L^*_{max}; L^*_{max}]^T$.*
3. *If $L^*_{max} < F_2 - 2C^*_{max}$ and $L^*_{max} < F_1 - C^*_{max}$ and $F_1 = F_2 - C^*_{max}$ then the set E defines in criteria space a single line segment with extreme points $[C^*_{max}; F_1 - C^*_{max}]^T$ and $[F_1 - L^*_{max}; L^*_{max}]^T$.*
4. *If $L^*_{max} < F_2 - 2C^*_{max}$ and $L^*_{max} < F_1 - C^*_{max}$ and $F_1 \neq F_2 - C^*_{max}$ then the set E defines in criteria space two connected line segments with*

extreme points $[C^*_{max}; \max(F_1; F_2 - C^*_{max}) - C^*_{max}]^T$, $[F_2 - F_1; -F_2]^T$ *and* $[C^+_{max}; L^*_{max}]^T$, *where* C^+_{max} *is the minimal value of the makespan of an optimal schedule for the* L_{max} *criterion. The value* C^+_{max} *can be obtained from the feasible schedule returned by Sahni's procedure for the* $P3|pmtn, \widetilde{d_i} = d_i + L^*_{max}|-$ *problem.*

Proof.
From lemma 40 we know that for a given ϵ value, $L^{\epsilon}_{max} = \max\{L^*_{max}; F_1 - \epsilon; F_2 - 2\epsilon\}$. We separate the proofs of the different cases.
Case 1: If the condition of case 1 holds then the expression of L^{ϵ}_{max} is now $L^{\epsilon}_{max} = \max\{L^*_{max}; F_2 - 2\epsilon\}$, since $\epsilon \geq C^*_{max}$. This means that the different values of the criterion L_{max} which correspond to strict Pareto optima are on a single line segment defined by $[C^*_{max}; F_2 - 2C^*_{max}]^T$, since $L^*_{max} < F_2 - 2C^*_{max}$, and $[\frac{1}{2}(F_2 - L^*_{max}); L^*_{max}]^T$. The value ϵ associated to L^*_{max} is obtained when $L^*_{max} = F_2 - 2\epsilon$.
Case 2: Is symetrical to case 1, since we have $L^{\epsilon}_{max} = \max\{L^*_{max}; F_1 - \epsilon\}$.
Case 3: This case reduces to case 2. As $F_1 = F_2 - C^*_{max}$, we have that $\forall \epsilon \geq C^*_{max}$ $F_1 - \epsilon \geq F_2 - 2\epsilon$ and thus we deduce that $\forall \epsilon \geq C^*_{max}$, $L^{\epsilon}_{max} = \max\{L^*_{max}; F_1 - \epsilon\}$.
Case 4: If the condition of case 4 holds, then we have values of ϵ such that $L^*_{max} < F_2 - 2\epsilon$ and $L^*_{max} < F_1 - \epsilon$. The first extreme point in criteria space is obtained for $\epsilon = C^*_{max}$ and due to the condition of case 4, we have the vector $[C^*_{max}; \max(F_1 - C^*_{max}; F_2 - 2C^*_{max})]^T$ which can be rewritten as $[C^*_{max}; \max(F_1; F_2 - C^*_{max}) - C^*_{max}]^T$. The second extreme point is obtained by considering that either $F_1 - C^*_{max} > F_2 - C^*_{max}$ or $F_1 - C^*_{max} < F_2 - C^*_{max}$. Thus, increasing C^*_{max} lets us be on a line segment until $F_1 - \epsilon = F_2 - 2\epsilon$. In this case we arrive at the second extreme point, defined by $[F_2 - F_1; -F_2]^T$. Continuing the increase in the value of the makespan will lead to the extreme point with a value of criterion L_{max} equal to L^*_{max}. To compute the corresponding value of the makespan, denoted by C^+_{max}, we only have to apply Sahni's algorithm with $\widetilde{d_i} = d_i + L^*_{max}$, $\forall i = 1, ..., n$. □

For any given criteria vector $[C; L]^T$ on one of the two line segments a corresponding schedule is obtained using Sahni's procedure with $\widetilde{d_i} = \min(d_i + L; C)$, $\forall i = 1, ..., n$.

Example.
We consider a problem for which $n = 5$.

i	1	2	3	4	5
p_i	3	7	4	8	10
d_i	8	10	12	13	15

(i) We have:
$C^*_{max} = \max\{\max(3; 7; 4; 8; 10); \frac{1}{3}(3 + 7 + 4 + 8 + 10)\} = \max\{10; \frac{32}{3}\} = \frac{32}{3}$,
$E_1 = 8$, $E_2 = \min(8 + 7; 10) = 10$, $E_3 = \min(8 + 7 + 4; 10 + 4; 12) = 12$, $E_4 = \min(8 + 7 + 4 + 8; 10 + 4 + 8; 12 + 8; 13) = 13$ and $E_5 = \min(8 + 7 + 4 + 8 + 10; 10 + 4 + 8 + 10; 12 + 8 + 10; 13 + 10; 15) = 15$ and ,
$L^*_{max} = \frac{1}{3}\max\{3 - 8; 10 - 10 - 8 - 0; 14 - 12 - \min(8 + 0 + 7; 10 + 8); 22 - 13 - \min(8+$

$0+11; 10+8+4; 12+10); 32-15-\min(8+0+19; 10+8+12; 12+10+8; 13+12)\}$
$= \frac{1}{3}\max\{-5; -8; -13; -10; -80\} = -\frac{5}{3}$.
(ii) $F_1 = \max\{3; 10-8-0; 14-\min(8+0+7; 10+8); 22-\min(8+0+11; 10+8+4; 12+10); 32-\min(8+0+19; 10+8+12; 12+10+8; 13+12)\}$
$= \max\{3; 2; -1; 3; 7\} = 7$,
$F_2 = \max\{3; 10-0; 14-\min(0+7; 8); 22-\min(0+11; 8+4; 10); 32-\min(0+19; 8+12; 10+8; 12)\}$
$= \max\{3; 10; 7; 12; 20\} = 20$.
We have $L^*_{max} = -\frac{5}{3} \geq F_1 - C^*_{max} = 7 - \frac{32}{3} = -\frac{11}{3}$ and $L^*_{max} = -\frac{5}{3} < F_2 - C^*_{max} = 20 - 2\frac{32}{3} = -\frac{4}{3}$ (case 1). Thus the set E is defined in the criteria space by a single line segment. The first end point of this line segment is $[C^*_{max}; F_2 - 2C^*_{max}]^T = [\frac{32}{3}; -\frac{4}{3}]^T$. The second end point is $[\frac{1}{2}(F_2 - L^*_{max}); L^*_{max}]^T = [\frac{65}{6}; -\frac{5}{3}]^T$. The shape of the set E in the criteria space is shown in figure 9.3.

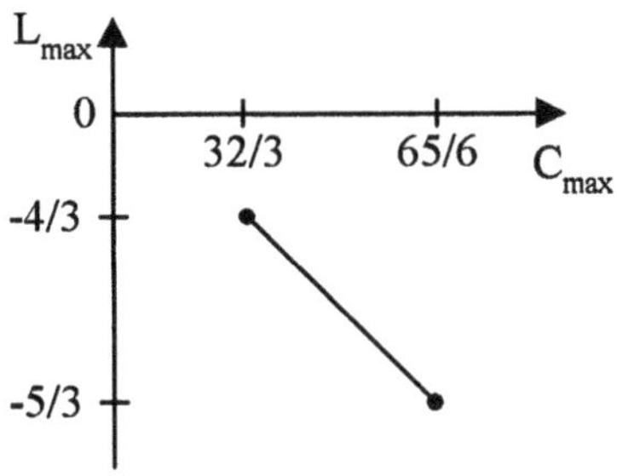

Fig. 9.3. The set E in criteria space

9.1.3 The $P2|d_i|Lex(T_{max}, \overline{U})$ problem

[Sarin and Hariharan, 2000] tackle the problem of scheduling n independent jobs on two parallel machines, when no preemption is allowed. The aim is to minimise the maximum tardiness and next the number of tardy jobs. Without loss of generality we assume that the jobs are such that $d_1 \leq d_2 \leq ... \leq d_n$ (break ties by indexing first the job with the smallest p_i). As the $P2|d_i|T_{max}$ problem is $\mathcal{NP}$-hard, the bicriteria problem is also. Sarin and Hariharan propose an heuristic to solve the bicriteria problem.

The first time, they only consider the minimisation of the T_{max} criterion of and propose a heuristic. They recall that there exists an optimal schedule for this criterion in which, on each machine, the jobs are sequenced in the order given by the rule EDD. Starting with this result they build an initial schedule by using the rule EDD-FAM, *i.e.* at each iteration the job with the smallest due date is assigned to the first available machine. This schedule is next improved by a neighbourhood procedure. Let us denote by T^1_{max} (respectively T^2_{max}) the value of the maximum tardiness restricted to the jobs scheduled on the first machine (respectively on the second machine). The improvement procedure can be broken down into two main steps. The first consists in trying to timeshift the interval $[T^1_{max}; T^2_{max}]$, *i.e.* to reduce T^1_{max} and T^2_{max} of the same quantity. If no pairwise interchange can lead to this relocation then the first step is completed. In the second step we try to decrease the size of the interval $[T^1_{max}; T^2_{max}]$ of the current solution. When no pairwise interchange can lead to this reduction then the second step is completed and we restart the first step. The heuristic stops when nothing can be done in both steps. Sarin and Hariharan provide numerous rules to do fruitful pairwise interchanges for these two steps. The outline of the heuristic is presented in figure 9.4.

```
                          ALGORITHM HSH1
Step 1:  Schedule the n jobs according to the rule EDD-FAM;
         CONTINUE=FALSE;
Step 2:  /* Timeshift step */
         While (there exists a two-job interchange leading to a timeshift) Do
             Using the theorem 2 of [Sarin and Hariharan, 2000]
             perform the two-job interchange identified;
             CONTINUE=TRUE;
         End While;
Step 3:  /* Reduction step */
         While (there exists an interchange leading to a reduction) Do
             Try to increase min(T^1_max; T^2_max) and/or to decrease
             max(T^1_max; T^2_max);
             CONTINUE=TRUE;
         End While;
Step 4:  If (CONTINUE=TRUE) Then
             CONTINUE=FALSE;
             Goto Step 2;
         End If;
         Print the current schedule and the corresponding value of T_max;
                    [Sarin and Hariharan, 2000]
```

Fig. 9.4. An heuristic algorithm for the $P2|d_i|T_{max}$ problem

For the bicriteria problem Sarin and Hariharan provide an enumeration algorithm based on a branch-and-bound scheme. Let us denote by T^H_{max} the maximum tardiness value computed by the heuristic HSH1 and by C^H_1 and C^H_2 the completion times of the last jobs on the first and second machine respectively. Without loss of generality we assume that $C^H_1 \geq C^H_2$. The heuristic works by maintaining $C^M_1 + C^M_2 = C^H_1 + C^H_2$ where C^M_1 and C^M_2 refer to the completion times of last jobs on the first and second machines for a schedule under construction. At the first attempt, the heuristic sets $C_1^M = C_1^H - 1$ and $C_2^M = C_2^H + 1$ and the problem becomes a feasability problem where for each job we introduce a deadline $\tilde{d}_i = d_i + T_{max}^H$. Next a backward branch-and-bound algorithm is applied. At the root node we branch from the set of jobs that can be scheduled either at C_1^M or C_2^M, *i.e.* such that $\tilde{d}_i \leq C_1^M$ or $\tilde{d}_i \leq C_2^M$. These jobs are the *candidate* jobs. A child node is created by scheduling a candidate job on a machine such that it does not violate its deadline. Possibly two nodes are created per job. Lower bounds and upper bounds on the criterion $\overline{U}$ are proposed by Sarin and Hariharan in order to shorten the search tree. At the end of the search the schedule with the lowest value of the criterion $\overline{U}$, if it exists, is retained and new values of C_1^M and C_2^M are tested. More accurately, we set $C_1^M = C_1^M - 1$ and $C_2^M = C_2^M + 1$. When $C_1^M - C_2^M \leq 1$ the heuristic stops and the schedule with the lowest value of the criterion $\overline{U}$ is returned.

Computational experiments on the $P2|d_i|T_{max}$ and $P2|d_i|Lex(T_{max}, \overline{U})$ problems are reported by Sarin and Hariharan. For the former, problems with up to 500 jobs are solved in a relatively short time. For the bicriteria problem, the heuristic seems quite limited in problem size since the time required to solve problems up to 100 jobs grows quickly.

9.1.4 The $P|d_i|\#(\overline{C}, \overline{U})$ problem

The minimisation of the criteria $\overline{C}$ and $\overline{U}$ on m identical machines has been tackled by [Ruiz-Torres et al., 1997] who tackle the enumeration of strict Pareto optima. As the $P|d_i|\overline{U}$ is $\mathcal{NP}$-hard the bicriteria problem is also and Ruiz-Torres, Enscore and Barton propose four heuristics to solve it.

The four heuristics proceed by iterative improvements of seed schedules. For each one of the heuristics, two searches are done starting from two different schedules. The first initial schedule is obtained by applying the rule SPT-FAM, *i.e.* at each iteration the job with the smallest processing time is assigned to the first available machine. The second initial schedule is obtained by applying the heuristics of [Ho and Chang, 1995] for the $P|d_i|\overline{U}$ problem. For each one of the four heuristics, the neighbourhood of the current solution is obtained by performing two-job permutations and single job insertions.

The two first improvement heuristics are deterministic ones and are denoted by G-NS and Q-NS.
The heuristic G-NS first performs a search starting with the first initial schedule. Among the whole neighbourhood of the current solution we consider solutions which have a lower value of the criterion $\overline{U}$ than the current solution. Among those neighbours we select the one with the lowest value of the criterion $\overline{C}$. The solution retained is put in a set of potential strict Pareto optima,

if it is not dominated by a solution of this set. If some potential strict Pareto optima are dominated by this new solution, they are deleted from this set. The heuristic stops when no neighbour improves the current solution. Next, the heuristic G-NS performs the improvement of the second initial schedule. In this case, the choice of the solution for the next iteration is done by considering in the neighbourhood of the current solution, the solutions which have a lower value of criterion $\overline{C}$. Among those solutions we select the one with the smallest value of criterion $\overline{U}$. Potential strict Pareto optima are added in the set computed at the first step. In each of the two runs, the heuristic G-NS stops when no neighbour can be selected according to the rules of choice presented above.
The heuristic Q-NS is similar to the heuristic G-NS except in the choice of the solution for the next iteration. When Q-NS starts with the first initial solution, which is optimal for the criterion $\overline{C}$, a neighbour is better than the current solution if it has a lower value of the criterion $\overline{U}$. Among those neighbours we select the one which has the lowest value of criterion $\overline{U}$. Ties are broken in favour of the schedule with the lowest value of criterion $\overline{C}$. When Q-NS starts with the second initial solution, the comparisons are done according to the $\overline{C}$ criterion.

The two last heuristics are simulated annealing heuristics and are denoted by G-SA and Q-SA. They are similar to G-NS and Q-NS respectively, except in the acceptance test of a better neighbor which is done according to the simulated annealing scheme. Computational results show that the heuristics Q-SA and G-SA slightly outperform the heuristics G-NS and Q-NS.

9.1.5 The $P|pmtn|Lex(\overline{C}, C_{max})$ problem

[Leung and Young, 1989] are interested in a bicriteria scheduling problem where the n jobs can be preempted at any (real) time. The aim is to schedule them in such a way that the makespan C_{max} and the average completion time $\overline{C}$ are minimised. More precisely, we search for a schedule S which is optimal for the lexicographical order $Lex(\overline{C}, C_{max})$. This problem is solvable in polynomial time.

The bicriteria problem without preemption is $\mathcal{NP}$-hard. We denote by S^{NP} an optimal solution to the problem without preemption and S^P an optimal solution to the problem when the preemption is allowed. We then have $\frac{C_{max}(S^{NP})}{C_{max}(S^P)} \leq \frac{2m}{m+1}$. This inequality shows that use of preemption enables us to reduce the optimal value of the criterion C_{max} for the $Lex(\overline{C}, C_{max})$ problem. The algorithm proposed by Leung and Young uses a procedure which is proposed by [Sahni, 1979] to solve the $P|pmtn, \tilde{d}_i|-$ problem. Without loss of generality we assume that $n = rm$ with $r \in \mathbb{N}$, *i.e.* the number of jobs is a multiple of the number of machines, and that $p_1 \leq p_2 \leq \ldots \leq p_n$. The proposed algorithm then schedules the $(r-1)m$ jobs $J_1, J_2, \ldots, J_{(r-1)m}$ according to the rule SPT-FAM. The value of the criterion C_{max} of an optimal schedule for the $P|pmtn|Lex(\overline{C}, C_{max})$ problem is given by:

$$C^*_{max} = \max_{k=1,\ldots,m} \left(\sum_{j=1}^{k} (C_j^M + p_{n-j+1})/k\right)$$

where C_j^M is the completion time of the last job on machine M_j when the jobs $J_1, \ldots, J_{(r-1)m}$ have been scheduled. Then, Sahni's procedure is used to solve the $P|pmtn, \tilde{d}_i = C^*_{max}|-$ problem for the m last jobs. The proposed algorithm, denoted by ELY1, is presented in figure 9.5. Its complexity is in $O(n\log(n))$ time.

Example.
We consider a problem for which $n = 6$ and $m = 2$.

i	1	2	3	4	5	6
p_i	3	5	7	9	11	13

(i) We have $r = 3$ and we schedule the jobs J_1, J_2, J_3 and J_4 according to the rule SPT-FAM and we obtain the partial schedule presented in figure 9.6.
(ii) $C_1^M = 10$, $C_2^M = 14$ and $C^*_{max} = \max((C_1^M + p_6)/1; (C_1^M + p_6 + C_2^M + p_5)/2)$ $= \max(23; 24) = 24$,
(iii) We place the remaining jobs in the order J_6 then J_5 according to the procedure for the $P|pmtn, \tilde{d}_i = 24|-$ problem. We obtain the schedule presented in figure 9.7.

To solve an ordinary problem for which $n \neq rm$, $n \in \mathbb{N}$, it is possible to reduce to the case $n = rm$ with $r \in \mathbb{N}$, by introducing dummy jobs with processing times equal to 0, and by using the algorithm ELY1.

9.2 Problems with uniform parallel machines

9.2.1 The $Q|p_i = p|\epsilon(f_{max}/g_{max})$ problem

[Tuzikov et al., 1998] study a scheduling problem where n jobs have to be scheduled on m machines M_j which have distinct processing speeds. The processing speed of machine M_j is denoted by k_j and the processing time of J_i on M_j is equal to $\frac{p_i}{k_j}$. The particularity of the problem is that all the jobs require the same processing time p. The aim is to minimise two maximum functions f_{max} and g_{max} defined by $f_{max} = \max_{i=1,\ldots,n}(\Phi_i(C_i))$ and $g_{max} = \max_{i=1,\ldots,n}(\Psi_i(C_i))$, where Φ_i and Ψ_i are increasing functions. Tuzikov,

ALGORITHM ELY1

/* We assume that $p_1 \leq \ldots \leq p_n$ */

Step 1: Schedule the jobs $J_1, \ldots, J_{(r-1)m}$ according to the rule SPT-FAM;

Step 2: /* We compute the minimal value of criterion C_{max} */

$$C_j^M = \sum_{k=1}^{r-1} p_{j+(k-1)m}, \ \forall j = 1, ..., m;$$

$$C_{max}^* = \max_{k=1,\ldots,m} \left(\sum_{\ell=1}^{k} (C_\ell^M + p_{n-\ell+1})/k\right);$$

Step 3: /* We apply the procedure of [Sahni, 1979] */

<u>For</u> $k = n$ <u>downto</u> $(n - m + 1)$ <u>Do</u>
- /* We schedule job J_k */
- $K = \{j / C_j^M < C_{max}^*\}$;
- Let $j_1 \in K$ be such that $C_{j_1}^M = \max_{j \in K}(C_j^M)$;
- <u>If</u> $(p_k \leq (C_{max}^* - C_{j_1}^M))$ <u>Then</u>
  - /* Schedule last job J_k on machine M_{j_1} */
  - $C_{j_1}^M = C_{j_1}^M + p_k$;
- <u>Else</u>
  - $L = \{\ell / C_\ell^M + p_k = C_{max}^*, \ell = 1, ..., (j_1 - 1)\}$;
  - <u>If</u> $(L \neq \emptyset)$ <u>Then</u>
    - Let $j_2 \in L$;
    - /* Schedule last job J_k on machine M_{j_2} */
    - $C_{j_2}^M = C_{j_2}^M + p_k$;
  - <u>Else</u>
    - Let j_2 and j_3 be such that $C_{max}^* - C_{j_2}^M < p_k < C_{max}^* - C_{j_3}^M$ and $\nexists j_4$ with $C_{j_4}^M \in [C_{j_2}^M; C_{j_3}^M]$;
    - /* Schedule last job J_k on machine M_{j_2} */
    - /* for $C_{max}^* - C_{j_2}^M$ time units */
    - /* Schedule last job J_k on machine M_{j_3} */
    - /* for $p_k - C_{max}^* + C_{j_2}^M$ time units */
    - $C_{j_3}^M = C_{j_3}^M + p_k - C_{max}^* + C_{j_2}^M$;
    - $C_{j_2}^M = C_{max}^*$;
  - <u>End If</u>;
- <u>End If</u>;

<u>End For</u>;

[Leung and Young, 1989]

Fig. 9.5. An optimal algorithm for the $P|pmtn|Lex(\overline{C}, C_{max})$ problem

Makhaniok and Manner propose an optimal polynomial time algorithm for the enumeration of the set of strict Pareto optima and which is based on the ϵ-constraint approach.

Firstly, they recall that the single criterion problem of minimising a maximum function, for instance f_{max}, is solvable in $O(n^2)$ time. As all jobs have the same processing time they are all equivalent except in their cost in the objective function. It is therefore possible to compute all the positional com-

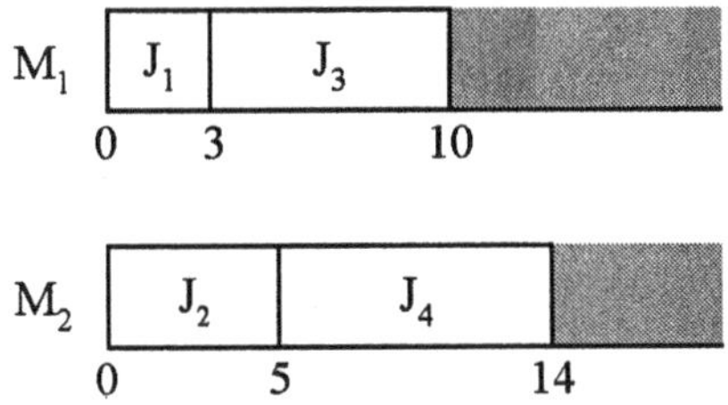

Fig. 9.6. A partial schedule

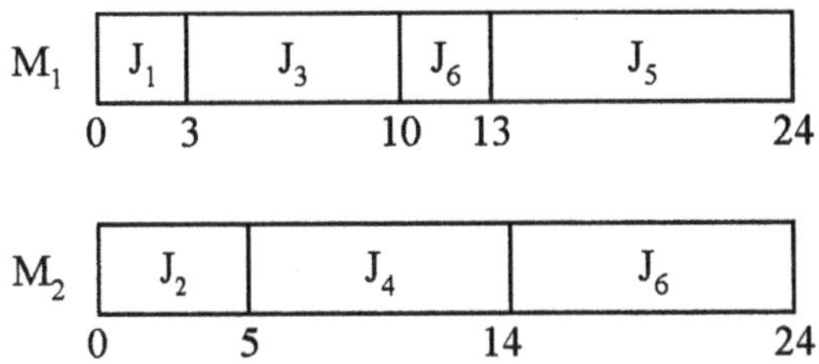

$C^*_{max} = 24$ and $\overline{C} = 80$

Fig. 9.7. The schedule calculated by the algorithm ELY1

pletion times on the machines. This can be achieved by starting with an arbitrary sequence of jobs and by applying the assignment rule ECT. This rule consists in assigning each job to the machine which completes it earlier. Thus we obtain $C_{[1]}$,...,$C_{[n]}$ where $C_{[u]}$ refers to the completion time of the job in position u. Next it remains to assign jobs to positions in order to minimise the criterion f_{max}. This can be done starting by the last position and by scheduling the job J_i such that $\Phi_i(C_{[n]}) = \min_{\ell=1,\dots,n} (\Phi_\ell(C_{[n]}))$. This process is iterated until each job has been assigned to a position.

To enumerate the set E, Tuzikov, Makhaniok and Manner solve iteratively the $Q|p_i = p|\epsilon(f_{max}/g_{max})$ and $Q|p_i = p|\epsilon(g_{max}/f_{max})$ problems in order to exclude from consideration the weak but not strict Pareto optima. The algorithm, denoted by ETMM1, is presented in figure 9.8. The resolution of a problem $Q|p_i = p, f_{max} \leq \epsilon|g_{max}$ can be done by applying an algorithm similar to the one used in the single criterion case. This algorithm, denoted by ETMM2, is presented in figure 9.9. It requires $O(n^2)$ time. Notice that the $Q|p_i = p, g_{max} < \epsilon|f_{max}$ problem can be solved by a slightly modified version of ETMM2, in which in the definition of the set $\mathcal{C}$ we consider a strict inequality and in which we swap the role of the functions Φ_i and Ψ_i.

Tuzikov, Makhaniok and Manner also show that there is at most $O(n^2)$ strict Pareto optima. This is due to the fact that there is at most n^2 different active schedules. They are all obtained by scheduling the jobs in all the possible positions. This implies that the algorithm ETMM1 requires $O(n^4)$ time.

ALGORITHM ETMM1

Step 1: Solve the $Q|p_i = p|f_{max}$ and $Q|p_i = p|g_{max}$ problems and let us denote by f^* and g^* the corresponding optimal values of the criteria; $\epsilon_1 = f^*$; $k = 1$; $E = \emptyset$;

Step 2: /* Enumeration of the set E */

Repeat

- Solve the $Q|p_i = p, f_{max} \leq \epsilon_1|g_{max}$ problem to obtain the schedule s^k;
- $E = E + \{s^k\}$;
- $\epsilon_2 = g_{max}(s^k)$;
- Solve the $Q|p_i = p, g_{max} < \epsilon_2|f_{max}$ problem to obtain the schedule s' (if it exists, otherwise set $s' = s^k$);
- $\epsilon_1 = f_{max}(s')$;
- $k = k + 1$;

Until $(\epsilon_2 = g^*)$;

Step 3: Print the set E;

[Tuzikov et al., 1998]

Fig. 9.8. An optimal algorithm for the $Q|p_i = p|\epsilon(f_{max}/g_{max})$ problem

Example.
We consider a problem for which $n = 5$, $m = 2$, $p = 6$, $k_1 = 1$, $k_2 = 3$ and the functions Ψ_i and Φ_i are defined as follows:
$\Psi_i(t) = t - d_i$ and $\Phi_i(t) = w_i t$, $\forall i = 1, ..., n$, where w_i and d_i are respectively a weight and a due date attached to job J_i. These data are detailed below.

i	1	2	3	4	5
d_i	6	8	12	13	16
w_i	1	2	3	4	5

(i) The algorithm ECT gives $C_{[i]} = [2; 4; 6; 6; 8]^T$,
We obtain $f^* = \max(8, 12, 18, 16, 10) = 18$ and,
$g^* = \max(-4, -4, -6, -7, -8) = -4$.
(ii) $\epsilon_1 = 18$, $k = 1$, $E = \emptyset$.
Resolution of the $Q|p_i = 6, f_{max} \leq 18|g_{max}$ problem by using the algorithm ETMM2:

$C_{[i]} = [2; 4; 6; 6; 8]^T$ and $\mu_{[i]} = [2; 2; 2; 1; 2]^T$,
$i = 5$, $\mathcal{C} = \{J_1, J_2\}$, $J_\ell = J_2$ is scheduled on M_2 and $C_2 = 8$,
$i = 4$, $\mathcal{C} = \{J_1, J_3\}$, $J_\ell = J_3$ is scheduled on M_1 and $C_3 = 6$,
$i = 3$, $\mathcal{C} = \{J_1\}$, $J_\ell = J_1$ is scheduled on M_2 and $C_1 = 6$,
$i = 2$, $\mathcal{C} = \{J_4\}$, $J_\ell = J_4$ is scheduled on M_2 and $C_4 = 4$,

```
ALGORITHM ETMM2
/* ε is the upper bound on the f_max criterion */
Step 1:  /* Computation of the positional completion times */
         C_j^M = 0, ∀j = 1, ..., m;
         T = {J_1, ..., J_n};
         For i = 1 to n Do
           | Let ℓ be such that (C_ℓ^M + p/k_ℓ) = max_{j=1,...,m} (C_j^M + p/k_j);
           | C_ℓ^M = C_ℓ^M + p/k_ℓ;
           | C_[i] = C_ℓ^M;
           | μ_[i] = ℓ;
         End For;
Step 2:  /* Assignment of jobs to positions */
         For i = n down to 1 Do
           | Let C = {J_u ∈ T/Φ_u(C_[i]) ≤ ε};
           | Let J_ℓ ∈ C be such that Ψ_ℓ(C_[i]) = min_{J_u∈C}(Ψ_u(C_[i]));
           | Schedule job J_ℓ on machine M_{μ_[i]} such that
           | it completes at time C_[i];
           | T = T − {J_ℓ};
         End For;
Step 3:  Print the obtained schedule;
[Tuzikov et al., 1998]
```

Fig. 9.9. An optimal algorithm for the $Q|p_i = p, f_{max} \leq \epsilon|g_{max}$ problem

$i = 1$, $\mathcal{C} = \{J_5\}$, $J_\ell = J_5$ is scheduled on M_2 and $C_5 = 2$,
$f_{max}(s^1) = 18$ and $g_{max}(s^1) = \max(0; -6; 0; -8; -14) = 0$.

$E = \{(18; 0)\}$ and $\epsilon_2 = 0$.

Resolution of the $Q|p_i = 6, g_{max} < 0|f_{max}$ problem by using a modified version of the algorithm ETMM2:

$C_{[i]} = [2; 4; 6; 6; 8]^T$ and $\mu_{[i]} = [2; 2; 2; 1; 2]^T$,
$i = 5$, $\mathcal{C} = \{J_3, J_4, J_5\}$, $J_\ell = J_3$ is scheduled on M_2 and $C_3 = 8$,
$i = 4$, $\mathcal{C} = \{J_2, J_4, J_5\}$, $J_\ell = J_2$ is scheduled on M_1 and $C_2 = 6$,
$i = 3$, $\mathcal{C} = \{J_4, J_5\}$, $J_\ell = J_4$ is scheduled on M_2 and $C_4 = 6$,
$i = 2$, $\mathcal{C} = \{J_1, J_5\}$, $J_\ell = J_1$ is scheduled on M_2 and $C_1 = 4$,
$i = 1$, $\mathcal{C} = \{J_5\}$, $J_\ell = J_5$ is scheduled on M_2 and $C_5 = 2$,
$f_{max}(s') = \max(4; 12; 24; 24; 10) = 24$ and
$g_{max}(s') = \max(-2; -2; -4; -7; -14) = -2$.

(iii) $\epsilon_1 = 24$, $k = 2$.

Resolution of the $Q|p_i = 6, f_{max} \leq 24|g_{max}$ problem by using the algorithm ETMM2:

$C_{[i]} = [2; 4; 6; 6; 8]^T$ and $\mu_{[i]} = [2; 2; 2; 1; 2]^T$,
$i = 5$, $\mathcal{C} = \{J_1, J_2, J_3\}$, $J_\ell = J_3$ is scheduled on M_2 and $C_3 = 8$,
$i = 4$, $\mathcal{C} = \{J_1, J_2, J_4\}$, $J_\ell = J_4$ is scheduled on M_1 and $C_4 = 6$,
$i = 3$, $\mathcal{C} = \{J_1, J_2\}$, $J_\ell = J_2$ is scheduled on M_2 and $C_2 = 6$,
$i = 2$, $\mathcal{C} = \{J_1, J_5\}$, $J_\ell = J_5$ is scheduled on M_2 and $C_5 = 4$,

$i = 1$, $\mathcal{C} = \{J_1\}$, $J_\ell = J_1$ is scheduled on M_2 and $C_1 = 2$,
$f_{max}(s^2) = 24$ and $g_{max}(s^2) = \max(-4; -2; -4; -7; -12) = -2$.

$E = \{(18; 0); (24; -2)\}$ and $\epsilon_2 = -2$.

Resolution of the $Q|p_i = 6, g_{max} < -2|f_{max}$ problem by using a modified version of the algorithm ETMM2:

$C_{[i]} = [2; 4; 6; 6; 8]^T$ and $\mu_{[i]} = [2; 2; 2; 1; 2]^T$,
$i = 5$, $\mathcal{C} = \{J_3, J_4, J_5\}$, $J_\ell = J_3$ is scheduled on M_2 and $C_3 = 8$,
$i = 4$, $\mathcal{C} = \{J_4, J_5\}$, $J_\ell = J_4$ is scheduled on M_1 and $C_4 = 6$,
$i = 3$, $\mathcal{C} = \{J_5\}$, $J_\ell = J_5$ is scheduled on M_2 and $C_5 = 6$,
$i = 2$, $\mathcal{C} = \{J_2\}$, $J_\ell = J_2$ is scheduled on M_2 and $C_2 = 4$,
$i = 1$, $\mathcal{C} = \{J_1\}$, $J_\ell = J_1$ is scheduled on M_2 and $C_1 = 2$,
$f_{max}(s') = \max(2; 8; 24; 24; 30) = 30$ and
$g_{max}(s') = \max(-4; -4; -4; -7; -10) = -4$.

(iv) $\epsilon_1 = 30$, $k = 3$.

Resolution of the $Q|p_i = 6, f_{max} \leq 30|g_{max}$ problem by using the algorithm ETMM2:

$C_{[i]} = [2; 4; 6; 6; 8]^T$ and $\mu_{[i]} = [2; 2; 2; 1; 2]^T$,
$i = 5$, $\mathcal{C} = \{J_1, J_2, J_3\}$, $J_\ell = J_3$ is scheduled on M_2 and $C_3 = 8$,
$i = 4$, $\mathcal{C} = \{J_1, J_2, J_4, J_5\}$, $J_\ell = J_5$ is scheduled on M_1 and $C_5 = 6$,
$i = 3$, $\mathcal{C} = \{J_1, J_2, J_4\}$, $J_\ell = J_4$ is scheduled on M_2 and $C_4 = 6$,
$i = 2$, $\mathcal{C} = \{J_1, J_2\}$, $J_\ell = J_2$ is scheduled on M_2 and $C_2 = 4$,
$i = 1$, $\mathcal{C} = \{J_1\}$, $J_\ell = J_1$ is scheduled on M_2 and $C_1 = 2$,
$f_{max}(s^3) = 30$ and $g_{max}(s^3) = -4$.

$E = \{(18; 0); (24; -2); (30; -4)\}$.

$\epsilon_2 = g^*$ and the algorithm ETMM1 stops after having found that no feasible solution to the $Q|p_i = 6, g_{max} < -4|f_{max}$ problem exists.

9.2.2 The $Q|p_i = p|\epsilon(\overline{g}/f_{max})$ problem

[Tuzikov et al., 1998] study a scheduling problem where n jobs have to be scheduled on m machines M_j which have distinct processing speeds denoted by k_j. The particularity of the problem is that all the jobs require the same processing time p. The aim is to minimise two functions f_{max} and $\overline{g}$ defined by $f_{max} = \max_{i=1,\dots,n}(\Phi_i(C_i))$ and $\overline{g} = \sum_{i=1}^{n}(\Psi_i(C_i))$, where Φ_i and Ψ_i are increasing functions. Tuzikov, Makhaniok and Manner propose an optimal polynomial time algorithm for the enumeration of the set of strict Pareto optima.

When only the criterion f_{max} is involved the problem is solvable in $O(n^2)$ time by an algorithm presented in section 9.2.1. When only the criterion $\overline{g}$ is involved the problem can be solved in $O(n^3)$ time by reduction to an assignment problem. Consider the positional completion times $C_{[i]}$ obtained using the rule ECT. The computation of a schedule can reduce to an assignment problem in which jobs are assigned to positional completion times. Thus the minimisation of the criterion $\overline{g}$ can be done in $O(n^3)$ time when the positional completion times are known. The latter can be achieved in $O(n\log(m))$ time.

The algorithm, denoted by ETMM3, which is proposed to enumerate the set of strict Pareto optima, is similar to the algorithm ETMM1. The main difference lies in that the algorithm ETMM3 does not solve the two possible ϵ-constraint problems, thus generating weak but not strict Pareto optima. These non desired solutions are deleted at the end of the enumeration. The algorithm ETMM3 is presented in figure 9.10. At each iteration, the $Q|p_i = p, f_{max} < \epsilon|\overline{g}$ problem is reduced to an assignment problem. Due to the constraint on criterion f_{max}, we set infinite costs when a job cannot occupy a position. As the maximum number of active schedules is at most n^2, the algorithm ETMM3 requires $O(n^5)$ time.

```
                         ALGORITHM ETMM3
Step 1:  Solve the Q|p_i = p|f_max and Q|p_i = p|g¯ problems and let us
         denote f* and g* the corresponding optimal values of the criteria;
         /* f+ refers to the value of the criterion f_max of the solution which
          gives g* */
         ε = f+ − 1; k = 1; E = ∅;
Step 2:  /* Enumeration of the set E */
         Repeat
           | Solve the Q|p_i = p, f_max < ε|g¯ problem to obtain the schedule s^k;
           | If (s^k exists) Then
           |    | E = E + {s^k};
           |    | ε = f_max(s^k);
           |    | k = k + 1;
           | End If;
         Until (s^k does not exist);
         Delete from the set E the solutions that are not strict Pareto optima;
Step 3:  Print the set E;
                      [Tuzikov et al., 1998]
```

Fig. 9.10. An optimal algorithm for the $Q|p_i = p|\epsilon(\overline{g}/f_{max})$ problem

9.2.3 The $Q|pmtn|\epsilon(\overline{C}/C_{max})$ problem

[Mc Cormick and Pinedo, 1995] study a scheduling problem where a processing speed k_j is associated with each machine M_j. The aim is to minimise the maximum completion time of jobs and the average completion time of jobs. Preemption of jobs is authorised at any real value t ($t \in \mathbb{R}$). We suppose that the jobs and machines are numbered such that $p_1 \leq p_2 \leq \ldots \leq p_n$ and

$k_1 \geq k_2 \geq \ldots \geq k_m$.

The $Q|pmtn|\overline{C}$ problem can be solved optimally by the rule SRPT-FM. This rule consists of scheduling the jobs with the smallest remaining processing time on the fastest machine, among those available, preempting when necessary.

The $Q|pmtn|C_{max}$ problem can be solved optimally by the rule LRPT-FM. This rule works differently to the rule SRPT-FM, since jobs having, at an instant t, the m most important processing times, are scheduled. Conversely to the previous algorithm the scheduled jobs can be preempted during a time greater than 0.

To solve the bicriteria problem, McCormick and Pinedo determine the set of strict Pareto optima. To do this they consider the ϵ-constraint approach and they solve the problem (P_ϵ) defined by:

$$\begin{aligned}&\text{Min } \overline{C}(s)\\&\text{with}\\&\qquad C_{max}(s) \leq \epsilon\\&\qquad s \in \mathcal{S}\end{aligned}$$

McCormick and Pinedo model this problem by a linear program. It shows that the set of solutions $\mathcal{S}$ is a compact polyhedron in $\mathbb{R}$. The criteria C_{max} and $\overline{C}$ being increasing convex functions on $\mathcal{S}$, they reach their respective minimum. Moreover, the set E is included in the frontier of $\mathcal{S}$, and is piecewise linear. We only have therefore to determine the set E to calculate the subset E_{ex} of the extreme strict Pareto optima. McCormick and Pinedo propose an algorithm to solve the (P_ϵ) problem. This algorithm, denoted by EMP1, looks for a schedule s^0 such that $C_{max}(s^0) = \epsilon$ and $\overline{C}(s^0)$ is the lowest possible. At a time t, the rule SRPT-FM is applied except if unscheduled jobs can only complete at the date ϵ. If this is the case the LRPT-FM rule is applied for these jobs.

We recall that jobs and machines are numbered such that $p_1 \leq p_2 \leq \ldots \leq p_n$ and $k_1 \geq k_2 \geq \ldots \geq k_m$. Let us consider figure 9.11 where the jobs J_1, J_2 and J_3 have been partially scheduled on machines M_1, M_2 and M_3. We define the processing capacities V_j, $\forall j = 1, ..., m$, for a given iteration of the algorithm by:

$$V_j = \sum_{\ell=0}^{m-j} (C_\ell^M - C_{\ell+1}^M) \times k_{j+\ell}$$

where C_j^M represents the completion time of the last job on machine M_j and $C_0^M = \epsilon$. If the rule LRPT-FM is applied at the next iteration for jobs J_n to J_{n-j+1}, these are processed in the capacities V_1 to V_j. McCormick and

Pinedo define the notion of latency, denoted by g_k, of a set of k capacities V_j by:

$$g_k = (V_1 + \ldots + V_k) - (p_n + p_{n-1} + \ldots + p_{n-k+1})$$

$\forall k = 1, ..., n$, by setting $V_j = 0$, $\forall j > m$.

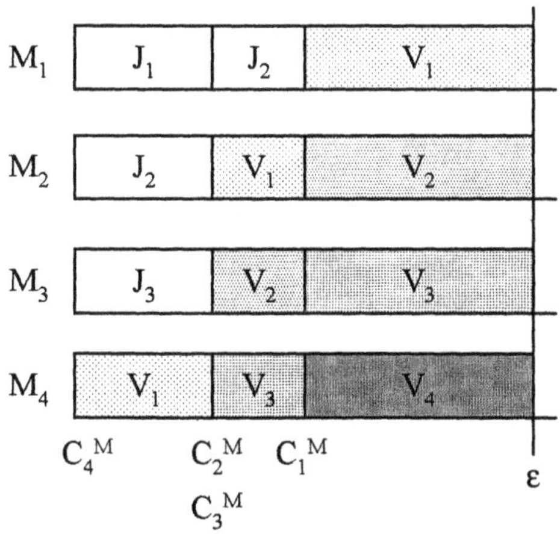

Fig. 9.11. A partial schedule and the corresponding processing capacities

A necessary and sufficient condition for the existence of a solution to the problem is that when the algorithm is initiated, we have $g_k \geq 0$, $\forall k = 1, ..., n$. The algorithm EMP1 uses the values g_k as follows: if at an iteration for a set k the value g_k equals 0, then the $n-k$ last jobs are scheduled according to the rule LRPT-FM. Otherwise, the algorithm applies the rule SRPT-FM. The job J_i with the lowest processing time p_i is then scheduled on the machine M_j such that $C_j^M = \min_{\ell=1,\ldots,m}(C_\ell^M)$. In the case where several machines satisfy this condition, we choose that having the greatest processing speed k_j. The duration x of job J_i on this machine is defined by:

$$x = \min\left(C_{j-1}^M - C_j^M, \frac{p_i}{k_j}, \frac{g_{n-i+1}}{k_j - k_m - 1}, \frac{\min_{\ell=i+1,\ldots,n}(g_\ell)}{k_j - k_m}\right)$$

In the case where $k_j = k_m$, we have $x = \min(\frac{p_i}{k_j}, C_{j-i}^M - C_j^M, g_{n-i+1})$.

Likewise, if $k_j - k_m = 1$, we have $x = \min(\frac{p_i}{k_j}, C_{j-i}^M - C_j^M, \min_{\ell=i+1,\ldots,n}(g_\ell))$.

If job J_i is not completed, we consider at the next iterations the remaining amount of job J_i.

Figure 9.14 presents a simplified version of algorithm EMP1. McCormick and

Pinedo propose an implementation in $O(mn)$ time and which assures that the maximum number of preemptions is in $O(mn)$.

Example.
We consider a problem for which $n = 10$, $m = 2$, $k_1 = 4$, $k_2 = 1$ and $\epsilon = 40$.

i	1	2	3	4	5	6	7	8	9	10
p_i	2	4	6	8	10	12	14	16	18	20

(i) $C_1^M = C_2^M = 0$, $C_0^M = 40$, $V_1 = 160$, $V_2 = 40$.
(ii) $g_1 = 160 - 20 = 140$, $g_2 = 162$, $g_3 = 146$, $g_4 = 132$, $g_5 = 120$, $g_6 = 110$, $g_7 = 102$, $g_8 = 96$, $g_9 = 92$, $g_{10} = 90$.
(iii) $g_k = 90$, $i = 1$, $M_j = M_1$, $x = \min(40; 2/4; 90/2; 92/3) = 0.5$. We obtain the partial schedule presented in figure 9.12.
(iv) By applying the next iterations, we obtain the schedule presented in figure 9.13.

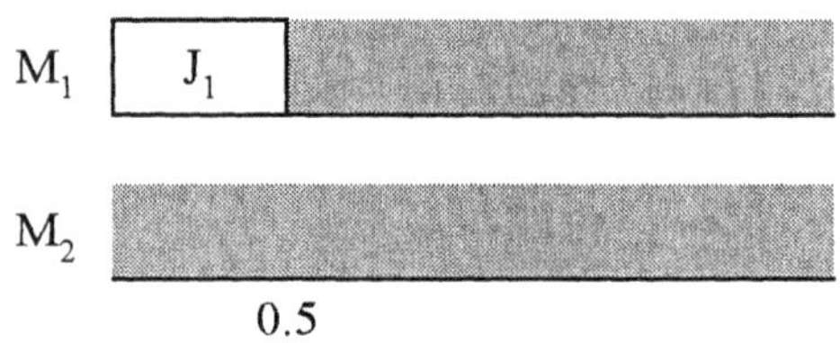

Fig. 9.12. A partial schedule

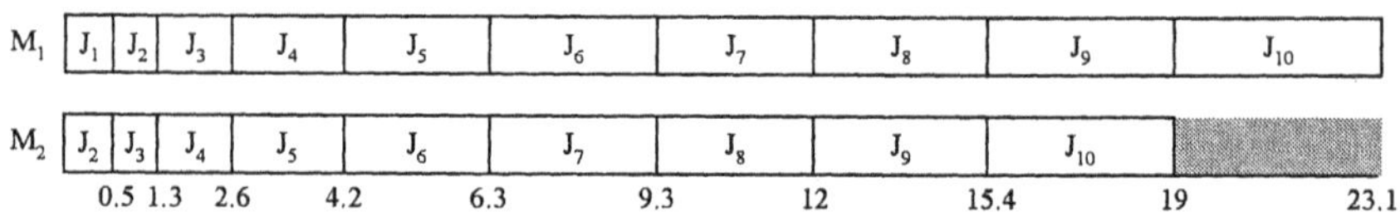

$C_{max} = 23.1$ and $\overline{C} = 93.7$

Fig. 9.13. The schedule calculated by the algorithm EMP1

McCormick and Pinedo present an algorithm, denoted by EMP2, for the enumeration of the set E, which uses the algorithm EMP1. Let s be an extreme strict Pareto optimum. Starting with this solution we can calculate $q(i)$ the number of jobs scheduled by the rule LRPT-FM before the job J_i, $\forall i = 1, ..., n$. We set $\kappa(i) = q(i+1) + 1$, the number of the machine on which the job J_i is completed and σ the number of the last job scheduled by the rule SRPT-FM, defined by $\sigma + q(\sigma + 1) = n$. $L_i = \{n - q(i), n - q(i) + 1, \ldots, n - q(i+1) - 1 = n - \kappa(i)\}$ is the list of jobs which have preempted the job J_i. These jobs have been scheduled by the rule LRPT-FM. We set $S_i = \sum_{j \in M_i^L} k_j$, $\forall i = 1, ..., \sigma$, with $M_i^L = \{M_j / \exists J_k \in L_i$ such that J_k is completed on $M_j\}$. The lists L_i depend on the values g_k of each iteration. Schedule s of value $(\epsilon, \overline{C})$ is an extreme strict Pareto optimum if and only if $\forall \epsilon > d > 0$ the running of the algorithm EMP1 for the value $\epsilon - d$ does not lead to the same lists L_i as those obtained during the construction of s. This is equivalent to considering that the weaker the value of the desired C_{max} is, the more likely the algorithm EMP1 will apply the rule LRPT-FM. Jobs that, for a more important value of C_{max}, were scheduled by SRPT-FM will preempt other jobs and be scheduled by LRPT-FM. The next value of $\epsilon' < \epsilon$ which is considered is obtained by calculation of the variations Δg_k of the latencies. This makes necessary the calculation of variations of the completion times of jobs in s scheduled by SRPT-FM. These latter variations are given by:

$$\Delta C_i = \frac{1}{k_{\kappa(i)}} \left(S_i + \sum_{e=1}^{i-1} (k_{q(i)+e} - k_{\kappa(i)+e}) \Delta C_{i-e} \right), \ \forall i = 1, ..., \sigma$$

We then obtain $\forall k = 1, ..., n - \sigma + 1$:

$$\Delta g_k = \sum_{a=\kappa(j-1)}^{k} k_a + \sum_{a=0}^{j-2} (k_{\kappa(j-1)+a} - k_{k+1+a}) \Delta C_{j-1-a}$$

with j such that $\kappa(j-1) \leq k < \kappa(j)$. Likewise we denote by $g_{k,j}$ the value of the latency when, applying the algorithm EMP1, we search to place job J_j according to the rule SRPT-FM: g_k is the value $g_{k,j}$ with j such that $\kappa(j-1) \leq k < \kappa(j)$. The value ϵ' of the criterion C_{max} of the next strict Pareto optimum to be determined is given by $\epsilon' = \epsilon - \min_{k=1,...,(n-\sigma+1)} (\frac{g_k}{\Delta g_k})$. The algorithm EMP2 is presented in figure 9.15. Its complexity is in $O(m^3 n)$ time.

We can show that the algorithm EMP2 only calculates the extreme strict Pareto optima in spite of the fact that weak, but non strict solutions can be obtained by using the ϵ-constraint approach. For a fixed value ϵ the solution determined by the algorithm EMP1 is a strict Pareto optimum because this is obtained by maximising C_{max} (under the constraint $C_{max} \leq \epsilon$) to minimise $\overline{C}$. This translates to the algorithm by alternatively applying the rules SRPT-FM and LRPT-FM. In other words, when we use the algorithm EMP1 in EMP2 we obtain an extreme strict Pareto optimum. To show that the algorithm EMP2 does not determine solutions belonging to the set $WE - E$, we just have to show that the initial solution determined by the rule SRPT-FM is a strict Pareto optimum, *i.e.* it is an optimal solution of the

```
ALGORITHM EMP1
/* We assume that p_1 <= ... <= p_n and k_1 >= ... >= k_m */
/* T is the set of remaining unscheduled jobs */
Step 1:  /*Initialisation and feasibility test */
         C_j^M = 0, ∀j = 1,...,m; C_0^M = ε;
         V_j = Σ_{ℓ=0}^{m-j} (C_ℓ^M - C_{ℓ+1}^M) × k_{j+ℓ}, ∀j = 1,...,m;
         For i=1 to n Do
         |  g_i = (V_1 + ... + V_i) - (p_n + p_{n-1} + ... + p_{n-i+1});
         |  /*V_i = 0, ∀i > m*/
         |  C_i = 0;
         |  If (g_i < 0) Then END; /* Unfeasible problem */ End If;
         End For
Step 2:  /* Main part of the algorithm */
         While (|T| ≠ 0) Do
         |  Let g_k = min_{i=1,...,|T|} (g_i);
         |  If (g_k > 0) Then
         |  |  /* We use the rule SRPT-FM */
         |  |  i = T[1];
         |  |  Let M_j be the machine such that C_j^M = min_{ℓ=1,...,m} (C_ℓ^M);
         |  |  /* Break ties by choosing the one with the greatest speed k_j */
         |  |  If (k_j = k_m) Then x = min(C_{j-1}^M - C_j^M, p_i/k_j, g_{|J|}); End If
         |  |  If (k_j - k_m = 1) Then
         |  |  |  x = min(C_{j-1}^M - C_j^M, p_i/k_j, min_{ℓ=1,...,|T|-1} (g_ℓ));
         |  |  End If
         |  |  If ((k_j - k_m ≠ 1) and (k_j ≠ k_m)) Then
         |  |  |  x = min(C_{j-1}^M - C_j^M, p_i/k_j, g_{|T|}/(k_j - k_m - 1),
         |  |  |          min_{ℓ=1,...,|T|-1} (g_ℓ)/(k_j - k_m));
         |  |  End If
         |  |  Schedule the job J_i in the time interval [C_j^M; C_j^M + x];
         |  |  If (x = k_j p_i) Then T = T - {J_i}; Else p_i = p_i - x/k_j; End If;
         |  |  Recompute V_j and g_k, ∀j = 1,...,m, ∀k = 1,...,n;
         |  Else
         |  |  Use the rule LRPT-FM on the jobs J_{|T|-k+1}, ..., J_{|T|};
         |  |  T = T - {J_{|T|-k+1}, ..., J_{|T|}};
         |  |  Recompute V_j and g_k, ∀j = 1,...,m, ∀k = 1,...,n;
         |  End If
         End While;
Step 3:  Print the resulting schedule;
[Mc Cormick and Pinedo, 1995]
```

Fig. 9.14. An optimal algorithm for the $Q|pmtn|\epsilon(\overline{C}/C_{max})$ problem

ALGORITHM EMP2

/* We assume that $p_1 \leq \ldots \leq p_n$ and $k_1 \geq \ldots \geq k_m$ */
/* ZE: the list of extreme strict Pareto optima in the criteria space */
/* w: the slope of the facet of the trade-off curve explored at a given iteration */
/* L_i: list of jobs which have preempted job J_i */

Step 1: /* Initialisation of the algorithm */
Compute a solution s^0 using the rule SRPT-FM;
$\epsilon = C_{max}(s^0)$; $g_1 = 0$; $Sj_1 = n$;
$ZE = \{(C_{max}(s^0), \overline{C}(s^0))\}$;
$w = 0$; $\sigma = n$; $L_j = \emptyset, q(j) = 0, \kappa(j) = 1, \forall j = 1, ..., n$;

Step 2: While ($w < \infty$) Do

$$\Delta C_i = \frac{1}{k_{\kappa(i)}}\left(S_i + \sum_{e=1}^{i-1}(k_{q(i)+e} - k_{\kappa(i)+e})\Delta C_{i-e}\right), \ \forall i = 1, ..., \sigma;$$

$$\Delta g_k = \sum_{a \in \kappa(j-1)}^{k} k_a + \sum_{a=0}^{j-2}(k_{\kappa(j-1)+a} - k_{k+1+a})\Delta C_{j-1-a}$$

with j such that $\kappa(j-1) \leq k < \kappa(j)$, $\forall k = 1, ..., n - \sigma + 1$;

$$\alpha^* = \min_{k=1,\ldots,(n-\sigma+1)}\left(\frac{g_k}{\Delta g_k}\right);$$

Let k^* be such that $\alpha^* = \frac{g_{k^*}}{\Delta g_{k^*}}$;
Let j^* be such that $\kappa(j^* - 1) \leq k^* < \kappa(j^*)$;
If ($j^* > 1$) Then
  $L_{j^*-1} = L_{j^*-1} + \{n - k^* + 1, n - k^* + 2, \ldots, n - q(j^*)\}$;
  $L_{j^*} = L_{j^*} - \{n - k^* + 1, n - k^* + 2, \ldots, n - q(j^*)\}$;
  If ($k^* = n - \sigma + 1$) Then
    $\sigma = \sigma - 1$; Compute $g_{n-\sigma+1}$; $Sj_{n-\sigma+1} = \sigma$;
  End If
  $\epsilon = \epsilon - \alpha^*$; $C_i = C_i + \Delta C_i$, $\forall i = 1, ..., n$;
  $g_e = g_e + \Delta g_e$, $\forall e = 1, ..., \kappa(j^* - 1) - 1$;
  Compute g_e, $\forall e = \kappa(j^* - 1), ..., k^*$;
  $Sj_e = j^* - 1$, $\forall e = \kappa(j^* - 1), ..., k^*$;
  Compute a solution s^0 using the algorithm EMP1 with the value ϵ;
  $ZE = ZE + \{s^0\}$;
Else
  $w = \infty$;
End If
End While

Step 3: Print the list ZE;

[Mc Cormick and Pinedo, 1995]

Fig. 9.15. An optimal algorithm for the $Q|pmtn|C_{max}, \overline{C}$ problem

$Q|pmtn|Lex(\overline{C}, C_{max})$ problem. The rule SRPT-FM is a necessary and sufficient condition for all optimal schedules for the criterion $\overline{C}$. Let two schedules s^1 and s^2 be optimal for the criterion $\overline{C}$. s^1 and s^2 verify the rule SRPT-FM and as $s^1 \neq s^2$ we deduce from this that at least two jobs J_i and J_k exist such that $p_i = p_k$. This implies that $C_{max}(s^1) = C_{max}(s^2)$. We conclude therefore from this that in criteria space there is only one point $(C_{max}(s); \overline{C}(s))$ such that $\overline{C}(s) = \min_{s' \in \mathcal{S}}(\overline{C}(s'))$. The rule SRPT-FM determines a schedule corresponding to this point and the solution which is found initially by the algorithm EMP2 is an extreme strict Pareto optimum.

9.3 Problems with unrelated parallel machines

9.3.1 The $R|p_{i,j} \in [\underline{p}_{i,j}, \overline{p}_{i,j}]|F_\ell(\overline{C}, \overline{CC}^w)$ problem

[Alidaee and Ahmadian, 1993] are interested in a scheduling problem where the processing times depend on the machine on which jobs are processed. Besides, these processing times are not data of the problem and we only have $p_{i,j} \in [\underline{p}_{i,j}, \overline{p}_{i,j}]$, $\forall i = 1, ..., n, \forall j = 1, ..., m$. The exact values $p_{i,j}$ have to be determined and we minimise a linear combination of the criteria $\overline{C}$ and $\overline{CC}^w$. The criterion $\overline{CC}^w$ is the total crashing time cost, defined by:

$$\overline{CC}^w = \sum_{i=1}^{n} \sum_{j=1}^{m} w_{i,j} x_{i,j}$$

with $w_{i,j}$ the cost of a unit of compression time of job J_i on machine M_j. $x_{i,j}$ is the number of compression time units of job J_i on M_j, which leads to $p_{i,j} = \overline{p}_{i,j} - x_{i,j}$. The complexity of this problem is open.

When $m = 1$ and the criterion $\overline{C}$ is replaced by the criterion $\overline{C}^w$, the problem is solvable in polynomial time ([Vickson, 1980b]). As for the $1|p_i \in [\underline{p}_i, \overline{p}_i]|F_\ell(\overline{C}, \overline{CC}^w)$ problem, an optimal schedule exists for the problem on unrelated machines in which all the jobs J_i are such that $p_{i,j} = \underline{p}_{i,j}$ or $\overline{p}_{i,j}$ if J_i is processed on M_j. Determination of the exact processing times when the schedule is known on each machine, can be reduced to an assignment problem. Let Q be the matrix $(mn \times n)$ composed of n successive matrices ρ_ℓ of dimension $(m \times n)$, where $\rho_\ell[i, j]$ is the maximum contribution to the objective function of job J_i if $(\ell - 1)$ jobs are scheduled on M_j after J_i. If we consider the matrix Q as the cost matrix of an assignment problem, then the optimal solution of this problem gives an optimal assignment and sequencing of jobs on machines. Next, determination of the optimal processing times can be achieved according to the following rule:

$$x_{i,j} = \begin{cases} \overline{p}_{i,j} - \underline{p}_{i,j} & \text{if } w_{i,j} < k \text{ and } J_i \text{ is processed on } M_j, \\ 0 & \text{if } w_{i,j} \geq k \text{ and } J_i \text{ is processed on } M_j, \\ \overline{p}_{i,j} & \text{otherwise.} \end{cases}$$

If M_j is the machine on which J_i is processed then k is the number of jobs processed after J_i.

9.3.2 The $R|pmtn|\epsilon(F_\ell(I_{max}, \overline{M})/C_{max})$ problem

[T'kindt et al., 2001] are interested in a scheduling problem connected with the production of glass bottles. The raw material is fused in several ovens and the molten glass produced is distributed to several moulding machines which process jobs simultaneously. The constraints associated with changing colour during production impose that the makespan is bounded by a date ϵ. We denote by b_i the quantity of glass associated with job J_i and $k_{i,j}$ the production rate when job J_i is processed on machine M_j. Preemption of jobs is authorised at any real time. We denote by C_{min} the minimal completion time of the last jobs on the machines and we seek to minimise the maximal loading difference, *i.e.* the criterion $I_{max} = C_{max} - C_{min}$. Each glass unit of job J_i has a fixed price, denoted by pr_i, which is independent from the production machines. The processing of job J_i on a machine M_j during one time unit, induces a production cost equal to $c_{i,j}$. Therefore, the production margin, denoted by $m_{i,j}$, saved for one time unit of processing of job J_i on machine M_j is equal to $m_{i,j} = k_{i,j}pr_i - c_{i,j}$. We want to maximise the actual profit, *i.e.* the criterion:

$$\overline{M} = \sum_{i=1}^{n}\sum_{j=1}^{m} p_{i,j} \times m_{i,j}$$

where $p_{i,j} = \frac{x_{i,j}}{k_{i,j}}$ is the processing time of job J_i on M_j and $x_{i,j}$ the associated quantity of glass. Calculation of a strict Pareto optimum for this problem can be achieved in polynomial time.

When the value ϵ of the period is fixed and when the weights of the criteria I_{max} and $\overline{M}$ are known, the algorithm proposed is similar to that presented by [Lawler and Labetoulle, 1978] and [Cochand et al., 1989] for the $R|pmtn|L_{max}$ problem. Firstly, the assignment of jobs on machines is determined by a linear program, denoted by ETBP1 (figure 9.16). In the obtained solution splitting of jobs can occur, but it is possible to deduce a solution where only the preemption is authorised. This calculation can be done by solving a colouring problem in a bipartite graph.

Characterisation of the set of strict Pareto optima is derived by calculating the set of strict Pareto optima which are extreme points in criteria space.

Mathematical formulation ETBP1	
Data:	n, number of jobs, m, number of machines, T, length of the scheduling period, b_i, $i = 1, ..., n$, quantity of glass associated to job J_i, α_1, α_2, parameters of the criteria, with $\alpha_1 + \alpha_2 = 1$, α_1 and $\alpha_2 \geq 0$, $k_{i,j}$, $i = 1, ..., n$, $j = 1, ..., m$, quantity of job J_i processed by machine M_j per time unit, $m_{i,j}$, $i = 1, ..., n$, $j = 1, ..., m$, production margin saved while processing one glass unit of job J_i on machine M_j.
Variables:	$x_{i,j}$, $i = 1, ..., n, j = 1, ..., m$, quantity of job J_i assigned on machine M_j, C_j, $j = 1, ..., m$, completion time of the last job on machine M_j, I_j, $j = 1, ..., m$, total idle time of machine M_j, C_{max}, makespan of the schedule, I_{max}, maximum idle time.
Objective:	Minimise $-\alpha_1 \sum_{i=1}^{n} \sum_{j=1}^{m} x_{i,j} \frac{m_{i,j}}{k_{i,j}} + \alpha_2 I_{max}$
Constraints:	$\sum_{j=1}^{m} x_{i,j} = b_i, \forall i = 1, ..., n$ $\sum_{j=1}^{m} \frac{x_{i,j}}{k_{i,j}} \leq C_{max}, \forall i = 1, ..., n$ $C_j = \sum_{i=1}^{n} \frac{x_{i,j}}{k_{i,j}}, \forall j = 1, ..., m$ $C_{max} = I_j + C_j, \forall j = 1, ..., m$ $I_{max} \geq I_j, \forall j = 1, ..., m$ $C_{max} \leq T$ $x_{i,j} \in \mathbb{R}^+, \forall i = 1, ..., n, \forall j = 1, ..., m$
[T'kindt et al., 2001]	

Fig. 9.16. A linear program for the $R|split|\epsilon(F_\ell(I_{max}, \overline{M})/C_{max})$ problem

Knowing these extreme points we can deduce the analytical expressions of the facets of the trade-off curve and therefore characterise the set of strict Pareto optima. The algorithm, denoted by ETBP2, which enumerates the extreme strict Pareto optima is presented in figure 9.17. It proceeds in two phases:

1. In the first phase we calculate the optimal solutions of the two lexicographical problems involving criteria I_{max} and $-\overline{M}$ minimisation problems.
2. In the second phase a new weights vector α for the criteria is calculated using the first two optima obtained. We determine the equation of the line

containing these two points to deduce the vector α. The new optimum calculated is added to the list of optima already obtained and the second phase is iterated with two new optima.

```
                         ALGORITHM ETBP2
/* T: list of current non dominated criteria vectors (criteria space) */
/* ZE: final set of non dominated criteria vectors (criteria space) */
/* E: final set of extreme strict Pareto optima (decision space) */
/* z^i = [-M̄(s^i); I_max(s^i)]; */;
Etape 1 : Solve (P_α) to obtain the assignment s^1 with criteria vector z^1
          which has an optimal value of I_max and a minimal value of -M̄;
          Solve (P_α) to obtain the assignment s^2 with criteria vector z^2
          which has an optimal value of -M̄ and a minimal value of I_max;
          If (z^1 = z^2) Then
          |  ZE = {z^1};
          |  Goto Step 3;
          End If;
Step 2:   T = (z^1; z^2);
          ZE = ∅;
          While (|T| ≠ 1) Do
          |  z^1 = T[1]; z^2 = T[2];
          |  δ_0 = (z_2^2 - z_2^1) / (z_1^1 - z_1^2);
          |  α = (δ_0/(δ_0 + 1); 1/(δ_0 + 1));
          |  Solve (P_α) to obtain the assignment s^0 with criteria vector
          |  z^0;
          |  If ((z^0 ≠ z^2) and (z^0 ≠ z^1)) Then
          |  |  T = T + {z^0};
          |  |  Sort vectors of T by increasing order of criterion I_max;
          |  Else
          |  |  ZE = ZE + {z^1};
          |  |  T = T - {z^1};
          |  End If;
          End While;
          ZE = ZE + T[1];
          Delete from ZE all non extreme points in criteria space;
Step 3:   For all vectors in ZE compute the corresponding schedules
          and put them in E;
                         [T'kindt et al., 2001]
```

Fig. 9.17. An optimal algorithm for the $R|pmtn|\epsilon(F_\ell(I_{max}, \overline{M})/C_{max})$ problem

Experimental results show that the number of extreme strict Pareto optima increases in proportion to the number of machines and jobs. Besides, problems containing the largest number of these solutions are the squared problems, *i.e.* those for which $n = m$. In conclusion, T'kindt, Billaut and Proust extend the algorithm ETBP2 to obtain an interactive algorithm which is more applicable in an industrial context.

10. Shop problems with assignment

10.1 A hybrid flowshop problem with three stages

[Fortemps et al., 1996] are interested in a scheduling problem which occurs in the chemical industry, denoted by $HF3,(P6,P3,1)|constr|\ F_\ell(C_{max},\gamma(T_i),\delta(VPI))$, where *constr* translates a set of constraints described hereafter. The shop comprises three stages. Each job J_i is defined by a release date, and a due date. Each machine M_j also has an availability date, denoted by R_j.

At the first stage, six identical machines process the jobs which require setup times which are independent of the sequence on each machine (constraint $S_{nsd}^{(1)}$). Besides, the setup times require the intervention of a unique resource (a team of men), making it impossible to perform several preparations at the same time. This additional resource leads to the consideration that certain operations require several resources for their processing (constraint $fix_j^{(1)}$). When an operation is completed, the resource is freed up when the operation is ready to be processed at the second stage, that is to say once the transportation is finished. This constraint is denoted by $block^{(1,2)}$. Finally, each machine M_j has an unavailability time period, denoted by $unavail_j - resumable^{(1)}$, corresponding for example to a period for maintenance.
At the second stage, three identical machines can process the jobs after leaving the first stage. At this stage, splitting of jobs is authorised (constraint $split^{(2)}$). The first two stages are connected by a network of pipes. Several pipes are connected by valves. Use of a valve at a time t for the transportation of a job J_i makes useless every pathway via this valve for transportation of a job J_j, until transportation of J_i is finished. This constraint is denoted by $pipe^{(2)}$.
At the third stage, a single machine distributes the materials flow corresponding to each job to different receptacles.

The field of constraints in the notation of the problem can take the expression: $constr = r_i^{(1)}, d_i^{(3)}, R_j, S_{nsd}^{(1)}, fix_j^{(1)}, block^{(1,2)}, pipe^{(2)}, unavail_j{-}resumable^{(1)}, split^{(2)}$

The aim is to compute a schedule that minimises a convex combination of three criteria. The criteria which are taken into account are:

1. the makespan, denoted by $C_{\max}$,
2. a penalty function $\gamma(T_1, \dots, T_n)$ of job tardiness,
3. a penalty function $\delta(VPI)$ which reflects violation of periods of machines unavailability at the first stage. The presence of this criterion is due to the complexity of the problem which led the authors to relax the unavailability constraints.

Since the problem is $\mathcal{NP}$-hard, the algorithm proposed to solve it is an heuristic which proceeds in two phases. The first calculates a sequence L of jobs, which reflects the order in which the latter are introduced into the shop. The second phase does the calculation of the final schedule and the assignment of jobs on the resources at each stage.
Two heuristics are proposed to determine the sequence L. The first is a simulated annealing algorithm and the second is a tabu search. The determination of this list is made by looking for a solution which minimises the convex combination of the criteria. The general idea of the assignment heuristic is to schedule the jobs as soon as possible on the machines at each stage, according to the rule FAM. These assignments are made whilst respecting the constraints at each stage.

10.2 Hybrid flowshop problems with k stages

10.2.1 The $HFk, (PM^{(\ell)})_{\ell=1}^{k}||F_\ell(C_{max}, \overline{C})$ problem

[Riane et al., 1997] are interested in a scheduling problem where the shop has k stages and each stage ℓ contains $M^{(\ell)}$ identical machines. The aim is to minimise the makespan and the sum of completion times. For this, Riane, Meskens and Artiba minimise a convex combination of the criteria. This problem is $\mathcal{NP}$-hard.

Figure 10.1 presents a mixed linear integer program, denoted by ERMA1. Constraints (A) express the fact that the jobs must be processed at every stage. Constraints (B) imply that there is at most one job in position ℓ on each machine. Constraints (C) and (D) enable us to calculate the completion times at each stage (both routing and disjunctive constraints on the machines). Finally, constraints (E) and (F) define the criteria $C_{\max}$ and $\overline{C}$ to be minimised.

Two tabu search heuristics are also proposed. The first randomly generates a sequence of jobs. Assignment at the first stage is made according to the rule FAM and the jobs are scheduled as soon as possible. We suppose that the assignments are made at the following stages using the same rule and by

Mathematical formulation ERMA1	
Data:	n, the number of jobs, k, the number of stages, $M^{(\ell)}$, $\ell = 1, ..., k$, the number of machines at stage ℓ, $p_i^{(\ell)}$, $i = 1, ..., n, \ell = 1, ..., k$, the processing time of job J_i at stage ℓ, α, $\alpha = 0, ..., 1$, a weight.
Variables:	$X_{i,j,u,v}$, $i, j = 1, ..., n$, $u = 1, ..., M^{(v)}$, $v = 1, ..., k$, boolean variable, equal to 1 if job J_i is processed in position j on machine M_u at stage v, 0 otherwise, $C_i^{(\ell)}$, $i = 1, ..., n, \ell = 1, ..., k$, the completion time of job J_i at stage ℓ, C_{max}, the makespan. $\overline{C}$, the sum of completion times.
Objective:	Minimise $\alpha\overline{C} + (1-\alpha)C_{max}$
Constraints:	$\sum_{m=1}^{M^{(v)}} \sum_{\ell=1}^{n} X_{i,\ell,m,v} = 1, \forall i = 1, ..., n, \forall v = 1, ..., k$ (A) $\sum_{i=1}^{n} X_{i,\ell,m,v} \leq 1, \forall m = 1, ..., M^{(v)}, \forall v = 1, ..., k, \forall \ell = 1, ..., n$ (B) $C_i^{(v)} \geq \sum_{\ell=1}^{u} \sum_{j=1}^{n} (X_{j,\ell,m,v} \times p_j^{(v)} + (X_{i,u,m,v} - 1) \times HV)$, $\forall m = 1, ..., M^{(v)}, \forall v = 1, ..., k, \forall i = 1, ..., n, \forall u = 1, ..., n$ (C) $C_i^{(v)} \geq C_i^{(v-1)} + p_i^{(v)}, \forall i = 1, ..., n, \forall v = 1, ..., k$ (D) $C_{max} \geq C_i^{(k)}, \forall i = 1, ..., n$ (E) $\overline{C} = \sum_{i=1}^{n} C_i^{(k)}$ (F)
[Riane et al., 1997]	

Fig. 10.1. An MIP model for the HFk, $(PM^{(\ell)})_{\ell=1}^{k}||F_\ell(C_{\max}, \overline{C})$ problem

considering the sequence of jobs sorted in non decreasing order of completion times at the previous stage. We apply a tabu search on the sequence of jobs of the first stage. The neighbourhood considered is obtained by permutations of any pair of jobs. For the second heuristic, the schedule is calculated according to the same scheme. The only difference lies in the fact that the initial sequence used at the first stage is generated by the heuristic of [Campbell et al., 1970].

10.2.2 The $HFk, (PM^{(\ell)})_{\ell=1}^{k}||\epsilon(\overline{C}/C_{max})$ problem

[Riane et al., 1997] are interested in a scheduling problem where the shop is made up of k stages, each stage ℓ comprising $M^{(\ell)}$ identical machines. The aim is to minimise the makespan and the sum of the completion time.
We consider minimisation of the criterion $\overline{C}$ under the constraint $C_{max} \leq \epsilon$. Figure 10.2 presents a mixed linear integer program, denoted by ERMA2, which solves this problem. Constraints (A) express the fact that the jobs must be processed at every stage. Constraints (B) imply that there is at most one job in position ℓ on each machine. Constraints (C) and (D) enable us to calculate the completion time at each stage (both routing and disjunctive constraints on the machines). Constraints (E) and (F) define the criteria $C_{\max}$ and $\overline{C}$ which are to be minimised. Finally, constraint (G) expresses the bound on the criterion $C_{\max}$ for the solution sought.

Three tabu search heuristics are presented for this problem. The principle of the first two is identical to that of the heuristic for the $HFk, (PM^{(\ell)})_{\ell=1}^{k}|| F_\ell(C_{\max}, \overline{C})$ problem. The third tabu algorithm improves an initial solution which is calculated by solving the $Lex(C_{max}, \overline{C})$ problem.

10.2.3 The $HFk, (PM^{(\ell)}(t))_{\ell=1}^{k}|r_i^{(1)}, d_i^{(k)}|\epsilon(C_{max}/T_{max})$ problem

[Vignier et al., 1996] are interested in a problem where unavailability constraints are imposed on the resources. The shop is made up of k stages, each stage ℓ containing $M^{(\ell)}$ identical machines. Each machine has its own periods during which it is not available to process. The number of machines available at an instant t at stage ℓ is denoted by $M^{(\ell)}(t)$ and we suppose that the machines have a "zig-zag" profile, *i.e.* $M^{(\ell)}(t) \in [M^{(\ell)} - 1; M^{(\ell)}]$, $\forall t$ (see [Sanlaville, 1992]). Each job J_i is defined by a release date at the first stage and a due date at the last stage. Preemption of jobs is forbidden except when a job cannot be completed before the start of the next unavailability period on the machine on which it is scheduled. We then speak of "resumable" machines (see [Lee et al., 1997]). The aim is to minimise the makespan knowing that the maximum lateness is bounded by a value ϵ (constraint $T_{max} \leq \epsilon$). This problem is equivalent to the problem $HFk, (PM^{(\ell)}(t))_{\ell=1}^{k}| r_i^{(1)}, \tilde{d}_i^{(k)}|C_{max}$, where $\tilde{d}_i^{(k)} = d_i^{(k)} + \epsilon, \forall i = 1, ..., n$.

To solve this problem a branch-and-bound procedure, inspired by the one proposed by [Brah and Hunsucker, 1991], is presented. At each node of the search tree we have to take two decisions: the next job to be scheduled and the machine to process it. Thus, at a given node, if the job J_i is scheduled on the same machine M_j as the job which was scheduled at the father node, then this node is a *circular node*. Otherwise, job J_i is scheduled on machine M_{j+1}, and the node is a *squared node*. This procedure assumes that all the

Mathematical formulation ERMA2	
Data:	n, the number of jobs, k, the number of stages, $M^{(\ell)}$, $\ell = 1, ..., k$, the number of machines at stage ℓ, $p_i^{(\ell)}$, $i = 1, ..., n, \ell = 1, ..., k$, the processing time of job J_i at stage ℓ, ϵ, an upper bound to criterion C_{max}.
Variables:	$X_{i,j,u,v}$, $i, j = 1, ..., n$, $u = 1, ..., M^{(v)}$, $v = 1, ..., k$, boolean variable, equal to 1 if job J_i is processed in position j on machine M_u of stage v, 0 otherwise, $C_i^{(\ell)}$, $i = 1, ..., n, \ell = 1, ..., k$, the completion time of job J_i at stage ℓ, C_{max}, the makespan. $\overline{C}$, the sum of completion times.
Objective:	Minimise $\overline{C}$
Constraints:	

$$\sum_{m=1}^{M^{(v)}} \sum_{\ell=1}^{n} X_{i,\ell,m,v} = 1, \ \forall i = 1, ..., n, \ \forall v = 1, ..., k \quad \text{(A)}$$

$$\sum_{i=1}^{n} X_{i,\ell,m,v} \leq 1, \ \forall m = 1, ..., M^{(v)}, \ \forall v = 1, ..., k, \ \forall \ell = 1, ..., n \quad \text{(B)}$$

$$C_i^{(v)} \geq \sum_{\ell=1}^{u} \sum_{j=1}^{n} (X_{j,\ell,m,v} \times p_j^{(v)} + (X_{i,u,m,v} - 1) \times HV), \ \forall m = 1, ..., M^{(v)}, \forall v = 1, ..., k, \forall i = 1, ..., n, \forall u = 1, ..., n \quad \text{(C)}$$

$$C_i^{(v)} \geq C_i^{(v-1)} + p_i^{(v)}, \ \forall i = 1, ..., n, \ \forall v = 1, ..., k \quad \text{(D)}$$

$$C_{max} \geq C_i^{(k)}, \ \forall i = 1, ..., n \quad \text{(E)}$$

$$\overline{C} = \sum_{i=1}^{n} C_i^{(k)} \quad \text{(F)}$$

$$C_{max} \leq \epsilon \quad \text{(G)}$$

[Riane et al., 1997]

Fig. 10.2. An MIP model for the $HFk, (PM^{(\ell)})_{\ell=1}^{k} || \epsilon(\overline{C}/C_{\max})$ problem

machines are numbered from 1 to $\sum_{\ell=1}^{k} M^{(\ell)}$, by considering firstly machines of stage 1, then those of stage 2, *etc.*
To be more precise, a certain number of rules must be respected when constructing nodes (see [Vignier, 1997] for a detailed description of these rules) to generate feasible solutions and to avoid redundant nodes in the search tree. At a node s_v, we can associate a stage ℓ and a set, denoted by Ω_v^ℓ, of unscheduled jobs at this stage. We therefore know a schedule of all the jobs at stages u, $\forall u = 1, ..., (\ell - 1)$. To verify at node s_v, the constraint $T_{\max} \leq \epsilon$, we

use a test of feasibility based on a result given by [Horn, 1974]. This test can be achieved by solving the $P|r_i, pmtn, \widetilde{d_i}|-$ problem. For stage ℓ, $\ell = 1, ..., k$, we set:

$$r_i = C_i^{(\ell-1)},\ \forall i \in \Omega_v^{(\ell)}, \text{ with } C_i^{(0)} = r_i^{(1)},$$
$$\text{and } d_i = d_i^{(k)} - \sum_{u=\ell+1}^{k} p_i^{(u)},\ \forall i \in \Omega_v^{(\ell)}.$$

Existence of a solution to the feasibility problem can be determined by constructing a bipartite graph G and by verifying that a flow of value $\sum_{i \in \Omega_v^{(\ell)}} p_i^{(\ell)}$ exists in this graph (see [Horn, 1974]). In order to take into account all the assignments already done at stage ℓ for node s_v, and the unavailability periods of the machines at stage ℓ, we only have to take into account the release dates of machines as well as the start times and the end times of unavailabilty periods on the machines when constructing the graph ([Drozdowski et al., 2000]). If a flow of value $\sum_{i \in \Omega_v^{(\ell)}} p_i^{(\ell)}$ does not exist in this graph, then node s_v is pruned. On the other hand, existence of such a flow does not guarantee that node s_v leads to a feasible solution. [Vignier et al., 1996] do not take account of jobs already scheduled at stage $S^{(\ell)}$ as mentionned above. They indicate that it is sufficient to impose on each vertex of the graph minimum capacities which are functions of jobs already assigned in time periods. The two approaches are equivalent from a theoretical point of view.
If node s_v is not pruned, then a lower bound on the criterion $C_{\max}$ is calculated. This bound is based on bounds LBJ and LBM, initially proposed by [Brah and Hunsucker, 1991], and improved by [Portmann et al., 1996] and [Portmann et al., 1998]. If the lower bound at node s_v is greater than the global upper bound then node s_v is pruned. The search strategy used to shorten the search space is the *depth* first strategy: let s_v be the node under consideration at an instant t, the next node to be processed is the child node of s_v with the lowest value of the lower bound (if there is one). The detailed algorithm, denoted by EVBP1, is presented in figure 10.3.

ALGORITHM EVBP1

```
/* ε is an upper bound to the maximum tardiness */
/* T is the set of n jobs to schedule */
Step 1:  /* Initialisation of the algorithm */
         Using an ordinary heuristic, compute an upper bound S_ref of value
         Cmax_ref;
         d̃_i^(ℓ) = (d_i^(k) + ε) − Σ_{u=ℓ+1}^{k} p_i^(u), ∀i = 1,...,n, ∀ℓ = 1,...,k;
         Create the root node s0: σ0 = ∅ ; Q = {s0};
Step 2:  /* Main part of the branch-and-bound */
         While (Q ≠ ∅) Do
           Choose a node s_v in Q by using the depth first search strategy;
           Q = Q − {s_i}; Ω = Ω_i;
           For v = 1 to |Ω_i| Do
             Choose a job J_j in Ω and create a child node s_{i+1}^(v) taking
             account of the generation rules of the tree;
             Search a maximal flot Φ in the bipartite graph associated
             with s_{i+1}^(v);
             If (Φ = Σ_{u∈Ω_k^(1)} p_u^(1)) Then
               Compute LB_Cmax(s_{i+1}^(v));
               If (LB_Cmax(s_{i+1}^(v)) < Cmax_ref) Then
                 If (Ω_{i+1} ≠ ∅) Then Q = Q + s_{i+1}^(v);
                 Else
                   S_ref = σ_{i+1}; Cmax_ref = LB_Cmax(s_{i+1}^(v));
                 End If;
               End If;
             End If;
           End For;
         End While;
Step 3:  Print S_ref and Cmax_ref;
```

[Vignier et al., 1996]

Fig. 10.3. An optimal algorithm for the $HFk, (PM^{(\ell)}(t))_{\ell=1}^{k}|r_i^{(1)}, d_i^{(k)}||\epsilon(C_{\max}/T_{\max})$ problem

A. Notations

A.1 Notation of data and variables

The notation of data and variables is now quite well normalised. We present in tables A.1 and A.2 the set of notations used throughout the book for the data and the variables respectively.

A.2 Usual notation of single criterion scheduling problems

Two notations exist to refer to scheduling problems. The older has been proposed by [Conway et al., 1967]. But as it is not the more used in the literature we present the one introduced by [Graham et al., 1979] and later detailled by [Blazewicz et al., 1996]. The notation is decomposed into three fields: $\alpha|\beta|\gamma$.
The field α directly refers to the typology presented in figure 1.1 and presents the structure of the scheduling problem (table A.3).
The field β contains the set of constraints of the problem (table A.4).
At last, in the field γ we put the criteria to optimise (table A.5). Concerning a more detailled presentation of the different classical criteria in scheduling, the reader is referred to [Rinnooy Kan, 1976].

Table A.1. Notation of data

Data of problems	
Notation	Meaning
n	number of jobs.
m	number of machines.
J_i	job number i, $i = 1, ..., n$.
n_i	number of operations of job J_i, we often have $n_i = m, \forall i$, $i = 1, ..., n$.
$m^{(\ell)}$ (or $M^{(\ell)}$)	number of machines at stage ℓ.
M_j	machine number j, $j = 1, ..., m$.
$O_{i,j}$	operation j of job J_i.
r_i ($r_{i,j}$)	release time of job J_i (respectively of operation $O_{i,j}$).
s_i ($s_{i,j}$)	desired start time of job J_i (respectively of operation $O_{i,j}$).
$p_{i,j}$ (or p_i^j)	processing time of operation $O_{i,j}$. When there is only one operation per job we use the notation p_i.
$\underline{p}_{i,j}$ ($\overline{p}_{i,j}$)	minimum processing time (respectively maximum) of operation $O_{i,j}$. When there is only one operation per job we use $\underline{p}_i$ (respectively $\overline{p}_i$). This data is generaly used in problems in which the processing times are variables to determine.
d_i ($d_{i,j}$)	due date of job J_i (respectively of operation $O_{i,j}$)
$\widetilde{d}_i$ ($\widetilde{d}_{i,j}$)	deadline of job J_i (respectively of operation $O_{i,j}$). The job J_i (resp. the operation $O_{i,j}$) cannot complete after this date.
w_i ($w_{i,j}$)	weight associated to job J_i (respectively to operation $O_{i,j}$).
k_j	production rate associated to machine M_j. This data is generaly used in uniform parallel machines scheduling problems.
$k_{i,j}$	production rate associated to the processing of job J_i on machine M_j. This data is generally used in unrelated parallel machines scheduling problems.
$S_{i,j}$	non sequence dependent setup time required before the processing of operation $O_{i,j}$.
$R_{i,j}$	non sequence dependent removal time required after the processing of operation $O_{i,j}$.

Table A.2. Notation of variables

Variables of problems	
Notation	Meaning
$t_{i,j}$	start time of operation $O_{i,j}$. When there is only one operation per job, we use the notation t_i.
$C_{i,j}$	completion time of operation $O_{i,j}$.
C_i	completion time of job J_i. $C_i = \max_{j=1,\dots,n_i}(C_{i,j})$.
T_i	tardiness of job J_i. We have $T_i = \max(0; C_i - d_i)$.
E_i	earliness of job J_i. We have $E_i = \max(0; d_i - C_i)$.
L_i	lateness of job J_i. We have $L_i = C_i - d_i$.
U_i	is equal to 1 if $C_i > d_i$ and 0 otherwise.

Table A.3. The field α

Field $\alpha = \alpha_1\alpha_2$			
sub-field α_1		sub-field α_2	
Value	Meaning	Value	Meaning
$\emptyset$	single machine.	$\emptyset$	the number of machines or pools is not fixed.
P, Q, R	identical, proportionnal or unrelated parallel machines.	$1, 2, 3$, *etc.*	the number of machines or stages is fixed and equal to $1, 2, 3$, *etc.*
F, J, O, X	flowshop, jobshop, openshop, mixed shop.	m	the number of machines or stages is unknown but fixed.
HF	hybrid flowshop.		
GO	general openshop.		
GJ	general jobshop.		
$\{P, Q, R\}MPM$	parallel machines (of type P or Q or R) with a general assignment problem.		
$GMPM$	shop problem with a general assignment problem.		
$OMPM$	openshop problem with a general assignment problem.		

Table A.4. The field β - (1)

Field β			
Value	Meaning	Value	Meaning
$prec$	there is general precedence constraints between operations.	$tree$	there is precedence constraint which forms a tree, between o erations.
$chains$	there is precedence constraints, which form a set of chains, between operations.	$in-tree$	there is precedence constraint which forms an in-tree, b tween operations.
$out-tree$	there is precedence constraints, which forms an out-tree, between operations.	$sp-graph$	There is precedence co straints, which forms serie-parallel graph, betwe operations.
r_i	jobs have distinct realease times.	s_i	jobs have desired start time.
$p_{i,j} = p$	jobs have a common processing time.	$p_i \in [\underline{p}_i; \overline{p}_i]$	the processing times of jobs a variables to determine and b long to the interval $[\underline{p}_i; \overline{p}_i]$.
d_i	jobs have a due date.	$d_i = d$	jobs have a common due dat
d_i $unknown$	jobs have a due date which is to be determined.	$d_i = d$ $unknown$	jobs have a common due da which is to be determined.
$\widetilde{d}_i$	jobs have a deadline.	a_{j_1,j_2}	there is a minimum time lag satisfy between the last oper tion of job J_{j_1} and the first o eration of job J_{j_2}.
$split$	the splitting of an operation into parts is allowed and several parts can be processed simultaneously.	$over$	the overlapping of two conse utive operations of a job is a lowed.
$pmtn$	the operations can be interrupted and resumed later on any machine.	$no-wait$	for each job, when an operatic completes the next one mu start.
			to follc

Table A.5. The field β - (2)

Field β *(second part)*			
Value	Meaning	Value	Meaning
$block$	the shop has storage areas, with a limited capacity, between the machines, which may leads an operation to be stored on a machine.	$recrc$	a job can be processed several times by the same machine.
$batch$	the operations can be gathered into batches during their processing.	$s-batch$	the operations can be gathered into batches and are processed in series in each batch.
$p-batch$	the operations can be gathered into batches and are processed in parallel in each batch.	$permu$ or $prmu$	we consider the set of permutation schedules (only available for flowshop scheduling problems).
$blcg$	the machines must complete their processing at the same time.	$unavail_j$	machine M_j can have unavailability periods, known in advance.
R_{sd} (R_{nsd})	there is a removal time after the processing of an operation. This one depends (respectively does not depend) on the sequence of operations on each machine.	S_{sd} (S_{nsd})	there is a setup time before the processing of an operation. This time depends (respectively does not depend) on the sequence of operations on each machine.
$nmit$	when a machine has started its processing, no idle time between operations is allowed.	$no-idle$	on each machine the processing of the operations is performed without idle time.

Table A.5. The field γ

Field γ		
Criterion	Expression	Meaning
C_{max}	$\max_{i=1,\dots,n}(C_i)$	Makespan, or maximum completion time.
T_{max}	$\max_{i=1,\dots,n}\big(\max(C_i - d_i; 0)\big)$	Maximum tardiness of jobs.
L_{max}	$\max_{i=1,\dots,n}(C_i - d_i)$	Maximum lateness of jobs.
E_{max}	$\max_{i=1,\dots,n}\big(\max(d_i - C_i; 0)\big)$	Maximum earliness of jobs.
F_{max}	$\max_{i=1,\dots,n}(C_i - r_i)$	Maximum flow time of jobs.
P_{max}	$\max_{i=1,\dots,n}\big(\max(s_i - t_i; 0)\big)$	Maximum promptness of jobs.
f_{max}	$\max_{i=1,\dots,n}(f_i)$	Generic maximum cost function. Generaly, it is assumed to be an increasing function of the completion times of jobs.
$\overline{C}$ ($\overline{C}^w$)	$\sum_{i=1}^{n} C_i$ ($\sum_{i=1}^{n} w_i C_i$)	(Weighted) Average completion time of jobs, or (weighted) average work-in-process.
$\overline{T}$ ($\overline{T}^w$)	$\sum_{i=1}^{n} T_i$ ($\sum_{i=1}^{n} w_i T_i$)	(Weighted) Average tardiness of jobs.
$\overline{U}$ ($\overline{U}^w$)	$\sum_{i=1}^{n} U_i$ ($\sum_{i=1}^{n} w_i U_i$)	(Weighted) Number of late jobs.
$\overline{E}$ ($\overline{E}^w$)	$\sum_{i=1}^{n} E_i$ ($\sum_{i=1}^{n} w_i E_i$)	(Weighted) Average earliness of jobs.
–		No criterion, it is a feasibility problem.

B. Synthesis on multicriteria scheduling problems

B.1 Single machine Just-in-Time scheduling problems

We present in this section the set of problems tackled in chapter 5. The first table details polynomially solvable problems, mentioning: the notation of the problem, the associated references and the resolution method as well as its complexity. The second table contains the set of $\mathcal{NP}$-hard problems. We distinguish the notation of the problem, its exact theoretical complexity and the associated references. The third table presents the set of open problems, mentioning: the notation of the problem and the associated references. In each table, in the column **Problem** we indicate between brackets the page number in this book where the corresponding problem is tackled.

POLYNOMIAL JUST-IN-TIME SCHEDULING PROBLEMS ON A SINGLE MACHINE

Problem [page]	Reference	Method & complexity
$1 \vert s_i, d_i, d_i - s_i \leq p_i, nmit \vert \epsilon(L_{max}/P_{max})$ [170]	[Hoogeveen, 1996]	Greedy $O(n\log(n))$
$1 \vert s_i, d_i, d_i - s_i \leq p_i \vert \epsilon(L_{max}/P_{max})$ [170]	[Hoogeveen, 1996]	Greedy $O(n^2\log(n))$
$1 \vert d_i, seq \vert F_\ell(\overline{E}, \overline{T})$ [147]	[Garey et al., 1988]	Greedy $O(n\log(n))$
$1 \vert p_i = 1, d_i \vert F_\ell(\overline{E}, \overline{T})$ [147]	[Garey et al., 1988]	Greedy $O(n\log(n))$
$1 \vert d_i, \text{chain} \vert F_\ell(\overline{E}, \overline{T})$ [147]	[Garey et al., 1988]	Greedy $O(n\log(n))$
$1 \vert d_i = d \geq \sum p_i \vert F_\ell(\overline{E}, \overline{T})$ [153]	[Kanet, 1981a]	Greedy $O(n^2)$
$1 \vert d_i = d \geq \delta \vert F_\ell(\overline{E}, \overline{T})$ [155]	[Bagchi et al., 1986]	Polynomial branch-and-bound
$1 \vert d_i = d, d\ unknown \vert F_\ell(\overline{E}, \overline{T})$ [171]	[Bector et al., 1988] [Webster et al., 1998]	Neighborhood
$1 \vert p_i = 1, d_i, nmit \vert \epsilon(E_{max}/\overline{U})$ [171]	[Kondakci et al., 1997]	Mixed integer programming
$1 \vert p_i = 1, d_i, nmit \vert \epsilon(\overline{E}/\overline{U})$ [171]	[Kondakci et al., 1997]	Mixed integer programming
$1 \vert d_i, seq \vert F_\ell(\overline{E}^\alpha, \overline{T}^\beta)$ [149]	[Szwarc and Mukhopadhyay, 1995]	Shifting ($O(cn)$, c number of blocks)
$1 \vert d_i = d \geq \sum p_i, w_i = p_i \vert F_\ell(\overline{E}^w, \overline{T}^w)$ [171]	[Ahmed and Sundararaghavan, 1990]	Greedy
$1 \vert p_i = 1, d_i \vert F(E_i, T_i)$ [147]	[Garey et al., 1988]	Greedy $O(n\log(n))$
$1 \vert s_i, d_i, \forall i \neq j, s_i \leq s_j \Leftrightarrow d_i \leq d_j \vert F(f(T_{max}), g(P_{max}))$ [172]	[Sidney, 1977] [Lakshminarayan et al., 1978]	Greedy $O(n^2)$ Greedy $O(n\log(n))$
$1 \vert d_i = d, A \geq M \vert F_\ell(\overline{U}^w, \overline{A})$ [172]	[De et al., 1991]	Greedy
$1 \vert p_i = 1, d_i, nmit \vert \epsilon(F_\ell(\overline{E}, \overline{T})/\overline{U})$ [171]	[Kondakci et al., 1997]	Mixed integer programming
$1 \vert d_i\ unknown, nmit, A \vert F_\ell(\overline{E}, \overline{T}, \overline{A})$ [172]	[Seidmann et al., 1981]	Greedy $O(n\log(n))$
$1 \vert d_i = d\ unknown, nmit \vert F_\ell(\overline{E}, \overline{T}, d)$ [155]	[Panwalker et al., 1982]	Dedicated $O(n\log(n))$
$1 \vert d_i = d\ unknown, nmit, classes \vert F_\ell(\overline{E}, \overline{T}, \overline{B}, d)$ [156]	[Chen, 1996]	Dynamic programming $O(n^5)$
$1 \vert d_i = d\ unknown, nmit \vert F_\ell(\overline{E}, \overline{T}, d, \overline{C})$ [155]	[Panwalker et al., 1982]	Dedicated $O(n\log(n))$
$1 \vert p_i \in [\underline{p}_i; \overline{p}_i] \cap \mathbb{N}, d_i = d\ non\ restrictive \vert F_\ell(\overline{E}, \overline{T}, \overline{CC}^w)$ [157]	[Chen et al., 1997]	Reduction to an assignment problem $O(n^3)$

$\mathcal{NP}$-HARD JUST-IN-TIME SCHEDULING PROBLEMS ON A SINGLE MACHINE

Problem	[page]	Complexity	Reference
$1\|d_i, nmit\|F_\ell(\overline{E}, \overline{T})$	[182]	$\mathcal{NP}$-hard	[Fry and Leong, 1986] [Azizoglu et al., 1991]
$1\|d_i\|F_\ell(\overline{E}, \overline{T})$	[182]	$\mathcal{NP}$-hard	[Szwarc, 1993] [Kim and Yano, 1994] [Fry et al., 1996]
$1\|d_i = d, nmit\|F_\ell(\overline{E}, \overline{T})$	[183]	$\mathcal{NP}$-hard	[Sundararaghavan and Ahmed, 1984]
$1\|d_i = d < \sum p_i, nmit\|F_\ell(\overline{E}, \overline{T})$	[183]	$\mathcal{NP}$-hard	[Bagchi et al., 1987a]
$1\|d_i = d < \delta, nmit\|F_\ell(\overline{E}, \overline{T})$	[184]	$\mathcal{NP}$-hard	[Bagchi et al., 1986] [Szwarc, 1989]
$1\|s_i, d_i\|F_\ell(\overline{P}, \overline{T})$	[184]	$\mathcal{NP}$-hard	[Koulamas, 1996]
$1\|d_i, nmit\|\epsilon(\overline{E}^w/\overline{U})$	[184]	$\mathcal{NP}$-hard	[Chand and Schneeberger, 1988]
$1\|d_i\|F_\ell(\overline{E}^\alpha, \overline{T}^\beta)$	[184]	strongly $\mathcal{NP}$-hard	[Fry et al., 1987a] [Fry and Blackstone, 1988] [James and Buchanan, 1997] [James and Buchanan, 1998]
$1\|r_i, d_i\|F_\ell(\overline{E}^\alpha, \overline{T}^\beta)$	[185]	strongly $\mathcal{NP}$-hard	[Yano and Kim, 1991] [Mazzini and Armentano, 2001]
$1\|d_i, nmit\|F_\ell(\overline{E}^\alpha, \overline{T}^\beta)$	[173]	strongly $\mathcal{NP}$-hard	[Ow and Morton, 1988] [Ow and Morton, 1989] [Li, 1997] [Almeida and Centeno, 1998] [Liaw, 1999]
$1\|d_i = d \geq \sum p_i, nmit\|F_\ell(\overline{E}^\alpha, \overline{T}^\beta)$	[186]	$\mathcal{NP}$-hard	[VandenAkker et al., 1998a]
$1\|d_i = d \geq \sum p_i, S_{sd}, nmit, classes\|F_\ell(\overline{E}^\alpha, \overline{T}^\beta)$	[186]	$\mathcal{NP}$-hard	[Azizoglu and Webster, 1997]
$1\|d_i = d\ unknown, S_{sd}, nmit\|F_\ell(\overline{E}^\alpha, \overline{T}^\beta)$	[186]	$\mathcal{NP}$-hard	[Webster et al., 1998]
$1\|d_i, nmit\|F(E_i, T_i)$	[187]	$\mathcal{NP}$-hard	[Gupta and Sen, 1983]
$1\|d_i = d, nmit\|F_\ell(\sum E_i^2, \sum T_i^2)$	[187]	$\mathcal{NP}$-hard	[Bagchi et al., 1987a]
$1\|d_i, nmit\|F(\overline{E}, \overline{T}, \overline{C})$	[187]	$\mathcal{NP}$-hard	[Dileepan and Sen, 1991]
$1\|d_i = d, nmit\|F(E_i, T_i)$	[187]	$\mathcal{NP}$-hard	[Bagchi et al., 1987b] [Kubiak, 1993]
$1\|d_i\|F_\ell(\overline{E}, \overline{T}, \overline{C})$	[188]	$\mathcal{NP}$-hard	[Fry et al., 1987b]

OPEN JUST-IN-TIME SCHEDULING PROBLEMS ON A SINGLE MACHINE

Problem	[page]	Reference
$1\|d_i\ unknown, nmit\|F_\ell(\overline{E}^\alpha, \overline{T}^\beta)$	[189]	[Adamopoulos and Pappis, 1996]
$1\|d_i, nmit\|F_\ell(L_{max}, -L_{min})$	[189]	[Gupta and Sen, 1984] [Tegze and Vlach, 1988] [Liao and Huang, 1991]
$1\|d_i, nmit\|F_\ell(\overline{C}, L_{max} - L_{min})$	[191]	[Sen et al., 1988]

B.2 Single machine problems

In this section we present the set of problems tackled in chapter 7. The first table details polynomially solvable problems, mentioning: the notation of the problem, the associated references and the resolution method as well as its complexity. The second table contains the set of $\mathcal{NP}$-hard problems. We distinguish the notation of the problem, its exact theoretical complexity and the associated references. The third table presents the set of open problems, mentioning: the notation of the problem and the associated references.

POLYNOMIAL SINGLE MACHINE SCHEDULING PROBLEMS (1/2)

Problem	[page]	Reference	Method & complexity
Minimisation of K increasing functions of the completion times			
$1\|\|\epsilon(f^1_{max}/f^2_{max},\dots,f^K_{max})$	[219]	[Hoogeveen, 1992b]	Greedy in $O(n^4)$ for $K=2$ and $O(n^{K(K+1)-6})$ otherwise.
Minimisation of the average completion time			
$1\|d_i\|\epsilon(\overline{C}/L_{max})$	[207]	[Smith, 1956] [Heck and Roberts, 1972] [VanWassenhove and Gelders, 1980] [Nelson et al., 1986] [Esswein et al., 2001]	Greedy $O(n\log(n))$ Greedy Greedy $O(n^2\overline{p}\log(n))$ Branch-and-Bound
$1\|d_i\|F_\ell(T_{max},\overline{C})$	[214]	[Sen and Gupta, 1983]	Branch-and-Bound
$1\|\|Lex(f_{max},\overline{C})$	[214]	[Emmons, 1975a]	Greedy
$1\|\|\epsilon(\overline{C}/f_{max})$	[207]	[John, 1984] [Hoogeveen and VandeVelde, 1995]	Neighbourhood $O(n\log(n))$ Greedy
$1\|s_i,pmtn,nmit\|F_\ell(\overline{C},P_{max})$	[215]	[Hoogeveen and van de Velde, 2001]	Neighbourhood $O(n\log(n))$
Minimisation of the weighted average completion time			
$1\|p_i=1,d_i\|Lex(T_{max},\overline{C}^w)$	[220]	[Chen and Bulfin, 1990]	Reduction to an assignment problem $O(n^3)$
$1\|p_i=1,d_i\|Lex(\overline{C}^w,T_{max})$	[220]	[Chen and Bulfin, 1990]	Greedy $O(n\log(n))$
$1\|p_i=1,d_i\|\epsilon(\overline{C}^w/T_{max})$	[220]	[Chen and Bulfin, 1990]	Reduction to an assignment problem $O(n^3)$
$1\|p_i=1,d_i\|Lex(\overline{C}^w,\overline{U})$	[220]	[Chen and Bulfin, 1990]	Greedy $O(n\log(n))$
$1\|p_i=1,d_i\|Lex(\overline{U},\overline{C}^w)$	[220]	[Chen and Bulfin, 1990]	Reduction to an assignment problem $O(n^3)$
$1\|p_i=1,d_i\|F_\ell(\overline{C}^w,\overline{U})$	[220]	[Chen and Bulfin, 1990]	Reduction to an assignment problem $O(n^3)$
$1\|p_i=1,d_i\|Lex(\overline{C}^w,\overline{U}^w)$	[220]	[Chen and Bulfin, 1990]	Greedy $O(n\log(n))$
$1\|p_i=1,d_i\|Lex(\overline{U}^w,\overline{C}^w)$	[220]	[Chen and Bulfin, 1990]	Reduction to an assignment problem $O(n^3)$
$1\|p_i=1,d_i\|F_\ell(\overline{C}^w,\overline{U}^w)$	[220]	[Chen and Bulfin, 1990]	Reduction to an assignment problem $O(n^3)$
$1\|p_i=1,d_i\|Lex(\overline{C}^w,\overline{T})$	[220]	[Chen and Bulfin, 1990]	Greedy $O(n\log(n))$
$1\|p_i=1,d_i\|Lex(\overline{T},\overline{C}^w)$	[220]	[Chen and Bulfin, 1990]	Greedy $O(n\log(n))$
$1\|p_i=1,d_i\|F_\ell(\overline{C}^w,\overline{T})$	[220]	[Chen and Bulfin, 1990]	Reduction to an assignment problem $O(n^3)$
$1\|p_i=1,d_i\|Lex(\overline{C}^w,\overline{T}^w)$	[220]	[Chen and Bulfin, 1990]	Greedy $O(n\log(n))$
$1\|p_i=1,d_i\|Lex(\overline{T}^w,\overline{C}^w)$	[220]	[Chen and Bulfin, 1990]	Reduction to an assignment problem $O(n^3)$
$1\|p_i=1,d_i\|F_\ell(\overline{C}^w,\overline{T}^w)$	[220]	[Chen and Bulfin, 1990]	Reduction to an assignment problem $O(n^3)$
Minimisation of crashing time costs			
$1\|p_i\in[\underline{p}_i;\overline{p}_i],d_i\|F_\ell(T_{max},\overline{CC}^w)$	[216]	[Vickson, 1980b]	Greedy $O(n^2)$
$1\|p_i\in[\underline{p}_i;\overline{p}_i],d_i\|\epsilon(T_{max}/\overline{CC}^w)$	[217]	[VanWassenhove and Baker, 1982]	Greedy $O(n^2)$
$1\|p_i\in[\underline{p}_i;\overline{p}_i]\|\epsilon(f_{max}/\overline{CC}^w)$	[217]	[VanWassenhove and Baker, 1982]	Greedy $O(n^2)$
$1\|p_i\in[\underline{p}_i;\overline{p}_i]\|F_\ell(\overline{C},\overline{CC}^w)$	[219]	[Vickson, 1980b]	Reduction to an assignment problem $O(n^3)$
$1\|p_i\in[\underline{p}_i;\overline{p}_i]\cap\mathbb{N}\|F_\ell(\overline{C},\overline{CC}^w)$	[219]	[Chen et al., 1997]	Reduction to an assignment problem $O(n^3)$
Minimisation of tool changing costs			
$1\|classes,orders,S_{sd}\|Lex(\overline{SC},\overline{AC})$	[221]	[Gupta et al., 1997]	Dedicated in $O(n\log(\mathcal{M}))$ with $\mathcal{M}$ the number of orders.
$1\|classes,commandes,S_{sd}\|Lex(\overline{AC},\overline{SC})$	[221]	[Gupta et al., 1997]	Dedicated $O(n)$
Minimisation of due date based criteria			
$1\|p_i=1,d_i\|Lex(T_{max},\overline{U})$	[222]	[Chen and Bulfin, 1990]	Reduction to an assignment problem $O(n^3)$
$1\|p_i=1,d_i\|\epsilon(\overline{U}/T_{max})$	[222]	[Chen and Bulfin, 1990]	Reduction to an assignment problem $O(n^3)$
$1\|p_i=1,d_i\|Lex(\overline{U}^w/T_{max})$	[222]	[Chen and Bulfin, 1990]	Reduction to an assignment problem $O(n^3)$
$1\|p_i=1,d_i\|\epsilon(T_{max},\overline{U}^w)$	[222]	[Chen and Bulfin, 1990]	Reduction to an assignment problem $O(n^3)$
$1\|p_i=1,d_i\|Lex(T_{max},\overline{T}^w)$	[222]	[Chen and Bulfin, 1990]	Reduction to an assignment problem $O(n^3)$

POLYNOMIAL SINGLE MACHINE SCHEDULING PROBLEMS (2/2)

Problem [page]	Reference	Method & complexity
$1\|p_i = 1, d_i\|\epsilon(\overline{T^w}/T_{max})$ [222]	[Chen and Bulfin, 1990]	Reduction to an assignment problem $O(n^3)$
$1\|p_i = 1, d_i\|Lex(\overline{T}, \overline{U})$ [222]	[Chen and Bulfin, 1990]	Greedy
$1\|p_i = 1, d_i\|Lex(\overline{U}, \overline{T})$ [222]	[Chen and Bulfin, 1990]	Reduction to an assignment problem $O(n^3)$
$1\|p_i = 1, d_i\|F_\ell(\overline{T}, \overline{U})$ [222]	[Chen and Bulfin, 1990]	Reduction to an assignment problem $O(n^3)$
$1\|p_i = 1, d_i\|Lex(\overline{T}, \overline{U^w})$ [222]	[Chen and Bulfin, 1990]	Greedy
$1\|p_i = 1, d_i\|Lex(\overline{U^w}, \overline{T})$ [222]	[Chen and Bulfin, 1990]	Reduction to an assignment problem $O(n^3)$
$1\|p_i = 1, d_i\|F_\ell(\overline{T}, \overline{U^w})$ [222]	[Chen and Bulfin, 1990]	Reduction to an assignment problem $O(n^3)$
$1\|p_i = 1, d_i\|Lex(\overline{U}, \overline{T^w})$ [222]	[Chen and Bulfin, 1990]	Reduction to an assignment problem $O(n^3)$
$1\|p_i = 1, d_i\|Lex(\overline{T^w}, \overline{U})$ [222]	[Chen and Bulfin, 1990]	Reduction to an assignment problem $O(n^3)$
$1\|p_i = 1, d_i\|F_\ell(\overline{T^w}, \overline{U})$ [222]	[Chen and Bulfin, 1990]	Reduction to an assignment problem $O(n^3)$
$1\|p_i = 1, d_i\|Lex(\overline{T^w}, \overline{U^w})$ [222]	[Chen and Bulfin, 1990]	Reduction to an assignment problem $O(n^3)$
$1\|p_i = 1, d_i\|Lex(\overline{U^w}, \overline{T^w})$ [222]	[Chen and Bulfin, 1990]	Reduction to an assignment problem $O(n^3)$
$1\|p_i = 1, d_i\|F_\ell(\overline{T^w}, \overline{U^w})$ [222]	[Chen and Bulfin, 1990]	Reduction to an assignment problem $O(n^3)$

$\mathcal{NP}$-HARD SINGLE MACHINE SCHEDULING PROBLEMS

Problem [page]	Complexity	Reference
Minimisation of the average completion time		
$1\|d_i, nmit\|\epsilon(\overline{C}/E_{max})$ [226]	stronlgy $\mathcal{NP}$-hard	[Azizoglu et al., 1997]
$1\|d_i\|\epsilon(\overline{C}/E_{max})$ [226]	stronlgy $\mathcal{NP}$-hard	[Della Croce and T'kindt, 2002] [Della Croce and T'kindt, 2003]
$1\|d_i\|Lex(\overline{U}, \overline{C})$ [227]	$\mathcal{NP}$-hard	[Emmons, 1975b]
$1\|d_i\|\epsilon(\overline{C}/\overline{U})$ [227]	$\mathcal{NP}$-hard	[Nelson et al., 1986] [Kiran and Unal, 1991]
$1\|d_i\|\#(\overline{C}, \overline{T})$ [222]	$\mathcal{NP}$-hard	[Lin, 1983]
$1\|d_i\|\epsilon(\overline{C}/\overline{U}, T_{max})$ [227]	$\mathcal{NP}$-hard	[Nelson et al., 1986]
Minimisation of the weighted average completion time		
$1\|d_i\|Lex(L_{max}, \overline{C^w})$ [227]	strongly $\mathcal{NP}$-hard	[Chand and Schneeberger, 1984] [Hoogeveen, 1992a]
$1\|d_i\|\epsilon(\overline{C^w}/L_{max})$ [228]	strongly $\mathcal{NP}$-hard	[Smith, 1956] [Bansal, 1980] [Chand and Schneeberger, 1986] [Heck and Roberts, 1972] [Burns, 1976] [Miyazaki, 1981]
$1\|d_i\|F_\ell(\overline{C^w}, \overline{T^w})$ [228]	strongly $\mathcal{NP}$-hard	[VanWassenhove and Gelders, 1978]
Minimisation of crashing time costs		
$1\|r_i, p_i \in [\underline{p}_i; \overline{p}_i] \cap \mathbb{N}\|F_\ell(C_{max}, \overline{CC^w})$ [223]	weakly $\mathcal{NP}$-hard	[Chen et al., 1997]
$1\|d_i, p_i \in [\underline{p}_i; \overline{p}_i] \cap \mathbb{N}\|F_\ell(\overline{U^w}, \overline{CC^w})$ [225]	weakly $\mathcal{NP}$-hard	[Chen et al., 1997]
$1\|d_i, p_i \in [\underline{p}_i; \overline{p}_i] \cap \mathbb{N}\|F_\ell(T_{max}, \overline{CC^w})$ [226]	weakly $\mathcal{NP}$-hard	[Chen et al., 1997]
Minimisation of tool changing costs		
$1\|d_i, S_{sd}\|F(\overline{SC}, T_{max})$ [229]	$\mathcal{NP}$-hard	[Bourgade et al., 1995]
$1\|C_{sd}\|F_\ell(\overline{C^w}, \overline{SC})$ [229]	$\mathcal{NP}$-hard	[Barnes and Vanston, 1981]

OPEN SINGLE MACHINE SCHEDULING PROBLEMS

Problem [page]	Reference
Minimisation of the average completion time	
$1\|d_i\|F_\ell(\overline{C}, \overline{E})$ [234]	[Fry and Leong, 1987]
Minimisation of crashing time costs	
$1\|p_i \in [\underline{p}_i; \overline{p}_i]\|F_\ell(\overline{C^w}, \overline{CC^w})$ [234]	[Vickson, 1980a]
Minimisation of due date based criteria	
$1\|d_i\|Lex(\overline{U}, T_{max})$ [230]	[Shantikumar, 1983] [Gupta et al., 1999a]
$1\|d_i\|\epsilon(\overline{U}/T_{max})$ [233]	[Nelson et al., 1986]

B.3 Shop problems

This section deals with the set of problems tackled in chapter 8. The first table present flowshop problems, mentioning: the notation of the problem, its complexity and the associated references. The last table is dedicated to jobshop and openshop problems.

FLOWSHOP SCHEDULING PROBLEMS

Problem	[page]	Complexity	Reference
Minimisation of maximum completion times			
$F2 \vert prmu \vert Lex(C_{max}, \overline{C})$	[235]	strongly $\mathcal{NP}$-hard	[Rajendran, 1992] [Neppalli et al., 1996] [Gupta et al., 2001] [Gupta et al., 2002] [Gupta et al., 1999b] [T'kindt et al., 2003]
$F2 \vert prmu \vert F_\ell(C_{max}, \overline{C})$	[250]	strongly $\mathcal{NP}$-hard	[Nagar et al., 1995b] [Serifoglu and Ulusoy, 1998] [Yeh, 1999]
$F2 \vert r_i, prmu \vert F_\ell(C_{max}, \overline{C})$	[256]	strongly $\mathcal{NP}$-hard	[Chou and Lee, 1999]
$F2 \vert prmu \vert \epsilon(\overline{C}/C_{max})$	[256]	strongly $\mathcal{NP}$-hard	[Sayin and Karabati, 1999]
$F \vert prmu \vert Lex(C_{max}, \overline{C})$	[270]	strongly $\mathcal{NP}$-hard	[Selen and Hott, 1986] [Wilson, 1989]
$F \vert prmu \vert \#(C_{max}, \overline{C})$	[272]	strongly $\mathcal{NP}$-hard	[Gangadharan and Rajendran, 1994] [Rajendran, 1994] [Rajendran, 1995]
$F2 \vert prmu, d_i \vert \#(C_{max}, T_{max})$	[262]	$\mathcal{NP}$-hard	[Daniels and Chambers, 1990]
$F \vert prmu, d_i \vert \epsilon(C_{max}/T_{max})$	[277]	$\mathcal{NP}$-hard	[Daniels and Chambers, 1990]
$F2 \vert prmu, d_i \vert \#(C_{max}, \overline{U})$	[265]	strongly $\mathcal{NP}$-hard	[Liao et al., 1997]
$F2 \vert prmu, d_i \vert \#(C_{max}, \overline{T})$	[267]	strongly $\mathcal{NP}$-hard	[Liao et al., 1997]
Minimisation of crashing time costs			
$F \vert p_{i,j} \in [\underline{p}_{i,j}; \overline{p}_{i,j}], prmu \vert F_\ell(C_{max}, \overline{CC}^w)$	[280]	$\mathcal{NP}$-hard	[Nowicki, 1993]
$F \vert p_{i,j} = p_i \in [\underline{p}_i; \overline{p}_i], prmu \vert \#(C_{max}, \overline{CC}^w)$	[281]	$\mathcal{P}$	[Cheng and Shakhlevich, 1999]
Minimisation of Just-in-Time criteria			
$F \vert prmu, d_i, nmit \vert F_\ell(\overline{E}^\alpha, \overline{T}^\beta)$	[176]	strongly $\mathcal{NP}$-hard	[Zegordi et al., 1995]

JOBSHOP AND OPENSHOP SCHEDULING PROBLEMS

Problem	[page]	Complexity	Reference
$J \vert\vert F_T(C_{max}, \overline{C}, \overline{I}, T_{max}, \overline{U})$	[284]	strongly $\mathcal{NP}$-hard	[Huckert et al., 1980]
$J \vert\vert GP(C_{max}, \overline{C}, \overline{E+T})$	[284]	strongly $\mathcal{NP}$-hard	[Deckro et al., 1982]
$O2 \vert\vert Lex(C_{max}, \overline{C})$	[284]	strongly $\mathcal{NP}$-hard	[Gupta and Werner, 1999] [Kyparisis and Koulamas, 2000]
$O3 \vert\vert Lex(C_{max}, \overline{C})$	[285]	strongly $\mathcal{NP}$-hard	[Kyparisis and Koulamas, 2000]

B.4 Parallel machines scheduling problems

We present in this section the set of problems tackled in chapter 9. The following table summarizes the problems, mentioning: the notation of the problem, its complexity and the associated references.

PARALLEL MACHINES SCHEDULING PROBLEMS

Problem	[page]	Complexity	Reference
Minimisation of increasing functions of the completion times			
$Q \mid p_i = p \mid \epsilon(f_{max}/g_{max})$	[297]	$\mathcal{P}$	[Tuzikov et al., 1998]
$Q \mid p_i = p \mid \epsilon(\overline{g}/f_{max})$	[302]	$\mathcal{P}$	[Tuzikov et al., 1998]
Minimisation of maximum completion times			
$P2 \mid pmtn, d_i \mid \epsilon(L_{max}/C_{max})$	[287]	$\mathcal{P}$	[Mohri et al., 1999]
$P3 \mid pmtn, d_i \mid \epsilon(L_{max}/C_{max})$	[290]	$\mathcal{P}$	[Mohri et al., 1999]
$P2 \mid d_i \mid Lex(T_{max}, \overline{U})$	[293]	$\mathcal{NP}$-hard	[Sarin and Hariharan, 2000]
$P \mid pmtn \mid Lex(\overline{C}, C_{max})$	[296]	$\mathcal{P}$	[Leung and Young, 1989]
$Q \mid pmtn \mid \epsilon(\overline{C}/C_{max})$	[303]	$\mathcal{P}$	[Mc Cormick and Pinedo, 1995]
$R \mid pmtn \mid \epsilon(F_\ell(I_{max}, -\overline{M})/C_{max})$	[311]	$\mathcal{P}$	[T'kindt et al., 2001]
Minimisation of crashing time costs			
$R \mid p_{i,j} \in [\underline{p}_{i,j}; \overline{p}_{i,j}] \mid F_\ell(\overline{C}, \overline{CC^w})$	[310]	Open	[Alidaee and Ahmadian, 1993]
$R \mid p_{i,j} \in [\underline{p}_{i,j}; \overline{p}_{i,j}], d_i = d$ $unknown \mid F_\ell(\overline{T}, \overline{E}, \overline{CC^w})$	[169]	$\mathcal{P}$	[Alidaee and Ahmadian, 1993]
Minimisation of Just-in-Time criteria			
$P \mid d_i = d$ non $restrictive, nmit \mid F_\ell(\overline{E}, \overline{T})$	[157]	$\mathcal{P}$	[Sundararaghavan and Ahmed, 1984]
$P \mid d_i = d$ $unknown, nmit \mid F_\ell(\overline{E}, \overline{T})$	[159]	$\mathcal{P}$	[Emmons, 1987]
$Q \mid d_i = d$ $unknown, nmit \mid F_\ell(\overline{E}, \overline{T})$	[188]	Open	[Emmons, 1987]
$P \mid d_i = d$ $nonrestrictive, nmit \mid fmax(\overline{E}^w, \overline{T}^w)$	[178]	strongly $\mathcal{NP}$-hard	[Li and Cheng, 1994]
$P \mid d_i = d$ $unknown, nmit \mid Lex(F_\ell(\overline{E}, \overline{T}), C_{max})$	[162]	Open	[Emmons, 1987]
$P \mid d_i = d$ $unknown, p_i = p, nmit \mid F_\ell(\overline{E}, \overline{T}, d)$	[165]	$\mathcal{P}$	[Cheng and Chen, 1994]

B.5 Shop scheduling problems with assignment

We collect in this section the set of problems tackled in chapter 10. The table below summarizes the set of problems met, mentioning: the notation of the problem, its complexity and the associated references.

HYBRID FLOWSHOP SCHEDULING PROBLEMS

Problem	[page]	Complexity	Reference
Minimisation of maximum completion times			
$HFk, (PM^{(\ell)})_{\ell=1}^k \mid\mid F_\ell(C_{max}, \overline{C})$	[316]	$\mathcal{NP}$-hard	[Riane et al., 1997]
$HFk, (PM^{(\ell)})_{\ell=1}^k \mid\mid \epsilon(\overline{C}/C_{max})$	[318]	$\mathcal{NP}$-hard	[Riane et al., 1997]
$HFk, (PM^{(\ell)}(t))_{\ell=1}^k \mid r_i^{(1)}, d_i^{(k)} \mid \epsilon(C_{max}/T_{max})$	[318]	$\mathcal{NP}$-hard	[Vignier et al., 1996]
$HF3, (P6, P3, 1) \mid constr \mid F_\ell(C_{max}, \gamma(T_i), delta(VPI))$	[315]	$\mathcal{NP}$-hard	[Fortemps et al., 1996]

References

[Achugbue and Chin, 1982] Achugbue, J. O. and Chin, F. Y. (1982). Scheduling the openshop to minimize mean flow time. *SIAM Journal on Computing*, 11:665–679.

[Adamopoulos and Pappis, 1996] Adamopoulos, G. L. and Pappis, C. P. (1996). Scheduling jobs with different job-dependent earliness and tardiness penalties using the SLK method. *European Journal of Operational Research*, 88:336–344.

[Ahmed and Sundararaghavan, 1990] Ahmed, M. S. and Sundararaghavan, P. S. (1990). Minimizing the weighted sum of late and early completion penalties in a single machine. *IIE Transactions*, 22(3):288–290.

[Alidaee and Ahmadian, 1993] Alidaee, B. and Ahmadian, A. (1993). Two parallel machine sequencing problems involving controllable job processing times. *European Journal of Operational Research*, 70:335–341.

[Allen, 1981] Allen, J. F. (1981). An interval-based representation of temporal knowledge. In *Proceedings of the IJCAI, Vancouver, Canada*, pages 221–226.

[Almeida and Centeno, 1998] Almeida, M. T. and Centeno, M. (1998). A composite heuristic for the single machine early/tardy job scheduling problem. *Computers and Operations Research*, 25(7/8):625–635.

[Aloulou, 2002] Aloulou, M. (2002). *Structure flexible d'ordonnancements à performances contrôlées pour le pilotage d'atelier en présence de perturbations (in french).* Phd thesis, Institut National Polytechnique de Lorraine, Nancy (France).

[Aloulou et al., 2004] Aloulou, M., Kovalyov, M., and Portmann, M. (2004). Maximization of single machine scheduling. *Annals of Operations Research*, 129:21–32.

[Aloulou and Portmann, 2003] Aloulou, M. A. and Portmann, M.-C. (2003). An efficient proactive reactive scheduling approach to hedge against shop floor disturbances. In *Proceedings of the 1st Multidisciplinary International Conference on Scheduling: Theory and Applications (MISTA'03), Nottingham, UK*, pages 337–362.

[Alves and Climaco, 2000] Alves, M. J. and Climaco, J. (2000). An interactive method for 0-1 multiobjective problems using simulated annealing and tabu search. *Journal of Heuristics*, 6(3):385–403.

[Aneja and Nair, 1979] Aneja, Y. P. and Nair, K. P. K. (1979). Bicriteria transportation problem. *Management Science*, 25:73–78.

[Artigues et al., 2005] Artigues, C., Billaut, J.-C., and Esswein, C. (2005). Maximization of solution flexibility for robust shop scheduling. *European Journal of Operational Research*, 165(2):314–328.

[Artigues and Roubellat, 2000] Artigues, C. and Roubellat, F. (2000). A polynomial activity insertion algorithm in a multi-resource schedule with cu-

mulative constraints and multiple modes. *European Journal of Operational Research*, 127:294–316.
[Ausiello et al., 1999] Ausiello, G., Crescenzi, P., Gambosi, G., Kann, V., Marchetti-Spaccamela, A., and Protasi, M. (1999). *Complexity and Approximation: Combinatorial Optimization Problems and Their Approximability Properties.* Springer, Heidelberg.
[Aytug et al., 2005] Aytug, H., Lawley, M. A., McKay, K., Mohan, S., and Uzsoy, R. (2005). Executing production schedules in the face of uncertainties: A review and some future directions. *European Journal of Operational Research*, 161(1):86–110.
[Azizoglu et al., 1991] Azizoglu, M., Kondakci, S. K., and Kirca, O. (1991). Bicriteria scheduling problem involving total tardiness and total earliness penalties. *International Journal of Production Economics*, 23:17–24.
[Azizoglu et al., 1997] Azizoglu, M., Kondakci, S. K., and Koksalan, M. (1997). *Bicriteria scheduling: minimizing flowtime and maximum earliness on a single machine*, pages 279–288. In [Climaco, 1997].
[Azizoglu and Webster, 1997] Azizoglu, M. and Webster, S. (1997). Scheduling job families about an unrestricted common due date on a single machine. *International Journal of Production Research*, 35:1321–1330.
[Bagchi et al., 1987a] Bagchi, U., Chang, Y.-L., and Sullivan, R. S. (1987a). Minimizing absolute and squared deviations of completion times with different earliness and tardiness penalties and a common due date. *Naval Research Logistics*, 34:739–751.
[Bagchi et al., 1986] Bagchi, U., Sullivan, R. S., and Chang, Y.-L. (1986). Minimizing mean absolute deviation of completion times about a common due date. *Naval Research Logistics Quarterly*, 33:227–240.
[Bagchi et al., 1987b] Bagchi, U., Sullivan, R. S., and Chang, Y.-L. (1987b). Minimizing mean squared deviation of completion times about a common due date. *Management Science*, 33(7):894–906.
[Baglin et al., 2001] Baglin, G., Bruel, O., Garreau, A., and Greif, M. (2001). *Management Industriel et Logistique.* Economica.
[Baker, 1974] Baker, K. R. (1974). *Introduction to sequencing and scheduling.* John Wiley & Sons, New-York.
[Baker and Scudder, 1990] Baker, K. R. and Scudder, G. D. (1990). Sequencing with earliness and tardiness penalties: a review. *Operations Research*, 38(1):22–36.
[Bansal, 1980] Bansal, S. P. (1980). Single machine scheduling to minimize weighted sum of completion times with secondary criterion - a branch and bound approach. *European Journal of Operational Research*, 5(3):177–181.
[Baptiste et al., 2001] Baptiste, P., Bloch, C., and Varnier, C. (2001). *Ordonnancement des lignes de traitement de surface (in french).* In F. Roubellat and P. Lopez (Eds.): Ordonnancement de la production, Traité IC2, Hermès (Paris), 259–289.
[Barnes and Vanston, 1981] Barnes, J. W. and Vanston, L. K. (1981). Scheduling jobs with linear delay penalties and sequence dependent setup costs. *Operations Research*, 29(1):146–160.
[Bartal et al., 2000] Bartal, Y., Leonardi, S., Marchetti-Spaccamela, A., Sgall, J., and Stougie, L. (2000). Multiprocessor scheduling with rejection. *SIAM Journal on Discrete Mathematics*, 13:64–78.
[Bector et al., 1988] Bector, C., Gupta, Y., and Gupta, M. (1988). Determination of an optimal common due date and optimal sequence in a sin-

gle machine job shop. *International Journal of Production Research*, 26(4):613–628.

[Benayoun et al., 1971] Benayoun, R., de Mongolfier, J., Tergny, J., and Laritchev, O. (1971). Linear programming with multiple objective functions: step method (STEM). *Mathematical Programming*, 1(3):366–375.

[Bentley and Wakefield, 1996] Bentley, P. J. and Wakefield, J. P. (1996). An analysis of multiobjective optimization within genetic algorithms. Technical Report ENGPJB96, University of Huddersfield, Huddersfield, England.

[Berge and Gouila-Houri, 1965] Berge, C. and Gouila-Houri, A. (1965). *Programming, Games and Transportation Networks, vol. 1.* Wiley, New York.

[Bertel and Billaut, 2004] Bertel, S. and Billaut, J.-C. (2004). A genetic algorithm for an industrial multiprocessor flow shop scheduling problem with recirculation. *European Journal of Operational Research*, 159:651–662.

[Billaut et al., 2005] Billaut, J.-C., Moukrim, A., and Sanlaville, E., editors (2005). *Flexibilité et robustesse en ordonnancement (in french).* Hermès, Paris.

[Billaut and Roubellat, 1996] Billaut, J.-C. and Roubellat, F. (1996). A new method for workshop real time scheduling. *International Journal of Production Research*, 34(6):1555–1579.

[Billaut et al., 1998] Billaut, J.-C., T'kindt, V., Richard, P., and Proust, C. (1998). Three exact methods and an efficient heuristic for solving a bicriteria flowshop scheduling problem. In *Multiconference on Computational Engineering in Systems Applications (CESA'98), IMACS/IEEE*, pages 371–377, Nabeul-Hammamet, Tunisia.

[Blazewicz et al., 1986] Blazewicz, J., Cellary, W., Slowinsky, R., and Weglarz, J. (1986). *Scheduling under resource constraints: deterministic models.* Baltzer Science Publishers.

[Blazewicz et al., 1996] Blazewicz, J., Ecker, K. H., Pesch, E., Schmidt, G., and Weglarz, J. (1996). *Scheduling Computer and Manufacturing Processes.* Springer, Berlin.

[Boldur, 1982] Boldur, G. (1982). L'analyse multicritère en perspective d'une théorie générale de la gestion des entreprises modernes (in french). *R.A.I.R.O. Recherche Opérationnelle/ Operations Research*, 16(1):1–19.

[Bonney and Gundry, 1976] Bonney, M. C. and Gundry, S. W. (1976). Solutions to the constrained flow-shop sequencing problem. *Operations Research Quarterly*, 27:869–883.

[Bourgade et al., 1995] Bourgade, V., Aguilera, L. M., Penz, B., and Binder, Z. (1995). Problème industriel d'ordonnancement bicritère sur machine unique : modélisation et aide à la décision (in french). *R.A.I.R.O.-APII*, 29(3):331–341.

[Bowman, 1976] Bowman, V. J. (1976). *On the relationship of the Tchebycheff norm and the efficient frontier of multiple-criteria objectives*, pages 76–85. In [Thiriez and Zionts, 1976].

[Brah and Hunsucker, 1991] Brah, S. A. and Hunsucker, J. L. (1991). Branch and bound algorithm for the flow shop with multiple processors. *European Journal of Operational Research*, 51:88–99.

[Briand et al., 2005] Briand, C., La, H. T., and Erschler, J. (2005). A new sufficient condition of optimality for the two-machine flowshop problem. *European Journal of Operational Research*, 169(3):712–722.

[Brightwell and Winkler, 1991] Brightwell, G. and Winkler, P. (1991). Counting linear extensions. *Order*, 8:225–242.

[Brucker, 2004] Brucker, P. (2004). *Scheduling Algorithms.* Springer, Berlin.

[Brucker et al., 1999] Brucker, P., Drexl, A., Mohring, R., Neumann, K., and Pesch, E. (1999). Resource-constrainted project scheduling: Notation, classification, models and methods. *European Journal of Operational Research*, 112:3–41.

[Burns, 1976] Burns, R. N. (1976). Scheduling to minimize the weighted sum of completion times with secondary criteria. *Naval Research Logistics Quarterly*, 23(1):125–129.

[Campbell et al., 1970] Campbell, H. G., Dudek, R. A., and Smith, M. L. (1970). A heuristic algorithm for the n-job, m-machine sequencing problem. *Management Science*, 16:630–637.

[Carlier, 1982] Carlier, J. (1982). The one machine sequencing problem. *European Journal of Operational Research*, 11:42–47.

[Carlier and Chrétienne, 1988] Carlier, J. and Chrétienne, P. (1988). *Problèmes d'ordonnancement : modélisation /complexité / algorithmes (in french).* Masson, Paris.

[Carlier and Latapie, 1991] Carlier, J. and Latapie, B. (1991). Une méthode arborescente pour résoudre les problèmes cumulatifs (in french). *R.A.I.R.O. - Recherche Opérationnelle / Operations Research*, 25(3):311–340.

[Chand and Schneeberger, 1984] Chand, S. and Schneeberger, H. (1984). Single machine scheduling to minimize weighted completion time with maximum allowable tardiness. Technical report, University of Purdue, U.S.A.

[Chand and Schneeberger, 1986] Chand, S. and Schneeberger, H. (1986). A note on the single machine scheduling problem with minimum weighted completion time and maximum allowable tardiness. *Naval Research Logistics Quarterly*, 33(3):551–557.

[Chand and Schneeberger, 1988] Chand, S. and Schneeberger, H. (1988). Single machine scheduling to minimize weighted earliness subject to no tardy jobs. *European Journal of Operational Research*, 34(2):221–230.

[Chang et al., 2000] Chang, Y., Yeh, C., and Shen, C. (2000). A multiobjective model for passenger train services planning: application to taiwan's high-speed rail line. *Transportation Research Part B: Policy and Practice*, 34:91–106.

[Charnes and Cooper, 1961] Charnes, A. and Cooper, W. W. (1961). *Management Models and Industrial Applications of Linear Programming.* John Wiley & Sons, vols. I and II, New York.

[Charnes et al., 1955] Charnes, A., Cooper, W. W., and Ferguson, R. O. (1955). Optimal estimation of executive compensation by linear programming. *Management Science*, 1(2):138–151.

[Chen and Bulfin, 1990] Chen, C.-L. and Bulfin, R. L. (1990). Scheduling unit processing time jobs on a single machine with multiple criteria. *Computers and Operations Research*, 17(1):1–7.

[Chen and Bulfin, 1993] Chen, C.-L. and Bulfin, R. L. (1993). Complexity of single machine, multi-criteria scheduling problems. *European Journal of Operational Research*, 70:115–125.

[Chen and Bulfin, 1994] Chen, C.-L. and Bulfin, R. L. (1994). Complexity of multiple machines, multi-criteria scheduling problems. In *3rd Industrial Engineering Research Conference (IERC'94)*, pages 662–665, Atlanta, U.S.A.

[Chen, 1996] Chen, Z.-L. (1996). Scheduling and common due date assignment with earliness and tardiness penalties and batch delivery costs. *European Journal of Operational Research*, 93:49–60.

[Chen et al., 1997] Chen, Z.-L., Lu, W., and Tang, G. (1997). Single machine scheduling with discretely controllable processing times. *Operations Research Letters*, 21:69–76.

[Cheng, 1989] Cheng, T. C. E. (1989). A heuristic for common due-date assignment and job scheduling on parallel machines. *Journal of the Operational Research Society*, 40:1129–1135.

[Cheng and Chen, 1994] Cheng, T. C. E. and Chen, Z.-L. (1994). Parallel-machine scheduling problems with earliness and tardiness penalties. *Journal of the Operational Research Society*, 45(6):685–695.

[Cheng and Kahlbacher, 1992] Cheng, T. C. E. and Kahlbacher, H. G. (1992). The parallel-machine common due-date assignment and scheduling problem is NP-hard. *Asia-Pacific Journal of Operational Research*, 9:235–238.

[Cheng and Shakhlevich, 1999] Cheng, T. C. E. and Shakhlevich, N. (1999). Proportionate flow shop with controllable processing times. *Journal of Scheduling*, 2:253–265.

[Chou and Lee, 1999] Chou, F. D. and Lee, C. Y. (1999). Two-machine flowshop scheduling with bicriteria problem. *Computers and Industrial Engineering*, 36(3):549–564.

[Chrétienne and Sourd, 2003] Chrétienne, P. and Sourd, F. (2003). PERT scheduling with convex cost functions. *Theoretical Computer Science*, 292:145–164.

[Chu, 1992] Chu, C. (1992). A branch-and-bound algorithm to minimize total flow time with unequal release dates. *Naval Research Logistics*, 39:859–875.

[Climaco, 1997] Climaco, J., editor (1997). *Multicriteria Analysis*. Springer-Verlag, Berlin.

[Climaco et al., 1997] Climaco, J., Ferreira, C., and Captivo, E. (1997). *Multicriteria Integer Programming: an Overview of the Different Algorithmic Approaches*, pages 248–258. In [Climaco, 1997].

[Cochand et al., 1989] Cochand, M., de Werra, D., and Slowinski, R. (1989). Preemptive scheduling with staircase and piecewise linear resource availability. *Zeitschrift fur Operations Research*, 33:297–313.

[Coello Coello, 1999] Coello Coello, C. A. (1999). A comprehensive survey of evolutionary-based multiobjective optimization techniques. *Knowledge and Information Syst. An International Journal*, 1(3):269–308.

[Connolly, 1990] Connolly, D. T. (1990). An improved annealing scheme for the QAP. *European Journal of Operational Research*, 46:93–100.

[Conway et al., 1967] Conway, R. W., Maxwell, W. L., and Miller, L. W. (1967). Theory of scheduling. *Addison-Wesley*.

[Cook, 1971] Cook, S. A. (1971). The complexity of theorem-proving procedures. In *Third Annual ACM Symposium on Theory of Computing*, pages 151–158, ACM-press, New York.

[Cowling, 2003] Cowling, P. (2003). A flexible decision support system for steel hot rolling mill scheduling. *Computers & Industrial Engineering*, 45:307–321.

[Cvetkovic and Parmee, 1998] Cvetkovic, D. and Parmee, I. (1998). Evolutionary design and multi-objective optimisation. In *6th European Congress on Intelligent Techniques and Soft Computing (EUFIT'98)*, pages 397–401, Aachen, Germany.

[Czyzak and Jaszkiewicz, 1997] Czyzak, P. and Jaszkiewicz, A. (1997). *Pareto Simulated Annealing*, pages 297–307. In [Fandel and Gal, 1997].

[Daniels and Chambers, 1990] Daniels, R. L. and Chambers, R. J. (1990). Multiobjective flow-shop scheduling. *Naval Research Logistics*, 37:981–995.

[Davenport and Beck, 2000] Davenport, A. J. and Beck, J. C. (2000). A survey of techniques for scheduling with uncertainty. *unpublished (available on web at http://www.mie.utoronto.ca/staff/profiles/beck/publications.html).*

[Davis and Kanet, 1993] Davis, J. S. and Kanet, J. J. (1993). Single machine scheduling with early and tardy completion costs. *Naval Research Logistics*, 40:85–101.

[De et al., 1991] De, P., Ghosh, J. B., and Wells, C. E. (1991). Scheduling to minimize weighted earliness and tardiness about a common due date. *Computers and Operations Research*, 18(5):465–475.

[Deckro et al., 1982] Deckro, R. F., Herbert, J. E., and Winkofsky, E. P. (1982). Multiple criteria job-shop scheduling. *Computers and Operations Research*, 9(4):279–285.

[Della Croce et al., 1996] Della Croce, F., Narayan, V., and Tadei, R. (1996). The two-machine total completion time flow shop problem. *European Journal of Operational Research*, 90:227–237.

[Della Croce and T'kindt, 2002] Della Croce, F. and T'kindt, V. (2002). A recovering beam search algorithm for the one-machine dynamic total completion time scheduling problem. *Journal of the Operational Research Society*, 53(11):1275–1280.

[Della Croce and T'kindt, 2003] Della Croce, F. and T'kindt, V. (2003). Improving the preemptive bound for the one-machine dynamic total completion time scheduling problem. *Operations Research Letters*, 31:142–148.

[Demeulemeester and Herroelen, 2002] Demeulemeester, E. and Herroelen, W. (2002). *Project scheduling - A Research Handbook, Vol.49 of International Series in Operations Research and Management Science.* Kluwer Academic Publishers, Boston.

[Dileepan and Sen, 1988] Dileepan, P. and Sen, T. (1988). Bicriterion static scheduling research for a single machine. *Omega*, 16(1):53–59.

[Dileepan and Sen, 1991] Dileepan, P. and Sen, T. (1991). Bicriterion jobshop scheduling with total flowtime and sum of squared lateness. *Engineering Costs and Production Economic*, 21:295–299.

[Dorigo et al., 1999] Dorigo, M., Di Caro, G., and Gambardella, L. (1999). Ant algorithms for discrete optimization. *Artificial Life*, 5(3):137–172.

[Drozdowski et al., 2000] Drozdowski, M., Blazewicz, J., and Formanowicz, P. (2000). Scheduling preemptable tasks on uniform processors with limited availability for maximum lateness criterion. In *7th International Workshop on Project Management and Scheduling (PMS 2000)*, pages 118–120, Osnabruck, Germany.

[Dyer et al., 1992] Dyer, J. S., Fishburn, F. C., Steuer, R. E., and Wallenius, J. (1992). Multiple criteria decision making, multiattribute utility theory: the next ten years. *Management Science*, 38(5):645–654.

[Ehrgott, 1997] Ehrgott, M. (1997). *Multiple Criteria Optimization: Classification and Methodology.* PhD thesis, University of Kaiserslautern, Germany.

[Ehrgott, 2000a] Ehrgott, M. (2000a). Approximation algorithms for combinatorial multicriteria optimization problems. *International Transactions in Operations Research*, 7:5–31.

[Ehrgott, 2000b] Ehrgott, M. (2000b). *Multicriteria Optimization.* Lecture Notes in Economics and Mathematical Systems, Springer-Verlag.

[Ehrgott and Gandibleux, 2000] Ehrgott, M. and Gandibleux, X. (2000). A survey and annotated bibliography of multiobjective combinatorial optimization. *OR Spektrum*, 22:425–460.

[Eilon and Chowdhury, 1977] Eilon, S. and Chowdhury, I. E. (1977). Minimizing waiting time variance in the single machine problem. *Management Science*, 23:567–675.

[Emmons, 1975a] Emmons, H. (1975a). A note on a scheduling problem with dual criteria. *Naval Research Logistics Quarterly*, 22(4):615–616.

[Emmons, 1975b] Emmons, H. (1975b). One machine sequencing to minimize mean flow time with minimum number tardy. *Naval Research Logistics Quarterly*, 22(4):585–592.

[Emmons, 1987] Emmons, H. (1987). Scheduling to a common due date on parallel uniform processors. *Naval Research Logistics*, 34:803–810.

[Erschler et al., 1983] Erschler, J., Fontan, G., Merce, C., and Roubellat, F. (1983). A new dominance concept in scheduling n jobs on a single machine with ready times and due dates. *Operations research*, 31(1):114–127.

[Erschler and Roubellat, 1989] Erschler, J. and Roubellat, F. (1989). *An Approach for real time scheduling for activities with time and resource constraints.* In [Slowinski and Weglarz, 1989].

[Esswein et al., 2005] Esswein, C., Billaut, J.-C., and Strusevich, V. A. (2005). Two-machine shop scheduling: compromise between flexibility and makespan value. *European Journal of Operational Research*, 167:796–809.

[Esswein et al., 2001] Esswein, C., T'kindt, V., and Billaut, J.-C. (2001). A polynomial time algorithm for solving a single machine bicriteria scheduling problem. Technical report, Laboratory of Computer Science, University of Tours (France).

[Estève et al., 2004] Estève, B., Aubijoux, C., Chartier, A., and T'kindt, V. (2004). A recovering beam search algorithm for the single machine just-in-time scheduling problem. *European Journal of Operational Research*, 39:27.

[Evans, 1984] Evans, G. W. (1984). An overview of techniques for solving multiobjective mathematical programs. *Management Science*, 30(11):1268–1282.

[Fandel and Gal, 1997] Fandel, G. and Gal, T. (1997). *Multiple Criteria Decision Making.* Lecture Notes in Economics and Mathematical Systems, Springer-Verlag, Berlin.

[Fargier and Lamothe, 2001] Fargier, H. and Lamothe, J. (2001). Handling soft constraints in hoist scheduling problems: the fuzzy approach. *Engineering Application of Artificial Intelligence*, 14:387–399.

[Faure, 1979] Faure, R. (1979). *Précis de Recherche Opérationnelle (in french).* Dunod, Paris.

[Fischer and Thompson, 1963] Fischer, H. and Thompson, L. (1963). *Probabilistic learning Combinations of local job-shop scheduling rules.* Prentice Hall, Englewood Cliffs, New Jersey.

[Fisher, 1976] Fisher, M. L. (1976). A dual algorithm for the one-machine scheduling problem. *Mathematical Programming*, 11:458–481.

[Fortemps et al., 1996] Fortemps, P., Ost, C., Pirlot, M., Teghem, J., and Tuyttens, D. (1996). Using metaheuristics for solving a production scheduling problem in a chemical firm: a case study. *International Journal of Production Economics*, 46–47:13–26.

[Francis and White, 1974] Francis, R. L. and White, J. A. (1974). *Facility Layout and Location: An Analytical Approach.* Prentice-Hall.

[Fry et al., 1987a] Fry, T. D., Armstrong, R. D., and Blackstone, R. H. (1987a). Minimizing weighted absolute deviation in single machine scheduling. *IIE Transactions*, 19(4):445–450.

[Fry et al., 1996] Fry, T. D., Armstrong, R. D., Darby-Dowman, K., and Philipoom, P. R. (1996). A branch and bound procedure to minimize mean absolute lateness on a single processor. *Computers and Operations Research*, 23(2):171–182.

[Fry et al., 1989] Fry, T. D., Armstrong, R. D., and Lewis, H. (1989). A framework for single machine multiple objective sequencing research. *Omega*, 17(6):595–607.

[Fry and Blackstone, 1988] Fry, T. D. and Blackstone, R. H. (1988). Planning for idle time: a rationale for underutilization of capacity. *International Journal of Production Research*, 26(12):1853–1859.

[Fry and Leong, 1986] Fry, T. D. and Leong, G. K. (1986). Bi-criterion single-machine scheduling with forbidden early shipments. *Engineering Costs and Production Science*, 10(2):133–137.

[Fry and Leong, 1987] Fry, T. D. and Leong, G. K. (1987). A bi-criterion approach to minimizing inventory costs on a single machine when early shipments are forbidden. *Computers and Operations Research*, 14(5):363–368.

[Fry et al., 1987b] Fry, T. D., Leong, G. K., and Rakes, T. R. (1987b). Single machine scheduling: a comparison of two solution procedures. *Omega*, 15(4):277–282.

[Fukuda, 1996] Fukuda, K. (1996). *Note on new complexity clases $\mathcal{ENP}$, $\mathcal{EP}$ and $\mathcal{CEP}$ - an extension of the classes $\mathcal{NP}$, co $-$ $\mathcal{NP}$ and $\mathcal{P}$.* http://www.ifor.math.ethz.ch/staff/fukuda/ENP_home/ENP_note.html.

[Fukuda et al., 1997] Fukuda, K., Liebling, T., and Margot, F. (1997). Analysis of backtrack algorithms for listing all vertices and all faces of a convex polyhedron. *Computational Geometry*, 8:1–12.

[Gabrel and Vanderpooten, 2002] Gabrel, V. and Vanderpooten, D. (2002). Enumeration and interactive selection of efficient paths in a multiple criteria graph for scheduling an earth observing satellite. *European Journal of Operational Research*, 139:533–542.

[Gandibleux and Fréville, 1998] Gandibleux, X. and Fréville, A. (1998). Potential efficient solutions generated by MOTS procedure on the 0/1 bi-objective knapsack problem compared with exact solutions. In *Multiconference on Computational Engineering in Systems Applications (CESA'98), IEEE-SMC/IMACS*, pages 291–300, Hammamet, Tunisia.

[Gandibleux et al., 1997] Gandibleux, X., Mezdaoui, N., and Fréville, A. (1997). *A Tabu Search Procedure to Solve MultiObjective Combinatorial Optimization Problems*, pages 291–300. Lecture Notes in Economics and Mathematical Systems, Springer-Verlag, Berlin.

[Gangadharan and Rajendran, 1994] Gangadharan, R. and Rajendran, C. (1994). A simulated annealing heuristic for scheduling in a flowshop with bicriteria. *Computers and Industrial Engineering*, 27(1–4):473–476.

[Gardiner and Vanderpooten, 1997] Gardiner, L. R. and Vanderpooten, D. (1997). *Interactive Multiple Criteria Procedures: Some Reflections*, pages 290–301. In [Climaco, 1997].

[Garey and Johnson, 1979] Garey, M. R. and Johnson, D. S. (1979). *Computers and intractability: a guide to the theory of $\mathcal{NP}$-Completeness.* W.H. Freeman and Company.

[Garey et al., 1988] Garey, M. R., Tarjan, R. E., and Wilfong, G. T. (1988). One-processor scheduling with symmetric earliness and tardiness penalties. *Mathematics of Operations Research*, 13(2):330–348.

[Gembicki, 1973] Gembicki, F. (1973). *Vector Optimization for Control with Performance and Parameter Sensitivity Indices.* PhD thesis, Case Western Reserve University, Cleveland, U.S.A.

[Geoffrion, 1968] Geoffrion, A. M. (1968). Proper efficiency and the theory of vector maximization. *Journal of Mathematical Analysis and Applications*, 22:618–630.

[Geoffrion et al., 1972] Geoffrion, A. M., Dyer, J., and Feinberg, A. (1972). An interactive approach for multi-criterion optimization, with an application to the operation of an academic department. *Management Science*, 19(4):357–368.

[Giard, 1988] Giard, V. (1988). *Gestion de la production (in french)*. Economica, Paris, 2nd edition.

[Goldratt, 1997] Goldratt, E. (1997). *The Critical chain*. The North River Press Publishing Corporation, Great Barrington.

[Goldratt and Cox, 1984] Goldratt, E. M. and Cox, J. (1984). *The goal*. North River Press.

[Gonzalez and Sahni, 1976] Gonzalez, S. and Sahni, T. (1976). Open shop scheduling to minimize finish time. *Journal of the Association of Computation Machinery*, 23:665–679.

[Gordon et al., 2002a] Gordon, V., Proth, J.-M., and Chu, C. (2002a). Due date assignment and scheduling: SLK, TWK and other due date assignement models. *Production Planning and Control*, 13(2):157–177.

[Gordon et al., 2002b] Gordon, V., Proth, J.-M., and Chu, C. (2002b). A survey of the state-of-the-art of common due date assignment and scheduling research. *European Journal of Operational Research*, 139(1):1–25.

[Gordon et al., 2004] Gordon, V., Proth, J.-M., and Strusevich, V. (2004). Scheduling with due-date assignment. In [Leung, 2004], chapter 21.

[Gotha, 1993] Gotha (1993). Les problèmes d'ordonnancement (in french). *R.A.I.R.O Recherche Operationnelle / Operations Research*, 27(1):77–150.

[Graham et al., 1979] Graham, R. L., Lawler, E. L., Lenstra, J. K., and Rinnooy Kan, A. H. G. (1979). Optimization and approximation in deterministic sequencing and scheduling: a survey. *Annals of Discrete Mathematics*, 5:287–326.

[Guitouni and Martel, 1997] Guitouni, A. and Martel, J.-M. (1997). Tentative guidelines to help choosing an appropriate MCDA method. *European Journal of Operational Research*, 109(2):501–521.

[Gupta et al., 1999a] Gupta, J., Hariri, A., and Potts, C. (1999a). Single-machine scheduling to minimize maximum tardiness with minimum number of tardy jobs. *Annals of Operations Research*, 92:107–123.

[Gupta and Ramnarayanan, 1996] Gupta, J. and Ramnarayanan, R. (1996). Single facility scheduling with dual criteria: Minimizing maximum tardiness subjectto minimum number of tardy jobs. *Production Planning and Control*, 7:190–196.

[Gupta, 1972] Gupta, J. N. D. (1972). Optimal scheduling in a multistage flowshop. *AIIE Transactions*, 4:238–243.

[Gupta et al., 2002] Gupta, J. N. D., Hennig, K., and Werner, F. (2002). Local search heuristic for the two-stage flowshop problems with secondary criterion. *Computers and Operations Research*, 29(2):113–149.

[Gupta et al., 1997] Gupta, J. N. D., Ho, J. C., and VanderVeen, A. A. A. (1997). Single machine hierarchical scheduling with customer orders and multiple job classes. *Annals of Operations Research*, 70:127–143.

[Gupta et al., 2001] Gupta, J. N. D., Neppalli, V. R., and Werner, F. (2001). Minimizing total flow time in a two-machine flowshop problem with minimum makespan. *International Journal of Production Economics*, 69(3):323–338.

[Gupta et al., 1999b] Gupta, J. N. D., Palanimuthu, N., and Chen, C.-L. (1999b). Designing a tabu search algorithm for the two-stage flowshop problem with secondary criterion. *Production Planning and Control*, 10(3):251–265.

[Gupta and Werner, 1999] Gupta, J. N. D. and Werner, F. (1999). On the solution of 2-machine flow and open shop scheduling problems with secondary criteria. In *15th ISPE/IEE International Conference on CAD/CAM, Robotics, and Factories of the Future*, Aguas de Lindoia, Sao Paulo, Brasil.

[Gupta and Sen, 1983] Gupta, S. K. and Sen, T. (1983). Minimizing a quadratic function of job lateness on a single machine. *Engineering costs of Production Economic*, 7(3):187–194.

[Gupta and Sen, 1984] Gupta, S. K. and Sen, T. (1984). Minimizing the range of lateness on a single machine. *Journal of Operational Research Society*, 35:853–857.

[Haimes et al., 1971] Haimes, Y., Ladson, L., and Wismer, D. (1971). On a bicriterion formulation of the problems of integrated system identification and system optimization. *IEEE Transactions on Systems, Man and Cybernetics*, 1:296–297.

[Haimes et al., 1975] Haimes, Y. Y., Hall, W. A., and Freedman, H. T. (1975). *Multiobjective Optimization in Water Resource Systems*. Elsevier Scientific Publishing, Amsterdam.

[Hall, 1986] Hall, N. G. (1986). Single-and multiple-processor models for minimizing completion time variance. *Naval Research Logistics Quarterly*, 33:49–54.

[Hall and Posner, 1991] Hall, N. G. and Posner, M. E. (1991). Earliness-tardiness scheduling problems, I: Weighted deviation of completion times about a common due date. *Operations Research*, 39:836–846.

[Haouari and Fawzan, 2002] Haouari, M. and Fawzan, M. A. (2002). A bi-objective model for maximizing the quality in project scheduling. Technical Report 2002-14, DIMACS.

[Hapke et al., 1998] Hapke, M., Jaszkiewicz, A., and Slowinski, R. (1998). Interactive analysis of multiple-criteria project scheduling problems. *European Journal of Operational Research*, 107:315–324.

[Heck and Roberts, 1972] Heck, H. and Roberts, S. (1972). A note on the extension of a result on scheduling with secondary criteria. *Naval Research Logistics Quarterly*, 19:59–66.

[Herroelen et al., 1998a] Herroelen, W., De Reyck, B., and Demeulemeester, E. (1998a). Resource-constrained project scheduling: a survey. *Computers and Operations Research*, 25(4):279–302.

[Herroelen et al., 1998b] Herroelen, W., Demeulemeester, E., and De Reyck, B. (1998b). *A classification scheme for project scheduling*. Kluwer Academic, Dordrecht, Germany.

[Herroelen et al., 2001] Herroelen, W., Demeulemeester, E., and De Reyck, B. (2001). A note on the paper "resource-constrainted project scheduling: notation, classification, models and methods" by brucker et al. *European Journal of Operational Research*, 128:679–688.

[Herroelen and Leus, 2004] Herroelen, W. and Leus, R. (2004). Robust and reactive project scheduling: a review and classification of procedures. *International Journal of Production Research*, 42(8):1599–1620.

[Herroelen and Leus, 2005] Herroelen, W. and Leus, R. (2005). Project scheduling under uncertainty: survey and research potentials. *European Journal of Operational Research*, 165(2):289–306.

[Ho and Chang, 1991] Ho, J. C. and Chang, Y.-L. (1991). A new heuristic for the n-job, m-machine flowshop problem. *European Journal of Operational Research*, 52:194–202.

[Ho and Chang, 1995] Ho, J. C. and Chang, Y.-L. (1995). Minimizing the number of tardy jobs for m parallel machines. *European Journal of Operational Research*, 84:343–355.

[Hoogeveen, 2005] Hoogeveen, H. (2005). Multicriteria scheduling. *European Journal of Operational Research*, 167:592–623.

[Hoogeveen and van de Velde, 2001] Hoogeveen, H. and van de Velde, S. (2001). Scheduling with target start times. *European Journal of Operational Research*, 129:87–94.

[Hoogeveen, 1992a] Hoogeveen, J. A. (1992a). *Single-Machine Bicriteria Scheduling*. PhD thesis, CWI, Amsterdam, The Netherlands.

[Hoogeveen, 1992b] Hoogeveen, J. A. (1992b). *Single machine scheduling to minimize a function of K maximum cost criteria*, pages 67–77. In [Hoogeveen, 1992a].

[Hoogeveen, 1996] Hoogeveen, J. A. (1996). Minimizing maximum promptness and maximum lateness on a single machine. *Mathematics of Operations Research*, 21(1):100–114.

[Hoogeveen and VandeVelde, 1995] Hoogeveen, J. A. and VandeVelde, S. L. (1995). Minimizing total completion time and maximum cost simultaneously is solvable in polynomial time. *Operations Research Letters*, 17:205–208.

[Hopcroft and Ullman, 1979] Hopcroft, J. E. and Ullman, J. D. (1979). *Introduction to automata theory, languages and computation.* Addison-Wesley.

[Horn, 1974] Horn, W. A. (1974). Some simple scheduling algorithms. *Naval Research Logistics Quarterly*, 21:177–185.

[Huckert et al., 1980] Huckert, K., Rhode, R., Roglin, O., and Weber, R. (1980). On the interactive solution to a multicriteria scheduling problem. *Zeitchrift fur Operations Research*, 24:47–60.

[Icmeli-Tukel and Rom, 1997] Icmeli-Tukel, O. and Rom, W. O. (1997). Ensuring quality in resource constrained project scheduling. *European Journal of Operational Research*, 103(3):483–496.

[Ignall and Schrage, 1965] Ignall, E. and Schrage, L. (1965). Application of the branch-and-bound technique to some flowshop problems. *Operations Research*, 13:400–412.

[Jacquet-Lagrèze et al., 1987] Jacquet-Lagrèze, E., Meziani, R., and Slowinski, R. (1987). MOLP with an interactive assessment of a piecewise utility function. *European Journal of Operational Research*, 31(3):350–357.

[James and Buchanan, 1997] James, R. J. W. and Buchanan, J. T. (1997). A neighbourhood scheme with a compressed solution space for the early/tardy scheduling problem. *European Journal of Operational Research*, 102:513–527.

[James and Buchanan, 1998] James, R. J. W. and Buchanan, J. T. (1998). Performance enhancements to tabu search for the early/tardy scheduling problem. *European Journal of Operational Research*, 106:254–265.

[Jaszkiewicz and Slowinski, 1997] Jaszkiewicz, A. and Slowinski, R. (1997). *Outranking-Driven Search Over a Nondominated Set*, pages 340–349. In [Fandel and Gal, 1997].

[Jensen and Hansen, 1999] Jensen, M. T. and Hansen, T. K. (1999). Robust solutions to job shop problems. In *Proceedings of the Congress of Evolutionary Computation, vol.2*, pages 1138–1144, Washington, U.S.A.

[John, 1984] John, T. C. (1984). Tradeoff solutions in single machine production scheduling for minimizing flow time and maximum penalty. *Computers and Operations Research*, 16(5):471–479.

[Johnson et al., 1988] Johnson, D., Yannakakis, M., and Papadimitriou, C. (1988). On generating all maximal independent sets. *Information Processing Letters*, 27:119–123.

[Johnson, 1954] Johnson, S. M. (1954). Optimal two and three stage production schedules with set-up time included. *Naval Research Logistics Quarterly*, 1:61–68.

[Jolai Ghazvini, 1998] Jolai Ghazvini, F. (1998). *Ordonnancement sous contrainte de groupage (in french)*. PhD thesis, Leibniz-Imag/INPG, Grenoble, France.

[Jozefowska et al., 1994] Jozefowska, J., Jurisch, B., and Kubiak, W. (1994). Scheduling shops to minimize the weighted number of late jobs. *Operations Research Letters*, 10:27–33.

[Kaliszewski, 2000] Kaliszewski, I. (2000). Using trade-off information in decision-making algorithms. *Computers and Operations Research*, 27:161–182.

[Kaminsky and Hochbaum, 2004] Kaminsky, P. and Hochbaum, D. (2004). Due-date quotation models and algorithms. In [Leung, 2004], chapter 20.

[Kanet, 1981a] Kanet, J. J. (1981a). Minimizing the average deviation of job completion times about a common due date. *Naval Research Logistics Quarterly*, 28(4):643–651.

[Kanet, 1981b] Kanet, J. J. (1981b). Minimizing variation of flow time in single machine systems. *Management Science*, 27(12):1453–1459.

[Karabati and Kouvelis, 1993] Karabati, S. and Kouvelis, P. (1993). The permutation flow shop problem with sum-of-completion times performance criterion. *Naval Research Logistics*, 40:843–862.

[Kawata et al., 2003] Kawata, Y., Morikawa, K., Takahashi, K., and Nakamura, N. (2003). Robustness optimisation of the minimum makespan schedules in a job shop. *Int. J. Manufacturing Technology and Management*, 5(1-2):1–9.

[Kim and Yano, 1994] Kim, Y.-D. and Yano, C. A. (1994). Minimizing mean tardiness and earliness in single-machine scheduling problems with unequal due dates. *Naval Research Logistics*, 41:913–933.

[Kiran and Unal, 1991] Kiran, A. and Unal, A. (1991). A single-machine problem with multiple criteria. *Naval Research Logistics*, 38:721–727.

[Klein and Hannan, 1982] Klein, D. and Hannan, E. (1982). An algorithm for the multiple objective integer linear programming problem. *European Journal of Operational Research*, (9):378–385.

[Kolisch and Padman, 2001] Kolisch, R. and Padman, R. (2001). An integrated survey of deterministic project scheduling. *Omega*, 29:249–272.

[Kondakci et al., 1997] Kondakci, S. K., Emre, E., and Koksalan, M. (1997). *Scheduling of Unit Processing Time Jobs on a Single Machine*, pages 654–660. In [Fandel and Gal, 1997].

[Korhonen and Laakso, 1986] Korhonen, P. and Laakso, J. (1986). A visual interactive method for solving the multicriteria problem. *European Journal of Operational Research*, 24(2):277–287.

[Koulamas, 1996] Koulamas, C. (1996). Single-machine scheduling with time windows and earliness/tardiness penalties. *European Journal of Operational Research*, 91:190–202.

[Kubiak, 1993] Kubiak, W. (1993). Completion time variance minimization on a single machine is difficult. *Operations Research Letters*, 14:49–59.

[Kyparisis and Koulamas, 2000] Kyparisis, G. J. and Koulamas, C. (2000). Open shop scheduling with makespan and total completion time criteria. *Computers and Operations Research*, 27:15–27.

[La, 2005] La, H. T. (2005). *Utilisation d'ordres partiels pour la caractérisation de solutions robustes en ordonnancement (in french)*. Phd thesis, LAAS-CNRS, Toulouse.

[Lakshminarayan et al., 1978] Lakshminarayan, S., Lakshmanan, R., Papineau, R. L., and Rochette, R. (1978). Optimal single-machine scheduling with earliness and tardiness penalties. *Operations Research*, 26(6):1079–1082.

[Lawler, 1973] Lawler, E. L. (1973). Optimal sequencing of a single machine subject to precedence constraints. *Management Science*, 19:544–546.

[Lawler and Labetoulle, 1978] Lawler, E. L. and Labetoulle, J. (1978). On preemptive scheduling of unrelated parallel processors by linear programming. *Journal of the Association of Computation Machinery*, 25(4):612–619.

[Lawler et al., 1989] Lawler, E. L., Lenstra, J. K., Rinnooy Kan, A. H. G., and Shmoys, D. B. (1989). Sequencing and scheduling: algorithms and complexity. Technical Report NFI 11.89/03, Eindhoven University of Technology, Eindhoven, The Netherlands.

[Lawler et al., 1975] Lawler, E. L., Rinnooy Kan, A. H. G., and Lageweg, B. (1975). Minimizing total costs in one-machine scheduling. *Operations Research*, 23:908–927.

[Lawrence, 1984] Lawrence, S. (1984). Resource constrained project scheduling: an experimental investigation of heuristic scheduling techniques (supplement). Technical Report (http://mscmga.ms.ic.ac.uk/info.html), Graduate School of Industrial Administration, Carnegie-Mellon University, Pittsburgh, Pennsylvania.

[Lee et al., 1997] Lee, C. Y., Lei, L., and Pinedo, M. (1997). Current trends in deterministic scheduling. *Annals of Operations Research*, 70:1–41.

[Lee and Vairaktarakis, 1996] Lee, C. Y. and Vairaktarakis, G. L. (1996). *Complexity of single machine hierarchical scheduling: A survey*, pages 269–298. World Scientific Publishing Co., Singapore.

[Lenstra et al., 1977] Lenstra, J.-K., Rinnooy Kan, A., and Brucker, P. (1977). Complexity of machine scheduling problems. *Annals of Discrete Mathematics*, 1:343–362.

[Leon et al., 1994] Leon, V. J., Wu, S. D., and Storer, R. H. (1994). Robustness measures and robust scheduling for job shops. *IIE Transactions*, 26(5):32–43.

[Leung, 2004] Leung, J.-T., editor (2004). *Handbook of Scheduling: Algorithms, Models and Performance Analysis*. Chapman & Hall/CRC Computer and Information Science serie, Volume 1.

[Leung and Young, 1989] Leung, J. Y. T. and Young, G. H. (1989). Minimizing schedule length subject to minimum flow time. *SIAM Journal on Computing*, 18(2):314–326.

[Lévine and Pomerol, 1986] Lévine, P. and Pomerol, J.-C. (1986). Priam, an interactive program for chosing among multiple attribute alternatives. *European Journal of Operational Research*, 25(2):272–280.

[Li and Cheng, 1994] Li, C. L. and Cheng, T. C. E. (1994). The parallel machine min-max weighted absolute lateness scheduling problem. *Naval Research Logistics*, 41:33–46.

[Li, 1997] Li, G. (1997). Single machine earliness and tardiness scheduling. *European Journal of Operational Research*, 96:546–558.

[Liao and Huang, 1991] Liao, C. J. and Huang, R. H. (1991). An algorithm for minimizing the range of lateness on a single machine. *Journal of the Operational Research Society*, 42(2):183–186.

[Liao et al., 1997] Liao, C. J., Yu, W. C., and Joe, C. B. (1997). Bicriterion scheduling in the two-machine flowshop. *Journal of the Operational Research Society*, 48:929–935.

[Liaw, 1999] Liaw, C. F. (1999). A branch-and-bound algorithm for the single machine earliness and tardiness scheduling problem. *Computers and Operations Research*, 26:679–693.

[Lin, 1983] Lin, K. S. (1983). Hybrid algorithm for sequencing with bicriteria. *Journal of Optimization Theory and Applications*, 39(1):105–124.

[Liu and MacCarthy, 1996] Liu, J. L. and MacCarthy, B. L. (1996). The classification of FMS scheduling problems. *International Journal of Production Research*, 34(3):647–656.

[Lofti et al., 1992] Lofti, V., Stewart, T., and Zionts, S. (1992). An aspiration-level interactive model for multiple criteria decision making. *Computers and Operations Research*, 19(7):671–681.

[Lofti and Zionts, 1990] Lofti, V. and Zionts, S. (1990). AIM, aspiration-level interactive method for multiple criteria decision making; user's guide. Technical report, University of New York, Buffalo, U.S.A.

[Lucic and Teodorovic, 1999] Lucic, P. and Teodorovic, D. (1999). Simulated annealing for the multi-objective aircrew rostering problem. *Transportation Research Part A: Policy and Practice*, 33(1):19–45.

[Mac Carthy and Liu, 1993] Mac Carthy, B. L. and Liu, J. L. (1993). Adressing the gap in scheduling research: a review of optimization and heuristic methods in production scheduling. *International Journal of Production Research*, 31(1):59–79.

[Martello and Toth, 1990] Martello, S. and Toth, P. (1990). *Knapsack Problems: Algorithm and Computer Implementations.* John Wiley & Sons, Chichester, England.

[Mazzini and Armentano, 2001] Mazzini, R. and Armentano, V. A. (2001). A heuristic for single machine scheduling with early and tardy costs. *European Journal of Operational Research*, 128:129–146.

[Mc Cormick and Pinedo, 1995] Mc Cormick, S. T. and Pinedo, M. L. (1995). Scheduling n independant jobs on m uniform machines with both flowtime and makespan objectives: a parametric analysis. *ORSA Journal on Computing*, 7(1):63–77.

[McKay et al., 1998] McKay, K. N., Safayeni, F. R., and Buzacott, J. A. (1998). Job-shop scheduling theory: what is relevant? *Interfaces*, 18(4):84–90.

[McNaughton, 1959] McNaughton, R. (1959). Scheduling with deadlines and loss functions. *Management Science*, 6:1–12.

[Mercé, 1987] Mercé, C. (1987). *Cohérence des décisions en planification hiérarchisée (in french).* PhD thesis, University Paul Sabatier, Toulouse, France.

[Merten and Muller, 1972] Merten, A. and Muller, M. (1972). Variance minimization in single machine sequencing problems. *Management Science*, 18(5):18–28.

[Miettinen, 1994] Miettinen, K. (1994). *On the Methodology of Multiobjective Optimization with Applications.* PhD thesis, University of Jyvaskyla, Department of Mathematics, Jyvaskyla, Finland.

[Miettinen, 1999] Miettinen, K. (1999). Comparative evaluation of some interactive reference point-based methods for multi-objective optimisation. *Journal of the Operational Research Society*, 50:949–959.

[Miyazaki, 1981] Miyazaki, S. (1981). One machine scheduling problem with dual criteria. *Journal of the Operational Research Society of Japan*, 24(1):37–50.

[Mohri et al., 1999] Mohri, S., Masuda, T., and Ishii, H. (1999). Bi-criteria scheduling problem on three identical parallel machines. *International Journal of Production Economics*, 60–61:529–536.

[Monden, 1998] Monden, Y. (1998). *Toyota Production System*. Engineering and Management Press, Norcross, GA.

[Moore, 1968] Moore, J. M. (1968). An n job, one machine sequencing algorithm for minimizing the number of late jobs. *Management Science*, 15(1):102–109.

[Morton and Pentico, 1993] Morton, T. and Pentico, D. (1993). *Heuristic scheduling systems*. John Wiley Interscience, New York.

[Mustafa and Goh, 1996] Mustafa, A. and Goh, M. (1996). Multicriterion models for higher education administration. *Omega*, 24(2):167–178.

[Nagar et al., 1995a] Nagar, A., Haddock, J., and Heragu, S. S. (1995a). Multiple and bicriteria scheduling: a literature survey. *European Journal of Operational Research*, 81:88–104.

[Nagar et al., 1995b] Nagar, A., Heragu, S. S., and Haddock, J. (1995b). A branch-and-bound approach for a two-machine flowshop scheduling problem. *Journal of the Operational Research Society*, 46:721–734.

[Nawaz et al., 1983] Nawaz, M., Enscore, E., and Ham, I. (1983). A heuristic algorithm for the m-machine, n-job flow-shop sequencing problem. *Management Science*, 11:91–95.

[Nelson et al., 1986] Nelson, R. T., Sarin, R. K., and Daniels, R. L. (1986). Scheduling with multiple performance measures: the one-machine case. *Management Science*, 32(4):464–479.

[Neppalli et al., 1996] Neppalli, V. R., Chen, C. L., and Gupta, J. N. D. (1996). Genetic algorithms for the two-stage bicriteria flowshop problem. *European Journal of Operational Research*, 95:356–373.

[Nollet et al., 1994] Nollet, J., Kélada, J., and Diorio, M. (1994). *La gestion des opérations et de la production*. Gatan Morin.

[Nowicki, 1993] Nowicki, E. (1993). An approximation algorithm for the m-machine permutation flow shop scheduling problem with controllable processing times. *European Journal of Operational Research*, 70:342–349.

[Nowicki and Zdrzalka, 1988] Nowicki, E. and Zdrzalka, S. (1988). Two-machine flow shop scheduling problem with controllable processing times. *European Journal of Operational Research*, 34:208–220.

[Nowicki and Zdrzalka, 1990] Nowicki, E. and Zdrzalka, S. (1990). A survey of results for sequencing problems with controllable processing times. *Discrete Applied Mathematics*, 26:271–287.

[Ogbu and Smith, 1990] Ogbu, F. A. and Smith, D. K. (1990). The application of simulated annealing algorithm to the solutions of the $n/m/Cmax$ flowshop problem. *Computers and Operations Research*, 17(3):243–253.

[Ogryczak, 1994] Ogryczak, W. (1994). A goal programming model of the reference point method. *Annals of Operation Research*, 51:33–44.

[Ogryczak, 1997] Ogryczak, W. (1997). *Preemptive Reference Point Method*, pages 156–167. In [Climaco, 1997].

[Olson et al., 1997] Olson, D. L., Mechitov, A., and Morshkovich, H. (1997). Comparison of MCDM paradigms. In *International Conference on Methods and Applications on Multicriteria Decision Making (MAMDM'97)*, pages 323–326, Fucam, Mons, Belgique.

[Oulamara, 2001] Oulamara, A. (2001). *Flowshops avec déterioration des tâches et groupement des tâches (in french).* PhD thesis, University Joseph Fournier of Grenoble (France).

[Ow and Morton, 1988] Ow, P. S. and Morton, T. E. (1988). Filtered beam search in scheduling. *International Journal of Production Research*, 26(1):35–62.

[Ow and Morton, 1989] Ow, P. S. and Morton, T. E. (1989). The single machine early/tardy problem. *Management Science*, 35(2):177–190.

[Page, 1961] Page, E. S. (1961). An approach to scheduling jobs on machines. *Journal of Royal Statistical Society*, B-23:484–492.

[Panwalker and Rajagopalan, 1982] Panwalker, S. S. and Rajagopalan, R. (1982). A single machine sequencing problem with controllable processing times. *European Journal of Operational Research*, 59:298–302.

[Panwalker et al., 1982] Panwalker, S. S., Smith, M. L., and Seidmann, A. (1982). Common due date assignment to minimize total penalty for the one machine scheduling problem. *Operations Research*, 30(2):391–399.

[Papadimitriou, 1995] Papadimitriou, C. H. (1995). *Computational Complexity.* Addison Wesley.

[Pinedo, 1995] Pinedo, M. (1995). *Scheduling - Theory, Algorithms, and Systems.* Prentice Hall, Englewood Cliffs.

[Pinedo and Chao, 1999] Pinedo, M. and Chao, X. (1999). *Operations Scheduling with applications in manufacturing and services.* Mc Graw Hill, Boston.

[Policella, 2005a] Policella, N. (2005a). *Scheduling with uncertainty. A proactive approach using partial order schedules.* Phd thesis, University of Rome, La Sapienza, Italy.

[Policella, 2005b] Policella, N. (2005b). Scheduling with uncertainty: a proactive approach using partial order schedules. *AI Communications*, 18:165–167.

[Policella et al., 2004] Policella, N., Oddi, A., Smith, S. F., and Cesta, A. (2004). Generating robust partial order schedules. In *Lecture Notes in Computer Science (LNCS), 3258*, pages 496–511.

[Portmann et al., 1996] Portmann, M. C., Vignier, A., Dardilhac, D., and Dezalay, D. (1996). Some hybrid flowshop scheduling by crossing branch and bound and genetic algorithms. In *5th International Workshop on Project Management and Scheduling (PMS'96), EURO*, pages 186–189, Poznan, Poland.

[Portmann et al., 1998] Portmann, M. C., Vignier, A., Dardilhac, D., and Dezalay, D. (1998). Some hybrid flowshop scheduling by crossing branch and bound and genetic algorithms. *European Journal of Operational Research*, 107:389–400.

[Potts and Kovalyov, 2000] Potts, C. and Kovalyov, M. (2000). Scheduling with batching: A review. *European Journal of Operational Research*, 120(2):228–249.

[Proust, 1992] Proust, C. (1992). Using Johnson's algorithm for solving flowshop scheduling problems. In *Summer school on scheduling theory and its applications, INRIA/C3/COMETT*, pages 297–342, Bonas, France. Invited talk.

[Ragatz and Mabert, 1984] Ragatz, G. L. and Mabert, V. A. (1984). A framework for the study of due date management in job shops. *International Journal of Production Research*, 22(4):685–695.

[Rajendran, 1992] Rajendran, C. (1992). Two-stage flowshop scheduling problem with bicriteria. *Journal of the Operational Research Society*, 43(9):871–884.

[Rajendran, 1994] Rajendran, C. (1994). A heuristic for scheduling in flowshop and flowline-based manufacturing cell with multi-criteria. *International Journal of Production Research*, 32(11):2541–2558.

[Rajendran, 1995] Rajendran, C. (1995). Heuristics for scheduling in flowshop with multiple objectives. *European Journal of Operational Research*, 82:540–555.

[Rajendran and Chaudhuri, 1991] Rajendran, C. and Chaudhuri, D. (1991). A flowshop scheduling algorithm to minimize total flowtime. *Journal of the Operational Research Society of Japan*, 34:28–46.

[Riane et al., 1997] Riane, F., Meskens, N., and Artiba, A. (1997). Bicriteria scheduling hybrid flowshop problems. In *International Conference on Industrial Engineering and Production Management (IEPM'97), Fucam*, pages 34–43, Lyon, France.

[Rinnooy Kan, 1976] Rinnooy Kan, A. H. G. (1976). *Machine Scheduling Problems: Classification, complexity and computations*. PhD thesis, Nihoff, La Hague, The Netherlands.

[Roy, 1976] Roy, B. (1976). From optimization to multicriteria decision aid: three main operational attitudes. In [Thiriez and Zionts, 1976], pages 130–132.

[Roy, 1985] Roy, B. (1985). *Méthodologie multicritère d'aide à la décision (in french)*. Economica, Paris.

[Roy, 1990] Roy, B. (1990). Decision aid and decision making. *European Journal of Operational Research*, 45:324–331.

[Roy and Bouyssou, 1993] Roy, B. and Bouyssou, D. (1993). *Aide multicritère à la décision: méthodes et cas (in french)*. Economica, Paris.

[Ruiz-Torres et al., 1997] Ruiz-Torres, A. J., Enscore, E. E., and Barton, R. R. (1997). Simulated annealing heuristics for the average flow-time and the number of tardy jobs bi-criteria identical parallel machine problem. *Computers and Industrial Engineering*, 33(1–2):257–260.

[Saaty, 1986] Saaty, T. L. (1986). Axiomatic foundation of the analytic hierarchy process. *Management Science*, 32(7):841–855.

[Sahni, 1979] Sahni, S. (1979). Preemptive scheduling with due dates. *Operations Research*, 27:925–934.

[Sanlaville, 1992] Sanlaville, E. (1992). *Conception et analyse d'algorithmes de liste en ordonnancement préemptif (in french)*. PhD thesis, University of Paris VI, Paris, France.

[Sarin and Hariharan, 2000] Sarin, S. C. and Hariharan, R. (2000). A two machine bicriteria scheduling problem. *International Journal of Production Economics*, 65:125–139.

[Sayin and Karabati, 1999] Sayin, S. and Karabati, S. (1999). A bicriteria approach to the two-machine flow shop scheduling problem. *European Journal of Operational Research*, 113:435–449.

[Schonberger, 1982] Schonberger, J. (1982). *Japanese manufacturing techniques: Nine hidden lessons in simplicity*. The Free Press (New York).

[Schwartz, 1967] Schwartz, L. (1967). *Cours d'Analyse (in french)*. Hermann.

[Seidmann et al., 1981] Seidmann, A., Panwalker, S. S., and Smith, M. L. (1981). Optimal assignment of due-dates for a single processor scheduling problem. *International Journal of Production Research*, 19(4):393–399.

[Selen and Hott, 1986] Selen, W. J. and Hott, D. D. (1986). A mixed integer goal-programming formulation of a flowshop scheduling problem. *Journal of the Operational Research Society*, 37:1121–1128.

[Sen et al., 1989] Sen, T., Dileepan, P., and Gupta, J. N. D. (1989). The two-machine flowshop scheduling problem with total tardiness. *Computers and Operations Research*, 16:333–340.

[Sen and Gupta, 1983] Sen, T. and Gupta, S. K. (1983). A branch-and-bound procedure to solve a bicriterion scheduling problem. *IIE Transactions*, 15(1):84–88.

[Sen et al., 1988] Sen, T., Raiszadeh, F. M. E., and Dileepan, P. (1988). A branch-and-bound approach to the bicriterion scheduling problem involving total flowtime and range of lateness. *Management Science*, 34(2):255–260.

[Serafini, 1987] Serafini, P. (1987). Some considerations about computational complexity for multi objective combinatorial problems. *Lecture Notes in Economics and Mathematical Systems*, 294:222–232.

[Serifoglu and Ulusoy, 1998] Serifoglu, F. S. and Ulusoy, G. (1998). A bicriteria two-machine permutation flowshop problem. *European Journal of Operational Research*, 107:414–430.

[Sevaux and Sorensen, 2004] Sevaux, M. and Sorensen, K. (2004). A genetic algorithm for robust schedules in a one-machine environment with ready times and due dates. *4OR*, 2(2):129–147.

[Shantikumar, 1983] Shantikumar, J. G. (1983). Scheduling n jobs on one machine to minimize the maxium tardiness with minimum number tardy. *Computers and Operations Research*, 10(3):255–266.

[Sidney, 1977] Sidney, J. B. (1977). Optimal single-machine scheduling with earliness and tardiness penalties. *Operations Research*, 25(1):62–69.

[Simon, 1977] Simon, J. (1977). On the difference between the one and the many. *Proceedings ICALP 1977, Lecture Notes in Computer Sciences*, 52:480–491.

[Sivrikaya-Serifoglu and Ulusoy, 1998] Sivrikaya-Serifoglu, F. S. and Ulusoy, G. (1998). A bicriteria two machine permutation flowshop problem. *European Journal of Operational Research*, 107:414–430.

[Slowinski and Weglarz, 1989] Slowinski, R. and Weglarz, J., editors (1989). *Advances in project scheduling.* Elsevier, Amsterdam.

[Smith, 1956] Smith, W. E. (1956). Various optimizers for single-stage production. *Naval Research Logistics Quarterly*, 3(1):59–66.

[Soland, 1979] Soland, R. M. (1979). Multicriteria optimization: a general characterization of efficient solutions. *Decision Sciences*, 10:27–38.

[Sourd, 2005] Sourd, F. (2005). Optimal timing of a sequence of tasks with general completion costs. *European Journal of Operational Research*, 165:82–96.

[Steuer, 1977] Steuer, R. (1977). An interactive multiple objective linear programming procedure. *TIMS Studies in the Management Science*, 6:225–239.

[Steuer, 1986] Steuer, R. (1986). *Multiple criteria optimization: theory, computation and application.* John Wiley, New York, U.S.A.

[Steuer and Choo, 1983] Steuer, R. and Choo, E. (1983). An interactive weighted Tchebycheff procedure for multiple objective programming. *Mathematical Programming*, 26:326–344.

[Steuer and Wood, 1986] Steuer, R. and Wood, E. F. (1986). A multiple objective Markov reservoir release policy model. Technical report, University of Georgia Athens, U.S.A.

[Stuztle, 1998] Stuztle, T. (1998). An ant approach to the flow shop problem. *Proceedings of EUFIT'98, Aachen (Germany)*, pages 1560–1564.

[Sundararaghavan and Ahmed, 1984] Sundararaghavan, P. S. and Ahmed, M. U. (1984). Minimizing the sum of absolute lateness in single-machine and multimachine scheduling. *Naval Research Logistics Quarterly*, 31(2):325–333.

[Szwarc, 1989] Szwarc, W. (1989). Single-machine scheduling to minimize absolute deviation of completion times from a common due date. *Naval Research Logistics*, 36:663–673.

[Szwarc, 1993] Szwarc, W. (1993). Adjacent orderings in single machine scheduling with earliness and tardiness penalties. *Naval Research Logistics*, 40:229–243.

[Szwarc and Mukhopadhyay, 1995] Szwarc, W. and Mukhopadhyay, S. K. (1995). Optimal timing schedules in earliness-tardiness single machine sequencing. *Naval Research Logistics*, 42:1109–1114.

[Tamiz et al., 1999] Tamiz, M., Mirrazavi, S. K., and Jones, D. F. (1999). Extensions of pareto efficiency analysis to integer goal programming. *Omega*, 27:179–188.

[Tanaev et al., 1994a] Tanaev, V., Gordon, V., and Shafransky, Y. (1994a). *Scheduling Theory. Single-Stage Systems.* The Netherlands, kluwer edition.

[Tanaev et al., 1994b] Tanaev, V. S., Sotskov, Y. N., and Strusevich, V. A. (1994b). *Scheduling Theory. Multi-Stage Systems.* Kluwer, The Netherlands.

[Tavares, 2002] Tavares, L. (2002). A review of the contribution of operational research to project management. *European Journal of Operational Research*, 136:1–18.

[Teghem, 1996] Teghem, J. (1996). *Programmation linéaire (in french).* collection SMA, Ellipses, University of Bruxelles, Belgique.

[Tegze and Vlach, 1988] Tegze, M. and Vlach, M. (1988). Improved bounds for the range of lateness on a single machine. *Journal of Operational Research Society*, 39:675–680.

[Thiriez and Zionts, 1976] Thiriez, H. and Zionts, S., editors (1976). *Multiple Criteria Decision Making.* Springer, Berlin.

[T'kindt et al., 2001] T'kindt, V., Billaut, J.-C., and Proust, C. (2001). Solving a bicriteria scheduling problem on unrelated parallel machines occurring in the glass bottle industry. *European Journal of Operational Research*, 135(1):42–49.

[T'kindt et al., 2005] T'kindt, V., Bouibede-Hocine, K., and Esswein, C. (2005). Counting and enumeration complexity with application to multicriteria scheduling. *4'OR*, 3(1):1–21.

[T'kindt et al., 2003] T'kindt, V., Gupta, J. N. D., and Billaut, J.-C. (2003). Two-machine flowshop scheduling problem with a secondary criterion. *Computers and Operations Research*, 30(4):505–526.

[T'kindt et al., 2002] T'kindt, V., Monmarché, N., Tercinet, F., and Laugt, D. (2002). An ant colony optimization algorithm to solve a 2-machine bicriteria flowshop scheduling problem. *European Journal of Operational Research*, 142(2):250–257.

[Tuyttens et al., 1999] Tuyttens, D., Teghem, J., Fortemps, P., and Van Nieuwenhuyse, K. (1999). Performance of the MOSA method for the bicriteria assignment problem. *Journal of Heuristics*, pages 295–310.

[Tuzikov et al., 1998] Tuzikov, A., Makhaniok, M., and Manner, R. (1998). Bicriterion scheduling of identical processing time jobs by uniform processors. *Computers and Operations Research*, 25(1):31–35.

[Ulungu and Teghem, 1994] Ulungu, E. L. and Teghem, J. (1994). Multi-objective combinatorial optimization problems: A survey. *Journal of Multi-Criteria Decision Analysis*, 3:83–104.

[Ulungu and Teghem, 1995] Ulungu, E. L. and Teghem, J. (1995). The two phases method: an efficient procedure to solve bi-objective combinatorial optimization problems. *Journal on Foundations of Computers and Decision Sciences*, 20(2):149–165.

[Ulungu and Teghem, 1997] Ulungu, E. L. and Teghem, J. (1997). *Solving Multi-Objective Knapsack Problem by a Branch-and-Bound Procedure*, pages 269–278. In [Climaco, 1997].

[Ulungu et al., 1995] Ulungu, E. L., Teghem, J., and Fortemps, P. (1995). *Heuristics for Multi-Objective Combinatorial Optimization Problem by Simulated Annealing*, pages 229–238. SCIence-TECHnics, Windsor, England.

[Ulungu et al., 1999] Ulungu, E. L., Teghem, J., Fortemps, P., and Tuyttens, D. (1999). Mosa method: A tool for solving multi-objective combinatorial optimization problems. *Journal of Multicriteria Decision Analysis*, 8:221–236.

[Ulungu et al., 1998] Ulungu, E. L., Teghem, J., and Ost, C. (1998). Efficiency of interactive multi-objective simulated annealing through a case study. *Journal of the Operational Research Society*, 49:1044–1050.

[Vadhan, 1995] Vadhan, S. (1995). The complexity of counting. *Thesis of Bachelor of Arts, Harvard College, Cambridge (USA)*, page 58.

[Valiant, 1979a] Valiant, L. (1979a). The complexity of computing the permanent. *Theoretical Computer Science*, 8:189–201.

[Valiant, 1979b] Valiant, L. (1979b). The complexity of enumeration and reliability problems. *SIAM Journal on Computing*, 8(3):410–421.

[Van de Vonder et al., 2005] Van de Vonder, S., Demeulemeester, E., Herroelen, W., and Leus, R. (2005). The trade-off between stability and makespan in resource-constrained project scheduling. *International Journal of Production Research*, to appear.

[VandenAkker et al., 1998a] VandenAkker, M., Hoogeveen, H., and VandeVelde, S. (1998a). A combined column generation and lagrangian relaxation algorithm for common due date scheduling. In *6th Workshop on Project Management and Scheduling (PMS'98), EURO*, Istanbul, Turkey.

[VandenAkker et al., 1998b] VandenAkker, M., Hoogeveen, H., and VandeVelde, S. (1998b). Combining column generation and lagrangean relaxation : an application to a single-machine common due date scheduling problem. Technical report, Department of Mathematics and Computing Science, Eindhoven University of Technology, Eindhoven, The Netherlands.

[Vanderpooten, 1988] Vanderpooten, D. (1988). A multicriteria interactive procedure supporting a directed learning of preferences. In *EURO IX, TIMS XXVIII*, Paris, France.

[Vanderpooten, 1990] Vanderpooten, D. (1990). *L'approche interactive dans l'aide multicritère à la décision (in french)*. PhD thesis, University of Paris IX, Dauphine, Paris, France.

[Vanderpooten, 1992] Vanderpooten, D. (1992). *Three basic conceptions underlying multiple criteria interactive procedures*, pages 441–448. Springer-Verlag.

[VandeVelde, 1990] VandeVelde, S. L. (1990). Minimizing the sum of the job completion times in the two-machine flow shop by lagrangian relaxation. *Annals of Operations Research*, 26:257–268.

[VanWassenhove and Baker, 1982] VanWassenhove, L. and Baker, K. R. (1982). A bicriterion approach to time/cost trade-offs in sequencing. *European Journal of Operational Research*, 11(1):48–54.

[VanWassenhove and Gelders, 1978] VanWassenhove, L. and Gelders, L. F. (1978). Four solution techniques for a general one machine scheduling problem: a comparative study. *European Journal of Operational Research*, 2(4):281–290.

[VanWassenhove and Gelders, 1980] VanWassenhove, L. and Gelders, L. F. (1980). Solving a bicriterion scheduling problem. *European Journal of Operational Research*, 4:42–48.

[Vickson, 1980a] Vickson, R. G. (1980a). Choosing the job sequence and processing times to minimize total processing plus flow cost on a single machine. *Operations Research*, 28(5):115–167.

[Vickson, 1980b] Vickson, R. G. (1980b). Two single machine sequencing problems involving controllable job processing times. *IIE Transactions*, 12(3):158–162.

[Vignier, 1997] Vignier, A. (1997). *Contribution à la résolution des problèmes d'ordonnancement de type monogamme, multimachine (Flow-shop hybride) (in french)*. PhD thesis, E3i, University of Tours, Tours, France.

[Vignier et al., 1996] Vignier, A., Billaut, J.-C., and Proust, C. (1996). Solving k-stage hybrid flowshop scheduling problems. In *Multiconference on Computational Engineering in Systems Applications (CESA'96), IEEE-SMC/IMACS*, pages 250–258, Lille, France.

[Vignier et al., 1999] Vignier, A., Billaut, J.-C., and Proust, C. (1999). Les flowshop hybrides : état de l'art (in french). *R.A.I.R.O. Recherche Opérationnelle/ Operations Research*, 33(2):117–183.

[Vincke, 1976] Vincke, P. (1976). Une méthode interactive en programmation linéaire à plusieurs fonctions économiques (in french). *Revue Francaise d'Informatique et de Recherche Opérationnelle*, 2:5–20.

[Vincke, 1989] Vincke, P. (1989). *Aide multicritère à la décision (in french)*. Collection SMA, Ellipse, Paris, France.

[Visée et al., 1998] Visée, M., Teghem, J., Pirlot, M., and Ulungu, E. (1998). Two-phases method and branch and bound procedures to solve the bi-objective knapsack problem. *Journal of Global Optimization*, 12:139–155.

[Viswanathkumar and Srinivasan, 2003] Viswanathkumar, G. and Srinivasan, G. (2003). A branch and bound algorithm to minimize completion time variance on a single processor. *Computers & Operations Research*, 30:1135–1150.

[VonNeumann and Morgenstern, 1954] VonNeumann, J. L. and Morgenstern, O. (1954). *Theory of games and economic behavior*. Wiley.

[Warburton, 1983] Warburton, A. (1983). Quasiconcave vector maximization : Connectedness of the sets of Pareto-optimal and weak pareto-optimal alternatives. *Journal of Optimization Theory and Applications*, 40:537–557.

[Webster et al., 1998] Webster, S., Job, P. D., and Gupta, A. (1998). A genetic algorithm for scheduling job families on a single machine with arbitrary earliness/tardiness penalties and an unrestricted common due date. *International Journal of Production Research*, 36(9):2543–2551.

[Wierzbicki, 1982] Wierzbicki, A. (1982). A mathematical basis for satisficing decision making. *Mathematical modelling*, 3:391–405.

[Wierzbicki, 1990] Wierzbicki, A. (1990). *The use of reference objectives in multiobjective optimization*, pages 468–486. In [Fandel and Gal, 1997].

[Wilhelm and Ward, 1987] Wilhelm, M. R. and Ward, T. L. (1987). Solving quadratic assignment problem by simulated annealing. *IIE Transactions*, 19:107–119.

[Wilson, 1989] Wilson, J. M. (1989). Alternative formulations of a flow-shop scheduling problem. *Journal of the Operational Research Society*, 40(4):395–399.

[Wright, 2005] Wright, M. (2005). Scheduling fixtures for basketball new zealand. *Computers & Operations Research*, to appear.

[Wu et al., 1999] Wu, S. D., Byeon, E. S., and Storer, R. H. (1999). A graph-theoretic decomposition of the job-shop scheduling problem to achieve scheduling robustness. *Operations Research*, 47(1):113–124.

[Wu et al., 1993] Wu, S. D., Storer, R. H., and Chang, P.-C. (1993). One-machine rescheduling heuristics with efficiency and stability as criteria. *Computers and Operations Research*, 20(1):1–14.

[Yano and Kim, 1991] Yano, C. A. and Kim, Y. D. (1991). Algorithms for a class of single machine weighted tardiness and earliness problems. *European Journal of Operational Research*, 52:167–178.

[Yeh, 1999] Yeh, W. C. (1999). A new branch-and-bound approach for the $n/2/\text{flowshop}/aF + bCmax$ flowshop scheduling problem. *Computers and Operations Research*, 26:1293–1310.

[Yu, 1978] Yu, P. (1978). Dynamic programming in finite-stage multicriteria decision problems. Technical Report 118, School of Business, University of Kansas, U.S.A.

[Yu, 1974] Yu, P. L. (1974). Cone convexity, cone extreme points and nondominated solutions in decision problems with multiobjectives. *Journal of Optimization Theory and Applications*, 14:319–377.

[Yu and Seiford, 1981] Yu, P. L. and Seiford, L. (1981). Multistage decision problems with multicriteria.

[Yu and Zeleny, 1975] Yu, P. L. and Zeleny, M. (1975). The set of all nondominated solutions in linear cases and a multicriteria simplex method. *Journal of Mathematical Analysis and Applications*, 49:430–468.

[Zegordi et al., 1995] Zegordi, S. H., Itoh, K., and Enkawa, T. (1995). A knowledgeable simulated annealing scheme for the early/tardy flow shop scheduling problem. *International Journal of Production Research*, 33(5):1449–1466.

[Zionts, 1997] Zionts, S. (1997). *Decision making: some experiences, myths and observations*, pages 233–241. In [Fandel and Gal, 1997].

[Zionts and Wallenius, 1976] Zionts, S. and Wallenius, J. (1976). An interactive programming method for solving the multiple criteria problem. *Management Science*, 22(6):652–663.

[Zionts and Wallenius, 1983] Zionts, S. and Wallenius, J. (1983). An interactive multiple objective linear programming method for a class of underlying non linear utility fonctions. *Management Science*, 29(5):519–529.

Index

Printing and Binding: Strauss GmbH, Mörlenbach

www.ingramcontent.com/pod-product-compliance
Lightning Source LLC
Chambersburg PA
CBHW071352220926
51613CB00008B/132
9783540282303